21 世纪英语专业系列教材

《圣经》与西方文化

The Bible and Western Culture

王 磊 编著

北京大学出版社
PEKING UNIVERSITY PRESS

图书在版编目(CIP)数据

《圣经》与西方文化 / 王磊编著. —北京：北京大学出版社，2012.6
（21 世纪英语专业系列教材）
ISBN 978-7-301-20724-6

Ⅰ.①圣… Ⅱ.①王… Ⅲ.①英语－高等学校－教材②《圣经》－关系－西方文化－研究 Ⅳ.①H31

中国版本图书馆 CIP 数据核字(2012)第 118268 号

书　　　名：《圣经》与西方文化
著作责任者：王　磊　编著
责 任 编 辑：叶　丹
标 准 书 号：ISBN 978-7-301-20724-6/H·3069
出 版 发 行：北京大学出版社
地　　　址：北京市海淀区成府路 205 号　100871
网　　　址：http://www.pup.cn　电子信箱：zbing@pup.pku.edu.cn
电　　　话：邮购部 62752015　发行部 62750672　编辑部 62754382　出版部 62754962
印 刷 者：北京鑫海金澳胶印有限公司
经 销 者：新华书店
　　　　　787 毫米×1092 毫米　16 开本　25 印张　780 千字
　　　　　2012 年 6 月第 1 版　2020 年 1 月第 4 次印刷
定　　　价：48.00 元

未经许可，不得以任何方式复制或抄袭本书之部分或全部内容。
版权所有，侵权必究
举报电话：(010)62752024　电子信箱：fd@pup.pku.edu.cn

《21世纪英语专业系列教材》
编写委员会

（以姓氏笔画排序）

王立非	王守仁	王克非
王俊菊	文秋芳	石　坚
申　丹	朱　刚	仲伟合
刘世生	刘意青	殷企平
孙有中	李　力	李正栓
张旭春	张庆宗	张绍杰
杨俊峰	陈法春	金　莉
封一函	胡壮麟	查明建
袁洪庚	桂诗春	黄国文
梅德明	董洪川	蒋洪新
程幼强	程朝翔	虞建华

No book in the whole history of mankind has had such a revolutionary influence, has so decisively affected the development of the western world, or had such a world-wide effect as the "Book of Books," the Bible.

Werner Keller, author of <u>The Bible as History</u>

序

《圣经》不仅是宗教文本，也是西方文明的一大渊源和基石，它以显性或隐性的方式存在于几千年西方文学、艺术、文化、政治和意识形态中，其重要性在我国改革开放后便逐渐得到了共识。除了从宗教、历史和《圣经》与文学、艺术的关系开展学术研究，发表文章和专著外，20世纪90年代中期我国高等院校同欧美高校一样，也开始设立了《圣经》课程，这是有深远意义的举措。欧美高等院校自上个世纪80年代开始普遍开设《圣经》的文学、文化阐释课程，其目的是为了挽救这部经典在年轻一代人中间逐渐失去的影响，因为不熟悉《圣经》他们就不可能理解从乔叟到乔伊斯的整个西方文学作品和艺术，就意味着西方文明传统将在未来年月丧失殆尽。一句话，开设《圣经》阐释课程对欧美国家来说是维护传统的大事。我国开设相关课程的目的自然不同，但也是当务之急，因为以新兴大国出现在世界舞台上的中国必须真正了解西方的思维逻辑、行事准则与方式。要达此目的，我国民众，特别是高校学生就必须熟悉《圣经》。当然，不同于欧美类似课程，我们主要是普及性的任务，授课程度比他们浅显得多。

进入21世纪后，随着对外学术交流的展开，围绕《圣经》研究的刊物、著作和论文增多，不止一所高校建立了《圣经》研究机构，设立相关课程的学校也多了起来。特别是近10年来，在开设课程的基础上，又先后出现了几套从《圣经》的文学阐释、文化内涵和对文化和艺术的影响等方面编写的教材，如《〈圣经〉文学阐释教程》（北京大学出版社）和《圣经文化导论》（上海外语教育出版社）等。这类教材的出版说明我国的《圣经》研习正式进入高校课堂，通过开设非宗教目的的《圣经》课，我们培养的学生将会改变对西方无知或表面化的认识，对西方过去和目前的文化及政治现象能够做到知根知底。具备这样知识结构的年轻一代将大大有利于我国在国际事务中施展身手，驾驭风云变幻。

正是在这样的大好形势下，我欣喜地又看到了一部高校《圣经》课教材，它就是北京大学出版社即将出版的《〈圣经〉与西方文化》，编者是上海外国语大学的教师王磊博士。王磊是一个科研和著述很有建树的年轻学者，不但教授课程涉及认知语言学、希腊罗马神话、莎士比亚及《圣经》，而且先后发表过这些方面的论文和著作。在编写《〈圣经〉与西方文化》之前，他已经成功地出版过"十一五"国家级规划教材《希腊罗马神话欣赏》（上海外语教育出版社）。这次的《圣经》教材是他多年教授和研究《圣经》的结晶，不仅在体例、结构和布局上充满新意，而且内容厚重，含金量很高，综合并深入地向学生和有兴趣的读者们介绍了这部经典文本。基于对这部教材的品质和意义的认识，我欣然同意为它作序。

开设《圣经》课的首要任务是让学生了解和熟悉该文本宣传的人类起源，上帝与人类的关系，希伯来民族的形成和发展，以色列建国和朝代更迭，它与周边民族和国家的争斗及亡国，还有耶稣生平和早期基督教会历史。这样的重点考虑，决定了教材一般以历史为主线，穿插关照一些希伯来诗歌、传记和哲理故事等精华内容，而割舍掉先知书和律法等与文学关系较远的卷章。当然，国内外也不乏有以神话、传奇、历史、短篇小说、智慧文学、诗歌、箴言、律法等文类为纲目来进行编排的教材。《〈圣经〉与西方文化》属于前者，它比较全面地涵括了上述重点内容，在章节编排上突显个人的成长和民族的历史发展，比如没有把第一部分《创世记》按文类编排分割为神话和传奇两部分，再比如教材的中段六个部分按时间顺序及族长和领袖的命运讲授了犹太人从出埃及到建国，再到以色列国分裂和灭亡的过程，呈现了一个较系统和完整的古代以色列民族史；最后用第八部分处理了四福音书，即耶稣的生平和早期的基督教会历史。这样的编排脉络清晰，重点突出，也符合我们学生的需求。

但是，这部教材既然称作《〈圣经〉与西方文化》，就不能只梳理历史。它不按照文类编排，又怎样来体现《圣经》的文学性和它与西方文学、艺术和文化的密切关系呢？这方面编者还是费了一番苦心的。（1）编者独出心裁地在每个单元设立了I."开篇"（Points of Departure）交代本单元的相关信息，背景和内容；II."选段"（Selected Readings），选自《钦定圣经》，一般每单元有数个选段，并配有内容标题、注释以及姓名和地名的音标；III."思考内容"（Food for Thought），即思考题；IV."圣经相关内容"（Biblical Relevance），包括"圣经典故"（Biblical Terms in Everyday English），"圣经对文学的影响"（Biblical References in Literature）和"圣经与艺术"（The Bible and Arts）；V. 最后还给出这一单元的音像和书籍等参考资料的名目。（2）教材配入了近两百幅插图，这本身就是《圣经》对西方艺术深远影响的明证，而且大大地提高了这部教材的趣味性。（3）最让我喜欢的是每单元以方框形式插入的"文化链接"（Cultural Connections）或"文学里的圣经"（The Bible in Literature）这种小栏目。它们形式灵活，内容丰富，既有我们熟悉的但丁的《神曲》和弥尔顿的《失乐园》，也有我们不大熟悉的巴比伦神话 The Enuma Elish 和不太注意的好莱坞电影《出埃及记》。这样的设置无疑大大拓宽了教材涵盖面，并以活泼的形式在进行选段解读的同时教授了《圣经》的文化和文学影响。（4）这部教材还有不少附加地图和表格，如十多幅古代近东、出埃及、以色列王国和保罗传教的地图，《圣经》各卷缩节名称表，《钦定圣经》英文的人称代词和动词变化表，《圣经》时期的历史年表等。这些设置给使用者提供了极大的方便，体现了编者严谨认真的学术态度。

这样一部丰富且潜力很大的教材，对教师们也是个挑战。首先，它不像其他同类教材除去选段是英文，其余用中文写就，而是全部用英文解释和注释的。因此，它要求教师具备较好的英语水平，甚至能相应地用英文授课。但正因为教材全部用英语写成，这门课程也就可以提高学生的英语阅读和表达能力。其次，处理与文学和文化链接的小方框时可深可浅，最简单的做法是仅仅解释所提供的知识信息，但也可以就比较重要的文学作品和文化现象进行拓宽和全面讨论。文学作品比如上面提到的《失乐园》，社会和文化现象比如诺亚儿子含被父亲诅咒、赶走后成为黑人的祖先，都是可以大做文章的议题。但讲解和阐释《圣经》文本选段才是此课程的核心，是开课成功与否的关键。做得好时，这门课不仅普及了历史和宗教知识，它还能综合训练学生细读文本和分析的能力，培养和熟悉西方的思维方式，学会使用西方现当代的语言、文化、文学和哲学理论，如神话原型理论、女权主义、解构主义、心理分析和叙事学理论等等。在这个意义上，《〈圣经〉与西方文化》提供给我们一个带领学生综合操练的平台，可以起到一石多鸟的作用。

19世纪，当英国资本主义大发展而带来社会精神和道德危机时，马修·阿诺德在《文化与无政府状态》一书中提倡希伯来精神和希腊精神并重，指出它们对规范英国社会言行和提升百姓素质的必要性。两希传统对西方无疑是不可或缺的，但它们也各有负面作用。希腊精神追求自由思想，阿诺德在强调它可以改变非利士人的物质主义的同时，也指出绝对的自由是有害于社会的。至于希伯来传统主要是以法律人，强调道德规范，阿诺德认为它有扼杀精神的危险。然而，进入20世纪和21世纪后，越来越多的人认识到《圣经》在国别关系和世界事务中的隐性作用，《圣经》里的选民思想和上帝赐地等宗教理念和意识形态不但长期存在于西方民族的集体潜意识中，并直接进入了当今世界的政治，比如在美国和西方的对外政策和态度及以色列和巴勒斯坦的矛盾斗争里都看得到《圣经》的影响。中国是东方古老的文明之乡，与西方在宗教和哲学、伦理和治国等理念上差异很大。正因如此，在中国快步迈进世界经济、政治格局的今天，我们的高等院校必须设置非宗教目的的《圣经》课程，以便彻底了解西方。而正是《〈圣经〉与西方文化》这样的教材为这类课程的普遍开设提供了条件，因此值得大力肯定和推广。

刘意青
2012年春，于北京

前　言

　　《圣经》之于西方文明史的意义不言而喻，其中所蕴含的知识和智慧应为欲了解中西文化交流来龙去脉，并有志于担当文化交流桥梁的人士所必备。但面对这样一本历经数千年，先经口口相传，后由多代作者、抄经人呕心沥血、锲而不舍所铸就的恢弘巨著，读者大多经历了由当初的摩拳擦掌、兴趣盎然到最后的偃旗息鼓、掩卷叹息的令人遗憾的阅读体验。究其原因，无外乎有这么几条：一是没做先行性的"功课"，不了解《圣经》的主要内容和意旨便贸然进入；二是仅仅把《圣经》当作犹太教或基督教的宗教文本进行阅读，忽略了该著作的文学性、历史性乃至现实性等的内涵。而这种《圣经》阅读中的缺失也就使得阅读本身枯燥乏味、举步维艰。实际上，对《圣经》的解读和研究早已不再囿于宗教和经院的视阈。左右18世纪西方学术、以重构作者及受众所处的历史环境为目标的高等批评（higher criticism），19世纪的圣经考古（biblical archaeology）以及繁荣于20世纪80年代的圣经文学研究（the Bible as literature）更是把我们的视野引向了生动真实的历史大世界和瑰丽多彩的文学百花园。作为《圣经》阅读难以为继的另一个原因是阅读的单一或单调性，即把对《圣经》的了解仅仅局限于文本的阅读，而疏于关注它在绘画、音乐、文学（the Bible in literature），甚至日常语言等西方文化诸方面的生动表现，也就失去了提高对西方文化敏感度，加强跨文化交流能力的良好机会。

　　基于以上认识，本书作者于六年前在任教的学校申请立项并开设了面向英语专业本科生的"《圣经》与西方文化"课程。该门课程基于英文《圣经》的文本阅读和讨论，同时兼顾《圣经》在文学、绘画、音乐、日常英语等文化方面的影响。随着课程年复一年的进行，作为课程讲义的《〈圣经〉与西方文化》也在不断的使用中得到逐步的完善，并最终能够由以"学术的尊严，精神的魅力"著称的北京大学出版社出版，从而能够在更大的范围内分享《圣经》文本及其文化的魅力。以下拟从教材材料的选择、编排特点、各章栏目等做几点说明。

　　教材的《圣经》原文部分选自被誉为"英语散文最伟岸的丰碑"（the noblest monument of English prose）的英文版《钦定圣经》（*King James Bible*），原因在于它作为迄今为止销量最大、流通最广、引用最多的圣经版本的深远和广泛的影响。2011年，英美两国的教会、大学及研究机构为纪念该《圣经》诞生四百周年所纷纷举办的系列讲座、展览等活动便充分地说明了这一点。《钦定圣经》行文晓畅，语言平易近人。据说，当初翻译的初衷之一是使即便是扶犁的农夫（the boy at the plow）听起来也毫无困难。该版本《圣经》影响了几个世纪的各代英美作家，不了解《圣经》实际上就很难理解充斥其作品的《圣经》的典故和习语的含义，甚至人物形象的寓意。限于篇幅，本教材选材的原则是以叙事文本为主，关照相关重要篇目，所以《旧约》"摩西五经"中的《利未记》、《民数记》和《申命记》，"先知书"中的《何西阿书》、《约珥书》、《阿莫司书》等"小先知书"，以及《新约》中的"书信"部分未加选录。同样的原因，记载着智勇双全的巾帼英雄犹滴（Judith）、受恶人诬告但终得昭雪的良家妇女苏撒娜（Susanna）和犹太民族英雄马卡比（Maccabees）等诸多生动故事的《次经》（Apocrypha）的相关篇目也只得忍痛割爱。

教材没有完全依据《圣经》通常的编排做法（即《旧约》和《新约》分别按"律法书"、"历史书"、"诗歌和智慧书"、"先知书"和"四福音书"、"书信"、"启示录"的顺序），而是在保持以上顺序基本不变的基础上，根据各部书所反映的时代情状，按照历史的顺序和内在的关联进行编排。这样做的好处是能够为所阅读的文本提供一个历史的参照纬度，从而加深对原文的理解。所以，原文本中"诗歌和智慧书"的《诗篇》、《箴言》、《传道书》和《雅歌》，因其与大卫王和所罗门王的关系而被分别调整至与这两位君王相关的部分中。时代划分的主要依据为Paul Roche (2001)。

教材各章按以下各部分编排：第一部分为《圣经》导读（Points of Departure），扼要介绍所选原文的主要内容以及需要重点关注的方面。第二部分（Selected Readings）为《圣经》原文阅读（节选）。该部分除《圣经》原文外，还设计以下内容：《圣经》题材西洋艺术插图；人名、地名、难点及文化等的脚注；相关《圣经》链接，包括：圣经典故（The Bible in Everyday English）、圣经文学（The Bible as Literature）、文学中的圣经（The Bible in Literature）、文化链接（Cultural Connections）（与圣经相关的文化提示）等栏目。第三部分（Food for Thought）根据选文的内容设计若干事实及延伸性的思考问题。第四部分（Biblical Relevance）为《圣经》在日常英语、文学及艺术作品中呈现形式的识别与赏析。最后一部分（Sources for Reference）提供深入探讨的书籍、音像资料及网站，为读者的自主学习提供便利。

最后，衷心感谢北京大学出版社将本人多年的心愿变成了现实，使得自己的这桩labor of love（语出1 Thessalonians 1:3；Hebrews 6:10）终究没有付之东流；感谢德高望重的刘意青教授奖掖后学，悉心指导并欣然为序。

王磊
2011年冬于上海外国语大学

THE BOOKS OF THE BIBLE

Old Testament (OT)[1]

Gen.	Genesis	2 Chr.	2 Chronicles	Dan.	Daniel
Exod.	Exodus	Ezr.	Ezra	Hos.	Hosea
Lev.	Leviticus	Neh.	Nehemiah	Jl.	Joel
Num.	Numbers	Est.	Esther	Am.	Amos
Dt.	Deuteronomy	Job	Job	Ob.	Obadiah
Jos.	Joshua	Ps.	Psalms	Jon.	Jonah
Jg.	Judges	Prov.	Proverbs	Mic.	Micah
Ru.	Ruth	Ec.	Ecclesiastes	Nah.	Nahum
1 Sam.	1 Samuel	S.	Song of Songs	Hab.	Habakkuk
2 Sam.	2 Samuel	Isa.	Isaiah	Zeph.	Zephaniah
1 Kg.	1 Kings	Jer.	Jeremiah	Hag.	Haggai
2 Kg.	2 Kings	Lam.	Lamentations	Zech.	Zechariah
1 Chr.	1 Chronicles	Ezek.	Ezekiel	Mal.	Malachi

New Testament (NT)

Mt.	Matthew	Eph.	Ephesians	Heb.	Hebrews
Mk.	Mark	Phil.	Philippians	Jas.	James
Lk.	Luke	Col.	Colossians	1 Pet.	1 Peter
Jn.	John	1 Th.	1 Thessalonians	2 Pet.	2 Peter
Ac.	Acts of the Apostles	2 Th.	2 Thessalonians	1 Jn.	1 John
Rom.	Romans	1 Tim.	1 Timothy	2 Jn.	2 John
1 C.	1 Corinthians	2 Tim.	2 Timothy	3 Jn.	3 John
2 C.	2 Corinthians	Tit.	Titus	Jude	Jude
Gal.	Galatians	Phm.	Philemon	Rev.	Revelation

---

1 Abbreviations of the books of the Bible are based on Black (2001:xiii).

PRONOUNS & VERBS IN THE *KING JAMES BIBLE*

1. 2nd Person Pronouns

	Singular	Plural
Subjective Case	*thou*	*you ye*
Possessive Case	*thy thine*	*your yours*
Objective Case	*thee*	*you ye*

NB.
Thine is often used
(1) before a word beginning with a vowel sound or the letter "*h*", as in: *thine eye, thine ass, thine head, thine heart*;
(2) as a possessive pronoun.

2. Verbs

to be	2nd person singular present: *art* 2nd person singular past: *wast*
to have	2nd person singular present: *hast* 3rd person singular present: *hath*

Normal verbs
2nd person singular present:
      verb+*st/est*, as in: *dost/doest, sayest, blessest, beholdest*
2nd person singular past:
      verb(past form)+*st/est*, as in: *didst, calledst, sawest, camest*
3rd person singular present:
      verb+*th/eth*, as in: *doth/doeth, seeth, cometh, liveth, goeth*
NB.
(1) For verbs ending with a vowel sound + y:
    y →i + th, as in: *saith*;
(2) When *thou* is used after *shall*, *shall* should be changed into *shalt*;
(3) When *thou* is used after *will*, *will* should be changed into *wilt*.

CONTENTS

PART ONE
IN THE BEGINNING (C. 40,000—1,700 B.C.E)
The Book of Genesis
  1. The Creation and the Fall of Man / 2
  2. From the Garden to the Tower / 10
  3. Abraham, the Progenitor / 20
  4. Jacob, the Deceiver / 32
  5. Joseph, a Dreamer / 40

PART TWO
THE EMERGENCE OF ISRAEL (C. 1,700—1,200 B.C.E.)
The Book of Exodus
  6. Bondage in Egypt / 56
  7. The Plagues of Egypt / 65
  8. The Escape from Egypt / 75
  9. The Covenant at Mount Sinai / 81

PART THREE
SETTLEMENT IN THE PROMISED LAND (C. 1,200—1,000 B.C.E.)
The Books of Joshua, Judges, Ruth
  10. Joshua, the Successor to Moses / 88
  11. Unlikely Heroes / 95
  12. Samson and the Philistines / 103
  13. Ruth / 111

PART FOUR
THE KINGDOMS OF SAUL AND DAVID (C. 1,020—900 B.C.E.)
The Books of 1 & 2 Samuel, Psalms
  14. Samuel and Saul / 118
  15. Saul and David / 126
  16. David the King / 138
  17. Psalms / 148

PART FIVE
THE KINGDOM OF SOLOMON (C. 962—922 B.C.E.)
The Books of 1 Kings, Proverbs, Song of Songs, Ecclesiastes
  18. Solomon / 154
  19. Proverbs / 163
  20. The Song of Songs / 170
  21. Ecclesiastes / 178

PART SIX
THE DIVIDED KINGDOM (C. 933—800 B.C.E.)
The Books of 1 & 2 Kings
  22. Elijah, the Ecstatic Prophet / 188
  23. Elisha / 200

PART SEVEN
PALESTINE DURING THE ASSYRIAN, BABYLONIAN, PERSIAN AND GREEK DOMINATION (C. 842—4 B. C. E.)
The Books of Esther, Job, Isaiah, Jeremiah, Ezekiel, Jonah, Daniel
  24. Esther / 212
  25. Job / 224
  26. The Prophets: Isaiah, Jeremiah, Ezekiel, Jonah / 234
  27. Daniel / 248

PART EIGHT
PALESTINE UNDER THE ROMANS (C. 4 B. C. E. —67 C. E.)
The Four Gospels, the Acts of Apostles, Revelation
THE FOUR GOSPELS
  28. Birth of John and Jesus / 258
  29. The Ministry of John and the Launch of Jesus' Career / 268
  30. Miracles and Healings / 278
  31. Jesus' Parables: the Kingdom of Heaven / 287
  32. The Church / 296
  33. The Final Judgment / 303
  34. The Passion / 311
  35. The Resurrection and Thereafter / 322
THE ACTS OF APOSTLES
  36. Apostles Empowered by the Holy Spirit / 329
  37. Preaching in Jerusalem / 333
  38. Preaching in Samaria and Judaea / 340
  39. The Journeys of Paul / 348
REVELATION
  40. Revelation / 361

BIBLIOGRAPHY / 369
APPENDICES / 371
  1. Maps / 371
    1.1 Map of the Ancient Near East
    1.2 Route of the Exodus of the Israelites from Egypt
    1.3 The Fertile Crescent
    1.4 The World of Patriarchs
    1.5 Map of the Kingdoms of David and Solomon
    1.6 The Divided Monarchy
    1.7 The Life and Ministry of Jesus Christ
    1.8 The Roman Empire at Its Zenith
    1.9 Paul's Missionary Journeys (1)
    1.10 Paul's Missionary Journeys (2)
    1.11 Paul's Missionary Journeys (3)
  2. A Chronology of Biblical Times / 377
    2.1 Ancient-United Kingdom
    2.2 Divided Monarchy-Exile
    2.3 The Greek Period
    2.4 The Roman Period/The New Testament
  3. An Overview of the Books of the Bible / 379

PART ONE

IN THE BEGINNING
(C. 40,000—1,700 B.C.E)
THE BOOK OF GENESIS

1. THE CREATION AND THE FALL OF MAN

I POINTS OF DEPARTURE

As the first book of the five books known as the Pentateuch (Greek for "five-volume" work, or 摩西五经 in Chinese), Genesis (Greek for "coming into being") begins with words that have now become famous: "In the beginning God created..." It relates the divine origin of the universe, but also skillfully anticipates the future story of Israel, with the events in Eden foreshadowing the life, travails, and hopes of the historical biblical community. As a matter of fact, the first three chapters of Genesis link to the last book of the Bible, Revelation, in that they are both like brackets of perfection around the sadness of life marked by sin, death, suffering and hatred, thus forming a U-shaped plot.

Genesis 1 divides creation into six days signifying a world carefully designed and imbued with order. This impression is further reinforced by a clear literary pattern appearing in all of the six days: (1) the announcement "and God said"; (2) a command "let there be" or some other forms of "let"; (3) the fulfillment; (4) the approval "God saw that it was good"; (5) the placement of time "the evening and the morning were the ____ day." Another pattern is the balanced pairing of days and works; God first creates three places or settings, and then he fills each setting with the appropriate creatures as shown below:

PAIRING OF DAYS AND WORKS	
Day One	**Day Four**
Light	Sun, moon, and stars
Day Two	**Day Five**
Sky and sea	Birds and sea creatures
Day Three	**Day Six**
Dry land and vegetation	Land animals and people

So, the world created by God was essentially good and orderly, that is, until human rebellion marred it. The place of man in the grand design of God merits an equal attention: he was made in the image of God and has dominion over other species — the crowning glory of God's creation.

Chapter 2, starting from 2:4, is not a duplicate of the creation story in the previous chapter: the order of creation, men and women's relation to it and their relation to each other, and the different names for God: Yahweh Elohim (the Lord God), the personal and covenant name of God, in Chapter 2, and the remote and detached name Elohim in Chapter 1. This suggests that there are two at least versions of the same story. Such phenomenon characterized by repetitions, inconsistencies and anachronisms keeps propping up throughout the first five books of the Bible. The consensus of scholarship (initiated by Julius Wellhausen with his Documentary hypothesis) is that the stories were taken from four different written sources and that these were brought together over the course of time to form the Pentateuch (or Torah, as it is known to Jews). The four sources are J, the Jahwist source (from the German transliteration of the Hebrew YHWH), E, the Elohist source, P, the Priestly source, and D, the Deuteronomist source.

The first few chapters of Genesis show a world in harmony, blessing, and goodness, with humanity and the natural world coexisting in peaceful abundance and delight. But everything was turned topsy-turvy after the first couple committed the original sin by eating of the tree of the knowledge of good and evil. All the ills from which the earthly Paradise had been exempt — toil, pain, aging, conflict, corruption, and loss — were now realities. The tempter was the "subtil" serpent, which has ever since been associated with the personification of evil later known as the Devil or Satan. And the forbidden fruit has long been linked with illicit sexual desire, suggesting a connection between tasting the fruit, awareness of nakedness, and shame. Jews and Christians differ in their interpretation of *Genesis 3*. Most Jews focus on such questions as "Is knowledge of good and evil preferable to innocence?" and regard moral choice as a step down from a state of innocence, where nobody is tempted to do evil. Others see in this narrative an affirmation of the importance of free will, of the capacity to choose between good and evil. Christians read this chapter as the story of "the fall" of human beings from God's presence and favor into suffering and sin; hence the original sin. In other words, it was Adam and Eve who through their disobedience brought physical and emotional suffering, moral evil, and death into the world (Schippe & Stetson, 2005:38).

For as by one man's disobedience many were made sinners, so by the obedience of one [*i.e. Jesus*] *shall many be made righteous.* (*Romans* 5:19)

II SELECTED READINGS

The Beginning

Genesis 1

¹ In the beginning God① created the heaven and the earth.

² And the earth was without form, and void; and darkness was upon the face of the deep. And the Spirit of God moved upon the face of the waters.

³ And God said, "Let there be light," and there was light. ⁴ And God saw the light, that it was good: and God divided the light from the darkness. ⁵ And God called the light Day, and the darkness he called Night. And the evening and the morning were the first day.

⁶ And God said, "Let there be a firmament② in the midst of the waters, and let it divide the waters from the waters." ⁷ And God made the firmament, and divided the waters which were under the firmament from the waters which were above the firmament: and it was so. ⁸ And God called the firmament Heaven.

And the evening and the morning were the second day.

⁹ And God said, "Let the waters under the heaven be gathered together unto one place, and let the dry land appear:" And it was so. ¹⁰ And God called the dry land Earth; and the gathering together of the waters called he Seas: and God saw that it was good. ¹¹ And God said, "Let the earth bring forth grass, the herb yielding seed, and the fruit tree yielding fruit after his kind, whose seed is in itself, upon the earth." And it

---

① **God** *Elohim* (the Mighty One) in Hebrew.
② **firmament** expanse or canopy.

Creation of Adam, the Sistine Chapel Ceiling paintings, Michelangelo (1475—1564)

was so. ^{12} And the earth brought forth grass, and herb yielding seed after his kind, and the tree yielding fruit, whose seed was in itself, after his kind: and God saw that it was good. ^{13} And the evening and the morning were the third day.

^{14} And God said, "Let there be lights in the firmament of the heaven to divide the day from the night; and let them be for signs, and for seasons, and for days, and years. ^{15} And let them be for lights in the firmament of the heaven to give light upon the earth: and it was so. ^{16} And God made two great lights; the greater light to rule the day, and the lesser light to rule the night: he made the stars also. ^{17} And God set them in the firmament of the heaven to give light upon the earth, ^{18} And to rule over the day and over the night, and to divide the light from the darkness: and God saw that it was good. ^{19} And the evening and the morning were the fourth day.

^{20} And God said, "Let the waters bring forth abundantly the moving creature that hath③ life, and fowl that may fly above the earth in the open firmament of heaven." ^{21} And God created great whales, and every living creature that moveth④, which the waters brought forth abundantly, after their kind, and every winged fowl after his kind: and God saw that it was good. ^{22} And God blessed them, saying, "Be fruitful, and multiply, and fill the waters in the seas, and let fowl multiply in the earth." ^{23} And the evening and the morning were the fifth day.

^{24} And God said, "Let the earth bring forth the living creature after his kind, cattle, and creeping thing, and beast of the earth after his kind." And it was so.

^{25} And God made the beast of the earth after his kind, and cattle after their kind, and every thing that creepeth upon the earth after his kind: and God saw that it was good.

Cultural Connections: *The Enuma Elish*

The *Enuma Elish* is a Babylonian or Mesopotamian myth of creation recounting the struggle between cosmic order and chaos. It was written sometime in the 12th century B.C.E. in cuneiform on seven clay tablets and brought to light through an archeological excavation made in the mid-19th century in the ruins of the palace of Ashurbanipal in Nineveh. The many parallels between this version and the Genesis account point to the great likelihood that biblical writers had drawn upon the cultural and religious legacy of their Ancient Near Eastern neighbors. In spite of the obvious similarities, differences are also salient.

^{26} And God said, "Let us make man in our image, after our likeness: and let them have dominion over the fish of the sea, and over the fowl of the air, and over the cattle, and over all the earth, and over every creeping thing that creepeth upon the earth."

^{27} So God created man in his own image, in the image of God created he him; male and female created he them.

^{28} And God blessed them, and God said unto them, "Be fruitful, and multiply, and replenish the earth, and subdue it: and have dominion over the fish of the sea, and over the fowl of the air, and over every living thing that moveth upon the earth."

---

③ **hath** *See* PRONOUNS & VERBS IN *KING JAMES BIBLE*.
④ **moveth** *ibid.*

²⁹ And God said, "Behold, I have given you every herb bearing seed, which is upon the face of all the earth, and every tree, in the which is the fruit of a tree yielding seed; to you it shall be for meat. ³⁰ And to every beast of the earth, and to every fowl of the air, and to every thing that creepeth upon the earth, wherein there is life, I have given every green herb for meat." And it was so.

³¹ And God saw every thing that he had made, and, behold, it was very good. And the evening and the morning were the sixth day.

Another Creation Story

Genesis 2

¹ Thus the heavens and the earth were finished, and all the host of them.

² And on the seventh day God ended his work which he had made; and he rested on the seventh day from all his work which he had made. ³ And God blessed the seventh day, and sanctified it: because that in it he had rested from all his work which God created and made.

Adam and Eve

⁴ These are the generations of the heavens and of the earth when they were created, in the day that the LORD God⑤ made the earth and the heavens.

⁵ And every plant of the field before it was in the earth, and every herb of the field before it grew: for the LORD God had not caused it to rain upon the earth, and there was not a man to till the ground. ⁶ But there went up a mist from the earth, and watered the whole face of the ground. ⁷ And the LORD God formed man⑥ of the dust of the ground, and breathed into his nostrils the breath of life; and man became a living soul.

⁸ And the LORD God planted a garden eastward in Eden⑦; and there he put the man whom he had formed. ⁹ And out of the ground made the LORD God to grow every tree that is pleasant to the sight, and good for food; the tree of life also in the midst of the garden, and the tree of knowledge of good and evil.

¹⁰ And a river went out of Eden to water the garden; and from thence it was parted, and became into four heads. ¹¹ The name of the first is Pison: that is it which compasseth the whole land of Havilah, where there is gold; ¹² And the gold of that land is good: there is bdellium and the onyx stone. ¹³ And the name of the second river is Gihon: the same is it that compasseth the whole land of Ethiopia. ¹⁴ And the name of the third river is Hiddekel: that is it which goeth toward the east of Assyria. And the fourth river is Euphrates.

Adam and Eve, Hans Grien Baldung (c. 1484—1545)

¹⁵ And the LORD God took the man, and put him into the garden of Eden to dress it and to keep it⑧. ¹⁶ And the LORD God commanded the man, saying, "Of every tree of the garden thou mayest freely eat: ¹⁷ But of the tree of the knowledge of good and evil, thou shalt not eat of it: for in the day that thou eatest thereof thou shalt surely die."

¹⁸ And the LORD God said, "It is not good that the man should be alone; I will make him an help meet

---

⑤ **the LORD God** *Yahweh Elohim* in Hebrew. *Yahweh* (/ˈjɑːveɪ/, 耶和华) came from the Hebrew Tetragrammaton representing the name of God with added vowels.
⑥ **man** The Hebrew for *man* (*Adam*) sounds like the Hebrew for *ground* (*adamah*); it is also the name *Adam*.
⑦ **a garden eastward in Eden** the Garden of Eden was possibly located in the Mesopotamian valley.
⑧ **to dress it and to keep it** to work it and take care of it.

for him."

^{19} And out of the ground the LORD God formed every beast of the field, and every fowl of the air; and brought them unto Adam to see what he would call them: and whatsoever Adam called every living creature, that was the name thereof. ^{20} And Adam gave names to all cattle, and to the fowl of the air, and to every beast of the field; but for Adam there was not found an help meet for⑨ him.

^{21} And the LORD God caused a deep sleep to fall upon Adam, and he slept: and he took one of his ribs, and closed up the flesh instead thereof; ^{22} And the rib, which the LORD God had taken from man, made he a woman, and brought her unto the man. ^{23} And Adam⑩ said, "This is now bone of my bones, and flesh of my flesh: she shall be called Woman⑪, because she was taken out of Man."

^{24} Therefore shall a man leave his father and his mother, and shall cleave unto his wife: and they shall be one flesh.

^{25} And they were both naked, the man and his wife, and were not ashamed.

The Bible in Literature: *Milton and the Bible*

John Milton (1608—1674), arguably the greatest English poet after Shakespeare, showed the direct influence of the Bible in his works. More than citing a few allusions to the Hebrew Scriptures and the New Testament, his works are permeated with scriptural images, echoes, stories, and themes. His great epics, *Paradise Lost* and *Paradise Regained*, though treating more or less the same theme as Genesis, make Satan an ever-evolving character, thus drastically transforming the way that tempter is perceived. Therefore, it can be rightfully said that Milton's vivid images not only have been profoundly influenced by the Bible, but also have influenced how the Bible is perceived in the Western world.

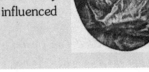

The Fall of Man

Genesis 3

^{1} Now the serpent was more subtil⑫ than any beast of the field which the LORD God had made. And he said unto the woman, "Yea, hath God said, ' Ye shall not eat of every tree of the garden' ?"

^{2} And the woman said unto the serpent, "We may eat of the fruit of the trees of the garden, ^{3} but of the fruit of the tree which is in the midst of the garden, God hath said, ' Ye shall not eat of it, neither shall ye touch it, lest ye die.' " ^{4} And the serpent said unto the woman, " Ye shall not surely die: ^{5} For God doth know that in the day ye eat thereof, then your eyes shall be opened, and ye shall be as gods, knowing good and evil." ^{6} And when the woman saw that the tree was good for food, and that it was pleasant to the eyes, and a tree to be desired to make one wise, she took of the fruit thereof, and did eat, and gave also unto her husband with her; and he did eat. ^{7} And the eyes of them both were opened, and they knew that they were naked; and

---

⑨ **an help meet for** a helper fit for.
⑩ **Adam** Or *the man*.
⑪ **Woman** The Hebrew for *woman* sounds like the Hebrew for *man*.
⑫ **subtil** = *subtile*, crafty.

they sewed fig leaves together, and made themselves aprons⑬.

⁸And they heard the voice of the LORD God walking in the garden in the cool of the day: and Adam and his wife hid themselves from the presence of the LORD God amongst the trees of the garden. ⁹And the LORD God called unto Adam, and said unto him, "Where art⑭ thou?"

¹⁰And he said, "I heard thy⑮ voice in the garden, and I was afraid, because I was naked; and I hid myself."

¹¹And he said, "Who told thee that thou wast naked? Hast thou eaten of the tree, whereof I commanded thee that thou shouldest not eat?"

¹²And the man said, "The woman whom thou gavest to be with me, she gave me of the tree, and I did eat."

¹³And the LORD God said unto the woman, "What is this that thou hast done?"

Temptation and the Original Sin, the Sistine Chapel Ceiling paintings, Michelangelo (1475—1564)

And the woman said, "The serpent beguiled me, and I did eat."

¹⁴And the LORD God said unto the serpent, "Because thou hast done this,
thou art cursed above all cattle,
and above every beast of the field;
upon thy belly shalt thou go,
and dust shalt thou eat
all the days of thy life:
¹⁵And I will put enmity between thee and the woman,
and between thy seed and her seed;
it shall bruise thy head,
and thou shalt bruise his heel."
¹⁶Unto the woman he said,
"I will greatly multiply thy sorrow and thy conception;
in sorrow thou shalt bring forth children;
and thy desire shall be to thy husband,
and he shall rule over thee."
¹⁷And unto Adam he said, "Because thou hast hearkened unto the voice of thy wife, and hast eaten of the tree, of which I commanded thee, saying, 'Thou shalt not eat of it,'
"Cursed is the ground for thy sake;
in sorrow shalt thou eat of it all the days of thy life;
¹⁸Thorns also and thistles shall it bring forth to thee;
and thou shalt eat the herb of the field;
¹⁹In the sweat of thy face
shalt thou eat bread,
till thou return unto the ground;
for out of it wast thou taken:
for dust thou art,
and unto dust shalt thou return."

---

⑬ **aprons** The 1560 edition of the *Geneva Bible* was notorious for its translation of *aprons* as *breeches*; hence *Breeches Bible* (马裤圣经).
⑭ **art** See PRONOUNS & VERBS IN *KING JAMES BIBLE*.
⑮ **thy** *ibid*.

²⁰ And Adam called his wife's name Eve⑯; because she was the mother of all living.

²¹ Unto Adam also and to his wife did the LORD God make coats of skins, and clothed them. ²² And the LORD God said, "Behold, the man is become as one of us, to know good and evil: and now, lest he put forth his hand, and take also of the tree of life, and eat, and live for ever:" ²³ Therefore the LORD God sent him forth from the garden of Eden, to till the ground from whence he was taken. ²⁴ So he drove out the man; and he placed at the east of the garden of Eden Cherubims, and a flaming sword which turned every way, to keep the way of the tree of life.

III FOOD FOR THOUGHT

1. What significance, if any, do you attach to the order of the creation?
2. What do you think is the meaning of man's having been made in the image of God?
3. In *Genesis 1—2*, there is not one creation account, but two, different in both content and style. Please elaborate. And how can you account for such heterogeneity (异文性) as exists throughout the Bible?
4. How is the serpent characterized? And how could it persuade Eve to eat the forbidden fruit?
5. What knowledge did Adam and Eve gain from eating the forbidden fruit?

IV BIBLICAL RELEVANCE

A. Biblical Terms in Everyday English

1. a daughter of Eve: _____
2. Adam's ale: _____
3. Adam and Eve's togs: _____
4. Adam's profession: _____
5. Adam's fig: _____
6. a fig leaf: _____
7. forbidden fruit: _____
8. by the sweat of one's brow (3:19): _____
9. For dust you are, and to dust you shall return (*ibid.*): _____

B. Biblical References in Literature

1. When Adam delved and Eve span
   Who was then a gentleman?
   (a slogan of the 1381 John Ball Peasants' Revolt in England)

2. Joanna the faithless, the betrayer: Joanna who mocked him whispered about him behind his back, trapped and tortured him. Joanna Eve.
   (Fay Weldon, *The Cloning of Joanna May*, 1989)

3. The fresh hill air had exhilarated my mind, and the aromatic scent of the evening gave the last touch of intoxication. Whatever serpent might lurk in it, it was a veritable Eden I had come to.
   (John Buchan, *Prester John*, 1910)

4. I do not actually remember the curtains of my room being touched by the summer wind although

---

⑯ **Eve** in Hebrew sounds like the Hebrew for *life-giver* and resembles the word for *living*.

I am sure they were; whenever I try to bring to mind this detail of the afternoon sensations it disappears, and I have knowledge of the image only as one who has swallowed some fruit of the Tree of Knowledge—its memory is usurped by the window of Mrs Van der Merwe's house and by the curtains disturbed, in the rainy season, by a trifling wind, unreasonably meaning a storm.

(Muriel Spark, "The Curtain Blows by the Breeze" in *Collected Stories*, 1961)

C. The Bible and Arts

1. The Sistine Chapel Ceiling paintings, 1508—1512, Michelangelo
   · *Fall and expulsion from the Garden of Eden*
2. *Adam and Eve*, Hans Grien Baldung (c. 1484—1545)
3. *The Creation*, oratorio composed by Franz Joseph Haydn (1732—1809)

V SOURCES FOR REFERENCE

1. (2003). *Testament: The Bible in Animation — Creation & the Flood*. (TV series)
2. (2006). *The Forbidden Book: The History of the English Bible*. (New Liberty Videos)
3. Sarna, H. (1966). *Understanding Genesis*. New York: Jewish Theological Seminary.
4. Schippe, C. & C. Stetson. (2005). *The Bible and Its Influence*. Front Royal, VA: BLP Publishing.

2. FROM THE GARDEN TO THE TOWER

I POINTS OF DEPARTURE

Genesis 4—11 show the consequences of the fall of Man that happened in the Garden of Eden and, like the first three chapters, take a big view of human society. Beginning at Chapter 12, lens is trained on a particular family — that of Abraham.

The fourth chapter recounts in a dramatic way the first murder ever committed. It is fratricide — the murder of a brother by a brother, thus introducing the archetypical narrative pattern of sibling rivalry that echoes throughout the Bible. The crime was committed simply because God favored Abel's sacrifice over his elder brother Cain's. Cain, fresh from the crime scene, responded to God's demand for Abel's whereabouts with the now famous rhetorical question, "Am I my brother's keeper?" According to the Bible, humans are responsible for one another and punished for evading that responsibility. This is what happened to Cain, but the punishment of him was mingled with mercy. So it can be said that the "mark of Cain" is not just a stigma of shame as popularly interpreted. Rather, it is a sign of protection. In fact, though a wanderer, Cain through his children became the grand avatar of farming, husbandry, metalworking, music, and the arts. And after the birth of his youngest son, Seth, God's name for the first time becomes "YHWH," usually translated as "The Lord God."

The story of Noah narrated in Chapters 6—9 of Genesis has been one of all-time children's favorites. Because of the increasing wickedness of man, God decided to wipe the race from the surface of the earth with a huge flood but intended to spare the family of Noah for his goodness of character. Noah was told to build an ark to survive the coming flood. In the ark in which the family huddled were also pairs (the P source) of other living species (or seven pairs of clean animals and two pairs of unclean animals, *Gen. 7:2—3*, the J source). After surviving the deluge, which was recorded universally in many other traditions, Noah emerged to offer sacrifice to God and to receive the promise confirmed by the sign of the rainbow that there would never be a similar cosmic catastrophe again. Noah also received the covenant with laws to apply to the whole future human race. The story of Noah has been a hero story up to this point — the story of an exemplary character whom God chose for extraordinary service. Then there is Noah's naked drunkenness in his tent that deheroizes him. The moral judgment that Noah pronounces on his three sons on the occasion of his waking up reaches its outworking in the genealogies of Chapter 10, which implies the unity and interrelatedness of all human beings only to be disrupted through the collapse of the Tower of Babel.

On the surface of it, the story of the Tower of Babel in Chapter 11 is etiological, explaining the diversity of human languages, dispersion of the human race over the earth, and of lesser but immediate importance, the ziggurats — a sort of stepped pyramids still dotting the landscape of

Mesopotamia. The Tower of Babel actually sketches a picture of utopian planning, symbolizing the human urge for fame and permanence, human self-reliance and aspiration, excitement about technology (the modern equivalent of skyscrapers) as the thing that will bring about the good life. So the key to interpreting the story is to ascertain whether God thinks the great architectural experiment would be bad rather than good for the human race.

II SELECTED READINGS

Cain and Abel

Genesis 4

Cain and Abel, Pietro Novelli
(1603—1647)

¹ And Adam knew① Eve his wife; and she conceived, and bare② Cain③, and said, "I have gotten a man from the LORD." ² And she again bare his brother Abel④. And Abel was a keeper of sheep, but Cain was a tiller of the ground. ³ And in process of time it came to pass, that Cain brought of the fruit of the ground an offering unto the LORD. ⁴ And Abel, he also brought of the firstlings of his flock and of the fat thereof. And the LORD had respect unto Abel and to his offering: ⁵ But unto Cain and to his offering he had not respect. And Cain was very wroth, and his countenance fell. ⁶ And the LORD said unto Cain, "Why art thou wroth? And why is thy countenance fallen? ⁷ If thou doest well, shalt thou not be accepted? And if thou doest not well, sin lieth at the door. And unto thee⑤ shall be his desire, and thou shalt rule over him."
⁸ And Cain talked with Abel his brother: and it came to pass, when they were in the field, that Cain rose up against Abel his brother, and slew him.
⁹ And the LORD said unto Cain, "Where is Abel thy brother?" And he said, "I know not: Am I my brother's keeper?" ¹⁰ And he said, "What hast thou done? The voice of thy brother's blood crieth unto me from the ground. ¹¹ And now art thou cursed from the earth, which hath opened her mouth to receive thy brother's blood from thy hand; ¹² When thou tillest the ground, it shall not henceforth yield unto thee her strength; a fugitive and a vagabond shalt thou be in the earth." ¹³ And Cain said unto the LORD, "My punishment is greater than I can bear. ¹⁴ Behold, thou hast driven me out this day from the face of the earth; and from thy face shall I be hid; and I shall be a fugitive and a vagabond in the earth; and it shall come to pass, that every one that findeth me shall slay me." ¹⁵ And the LORD said unto him, "Therefore whosoever slayeth Cain, vengeance shall be taken on him sevenfold." And the LORD set a mark upon Cain, lest any finding him should kill him. ¹⁶ And Cain went out from the presence of the LORD, and dwelt in the land of Nod⑥, on the east of Eden.
¹⁷ And Cain knew his wife; and she conceived, and bare Enoch: and he builded a city, and called the name of the city, after the name of his son, Enoch. ¹⁸ And unto Enoch was born Irad: and Irad begat Mehujael: and Mehujael begat Methusael: and Methusael begat Lamech. ¹⁹ And Lamech took unto him two wives: the name of

---

① **knew** *archaic* have sexual intercourse with → *know in the biblical sense*.
② **bare** *archaic* past tense of *bear*.
③ **Cain** (/kein/, 该隐) sounds like the Hebrew for *brought forth* or *acquired*.
④ **Abel** /ˈeibəl/, 亚伯.
⑤ **thee** See PRONOUNS & VERBS IN *KING JAMES BIBLE*.
⑥ **Nod** (/nɔd/, 挪得) means *wandering*.

the one was Adah, and the name of the other Zillah.

The Bible in Literature: *Dante's Divine Comedy*

In *The Divine Comedy*(神曲), one of the great epics of Western literature, Dante Alighieri (1265—1321) consigned those who have committed the worst crime of murdering their family members to the ninth circle of "lower hell," called "Caina," where they are placed in ice up to their necks with their heads bent forward.

^{20} And Adah bare Jabal: he was the father of such as dwell in tents, and of such as have cattle. ^{21} And his brother's name was Jubal: he was the father of all such as handle the harp and organ. ^{22} And Zillah, she also bare Tubalcain, an instructor of every artificer in brass and iron: and the sister of Tubalcain was Naamah.

^{23} And Lamech said unto his wives, Adah and Zillah,

"Hear my voice; ye wives of Lamech, hearken⑦ unto my speech:

for I have slain a man to my wounding⑧,

and a young man to my hurt.

^{24} If Cain shall be avenged sevenfold,

truly Lamech seventy and sevenfold."

^{25} And Adam knew his wife again; and she bare a son, and called his name Seth⑨: "For God," said she, "hath appointed me another seed instead of Abel, whom Cain slew." ^{26} And to Seth, to him also there was born a son; and he called his name Enos: then began men to call upon the name of the LORD.

Noah and the Flood

Genesis 6

^{1} And it came to pass, when men began to multiply on the face of the earth, and daughters were born unto them, ^{2} That the sons of God saw the daughters of men that they were fair; and they took them wives of all which they chose.

^{3} And the LORD said, "My spirit shall not always strive with man, for that he also is flesh: yet his days shall be an hundred and twenty years." ^{4} There were giants in the earth in those days; and also after that, when the sons of God came in unto the daughters of men, and they bare children to them, the same became mighty men which were of old, men of renown.

^{5} And GOD saw that the wickedness of man was great in the earth, and that every imagination of the thoughts of his heart was only evil continually. ^{6} And it repented the LORD that he had made man on the earth, and it grieved him at his heart. ^{7} And the LORD said, "I will destroy man whom I have created from the face of the earth; both man, and beast, and the creeping thing, and the fowls of the air; for it repenteth me that I have made them." ^{8} But Noah⑩ found grace in the eyes of the LORD.

^{9} These are the generations of Noah: Noah was a just man and perfect in his generations, and Noah

---

⑦ **hearken** *archaic* listen to; hear.
⑧ **I have slain a man to my wounding** I have killed a man for wounding me.
⑨ **Seth** (/seθ/, 塞特) probably means *he appointed*.
⑩ **Noah** (/'nəuə/, 诺亚) sounds like the Hebrew for *comfort*. He was the son of Lamech (4:18).

walked with God. ¹⁰ And Noah begat three sons, Shem, Ham, and Japheth⑪.

¹¹ The earth also was corrupt before God, and the earth was filled with violence. ¹² And God looked upon the earth, and, behold, it was corrupt; for all flesh had corrupted his way upon the earth. ¹³ And God said unto Noah, " The end of all flesh is come before me; for the earth is filled with violence through them; and, behold, I will destroy them with the earth. ¹⁴ Make thee an ark of gopher wood; rooms shalt thou make in the ark, and shalt pitch it within and without with pitch.¹⁵ And this is the fashion which thou shalt make it of: The length of the ark shall be 300 cubits, the breadth of it 50 cubits, and the height of it 30 cubits⑫.

Noah's Ark, Edward Hicks(1780—1849)

¹⁶ A window shalt thou make to the ark, and in a cubit shalt thou finish it above; and the door of the ark shalt thou set in the side thereof; with lower, second, and third stories shalt thou make it.¹⁷ And, behold, I, even I, do bring a flood of waters upon the earth, to destroy all flesh, wherein is the breath of life, from under heaven; and every thing that is in the earth shall die. ¹⁸ But with thee will I establish my covenant; and thou shalt come into the ark, thou, and thy sons, and thy wife, and thy sons' wives with thee. ¹⁹ And of every living thing of all flesh, two of every sort shalt thou bring into the ark, to keep them alive with thee; they shall be male and female. ²⁰ Of fowls after their kind, and of cattle after their kind, of every creeping thing of the earth after his kind, two of every sort shall come unto thee, to keep them alive.²¹ And take thou unto thee of all food that is eaten, and thou shalt gather it to thee; and it shall be for food for thee, and for them."

²² Thus did Noah; according to all that God commanded him, so did he.

Genesis 7

¹ And the LORD said unto Noah, " Come thou and all thy house into the ark; for thee have I seen righteous before me in this generation. ² Of every clean beast thou shalt take to thee by sevens, the male and his female: and of beasts that are not clean by two, the male and his female. ³ Of fowls also of the air by sevens, the male and the female; to keep seed alive upon the face of all the earth. ⁴ For yet seven days⑬, and I will cause it to rain upon the earth forty days and forty nights; and every living substance that I have made will I destroy from off the face of the earth." ⁵ And Noah did according unto all that the LORD commanded him.

⁶ And Noah was six hundred years old when the flood of waters was upon the earth. ⁷ And Noah went in, and his sons, and his wife, and his sons' wives with him, into the ark, because of the waters of the flood. ⁸ Of clean beasts, and of beasts that are not clean, and of fowls, and of every thing that creepeth upon the earth.⁹ There went in two and two unto Noah into the ark, the male and the female, as God had commanded Noah. ¹⁰ And it came to pass after seven days, that the waters of the flood were upon the earth, ¹¹ In the six hundredth year of Noah's life, in the second month, the seventeenth day of the month, the same day were all the fountains of the great deep broken up, and the windows of heaven were opened. ¹² And the rain was upon the earth forty days and forty nights. ¹³ In the selfsame day entered Noah, and Shem, and Ham, and Japheth, the sons of Noah, and Noah's wife, and the three wives of his sons with them, into the ark; ¹⁴ They, and every beast after his kind, and all the cattle after their kind, and every creeping thing that creepeth upon the earth after his kind, and every fowl after his kind, every bird of every sort. ¹⁵ And they went in unto Noah into the ark, two and two of all flesh, wherein is the breath of life. ¹⁶ And they that went in, went in male and

---

⑪ **Shem** /ʃem/, 闪。**Ham** /hæm/, 含。**Japheth** /ˈdʒeifiθ/, 雅弗。

⑫ 300 cubits ≈ 140 metres, 50 cubits ≈ 23 metres, 30 cubits ≈ 13.5 metres. A cubit was an ancient unit of linear measure, originally equal to the length of the forearm from the tip of the middle finger to the elbow, or about 17 to 22 inches (43 to 56 centimeters).

⑬ **For yet seven days** seven days from now.

female of all flesh, as God had commanded him: and the LORD shut him in.

¹⁷ And the flood was forty days upon the earth; and the waters increased, and bare up the ark, and it was lift up above the earth. ¹⁸ And the waters prevailed, and were increased greatly upon the earth; and the ark went upon the face of the waters. ¹⁹ And the waters prevailed exceedingly upon the earth; and all the high hills, that were under the whole heaven, were covered. ²⁰ Fifteen cubits⑭ upward did the waters prevail; and the mountains were covered.

²¹ And all flesh died that moved upon the earth, both of fowl, and of cattle, and of beast, and of every creeping thing that creepeth upon the earth, and every man:²² All in whose nostrils was the breath of life, of all that was in the dry land, died. ²³ And every living substance was destroyed which was upon the face of the ground, both man, and cattle, and the creeping things, and the fowl of the heaven; and they were destroyed from the earth: and Noah only remained alive, and they that were with him in the ark. ²⁴ And the waters prevailed upon the earth an hundred and fifty days.

Cultural Connections: *Ships Named "Noah"*

It has been ship-builders' unfulfilled dream to design and construct a vessel as colossal and virtually unsinkable as Noah's Ark. Naming their ships as such is at least an expression of the spirit of that undaunted and soaring ambition of human beings. In fact, in Britain's navy history, there used to be five ships that borne the names of Ark Royal (1587), HMS Royal Ark (1914, 1937, 1950 and 1981).

1587　　　1914　　　1937　　　1950　　　1981

Genesis 8

¹ And God remembered Noah, and every living thing, and all the cattle that was with him in the ark; and God made a wind to pass over the earth, and the waters assuaged; ² The fountains also of the deep and the windows of heaven were stopped, and the rain from heaven was restrained; ³ And the waters returned from off the earth continually: and after the end of the hundred and fifty days the waters were abated.⁴ And the ark rested in the seventh month, on the seventeenth day of the month, upon the mountains of Ararat⑮. ⁵ And the waters decreased continually until the tenth month: in the tenth month, on the first day of the month, were the tops of the mountains seen.

⁶ And it came to pass at the end of forty days, that Noah opened the window of the ark which he had made: ⁷ And he sent forth a raven, which went forth to and fro, until the waters were dried up from off the earth. ⁸ Also he sent forth a dove from him, to see if the waters were abated from off the face of the ground; ⁹ But the dove found no rest for the sole of her foot, and she returned unto him into the ark, for the waters were on the face of the whole earth: then he put forth his hand, and took her, and pulled her in unto him into the ark. ¹⁰ And he stayed yet other seven days; and again he sent forth the dove out of the ark; ¹¹ And the dove came in to him in the evening; and, lo, in her mouth was an olive leaf plucked off: so Noah knew that the

---

⑭　**Fifteen cubits** ≈ 6.9 metres.
⑮　**Ararat** (/ˈærəˌræt/, 亚拉腊山) a massif in easternmost Turkey near the Iranian border with a height of about 5,168 m.

waters were abated from off the earth. ¹² And he stayed yet other seven days; and sent forth the dove; which returned not again unto him any more.

¹³ And it came to pass in the six hundredth and first year, in the first month, the first day of the month, the waters were dried up from off the earth: and Noah removed the covering of the ark, and looked, and, behold, the face of the ground was dry. ¹⁴ And in the second month, on the seven and twentieth day of the month, was the earth dried. ¹⁵ And God spake unto Noah, saying,

Dove Back to the Ark, a modern graphic

¹⁶ " Go forth of the ark, thou, and thy wife, and thy sons, and thy sons' wives with thee. ¹⁷ Bring forth with thee every living thing that is with thee, of all flesh, both of fowl, and of cattle, and of every creeping thing that creepeth upon the earth; that they may breed abundantly in the earth, and be fruitful, and multiply upon the earth." ¹⁸ And Noah went forth, and his sons, and his wife, and his sons' wives with him: ¹⁹ Every beast, every creeping thing, and every fowl, and whatsoever creepeth upon the earth, after their kinds, went forth out of the ark.

²⁰ And Noah builded an altar unto the LORD; and took of every clean beast, and of every clean fowl, and offered burnt offerings on the altar. ²¹ And the LORD smelled a sweet savour; and the LORD said in his heart, " I will not again curse the ground any more for man's sake; for the imagination of man's heart is evil from his youth; neither will I again smite any more every thing living, as I have done. ²² While the earth remaineth, seedtime and harvest, and cold and heat, and summer and winter, and day and night shall not cease."

God's Covenant with Noah

Genesis 9

¹ And God blessed Noah and his sons, and said unto them, " Be fruitful, and multiply, and replenish the earth. ² And the fear of you and the dread of you shall be upon every beast of the earth, and upon every fowl of the air, upon all that moveth upon the earth, and upon all the fishes of the sea; into your hand are they delivered. ³ Every moving thing that liveth shall be meat for you; even as the green herb have I given you all things.

⁴ But flesh with the life thereof, which is the blood thereof, shall ye not eat. ⁵ And surely your blood of your lives will I require; at the hand of every beast will I require it, and at the hand of man; at the hand of every man's brother will I require the life of man.

⁶ Whoso sheddeth man's blood,
by man shall his blood be shed:
for in the image of God made he man.

⁷ And you, be ye fruitful, and multiply; bring forth abundantly in the earth, and multiply therein."

⁸ And God spake unto Noah, and to his sons with him, saying, ⁹ " And I, behold, I establish my covenant with you, and with your seed after you; ¹⁰ And with every living creature that is with you, of the fowl, of the cattle, and of every beast of the earth with you; from all that go out of the ark, to every beast of the earth. ¹¹ And I will establish my covenant with you; neither shall all flesh be cut off any more by the waters of a flood; neither shall there any more be a flood to destroy the earth."

¹² And God said, " This is the token of the covenant which I make between me and you and every living creature that is with you, for perpetual generations: ¹³ I do set my bow in the cloud, and it shall be for a token of a covenant between me and the earth. ¹⁴ And it shall come to pass, when I bring a cloud over the earth, that the bow shall be seen in the cloud: ¹⁵ And I will remember my covenant, which is between me and you and every living creature of all flesh; and the waters shall no more become a flood to destroy all flesh. ¹⁶ And the bow shall be in the cloud; and I will look upon it, that I may remember the everlasting covenant between God and

every living creature of all flesh that is upon the earth."

¹⁷ And God said unto Noah, "This is the token of the covenant, which I have established between me and all flesh that is upon the earth."

The Sons of Noah

¹⁸ And the sons of Noah, that went forth of the ark, were Shem, and Ham, and Japheth: and Ham is the father of Canaan⑯. ¹⁹ These are the three sons of Noah: and of them was the whole earth overspread.

Noah's Drunkenness

²⁰ And Noah began to be an husbandman, and he planted a vineyard: ²¹ And he drank of the wine, and was drunken; and he was uncovered within his tent. ²² And Ham, the father of Canaan, saw the nakedness of his father, and told his two brethren without. ²³ And Shem and Japheth took a garment, and laid it upon both their shoulders, and went backward, and covered the nakedness of their father; and their faces were backward, and they saw not their father's nakedness.

Drunkenness of Noah, the Sistine Chapel Ceiling paintings, Michelangelo (1475—1564)

²⁴ And Noah awoke from his wine, and knew what his younger son had done unto him. ²⁵ And he said,
"Cursed be Canaan;
a servant of servants shall he be unto his brethren."
²⁶ And he said,
"Blessed be the LORD God of Shem;
and Canaan shall be his servant.
²⁷ God shall enlarge Japheth,
and he shall dwell in the tents of Shem;
and Canaan shall be his servant."
²⁸ And Noah lived after the flood three hundred and fifty years. ²⁹ And all the days of Noah were nine hundred and fifty years: and he died.

Cultural Connections: *Slavery*

The curse of Ham's sons for their father's having seen Noah's drunken nakedness was sometimes used by 19th-century Christians to argue for the Bible's condonement of African slavery, for according to Jewish tradition (incorporated into Christian thought), Ham and his children were the ancestors of Africans, but this has not been borne out by the Bible. As so often happens, the Bible has been used to justify both sides in many public controversies, local and international, speaking eloquently for William Shakespeare's witticism that "[t]he devil can cite Scripture for his own purpose." (*The Merchant of Venice*, Act 1, scene iii: 97)

---

⑯ **Canaan** (/ˈkeɪnən/, 迦南) an ancient region between the Jordan River and the Mediterranean Sea.

The Tower of Babel

Genesis 11

¹ And the whole earth was of one language, and of one speech. ² And it came to pass, as they journeyed from the east, that they found a plain in the land of Shinar; and they dwelt there.

³ And they said one to another, "Go to, let us make brick, and burn them throughly." And they had brick for stone, and slime had they for morter. ⁴ And they said, "Go to, let us build us a city and a tower, whose top may reach unto heaven; and let us make us a name, lest we be scattered abroad upon the face of the whole earth."

⁵ And the LORD came down to see the city and the tower, which the children of men builded. ⁶ And the LORD said, "Behold, the people is one, and they have all one language; and this they begin to do: and now nothing will be restrained from them, which they have imagined to do. ⁷ Go to, let us go down, and there confound their language, that they may not understand one another's speech."

The Tower of Babel, Pieter Bruegel the Elder (1525—1569)

⁸ So the LORD scattered them abroad from thence upon the face of all the earth: and they left off to build the city. ⁹ Therefore is the name of it called Babel⑰; because the LORD did there confound the language of all the earth: and from thence did the LORD scatter them abroad upon the face of all the earth.

From Shem to Abram

¹⁰ These are the generations of Shem: Shem was an hundred years old, and begat Arphaxad two years after the flood: ¹¹ And Shem lived after he begat Arphaxad five hundred years, and begat sons and daughters.

¹² And Arphaxad lived five and thirty years, and begat Salah: ¹³ And Arphaxad lived after he begat Salah four hundred and three years, and begat sons and daughters. ¹⁴ And Salah lived thirty years, and begat Eber: ¹⁵ And Salah lived after he begat Eber four hundred and three years, and begat sons and daughters.

¹⁶ And Eber lived four and thirty years, and begat Peleg: ¹⁷ And Eber lived after he begat Peleg four hundred and thirty years, and begat sons and daughters.

¹⁸ And Peleg lived thirty years, and begat Reu: ¹⁹ And Peleg lived after he begat Reu two hundred and nine years, and begat sons and daughters.

²⁰ And Reu lived two and thirty years, and begat Serug: ²¹ And Reu lived after he begat Serug two hundred and seven years, and begat sons and daughters.

²² And Serug lived thirty years, and begat Nahor: ²³ And Serug lived after he begat Nahor two hundred years, and begat sons and daughters.

²⁴ And Nahor lived nine and twenty years, and begat Terah: ²⁵ And Nahor lived after he begat Terah an hundred and nineteen years, and begat sons and daughters.

²⁶ And Terah lived seventy years, and begat Abram, Nahor, and Haran.

²⁷ Now these are the generations of Terah: Terah begat Abram, Nahor, and Haran; and Haran begat Lot. ²⁸ And Haran died before his father Terah in the land of his nativity, in Ur⑱ of the Chaldees. ²⁹ And Abram and Nahor took them wives: the name of Abram's wife was Sarai; and the name of Nahor's wife, Milcah, the daughter of Haran, the father of Milcah, and the father of Iscah. ³⁰ But Sarai was barren; she had no child.

---

⑰ **Babel** (/ˈbeɪbəl/, 巴别塔) sounds like the Hebrew for *confused*.
⑱ **Ur** (/ˈʊər/, 吾珥) one of the oldest cities in Mesopotamia in what is now southeast Iraq.

³¹ *And Terah took Abram his son, and Lot the son of Haran his son's son, and Sarai his daughter in law, his son Abram's wife; and they went forth with them from Ur of the Chaldees, to go into the land of Canaan; and they came unto Haran, and dwelt there.* ³² *And the days of Terah were two hundred and five years: and Terah died in Haran.*

III FOOD FOR THOUGHT

1. What is the motif of Cain's fratricide?
2. Why did Cain ask God, "Am I my brother's keeper?"
3. It is said that the Noah story is an interweaving of two stories by two different writers. What inconsistencies can you find to support this assumption?
4. Why did God need to confuse the languages and scatter the people?
5. Is there a common line that ties the Tower of Babel to the stories of Adam and Eve, Cain and Abel, and Noah?

IV BIBLICAL RELEVANCE

A. Biblical Terms in Everyday English
1. the brand/mark of Cain (4:15): _____
2. land of nod (4:16): _____
3. after me the deluge: _____
4. Noah's ark: _____
5. the Tower of Babel: _____

B. Biblical References in Literature
1. "If I had only got her with me — if I only had!" he said. "Hard work would be nothing to me then! But that was not to be. I — Cain — go alone as I deserve — an outcast and a vagabond."
   (Thomas Hardy, *The Mayor of Casterbridge*, 1886)
2. He had research assistants, in fluctuating numbers, whom he dispatched like Noah's doves and ravens into the libraries of the world, clutching numbered slips of paper, like cloakroom tickets or luncheon vouchers, each containing a query, a half-line of possible quotation, a proper name to be located.
   (A. S. Byatt, *Possession*, 1990)
3. And it would balance her table, thought Mair, although that was hardly likely to have been a consideration. She despised the Noah's Ark convention which decreed that a superfluous man, however unattractive or stupid, was acceptable; a superfluous woman, however witty and well-informed, a social embarrassment.
   (P. D. James, *Devices and Desires*, 1989)
4. He woke to a babel the next morning, and when he went down to the hall found the sisters getting their children ready for school.
   (V. S. Naipaul, *A House for Mr Biswas*, 1961)
5. The crew's mess on board the Kronos is a Tower of Babel of English, French, Filipino, Danish, and German.
   (Peter Høeg, *Miss Smilla's Feeling for Snow*, 1992)

C. The Bible and Arts
1. The Sistine Chapel Ceiling paintings, 1508—1512, Michelangelo
    · *The Deluge* · *Sacrifice of Noah* · *Drunkenness of Noah*
2. *The Tower of Babel*, Pieter Bruegel the Elder (1525—1569)
3. *Cain and Abel*, Pietro Novelli (1603—1647)
4. *Noah's Ark*, Edward Hicks (1780—1849)

V SOURCES FOR REFERENCE

1. (1999). *Noah's Ark*, a TV Film directed by John Irvin and starring Jon Voight and Mary Steenburgen.
2. Levine, J. (1999). "Pomp and Circumstance, Marches" in *Fantasia* 2000. (Animated film by Walt Disney based on the story of Noah's Ark).
3. Ryken, L. & P. G. Ryken. (2007). *The Literary Study Bible*. Wheaton, Illinois: Crossway Bibles.
4. Keller, W. (transl.) (1974). *The Bible as History*. New York: Bantam Books.

3. ABRAHAM, THE PROGENITOR

I. POINTS OF DEPARTURE

At Chapter 12, Genesis changes dramatically by leaving the big picture of world history for a minute focus on one lonely family, a childless nomad, Abram (later called Abraham, symbolizing his complete change of heart towards his God). The Abram saga begins with a call from God for Abram and Sarai to go from Ur, a great center of ancient Mesopotamian civilization, to a land where Abram would be made patriarch of a great nation.

On this journey of faith, Abram and Sarai (later renamed Sarah) are portrayed as flesh-and-blood humans, true to life, full of bad moments and good ones. During their sojourn in Egypt, Abram, for the sake of his own life, passed his beautiful wife off as his sister, though he was telling half the truth, for she was indeed his half sister. But it was not his cunning that saved him. Rather, it was God in the form of plagues that prevented Pharaoh from committing murder against him and adultery against his wife. Ironically, in the conflict between faith and expediency, the latter scores an ignominious victory in this episode. Later, the barren Sarai persuaded her husband to take Hagar, her Egyptian maid as his concubine, but when Hagar got pregnant, she had a fit of jealousy and obtained Abram's permission to drive both the mother and her baby away, providing another round of ammunition to those who are pro-slavery (See **Cultural Connections: Slavery**, in the previous chapter). Before the destruction of the wicked cities of Sodom and Gomorrah, Abraham again shows his true color through his negotiations with God for Sodom. Obviously, the heroes in Genesis are not cardboard characters of perfect virtue. Great faithfulness to God is shown side by side with human feelings and failings. Where biblical characters are judged, our familiar moral standards do not apply. The flawed humanity of these characters is one reason Genesis continues to intrigue and inspire readers throughout the world.

Sodom and Gomorrah, the two wicked cities destroyed by God, have now become synonymous with a metropolis famous for its vice and corruption. Though the derivatives "sodomy" and "sodomite" both pinpoint a particular evil of Sodom, *Ezekiel 16:49* describes the Sodomites as arrogant, overfed and unconcerned about the poor and needy. Lot and his family were the only people who survived the destruction, but his wife forgetting the angel messengers' warning looked back and turned into a pillar of salt, contributing another familiar idiom to the English language. The father-daughters incest sounds reasonably unsavory, but it was less prompted by lust than by the paramount necessity of maintaining the bloodline when the males around them had been annihilated.

The Akedah, the story of Abraham's binding of Isaac in *Genesis 22*, is of strange violence and tenderness, of a father ordered by his God to sacrifice his only son. Only at the last moment were Abraham and Isaac rescued from the approaching horror by the intervention of an angel. This story has touched a deep nerve in Jewish and Christian sensibilities. Both view it as evidence of the patriarch's unquestioning faithfulness to God, but the Jewish tradition stresses the test of Abraham's faith and the affirmation of God's mercy in releasing Abraham from the horror of human sacrifice, while the Christian tradition sees in the willingness of Abraham to sacrifice his beloved son a foreshadowing of the sacrifice of Jesus by God, his father.

II SELECTED READINGS

The Call of Abram

Genesis 12

¹ Now the LORD had said unto Abram①, "Get thee out of thy country, and from thy kindred, and from thy father's house, unto a land that I will shew② thee:
² And I will make of thee a great nation,
    and I will bless thee,
and make thy name great;
    and thou shalt be a blessing:
³ And I will bless them that bless thee,
    and curse him that curseth thee:
and in thee shall all families of the earth be blessed."
⁴ So Abram departed, as the LORD had spoken unto him; and Lot went with him: and Abram was seventy and five years old when he departed out of Haran. ⁵ And Abram took Sarai③ his wife, and Lot his brother's son, and all their substance that they had gathered, and the souls that they had gotten in Haran; and they went forth to go into the land of Canaan; and into the land of Canaan they came.
⁶ And Abram passed through the land unto the place of Sichem, unto the plain of Moreh. And the Canaanite was then in the land. ⁷ And the LORD appeared unto Abram, and said, "Unto thy seed will I give this land: and there builded he an altar unto the LORD, who appeared unto him."
⁸ And he removed from thence unto a mountain on the east of Bethel, and pitched his tent, having Bethel on the west, and Hai on the east: and there he builded an altar unto the LORD, and called upon the name of the LORD. ⁹ And Abram journeyed, going on still toward the south.

Abram in Egypt

¹⁰ And there was a famine in the land: and Abram went down into Egypt to sojourn there; for the famine was grievous in the land. ¹¹ And it came to pass, when he was come near to enter into Egypt, that he said unto Sarai his wife, "Behold now, I know that thou art a fair woman to look upon: ¹² Therefore it shall come to pass, when the Egyptians shall see thee, that they shall say, 'This is his wife:' and they will kill me, but they will save thee alive. ¹³ Say, I pray thee, thou art my sister: that it

The Fertile Crescent and the Outline
of Abraham's Migration

---

① **Abram** /ˈeibrəm/, 亚伯兰。
② **shew** *archaic* variant of *show*.
③ **Sarai** /ˈseərai/, 撒莱。

may be well with me for thy sake; and my soul shall live because of thee."

¹⁴ And it came to pass, that, when Abram was come into Egypt, the Egyptians beheld the woman that she was very fair. ¹⁵ The princes also of Pharaoh saw her, and commended her before Pharaoh: and the woman was taken into Pharaoh's house. ¹⁶ And he entreated Abram well for her sake: and he had sheep, and oxen, and he asses, and menservants, and maidservants, and she asses, and camels.

¹⁷ And the LORD plagued Pharaoh and his house with great plagues because of Sarai Abram's wife. ¹⁸ And Pharaoh called Abram, and said, "What is this that thou hast done unto me? Why didst thou not tell me that she was thy wife?

¹⁹ Why saidst thou, She is my sister? so I might have taken her to me to wife: now therefore behold thy wife, take her, and go thy way." ²⁰ And Pharaoh commanded his men concerning him: and they sent him away, and his wife, and all that he had.

God's Covenant with Abraham

Genesis 15

¹ After these things the word of the LORD came unto Abram in a vision, saying,
"Fear not, Abram:
I am thy shield,
and thy exceeding great reward."
² And Abram said, "LORD God, what wilt thou give me, seeing I go childless, and the steward of my house is this Eliezer of Damascus?" ³ And Abram said, "Behold, to me thou hast given no seed: and, lo, one born in my house is mine heir."

⁴ And, behold, the word of the LORD came unto him, saying, "This shall not be thine heir; but he that shall come forth out of thine own bowels shall be thine heir." ⁵ And he brought him forth abroad, and said, "Look now toward heaven, and tell the stars, if thou be able to number them." And he said unto him, "So shall thy seed be."

⁶ And he believed in the LORD; and he counted it to him for righteousness.

⁷ And he said unto him, "I am the LORD that brought thee out of Ur of the Chaldees, to give thee this land to inherit it."

⁸ And he said, "LORD God, whereby shall I know that I shall inherit it?"

⁹ And he said unto him, "Take me an heifer of three years old, and a she goat of three years old, and a ram of three years old, and a turtledove, and a young pigeon."

¹⁰ And he took unto him all these, and divided them in the midst, and laid each piece one against another: but the birds divided he not. ¹¹ And when the fowls came down upon the carcasses, Abram drove them away.

¹² And when the sun was going down, a deep sleep fell upon Abram; and, lo, an horror of great darkness fell upon him. ¹³ And he said unto Abram, "Know of a surety④ that thy seed shall be a stranger in a land that is not their's, and shall serve them; and they shall afflict them four hundred years; ¹⁴ And also that nation, whom they shall serve, will I judge: and afterward shall they come out with great substance. ¹⁵ And thou shalt go to thy fathers in peace; thou shalt be buried in a good old age. ¹⁶ But in the fourth generation they shall come hither again: for the iniquity of the Amorites is not yet full."

¹⁷ And it came to pass, that, when the sun went down, and it was dark, behold a smoking furnace, and a burning lamp that passed between those pieces. ¹⁸ In the same day the LORD made a covenant with Abram, saying, "Unto thy seed have I given this land, from the river of Egypt unto the great river, the river Euphrates: ¹⁹ The Kenites, and the Kenizzites, and the Kadmonites, ²⁰ And the Hittites, and the Perizzites, and the Rephaims, ²¹ And the Amorites, and the Canaanites, and the Girgashites, and the Jebusites."

---

④ **of a surety** for certain.

Hagar and Ishmael

Genesis 16

¹ Now Sarai Abram's wife bare him no children: and she had an handmaid, an Egyptian, whose name was Hagar⑤. ² And Sarai said unto Abram, "Behold now, the LORD hath restrained me from bearing: I pray thee, go in unto my maid; it may be that I may obtain children by her."

And Abram hearkened to the voice of Sarai. ³ And Sarai Abram's wife took Hagar her maid the Egyptian, after Abram had dwelt ten years in the land of Canaan, and gave her to her husband Abram to be his wife. ⁴ And he went in unto Hagar, and she conceived: and when she saw that she had conceived, her mistress was despised in her eyes. ⁵ And Sarai said unto Abram, "My wrong be upon thee: I have given my maid into thy bosom; and when she saw that she had conceived, I was despised in her eyes: the LORD judge between me and thee."

⁶ But Abram said unto Sarai, "Behold, thy maid is in thy hand; do to her as it pleaseth thee." And when Sarai dealt hardly with her, she fled from her face.

⁷ And the angel of the LORD found her by a fountain of water in the wilderness, by the fountain in the way to Shur. ⁸ And he said, "Hagar, Sarai's maid, whence camest thou? And whither wilt thou go?"

And she said, "I flee from the face of my mistress Sarai."

⁹ And the angel of the LORD said unto her, "Return to thy mistress, and submit thyself under her hands." ¹⁰ And the angel of the LORD said unto her, "I will multiply thy seed exceedingly, that it shall not be numbered for multitude."

¹¹ And the angel of the LORD said unto her,
"Behold, thou art with child,
and shalt bear a son,
and shalt call his name Ishmael⑥;
because the LORD hath heard thy affliction.
¹² And he will be a wild man;
his hand will be against every man,
and every man's hand against him;

Hagar Leaves the Home of Abraham, 1615—1617, Peter Paul Rubens

and he shall dwell in the presence of all his brethren."

¹³ And she called the name of the LORD that spake unto her, "Thou God seest me," for she said, "Have I also here looked after him that seeth me?" ¹⁴ Wherefore the well was called Beerlahairoi⑦; behold, it is between Kadesh and Bered.

¹⁵ And Hagar bare Abram a son: and Abram called his son's name, which Hagar bare, Ishmael. ¹⁶ And Abram was fourscore and six years old, when Hagar bare Ishmael to Abram.

The Covenant of Circumcision

Genesis 17

¹ And when Abram was ninety years old and nine, the LORD appeared to Abram, and said unto him, "I am the Almighty God; walk before me, and be thou perfect. ² And I will make my covenant between me and thee, and will multiply thee exceedingly."

---

⑤ **Hagar** /ˈheigɑː/, 夏甲。
⑥ **Ishmael** (/ˈiʃmeiəl/, 以实玛利) means *God hears*.
⑦ **Beerlahairoi** means *the well of the Living One who sees me*.

³ And Abram fell on his face: and God talked with him, saying, ⁴ "As for me, behold, my covenant is with thee, and thou shalt be a father of many nations.

⁵ Neither shall thy name any more be called Abram⑧, but thy name shall be Abraham⑨; for a father of many nations have I made thee. ⁶ And I will make thee exceeding fruitful, and I will make nations of thee, and kings shall come out of thee. ⁷ And I will establish my covenant between me and thee and thy seed after thee in their generations for an everlasting covenant, to be a God unto thee, and to thy seed after thee. ⁸ And I will give unto thee, and to thy seed after thee, the land wherein thou art a stranger, all the land of Canaan, for an everlasting possession; and I will be their God."

⁹ And God said unto Abraham, "Thou shalt keep my covenant therefore, thou, and thy seed after thee in their generations. ¹⁰ This is my covenant, which ye shall keep, between me and you and thy seed after thee; Every man child among you shall be circumcised. ¹¹ And ye shall circumcise the flesh of your foreskin; and it shall be a token of the covenant betwixt me and you. ¹² And he that is eight days old shall be circumcised among you, every man child in your generations, he that is born in the house, or bought with money of any stranger, which is not of thy seed. ¹³ He that is born in thy house, and he that is bought with thy money, must needs be circumcised: and my covenant shall be in your flesh for an everlasting covenant. ¹⁴ And the uncircumcised man child whose flesh of his foreskin is not circumcised, that soul shall be cut off from his people; he hath broken my covenant."

¹⁵ And God said unto Abraham, "As for Sarai thy wife, thou shalt not call her name Sarai, but Sarah⑩ shall her name be. ¹⁶ And I will bless her, and give thee a son also of her: yea, I will bless her, and she shall be a mother of nations; kings of people shall be of her."

¹⁷ Then Abraham fell upon his face, and laughed, and said in his heart, "Shall a child be born unto him that is an hundred years old? And shall Sarah, that is ninety years old, bear?" ¹⁸ And Abraham said unto God, "O that Ishmael might live before thee!"

¹⁹ And God said, "Sarah thy wife shall bear thee a son indeed; and thou shalt call his name Isaac: and I will establish my covenant with him for an everlasting covenant, and with his seed after him. ²⁰ And as for Ishmael, I have heard thee: Behold, I have blessed him, and will make him fruitful, and will multiply him exceedingly; twelve princes shall he beget, and I will make him a great nation. ²¹ But my covenant will I establish with Isaac, which Sarah shall bear unto thee at this set time in the next year." ²² And he left off talking with him, and God went up from Abraham.

²³ And Abraham took Ishmael his son, and all that were born in his house, and all that were bought with his money, every male among the men of Abraham's house; and circumcised the flesh of their foreskin in the selfsame day, as God had said unto him. ²⁴ And Abraham was ninety years old and nine, when he was circumcised in the flesh of his foreskin. ²⁵ And Ishmael his son was thirteen years old, when he was circumcised in the flesh of his foreskin. ²⁶ In the selfsame day was Abraham circumcised, and Ishmael his son. ²⁷ And all the men of his house, born in the house, and bought with money of the stranger, were circumcised with him.

Genesis 18
Entertaining Angels Unawares⑪

¹ And the LORD appeared unto him in the plains of Mamre: and he sat in the tent door in the heat of the day; ² And he lift up his eyes and looked, and, lo, three men stood by him: and when he saw them, he ran to meet them from the tent door, and bowed himself toward the ground.

³ And said, "My Lord, if now I have found favour in thy sight, pass not away, I pray thee, from thy

---

⑧ **Abram** means *exalted father*.
⑨ **Abraham** means *father of a multitude*.
⑩ **Sarah** means *princess*.
⑪ Hospitality was well treasured in ancient times largely as a result of nomadic conditions. Abraham's hospitality here and that of Lot's in *Genesis 19* are frequently alluded to, whose significance is summarized in *Hebrews 13:2*: "Be not forgetful to entertain strangers: for thereby some have entertained angels unawares."

servant: ⁴ *Let a little water, I pray you, be fetched, and wash your feet, and rest yourselves under the tree:* ⁵ *And I will fetch a morsel of bread, and comfort ye your hearts; after that ye shall pass on: for therefore are ye come to your servant."*

And they said, *"So do, as thou hast said."*

⁶ *And Abraham hastened into the tent unto Sarah, and said, "Make ready quickly three measures of fine meal, knead it, and make cakes upon the hearth."*

⁷ *And Abraham ran unto the herd, and fetcht a calf tender and good, and gave it unto a young man; and he hasted to dress it.* ⁸ *And he took butter, and milk, and the calf which he had dressed, and set it before them; and he stood by them under the tree, and they did eat.*

⁹ *And they said unto him, "Where is Sarah thy wife?"*

And he said, *"Behold, in the tent."*

¹⁰ *And he said, "I will certainly return unto thee according to the time of life; and, lo, Sarah thy wife shall have a son."*

And Sarah heard it in the tent door, which was behind him. ¹¹ *Now Abraham and Sarah were old and well stricken in age; and it ceased to be with Sarah after the manner of women⑫.* ¹² *Therefore Sarah laughed within herself, saying, "After I am waxed old shall I have pleasure, my lord being old also?"*

¹³ *And the LORD said unto Abraham, "Wherefore did Sarah laugh, saying, 'Shall I of a surety bear a child, which am old?'* ¹⁴ *Is any thing too hard for the LORD? At the time appointed I will return unto thee, according to the time of life, and Sarah shall have a son."*

¹⁵ *Then Sarah denied, saying, "I laughed not;" for she was afraid. And he said, "Nay; but thou didst laugh."*

Abraham Pleads for Sodom

¹⁶ *And the men rose up from thence, and looked toward Sodom: and Abraham went with them to bring them on the way.* ¹⁷ *And the LORD said, "Shall I hide from Abraham that thing which I do;* ¹⁸ *Seeing that Abraham shall surely become a great and mighty nation, and all the nations of the earth shall be blessed in him?* ¹⁹ *For I know him, that he will command his children and his household after him, and they shall keep the way of the LORD, to do justice and judgment; that the LORD may bring upon Abraham that which he hath spoken of him."*

²⁰ *And the LORD said, "Because the cry of Sodom and Gomorrah is great, and because their sin is very grievous;* ²¹ *I will go down now, and see whether they have done altogether according to the cry⑬ of it, which is come unto me; and if not, I will know."*

²² *And the men turned their faces from thence, and went toward Sodom: but Abraham stood yet before the LORD.* ²³ *And Abraham drew near, and said, "Wilt thou also destroy the righteous with the wicked?* ²⁴ *Peradventure⑭ there be fifty righteous within the city: wilt thou also destroy and not spare the place for the fifty righteous that are therein?* ²⁵ *That be far from thee to do after this manner, to slay the righteous with the wicked: and that the righteous should be as the wicked, that be far from thee: Shall not the Judge of all the earth do right?"*

²⁶ *And the LORD said, "If I find in Sodom fifty righteous within the city, then I will spare all the place for their sakes."*

²⁷ *And Abraham answered and said, "Behold now, I have taken upon me to speak unto the Lord, which am but dust and ashes:* ²⁸ *Peradventure there shall lack five of the fifty righteous: wilt thou destroy all the city for lack of five?" And he said, "If I find there forty and five, I will not destroy it."*

²⁹ *And he spake unto him yet again, and said, "Peradventure there shall be forty found there." And he*

---

⑫ **after the manner of women** past the age of childbearing.
⑬ **cry** outcry.
⑭ **Peradventure** suppose.

said, "I will not do it for forty's sake."

 ³⁰ And he said unto him, "Oh let not the Lord be angry, and I will speak: Peradventure there shall thirty be found there." And he said, "I will not do it, if I find thirty there."

 ³¹ And he said, "Behold now, I have taken upon me to speak unto the Lord: Peradventure there shall be twenty found there." And he said, "I will not destroy it for twenty's sake."

 ³² And he said, "Oh let not the Lord be angry, and I will speak yet but this once: Peradventure ten shall be found there." And he said, "I will not destroy it for ten's sake."

 ³³ And the LORD went his way, as soon as he had left communing with Abraham: and Abraham returned unto his place.

Sodom⑮ and Gomorrah⑯ Destroyed

Genesis 19

 ¹ And there came two angels to Sodom at even; and Lot⑰ sat in the gate of Sodom: and Lot seeing them rose up to meet them; and he bowed himself with his face toward the ground; ² And he said, "Behold now, my lords, turn in, I pray you, into your servant's house, and tarry all night, and wash your feet, and ye shall rise up early, and go on your ways." And they said,

"Nay; but we will abide in the street all night."

 ³ And he pressed upon them greatly; and they turned in unto him, and entered into his house; and he made them a feast, and did bake unleavened bread, and they did eat. ⁴ But before they lay down, the men of the city, even the men of Sodom, compassed the house round, both old and young, all the people from every quarter: ⁵ And they called unto Lot, and said unto him, "Where are the men which came in to thee this night? bring them out unto us, that we may know⑱ them."

 ⁶ And Lot went out at the door unto them, and shut the door after him, ⁷ And said, "I pray you, brethren, do not so wickedly. ⁸ Behold now, I have two daughters which have not known man; let me, I pray you, bring them out unto you, and do ye to them as is good in your eyes: only unto these men do nothing; for therefore came they under the shadow of my roof."

 ⁹ And they said, "Stand back." And they said again, "This one fellow came in to sojourn, and he will needs be a judge⑲: now will we deal worse with thee, than with them." And they pressed sore upon the man, even Lot, and came near to break the door.

 ¹⁰ But the men put forth their hand, and pulled Lot into the house to them, and shut to the door. ¹¹ And they smote the men that were at the door of the house with blindness, both small and great: so that they wearied themselves to find the door.

 ¹² And the men said unto Lot, "Hast thou here any besides? Son in law, and thy sons, and thy daughters, and whatsoever thou hast in the city, bring them out of this place: ¹³ For we will destroy this place, because the cry of them is waxen great before the face of the LORD; and the LORD hath sent us to destroy it."

 ¹⁴ And Lot went out, and spake unto his sons in law, which married his daughters, and said, "Up, get you out of this place; for the LORD will destroy this city." But he seemed as one that mocked unto his sons in law⑳.

 ¹⁵ And when the morning arose, then the angels hastened Lot, saying, "Arise, take thy wife, and thy two daughters, which are here; lest thou be consumed in the iniquity of the city㉑."

---

⑮ **Sodom** /ˈsɔdəm/, 所多玛。
⑯ **Gomorrah** /gəˈmɔrə/, 蛾摩拉。
⑰ **Lot** 罗得。
⑱ **know** in the biblical sense. *See* fn. 1, Chapter 2.
⑲ **will needs be a judge** wants to play the judge.
⑳ **seemed as one that mocked unto his sons in law** seemed to his sons-in-law to be joking.
㉑ **in the iniquity of the city** in the punishment of the city.

¹⁶ And while he lingered, the men laid hold upon his hand, and upon the hand of his wife, and upon the hand of his two daughters; the LORD being merciful unto him: and they brought him forth, and set him without the city. ¹⁷ And it came to pass, when they had brought them forth abroad, that he said, "Escape for thy life; look not behind thee, neither stay thou in all the plain; escape to the mountain, lest thou be consumed."

¹⁸ And Lot said unto them, "Oh, not so, my Lord: ¹⁹ Behold now, thy servant hath found grace in thy sight, and thou hast magnified thy mercy, which thou hast shewed unto me in saving my life; and I cannot escape to the mountain, lest some evil take me, and I die: ²⁰ Behold now, this city is near to flee unto, and it is a little one: Oh, let me escape thither, (is it not a little one?) and my soul shall live."

²¹ And he said unto him, "See, I have accepted thee concerning this thing also, that I will not overthrow this city, for the which thou hast spoken. ²² Haste thee, escape thither; for I cannot do any thing till thou be come thither." Therefore the name of the city was called Zoar㉒.

A Pillar of Salt

²³ The sun was risen upon the earth when Lot entered into Zoar. ²⁴ Then the LORD rained upon Sodom and upon Gomorrah brimstone and fire from the LORD out of heaven; ²⁵ And he overthrew those cities, and all the plain, and all the inhabitants of the cities, and that which grew upon the ground. ²⁶ But his wife looked back from behind him, and she became a pillar of salt.

²⁷ And Abraham gat up early in the morning to the place where he stood before the LORD: ²⁸ And he looked toward Sodom and Gomorrah, and toward all the land of the plain, and beheld, and, lo, the smoke of the country went up as the smoke of a furnace.

²⁹ And it came to pass, when God destroyed the cities of the plain, that God remembered Abraham, and sent Lot out of the midst of the overthrow, when he overthrew the cities in the which Lot dwelt.

Lot and His Daughters

³⁰ And Lot went up out of Zoar, and dwelt in the mountain, and his two daughters with him; for he feared to dwell in Zoar: and he dwelt in a cave, he and his two daughters. ³¹ And the firstborn said unto the younger, "Our father is old, and there is not a man in the earth to come in unto us after the manner of all the earth: ³² Come, let us make our father drink wine, and we will lie with him, that we may preserve seed of our father."

³³ And they made their father drink wine that night: and the firstborn went in, and lay with her father; and he perceived not when she lay down, nor when she arose.

³⁴ And it came to pass on the morrow, that the firstborn said unto the younger, "Behold, I lay yesternight with my father: let us make him drink wine this night also; and go thou in, and lie with him, that we may preserve seed of our father." ³⁵ And they made their father drink wine that night also: and the younger arose, and lay with him; and he perceived not when she lay down, nor when she arose.

³⁶ Thus were both the daughters of Lot with child by their father. ³⁷ And the firstborn bare a son, and called his name Moab㉓: the same is the

Lot and His Daughters, Leyden van Lucas (1494—1533)

㉒ **Zoar**（琐珥）means *little*.
㉓ **Moab**（/ˈməuæb/, 摩押）sounds like the Hebrew for *from father*.

father of the Moabites unto this day. ³⁸ And the younger, she also bare a son, and called his name Benammi㉔: the same is the father of the children of Ammon unto this day.

Abraham and Isaac

Genesis 21

The Birth of Isaac

¹ And the LORD visited Sarah as he had said, and the LORD did unto Sarah as he had spoken. ² For Sarah conceived, and bare Abraham a son in his old age, at the set time of which God had spoken to him. ³ And Abraham called the name of his son that was born unto him, whom Sarah bare to him, Isaac㉕.

⁴ And Abraham circumcised his son Isaac being eight days old, as God had commanded him. ⁵ And Abraham was an hundred years old, when his son Isaac was born unto him.

⁶ And Sarah said, "God hath made me to laugh, so that all that hear will laugh with me." ⁷ And she said, "Who would have said unto Abraham, that Sarah should have given children suck? For I have born him a son in his old age."

Hagar and Ishmael Sent Away

⁸ And the child grew, and was weaned: and Abraham made a great feast the same day that Isaac was weaned. ⁹ And Sarah saw the son of Hagar the Egyptian, which she had born unto Abraham, mocking. ¹⁰ Wherefore she said unto Abraham, "Cast out this bondwoman and her son: for the son of this bondwoman shall not be heir with my son, even with Isaac."

¹¹ And the thing was very grievous in Abraham's sight㉖ because of his son. ¹² And God said unto Abraham, "Let it not be grievous in thy sight because of the lad, and because of thy bondwoman; in all that Sarah hath said unto thee, hearken unto her voice; for in Isaac shall thy seed be called. ¹³ And also of the son of the bondwoman will I make a nation, because he is thy seed."

¹⁴ And Abraham rose up early in the morning, and took bread, and a bottle of water, and gave it unto Hagar, putting it on her shoulder, and the child, and sent her away: and she departed, and wandered in the wilderness of Beersheba. ¹⁵ And the water was spent in the bottle, and she cast the child under one of the shrubs. ¹⁶ And she went, and sat her down over against him a good way off, as it were a bowshot: for she said, "Let me not see the death of the child." And she sat over against him, and lift up her voice, and wept.

¹⁷ And God heard the voice of the lad; and the angel of God called to Hagar out of heaven, and said unto her, "What aileth thee, Hagar? Fear not; For God hath heard the voice of the lad where he is. ¹⁸ Arise, lift up the lad, and hold him in thine hand; For I will make him a great nation."

¹⁹ And God opened her eyes, and she saw a well of water; and she went, and filled the bottle with water, and gave the lad drink.

²⁰ And God was with the lad; and he grew, and dwelt in the wilderness, and became an archer. ²¹ And he dwelt in the wilderness of Paran: and his mother took him a wife out of the land of Egypt. ...

The Akedah: the Binding of Isaac

Genesis 22

¹ And it came to pass after these things, that God did tempt Abraham, and said unto him, Abraham: and he said, "Behold, here I am." ² And he said, "Take now thy son, thine only son Isaac, whom thou lovest, and get thee into the land of Moriah; and offer him there for a burnt offering upon one of the mountains which I

㉔ **Benammi**（便亚米）means *son of my people*.
㉕ **Isaac**（/ˈaizək/, 以撒）means *he laughs*.
㉖ **grievous in Abraham's sight** displeasing to Abraham.

will tell thee of."

³ And Abraham rose up early in the morning, and saddled his ass, and took two of his young men with him, and Isaac his son, and clave the wood for the burnt offering, and rose up, and went unto the place of which God had told him. ⁴ Then on the third day Abraham lifted up his eyes, and saw the place afar off. ⁵ And Abraham said unto his young men, "Abide ye here with the ass; and I and the lad will go yonder and worship, and come again to you."

Sacrifice of Isaac, 1601—1602, Caravaggio

⁶ And Abraham took the wood of the burnt offering, and laid it upon Isaac his son; and he took the fire in his hand, and a knife; and they went both of them together. ⁷ And Isaac spake unto Abraham his father, and said, "My father:" and he said, "Here am I, my son." And he said, "Behold the fire and the wood: but where is the lamb for a burnt offering?"

⁸ And Abraham said, "My son, God will provide himself a lamb for a burnt offering:" so they went both of them together.

⁹ And they came to the place which God had told him of; and Abraham built an altar there, and laid the wood in order, and bound Isaac his son, and laid him on the altar upon the wood. ¹⁰ And Abraham stretched forth his hand, and took the knife to slay his son. ¹¹ And the angel of the LORD called unto him out of heaven, and said, "Abraham, Abraham:" and he said, "Here am I."

¹² And he said, "Lay not thine hand upon the lad, neither do thou any thing unto him: for now I know that thou fearest God, seeing thou hast not withheld thy son, thine only son from me."

¹³ And Abraham lifted up his eyes, and looked, and behold behind him a ram caught in a thicket by his horns: and Abraham went and took the ram, and offered him up for a burnt offering in the stead of his son. ¹⁴ And Abraham called the name of that place Jehovahjireh⑳: as it is said to this day, in the mount of the LORD it shall be seen.

¹⁵ And the angel of the LORD called unto Abraham out of heaven the second time. ¹⁶ And said, "By myself have I sworn, saith the LORD, for because thou hast done this thing, and hast not withheld thy son, thine only son: ¹⁷ That in blessing I will bless thee, and in multiplying I will multiply thy seed as the stars of the heaven, and as the sand which is upon the sea shore; and thy seed shall possess the gate of his enemies; ¹⁸ And in thy seed shall all the nations of the earth be blessed; because thou hast obeyed my voice."

¹⁹ So Abraham returned unto his young men, and they rose up and went together to Beersheba; and Abraham dwelt at Beersheba.

²⁰ And it came to pass after these things, that it was told Abraham, saying, "Behold, Milcah, she hath also born children unto thy brother Nahor; ²¹ Huz his firstborn, and Buz his brother, and Kemuel the father of Aram, ²² And Chesed, and Hazo, and Pildash, and Jidlaph, and Bethuel. ²³ And Bethuel begat Rebekah: these eight Milcah did bear to Nahor, Abraham's brother. ²⁴ And his concubine, whose name was Reumah, she bare also Tebah, and Gaham, and Thahash, and Maachah."

III FOOD FOR THOUGHT

1. How was Ishmael treated by God?
2. What is the exact nature of the covenant God made with Abraham? How can you compare the Abrahamic covenant and the Noahic covenant?

---

⑳ **Jehovahjireh**（耶和华以勒）means *The Lord will provide*.

3. On what ground were the two cities destroyed?
4. Why did Lot's wife become a pillar of salt, not of sugar or flour or anything else?
5. How did Abraham's reaction to God's command to sacrifice Isaac reinforce our understanding of Abraham's character?

IV BIBLICAL RELEVANCE

A. Biblical Terms in Everyday English
1. of a surety (15:13): _____
2. Ishmael (16:11): _____
3. promised land/ land of promise: _____
4. entertain an angel/angels unawares (18:1—15): _____
5. brimstone and fire (19:24): _____
6. as curious as Lot's wife: _____
7. Sodom and Gomorrah: _____
8. the sin of Sodom: _____
9. sodomy: _____
10. sodomize: _____

B. Biblical References in Literature
1. In the latter quarter of each year cattle were at once the mainstay and the terror of families about Casterbridge and its neighbourhood, where breeding was carried on with Abrahamic success.
   (Thomas Hardy, *The Mayor of Casterbridge*, 1886)
2. Beside the milk-bush sat the Kaffir woman still — like Hagar, he thought, thrust out by her mistress in the wilderness to die.
   (Olive Schreiner, *The Story of an African Farm*, 1883)
3. Years ago, when we were in trouble, we thought we could one day go north. Well, we are north now. We are at that Promised Land.
   (Studs Terkel, *American Dreams: Lost and Found*, 1980)
4. "Be serious. It's not just the wife Dunny, we have to face it. You're queer." "The sin of Sodom, you mean? If you knew boys as I do, you would not suggest anything so grotesque. If Oscar Wilde had pleaded insanity, he would have walked out of court a free man."
   (Robertson Davies, *Fifth Business*, 1970)
5. "I shall walk out of the office and never step into it again. I shall not even bestow the backwardest of glances upon it. Let Sodom and Gomorrah be razed — but I shall not be turned into a pillar of salt." "Is it Macao and Hong Kong you mean, when you talk of Sodom and Gomorrah? or perhaps Canton? I trust I am not to be cast in the role of Lot's wife."
   (Timothy Mo, *An Insular Possession*, 1986)

C. The Bible and Arts
1. *Abraham's Journey to Canaan*, 1614, Pieter Pietersz Lastman
2. *Sarah Presenting Hagar to Abraham*, 1699, Adriaen van der Werff (1659—1722)
3. *The Expulsion of Hagar*, Lorrain Claude (1600—1682)
4. *Hagar Leaves the Home of Abraham*, 1615—1617, Peter Paul Rubens
5. *Lot and His Daughters*, Leyden van Lucas (1494—1533)

6. *Sacrifice of Isaac*, 1601—1602, Caravaggio
7. *Isaac Meeting Rebecca*, c. 1640, Castiglione, Giovanni Benedetto (Il Grechetto)

V SOURCES FOR REFERENCE

1. (1994). *The Bible Collection: Abraham*, a TV play by Turner Home Entertainment.
2. Roche, P. (2001). *The Bible's Greatest Stories*. New York: New American Library.
3. Riches, J. (2000). *The Bible: A Very Short Introduction*. Oxford: Oxford University Press.

4. JACOB, THE DECEIVER

I POINTS OF DEPARTURE

Genesis 25:19 to the end of the book narrates the stories of Jacob and his sons, a gallery of characters least expected to be God's chosen people. The Genesis account of the lives of Jacob and his wives, and Joseph and his brothers offers a gripping family saga replete with love and envy, anger and reconciliation, deceit and integrity.

Different from his father Isaac noted for his faith, Jacob is known as a con man in God's family. Jacob's character trait of trickery is even foreshadowed at birth through his name (meaning *he grasps the heel*; figuratively *he deceives*). This foreshadowing is very soon confirmed by the stories of exchanged birthright and the subsequent theft of the aged, dim-sighted Isaac's blessing. The former implies spiritual values (in the form of birthright) are weightier than momentary physical appetite, while the latter, full of familiar elements found in a story — conflict, suspense, intrigue, dramatic irony, constitutes an engaging literary study. As the ancient Chinese wisdom "即以其人之道,还治其人之身" (dose sb. with his own physique) suggests, Jacob's trick backfired when he was outsmarted by another trickster — his uncle and father-in-law, Laban in Haran and had to serve him for 20 years before he could marry Rachel, the girl of his heart's desire. Here again poetic justice is at work, because before his marriage to Rachel, Jacob, who impersonated his brother Esau's appearance to steal his father's blessing, was tricked into marrying Rachel's older sister, Leah. With two wives living under the same roof, Jacob's marriage was dominated again by sibling rivalry, this time, between two sisters, for the favor of their common husband. The two women together with their maids offered to Jacob as concubines begot 12 sons, who were to become the ancestors of the 12 tribes of Israel.

The unattractive portrayal of Jacob is typical of the Old Testament narrative, suggesting how the ways of God often differ from human expectations. Jacob is mentioned time and again in the New Testament, for example, in *Rom. 9:13* to illustrate the sovereign grace of God, and in *Heb. 11:9* as one of the exemplars of true faith. The story of Jacob also contributes some memorable expressions, among which is "a mess of pottage," used by the Russian revolutionary leader Vladimir Ilyich Lenin (1870—1924) in his *The State and Revolution* (1918) to criticize the workers' party for "sell[ing] their birthright for a mess of pottage," that is, renouncing their leadership role in the struggle against the bourgeoisie.

II SELECTED READINGS

Jacob and Esau

Genesis 25

...

¹⁹ And these are the generations of Isaac, Abraham's son:

Abraham begat Isaac: ²⁰ And Isaac was forty years old when he took Rebekah to wife, the daughter of Bethuel the Syrian of Padanaram, the sister to Laban the Syrian.

²¹ And Isaac intreated the LORD for his wife, because she was barren: and the LORD was intreated of him, and Rebekah his wife conceived. ²² And the children struggled together within her; and she said, "If it be so, why am I thus?" And she went to enquire of the LORD.

²³ And the LORD said unto her, "Two nations are in thy womb, and two manner of people shall be separated from thy bowels; and the one people shall be stronger than the other people; and the elder shall serve the younger."

²⁴ And when her days to be delivered were fulfilled, behold, there were twins in her womb. ²⁵ And the first came out red, all over like an hairy garment; and they called his name Esau①. ²⁶ And after that came his brother out, and his hand took hold on Esau's heel; and his name was called Jacob②: and Isaac was threescore years old when she bare them.

²⁷ And the boys grew: and Esau was a cunning hunter, a man of the field; and Jacob was a plain man, dwelling in tents. ²⁸ And Isaac loved Esau, because he did eat of his venison: but Rebekah loved Jacob.

²⁹ And Jacob sod pottage: and Esau came from the field, and he was faint: ³⁰ And Esau said to Jacob, "Feed me, I pray thee, with that same red pottage; for I am faint." Therefore was his name called Edom.

³¹ And Jacob said, "Sell me this day thy birthright." ³² And Esau said, "Behold, I am at the point to die: and what profit shall this birthright do to me?" ³³ And Jacob said, "Swear to me

Esau and Jacob, 1640s, Matthias Stom

this day." And he sware unto him: and he sold his birthright unto Jacob. ³⁴ Then Jacob gave Esau bread and pottage of lentiles; and he did eat and drink, and rose up, and went his way: thus Esau despised his birthright.

Jacob Gets Isaac's Blessing

Genesis 27

¹ And it came to pass, that when Isaac was old, and his eyes were dim, so that he could not see, he called Esau his eldest son, and said unto him, "My son." and he said unto him, "Behold, here am I."

² And he said, "Behold now, I am old, I know not the day of my death. ³ Now therefore take, I pray thee, thy weapons, thy quiver and thy bow, and go out to the field, and take me some venison; ⁴ And make me savoury meat, such as I love, and bring it to me, that I may eat; that my soul may bless thee before I die."

---

① **Esau** (/ˈiːsɔː/, 以扫) may mean *hairy*; he was also called Edom, which means *red*.
② **Jacob** (/ˈdʒeikəb/, 雅各) means *He takes by the heel*, or *He cheats*.

⁵ And Rebekah heard when Isaac spake to Esau his son. And Esau went to the field to hunt for venison, and to bring it. ⁶ And Rebekah spake unto Jacob her son, saying, "Behold, I heard thy father speak unto Esau thy brother, saying, '⁷ Bring me venison, and make me savoury meat, that I may eat, and bless thee before the LORD before my death.' ⁸ Now therefore, my son, obey my voice according to that which I command thee. ⁹ Go now to the flock, and fetch me from thence two good kids of the goats; and I will make them savoury meat for thy father, such as he loveth. ¹⁰ And thou shalt bring it to thy father, that he may eat, and that he may bless thee before his death."

¹¹ And Jacob said to Rebekah his mother, "Behold, Esau my brother is a hairy man, and I am a smooth man. ¹² My father peradventure will feel me, and I shall seem to him as a deceiver; and I shall bring a curse upon me, and not a blessing."

¹³ And his mother said unto him, "Upon me be thy curse, my son; only obey my voice, and go fetch me them."

Isaac Blessing Jacob, Jean-Baptiste Jouvenet
(1644—1717)

¹⁴ And he went, and fetched, and brought them to his mother: and his mother made savoury meat, such as his father loved. ¹⁵ And Rebekah took goodly raiment of her eldest son Esau, which were with her in the house, and put them upon Jacob her younger son. ¹⁶ And she put the skins of the kids of the goats upon his hands, and upon the smooth of his neck. ¹⁷ And she gave the savoury meat and the bread, which she had prepared, into the hand of her son Jacob.

¹⁸ And he came unto his father, and said, "My father." And he said, "Here am I; who art thou, my son?"

¹⁹ And Jacob said unto his father, "I am Esau thy firstborn; I have done according as thou badest me: arise, I pray thee, sit and eat of my venison, that thy soul may bless me."

²⁰ And Isaac said unto his son, "How is it that thou hast found it so quickly, my son?"

And he said, "Because the LORD thy God brought it to me."

²¹ And Isaac said unto Jacob, "Come near, I pray thee, that I may feel thee, my son, whether thou be my very son Esau or not."

²² And Jacob went near unto Isaac his father; and he felt him, and said, "The voice is Jacob's voice, but the hands are the hands of Esau." ²³ And he discerned him not, because his hands were hairy, as his brother Esau's hands: so he blessed him. ²⁴ And he said, "Art thou my very son Esau?"

And he said, "I am."

²⁵ And he said, "Bring it near to me, and I will eat of my son's venison, that my soul may bless thee." And he brought it near to him, and he did eat: and he brought him wine, and he drank. ²⁶ And his father Isaac said unto him, "Come near now, and kiss me, my son."

²⁷ And he came near, and kissed him: and he smelled the smell of his raiment, and blessed him, and said, "See, the smell of my son
is as the smell of a field which the LORD hath blessed.
²⁸ Therefore God give thee of the dew of heaven,
and the fatness of the earth, and plenty of corn and wine.
²⁹ Let people serve thee,
and nations bow down to thee.
Be lord over thy brethren,
and let thy mother's sons bow down to thee.
Cursed be every one that curseth thee,
and blessed be he that blesseth thee."

³⁰ And it came to pass, as soon as Isaac had made an end of blessing Jacob, and Jacob was yet scarce gone

out from the presence of Isaac his father, that Esau his brother came in from his hunting. ³¹ And he also had made savoury meat, and brought it unto his father, and said unto his father, " Let my father arise, and eat of his son's venison, that thy soul may bless me."

³² And Isaac his father said unto him, " Who art thou?" And he said, " I am thy son, thy firstborn Esau."

³³ And Isaac trembled very exceedingly, and said, " Who? where is he that hath taken venison, and brought it me, and I have eaten of all before thou camest, and have blessed him? Yea, and he shall be blessed."

³⁴ And when Esau heard the words of his father, he cried with a great and exceeding bitter cry, and said unto his father, " Bless me, even me also, O my father."

³⁵ And he said, " Thy brother came with subtilty, and hath taken away thy blessing."

³⁶ And he said, " Is not he rightly named Jacob? For he hath supplanted me these two times: he took away my birthright; and, behold, now he hath taken away my blessing." And he said, " Hast thou not reserved a blessing for me?"

³⁷ And Isaac answered and said unto Esau, " Behold, I have made him thy lord, and all his brethren have I given to him for servants; and with corn and wine have I sustained him: and what shall I do now unto thee, my son?"

³⁸ And Esau said unto his father, " Hast thou but one blessing, my father? Bless me, even me also, O my father." And Esau lifted up his voice, and wept.

³⁹ And Isaac his father answered and said unto him,
" Behold, thy dwelling shall be the fatness of the earth,
and of the dew of heaven from above;
⁴⁰ And by thy sword shalt thou live,
and shalt serve thy brother;
and it shall come to pass when thou shalt have the dominion,
that thou shalt break his yoke from off thy neck."

Jacob Flees to Laban

⁴¹ And Esau hated Jacob because of the blessing wherewith his father blessed him: and Esau said in his heart, " The days of mourning for my father are at hand; then will I slay my brother Jacob."

⁴² And these words of Esau her elder son were told to Rebekah: and she sent and called Jacob her younger son, and said unto him, " Behold, thy brother Esau, as touching thee, doth comfort himself, purposing to kill thee. ⁴³ Now therefore, my son, obey my voice; and arise, flee thou to Laban my brother to Haran; ⁴⁴ And tarry with him a few days, until thy brother's fury turn away; ⁴⁵ Until thy brother's anger turn away from thee, and he forget that which thou hast done to him: then I will send, and fetch thee from thence: why should I be deprived also of you both in one day?"

⁴⁶ And Rebekah said to Isaac, " I am weary of my life because of the daughters of Heth: if Jacob take a wife of the daughters of Heth, such as these which are of the daughters of the land, what good shall my life do me?"

Genesis 28

¹ And Isaac called Jacob, and blessed him, and charged him, and said unto him, " Thou shalt not take a wife of the daughters of Canaan. ² Arise, go to Padanaram, to the house of Bethuel thy mother's father; and take thee a wife from thence of the daughters of Laban thy mother's brother. ³ And God Almighty bless thee, and make thee fruitful, and multiply thee, that thou mayest be a multitude of people; ⁴ And give thee the blessing of Abraham, to thee, and to thy seed with thee; that thou mayest inherit the land wherein thou art a stranger, which God gave unto Abraham." ⁵ And Isaac sent away Jacob: and he went to Padanaram unto Laban, son of Bethuel the Syrian, the brother of Rebekah, Jacob's and Esau's mother.

⁶ When Esau saw that Isaac had blessed Jacob, and sent him away to Padanaram, to take him a wife from thence; and that as he blessed him he gave him a charge, saying, "Thou shalt not take a wife of the daughters of Canaan." ⁷ And that Jacob obeyed his father and his mother, and was gone to Padanaram. ⁸ And Esau seeing that the daughters of Canaan pleased not Isaac his father; ⁹ Then went Esau unto Ishmael, and took unto the wives which he had Mahalath the daughter of Ishmael Abraham's son, the sister of Nebajoth, to be his wife.

Jacob's Dream at Bethel

¹⁰ And Jacob went out from Beersheba, and went toward Haran. ¹¹ And he lighted upon a certain place, and tarried there all night, because the sun was set; and he took of the stones of that place, and put them for his pillows, and lay down in that place to sleep. ¹² And he dreamed, and behold a ladder set up on the earth, and the top of it reached to heaven: and behold the angels of God ascending and descending on it. ¹³ And, behold, the LORD stood above it, and said, "I am the LORD God of Abraham thy father, and the God of Isaac: the land whereon thou liest, to thee will I give it, and to thy seed; ¹⁴ And thy seed shall be as the dust of the earth, and thou shalt spread abroad to the west, and to the east, and to the north, and to the south: and in thee and in thy seed shall all the families of the earth be blessed. ¹⁵ And, behold, I am with thee, and will keep thee in all places whither thou goest, and will bring thee again into this land; for I will not leave thee, until I have done that which I have spoken to thee of." ¹⁶ And Jacob awaked out of his sleep, and he said, " Surely the LORD is in this place; and I knew it not." ¹⁷ And he was afraid, and said, " How dreadful is this place! This is none other but the house of God, and this is the gate of heaven."

Jacob's Dream, 1726—1729,
Giovanni Battista Tiepolo

¹⁸ And Jacob rose up early in the morning, and took the stone that he had put for his pillows, and set it up for a pillar, and poured oil upon the top of it. ¹⁹ And he called the name of that place Bethel③: but the name of that city was called Luz at the first.
²⁰ And Jacob vowed a vow, saying, " If God will be with me, and will keep me in this way that I go, and will give me bread to eat, and raiment to put on, ²¹ So that I come again to my father's house in peace; then shall the LORD be my God: ²² And this stone, which I have set for a pillar, shall be God's house: and of all that thou shalt give me I will surely give the tenth unto thee."

Genesis 29

...

¹² And Jacob told Rachel that he was her father's brother, and that he was Rebekah's son: and she ran and told her father.
¹³ And it came to pass, when Laban heard the tidings of Jacob his sister's son, that he ran to meet him, and embraced him, and kissed him, and brought him to his house. And he told Laban all these things. ¹⁴ And Laban said to him, " Surely thou art my bone and my flesh."

Jacob Marries Leah and Rachel

And he abode with him the space of a month. ¹⁵ And Laban said unto Jacob, " Because thou art my

---

③ **Bethel** (/ˈbeθəl/, 伯特利) means *the house of God*.

brother, shouldest thou therefore serve me for nought? Tell me, what shall thy wages be?"

^{16} *And Laban had two daughters: the name of the elder was Leah, and the name of the younger was Rachel.* ^{17} *Leah was tender eyed; but Rachel was beautiful and well favoured.*

^{18} *And Jacob loved Rachel; and said, "I will serve thee seven years for Rachel thy younger daughter."*

^{19} *And Laban said, "It is better that I give her to thee, than that I should give her to another man: abide with me."* ^{20} *And Jacob served seven years for Rachel; and they seemed unto him but a few days, for the love he had to her.*

^{21} *And Jacob said unto Laban, "Give me my wife, for my days are fulfilled, that I may go in unto her."*

Jacob and Rachel, William Dyce (1806—1864)

^{22} *And Laban gathered together all the men of the place, and made a feast.* ^{23} *And it came to pass in the evening, that he took Leah his daughter, and brought her to him; and he went in unto her.* ^{24} *And Laban gave unto his daughter Leah Zilpah his maid for an handmaid.*

^{25} *And it came to pass, that in the morning, behold, it was Leah: and he said to Laban, "What is this thou hast done unto me? Did not I serve with thee for Rachel? Wherefore then hast thou beguiled me?"*

^{26} *And Laban said, "It must not be so done in our country, to give the younger before the firstborn.* ^{27} *Fulfil her week, and we will give thee this also for the service which thou shalt serve with me yet seven other years."*

^{28} *And Jacob did so, and fulfilled her week; and he gave him Rachel his daughter to wife also.* ^{29} *And Laban gave to Rachel his daughter Bilhah his handmaid to be her maid.* ^{30} *And he went in also unto Rachel, and he loved also Rachel more than Leah, and served with him yet seven other years.*

Jacob's Children

^{31} *And when the LORD saw that Leah was hated, he opened her womb: but Rachel was barren.* ^{32} *And Leah conceived, and bare a son, and she called his name Reuben*[④]*: for she said, "Surely the LORD hath looked upon my affliction; now therefore my husband will love me."*

^{33} *And she conceived again, and bare a son; and said, "Because the LORD hath heard I was hated, he hath therefore given me this son also," and she called his name Simeon*[⑤]*.*

^{34} *And she conceived again, and bare a son; and said, "Now this time will my husband be joined unto me, because I have born him three sons: therefore was his name called Levi*[⑥]*."*

^{35} *And she conceived again, and bare a son: and she said, "Now will I praise the LORD: therefore she called his name Judah*[⑦]*," and left bearing.*

* * * * * * * * * * * *

Jacob's Other Children (30:1—24, 35:16—18)

The sons of Rachel's maidservant Bilhah: Dan[⑧] and Naphtali[⑨].
The sons of Leah's maidservant Zilpah: Gad[⑩] and Asher[⑪].

---

④ **Reuben** (/ˈruːbən/, 流便) means *see, a son*.
⑤ **Simeon** (/ˈsimiən/, 西缅) sounds like the Hebrew for *one who hears*.
⑥ **Levi** (/ˈliːvai/, 利未) may be derived from the Hebrew for *attached*.
⑦ **Judah** (/ˈdʒuːdə/, 犹大) sounds like the Hebrew for *praise*.
⑧ **Dan** (/dæn/, 但) sounds like the Hebrew for *judged*.
⑨ **Naphtali** (/ˈnæftəlai/, 拿弗他利) means *my struggle*.
⑩ **Gad** (/gæd/, 迦得) sounds like the Hebrew for *good fortune* or *a troop*.
⑪ **Asher** (/ˈæʃə/, 亚设) means *happy*.

The sons of Leah: Issachar⑫ and Zebulun⑬.
The sons of Rachel: Joseph⑭ and Benjamin⑮.

Other Events of Significance
Fleeing from Laban (31)
  After robbing Esau of his birthright through trickery, Jacob had to run for his life and spent 20 years in exile. During this period, he was time and again given a dose of his own physic by Uncle Laban. First, there was Laban's palming off his older daughter Leah on Jacob. Then there were frequent changes of Jacob's wages. Meanwhile, Jacob schemed to get the biggest and best flock by allowing the stronger flock to mate in front of peeled sticks of trees and produce streaked, speckled or spotted goats. With his wealth multiplied so abundantly and his house growing, Jacob now saw the time for returning to his native land.

Wrestling with God (32:22—32)
  In this late night encounter, Jacob found himself wrestling with God himself. God touched the socket of his hip and his hip was out of joint. After this strange light, Jacob always walked with a limp, and what is more important, he was given a new name—Israel, meaning "struggle"—a name that bears God's grace. Thus Jacob became the namesake of God's chosen people, the "Israelites."

The Meeting of Jacob and Esau (32:4—33, 33:1—11)
  Surface reconciliation can not hide mistrust underneath it, at least on the part of Jacob.

III FOOD FOR THOUGHT

1. How did the Lord explain to Rebekah why her unborn children were struggling in her body?
2. How did Jacob and Esau differ in appearance and inclination?
3. What two reasons does the account give for Jacob's leaving and going to Laban's house?
4. What irony is involved in Laban's deception?
5. How can you comment on the women of *Genesis* with Sarah, Hagar, Rebekah, Rachel and Leah as examples?

IV BIBLICAL RELEVANCE

A. Biblical Terms in Everyday English
1. an Esau: _____
2. Jacob's ladder: _____
3. Jacob's stone: _____
4. Jacob's voice and Esau's hand: _____
5. sell one's birthright for a mess of pottage (of lentils): _____

---

⑫ **Issachar** (/ˈisəˌkɑː/, 以萨迦) sounds like the Hebrew for *wages*, or *hire*.
⑬ **Zebulun** (/ˈzebjulən/, 西布伦) probably means *honour*.
⑭ **Joseph** (/ˈdʒəuzif/, 约瑟) means *may he add*.
⑮ **Benjamin** (/ˈbendʒəmin/, 便雅悯) means *son of my right hand*.

B. Biblical References in Literature

1. New Deliverance was borderline charismatic and not the sort of church I felt comfortable attending; but at lunch the day before, Nadine had caught me off guard — a fudge delight cookies has the power to cloud minds — and laid on the guilt. "Isabel says you went to her and Haywood's church last Sunday and to Seth and Minnie's Sunday before last, but you haven't been to ours in almost two years." With Jacob's pottage rich and chocolaty on my tongue, I had no quick words with which to resist.

   (Margaret Maron, *Southern Discomfort*, 1993)

2. In our dreams we sometimes struggle from the oceans of desire up Jacob's ladder to that orderly place. Then human voices wake us and we drown.

   (Jeanette Winterson, *The Passion*, 1987)

3. Six years were a long time, but how much shorter than never, the idea he had for so long been obliged to endure! Jacob had served twice seven years for Rachel: what were six for such a woman as this?

   (Thomas Hardy, *Far from the Madding Crowd*, 1874)

4. Sometimes their hearts failed them and they felt that they could not resist the passion that burned the marrow of their bones. They resisted. They wrestled with evil as Jacob wrestled with the angel of God and at last they conquered.

   (W. Somerset Maugham, *The Judgment Seat*, 1957)

C. The Bible and Arts

1. *Esau and Jacob*, 1640s, Matthias Stom
2. *Isaac Blessing Jacob*, Jean-Baptiste Jouvenet (1644—1717)
3. *Jacob's Dream*, 1726—1729, Giovanni Battista Tiepolo
4. *Jacob and Rachel*, William Dyce (1806—1864)
5. *Fight between Jacob and the Angel*, Eugene Delacroix (1798—1863)

V SOURCES FOR REFERENCE

1. (1994). *The Bible Collection: Jacob*, a TV play by Turner Home Entertainment.
2. Yancey, P. & T. Stafford (notes by) (1989). *The New Student Bible*, New International Version. Grand Rapids, Mich: Zondervan Publishing House.
3. Browning, W. R. E. (ed.) (2009). *A Dictionary of Bible*. Oxford: Oxford University Press.

5. JOSEPH, A DREAMER

I   POINTS OF DEPARTURE

With the saga of Joseph, we are moving steadily from the primordial narrative of early Genesis to the far more historical territory of the Middle Bronze Age (2200 B.C.E. — 1570 B.C.E.). Joseph was the apple of Jacob's eye, evidenced by the coat of many colors and privileges attached to it. What's more, Joseph was a dreamer and foolish enough to tell everything to his brothers. Naturally, he became the victim of his brothers' jealousy, and was sold by them to merchants on their way to Egypt. There, in the house of Potiphar, however, Joseph was so successful that he became his master's right-hand man, in complete charge of his household and possessions. But the love-forlorn Potiphar's wife seduced and then slandered him, which led to his imprisonment. Then his amazing feat to interpret dreams accurately earned him freedom and above all elevation to a rank second only to that of Pharaoh. When the brothers came to buy corn during a famine, a dramatic reconciliation followed, and the whole family moved to Egypt.

That is the basic outline of the story of Joseph and his brothers, but one of the important themes is the theme of God's providence. That is, the petty jealousies, murderous conspiracy of Joseph's brothers and his own evolution from a spoiled brat to an upright, confident and tactful administrator were all the unwitting instruments of a larger divine plan. Just as Joseph said to his brothers in *Genesis 50:20*, "But as for you, ye thought evil against me; but God meant it unto good, to bring to pass, as it is this day, to save much people alive."

So, the story probably typifies the constant internecine conflict amongst the twelve tribes but also the hope of an ultimate reconciliation. There may also be a dim recollection of a historical fact that the parties of Hebrews of different tribes had temporarily settled in Egypt at different times. In this sense, the story of Joseph serves as a link between the cycle of sagas of the early period of Hebrew settlement in Canaan in the Book of Genesis and the cycle of sagas in the Book of Exodus which have Moses for their central figure, thus unifying two divergent traditions concerning the call of Israel.

II   SELECTED READINGS

The Coat of Many Colors

Genesis 37

¹ And Jacob dwelt in the land wherein his father was a stranger, in the land of Canaan.
² These are the generations of Jacob.
Joseph, being seventeen years old, was feeding the flock with his brethren; and the lad was with the sons

of Bilhah, and with the sons of Zilpah, his father's wives: and Joseph brought unto his father their evil report①. ³ Now Israel loved Joseph more than all his children, because he was the son of his old age: and he made him a coat of many colours. ⁴ And when his brethren saw that their father loved him more than all his brethren, they hated him, and could not speak peaceably unto him.

A Dream of Sheaves in the Field

Richly Ornamented Robe

⁵ And Joseph dreamed a dream, and he told it his brethren: and they hated him yet the more. ⁶ And he said unto them, "Hear, I pray you, this dream which I have dreamed: ⁷ For, behold, we were binding sheaves in the field, and, lo, my sheaf arose, and also stood upright; and, behold, your sheaves stood round about, and made obeisance to my sheaf." ⁸ And his brethren said to him, "Shalt thou indeed reign over us? Or shalt thou indeed have dominion over us?" And they hated him yet the more for his dreams, and for his words.

A Dream of the Sun, the Moon, and the 11 Stars

⁹ And he dreamed yet another dream, and told it his brethren, and said, "Behold, I have dreamed a dream more; and, behold, the sun and the moon and the eleven stars made obeisance to me." ¹⁰ And he told it to his father, and to his brethren: and his father rebuked him, and said unto him, "What is this dream that thou hast dreamed? Shall I and thy mother and thy brethren indeed come to bow down ourselves to thee to the earth?" ¹¹ And his brethren envied him; but his father observed the saying②.

Joseph's Dreams

¹² And his brethren went to feed their father's flock in Shechem. ¹³ And Israel said unto Joseph, "Do not thy brethren feed the flock in Shechem? Come, and I will send thee unto them." And he said to him, "Here am I." ¹⁴ And he said to him, "Go, I pray thee, see whether it be well with thy brethren, and well with the flocks; and bring me word again." So he sent him out of the vale of Hebron, and he came to Shechem. ¹⁵ And a certain man found him, and, behold, he was wandering in the field: and the man asked him, saying, "What seekest thou?"

¹⁶ And he said, "I seek my brethren: tell me, I pray thee, where they feed their flocks." ¹⁷ And the man said, "They are departed hence; for I heard them say, Let us go to Dothan." And Joseph went after his brethren, and found them in Dothan.

¹⁸ And when they saw him afar off, even before he came near unto them, they conspired against him to slay him. ¹⁹ And they said one to another, "Behold, this dreamer cometh. ²⁰ Come now therefore, and let us slay him, and cast him into some pit, and we will say, "Some evil beast hath devoured him: and we shall see what will become of his dreams." ²¹ And Reuben heard it, and he delivered him out of their hands; and said, "Let us not kill him." ²² And Reuben said unto them, "Shed no blood, but cast him into this pit that is in the wilderness, and lay no hand upon him; that he might rid him out of their hands, to deliver him to his father again." ²³ And

---

① **their evil report** a bad report of them.
② **observed the saying** kept the saying in mind.

it came to pass, when Joseph was come unto his brethren, that they stript Joseph out of his coat, his coat of many colours that was on him; ²⁴ And they took him, and cast him into a pit: and the pit was empty, there was no water in it.

Joseph Being Sold by His Brothers, 1816, Johann Friedrich Overbeck

²⁵ And they sat down to eat bread: and they lifted up their eyes and looked, and, behold, a company of Ishmeelites came from Gilead with their camels bearing spicery and balm and myrrh, going to carry it down to Egypt. ²⁶ And Judah said unto his brethren, "What profit is it if we slay our brother, and conceal his blood? ²⁷ Come, and let us sell him to the Ishmeelites, and let not our hand be upon him; for he is our brother and our flesh." And his brethren were content. ²⁸ Then there passed by Midianites merchantmen; and they drew and lifted up Joseph out of the pit, and sold Joseph to the Ishmeelites for twenty pieces of silver: and they brought Joseph into Egypt.

²⁹ And Reuben returned unto the pit; and, behold, Joseph was not in the pit; and he rent his clothes. ³⁰ And he returned unto his brethren, and said, "The child is not; and I, whither shall I go?" ³¹ And they took Joseph's coat, and killed a kid of the goats, and dipped the coat in the blood; ³² And they sent the coat of many colours, and they brought it to their father; and said, "This have we found: know now whether it be thy son's coat or no." ³³ And he knew it, and said, "It is my son's coat; an evil beast hath devoured him; Joseph is without doubt rent in pieces." ³⁴ And Jacob rent his clothes, and put sackcloth upon his loins, and mourned for his son many days. ³⁵ And all his sons and all his daughters rose up to comfort him; but he refused to be comforted; and he said, "For I will go down into the grave unto my son mourning." Thus his father wept for him. ³⁶ And the Midianites sold him into Egypt unto Potiphar, an officer of Pharaoh's, and captain of the guard.

Judah and Tamar③

Genesis 38

¹ And it came to pass at that time, that Judah went down from his brethren, and turned in to a certain Adullamite, whose name was Hirah. ² And Judah saw there a daughter of a certain Canaanite, whose name was Shuah; and he took her, and went in unto her. ³ And she conceived, and bare a son; and he called his name Er. ⁴ And she conceived again, and bare a son; and she called his name Onan. ⁵ And she yet again conceived, and bare a son; and called his name Shelah: and he was at Chezib, when she bare him.

A Brother's Duty④

⁶ And Judah took a wife for Er his firstborn, whose name was Tamar. ⁷ And Er, Judah's firstborn, was wicked in the sight of the LORD; and the LORD slew him. ⁸ And Judah said unto Onan, "Go in unto thy brother's wife, and marry her, and raise up seed to thy brother." ⁹ And Onan knew that the seed should not be his; and it came to pass, when he went in unto his brother's wife, that he spilled it on the ground, lest that he should give seed to his brother. ¹⁰ And the thing which he did displeased the LORD: wherefore he slew him also.

¹¹ Then said Judah to Tamar his daughter-in-law, "Remain a widow at thy father's house, till Shelah my son be grown." For he said, "Lest peradventure he die also, as his brethren did." And Tamar went and dwelt in her father's house.

---

③ **Tamar** /ˈteimɑː(r)/, 他玛。Compare another Tamar in 2 Sam. 13.
④ See Dt. 25:5—10.

¹²And in process of time the daughter of Shuah, Judah's wife died; and Judah was comforted, and went up unto his sheepshearers to Timnath, he and his friend Hirah the Adullamite.

A Roadside "Harlot"

¹³And it was told Tamar, saying, "Behold thy father in law goeth up to Timnath to shear his sheep." ¹⁴And she put her widow's garments off from her, and covered her with a vail, and wrapped herself, and sat in an open place, which is by the way to Timnath; for she saw that Shelah was grown, and she was not given unto him to wife.

¹⁵When Judah saw her, he thought her to be an harlot; because she had covered her face. ¹⁶And he turned unto her by the way, and said, "Go to, I pray thee, let me come in unto thee." ¹⁶(For he knew not that she was his daughter-in-law.)

And she said, "What wilt thou give me, that thou mayest come in unto me?" ¹⁷And he said, "I will send thee a kid from the flock."

And she said, "Wilt thou give me a pledge, till thou send it?"

¹⁸And he said, "What pledge shall I give thee?"

And she said, "Thy signet, and thy bracelets, and thy staff that is in thine hand." And he gave it her, and came in unto her, and she conceived by him. ¹⁹And she arose, and went away, and laid by her vail from her, and put on the garments of her widowhood.

²⁰And Judah sent the kid by the hand of his friend the Adullamite, to receive his pledge from the woman's hand: but he found her not. ²¹Then he asked the men of that place, saying, "Where is the harlot, that was openly by the way side?"

And they said, "There was no harlot in this place."

²²And he returned to Judah, and said, "I cannot find her," and also the men of the place said, that there was no harlot in this place.

²³And Judah said, "Let her take it to her, lest we be shamed: behold, I sent this kid, and thou hast not found her."

²⁴And it came to pass about three months after, that it was told Judah, saying, "Tamar thy daughter-in-law hath played the harlot; and also, behold, she is with child by whoredom."

And Judah said, "Bring her forth, and let her be burnt."

Judah and Tamar, Emile Jean Horace Vernet (1789—1863)

²⁵When she was brought forth, she sent to her father-in-law, saying, "By the man, whose these are, am I with child," and she said, "Discern, I pray thee, whose are these, the signet, and bracelets, and staff."

²⁶And Judah acknowledged them, and said, "She hath been more righteous than I; because that I gave her not to Shelah my son." And he knew her again no more.

²⁷And it came to pass in the time of her travail⑤, that, behold, twins were in her womb. ²⁸And it came to pass, when she travailed, that the one put out his hand: and the midwife took and bound upon his hand a scarlet thread, saying, "This came out first." ²⁹And it came to pass, as he drew back his hand, that, behold, his brother came out: and she said, "How hast thou broken forth? This breach be upon thee." Therefore his name was called Pharez⑥. ³⁰And afterward came out his brother, that had the scarlet thread upon his hand: and his name was called Zarah⑦.

---

⑤ **travail** the labor of childbirth.
⑥ **Pharez** (/ˈfɑːrez/,法勒斯) means *breaking out*.
⑦ **Zarah** (/ˈzærə/,谢拉) means *scarlet* or *brightness*.

Joseph and Potiphar's Wife

Genesis 39

*Joseph and Potiphar's Wife,
c. 1631, Guido Reni*

¹ And Joseph was brought down to Egypt; and Potiphar⑧, an officer of Pharaoh, captain of the guard, an Egyptian, bought him of the hands of the Ishmeelites, which had brought him down thither. ² And the LORD was with Joseph, and he was a prosperous man; and he was in the house of his master the Egyptian. ³ And his master saw that the LORD was with him, and that the LORD made all that he did to prosper in his hand. ⁴ And Joseph found grace in his sight, and he served him: and he made him overseer over his house, and all that he had he put into his hand. ⁵ And it came to pass from the time that he had made him overseer in his house, and over all that he had, that the LORD blessed the Egyptian's house for Joseph's sake; and the blessing of the LORD was upon all that he had in the house, and in the field. ⁶ And he left all that he had in Joseph's hand; and he knew not ought he had, save the bread which he did eat⑨.

And Joseph was a goodly person, and well favoured. ⁷ And it came to pass after these things, that his master's wife cast her eyes upon Joseph; and she said, "Lie with me." ⁸ But he refused, and said unto his master's wife, "Behold, my master wotteth not what is with me in the house⑩, and he hath committed all that he hath to my hand; ⁹ There is none greater in this house than I; neither hath he kept back any thing from me but thee, because thou art his wife: how then can I do this great wickedness, and sin against God?" ¹⁰ And it came to pass, as she spake to Joseph day by day, that he hearkened not unto her, to lie by her, or to be with her.

¹¹ And it came to pass about this time, that Joseph went into the house to do his business; and there was none of the men of the house there within. ¹² And she caught him by his garment, saying, "Lie with me." And he left his garment in her hand, and fled, and got him out. ¹³ And it came to pass, when she saw that he had left his garment in her hand, and was fled forth, ¹⁴ That she called unto the men of her house, and spake unto them, saying, "See, he hath brought in an Hebrew unto us to mock us; he came in unto me to lie with me, and I cried with a loud voice. ¹⁵ And it came to pass, when he heard that I lifted up my voice and cried, that he left his garment with me, and fled, and got him out." ¹⁶ And she laid up his garment by her, until his lord came home. ¹⁷ And she spake unto him according to these words, saying, "The Hebrew servant, which thou hast brought unto us, came in unto me to mock me. ¹⁸ And it came to pass, as I lifted up my voice and cried, that he left his garment with me, and fled out."

¹⁹ And it came to pass, when his master heard the words of his wife, which she spake unto him, saying, "After this manner did thy servant to me," that his wrath was kindled. ²⁰ And Joseph's master took him, and put him into the prison, a place where the king's prisoners were bound: and he was there in the prison. ²¹ But the LORD was with Joseph, and shewed him mercy, and gave him favour in the sight of the keeper of the prison. ²² And the keeper of the prison committed to Joseph's hand all the prisoners that were in the prison; and whatsoever they did there, he was the doer of it. ²³ The keeper of the prison looked not to any thing that was under his hand; because the LORD was with him, and that which he did, the LORD made it to prosper.

---

⑧ **Potiphar** (/ˈpɒtifə/, 波提乏) *Pa-di-pa-rê* in Egyptian, meaning *the gift of the god Rê*. (Keller, 1982:89)
⑨ **knew not ought he had, save the bread which he did eat** did not concern himself with anything except the food he ate.
⑩ **wotteth not what is with me in the house** does not concern himself with anything in the house because of me.

The Bible and Western Culture

Cultural Connections: *The Tale of the Two Brothers*

"The Tale of the Two Brothers" preserved on the Papyrus D'Orbiney might have been the prototype of the story of Joseph and Potiphar's wife except that Potiphar becomes Anubis, the elder one who has a wife, Joseph, the younger who lived with his brother, and the adulteress, Anubis's wife. And instead of being thrown into prison, the younger brother ran away when his elder brother intended to kill him. (Keller, 1980:84—85)

Interpreting the Prisoners' Dreams

Genesis 40

¹And it came to pass after these things, that the butler of the king of Egypt and his baker had offended their lord the king of Egypt. ²And Pharaoh was wroth against two of his officers, against the chief of the butlers, and against the chief of the bakers. ³And he put them in ward in the house of the captain of the guard, into the prison, the place where Joseph was bound. ⁴And the captain of the guard charged Joseph with them, and he served them: and they continued a season in ward.

⁵And they dreamed a dream both of them, each man his dream in one night, each man according to the interpretation of his dream, the butler and the baker of the king of Egypt, which were bound in the prison. ⁶And Joseph came in unto them in the morning, and looked upon them, and, behold, they were sad. ⁷And he asked Pharaoh's officers that were with him in the ward of his lord's house, saying, "Wherefore look ye so sadly to day?" ⁸And they said unto him, "We have dreamed a dream, and there is no interpreter of it." And Joseph said unto them, "Do not interpretations belong to God? Tell me them, I pray you."

⁹And the chief butler told his dream to Joseph, and said to him, "In my dream, behold, a vine was before me; ¹⁰And in the vine were three branches: and it was as though it budded, and her blossoms shot forth; and the clusters thereof brought forth ripe grapes. ¹¹And Pharaoh's cup was in my hand: and I took the grapes, and pressed them into Pharaoh's cup, and I gave the cup into Pharaoh's hand." ¹²And Joseph said unto him, "This is the interpretation of it: The three branches are three days.

The Dreams of the Cupbearer and the Baker, 1626, Bernardo Strozzi

¹³Yet within three days shall Pharaoh lift up thine head, and restore thee unto thy place: and thou shalt deliver Pharaoh's cup into his hand, after the former manner when thou wast his butler. ¹⁴But think on me when it shall be well with thee, and shew kindness, I pray thee, unto me, and make mention of me unto Pharaoh, and bring me out of this house. ¹⁵For indeed I was stolen away out of the land of the Hebrews: and here also have I done nothing that they should put me into the dungeon."

¹⁶When the chief baker saw that the interpretation was good, he said unto Joseph, "I also was in my dream, and, behold, I had three white baskets on my head. ¹⁷And in the uppermost basket there was of all manner of bakemeats for Pharaoh; and the birds did eat them out of the basket upon my head." ¹⁸And Joseph

answered and said, "This is the interpretation thereof: The three baskets are three days. ¹⁹ Yet within three days shall Pharaoh lift up thy head from off thee, and shall hang thee on a tree; and the birds shall eat thy flesh from off thee."

²⁰ And it came to pass the third day, which was Pharaoh's birthday, that he made a feast unto all his servants: and he lifted up the head of the chief butler and of the chief baker among his servants. ²¹ And he restored the chief butler unto his butlership again; and he gave the cup into Pharaoh's hand. ²² But he hanged the chief baker: as Joseph had interpreted to them. ²³ Yet did not the chief butler remember Joseph, but forgat him.

Interpreting Pharaoh's Dreams

Genesis 41

¹ And it came to pass at the end of two full years, that Pharaoh dreamed: and, behold, he stood by the river. ² And, behold, there came up out of the river seven well favoured kine and fatfleshed; and they fed in a meadow. ³ And, behold, seven other kine came up after them out of the river, ill favoured and leanfleshed; and stood by the other kine upon the brink of the river. ⁴ And the ill favoured and leanfleshed kine did eat up the seven well favoured and fat kine. So Pharaoh awoke. ⁵ And he slept and dreamed the second time: and, behold, seven ears of corn came up upon one stalk, rank and good. ⁶ And, behold, seven thin ears and blasted with the east wind sprung up after them. ⁷ And the seven thin ears devoured the seven rank and full ears. And Pharaoh awoke, and, behold, it was a dream. ⁸ And it came to pass in the morning that his spirit was troubled; and he sent and called for all the magicians of Egypt, and all the wise men thereof: and Pharaoh told them his dream; but there was none that could interpret them unto Pharaoh.

Joseph Interpreting Pharaoh's Dreams, 1816—1817, Peter Cornelius

⁹ Then spake the chief butler unto Pharaoh, saying, "I do remember my faults this day. ¹⁰ Pharaoh was wroth with his servants, and put me in ward in the captain of the guard's house, both me and the chief baker. ¹¹ And we dreamed a dream in one night, I and he; we dreamed each man according to the interpretation of his dream. ¹² And there was there with us a young man, an Hebrew, servant to the captain of the guard; and we told him, and he interpreted to us our dreams; to each man according to his dream he did interpret. ¹³ And it came to pass, as he interpreted to us, so it was; me he restored unto mine office, and him he hanged."

¹⁴ Then Pharaoh sent and called Joseph, and they brought him hastily out of the dungeon: and he shaved himself, and changed his raiment, and came in unto Pharaoh. ¹⁵ And Pharaoh said unto Joseph, "I have dreamed a dream, and there is none that can interpret it: and I have heard say of thee, that thou canst understand a dream to interpret it." ¹⁶ And Joseph answered Pharaoh, saying, "It is not in me: God shall give Pharaoh an answer of peace." ¹⁷ And Pharaoh said unto Joseph, "In my dream, behold, I stood upon the bank of the river: ¹⁸ And, behold, there came up out of the river seven kine, fatfleshed and well favoured; and they fed in a meadow: ¹⁹ And, behold, seven other kine came up after them, poor and very ill favoured and leanfleshed, such as I never saw in all the land of Egypt for badness: ²⁰ And the lean and the ill favoured kine did eat up the first seven fat kine: ²¹ And when they had eaten them up, it could not be known that they had eaten them; but they were still ill favoured, as at the beginning. So I awoke. ²² And I saw in my dream, and, behold, seven ears came up in one stalk, full and good: ²³ And, behold, seven ears, withered, thin, and blasted with the east wind, sprung up after them: ²⁴ And the thin ears devoured the seven good ears: and I told this unto the magicians; but there was none that could declare it to me."

²⁵ And Joseph said unto Pharaoh, "The dream of Pharaoh is one: God hath shewed Pharaoh what he is

about to do. ²⁶ The seven good kine are seven years; and the seven good ears are seven years: the dream is one. ²⁷ And the seven thin and ill favoured kine that came up after them are seven years; and the seven empty ears blasted with the east wind shall be seven years of famine. ²⁸ This is the thing which I have spoken unto Pharaoh: What God is about to do he sheweth unto Pharaoh. ²⁹ Behold, there come seven years of great plenty throughout all the land of Egypt: ³⁰ And there shall arise after them seven years of famine; and all the plenty shall be forgotten in the land of Egypt; and the famine shall consume the land; ³¹ And the plenty shall not be known in the land by reason of that famine following; for it shall be very grievous. ³² And for that the dream was doubled unto Pharaoh twice; it is because the thing is established by God, and God will shortly bring it to pass. ³³ Now therefore let Pharaoh look out a man discreet and wise, and set him over the land of Egypt. ³⁴ Let Pharaoh do this, and let him appoint officers over the land, and take up the fifth part of the land of Egypt in the seven plenteous years. ³⁵ And let them gather all the food of those good years that come, and lay up corn under the hand of Pharaoh, and let them keep food in the cities. ³⁶ And that food shall be for store to the land against the seven years of famine, which shall be in the land of Egypt; that the land perish not through the famine."

Joseph Interprets Pharaoh's Dream
⟨ http://lavistachurchofchrist.org⟩

³⁷ And the thing was good in the eyes of Pharaoh, and in the eyes of all his servants. ³⁸ And Pharaoh said unto his servants, " Can we find such a one as this is, a man in whom the Spirit of God is?" ³⁹ And Pharaoh said unto Joseph, " Forasmuch as God hath shewed thee all this, there is none so discreet and wise as thou art: ⁴⁰ Thou shalt be over my house, and according unto thy word shall all my people be ruled: only in the throne will I be greater than thou."

Joseph in Charge of Egypt

⁴¹ And Pharaoh said unto Joseph, " See, I have set thee over all the land of Egypt." ⁴² And Pharaoh took off his ring from his hand, and put it upon Joseph's hand, and arrayed him in vestures of fine linen, and put a gold chain about his neck; ⁴³ And he made him to ride in the second chariot which he had; and they cried before him, " Bow the knee!" And he made him ruler over all the land of Egypt. ⁴⁴ And Pharaoh said unto Joseph, " I am Pharaoh, and without thee shall no man lift up his hand or foot in all the land of Egypt." ⁴⁵ And Pharaoh called Joseph's name Zaphnathpaaneah; and he gave him to wife Asenath the daughter of Potipherah priest of On. And Joseph went out over all the land of Egypt.

⁴⁶ And Joseph was thirty years old when he stood before Pharaoh king of Egypt. And Joseph went out from the presence of Pharaoh, and went throughout all the land of Egypt. ⁴⁷ And in the seven plenteous years the earth brought forth by handfuls. ⁴⁸ And he gathered up all the food of the seven years, which were in the land of Egypt, and laid up the food in the cities: the food of the field, which was round about every city, laid he up in the same. ⁴⁹ And Joseph gathered corn as the sand of the sea, very much, until he left numbering; for it was without number.

⁵⁰ And unto Joseph were born two sons before the years of famine came, which Asenath the daughter of Potipherah priest of On bare unto him. ⁵¹ And Joseph called the name of the firstborn Manasseh⑪: For God, said he, hath made me forget all my toil, and all my father's house. ⁵² And the name of the second called he Ephraim⑫: For God hath caused me to be fruitful in the land of my affliction.

⁵³ And the seven years of plenteousness, that was in the land of Egypt, were ended. ⁵⁴ And the seven years

---

⑪ **Manasseh** (/məˈnæsə/, 玛拿西) sounds like the Hebrew for *forget*.
⑫ **Ephraim** (/ˈiːfreiim/, 以法莲) sounds like the Hebrew for *twice fruitful*.

of dearth began to come, according as Joseph had said: and the dearth was in all lands; but in all the land of Egypt there was bread. ⁵⁵ And when all the land of Egypt was famished, the people cried to Pharaoh for bread: and Pharaoh said unto all the Egyptians, " Go unto Joseph; what he saith to you, do."

⁵⁶ And the famine was over all the face of the earth: And Joseph opened all the storehouses, and sold unto the Egyptians; and the famine waxed sore in the land of Egypt. ⁵⁷ And all countries came into Egypt to Joseph for to buy corn; because that the famine was so sore in all lands.

The Arrival of Joseph's Brothers

Genesis 42

¹ Now when Jacob saw that there was corn in Egypt, Jacob said unto his sons, " Why do ye look one upon another?" ² And he said, " Behold, I have heard that there is corn in Egypt: get you down thither, and buy for us from thence; that we may live, and not die." ³ And Joseph's ten brethren went down to buy corn in Egypt. ⁴ But Benjamin, Joseph's brother, Jacob sent not with his brethren; for he said, " Lest peradventure mischief befall him." ⁵ And the sons of Israel came to buy corn among those that came: for the famine was in the land of Canaan.

⁶ And Joseph was the governor over the land, and he it was that sold to all the people of the land: and Joseph's brethren came, and bowed down themselves before him with their faces to the earth. ⁷ And Joseph saw his brethren, and he knew them, but made himself strange unto them, and spake roughly unto them; and he said unto them, " Whence come ye?" And they said, " From the land of Canaan to buy food." ⁸ And Joseph knew his brethren, but they knew not him. ⁹ And Joseph remembered the dreams which he dreamed of them, and said unto them, " Ye are spies; to see the nakedness of the land ye are come⑬." ¹⁰ And they said unto him, " Nay, my lord, but to buy food are thy servants come. ¹¹ We are all one man's sons; we are true men, thy servants are no spies."

¹² And he said unto them, " Nay, but to see the nakedness of the land ye are come." ¹³ And they said, " Thy servants are twelve brethren, the sons of one man in the land of Canaan; and, behold, the youngest is this day with our father, and one is not." ¹⁴ And Joseph said unto them, " That is it that I spake unto you, saying, ' Ye are spies.' ¹⁵ Hereby ye shall be proved: By the life of Pharaoh ye shall not go forth hence, except your youngest brother come hither. ¹⁶ Send one of you, and let him fetch your brother, and ye shall be kept in prison, that your words may be proved, whether there be any truth in you: or else by the life of Pharaoh surely ye are spies." ¹⁷ And he put them all together into ward three days.

¹⁸ And Joseph said unto them the third day, " This do, and live; for I fear God: ¹⁹ If ye be true men, let one of your brethren be bound in the house of your prison: go ye, carry corn for the famine of your houses: ²⁰ But bring your youngest brother unto me; so shall your words be verified, and ye shall not die." And they did so. ²¹ And they said one to another, " We are verily guilty concerning our brother, in that we saw the anguish of his soul, when he besought us, and we would not hear; therefore is this distress come upon us." ²² And Reuben answered them, saying, " Spake I not unto you, saying, ' Do not sin against the child;' and ye would not hear? therefore, behold, also his blood is required." ²³ And they knew not that Joseph understood them; for he spake unto them by an interpreter. ²⁴ And he turned himself about from them, and wept; and returned to them again, and communed with them, and took from them Simeon, and bound him before their eyes. ²⁵ Then Joseph commanded to fill their sacks with corn, and to restore every man's money into his sack, and to give them provision for the way: and thus did he unto them.

²⁶ And they laded their asses with the corn, and departed thence. ²⁷ And as one of them opened his sack to give his ass provender in the inn, he espied his money; for, behold, it was in his sack's mouth. ²⁸ And he said unto his brethren, " My money is restored; and, lo, it is even in my sack." And their heart failed them, and they were afraid, saying one to another, " What is this that God hath done unto us?"

---

⑬ **to see the nakedness of the land ye are come** you have come to see where our land is unprotected.

²⁹ And they came unto Jacob their father unto the land of Canaan, and told him all that befell unto them; saying, ³⁰ "The man, who is the lord of the land, spake roughly to us, and took us for spies of the country. ³¹ And we said unto him, 'We are true men; we are no spies:' ³² We be twelve brethren, sons of our father; one is not, and the youngest is this day with our father in the land of Canaan.' ³³ And the man, the lord of the country, said unto us, 'Hereby shall I know that ye are true men; leave one of your brethren here with me, and take food for the famine of your households, and be gone: ³⁴ And bring your youngest brother unto me: then shall I know that ye are no spies, but that ye are true men: so will I deliver you your brother, and ye shall traffick in the land.'"

³⁵ And it came to pass as they emptied their sacks, that, behold, every man's bundle of money was in his sack; and when both they and their father saw the bundles of money, they were afraid. ³⁶ And Jacob their father said unto them, "Me have ye bereaved of my children: Joseph is not⑭, and Simeon is not, and ye will take Benjamin away: all these things are against me." ³⁷ And Reuben spake unto his father, saying, "Slay my two sons, if I bring him not to thee: deliver him into my hand, and I will bring him to thee again." ³⁸ And he said, "My son shall not go down with you; for his brother is dead, and he is left alone: if mischief befall him by the way in the which ye go, then shall ye bring down my gray hairs with sorrow to the grave."

The Second Journey of the Brothers

Genesis 43

¹ And the famine was sore in the land. ² And it came to pass, when they had eaten up the corn which they had brought out of Egypt, their father said unto them, "Go again, buy us a little food." ³ And Judah spake unto him, saying, "The man did solemnly protest unto us, saying, 'Ye shall not see my face, except your brother be with you.' ⁴ If thou wilt send our brother with us, we will go down and buy thee food. ⁵ But if thou wilt not send him, we will not go down: for the man said unto us, 'Ye shall not see my face, except your brother be with you.'" ⁶ And Israel said, "Wherefore dealt ye so ill with me, as to tell the man whether ye had yet a brother?" ⁷ And they said, "The man asked us straitly of our state, and of our kindred, saying, 'Is your father yet alive? Have ye another brother?' And we told him according to the tenor of these words: could we certainly know that he would say, 'Bring your brother down?'" ⁸ And Judah said unto Israel his father, "Send the lad with me, and we will arise and go; that we may live, and not die, both we, and thou, and also our little ones. ⁹ I will be surety for him⑮; of my hand shalt thou require him: if I bring him not unto thee, and set him before thee, then let me bear the blame for ever: ¹⁰ For except we had lingered, surely now we had returned this second time."

¹¹ And their father Israel said unto them, "If it must be so now, do this; take of the best fruits in the land in your vessels, and carry down the man a present, a little balm, and a little honey, spices, and myrrh, nuts, and almonds: ¹² And take double money in your hand; and the money that was brought again in the mouth of your sacks, carry it again in your hand; peradventure it was an oversight. ¹³ Take also your brother, and arise, go again unto the man: ¹⁴ And God Almighty give you mercy before the man, that he may send away your other brother, and Benjamin. If I be bereaved of my children, I am bereaved."

¹⁵ And the men took that present, and they took double money in their hand, and Benjamin; and rose up, and went down to Egypt, and stood before Joseph. ¹⁶ And when Joseph saw Benjamin with them, he said to the ruler of his house, "Bring these men home, and slay, and make ready; for these men shall dine with me at noon." ¹⁷ And the man did as Joseph bade; and the man brought the men into Joseph's house. ¹⁸ And the men were afraid, because they were brought into Joseph's house; and they said, "Because of the money that was returned in our sacks at the first time are we brought in; that he may seek occasion against us, and fall upon us, and take us for bondmen, and our asses." ¹⁹ And they came near to the steward of Joseph's house, and they

---

⑭ **is not** no more.
⑮ **I will be surety for him** I will guarantee his safety.

communed with him at the door of the house, ^{20} And said, "O sir, we came indeed down at the first time to buy food: ^{21} And it came to pass, when we came to the inn, that we opened our sacks, and, behold, every man's money was in the mouth of his sack, our money in full weight: and we have brought it again in our hand. ^{22} And other money have we brought down in our hands to buy food: we cannot tell who put our money in our sacks." ^{23} And he said, "Peace be to you, fear not: your God, and the God of your father, hath given you treasure in your sacks. I had your money." And he brought Simeon out unto them. ^{24} And the man brought the men into Joseph's house, and gave them water, and they washed their feet; and he gave their asses provender. ^{25} And they made ready the present against Joseph came at noon: for they heard that they should eat bread there.

^{26} And when Joseph came home, they brought him the present which was in their hand into the house, and bowed themselves to him to the earth. ^{27} And he asked them of their welfare, and said, "Is your father well, the old man of whom ye spake? Is he yet alive?" ^{28} And they answered, "Thy servant our father is in good health, he is yet alive." And they bowed down their heads, and made obeisance. ^{29} And he lifted up his eyes, and saw his brother Benjamin, his mother's son, and said, "Is this your younger brother, of whom ye spake unto me?" And he said, "God be gracious unto thee, my son." ^{30} And Joseph made haste; for his bowels did yearn upon his brother: and he sought where to weep; and he entered into his chamber, and wept there. ^{31} And he washed his face, and went out, and refrained himself, and said, "Set on bread." ^{32} And they set on for him by himself, and for them by themselves, and for the Egyptians, which did eat with him, by themselves: because the Egyptians might not eat bread with the Hebrews; for that is an abomination unto the Egyptians. ^{33} And they sat before him, the firstborn according to his birthright, and the youngest according to his youth: and the men marvelled one at another. ^{34} And he took and sent messes unto them from before him: but Benjamin's mess was five times so much as any of theirs. And they drank, and were merry with him.

A Silver Cup in a Sack

Genesis 44

^{1} And he commanded the steward of his house, saying, "Fill the men's sacks with food, as much as they can carry, and put every man's money in his sack's mouth. ^{2} And put my cup, the silver cup, in the sack's mouth of the youngest, and his corn money." And he did according to the word that Joseph had spoken.

^{3} As soon as the morning was light, the men were sent away, they and their asses. ^{4} And when they were gone out of the city, and not yet far off, Joseph said unto his steward, "Up, follow after the men; and when thou dost overtake them, say unto them, 'Wherefore have ye rewarded evil for good? ^{5} Is not this it in which my lord drinketh, and whereby indeed he divineth? Ye have done evil in so doing.'"

^{6} And he overtook them, and he spake unto them these same words. ^{7} And they said unto him, "Wherefore saith my lord these words? God forbid that thy servants should do according to this thing: ^{8} Behold, the money, which we found in our sacks' mouths, we brought again unto thee out of the land of Canaan: how then should we steal out of thy lord's house silver or gold? ^{9} With whomsoever of thy servants it be found, both let him die, and we also will be my lord's bondmen." ^{10} And he said, "Now also let it be according unto your words: he with whom it is found shall be my servant; and ye shall be blameless." ^{11} Then they speedily took down every man his sack to the ground, and opened every man his sack. ^{12} And he searched, and began at the eldest, and left at the youngest: and the cup was found in Benjamin's sack. ^{13} Then they rent their clothes, and laded every man his ass, and returned to the city.

^{14} And Judah and his brethren came to Joseph's house; for he was yet there: and they fell before him on the ground. ^{15} And Joseph said unto them, "What deed is this that ye have done? Wot ye not that such a man as I can certainly divine?⑯" ^{16} And Judah said, "What shall we say unto my lord? what shall we speak? or

---

⑯ **wot ye not that such a man as I can certainly divine**? Don't you know that a man like me can find things out by divination?

how shall we clear ourselves? God hath found out the iniquity of thy servants: behold, we are my lord's servants, both we, and he also with whom the cup is found." ¹⁷ And he said, " God forbid that I should do so: but the man in whose hand the cup is found, he shall be my servant; and as for you, get you up in peace unto your father."

¹⁸ Then Judah came near unto him, and said, " Oh my lord, let thy servant, I pray thee, speak a word in my lord's ears, and let not thine anger burn against thy servant: for thou art even as Pharaoh. ¹⁹ My lord asked his servants, saying, ' Have ye a father, or a brother?' ²⁰ And we said unto my lord, ' We have a father, an old man, and a child of his old age, a little one; and his brother is dead, and he alone is left of his mother, and his father loveth him.' ²¹ And thou saidst unto thy servants, ' Bring him down unto me, that I may set mine eyes upon him.' ²² And we said unto my lord, ' The lad cannot leave his father: for if he should leave his father, his father would die.' ²³ And thou saidst unto thy servants, ' Except your youngest brother come down with you, ye shall see my face no more.'

²⁴ And it came to pass when we came up unto thy servant my father, we told him the words of my lord. ²⁵ And our father said, ' Go again, and buy us a little food.' ²⁶ And we said, ' We cannot go down: if our youngest brother be with us, then will we go down: for we may not see the man's face, except our youngest brother be with us.' ²⁷ And thy servant my father said unto us, ' Ye know that my wife bare me two sons: ²⁸ And the one went out from me, and I said, Surely he is torn in pieces; and I saw him not since: ²⁹ And if ye take this also from me, and mischief befall him, ye shall bring down my gray hairs with sorrow to the grave.'

³⁰ Now therefore when I come to thy servant my father, and the lad be not with us; seeing that his life is bound up in the lad's life; ³¹ It shall come to pass, when he seeth that the lad is not with us, that he will die: and thy servants shall bring down the gray hairs of thy servant our father with sorrow to the grave. ³² For thy servant became surety for the lad unto my father, saying, ' If I bring him not unto thee, then I shall bear the blame to my father for ever.' ³³ Now therefore, I pray thee, let thy servant abide instead of the lad a bondman to my lord; and let the lad go up with his brethren. ³⁴ For how shall I go up to my father, and the lad be not with me? lest peradventure I see the evil that shall come on my father."

Joseph Made Himself Known

Genesis 45

¹ Then Joseph could not refrain himself before all them that stood by him; and he cried, " Cause every man to go out from me." And there stood no man with him, while Joseph made himself known unto his brethren. ² And he wept aloud: and the Egyptians and the house of Pharaoh heard. ³ And Joseph said unto his brethren, " I am Joseph; doth my father yet live? And his brethren could not answer him; for they were troubled at his presence." ⁴ And Joseph said unto his brethren, " Come near to me, I pray you." And they came near. And he said, " I am Joseph your brother, whom ye sold into Egypt. ⁵ Now therefore be not grieved, nor angry with yourselves, that ye sold me hither: for God did send me before you to preserve life. ⁶ For these two years hath the famine been in the land: and yet there are five years, in the which there shall neither be earing nor harvest. ⁷ And God sent me before you to preserve you a posterity in the earth, and to save your lives by a great deliverance. ⁸ So now it was not you that sent me hither, but God: and he hath made me a father to Pharaoh, and lord of all his house, and a ruler throughout all the land of Egypt. ⁹ Haste ye, and go up to my father, and say unto him, ' Thus saith thy son Joseph, God hath made me lord of all Egypt: come down unto me, tarry not: ¹⁰ And thou shalt dwell in the

Joseph Recognized by His Brothers,
Peter Cornelius (1784—1867)

land of Goshen⑰, and thou shalt be near unto me, thou, and thy children, and thy children's children, and thy flocks, and thy herds, and all that thou hast: ¹¹ And there will I nourish thee; for yet there are five years of famine; lest thou, and thy household, and all that thou hast, come to poverty. ¹² And, behold, your eyes see, and the eyes of my brother Benjamin, that it is my mouth that speaketh unto you. ¹³ And ye shall tell my father of all my glory in Egypt, and of all that ye have seen; and ye shall haste and bring down my father hither." ¹⁴ And he fell upon his brother Benjamin's neck, and wept; and Benjamin wept upon his neck. ¹⁵ Moreover he kissed all his brethren, and wept upon them: and after that his brethren talked with him.

¹⁶ And the fame thereof was heard in Pharaoh's house, saying, "Joseph's brethren are come." And it pleased Pharaoh well, and his servants. ¹⁷ And Pharaoh said unto Joseph, "Say unto thy brethren, this do ye; Lade your beasts, and go, get you unto the land of Canaan; ¹⁸ And take your father and your households, and come unto me: and I will give you the good of the land of Egypt, and ye shall eat the fat of the land. ¹⁹ Now thou art commanded, this do ye; take you wagons out of the land of Egypt for your little ones, and for your wives, and bring your father, and come. ²⁰ Also regard not your stuff; for the good of all the land of Egypt is yours."

Cultural Connections: *Joseph and the Amazing Technicolor Dreamcoat*

Joseph and the Amazing Technicolor Dreamcoat is an Andrew Lloyd Webber musical with lyrics by Tim Rice. It is one of the most popular musicals for schools and amateur theatre groups, acclaimed for its family-friendly storyline, universal themes and a variety of musical styles like French ballads ("Those Canaan Days"), Elvis-inspired rock'n roll ("Song of the King"), western ("One More Angel in Heaven"), 1920s Charleston ("Potiphar"), Reggae ("Benjamin Calypso") and disco ("Go, Go, Go Joseph"). The amusing and idiomatic lyrics are equally entertaining.

²¹ And the children of Israel did so: and Joseph gave them wagons, according to the commandment of Pharaoh, and gave them provision for the way. ²² To all of them he gave each man changes of raiment; but to Benjamin he gave three hundred pieces of silver, and five changes of raiment. ²³ And to his father he sent after this manner; ten asses laden with the good things of Egypt, and ten she asses laden with corn and bread and meat for his father by the way. ²⁴ So he sent his brethren away, and they departed: and he said unto them, "See that ye fall not out by the way."

²⁵ And they went up out of Egypt, and came into the land of Canaan unto Jacob their father, ²⁶ And told him, saying, "Joseph is yet alive, and he is governor over all the land of Egypt." And Jacob's heart fainted, for he believed them not. ²⁷ And they told him all the words of Joseph, which he had said unto them: and when he saw the wagons which Joseph had sent to carry him, the spirit of Jacob their father revived: ²⁸ And Israel said, "It is enough; Joseph my son is yet alive: I will go and see him before I die."

III FOOD FOR THOUGHT

1. Did Joseph encourage the hostility that existed between his brothers and himself? How?
2. What reason did Joseph give for ignoring Potiphar's wife?

---

⑰ Goshen /ˈɡəʊʃən/, 歌珊地。

3. What was the relationship between Joseph and Pharaoh's butler and baker as the story began? And how did it change as the story developed?
4. How did Joseph's advice to Pharaoh work to his own advantage?
5. What might have been Joseph's motive in putting his brothers through these "tests"?

IV BIBLICAL RELEVANCE

A. Biblical Terms in Everyday English
1. coat of many colors: _____
2. Joseph's coat: _____
3. Potiphar's wife syndrome: _____
4. Pharaoh's fat/gaunt cows: _____
5. Benjamin's mess: _____

B. Biblical References in Literature
1. I don't believe you ever knew what a sore touch it was with Boy that you were such a Joseph about women. He felt it put him in the wrong. He always felt that the best possible favour you could do a woman was to push her into bed.
   (Robertson Davies, *The Manticore*, 1972)
2. So pressing an issue is it [the sexual harassment of men by women] ... that the European Union considered it necessary to produce a 93-page booklet on what it described as "the Potiphar's wife syndrome."
   (*The Guardian*, 1994)
3. I suppose he is interested in my dreams because a dream can mean something, or so it says in the Bible, such as Pharaoh and the fat kine and the lean kine, and Jacob with the angels going up and down the ladder.
   (Margaret Atwood, *Alias Grace*, 1996)
4. The honour and love you bear him is nothing but meet, for God has given him great gifts, and he uses them as the patriarch Joseph did, who, when he was exalted to a place of power and trust, yet yearned with tenderness towards his parents, and his younger brother.
   (George Eliot, *Adam Bede*, 1859)
5. It's a bleak and barren country there, not like this land of Goshen you've been used to.
   (George Eliot, *Adam Bede*, 1859)

C. The Bible and Arts
1. *Joseph Being Sold by His Brothers*, 1816, Johann Friedrich Overbeck
2. *Judah and Tamar*, Emile Jean Horace Vernet (1789—1863)
3. *Joseph and Potiphar's Wife*, c. 1631, Guido Reni
4. *The Dreams of the Cupbearer and the Baker*, 1626, Bernardo Strozzi
5. *Joseph Recognized by His Brothers*, Peter von Cornelius (1784—1867)
6. *Stories of Joseph*, c. 1520, Andrea del Sarto

V SOURCES FOR REFERENCE

1. (2000). *Joseph and the Amazing Technicolor Dreamcoat*. A straight-to-video musical film by Andrew Lloyd Webber, Universal Studios.
2. Keller, W., (transl.) (1980). *The Bible as History*. New York: Bantam Books.

PART TWO

THE EMERGENCE OF ISRAEL
(C. 1,700—1,200 B.C.E.)
THE BOOK OF EXODUS

6. BONDAGE IN EGYPT

1 POINTS OF DEPARTURE

As the second book of the Pentateuch, Exodus is not to be taken as a book of history. It is a description of events in Hebrew memory, narrated in such a way that the nation could understand and value itself. Taking its title from the Greek LXX[①], it means "departure" and consists of some of the most memorable stories ever told: the birth and calling of Moses (*Exod.* 2—6), the contest between Moses and Pharaoh, and the ten plagues, culminating in the death of the first-born (*Exod.* 7—12), the march out of Egypt including the dramatic parting of the Red Sea (*Exod.* 13—15), wanderings in the wilderness (*Exod.* 15:22—18), and the meetings at the mountain (*Exod.* 19—40).

Nothing makes a nation's blood boil like a liberator: George Washington and Abraham Lincoln in the United States, Mahatma Gandhi in India and Nelson Mandela in South Africa, the controversial revolutionary Guevara in Cuba, and of course, Dr. Sun Yet-sat and Mao Zedong in China. In these charismatic leaders we see such shared qualities as vision, faith, devotion, courage and resourcefulness. But most of these qualities were found lacking in Moses, at least in the beginning of his career, when he was uncertain about his ability to lead, citing the four difficulties of his when facing his God: his unworthiness and lack of authority, his fear of the people's distrust, his speech difficulties and his sheer cowardice (*Exod.* 4:1—13). But with God's assurance of his continuing presence, Moses went forward to meet his challenges and developed from a fumbling start to his emergence as one of history's most decisive and powerful leaders and is named in the New Testament as the giver of the Law (*Mk.* 7:10; *Rom.* 9:15; 2 *Cor.* 3:13), as one whose faith is an example to the Church (*Heb.* 3:2; 11:24), and as the prophet of the Messiah (*Ac.* 3:22). In Matthew, Jesus is portrayed as the "second Moses," who proclaims the New Law (*Mt.* 5—7). At the Transfiguration, Moses is said to be present and so authenticates Jesus' claim as uttered by the heavenly voice (*Mk.* 9:7).

Speaking of the influence of the Book of Exodus, we are again mindful of William Shakespeare's "The devil can cite Scripture for his purpose." Indeed, people had kept coming back to the Bible in search of evidences either to support or condemn slavery until it got generally abolished in the 19th century in England, thanks to the unremitting efforts of William Wilberforce (1759—1833). Ever since then, the Exodus story has provided inspiration, metaphor, and support to the downtrodden in their struggle for freedom. Take Afro-Americans. Just as the Hebrews who were slaves in Egypt escaped with God's help, and eventually entered the Promised Land, so the African American slaves eventually were freed and have slowly struggled for civil rights. The Exodus story just resonates throughout African American spirituals, abolitionist

---

① **LXX** the symbol employed for the Septuagint (七十士译本), an Ancient Greek translation of the Hebrew Bible (the Old Testament), based on the legend that it was the many days' work of seventy (or seventy-two) scholars in Alexandria, Egypt. More probably, it was done less hurriedly sometime between 285 B.C.E. and 150 B.C.E.

writings, e. g. of the former slave Frederick Douglas, and the speeches of Dr. Martin Luther King, Jr., who in his last speech made a parallel between Moses who did not live to enter the Promised Land and him himself who was to be assassinated by saying, "... And I've seen the Promised Land. I may not get there with you. But I want you to know tonight, that we, as a people will get to the Promised Land. ..."

II SELECTED READINGS

The Waxing and Suffering of the Israelites

Exodus 1

¹ Now these are the names of the children of Israel, which came into Egypt; every man and his household came with Jacob.² Reuben, Simeon, Levi, and Judah, ³ Issachar, Zebulun, and Benjamin, ⁴ Dan, and Naphtali, Gad, and Asher. ⁵ And all the souls that came out of the loins of Jacob were seventy souls: for Joseph was in Egypt already.

⁶ And Joseph died, and all his brethren, and all that generation. ⁷ And the children of Israel were fruitful, and increased abundantly, and multiplied, and waxed exceeding mighty; and the land was filled with them.

⁸ Now there arose up a new king over Egypt, who knew not Joseph. ⁹ And he said unto his people, "Behold, the people of the children of Israel are more and mightier than we. ¹⁰ Come on, let us deal wisely with them, lest they multiply and it come to pass, when there befalleth any war, that they join also unto our enemies and fight against us, and so get them up out of the land."

¹¹ Therefore they set over them taskmasters to afflict them with their burdens. And they built for Pharaoh treasure cities, Pithom and Raamses.¹² But the more they afflicted them, the more they multiplied and grew; and they were grieved because of the children of Israel. ¹³ And the Egyptians made the children of Israel to serve with rigor. ¹⁴ And they made their lives bitter with hard bondage, in mortar and in brick, and in all manner of service in the field; all their service wherein they made them serve was with rigor.

The Wisdom of the Hebrew Midwives

¹⁵ And the king of Egypt spoke to the Hebrew midwives, of whom the name of one was Shiphrah, and the name of the other Puah. ¹⁶ And he said, "When ye do the office of a midwife to the Hebrew women and see them upon the birthstools, if it be a son then ye shall kill him; but if it be a daughter then she shall live." ¹⁷ But the midwives feared God, and did not do as the king of Egypt commanded them, but saved the men children alive. ¹⁸ And the king of Egypt called for the midwives and said unto them, "Why have ye done this thing, and have saved the men children alive?"

¹⁹ And the midwives said unto Pharaoh, "Because the Hebrew women are not as the Egyptian women; for they are lively, and are delivered ere the midwives come in unto them."

²⁰ Therefore God dealt well with the midwives, and the people multiplied and waxed very mighty. ²¹ And it came to pass, because the midwives feared God, that He made them houses.

²² And Pharaoh charged all his people, saying, "Every son who is born ye shall cast into the river, and every daughter ye shall save alive."

The Hebrew Midwives

The Birth of Moses

Exodus 2

¹ And there went a man of the house of Levi, and took for a wife a daughter of Levi. ² And the woman conceived and bore a son; and when she saw that he was a goodly child, she hid him three months. ³ And when she could no longer hide him, she took for him an ark of bulrushes, and daubed it with slime and with pitch, and put the child therein; and she laid it in the reeds by the river's brink. ⁴ And his sister stood afar off to learn what would be done to him.

Moses Saved from the Water, 1518—1519, Raphael

⁵ And the daughter of Pharaoh came down to wash herself at the river, and her maidens walked along by the riverside; and when she saw the ark among the reeds, she sent her maid to fetch it. ⁶ And when she had opened it, she saw the child; and behold, the babe wept. And she had compassion on him and said, "This is one of the Hebrews' children."

⁷ Then said his sister to Pharaoh's daughter, "Shall I go and call to thee a nurse of the Hebrew women, that she may nurse the child for thee?"

⁸ And Pharaoh's daughter said to her, "Go." And the maid went and called the child's mother. ⁹ And Pharaoh's daughter said unto her, "Take this child away and nurse it for me, and I will give thee thy wages." And the woman took the child, and nursed it. ¹⁰ And the child grew, and she brought him unto Pharaoh's daughter, and he became her son. And she called his name Moses②, and she said, "Because I drew him out of the water."

Moses Flees to Midian

¹¹ And it came to pass in those days, when Moses was grown, that he went out unto his brethren and looked on their burdens; and he spied an Egyptian smiting a Hebrew, one of his brethren. ¹² And he looked this way and that way, and when he saw that there was no man, he slew the Egyptian and hid him in the sand. ¹³ And when he went out the second day, behold, two men of the Hebrews strove together; and he said to him that did the wrong, "Why smitest thou thy fellow?"

¹⁴ And he said, "Who made thee a prince and a judge over us? Intendest thou to kill me as thou killed the Egyptian?" And Moses feared and said, "Surely this thing is known."

¹⁵ Now when Pharaoh heard this thing, he sought to slay Moses. But Moses fled from the face of Pharaoh, and dwelt in the land of Midian; and he sat down by a well. ¹⁶ Now the priest of Midian had seven daughters; and they came and drew water, and filled the troughs to water their father's flock. ¹⁷ And the shepherds came and drove them away; but Moses stood up and helped them, and watered their flock.

¹⁸ And when they came to Reuel their father, he said, "How is it that ye have come so soon today?"

¹⁹ And they said, "An Egyptian delivered us out of the hand of the shepherds, and also drew water enough for us and watered the flock."

²⁰ And he said unto his daughters, "And where is he? Why is it that ye have left the man? Call him, that he may eat bread."

²¹ And Moses was content to dwell with the man; and he gave Moses Zipporah his daughter. ²² And she bore him a son, and he called his name Gershom③; for he said, "I have been a stranger in a strange land."

²³ And it came to pass in process of time that the king of Egypt died. And the children of Israel sighed by

---

② **Moses** (/ˈməʊzɪz/, 摩西) sounds like the Hebrew for *draw out*.
③ **Gershom** (/ˈɡəʃɔm/, 革舜) sounds like the Hebrew for *a stranger there*.

reason of the bondage, and they cried; and their cry came up unto God by reason of the bondage. ²⁴ And God heard their groaning, and God remembered His covenant with Abraham, with Isaac, and with Jacob. ²⁵ And God looked upon the children of Israel, and God had respect unto them.

Moses and the Burning Bush

Exodus 3

¹ Now Moses kept the flock of Jethro his father-in-law, the priest of Midian; and he led the flock to the back side of the desert and came to the mountain of God, even to Horeb. ² And the angel of the LORD appeared unto him in a flame of fire out of the midst of a bush; and he looked and, behold, the bush burned with fire, and the bush was not consumed. ³ And Moses said, " I will now turn aside and see this great sight, why the bush is not burnt."

⁴ And when the LORD saw that he turned aside to see, God called unto him out of the midst of the bush and said, " Moses, Moses."

And he said, " Here am I."

⁵ And He said, " Draw not nigh hither. Put off thy shoes from off thy feet, for the place whereon thou standest is holy ground." ⁶ Moreover He said, " I am the God of thy father, the God of Abraham, the God of Isaac, and the God of Jacob." And Moses hid his face, for he was afraid to look upon God.

Burning Bush, Sebastien Bourdon (1616—1671)

⁷ And the LORD said, " I have surely seen the affliction of My people who are in Egypt, and have heard their cry by reason of their taskmasters, for I know their sorrows. ⁸ And I have come down to deliver them out of the hand of the Egyptians, and to bring them up out of that land unto a good land and a large, unto a land flowing with milk and honey, unto the place of the Canaanites and the Hittites, and the Amorites and the Perizzites, and the Hivites and the Jebusites. ⁹ Now therefore behold, the cry of the children of Israel hath come unto Me, and I have also seen the oppression wherewith the Egyptians oppress them. ¹⁰ Come now therefore, and I will send thee unto Pharaoh, that thou mayest bring forth My people, the children of Israel, out of Egypt."

¹¹ And Moses said unto God, " Who am I, that I should go unto Pharaoh, and that I should bring forth the children of Israel out of Egypt?"

¹² And He said, " Certainly I will be with thee; and this shall be a token unto thee that I have sent thee: when thou hast brought forth the people out of Egypt, ye shall serve God upon this mountain."

¹³ And Moses said unto God, " Behold, when I come unto the children of Israel and shall say unto them, ' The God of your fathers hath sent me unto you,' and they shall say to me, ' What is His name?' what shall I say unto them?"

¹⁴ And God said unto Moses, " I AM THAT I AM."④ And He said, " Thus shalt thou say unto the children of Israel, ' I AM hath sent me unto you.' "

¹⁵ And God said moreover unto Moses, " Thus shalt thou say unto the children of Israel: The LORD God of your fathers, the God of Abraham, the God of Isaac, and the God of Jacob hath sent me unto you.' This is My name for ever, and this is My memorial unto all generations.

¹⁶ " Go, and gather the elders of Israel together, and say unto them, ' The LORD God of your fathers, the God of Abraham, of Isaac, and of Jacob appeared unto me, saying, I have surely visited you and seen that which is done to you in Egypt; ¹⁷ And I have said I will bring you up out of the affliction of Egypt unto the

---

④ **I AM THAT I AM** literal translation of the Hebrew Tetragrammaton YHWH or *Yahweh* when vowels are added. Though there is no agreement as to the exact meaning of the name, four views are suggested: (a) *He who falls.* (b) *He who causes to be.* (c) *He who will be what he will be.* (d) The name developed from an exclamation or an ejaculation used in the cult. (Black, 2001:212—213)

land of the Canaanites and the Hittites, and the Amorites and the Perizzites, and the Hivites and the Jebusites, unto a land flowing with milk and honey.'

^{18} "And they shall hearken to thy voice; and thou shalt come, thou and the elders of Israel, unto the king of Egypt, and ye shall say unto him, ' The LORD God of the Hebrews hath met with us; and now let us go, we beseech thee, three days' journey into the wilderness, that we may sacrifice to the LORD our God.'

^{19} "And I am sure that the king of Egypt will not let you go, no, not by a mighty hand. ^{20} And I will stretch out My hand and smite Egypt with all My wonders which I will do in the midst thereof; and after that he will let you go.

^{21} "And I will give this people favor in the sight of the Egyptians. And it shall come to pass that, when ye go, ye shall not go empty, ^{22} But every woman shall borrow of her neighbor and of her that sojourneth in her house jewels of silver and jewels of gold and raiment; and ye shall put them upon your sons and upon your daughters, and ye shall despoil the Egyptians."

Signs for Moses

Exodus 4

^{1} And Moses answered and said, "But, behold, they will not believe me, nor hearken unto my voice; for they will say, ' The LORD hath not appeared unto thee.' " ^{2} And the LORD said unto him, "What is that in thine hand?" And he said, "A rod." ^{3} And He said, " Cast it on the ground." And he cast it on the ground, and it became a serpent; and Moses fled from before it. ^{4} And the LORD said unto Moses, " Put forth thine hand and take it by the tail." And he put forth his hand and caught it, and it became a rod in his hand — ^{5} " That they may believe that the LORD God of their fathers, the God of Abraham, the God of Isaac, and the God of Jacob hath appeared unto thee." ^{6} And the LORD said furthermore unto him, " Put now thine hand into thy bosom." And he put his hand into his bosom; and when he took it out, behold, his hand was leprous as snow. ^{7} And He said, " Put thine hand into thy bosom again." And he put his hand into his bosom again and plucked it out of his bosom, and behold, it was turned again as his other flesh. ^{8} " And it shall come to pass, if they will not believe thee, neither hearken to the voice of the first sign, that they will believe the voice of the latter sign. ^{9} And it shall come to pass, if they will not believe also these two signs, neither hearken unto thy voice, that thou shalt take of the water of the river and pour it upon the dry land; and the water which thou takest out of the river shall become blood upon the dry land."

^{10} And Moses said unto the LORD, " O my Lord, I am not eloquent, neither heretofore nor since Thou hast spoken unto Thy servant; but I am slow of speech and of a slow tongue." ^{11} And the LORD said unto him, " Who hath made man's mouth? Or who maketh the dumb or deaf, or the seeing or the blind? Have not I, the LORD? ^{12} Now therefore go, and I will be with thy mouth and teach thee what thou shalt say." ^{13} And he said, " O my Lord, send, I pray Thee, by the hand of him whom Thou wilt send." ^{14} And the anger of the LORD was kindled against Moses, and He said, " Is not Aaron the Levite thy brother? I know that he can speak well. And also, behold, he cometh forth to meet thee; and when he seeth thee, he will be glad in his heart. ^{15} And thou shalt speak unto him and put words in his mouth; and I will be with thy mouth and with his mouth, and will teach you what ye shall do. ^{16} And he shall be thy spokesman unto the people; and he shall be, even he shall be to thee instead of a mouth, and thou shalt be to him instead of God. ^{17} And thou shalt take this rod in thine hand, wherewith thou shalt do signs."

Moses Returns to Egypt

^{18} And Moses went and returned to Jethro his father-in-law, and said unto him, " Let me go, I pray thee, and return unto my brethren who are in Egypt and see whether they are yet alive." And Jethro said to Moses, " Go in peace." ^{19} And the LORD said unto Moses in Midian, " Go, return into Egypt; for all the men are dead who sought thy life." ^{20} And Moses took his wife and his sons, and set them upon an ass, and he returned to the land of Egypt. And Moses took the rod of God in his hand.

²¹ And the LORD said unto Moses, "When thou goest to return into Egypt, see that thou do all those wonders before Pharaoh which I have put in thine hand; but I will harden his heart, that he shall not let the people go. ²² And thou shalt say unto Pharaoh, 'Thus saith the LORD: Israel is My son, even My firstborn. ²³ And I say unto thee, "Let My son go, that he may serve Me." And if thou refuse to let him go, behold, I will slay thy son, even thy firstborn.'"

²⁴ And it came to pass, on the way at the inn, that the LORD met him and sought to kill him. ²⁵ Then Zipporah took a sharp stone and cut off the foreskin of her son, and cast it at his feet and said, "Surely a bloody husband art thou to me." ²⁶ So He let him go; then she said, "A bloody husband thou art, because of the circumcision."

²⁷ And the LORD said to Aaron, "Go into the wilderness to meet Moses." And he went and met him on the mount of God, and kissed him. ²⁸ And Moses told Aaron all the words of the LORD who had sent him, and all the signs which He had commanded him. ²⁹ And Moses and Aaron went and gathered together all the elders of the children of Israel. ³⁰ And Aaron spoke all the words which the LORD had spoken unto Moses, and did the signs in the sight of the people. ³¹ And the people believed; and when they heard that the LORD had visited the children of Israel, and that He had looked upon their affliction, then they bowed their heads and worshiped.

Bricks without Straw

Exodus 5

¹ And afterward Moses and Aaron went in and told Pharaoh, "Thus saith the LORD God of Israel: 'Let My people go, that they may hold a feast unto Me in the wilderness.'"

² And Pharaoh said, "Who is the LORD, that I should obey his voice to let Israel go? I know not the LORD, neither will I let Israel go." ³ And they said, "The God of the Hebrews hath met with us. Let us go, we pray thee, three days' journey into the desert and sacrifice unto the LORD our God, lest He fall upon us with pestilence or with the sword."

⁴ And the king of Egypt said unto them, "Why do ye, Moses and Aaron, delay the people from their work? Get you unto your burdens!" ⁵ And Pharaoh said, "Behold, the people of the land now are many, and ye make them rest from their burdens!"

⁶ And Pharaoh commanded the same day the taskmasters of the people and their officers, saying, ⁷ "Ye shall no more give the people straw to make brick, as heretofore. Let them go and gather straw for themselves. ⁸ And the tally of bricks which they made heretofore, ye shall lay upon them; ye shall not diminish any thereof. For they are idle; therefore they cry, saying, 'Let us go and sacrifice to our God.' ⁹ Let there more work be laid upon the men, that they may labor therein, and let them not regard vain words."

The Bible in Everyday English: *making bricks without straw*

Ordering the Israelites to make bricks but denying them the use of straw is comparable to requesting the cleverest Chinese housewife to cook a meal without rice (巧妇难为无米之炊). The proverb *you can not make bricks without straw* then means "one can not make something without the necessary materials."

^{10} And the taskmasters of the people went out, and their officers, and they spoke to the people, saying, "Thus saith Pharaoh: ' I will not give you straw. ^{11} Go ye, get you straw where ye can find it; yet not any of your work shall be diminished.' " ^{12} So the people were scattered abroad throughout all the land of Egypt to gather stubble instead of straw. ^{13} And the taskmasters hastened them, saying, " Fulfill your works, your daily tasks, as when there was straw." ^{14} And the officers of the children of Israel, whom Pharaoh's taskmasters had set over them, were beaten and were demanded, " Why have ye not fulfilled your task in making brick both yesterday and today, as heretofore?"

^{15} Then the officers of the children of Israel came and cried unto Pharaoh, saying, " Why dealest thou thus with thy servants? ^{16} There is no straw given unto thy servants, and they say to us, ' Make brick!' And behold, thy servants are beaten, but the fault is in thine own people."

^{17} But he said, " Ye are idle, ye are idle! Therefore ye say, ' Let us go and do sacrifice to the LORD.' ^{18} Go therefore now and work; for there shall no straw be given you, yet shall ye deliver the tally of bricks."

^{19} And the officers of the children of Israel saw that they were in evil straits after it was said, " Ye shall not diminish any from your bricks of your daily task." ^{20} And they met Moses and Aaron, who stood in the way as they came forth from Pharaoh. ^{21} And they said unto them, " The LORD look upon you and judge, because ye have made our savor to be abhorred in the eyes of Pharaoh and in the eyes of his servants, to put a sword in their hand to slay us." ...

Questioning with God

Exodus 6

^{1} Then the LORD said unto Moses, " Now shalt thou see what I will do to Pharaoh; for with a strong hand shall he let them go, and with a strong hand shall he drive them out of his land." ^{2} And God spoke unto Moses and said unto him, " I am the LORD. ^{3} And I appeared unto Abraham, unto Isaac, and unto Jacob by the name of God Almighty, but by My name JEHOVAH was I not known to them. ^{4} And I have also established My covenant with them, to give them the land of Canaan, the land of their pilgrimage, wherein they were strangers. ^{5} And I have also heard the groaning of the children of Israel, whom the Egyptians keep in bondage; and I have remembered My covenant.

^{6} Therefore say unto the children of Israel: ' I am the LORD, and I will bring you out from under the burdens of the Egyptians, and I will rid you out from their bondage, and I will redeem you with an outstretched arm and with great judgments. ^{7} And I will take you to Me for a people, and I will be to you a God; and ye shall know that I am the LORD your God, who bringeth you out from under the burdens of the Egyptians. ^{8} And I will bring you in unto the land, concerning which I swore to give to Abraham, to Isaac, and to Jacob; and I will give it to you for a heritage: I am the LORD.' "

^{9} And Moses spoke so unto the children of Israel, but they hearkened not unto Moses from anguish of spirit and from cruel bondage.

^{10} And the LORD spoke unto Moses, saying, ^{11} " Go in, speak unto Pharaoh king of Egypt, that he let the children of Israel go out of his land."

^{12} And Moses spoke before the LORD, saying, " Behold, the children of Israel have not hearkened unto me. How then shall Pharaoh hear me, who am of uncircumcised lips?"

^{13} And the LORD spoke unto Moses and unto Aaron, and gave them a charge unto the children of Israel and unto Pharaoh king of Egypt to bring the children of Israel out of the land of Egypt.

...

The Bible and Western Culture

Cultural Connections: *Michelangelo's Moses*

One of the best-known artwork of Moses is the statue by Michelangelo commissioned for San Pietro in Vincoli (Saint Peter in Chains), a Roman Catholic church in Rome, Italy. Moses is depicted with horns, connoting "the radiance of the Lord," due to the similarity in the Hebrew words for "beams of light" and "horns." Such representation had another, more expedient consideration: horns are easier to chisel than rays of light!

Aaron to Speak for Moses

Exodus 7

¹ And the LORD said unto Moses, "See, I have made thee a god to Pharaoh, and Aaron thy brother shall be thy prophet. ² Thou shalt speak all that I command thee; and Aaron thy brother shall speak unto Pharaoh, that he send the children of Israel out of his land. ³ And I will harden Pharaoh's heart, and multiply My signs and My wonders in the land of Egypt. ⁴ But Pharaoh shall not hearken unto you, that I may lay My hand upon Egypt and bring forth Mine armies and My people, the children of Israel, out of the land of Egypt by great judgments. ⁵ And the Egyptians shall know that I am the LORD, when I stretch forth Mine hand upon Egypt and bring out the children of Israel from among them."

⁶ And Moses and Aaron did as the LORD commanded them; so did they. ⁷ And Moses was fourscore years old, and Aaron fourscore and three years old when they spoke unto Pharaoh.

Aaron's Staff Becomes a Snake

⁸ And the LORD spoke unto Moses and unto Aaron, saying, ⁹ "When Pharaoh shall speak unto you, saying, 'Show a miracle for yourselves,' then thou shalt say unto Aaron, 'Take thy rod and cast it before Pharaoh, and it shall become a serpent.'"

¹⁰ And Moses and Aaron went in unto Pharaoh, and they did so as the LORD had commanded; and Aaron cast down his rod before Pharaoh and before his servants, and it became a serpent. ¹¹ Then Pharaoh also called the wise men and the sorcerers. Now the magicians of Egypt, they also did in like manner with their enchantments. ¹² For they cast down every man his rod, and they became serpents; but Aaron's rod swallowed up their rods. ¹³ And He hardened Pharaoh's heart, that he hearkened not unto them, as the LORD had said. (To be continued)

Moses and Aaron before Pharaoh, Paul Hardy

III FOOD FOR THOUGHT

1. Exodus is held to be a continuation of Genesis. Then how does the narrator make the transition between these two books?
2. What are the ironies concerning the birth and upbringing of Moses?
3. What character traits of Moses are shown in his dialogue with his God in *Exodus 4:1—17*?
4. How did Pharaoh react when asked to let the Israelites go?
5. What role was Aaron to play in Exodus?

IV BIBLICAL RELEVANCE

A. Biblical Terms in Everyday English
1. a stranger in a strange land (2:22): _____
2. the bush burned with fire but not consumed (3:2): _____
3. a land flowing with milk and honey (3:8): _____
4. I AM THAT I AM (3:14): _____
5. harden one's heart (4:21): _____
6. make bricks without straw (5:7): _____

B. Biblical References in Literature
1. "If I go furze-cutting we shall be fairly well off." "In comparison with slaves, and the Israelites in Egypt, and such people!"
   (Thomas Hardy, *The Return of the Native*, 1880)
2. But going back to what's fundamental, Vic, it seems to me you guard everything you do like you were protecting baby Moses from the Pharaoh.
   (Sara Paretsky, *Tunnel Vision*, 1994)
3. She has revelations. All this stuff about Darcy's Utopia is dictated to her, she claims, by a kind of shining cloud. I laughed. I couldn't help it. "Like God appearing to Moses in a burning bush, or the Archangel Gabriel to Mohammed as a shining pillar?" I asked.
   (Fay Weldon, *Darcy's Utopia*, 1990)

C. The Bible and Arts
1. *Moses*, 1515, Michelangelo, St. Pietro in Vincoli, Rome
2. *Moses Saved from the Water*, 1518—1519, Raphael
3. *Pharaoh's Daughter Finds Baby Moses*, 1638, Nicolas Poussin
4. *Moses and Aaron before Pharaoh*, Paul Hardy

V SOURCES FOR REFERENCE

1. (1960). *Exodus*, a film by Otto Preminger based on the novel by Leon Uris about a Jewish refugee ship by that name.
2. (2006). *The Exodus Decoded*, a documentary produced by Simcha Jacobovici attempting to verify the biblical story.
3. Black, M. (ed.) (2001). *Peake's Commentary on the Bible*. London: Routledge.

7. THE PLAGUES OF EGYPT

I POINTS OF DEPARTURE

The ten cataclysmic plagues descending upon the land of Egypt have always filled people with wonder and tested the tech-savvy Hollywood directors time and again. Though all but the last were phenomena or diseases indigenous to Egypt, they were larger than life and served to establish Moses' authority and the connection which the faith of God made between Israelites and God.

A set narrative pattern that emerges through the story of the Ten Plagues can be summarized as follows: 1) Yahweh's instruction for Moses to confront Pharaoh with the ultimatum of letting his people go, 2) Moses' request and Pharaoh's refusal to comply, 3) the visit of a plague, 4) Pharaoh's repentance, 5) the halt of the plague, and 6) the hardening of Pharaoh's heart, and the cycle begins again. With each plague unfolding and abated, we see the Pharaoh's stubbornness represented in various ways: sometimes God "hardened Pharaoh's heart" (7:13); sometimes Pharaoh himself "hardened his heart" (8:15) and also God "hardened his heart" (10:1). Then, a question arises: Since God held such sway, why wasn't Pharaoh impressed to let the Israelites go in the first place?

Three rites derive their origin from *Exodus*: the Passover, the Feast of Unleavened Bread, and the Dedication of the First-born to Yahweh. Among all the plagues, the last was the deadliest, and also the one that proved effective for Israel's deliverance. Sacrificed lamb's blood was sprinkled at the entrance to dwellings of the Israelites so that the death angel passed over their firstborns. God's instructions for the Passover food stressed the need for haste. The unleavened bread were a kind of biscuits that could be baked quickly, also known as "the bread of affliction" (*Dt.* 16:3). The "bitter herbs," another food of necessity, are probably some kind of medicinal ones taken as a preventative against common diseases likely to be contracted during trips.

Today, the Passover is still annually observed as *Pesach* by Jews around the world and each family usually has a memorial meal (called *Seder*) of unleavened bread and bitter herbs, recalling the Israelites' sufferings in slavery and their deliverance. Though Christians do not celebrate this festival, some of its elements have been incorporated into a new Christian festival called the Eucharist, or the Lord's Supper, with Christ representing the Passover Lamb. Apart from the coincidence in timing of Jesus' crucifixion with Passover, the Lord's Supper also memorializes a time of pain and of bloodshed, a time of freedom and deliverance.

II SELECTED READINGS

The Plague of Blood

Exodus 7 (Continued)

Moses stretched forth his rod over the land of Egypt, and the LORD brought an east wind upon the land all that day and all that night; and when it was morning, the east wind brought the locusts. ¹⁴ And the locusts went up over all the land of Egypt, and rested in all the borders of Egyp.¹⁴ And the LORD said unto Moses, " Pharaoh's heart is hardened; he refuseth to let the people go.¹⁵ Get thee unto Pharaoh in the morning. Lo, he goeth out unto the water, and thou shalt stand by the river's brink until he come; and the rod which was turned to a serpent shalt thou take in thine hand.¹⁶ And thou shalt say unto him, ' The LORD God of the Hebrews hath sent me unto thee, saying, Let My people go, that they may serve Me in the wilderness; and behold, hitherto thou wouldest not hear. ¹⁷ Thus saith the LORD: " In this thou shalt know that I am the LORD: Behold, I will smite with the rod that is in mine hand upon the waters which are in the river, and they shall be turned to blood. ¹⁸ And the fish that are in the river shall die, and the river shall stink; and the Egyptians shall loathe to drink of the water of the river."

Moses and Aaron Chonging the Rivers of Egypt to Blood, 1631, Bartholomeus Breenbergh

¹⁹ And the LORD spoke unto Moses, " Say unto Aaron, ' Take thy rod and stretch out thine hand upon the waters of Egypt, upon their streams, upon their rivers, and upon their ponds, and upon all their pools of water, that they may become blood; and that there may be blood throughout all the land of Egypt, both in vessels of wood and in vessels of stone.' "

²⁰ And Moses and Aaron did so, as the LORD commanded; and he lifted up the rod and smote the waters that were in the river, in the sight of Pharaoh and in the sight of his servants; and all the waters that were in the river were turned to blood. ²¹ And the fish that were in the river died; and the river stank, and the Egyptians could not drink of the water of the river; and there was blood throughout all the land of Egypt.

²² And the magicians of Egypt did so with their enchantments; and Pharaoh's heart was hardened, neither did he hearken unto them, as the LORD had said. ²³ And Pharaoh turned and went into his house, neither did he set his heart to this also. ²⁴ And all the Egyptians dug round about the river for water to drink, for they could not drink of the water of the river.

The Plague of Frogs

²⁵ And seven days were fulfilled after the LORD had smitten the river.

Exodus 8

¹ And the LORD spoke unto Moses, " Go unto Pharaoh and say unto him, ' Thus saith the LORD: Let My people go, that they may serve Me. ² And if thou refuse to let them go, behold, I will smite all thy borders with frogs.³ And the river shall bring forth frogs abundantly, which shall go up and come into thine house, and into thy bedchamber and upon thy bed, and into the house of thy servants and upon thy people, and into thine ovens and into thy kneading troughs. ⁴ And the frogs shall come up both on thee and upon thy people and upon all thy servants.' "

The Bible and Western Culture

⁵ And the LORD spoke unto Moses, "Say unto Aaron, 'Stretch forth thine hand with thy rod over the streams, over the rivers and over the ponds, and cause frogs to come up upon the land of Egypt.'"

Plague of Frogs, Ted Larson

⁶ And Aaron stretched out his hand over the waters of Egypt, and the frogs came up and covered the land of Egypt. ⁷ And the magicians did so with their enchantments, and brought up frogs upon the land of Egypt.

⁸ Then Pharaoh called for Moses and Aaron and said, "Entreat the LORD, that he may take away the frogs from me and from my people; and I will let the people go, that they may do sacrifice unto the LORD."

⁹ And Moses said unto Pharaoh, "Glory over me: When shall I entreat for thee and for thy servants and for thy people to destroy the frogs from thee and thy houses, that they may remain in the river only?"

¹⁰ And he said, "Tomorrow." And Moses said, "Be it according to thy word, that thou mayest know that there is none like unto the LORD our God. ¹¹ And the frogs shall depart from thee, and from thy houses and from thy servants and from thy people. They shall remain in the river only."

¹² And Moses and Aaron went out from Pharaoh; and Moses cried unto the LORD because of the frogs which He had brought against Pharaoh. ¹³ And the LORD did according to the word of Moses; and the frogs died out of the houses, out of the villages, and out of the fields. ¹⁴ And they gathered them together upon heaps, and the land stank. ¹⁵ But when Pharaoh saw that there was respite, he hardened his heart and hearkened not unto them, as the LORD had said.

The Plague of Gnats

¹⁶ And the LORD said unto Moses, "Say unto Aaron, 'Stretch out thy rod and smite the dust of the land, that it may become lice throughout all the land of Egypt.'" ¹⁷ And they did so; for Aaron stretched out his hand with his rod and smote the dust of the earth, and it became lice on man and on beast. All the dust of the land became lice throughout all the land of Egypt. ¹⁸ And the magicians so did with their enchantments to bring forth lice, but they could not; so there were lice upon man and upon beast.

¹⁹ Then the magicians said unto Pharaoh, "This is the finger of God." And Pharaoh's heart was hardened, and he hearkened not unto them, as the LORD had said.

The Plague of Flies

²⁰ And the LORD said unto Moses, "Rise up early in the morning and stand before Pharaoh. Lo, he cometh forth to the water, and say unto him, 'Thus saith the LORD: Let My people go, that they may serve Me. ²¹ Else, if thou wilt not let My people go, behold, I will send swarms of flies upon thee, and upon thy servants and upon thy people and into thy houses; and the houses of the Egyptians shall be full of swarms of flies, and also the ground whereon they are.

²² And I will sever in that day the land of Goshen in which My people dwell, that no swarms of flies shall be there, to the end thou mayest know that I am the LORD in the midst of the earth. ²³ And I will put a division between My people and thy people. Tomorrow shall this sign be.'"

²⁴ And the LORD did so; and there came a grievous swarm of flies into the house of Pharaoh, and into his servants' houses and into all the land of Egypt. The land was corrupted by reason of the swarm of flies.

²⁵ And Pharaoh called for Moses and for Aaron and said, "Go ye, sacrifice to your God in the land."

²⁶ And Moses said, "It is not meet so to do; for we shall sacrifice the abomination of the Egyptians to the LORD our God. Lo, shall we sacrifice the abomination of the Egyptians before their eyes, and will they not stone us? ²⁷ We will go three days' journey into the wilderness and sacrifice to the LORD our God, as He shall

command us."

^{28} And Pharaoh said, " I will let you go, that ye may sacrifice to the LORD your God in the wilderness; only ye shall not go very far away. Entreat for me."

^{29} And Moses said, " Behold, I go out from thee, and I will entreat the LORD that the swarms of flies may depart from Pharaoh, from his servants and from his people tomorrow; but let not Pharaoh deal deceitfully any more in not letting the people go to sacrifice to the LORD."

^{30} And Moses went out from Pharaoh and entreated the LORD. ^{31} And the LORD did according to the word of Moses, and He removed the swarms of flies from Pharaoh, from his servants, and from his people; there remained not one.

^{32} And Pharaoh hardened his heart at this time also, neither would he let the people go.

The Plague of Livestock

Exodus 9

^{1} Then the LORD said unto Moses, " Go in unto Pharaoh and tell him, ' Thus saith the LORD God of the Hebrews: Let My people go, that they may serve Me. ^{2} For if thou refuse to let them go and wilt hold them still, ^{3} Behold, the hand of the LORD is upon thy cattle which are in the field, upon the horses, upon the asses, upon the camels, upon the oxen, and upon the sheep. There shall be a very grievous pestilence. ^{4} And the LORD shall distinguish between the cattle of Israel and the cattle of Egypt; and there shall nothing die of all that belong to the children of Israel.' "

^{5} And the LORD appointed a set time, saying, " Tomorrow the LORD shall do this thing in the land." ^{6} And the LORD did that thing on the morrow; and all the cattle of Egypt died, but of the cattle of the children of Israel died not one. ^{7} And Pharaoh sent, and behold, there was not one of the cattle of the Israelites dead. And the heart of Pharaoh was hardened, and he did not let the people go.

The Plague of Boils

^{8} And the LORD said unto Moses and unto Aaron, " Take to you handfuls of ashes from the furnace, and let Moses sprinkle it toward the heaven in the sight of Pharaoh. ^{9} And it shall become small dust in all the land of Egypt, and shall be a boil breaking forth with blains, upon man and upon beast throughout all the land of Egypt."

^{10} And they took ashes from the furnace and stood before Pharaoh, and Moses sprinkled it up toward heaven; and it became boils breaking forth with blains upon man and upon beast. ^{11} And the magicians could not stand before Moses because of the boils, for the boils were upon the magicians and upon all the Egyptians. ^{12} And the LORD hardened the heart of Pharaoh, and he hearkened not unto them, as the LORD had spoken unto Moses.

The Plague of Hail

^{13} And the LORD said unto Moses, " Rise up early in the morning, and stand before Pharaoh and say unto him, ' Thus saith the LORD God of the Hebrews: Let My people go, that they may serve Me. ^{14} For I will at this time send all My plagues upon thine heart, and upon thy servants and upon thy people, that thou mayest know that there is none like Me in all the earth. ^{15} For now I will stretch out My hand, that I may smite thee and thy people with pestilence, and thou shalt be cut off from the earth. ^{16} And in very deed, for this cause have I raised thee up: to show in thee My power, and that My name may be declared throughout all the earth. ^{17} As yet exaltest thou thyself against My people, that thou wilt not let them go? ^{18} Behold, tomorrow about this time I will cause it to rain a very grievous hail, such as hath not been in Egypt since the foundation thereof even until now. ^{19} Send therefore now, and gather thy cattle and all that thou hast in the field, for upon every man and beast which shall be found in the field and shall not be brought home, the hail shall come down upon them, and they shall die.'"

²⁰ He that feared the word of the LORD among the servants of Pharaoh made his servants and his cattle flee into the houses, ²¹ And he that regarded not the word of the LORD left his servants and his cattle in the field.

²² And the LORD said unto Moses, "Stretch forth thine hand toward heaven, that there may be hail in all the land of Egypt, upon man and upon beast and upon every herb of the field, throughout the land of Egypt." ²³ And Moses stretched forth his rod toward heaven; and the LORD sent thunder and hail, and the fire ran along upon the ground; and the LORD rained hail upon the land of Egypt. ²⁴ So there was

The Seventh Plague, 1823, John Martin

hail and fire mingled with the hail, very grievous, such as there was none like it in all the land of Egypt since it became a nation. ²⁵ And the hail smote throughout all the land of Egypt all that was in the field, both man and beast; and the hail smote every herb of the field and broke every tree of the field. ²⁶ Only in the land of Goshen, where the children of Israel were, was there no hail.

²⁷ And Pharaoh sent and called for Moses and Aaron, and said unto them, "I have sinned this time. The LORD is righteous, and I and my people are wicked.

²⁸ Entreat the LORD (for it is enough), that there be no more mighty thunderings and hail; and I will let you go, and ye shall stay no longer."

²⁹ And Moses said unto him, "As soon as I have gone out of the city, I will spread abroad my hands unto the LORD; and the thunder shall cease, neither shall there be any more hail, that thou mayest know that the earth is the LORD's. ³⁰ But as for thee and thy servants, I know that ye will not yet fear the LORD God."

³¹ And the flax and the barley were smitten; for the barley was in the ear, and the flax was in bolls. ³² But the wheat and the rye were not smitten, for they were not grown up. ³³ And Moses went out of the city from Pharaoh, and spread abroad his hands unto the LORD; and the thunder and hail ceased, and the rain was not poured upon the earth. ³⁴ And when Pharaoh saw that the rain and the hail and the thunder had ceased, he sinned yet more and hardened his heart, he and his servants. ³⁵ And the heart of Pharaoh was hardened, neither would he let the children of Israel go, as the LORD had spoken by Moses.

The Plague of Locusts

Exodus 10

¹ And the LORD said unto Moses, "Go in unto Pharaoh; for I have hardened his heart and the heart of his servants, that I might show these My signs before him; ² And that thou mayest tell in the ears of thy son and of thy son's son what things I have wrought in Egypt, and My signs which I have done among them, that ye may know that I am the LORD."

³ And Moses and Aaron came in unto Pharaoh and said unto him, "Thus saith the LORD God of the Hebrews: 'How long wilt thou refuse to humble thyself before Me? Let My people go, that they may serve me. ⁴ Else, if thou refuse to let My people go, behold, tomorrow will I bring the locusts into thy border. ⁵ And they shall cover the face of the earth, that one shall not be able to see the earth; and they shall eat the residue of that which has escaped, which remaineth unto you from the hail, and shall eat every tree which groweth for you out of the field. ⁶ And they shall fill thy houses and the houses of all thy servants and the houses of all the Egyptians — which neither thy fathers nor thy fathers' fathers have seen since the day that they were upon the earth unto this day.'" And he turned himself, and went out from Pharaoh.

⁷ And Pharaoh's servants said unto him, "How long shall this man be a snare unto us? Let the men go,

Moses and Aaron Watching a Plague of Locusts Attack the Land, the British Library

that they may serve the LORD their God. Knowest thou not yet that Egypt is destroyed?"

⁸ And Moses and Aaron were brought again unto Pharaoh; and he said unto them, " Go, serve the LORD your God. But who are they that shall go?"

⁹ And Moses said, " We will go with our young and with our old, with our sons and with our daughters, with our flocks and with our herds will we go, for we must hold a feast unto the LORD."

¹⁰ And he said unto them, " Let the LORD be so with you, as I will let you go, and your little ones. Look to it, for evil is before you. ¹¹ Not so! Go now ye that are men, and serve the LORD, for that ye did desire." And they were driven out from Pharaoh's presence.

¹² And the LORD said unto Moses, " Stretch out thine hand over the land of Egypt for the locusts, that they may come up upon the land of Egypt and eat every herb of the land, even all that the hail hath left."

¹³ And Moses stretched forth his rod over the land of Egypt, and the LORD brought an east wind upon the land all that day, and all that night; and when it was morning, the east wind brought the locusts. ¹⁴ And the locust went up over all the land of Egypt, and rested in all the coasts of Egypt: very grievous were they; before them there were no such locusts as they, neither after them shall be such. ¹⁵ For they covered the face of the whole earth, so that the land was darkened; and they ate every herb of the land and all the fruit of the trees which the hail had left, and there remained not any green thing in the trees or in the herbs of the field through all the land of Egypt.

¹⁶ Then Pharaoh called for Moses and Aaron in haste, and he said, " I have sinned against the LORD your God, and against you. ¹⁷ Now therefore forgive, I pray thee, my sin only this once, and entreat the LORD your God, that he may take away from me this death only."

¹⁸ And he went out from Pharaoh and entreated the LORD. ¹⁹ And the LORD turned a mighty, strong west wind, which took away the locusts and cast them into the Red Sea. There remained not one locust in all the borders of Egypt. ²⁰ But the LORD hardened Pharaoh's heart, so that he would not let the children of Israel go.

The Plague of Darkness

²¹ And the LORD said unto Moses, " Stretch out thine hand toward heaven, that there may be darkness over the land of Egypt, even darkness which may be felt." ²² And Moses stretched forth his hand toward heaven, and there was a thick darkness in all the land of Egypt three days. ²³ They saw not one another, neither rose any from his place for three days; but all the children of Israel had light in their dwellings.

²⁴ And Pharaoh called unto Moses and said, " Go ye, serve the LORD; only let your flocks and your herds be stayed. Let your little ones also go with you."

²⁵ And Moses said, " Thou must give us also sacrifices and burnt offerings, that we may sacrifice unto the LORD our God. ²⁶ Our cattle also shall go with us. There shall not a hoof be left behind; for thereof must we take to serve the LORD our God, and we know not with what we must serve the LORD until we come thither."

²⁷ But the LORD hardened Pharaoh's heart, and he would not let

The Plague of Darkness, the British Library

them go. ²⁸ And Pharaoh said unto him, " Get thee from me! Take heed to thyself! See my face no more, for in that day thou seest my face thou shalt die!" ²⁹ And Moses said, " Thou hast spoken well. I will see thy face again no more."

The Plague on the Firstborn

Exodus 11

¹ And the LORD said unto Moses, " Yet will I bring one plague more upon Pharaoh and upon Egypt. Afterwards he will let you go hence. When he shall let you go, he shall surely thrust you out hence altogether.² Speak now in the ears of the people, and let every man borrow from his neighbor, and every woman from her neighbor, jewels of silver and jewels of gold." ³ And the LORD gave the people favor in the sight of the Egyptians. Moreover the man Moses was very great in the land of Egypt in the sight of Pharaoh's servants and in the sight of the people.

⁴ And Moses said, " Thus saith the LORD: ' About midnight will I go out into the midst of Egypt; ⁵ And all the firstborn in the land of Egypt shall die, from the firstborn of Pharaoh who sitteth upon his throne, even unto the firstborn

The Plague on the Firstborn

of the maidservant who is behind the mill, and all the firstborn of beasts.⁶ And there shall be a great cry throughout all the land of Egypt, such as there was none like it, nor shall be like it any more. ⁷ But against any of the children of Israel shall not a dog move his tongue, against man or beast, that ye may know how the LORD doth put a difference between the Egyptians and Israel.' ⁸ And all these thy servants shall come down unto me and bow down themselves unto me, saying, ' Get thee out, and all the people who follow thee!' And after that I will go out." And he went out from Pharaoh in a great anger.

⁹ And the LORD said unto Moses, " Pharaoh shall not hearken unto you, that My wonders may be multiplied in the land of Egypt." ¹⁰ And Moses and Aaron did all these wonders before Pharaoh; and the LORD hardened Pharaoh's heart, so that he would not let the children of Israel go out of his land.

The Passover①

Exodus 12

¹ And the LORD spoke unto Moses and Aaron in the land of Egypt, saying, ² " This month shall be unto you the beginning of months; it shall be the first month of the year to you. ³ Speak ye unto all the congregation of Israel, saying, ' On the tenth day of this month they shall take for themselves every man a lamb, according to the house of their fathers, a lamb for a house. ⁴ And if the household be too little for the lamb, let him and his neighbor next unto his house take it according to the number of the souls; every man according to his eating shall make your count for the lamb. ⁵ Your lamb shall be without blemish, a male of the first year; ye shall take it out from the sheep, or from the goats. ⁶ And ye shall keep it up until the fourteenth day of the same month, and the whole assembly of the congregation of Israel shall kill it in the evening. ⁷ And they shall take of the blood, and strike it on the two side posts and on the upper door post of the houses wherein they shall eat it. ⁸ And they shall eat the flesh in that night, roasted with fire; and with unleavened bread and with bitter herbs they shall eat it. ⁹ Eat not of it raw, nor boiled at all with water, but roasted with fire — his head with his

---

① **The Passover** (逾越节) the major Jewish spring festival lasting seven or eight days from the 14th of the seventh month of the year in the Jewish calendar, commemorating the exodus of the Jews from Egypt. The term *pass over* refers to the exemption of the Israelites from the death of their firstborn.

legs and with the viscera thereof. ¹⁰ *And ye shall let nothing of it remain until the morning, and that which remaineth of it until the morning ye shall burn with fire.* ¹¹ *And thus shall ye eat it: with your loins girded, your shoes on your feet, and your staff in your hand; and ye shall eat it in haste; it is the LORD's Passover.'*

¹² *For I will pass through the land of Egypt this night, and will smite all the firstborn in the land of Egypt, both man and beast; and against all the gods of Egypt I will execute judgment: I am the LORD.* ¹³ *And the blood shall be to you for a token upon the houses where ye are; and when I see the blood, I will pass over you, and the plague shall not be upon you to destroy you when I smite the land of Egypt."*

¹⁴ *" ' And this day shall be unto you for a memorial, and ye shall keep it a feast to the LORD throughout your generations; ye shall keep it a feast by an ordinance for ever.* ¹⁵ *Seven days shall ye eat unleavened bread. Even the first day ye shall put away leaven out of your houses; for whosoever eateth leavened bread from the first day until the seventh day, that soul shall be cut off from Israel.* ¹⁶ *And in the first day there shall be a holy convocation, and in the seventh day there shall be a holy convocation to you. No manner of work shall be done in them, save that which every man must eat, that only may be done by you.*

¹⁷ *And ye shall observe the Feast of Unleavened Bread, for in this selfsame day have I brought your armies out of the land of Egypt. Therefore shall ye observe this day in your generations by an ordinance for ever.* ¹⁸ *In the first month, on the fourteenth day of the month at evening, ye shall eat unleavened bread until the one and twentieth day of the month at evening.* ¹⁹ *Seven days shall there be no leaven found in your houses; for whosoever eateth that which is leavened, even that soul shall be cut off from the congregation of Israel, whether he be a stranger or born in the land.* ²⁰ *Ye shall eat nothing leavened; in all your habitations shall ye eat unleavened bread.' "*

²¹ *Then Moses called for all the elders of Israel and said unto them, " Draw out and take you a lamb according to your families, and kill the Passover.* ²² *And ye shall take a bunch of hyssop, and dip it in the blood that is in the basin, and strike the lintel and the two side posts with the blood that is in the basin; and none of you shall go out from the door of his house until the morning.* ²³ *For the LORD will pass through to smite the Egyptians; and when He seeth the blood upon the lintel and on the two side posts, the LORD will pass over the door and will not suffer the destroyer to come in unto your houses to smite you.*

²⁴ *And ye shall observe this thing as an ordinance to thee and to thy sons for ever.* ²⁵ *And it shall come to pass, when ye come to the land which the LORD will give you, according as He hath promised, that ye shall keep this service.* ²⁶ *And it shall come to pass, when your children shall say unto you, ' What mean ye by this service?'* ²⁷ *That ye shall say, ' It is the sacrifice of the LORD's Passover, who passed over the houses of the children of Israel in Egypt when He smote the Egyptians and delivered our houses.' "And the people bowed their heads and worshiped.* ²⁸ *And the children of Israel went away, and did as the LORD had commanded Moses and Aaron; so did they.*

²⁹ *And it came to pass, that at midnight the LORD smote all the firstborn in the land of Egypt, from the firstborn of Pharaoh who sat on his throne, unto the firstborn of the captive who was in the dungeon, and all the firstborn of cattle.*

³⁰ *And Pharaoh rose up in the night, he and all his servants and all the Egyptians; and there was a great cry in Egypt, for there was not a house where there was not one dead.*

The Exodus

³¹ *And he called for Moses and Aaron by night and said, " Rise up, and get you forth from among my people, both ye and the children of Israel! And go, serve the LORD, as ye have said.* ³² *Also take your flocks and your herds, as ye have said; and be gone, and bless me also."*

³³ *And the Egyptians were urgent upon the people, that they might send them out of the land in haste; for they said, " We are all dead men."* ³⁴ *And the people took their dough before it was leavened, their kneading troughs being bound up in their clothes upon their shoulders.* ³⁵ *And the children of Israel did according to the word of Moses, and they borrowed from the Egyptians jewels of silver and jewels of gold and raiment.* ³⁶ *And*

the LORD gave the people favor in the sight of the Egyptians, so that they lent unto them such things as they required. And they despoiled the Egyptians.

⁳⁷ And the children of Israel journeyed from Rameses to Succoth, about six hundred thousand on foot who were men, besides children. ³⁸ And a mixed multitude went up also with them, and flocks and herds, even very much cattle.

³⁹ And they baked unleavened cakes of the dough which they brought forth out of Egypt; for it was not leavened because they were thrust out of Egypt and could not tarry, neither had they prepared for themselves any victual.

⁴⁰ Now the sojourning of the children of Israel who dwelt in Egypt was four hundred and thirty years. ⁴¹ And it came to pass at the end of the four hundred and thirty years, even on the selfsame day it came to pass, that all the hosts of the LORD went out from the land of Egypt. ...

Cultural Connections: *the movie Exodus*

The 1960 film directed by Otto Preminger and starring Paul Newman is based on the events that happened on the ship *Exodus* in 1947 and deals with the founding of the state of Israel in 1948. Its political influence aside, the film is noted for its main theme which has been widely remixed, covered and even sung with lyrics by many artists, ranging in genre from jazz, hip-hop to classical. The charismatic Croatian pianist, Maksim Mrvica's interpretation of the same piece was yet another feather in his musical cap.

III FOOD FOR THOUGHT

1. What is indicated about the power of God and the power of Pharaoh in the incident with the rods?
2. How did Pharaoh react to the waters of Egypt being turned to blood? Why?
3. What was the final plague by which the Israelites' bondage was ended?
4. Can you see any controversy in the "hardening of Pharaoh's heart" tradition?
5. How can you explain the significance of the Passover with a discussion of its constitutive elements?

IV BIBLICAL RELEVANCE

A. Biblical Terms in Everyday English
1. This is the finger of God (8:19): _____
2. Passover (12:14): _____
3. (de)spoil/plunder the Egyptians (3:22, 12:36): _____
4. the subtle doom fell on Egyptian firstborn: _____

B. Biblical References in Literature

1. By reason of the density of the interwoven foliage overhead, it was gloomy there at cloudless noontide, twilight in the evening, dark as midnight at dusk, and black as the ninth plague of Egypt at midnight.

   (Thomas Hardy, *Far from the Madding Crowd*, 1874)

2. If Mr Thurle's so ready to take farms under you, it's a pity but what he should take this, and see if he likes to live in a house wi'all the plagues o'Egypt in't—wi'the cellar full o'water, and the frogs and toads hoppin'up the steps by dozens—and the floors rotten, and the rats and mice gnawing every bit o'cheese, and runnin' over our heads as we lie i'bed till we expect'em to eat us up alive.

   (George Eliot, *Adam Bede*, 1859)

3. My hopes were all dead - struck with a subtle doom, such as, in one night, fell on all the first-born in the land of Egypt.

   (Charlotte Brontë, *Jane Eyre*, 1847)

C. The Bible and Arts

1. *Moses and Aaron Changing the Rivers of Egypt to Blood*, 1631, Bartholomeus Breenbergh
2. *The Fifth Plague of Egypt*, 1800, Joseph Mallord William Turner
3. *The Seventh Plague*, 1823, John Martin
4. *The Tenth Plague of Egypt*, Exhibited 1802, Joseph Mallord William Turner

V SOURCES FOR REFERENCE

1. "The Ten Plagues," a song from the 1998 DreamWorks animated film *The Prince of Egypt*.
2. "When You Believe," an Academy Award-winning song by American recording artists Mariah Carey and Whitney Houston written for the animated film *The Prince of Egypt*.
3. Schippe, C. & C. Stetson. (2005). *The Bible and Its Influence*. Front Royal, VA: BLP Publishing.
4. Browning, W. R. E. (2009). *A Dictionary of the Bible*. Oxford: Oxford University Press.

8. THE ESCAPE FROM EGYPT

I POINTS OF DEPARTURE

Here comes the Exodus, the great constitutive event of Hebrew history, comparable to the "aburbe condita" for the Romans and the "anno domini" for the Christians, and the remembrance and the wonder of it echo through the whole of the Old Testament. Caught hopelessly between the imperial army of Pharaoh and the Red Sea, or more accurately the Reed Sea, probably the marshes of the Lake Timsah which are now part of the Suez Canal (Browning, 2009:310), the Israelites were amazed to find a pillar of cloud by day and a pillar of fire by night setting them and the Egyptians apart. What was more miraculous was the parting of the Red Sea for the Israelites to pass on solid ground. This miracle was sufficient to appease the grumbling Israelites and establish the Lord as the Israelites' God and Moses his prophet. History repeats itself. So does this miracle, twice a year near the Jindo Island, in South Korea, which reveals a land path 2.8 kilometers long and 40 meters wide in the sea for a period of one hour, attracting a growing tide of enthusiastic tourists worldwide.

Miracles did not stop beyond the Red Sea yet; more were coming. In fact, the Book of Exodus contains more miracles than any other part of the Bible except the four Gospels where Jesus Christ is to be master of this supernatural feat. While wondering through the wilderness, the Israelites were provided with manna and quail. When they were thirsty for water, Moses struck the rock and water gushed out. But intriguing enough, it was this very act that led to the condemnation of Moses that he could only see the Promised Land from a distance instead of entering it (*Num. 20:12*). There are three suggestions: first, his words to his people were rash (*Num. 20:10*; *Ps. 106:32f*); second, Moses was told to speak to the rock but he struck it, and third, he was bidden to strike it once, but he struck it twice (Black, 2001:264). So Moses' sin was disobedience against and lack of trust in his God. Actually, it was not Moses alone who failed to enter the Promised Land; all of the older generation were similarly cursed. The reason for this, and the 40-year wandering of the Israelites is given in *Numbers 32:10—13*:

"*Surely none of the men that came up out of Egypt, from twenty years old and upward, shall see the land which I sware unto Abraham, unto Isaac, and unto Jacob; because they have not wholly followed me: Save Caleb the son of Jephunneh the Kenezite, and Joshua the son of Nun: for they have wholly followed the LORD. And the LORD's anger was kindled against Israel, and he made them wander in the wilderness forty years, until all the generation, that had done evil in the sight of the LORD, was consumed.*"

II SELECTED READINGS

A Path through the Red Sea①

Exodus 14

¹ And the LORD spake unto Moses, saying, ² "Speak unto the children of Israel, that they turn and encamp before Pihahiroth, between Migdol and the sea, over against Baalzephon: before it shall ye encamp by the sea. ³ For Pharaoh will say of the children of Israel, ' They are entangled in the land, the wilderness hath shut them in.' ⁴ And I will harden Pharaoh's heart, that he shall follow after them; and I will be honoured upon Pharaoh, and upon all his host②; that the Egyptians may know that I am the LORD." And they did so.

⁵ And it was told the king of Egypt that the people fled; and the heart of Pharaoh and of his servants was turned against the people, and they said, " Why have we done this, that we have let Israel go from serving us?" ⁶ And he made ready his chariot and took his people with him, ⁷ And he took six hundred chosen chariots and all the chariots of Egypt and captains over every one of them. ⁸ And the LORD hardened the heart of Pharaoh king of Egypt, and he pursued after the children of Israel; and the children of Israel went out with a high hand③. ⁹ But the Egyptians pursued after them, all the horses and chariots of Pharaoh, and his horsemen and his army, and overtook them encamping by the sea beside Pihahiroth, before Baalzephon.

Crossing of the Red Sea, Cosimo Rosselli (1439—1507)

¹⁰ And when Pharaoh drew nigh, the children of Israel lifted up their eyes, and behold, the Egyptians marched after them; and they were sore afraid; and the children of Israel cried out unto the LORD. ¹¹ And they said unto Moses, " Because there were no graves in Egypt, hast thou taken us away to die in the wilderness? Why hast thou dealt thus with us, to carry us forth out of Egypt?

¹² Is not this the word that we told thee in Egypt, saying, ' Let us alone, that we may serve the Egyptians' ? For it had been better for us to serve the Egyptians, than that we should die in the wilderness."

¹³ And Moses said unto the people, " Fear ye not. Stand still, and see the salvation of the LORD, which He will show to you today; for the Egyptians whom ye have seen today, ye shall see them again no more for ever. ¹⁴ The LORD shall fight for you, and ye shall hold your peace."

¹⁵ And the LORD said unto Moses, " Why criest thou unto Me? Speak unto the children of Israel, that they go forward. ¹⁶ But lift thou up thy rod, and stretch out thine hand over the sea and divide it; and the children of Israel shall go on dry ground through the midst of the sea. ¹⁷ And I, behold, I will harden the hearts of the Egyptians, and they shall follow them; and I will get Myself honor above Pharaoh and above all his host, above his chariots and above his horsemen. ¹⁸ And the Egyptians shall know that I am the LORD when I have gotten Myself honor above Pharaoh, above his chariots, and above his horsemen." ¹⁹ And the angel of God, who went before the camp of Israel, removed and went behind them; and the pillar of the cloud went

---

① **The Red Sea** Hebrew *Yam Suph*, meaning Reed Sea or Papyrus Marsh, sometimes translated as the *Red Sea*, sometimes as the *Reed Sea*. Given the fact that on the shores of the Red Sea there are no reeds, the flight from Egypt may not have taken place there; rather over a Sea of Reeds which disappeared when the Suez Canal was constructed in the 19th century.

② **I will be honoured upon Pharaoh, and upon all his host** I will get glory over Pharaoh and all his army.

③ **with a high hand** boldly or defiantly.

from before their face and stood behind them. ²⁰ *And it came between the camp of the Egyptians and the camp of Israel; and it was a cloud and darkness to them, but it gave light by night to these, so that the one came not near the other all the night.*

²¹ *And Moses stretched out his hand over the sea; and the LORD caused the sea to go back by a strong east wind all that night and made the sea dry land, and the waters were divided.* ²² *And the children of Israel went into the midst of the sea upon the dry ground, and the waters were a wall unto them on their right hand and on their left.*

²³ *And the Egyptians pursued, and went in after them to the midst of the sea, even all Pharaoh's horses, his chariots, and his horsemen.* ²⁴ *And it came to pass that in the morning watch the LORD looked unto the host of the Egyptians through the pillar of fire and of the cloud, and troubled the host of the Egyptians.* ²⁵ *And He took off their chariot wheels, that they drove them heavily, so that the Egyptians said, " Let us flee from the face of Israel, for the LORD fighteth for them against the Egyptians."*

²⁶ *And the LORD said unto Moses, " Stretch out thine hand over the sea, that the waters may come again upon the Egyptians, upon their chariots, and upon their horsemen."* ²⁷ *And Moses stretched forth his hand over the sea, and the sea returned to his strength when the morning appeared. And the Egyptians fled against it, and the LORD overthrew the Egyptians in the midst of the sea.* ²⁸ *And the waters returned, and covered the chariots and the horsemen and all the host of Pharaoh that came into the sea after them. There remained not so much as one of them.*

Israelites Passing through the Wilderness,
William West (1801—1861)

²⁹ *But the children of Israel walked upon dry land in the midst of the sea, and the waters were a wall unto them on their right hand and on their left.* ³⁰ *Thus the LORD saved Israel that day out of the hand of the Egyptians, and Israel saw the Egyptians dead upon the seashore.* ³¹ *And Israel saw that great work which the LORD did upon the Egyptians; and the people feared the LORD, and believed the LORD and His servant Moses.*

Manna and Quail from Heaven

Exodus 16

¹ *And they took their journey from Elim, and all the congregation of the children of Israel came unto the Wilderness of Sin, which is between Elim and Sinai, on the fifteenth day of the second month after their departing out of the land of Egypt.* ² *And the whole congregation of the children of Israel murmured against Moses and Aaron in the wilderness.* ³ *And the children of Israel said unto them, " Would to God we had died by the hand of the LORD in the land of Egypt, when we sat by the fleshpots and when we ate bread to the full! For ye have brought us forth into this wilderness to kill this whole assembly with hunger."*

California Quail

⁴ *Then said the LORD unto Moses, " Behold, I will rain bread from heaven for you; and the people shall go out and gather a certain rate every day, that I may put them to the proof, whether they will walk in My law, or no.* ⁵ *And it shall come to pass that on the sixth day they shall prepare that which they bring in, and it shall be twice as much as they gather daily."*

⁶ *And Moses and Aaron said unto all the children of Israel, " At evening, then ye shall know that the LORD hath brought you out from the land of Egypt;* ⁷ *And in the morning, then ye shall see the glory of the*

LORD, for He heareth your murmurings against the LORD. And what are we, that ye murmur against us?" ⁸ And Moses said, "This shall be when the LORD shall give you in the evening flesh to eat and in the morning bread to the full, for the LORD heareth your murmurings which ye murmur against Him. And what are we? Your murmurings are not against us, but against the LORD."

⁹ And Moses spoke unto Aaron, "Say unto all the congregation of the children of Israel, 'Come near before the LORD, for He hath heard your murmurings.'"

¹⁰ And it came to pass, as Aaron spoke unto the whole congregation of the children of Israel, that they looked toward the wilderness, and behold, the glory of the LORD appeared in the cloud.

¹¹ And the LORD spoke unto Moses, saying, ¹² "I have heard the murmurings of the children of Israel. Speak unto them, saying, 'At evening ye shall eat flesh, and in the morning ye shall be filled with bread; and ye shall know that I am the LORD your God.'"

¹³ And it came to pass that at evening the quails④ came up and covered the camp, and in the morning the dew lay round about the host. ¹⁴ And when the dew that lay had gone up, behold, upon the face of the wilderness there lay a small round thing, as small as the hoarfrost on the ground. ¹⁵ And when the children of Israel saw it, they said one to another, It is manna⑤; for they wist not what it was.

The Gathering of the Manna, 1470

And Moses said unto them, "This is the bread which the LORD hath given you to eat." ¹⁶ This is the thing which the LORD hath commanded, Gather of it every man according to his eating, an omer for man, according to the number of your persons; take ye every man for them which are in his tents.

¹⁷ And the children of Israel did so, and gathered, some more, some less. ¹⁸ And when they did mete it with an omer, he that gathered much had nothing over, and he that gathered little had no lack; they gathered every man according to his eating.

¹⁹ And Moses said, "Let no man leave of it till the morning."

²⁰ Notwithstanding they hearkened not unto Moses; but some of them left of it until the morning, and it bred worms, and stank; and Moses was wroth with them.

²¹ And they gathered it every morning, every man according to his eating: and when the sun waxed hot, it melted. ²² And it came to pass, that on the sixth day they gathered twice as much bread, two omers for one man: and all the rulers of the congregation came and told Moses. ²³ And he said unto them, "This is that which the LORD hath said, To morrow is the rest of the holy sabbath unto the LORD: bake that which ye will bake to day, and seethe that ye will seethe; and that which remaineth over lay up for you to be kept until the morning."

²⁴ And they laid it up till the morning, as Moses bade: and it did not stink, neither was there any worm therein. ²⁵ And Moses said, "Eat that to day; for to day is a sabbath unto the LORD: to day ye shall not find it in the field. ²⁶ Six days ye shall gather it; but on the seventh day, which is the sabbath, in it there shall be none."

²⁷ And it came to pass, that there went out some of the people on the seventh day for to gather, and they found none. ²⁸ And the LORD said unto Moses, "How long refuse ye to keep my commandments and my laws? ²⁹ See, for that the LORD hath given you the sabbath, therefore he giveth you on the sixth day the bread of two days; abide ye every man in his place, let no man go out of his place on the seventh day." ³⁰ So the

---

④ **quails** (/kweil/, 鹌鹑) migrate across the Sinai peninsula in great flocks between Europe and Arabia. Exhausted by their long flight, they roost on the ground or in low bushes, making their capture fairly easy.

⑤ **manna** (/ˈmænə/, 吗哪) ("what is it") As asserted by the German botanist G. Ehrenberg in 1823 and confirmed later through an organized manna expedition by Friedrich Simon Bodenheimer and Oskar Theodor from the Hebrew University at Jerusalem, manna is a secretion exuded by tamarisk trees and bushes when they are pierced by a certain type of plant-louse found in Sinai (Keller, 1982: 123—124).

people rested on the seventh day.

³¹ And the house of Israel called the name thereof Manna: and it was like coriander seed, white; and the taste of it was like wafers made with honey. ³² And Moses said, "This is the thing which the LORD commandeth, Fill an omer of it to be kept for your generations; that they may see the bread wherewith I have fed you in the wilderness, when I brought you forth from the land of Egypt."

³³ And Moses said unto Aaron, "Take a pot, and put an omer full of manna therein, and lay it up before the LORD, to be kept for your generations."

³⁴ As the LORD commanded Moses, so Aaron laid it up before the Testimony, to be kept. ³⁵ And the children of Israel did eat manna forty years, until they came to a land inhabited; they did eat manna, until they came unto the borders of the land of Canaan. ³⁶ Now an omer is the tenth part of an ephah.

Water from the Rock

Exodus 17

¹ And all the congregation of the children of Israel journeyed from the wilderness of Sin, after their journeys, according to the commandment of the LORD, and pitched in Rephidim: and there was no water for the people to drink. ² Wherefore the people did chide with Moses, and said, "Give us water that we may drink."

And Moses said unto them, "Why chide ye with me? Wherefore do ye tempt the LORD?"

³ And the people thirsted there for water; and the people murmured against Moses, and said, "Wherefore is this that thou hast brought us up out of Egypt, to kill us and our children and our cattle with thirst?"

Moses Bringing forth Water from the Rock, 1649, Nicolas Poussin

⁴ And Moses cried unto the LORD, saying, "What shall I do unto this people? they be almost ready to stone me."

The Trials of Moses, 1481—1482, Sandro Botticelli

⁵ And the LORD said unto Moses, "Go on before the people, and take with thee of the elders of Israel; and thy rod, wherewith thou smotest the river, take in thine hand, and go. ⁶ Behold, I will stand before thee there upon the rock in Horeb; and thou shalt smite the rock, and there shall come water out of it, that the people may drink." And Moses did so in the sight of the elders of Israel. ⁷ And he called the name of the place Massah^⑥, and Meribah^⑦, because of the chiding of the children of Israel, and because they tempted the LORD, saying, "Is the LORD among us, or not?" ...

III FOOD FOR THOUGHT

1. Why didn't the Israelites follow the shortest route to the Promised Land?
2. How might we explain the "pillar of cloud" and the "pillar of fire"?

---

⑥ **Massah** means *testing*.
⑦ **Meribah** means *quarreling*.

3. What seems to be the emerging pattern of the Israelites' response to their leader Moses as they proceeded through the wilderness?
4. This is what the Israelites said to Moses and Aaron, "Would that we had died by the hand of the Lord in the land of Egypt, when we sat by the fleshpots and ate bread to the full; for you have brought us out into this wilderness to kill this whole assembly with hunger." (*Exodus 16: 3*) How can you argue for or against this statement?

IV BIBLICAL RELEVANCE

A. Biblical Terms in Everyday English
1. the flesh/meat-pots of Egypt (16:3): _____
2. pillar of cloud and pillar of fire (13:21—22): _____
3. manna from heaven (16:15): _____

B. Biblical References in Literature
1. The English Department had changed its quarters since his arrival at Rummidge. The changeover had taken place in the Easter vacation amid much wailing and gnashing of teeth. Oy, oy, Exodus was nothing in comparison.
   (David Lodge, *Changing Places*, 1975)
2. The word is not prepared beforehand; it falls on my mind like the manna fell from heaven into the bellies of the starving Israelites.
   (Stella Gibbons, *Cold Comfort Farm*, 1932)
3. They hurry after the Plenipo. Moses going through the Red Sea, thinks Gideon of Elliot's progress through the crowd.
   (Timothy Mo, *An Insular Possession*, 1986)

C. The Bible and Arts
1. *Crossing of the Red Sea*, Cosimo Rosselli (1439 — 1507)
2. *Israelites Passing through the Wilderness*, William West (1801 — 1861)
3. *The Israelites in the Desert*, c. 1593, Tintoretto
4. *Moses Bringing forth Water from the Rock*, 1649, Nicolas Poussin
5. *The Trials of Moses*, 1481—1482, Sandro Botticelli

V SOURCES FOR REFERENCE

1. Black, M. (ed.) (2001). *Peake's Commentary on the Bible*. London: Routledge.
2. Browning, W. R. E. (2009). *A Dictionary of the Bible*. Oxford: Oxford University Press.
3. Keller, W. (1974). *The Bible as History*. New York: Bantam Books.

9. THE COVENANT AT MOUNT SINAI

I   POINTS OF DEPARTURE

The Hebrew word *berith* for "covenant" denotes an arrangement between two parties and in the Old Testament it is a series of solemn promises or vows between God and the people of Israel. The patriarchal covenants are mostly unilateral, stressing the element of grace on the part of God embodied through the rainbow. The Noahide covenant (*Gen. 9:1—17*), for example, promised Noah that God would never send a universal flood to destroy his people again, while the Abrahamaic covenant (*Gen. 15; 17:1—14*) granted the titular patriarch land and more children than he could count and was sealed with the promise of circumcision (*Gen. 17: 23*). In both covenants, God made no promises beyond being the patron or protector of Israel. But the covenant concluded at Mount Sinai with Moses (*Exod. 20:1—17; Dt. 5:4—21*), the Mosaic covenant, marks a radical departure, which is comparable to a mutual and conditional suzerainty treaty binding a suzerain and a vassal (Mendenhall, 1955: 32—34).

Most of the Mosaic covenant is couched in the Ten Commandments, also known as the Decalogue. The Ten Commandments prohibit idolatry and call for a total cessation of work on the Sabbath Day. They demand respect for individuals and for the life of the nation. They provide an ethical basis for a secure existence. As the foundation principles for the Hebrews' community life, the Ten Commandments are a constitution ordering their political, social and spiritual lives, a birth certificate establishing its birth as a nation, and a marriage certificate expressing God's love for His people who are expected to be pious in return — idolatry is tantamount to adultery (Philip and Stafford, 2002: 63). The Ten Commandments lie at the core of Judaism, constituting the basic moral and ritual code later expanded by the other commandments.

The Ten Commandments inscribed on a stone tablet were taken down from Mount Sinai by Moses, deposited in the Ark of the Covenant which was carried in the wilderness until it was installed by King Solomon in the Holy of Holies of his new Temple (*1 Kgs. 8:4—7*). It was believed that its presence, i.e. that of God, would protect the city of Jerusalem from its enemies, but in fact the ark was probably part of the loot in the wake of the destruction of that city by the Babylonians in 586 B.C.E. In spite of all the skepticism concerning its historicity, the Ark of Covenant has remained fresh as ever in the Western imagination and the huge success of *Indiana Jones and the Raiders of the Lost Ark* directed by Steven Spielberg, produced by George Lucas, and starring Harrison Ford was a more recent proof.

II SELECTED READINGS

The Calling on Mount Sinai

Exodus 19

¹ In the third month after the children of Israel had gone forth out of the land of Egypt, the same day came they into the Wilderness of Sinai. ² For they had departed from Rephidim, and had come to the desert of Sinai and had pitched camp in the wilderness; and there Israel camped before the mount.

³ And Moses went up unto God, and the LORD called unto him out of the mountain, saying, "Thus shalt thou say to the house of Jacob, and tell the children of Israel: ⁴ 'Ye have seen what I did unto the Egyptians, and how I bore you on eagles' wings and brought you unto Myself. ⁵ Now therefore, if ye will obey My voice indeed and keep My covenant, then ye shall be a peculiar treasure unto Me above all people; for all the earth is Mine. ⁶ And ye shall be unto Me a kingdom of priests and a holy nation.' These are the words which thou shalt speak unto the children of Israel."

⁷ And Moses came and called for the elders of the people, and laid before their faces all these words which the LORD commanded him. ⁸ And all the people answered together, and said, "All that the LORD hath spoken we will do." And Moses returned the words of the people unto the LORD. ⁹ And the LORD said unto Moses, "Lo, I come unto thee in a thick cloud, that the people may hear when I speak with thee, and believe thee for ever." And Moses told the words of the people unto the LORD.

¹⁰ And the LORD said unto Moses, "Go unto the people, and sanctify them to day and to morrow, and let them wash their clothes, ¹¹ And be ready against the third day: for the third day the LORD will come down in the sight of all the people upon Mount Sinai. ¹² And thou shalt set bounds unto the people round about, saying, 'Take heed to yourselves, that ye go not up into the mount, or touch the border of it: whosoever toucheth the mount shall be surely put to death: ¹³ There shall not an hand touch it, but he shall surely be stoned, or shot through; whether it be beast or man, it shall not live.' When the trumpet soundeth long, they shall come up to the mount."

¹⁴ And Moses went down from the mount unto the people, and sanctified the people; and they washed their clothes. ¹⁵ And he said unto the people, "Be ready against the third day: come not at your wives."

¹⁶ And it came to pass on the third day in the morning, that there were thunders and lightnings, and a thick cloud upon the mount, and the voice of the trumpet exceeding loud; so that all the people that was in the camp trembled. ¹⁷ And Moses brought forth the people out of the camp to meet with God; and they stood at the nether part of the mount. ¹⁸ And Mount Sinai was altogether on a smoke, because the LORD descended upon it in fire: and the smoke thereof ascended as the smoke of a furnace, and the whole mount quaked greatly. ¹⁹ And when the voice of the trumpet sounded long, and waxed louder and louder, Moses spake, and God answered him by a voice.

²⁰ And the LORD came down upon Mount Sinai, on the top of the mount: and the LORD called Moses up to the top of the mount; and Moses went up. ²¹ And the LORD said unto Moses, "Go down, charge the people, lest they break through unto the LORD to gaze, and many of them perish. ²² And let the priests also, which come near to the LORD, sanctify themselves, lest the LORD break forth upon them."

²³ And Moses said unto the LORD, "The people cannot come up to Mount Sinai: for thou chargedst us, saying, 'Set bounds about the mount, and sanctify it.'"

²⁴ And the LORD said unto him, "Away, get thee down, and thou shalt come up, thou, and Aaron with thee: but let not the priests and the people break through to come up unto the LORD, lest he break forth upon them." ²⁵ So Moses went down unto the people, and spake unto them.

The Ten Commandments

Exodus 20

¹ And God spake all these words, saying,

² " I am the LORD thy God, which have brought thee out of the land of Egypt, out of the house of bondage.

³ Thou shalt have no other gods before me.

⁴ Thou shalt not make unto thee any graven image, or any likeness of any thing that is in heaven above, or that is in the earth beneath, or that is in the water under the earth. ⁵ Thou shalt not bow down thyself to them, nor serve them: for I the LORD thy God am a jealous God, visiting the iniquity of the fathers upon the children unto the third and fourth generation of them that hate me; ⁶ And shewing mercy unto thousands of them that love me, and keep my commandments.

⁷ " Thou shalt not take the name of the LORD thy God in vain; for the LORD will not hold him guiltless that taketh his name in vain.

⁸ " Remember the sabbath day, to keep it holy. ⁹ Six days shalt thou labour, and do all thy work; ¹⁰ But the seventh day is the sabbath of the LORD thy God: in it thou shalt not do any work, thou, nor thy son, nor thy daughter, thy manservant, nor thy maidservant, nor thy cattle, nor thy stranger that is within thy gates: ¹¹ For in six days the LORD made heaven and earth, the sea, and all that in them is, and rested the seventh day: wherefore the LORD blessed the sabbath day, and hallowed it.

The Ten Commandments, 1936

¹² " Honour thy father and thy mother: that thy days may be long upon the land which the LORD thy God giveth thee.

¹³ " Thou shalt not kill.

¹⁴ " Thou shalt not commit adultery.

¹⁵ " Thou shalt not steal.

¹⁶ " Thou shalt not bear false witness against thy neighbour.

¹⁷ " Thou shalt not covet thy neighbour's house, thou shalt not covet thy neighbour's wife, nor his manservant, nor his maidservant, nor his ox, nor his ass, nor any thing that is thy neighbour's."

¹⁸ And all the people saw the thunderings, and the lightnings, and the noise of the trumpet, and the mountain smoking: and when the people saw it, they removed, and stood afar off. ¹⁹ And they said unto Moses, " Speak thou with us, and we will hear: but let not God speak with us, lest we die."

²⁰ And Moses said unto the people, " Fear not: for God is come to prove you, and that his fear may be before your faces, that ye sin not." ²¹ And the people stood afar off, and Moses drew near unto the thick darkness where God was.

²² And the LORD said unto Moses, " Thus thou shalt say unto the children of Israel, ' Ye have seen that I have talked with you from heaven. ²³ Ye shall not make with me gods of silver, neither shall ye make unto you gods of gold. ²⁴ An altar of earth thou shalt make unto me, and shalt sacrifice thereon thy burnt offerings, and thy peace offerings, thy sheep, and thine oxen: in all places where I record my name I will come unto thee, and I will bless thee. ²⁵ And if thou wilt make me an altar of stone, thou shalt not build it of hewn stone: for if thou lift up thy tool upon it, thou hast polluted it. ²⁶ Neither shalt thou go up by steps unto mine altar, that thy nakedness be not discovered thereon.' "

Aaron and the Golden Calf

Exodus 32

¹And when the people saw that Moses delayed to come down out of the mount, the people gathered themselves together unto Aaron, and said unto him, "Up, make us gods, which shall go before us; for as for this Moses, the man that brought us up out of the land of Egypt, we wot not what is become of him."

The Adoration of the Golden Calf, Nicolas Poussin (1594—1665)

²And Aaron said unto them, "Break off the golden earrings, which are in the ears of your wives, of your sons, and of your daughters, and bring them unto me." ³And all the people brake off the golden earrings which were in their ears, and brought them unto Aaron. ⁴And he received them at their hand, and fashioned it with a graving tool, after he had made it a molten calf: and they said, "These be thy gods, O Israel, which brought thee up out of the land of Egypt."

⁵And when Aaron saw it, he built an altar before it; and Aaron made proclamation, and said, "To morrow is a feast to the LORD." ⁶And they rose up early on the morrow, and offered burnt offerings, and brought peace offerings; and the people sat down to eat and to drink, and rose up to play.

⁷And the LORD said unto Moses, "Go, get thee down; for thy people, which thou broughtest out of the land of Egypt, have corrupted themselves: ⁸They have turned aside quickly out of the way which I commanded them: they have made them a molten calf, and have worshipped it, and have sacrificed thereunto, and said, 'These be thy gods, O Israel, which have brought thee up out of the land of Egypt.'"

⁹And the LORD said unto Moses, "I have seen this people, and, behold, it is a stiffnecked people. ¹⁰Now therefore let me alone, that my wrath may wax hot against them, and that I may consume them: and I will make of thee a great nation."

¹¹And Moses besought the LORD his God, and said, "LORD, why doth thy wrath wax hot against thy people, which thou hast brought forth out of the land of Egypt with great power, and with a mighty hand? ¹²Wherefore should the Egyptians speak, and say, 'For mischief did he bring them out, to slay them in the mountains, and to consume them from the face of the earth?' Turn from thy fierce wrath, and repent of this evil against thy people. ¹³Remember Abraham, Isaac, and Israel, thy servants, to whom thou swarest by thine own self, and saidst unto them, 'I will multiply your seed as the stars of heaven, and all this land that I have spoken of will I give unto your seed, and they shall inherit it for ever.'" ¹⁴And the LORD repented of the evil which he thought to do unto his people.

¹⁵And Moses turned, and went down from the mount, and the two tables of the testimony were in his hand: the tables were written on both their sides; on the one side and on the other were they written. ¹⁶And the tables were the work of God, and the writing was the writing of God, graven upon the tables.

¹⁷And when Joshua heard the noise of the people as they shouted, he said unto Moses, "There is a noise of war in the camp."

¹⁸And he said,

"It is not the voice of them that shout for mastery,
neither is it the voice of them that cry for being overcome:
but the noise of them that sing do I hear."

¹⁹And it came to pass, as soon as he came nigh unto the camp, that he saw the calf, and the dancing: and Moses' anger waxed hot, and he cast the tables out of his hands, and brake them beneath the mount. ²⁰And he took the calf which they had made, and burnt it in the fire, and ground it to powder, and strawed it upon the water, and made the children of Israel drink of it.

^{21} And Moses said unto Aaron, "What did this people unto thee, that thou hast brought so great a sin upon them?"

^{22} And Aaron said, "Let not the anger of my lord wax hot: thou knowest the people, that they are set on mischief. ^{23} For they said unto me, 'Make us gods, which shall go before us: for as for this Moses, the man that brought us up out of the land of Egypt, we wot not what is become of him.' ^{24} And I said unto them, 'Whosoever hath any gold, let them break it off.' so they gave it me: then I cast it into the fire, and there came out this calf."

^{25} And when Moses saw that the people were naked; (for Aaron had made them naked unto their shame among their enemies①.) ^{26} Then Moses stood in the gate of the camp, and said, "Who is on the LORD's side? Let him come unto me." And all the sons of Levi gathered themselves together unto him.

^{27} And he said unto them, thus saith the LORD God of Israel, "Put every man his sword by his side, and go in and out from gate to gate throughout the camp, and slay every man his brother, and every man his companion, and every man his neighbour." ^{28} And the children of Levi did according to the word of Moses: and there fell of the people that day about three thousand men. ^{29} For Moses had said, "Consecrate yourselves today to the LORD, even every man upon his son, and upon his brother; that he may bestow upon you a blessing this day."

^{30} And it came to pass on the morrow, that Moses said unto the people, "Ye have sinned a great sin: and now I will go up unto the LORD; peradventure I shall make an atonement for your sin."

^{31} And Moses returned unto the LORD, and said, "Oh, this people have sinned a great sin, and have made them gods of gold. ^{32} Yet now, if thou wilt forgive their sin—; and if not, blot me, I pray thee, out of thy book which thou hast written." ^{33} And the LORD said unto Moses, "Whosoever hath sinned against me, him will I blot out of my book. ^{34} Therefore now go, lead the people unto the place of which I have spoken unto thee: behold, mine Angel shall go before thee: nevertheless in the day when I visit I will visit their sin upon them②."

^{35} And the LORD plagued the people, because they made the calf, which Aaron made.

III FOOD FOR THOUGHT

1. What is Moses' role in the covenant?
2. How does the covenant at Mount Sinai contrast with the one God made with Noah and the one with Abraham in Genesis?
3. What sin did the Israelites commit while Moses was still up in the mountain? What was Aaron's role in it?
4. What persuaded Yahweh not to destroy the people?
5. What characteristics of a great leader were displayed by Moses in his experiences throughout the Book of Exodus?

IV BIBLICAL RELEVANCE

A. Biblical Terms in Everyday English
1. golden calf: _____

---

① **for Aaron had made them naked unto their shame among their enemies** for Aaron had let them run wild and so become a laughing stock to their enemies.
② **I will visit their sin upon them** I will punish them for their sin.

2. thunders on the Mount Sinai (19:16): _____

B. Biblical References in Literature
1. Duchess of Gloucester: ... Could I come near your beauty with my nails, I'd set my ten commandments in your face.
(W. Shakespeare, *1 Henry VI*, Act I, Scene 3)
2. He hummed as he filled the kettle, it was a good sign to use the big brown pot. They took the big pot round with them from job to job, it was their Ark of the Covenant almost.
(Gwendoline Butlter, *A Dark Coffin*, 1995)

C. The Bible and Arts
1. *Moses Receives the Tablets of the Law*, Marc Chagall (1887—1985)
2. *The Adoration of the Golden Calf*, Nicolas Poussin (1594—1665)
3. *Moses and the Golden Calf*, Domenico Beccafumi (1486—1551)
4. *Moses Destroyeth the Tablets of the Ten Commandments*, James Tissot (1836—1902)

V SOURCES FOR REFERENCE

1. Hayes, C. (2006). "Exodus: From Egypt to Sinai." In *Introduction to the Old Testament*. Open Yale Course retrievable at 〈http://oyc.yale.edu/religious-studies/introduction-to-the-old-testament-hebrew-bible/content/downloads.〉
2. Mendenhall, George E. (1955). *Law and Covenant in Israel and the Ancient Near East*. Pittsburgh, PA: Biblical Colloquium.

PART THREE

SETTLEMENT IN THE PROMISED LAND
(C.1,200 — 1,000 B.C.E.)
THE BOOKS OF JOSHUA, JUDGES, RUTH

10. JOSHUA, THE SUCCESSOR TO MOSES

I POINTS OF DEPARTURE

With the Book of Exodus (and Genesis, Leviticus, Numbers and Deuteronomy), we wind up the first part of the Hebrew Bible (the Tanakh), Torah ("Law") or Pentateuch ("five scrolls"), with which Moses is credited. Apart from those memorable stories, this part is a body of statutes, instructions for worship, sacrificial procedure, right conduct, and precautions to preserve purity. And now from this chapter, we are entering the second part, known as Nebi'im ("Prophets"), consisting of the Former Prophets of the books of Joshua, Judges, 1 and 2 Samuel, and 1 and 2 Kings, and the Latter Prophets of Isaiah, Jeremiah, Ezekiel, and the Twelve Minor Prophets[①]. The Former Prophets is a continuation from the Pentateuch which leaves without God's promise being fulfilled. It introduces the idea of a *prophet* ("to speak on behalf of another"), a messenger of God, which is not seen in the Pentateuch. The recurrent message is obedience to God leads to a blessing, and disobedience will lead to a punishment. The role of the prophet evolved from the anointment (by Samuel) of kings during the reigns of King David and King Solomon to social and religious criticism.

As the sixth book in the Old Testament, the Book of Joshua describes the occupation of the Promised Land under Joshua, Moses' successor, representing the last phase in the history of God's promise to Israel first mentioned in *Genesis 12:1—3*. Rahab, a prostitute of Jericho to be taken by Joshua, entertained two Israelite spies and helped them escape their pursuers. As a reward, she and her household were spared when the city was sacked. In the New Testament, she is mentioned as a direct ancestor of Jesus Christ (*Mt. 1:5*) and commended for her faith (*Heb. 11:31*; *Jas 2:25*). Joshua's damming of the Jordan River, echoing the crossing of the Red Sea 40 years earlier, served to establish the hero as a worthy successor of Moses. Trumpets blaring, people shouting and marching, the wall of Jericho crumpled, making it an easy prey for the land-hungry Israelites. In spite of the lack of archeological support, the conquest of Jericho serves to impress the view that so long as the people were faithful to the covenant, they would be invincible.

"Joshua" becomes "Jesus" in Greek; hence the misleading *Acts 7:45* and *Heb. 4:8* in the King James Bible (Browning, 2009: 171, 177). Joshua was known as one of the Nine Worthies[②] in the Middle Ages.

---

① **The Twelve Minor Prophets** includes Hosea, Joel, Amos, Obadiah, Jonah, Micah, Nahum, Habakkuk, Zephaniah, Haggai, Zechariah, Malachi.

② **The Nine Worthies** are nine historical, scriptural and legendary personages who personify the ideals of chivalry in the Middle Ages, the others being Hector, Alexander the Great and Julius Caesar (Pagans); Joshua, David and Judas Maccabeus (Old Testament Jews); King Arthur, Charlemagne and Godfrey of Bouillon (Chivalric Christian Heroes). (http://en.wikipedia.org/wiki/Nine_Worthies).

II SELECTED READINGS

The Lord Commands Joshua

Joshua 1

¹ Now after the death of Moses the servant of the LORD, it came to pass that the LORD spoke unto Joshua the son of Nun, Moses' minister, saying, ² "Moses My servant is dead. Now therefore arise, go over this Jordan, thou and all this people, unto the land which I give to them, even to the children of Israel. ³ Every place that the sole of your foot shall tread upon, that have I given unto you, as I said unto Moses. ⁴ From the wilderness and this Lebanon even unto the great river, the River Euphrates, all the land of the Hittites, and unto the great sea toward the going down of the sun, shall be your border. ⁵ There shall not any man be able to stand before thee all the days of thy life. As I was with Moses, so I will be with thee: I will not fail thee nor forsake thee."

⁶ "Be strong and of a good courage, for unto this people shalt thou divide for an inheritance the land which I swore unto their fathers to give them. ⁷ Only be thou strong and very courageous, that thou mayest observe to do according to all the law, which Moses My servant commanded thee. Turn not from it to the right hand or to the left, that thou mayest prosper whithersoever thou goest. ⁸ This Book of the Law shall not depart out of thy mouth, but thou shalt meditate therein day and night, that thou mayest observe to do according to all that is written therein. For then thou shalt make thy way prosperous, and then thou shalt have good success. ⁹ Have not I commanded thee? Be strong and of a good courage; be not afraid, neither be thou dismayed, for the LORD thy God is with thee whithersoever thou goest."

¹⁰ Then Joshua commanded the officers of the people, saying, ¹¹ "Pass through the host and command the people, saying, 'Prepare you victuals, for within three days ye shall pass over this Jordan to go in to possess the land which the LORD your God giveth you to possess it.'"

¹² And to the Reubenites and to the Gadites and to half the tribe of Manasseh spoke Joshua, saying, ¹³ "Remember the word which Moses the servant of the LORD commanded you, saying, 'The LORD your God hath given you rest and hath given you this land.' ¹⁴ Your wives, your little ones, and your cattle shall remain in the land which Moses gave you on this side of the Jordan. But ye shall pass before your brethren armed, all the mighty men of valor, and help them; ¹⁵ Until the LORD shall have given your brethren rest, as He hath given you, and they also have possessed the land which the LORD your God giveth them. Then ye shall return unto the land of your possession and enjoy it, which Moses the LORD's servant gave you on this side of the Jordan toward the sunrising."

¹⁶ And they answered Joshua, saying, "All that thou commandest us we will do, and whithersoever thou sendest us we will go. ¹⁷ According as we hearkened unto Moses in all things, so will we hearken unto thee; only the LORD thy God be with thee, as He was with Moses. ¹⁸ Whosoever he be that doth rebel against thy commandment and will not hearken unto thy words in all that thou commandest him, he shall be put to death. Only be strong and of a good courage."

Rahab and the Spies

Joshua 2

¹ And Joshua the son of Nun sent out of Shittim two men to spy secretly, saying, "Go, view the land, even Jericho." And they went and came into a harlot's house, named Rahab[3], and lodged there.

---

③ **Rahab** (/ˈrɑːhæb/, 喇合) became a direct ancestor of Jesus Christ (*Mt.* 1:5) by marrying a man named Salmon.

Rahab Helping the Two Israelite Spies, 1897, Frederick Richard Pickersgill

² And it was told the king of Jericho, saying, "Behold, there came men in hither tonight of the children of Israel to search out④ the country." ³ And the king of Jericho sent unto Rahab, saying, "Bring forth the men who have come to thee, who have entered into thine house, for they have come to search out all the country."

⁴ And the woman took the two men and hid them, and said thus, "There came men unto me, but I knew not from whence they came. ⁵ And it came to pass about the time of shutting of the gate, when it was dark, that the men went out. Whither the men went I know not. Pursue after them quickly, for ye shall overtake them." ⁶ But she had brought them up to the roof of the house and hid them with the stalks of flax which she had laid in order upon the roof. ⁷ And the men pursued after them on the way to the Jordan unto the fords; and as soon as those who pursued after them had gone out, they shut the gate.

⁸ And before they lay down, she came up unto them upon the roof. ⁹ And she said unto the men, "I know that the LORD hath given you the land, and that your terror has fallen upon us, and that all the inhabitants of the land faint because of you. ¹⁰ For we have heard how the LORD dried up the water of the Red Sea for you when ye came out of Egypt, and what ye did unto the two kings of the Amorites who were on the other side of the Jordan, Sihon and Og, whom ye utterly destroyed. ¹¹ And as soon as we had heard these things, our hearts did melt, neither did there remain any more courage in any man because of you; for the LORD your God, He is God in heaven above and on earth beneath. ¹² Now therefore, I pray you, swear unto me by the LORD, since I have shown you kindness, that ye will also show kindness unto my father's house, and give me a true token. ¹³ And that ye will save alive my father and my mother, and my brethren and my sisters, and all that they have, and deliver our lives from death."

¹⁴ And the men answered her, "Our life for yours, if ye utter not this our business. And it shall be, when the LORD hath given us the land, that we will deal kindly and truly with thee."

¹⁵ Then she let them down by a cord through the window, for her house was upon the town wall, and she dwelt upon the wall. ¹⁶ And she said unto them, "Get you to the mountain, lest the pursuers meet you; and hide yourselves there three days until the pursuers have returned, and afterward may ye go your way."

¹⁷ And the men said unto her, "We will be blameless of this thine oath which thou hast made us swear. ¹⁸ Behold, when we come into the land, thou shalt bind this line of scarlet thread in the window which thou didst let us down by; and thou shalt bring thy father, and thy mother, and thy brethren, and all thy father's household home unto thee. ¹⁹ And it shall be that whosoever shall go out of the doors of thy house into the street, his blood shall be upon his head, and we will be guiltless; and whosoever shall be with thee in the house, his blood shall be on our head if any hand be upon him.

²⁰ And if thou utter this our business, then we will be free of thine oath which thou hast made us to swear."

²¹ And she said, "According unto your words, so be it." And she sent them away, and they departed; and she bound the scarlet line in the window.

Rahab and the Spies, 1893, Henry Davenport

²² And they went and came unto the mountain, and abode there three days until the pursuers had returned; and the pursuers sought them throughout all the way, but found them not. ²³ So the two men returned and

---

④ **search out** spy out.

descended from the mountain, and passed over and came to Joshua the son of Nun, and told him all things that befell them. ²⁴ And they said unto Joshua, "Truly the LORD hath delivered into our hands all the land, for even all the inhabitants of the country do faint because of us."

Crossing the Jordan

Joshua 3

¹ And Joshua rose early in the morning; and they removed from Shittim and came to the Jordan, he and all the children of Israel, and lodged there before they passed over. ² And it came to pass after three days that the officers went through the host. ³ And they commanded the people, saying, "When ye see the ark of the covenant⑤ of the LORD your God and the priests the Levites bearing it, then ye shall remove from your place and go after it. ⁴ Yet there shall be a space between you and it, about two thousand cubits by measure. Come not near unto it, that ye may know the way by which ye must go, for ye have not passed this way heretofore."

⁵ And Joshua said unto the people, "Sanctify yourselves, for tomorrow the LORD will do wonders among you."

⁶ And Joshua spoke unto the priests, saying, "Take up the ark of the covenant, and pass over before the people." And they took up the ark of the covenant, and went before the people.

⁷ And the LORD said unto Joshua, "This day will I begin to magnify thee in the sight of all Israel, that they may know that as I was with Moses, so I will be with thee. ⁸ And thou shalt command the priests who bear the ark of the covenant, saying, 'When ye have come to the brink of the water of the Jordan, ye shall stand still in the Jordan.' "

⁹ And Joshua said unto the children of Israel, "Come hither, and hear the words of the LORD your God." ¹⁰ And Joshua said, "Hereby ye shall know that the living God is among you, and that He will without fail drive out from before you the Canaanites and the Hittites and the Hivites and the Perizzites and the Girgashites and the Amorites and the Jebusites. ¹¹ Behold, the ark of the covenant of the Lord of all the earth passeth over before you into the Jordan. ¹² Now therefore, take for yourselves twelve men out of the tribes of Israel, out of every tribe a man. ¹³ And it shall come to pass, as soon as the soles of the feet of the priests who bear the ark of the LORD, the Lord of all the earth, shall rest in the waters of the Jordan, that the waters of the Jordan shall be cut off from the waters that come down from above; and they shall stand up in a heap."

The Priests Who Carried the Ark of the Covenant of the Lord Stood Firm on Dry Ground, Nurit Tzarfati

¹⁴ And it came to pass, when the people removed from their tents to pass over the Jordan, and the priests bearing the ark of the covenant before the people. ¹⁵ And as those who bore the ark had come unto the Jordan, and the feet of the priests who bore the ark were dipped in the brim of the water (for the Jordan overfloweth all his banks all the time of harvest). ¹⁶ That the waters which came down from above stood and rose up in a heap very far from the city Adam, that is beside Zaretan. And those who came down toward the sea of the plain, even the Salt Sea, failed and were cut off; and the people passed over right against Jericho. ¹⁷ And the priests who bore the ark of the covenant of the LORD stood firm on dry ground in the midst of the Jordan, and all the Israelites passed over on dry ground, until all the people had passed clean over the Jordan.

---

⑤ **the ark of the covenant** (约柜) was the holiest sign of God's presence. In or near it were placed several important mementos of the journey to the Promised Land including the stone tablets of the Law of Moses, a jar of the miraculous manna and Aaron's sprouted staff.

The Fall of Jericho

Joshua 6

¹ Now Jericho⑥ was securely shut up because of the children of Israel: none went out, and none came in.
² And the LORD said unto Joshua, "See, I have given into thine hand Jericho, and the king thereof and the mighty men of valor. ³ And ye shall compass the city, all ye men of war, and go round about the city once. Thus shalt thou do six days. ⁴ And seven priests shall bear before the ark seven trumpets of rams' horns; and the seventh day ye shall compass the city seven times, and the priests shall blow with the trumpets. ⁵ And it shall come to pass, when they make a long blast with the ram's horn and when ye hear the sound of the trumpet, that all the people shall shout with a great shout; and the wall of the city shall fall down flat, and the people shall ascend up every man straight before him."

⁶ And Joshua the son of Nun called the priests and said unto them, "Take up the ark of the covenant, and let seven priests bear seven trumpets of rams' horns before the ark of the LORD." ⁷ And he said unto the people, "Pass on, and compass the city, and let him that is armed pass on before the ark of the LORD."

Taking Jericho, ca. 1455, Jean Fouquet

⁸ And it came to pass, when Joshua had spoken unto the people, that the seven priests bearing the seven trumpets of rams' horns passed on before the LORD and blew with the trumpets; and the ark of the covenant of the LORD followed them. ⁹ And the armed men went before the priests who blew with the trumpets, and the rearward came after the ark, the priests going on and blowing with the trumpets. ¹⁰ And Joshua had commanded the people, saying, "Ye shall not shout nor make any noise with your voice, neither shall any word proceed out of your mouth until the day I bid you shout. Then shall ye shout."

¹¹ So the ark of the LORD compassed the city, going about it once; and they came into the camp and lodged in the camp.

¹² And Joshua rose early in the morning, and the priests took up the ark of the LORD. ¹³ And seven priests bearing seven trumpets of rams' horns before the ark of the LORD went on continually and blew with the trumpets; and the armed men went before them, but the rearward came after the ark of the LORD, the priests going on and blowing with the trumpets. ¹⁴ And the second day they compassed the city once and returned into the camp. So they did six days.

¹⁵ And it came to pass on the seventh day that they rose early, about the dawning of the day, and compassed the city in the same manner seven times. Only on that day they compassed the city seven times. ¹⁶ And it came to pass at the seventh time, when the priests blew with the trumpets, Joshua said unto the people, "Shout! For the LORD hath given you the city. ¹⁷ And the city shall be accursed, even it and all who are therein, to the LORD. Only Rahab the harlot shall live, she and all who are with her in the house, because she hid the messengers that we sent. ¹⁸ And ye, in all ways keep yourselves from the accursed thing, lest ye make yourselves accursed when ye take of the accursed thing, and make the camp of Israel a curse and trouble it. ¹⁹ But all the silver and gold and vessels of brass and iron are consecrated unto the LORD. They shall come into the treasury of the LORD."

²⁰ So the people shouted when the priests blew with the trumpets. And it came to pass, when the people heard the sound of the trumpet and the people shouted with a great shout, that the wall fell down flat, so that the people went up into the city, every man straight before him; and they took the city. ²¹ And they utterly destroyed all that was in the city, both man and woman, young and old, and ox and sheep and ass, with the edge of the sword. ²² But Joshua had said unto the two men who had spied out the country, "Go into the

---

⑥ **Jericho** (/ˈdʒerikəʊ/, 耶利哥) a stronghold near the northwest shore of the Dead Sea, commanding the valley of the lower Jordan River.

harlot's house, and bring out from thence the woman and all that she hath, as ye swore unto her." ²³ And the young men who were spies went in and brought Rahab and her father and her mother and her brethren, and all that she had; and they brought out all her kindred and left them outside the camp of Israel.

²⁴ And they burned the city with fire and all that was therein. Only the silver and the gold and the vessels of brass and of iron they put into the treasury of the house of the LORD. ²⁵ And Joshua saved Rahab the harlot alive, and her father's household and all that she had; and she dwelleth in Israel even unto this day, because she hid the messengers whom Joshua sent to spy out Jericho.

²⁶ And Joshua adjured them at that time, saying, " Cursed be the man before the LORD who riseth up and buildeth this city Jericho."

"He shall lay the foundation thereof in his firstborn,
and in his youngest son shall he set up the gates of it." ⑦

²⁷ So the LORD was with Joshua, and his fame was noised throughout all the country.

The Sun Stands Still

Joshua 10

¹ Now it came to pass, when Adonizedec king of Jerusalem had heard how Joshua had taken Ai, and had utterly destroyed it; as he had done to Jericho and her king, so he had done to Ai and her king; and how the inhabitants of Gibeon had made peace with Israel, and were among them; ² That they feared greatly, because Gibeon was a great city, as one of the royal cities, and because it was greater than Ai, and all the men thereof were mighty. ³ Wherefore Adonizedec king of Jerusalem, sent unto Hoham king of Hebron, and unto Piram king of Jarmuth, and unto Japhia king of Lachish, and unto Debir king of Eglon, saying, ⁴ " Come up unto me, and help me, that we may smite Gibeon: for it hath made peace with Joshua and with the children of Israel."

⁵ Therefore the five kings of the Amorites, the king of Jerusalem, the king of Hebron, the king of Jarmuth, the king of Lachish, the king of Eglon, gathered themselves together, and went up, they and all their hosts, and encamped before Gibeon, and made war against it.

⁶ And the men of Gibeon sent unto Joshua to the camp to Gilgal, saying, " Slack not thy hand from thy servants; come up to us quickly, and save us, and help us: for all the kings of the Amorites that dwell in the mountains are gathered together against us."

⁷ So Joshua ascended from Gilgal, he, and all the people of war with him, and all the mighty men of valour. ⁸ And the LORD said unto Joshua, " Fear them not: for I have delivered them into thine hand; there shall not a man of them stand before thee."

⁹ Joshua therefore came unto them suddenly, and went up from Gilgal all night. ¹⁰ And the LORD discomfited them before Israel, and slew them with a great slaughter at Gibeon, and chased them along the way that goeth up to Bethhoron, and smote them to Azekah, and unto Makkedah. ¹¹ And it came to pass, as they fled from before Israel, and were in the going down to Bethhoron, that the LORD cast down great stones from heaven upon them unto Azekah, and they died: they were more which died with hailstones than they whom the children of Israel slew with the sword.

¹² Then spake Joshua to the LORD in the day when the LORD delivered up the Amorites before the children of Israel, and he said in the sight of Israel,

" Sun, stand thou still upon Gibeon;
and thou, Moon, in the valley of Ajalon.

¹³ And the sun stood still,
and the moon stayed,
until the people had avenged themselves upon their enemies.
Is not this written in the book of Jasher?

---

⑦ This curse had tragic consequence for Hiel (*1 Kg. 16:34*).

So the sun stood still in the midst of heaven, and hasted not to go down about a whole day. ¹⁴ *And there was no day like that before it or after it, that the LORD hearkened unto the voice of a man: for the LORD fought for Israel.* ¹⁵ *And Joshua returned, and all Israel with him, unto the camp to Gilgal.*

III FOOD FOR THOUGHT

1. What did Joshua promise the people after his encounter with God?
2. What characteristics would you attribute to Rahab?
3. What is the Ark of Covenant?
4. What instructions did Joshua receive for the siege of Jericho?

IV BIBLICAL RELEVANCE

A. Biblical Terms in Everyday English
1. from Jericho to June: _____
2. Go to Jericho!: _____
3. has/have been to Jericho: _____

B. Biblical References in Literature
1. As Jenny Long drove to the hospital the next morning she sang softly to herself. She was quite confident that it wouldn't be long before Harry gave in and said it was time they got married. After all, even Jericho fell in the end.
   (Marx Marquis, *Written in Blood*, 1995)
2. We were gaining about twenty minutes every day, because we were going east so fast—we gained just about enough every day to keep along with the moon. It was becoming an old moon to the friends we had left behind us, but to us Joshuas it stood still.
   (Mark Twain, *The Innocents Abroad*, 1869)

C. The Bible and Arts
1. *Eleazar Commissioning Joshua*, 1851—1860, Julius Schnorr von Carolsfeld
2. *The Flight of the Spies*, 1896—1900, James Tissot
3. *The Priests Who Carried the Ark of the Covenant of the Lord Stood Firm on Dry Ground*, Nurit Tzarfati
4. *The Taking of Jericho*, 1896—1900, James Tissot
5. *The Victory of Joshua over Amorites*, 1624—1626, Nicolas Poussin

V SOURCES FOR REFERENCE

1. http://en.wikipedia.org/wiki/Joshua
2. (2004). "Episode 6: Joshua and the Walls of Jericho," *Bible Mysteries*, a series of BBC TV programs exploring great figures and events from biblical times.
3. Browning, W. R. E. (2009). *A Dictionary of the Bible*. Oxford: Oxford University Press.

11. UNLIKELY HEROES

I. POINTS OF DEPARTURE

The Book of Judges sets out some of Israel's traditions from the death of Joshua to the advent of Samuel, covering a historical span of approximately 300 years. During this period of anarchy, the 12 tribes of Israel were independent of one another, fending against hostile neighboring tribes single-handedly and mostly fighting among themselves. And what is worse, they learned to live with their sophisticated neighbours and adopted their worship of the local idol Baal, committing the sin of apostasy. Then a pattern emerges of the Israelites' apostasy, their suffering at the hands of foreign invaders, and their subsequent deliverance by a certain judge sent by God. This pattern repeats itself again and again throughout the book.

The judges sent by God to deliver the people of Israel were unheroic "heroes," each made up of certain unseemly stuff. Take Ehud for example. As the left-handed son of Gera the Benjamite, he murdered the king of Moab with a double-edged sword concealed under his clothing (*Jg. 15—23*). It is reminiscent of a Chinese legend about an aborted assassination attempt involving a dagger hidden in the scroll of a map presented by a hero named Jing Ke (荆轲) (Kuo, 1990: 89), but will surely cause a few raised eyebrows among Jewish and Christian readers who are familiar with the commandment against murder. Deborah, though notable for her gender and virtues of wisdom and courage, had a female follower of dubious character: Jael, who, to assist Deborah in her battle, lured the enemy general, Sisera of Canaan into her tent with feigned hospitality, and then killed him in the most gruesome way possible, by driving a peg through his temple into the ground (*Jg. 4:17—22*). Gideon, another unlikely leader, started out as a member of a family who worshipped Baal instead of God, a milksop who seemed to be forever asking for miracles in order to believe. But God accepted what he was and gave him the signs and eventually made a courageous leader out of this cast-off material. Jephthah was the son of a prostitute, driven away by his half brothers — a social outcast. And he betrayed his lack of wisdom through his rash vow to God (*Jg. 11:31*) and his harsh answer to a complaint (*Jg. 12:3*), both of which had destructive consequences. Samson, the most famous hero during the time of the judges, was, apart from his supernatural physical strength, given to lust for women.

The selection of this motley band of unlikely heroes together with their equally incredible against-all-odds victories serves to reiterate that all glory belongs to God and God alone. This is borne out by Paul in *1 Corinthians 1:26—27, 31*:

For ye see your calling, brethren, how that not many wise men after the flesh, not many mighty, not many noble, are called. But God hath chosen the foolish things of the world to confound the wise; and God hath chosen the weak things of the world to confound the things which are mighty. That, according as it is written, He that glorieth, let him glory in the Lord.

II SELECTED READINGS

God Promises Deliverance

Judges 6

¹ And the children of Israel did evil in the sight of the LORD: and the LORD delivered them into the hand of Midian seven years. ² And the hand of Midian prevailed against Israel: and because of the Midianites the children of Israel made them the dens which are in the mountains, and caves, and strong holds. ³ And so it was, when Israel had sown, that the Midianites came up, and the Amalekites, and the children of the east, even they came up against them; ⁴ And they encamped against them, and destroyed the increase of the earth, till thou come unto Gaza, and left no sustenance for Israel, neither sheep, nor ox, nor ass. ⁵ For they came up with their cattle and their tents, and they came as grasshoppers for multitude; for both they and their camels were without number: and they entered into the land to destroy it. ⁶ And Israel was greatly impoverished because of the Midianites; and the children of Israel cried unto the LORD.

⁷ And it came to pass, when the children of Israel cried unto the LORD because of the Midianites, ⁸ that the LORD sent a prophet unto the children of Israel, which said unto them. Thus saith the LORD God of Israel, "I brought you up from Egypt, and brought you forth out of the house of bondage; ⁹ And I delivered you out of the hand of the Egyptians, and out of the hand of all that oppressed you, and drave them out from before you, and gave you their land; ¹⁰ And I said unto you, 'I am the LORD your God; fear not the gods of the Amorites, in whose land ye dwell: but ye have not obeyed my voice.'"

The Call of Gideon

¹¹ And there came an angel of the LORD, and sat under an oak which was in Ophrah, that pertained unto Joash the Abiezrite: and his son Gideon① threshed wheat by the winepress, to hide it from the Midianites. ¹² And the angel of the LORD appeared unto him, and said unto him, "The LORD is with thee, thou mighty man of valour."

Gideon and the Angel
〈http://lavistachurchofchrist.org〉

¹³ And Gideon said unto him, "Oh my Lord, if the LORD be with us, why then is all this befallen us? And where be all his miracles which our fathers told us of, saying, 'Did not the LORD bring us up from Egypt?' But now the LORD hath forsaken us, and delivered us into the hands of the Midianites." ¹⁴ And the LORD looked upon him, and said, "Go in this thy might, and thou shalt save Israel from the hand of the Midianites: have not I sent thee?"

¹⁵ And he said unto him, "Oh my Lord, wherewith shall I save Israel? Behold, my family is poor in Manasseh, and I am the least in my father's house."

¹⁶ And the LORD said unto him, "Surely I will be with thee, and thou shalt smite the Midianites as one man."

¹⁷ And he said unto him, "If now I have found grace in thy sight, then shew me a sign that thou talkest with me." ¹⁸ Depart not hence, I pray thee, until I come unto thee, and bring forth my present, and set it before thee.

---

① **Gideon** /ˈgidiən/,基甸。

And he said, "I will tarry until thou come again."

¹⁹ And Gideon went in, and made ready a kid, and unleavened cakes of an ephah of flour: the flesh he put in a basket, and he put the broth in a pot, and brought it out unto him under the oak, and presented it.

²⁰ And the angel of God said unto him, "Take the flesh and the unleavened cakes, and lay them upon this rock, and pour out the broth." And he did so. ²¹ Then the angel of the LORD put forth the end of the staff that was in his hand, and touched the flesh and the unleavened cakes; and there rose up fire out of the rock, and consumed the flesh and the unleavened cakes. Then the angel of the LORD departed out of his sight. ²² And when Gideon perceived that he was an angel of the LORD, Gideon said, "Alas, O LORD God! For because I have seen an angel of the LORD face to face."

²³ And the LORD said unto him, "Peace be unto thee; fear not: thou shalt not die." ²⁴ Then Gideon built an altar there unto the LORD, and called it Jehovahshalom: unto this day it is yet in Ophrah of the Abiezrites.

²⁵ And it came to pass the same night, that the LORD said unto him, "Take thy father's young bullock, even the second bullock of seven years old, and throw down the altar of Baal② that thy father hath, and cut down the grove that is by it: ²⁶ And build an altar unto the LORD thy God upon the top of this rock, in the ordered place, and take the second bullock, and offer a burnt sacrifice with the wood of the grove which thou shalt cut down."

²⁷ Then Gideon took ten men of his servants, and did as the LORD had said unto him: and so it was, because he feared his father's household, and the men of the city, that he could not do it by day, that he did it by night.

²⁸ And when the men of the city arose early in the morning, behold, the altar of Baal was cast down, and the grove was cut down that was by it, and the second bullock was offered upon the altar that was built.

²⁹ And they said one to another, "Who hath done this thing?" And when they enquired and asked, they said, "Gideon the son of Joash hath done this thing." ³⁰ Then the men of the city said unto Joash, "Bring out thy son, that he may die: because he hath cast down the altar of Baal, and because he hath cut down the grove that was by it."

³¹ And Joash said unto all that stood against him, "Will ye plead for Baal? Will ye save him? He that will plead for him, let him be put to death whilst it is yet morning: if he be a god, let him plead for himself, because one hath cast down his altar." ³² Therefore on that day he called him Jerubbaal, saying, "Let Baal plead against him, because he hath thrown down his altar."

³³ Then all the Midianites and the Amalekites and the children of the east were gathered together, and went over, and pitched in the valley of Jezreel. ³⁴ But the Spirit of the LORD came upon Gideon, and he blew a trumpet; and Abiezer was gathered after him. ³⁵ And he sent messengers throughout all Manasseh; who also was gathered after him: and he sent messengers unto Asher, and unto Zebulun, and unto Naphtali; and they came up to meet them.

The Miracle of the Fleece

³⁶ And Gideon said unto God, "If thou wilt save Israel by mine hand, as thou hast said. ³⁷ Behold, I will put a fleece of wool in the floor; and if the dew be on the fleece only, and it be dry upon all the earth beside, then shall I know that thou wilt save Israel by mine hand, as thou hast said." ³⁸ And it was so: for he rose up early on the morrow, and thrust the fleece together, and wringed the dew out of the fleece, a bowl full of water.

³⁹ And Gideon said unto God, "Let not thine anger be hot against me, and I will speak but this once: let me prove, I pray thee, but this once with the fleece; let it now be dry only upon the fleece, and upon all the ground let there be dew." ⁴⁰ And God did so that night: for it was dry upon the fleece only, and there was dew on all the ground.

---

② **Baal** (/ˈbeɪəl/, 巴力) fertility and nature god of the Phoenicians and Canaanites worshiped in Israel.

Gideon Defeats the Midianites

Judges 7

¹ Then Jerubbaal, who is Gideon, and all the people that were with him, rose up early, and pitched beside the well of Harod: so that the host of the Midianites were on the north side of them, by the hill of Moreh, in the valley.

Sifting the Soldiers

² And the LORD said unto Gideon, "The people that are with thee are too many for me to give the Midianites into their hands, lest Israel vaunt themselves against me, saying, ' Mine own hand hath saved me.' ³ Now therefore go to, proclaim in the ears of the people, saying, ' Whosoever is fearful and afraid, let him return and depart early from mount Gilead.' " And there returned of the people twenty and two thousand; and there remained ten thousand.

Gideon Sifting His Soldiers ⟨http://scripturelady.com⟩

⁴ And the LORD said unto Gideon, "The people are yet too many; bring them down unto the water, and I will try them for thee there: and it shall be, that of whom I say unto thee. This shall go with thee, the same shall go with thee; and of whomsoever I say unto thee. This shall not go with thee, the same shall not go." ⁵ So he brought down the people unto the water: and the LORD said unto Gideon, " Every one that lappeth of the water with his tongue, as a dog lappeth, him shalt thou set by himself; likewise every one that boweth down upon his knees to drink." ⁶ And the number of them that lapped, putting their hand to their mouth, were three hundred men: but all the rest of the people bowed down upon their knees to drink water.

⁷ And the LORD said unto Gideon, " By the three hundred men that lapped will I save you, and deliver the Midianites into thine hand: and let all the other people go every man unto his place." ⁸ So the people took victuals in their hand, and their trumpets: and he sent all the rest of Israel every man unto his tent, and retained those three hundred men.

And the host of Midian was beneath him in the valley. ⁹ And it came to pass the same night, that the LORD said unto him, " Arise, get thee down unto the host; for I have delivered it into thine hand. ¹⁰ But if thou fear to go down, go thou with Phurah thy servant down to the host: ¹¹ And thou shalt hear what they say; and afterward shall thine hands be strengthened to go down unto the host. Then went he down with Phurah his servant unto the outside of the armed men that were in the host." ¹² And the Midianites and the Amalekites and all the children of the east lay along in the valley like grasshoppers for multitude; and their camels were without number, as the sand by the sea side for multitude.

¹³ And when Gideon was come, behold, there was a man that told a dream unto his fellow, and said, " Behold, I dreamed a dream, and, lo, a cake of barley bread tumbled into the host of Midian, and came unto a tent, and smote it that it fell, and overturned it, that the tent lay along."

A Trumpet-and-Jar Strategy

¹⁴ And his fellow answered and said, " This is nothing else save the sword of Gideon the son of Joash, a man of Israel: for into his hand hath God delivered Midian, and all the host." ¹⁵ And it was so, when Gideon heard the telling of the dream, and the interpretation thereof, that he worshipped, and returned into the host of Israel, and said, " Arise; for the LORD hath delivered into your hand the host of Midian." ¹⁶ And he divided

the three hundred men into three companies, and he put a trumpet in every man's hand, with empty pitchers, and lamps within the pitchers. ¹⁷ And he said unto them, "Look on me, and do likewise: and, behold, when I come to the outside of the camp, it shall be that, as I do, so shall ye do." ¹⁸ When I blow with a trumpet, I and all that are with me, then blow ye the trumpets also on every side of all the camp, and say, "The sword of the LORD, and of Gideon." ¹⁹ So Gideon, and the hundred men that were with him, came unto the outside of the camp in the beginning of the middle watch; and they had but newly set the watch: and they blew the trumpets, and brake the pitchers that were in their hands. ²⁰ And the three companies blew the trumpets, and brake the pitchers, and held

Gideon Defeats the Midianites by Trickery

the lamps in their left hands, and the trumpets in their right hands to blow withal: and they cried, "The sword of the LORD, and of Gideon." ²¹ And they stood every man in his place round about the camp; and all the host ran, and cried, and fled.

²² And the three hundred blew the trumpets, and the LORD set every man's sword against his fellow, even throughout all the host: and the host fled to Bethshittah in Zererath, and to the border of Abelmeholah, unto Tabbath. ²³ And the men of Israel gathered themselves together out of Naphtali, and out of Asher, and out of all Manasseh, and pursued after the Midianites. ²⁴ And Gideon sent messengers throughout all mount Ephraim, saying, "Come down against the Midianites, and take before them the waters unto Bethbarah and Jordan."

Then all the men of Ephraim gathered themselves together, and took the waters unto Bethbarah and Jordan. ²⁵ And they took two princes of the Midianites, Oreb and Zeeb; and they slew Oreb upon the rock Oreb, and Zeeb they slew at the winepress of Zeeb, and pursued Midian, and brought the heads of Oreb and Zeeb to Gideon on the other side Jordan.

Gideon's Ephod③

²² Then the men of Israel said unto Gideon, "Rule thou over us, both thou, and thy son, and thy son's son also: for thou hast delivered us from the hand of Midian."

²³ And Gideon said unto them, "I will not rule over you, neither shall my son rule over you: the LORD shall rule over you." ²⁴ And Gideon said unto them, "I would desire a request of you, that ye would give me every man the earrings of his prey." (For they had golden earrings, because they were Ishmaelites.)

²⁵ And they answered, "We will willingly give them." And they spread a garment, and did cast therein every man the earrings of his prey. ²⁶ And the weight of the golden earrings that he requested was a thousand and seven hundred shekels of gold; beside ornaments, and collars, and purple raiment that was on the kings of Midian, and beside the chains that were about their camels' necks. ²⁷ And Gideon made an ephod thereof, and put it in his city, even in Ophrah: and all Israel went thither a whoring after it: which thing became a snare unto Gideon, and to his house.

Gideon's Death

²⁸ Thus was Midian subdued before the children of Israel, so that they lifted up their heads no more. And the country was in quietness forty years in the days of Gideon.

²⁹ And Jerubbaal the son of Joash went and dwelt in his own house. ³⁰ And Gideon had threescore and

---

③ **Ephod** /ˈiːfɒd/, a sleeveless garment worn by Jewish priests.

ten sons of his body begotten: for he had many wives. ³¹And his concubine that was in Shechem, she also bare him a son, whose name he called Abimelech. ³²And Gideon the son of Joash died in a good old age, and was buried in the sepulchre of Joash his father, in Ophrah of the Abiezrites.

³³And it came to pass, as soon as Gideon was dead, that the children of Israel turned again, and went a whoring after Baalim④, and made Baalberith their god. ³⁴And the children of Israel remembered not the LORD their God, who had delivered them out of the hands of all their enemies on every side. ³⁵Neither shewed they kindness to the house of Jerubbaal, namely, Gideon, according to all the goodness which he had shewed unto Israel.

Cultural Connections: *Gideon International*

Inspired by the humility, faith, and obedience of Gideon, Gideon International was established in 1899, an evangelical Christian organization dedicated to distributing copies of the Bible in English(especially the *King James Bible*) and many other languages in 194 countries of the world, most famously in hotel and motel rooms. The symbol of the Gideons is a two-handled pitcher and torch, recalling Gideon's victory over the Midianites (*Jg. 7: 19—21*).

The Gideons International

Jephthah's Dilemma

Judges 11

¹Now Jephthah⑤ the Gileadite was a mighty man of valour, and he was the son of an harlot: and Gilead begat Jephthah. ²And Gilead's wife bare him sons; and his wife's sons grew up, and they thrust out Jephthah, and said unto him, "Thou shalt not inherit in our father's house; for thou art the son of a strange woman." ³Then Jephthah fled from his brethren, and dwelt in the land of Tob: and there were gathered vain men to Jephthah, and went out with him.

⁴And it came to pass in process of time, that the children of Ammon made war against Israel. ⁵And it was so, that when the children of Ammon made war against Israel, the elders of Gilead went to fetch Jephthah out of the land of Tob. ⁶And they said unto Jephthah, "Come, and be our captain, that we may fight with the children of Ammon." ⁷And Jephthah said unto the elders of Gilead, "Did not ye hate me, and expel me out of my father's house? And why are ye come unto me now when ye are in distress?"

⁸And the elders of Gilead said unto Jephthah, "Therefore we turn again to thee now, that thou mayest go with us, and fight against the children of Ammon, and be our head over all the inhabitants of Gilead." ⁹And Jephthah said unto the elders of Gilead, "If ye bring me home again to fight against the children of Ammon, and the LORD deliver them before me, shall I be your head?" ¹⁰And the elders of Gilead said unto Jephthah, "The LORD be witness between us, if we do not so according to thy words." ¹¹Then Jephthah went with the elders of Gilead, and the people made him head and captain over them: and Jephthah uttered all his words before the LORD in Mizpeh.

...

²⁹Then the Spirit of the LORD came upon Jephthah, and he passed over Gilead, and Manasseh, and passed over Mizpeh of Gilead, and from Mizpeh of Gilead he passed over unto the children of Ammon. ³⁰And Jephthah vowed a vow unto the LORD, and said, "If thou shalt without fail deliver the children of Ammon

---

④ **went a whoring after Baalim** prostituted themselves to the Baals.
⑤ **Jephthah** /ˈdʒefθə/, 耶弗他。

into mine hands. ³¹ Then it shall be, that whatsoever cometh forth of the doors of my house to meet me, when I return in peace from the children of Ammon, shall surely be the LORD's, and I will offer it up for a burnt offering."

³² So Jephthah passed over unto the children of Ammon to fight against them; and the LORD delivered them into his hands. ³³ And he smote them from Aroer, even till thou come to Minnith, even twenty cities, and unto the plain of the vineyards, with a very great slaughter. Thus the children of Ammon were subdued before the children of Israel.

³⁴ And Jephthah came to Mizpeh unto his house, and, behold, his daughter came out to meet him with timbrels and

Jephthah's Daughter, Bon Boullogne, the Elder (1609—1674)

with dances: and she was his only child; beside her he had neither son nor daughter. ³⁵ And it came to pass, when he saw her, that he rent his clothes, and said, "Alas, my daughter! Thou hast brought me very low, and thou art one of them that trouble me: for I have opened my mouth unto the LORD, and I cannot go back."

³⁶ And she said unto him, "My father, if thou hast opened thy mouth unto the LORD, do to me according to that which hath proceeded out of thy mouth; forasmuch as the LORD hath taken vengeance for thee of thine enemies, even of the children of Ammon." ³⁷ And she said unto her father, "Let this thing be done for me: let me alone two months, that I may go up and down upon the mountains, and bewail my virginity, I and my fellows."

³⁸ And he said, "Go. And he sent her away for two months: and she went with her companions, and bewailed her virginity upon the mountains." ³⁹ And it came to pass at the end of two months, that she returned unto her father, who did with her according to his vow which he had vowed: and she knew no man.

And it was a custom in Israel, ⁴⁰ that the daughters of Israel went yearly to lament the daughter of Jephthah the Gileadite four days in a year.

"Shibboleth[6]!"

Judges 12

¹ And the men of Ephraim gathered themselves together, and went northward, and said unto Jephthah, "Wherefore passedst thou over to fight against the children of Ammon, and didst not call us to go with thee? We will burn thine house upon thee with fire."

² And Jephthah said unto them, "I and my people were at great strife with the children of Ammon; and when I called you, ye delivered me not out of their hands. ³ And when I saw that ye delivered me not, I put my life in my hands, and passed over against the children of Ammon, and the LORD delivered them into my hand: wherefore then are ye come up unto me this day, to fight against me?"

⁴ Then Jephthah gathered together all the men of Gilead, and fought with Ephraim: and the men of Gilead smote Ephraim, because they said, Ye Gileadites are fugitives of Ephraim among the Ephraimites, and among the Manassites. ⁵ And the Gileadites took the passages of Jordan before the Ephraimites: and it was so, that when those Ephraimites which were escaped said, "Let me go over; that the men of Gilead said unto him, Art thou an Ephraimite? If he said, "Nay;" ⁶ Then said they unto him, "Say now 'Shibboleth.'" And he said "Sibboleth," for he could not frame to pronounce it right. Then they took him, and slew him at the passages of Jordan: and there fell at that time of the Ephraimites forty and two thousand.

⁷ And Jephthah judged Israel six years. Then died Jephthah the Gileadite, and was buried in one of the cities of Gilead. ...

---

⑥ **Shibboleth** (/ˈʃɪbəliθ/, 示播列) means *stream*, or *an ear of grain*.

Cultural Connections: *shibboleth*

Judges 12 contributes a word, *shibboleth*, which now refers to "a manner of speaking that is distinctive of a particular group of people" and is often employed to identify its speaker as being a member or not a member of a particular group. Shibboleths of this kind are found galore in the Chinese novel *Tracks in the Snowy Forest* (《林海雪原》), a typical example cited as follows:

座山雕：脸红什么？/杨子荣：精神焕发！
座山雕：怎么又黄了？/杨子荣：防冷，涂的蜡！

III FOOD FOR THOUGHT

1. How were the Israelites threatened in *Judges 6:1—5*?
2. What did Gideon ask the Lord to do before he led the Israelites against the Midianites?
3. Why did Gideon reduce the size of his fighting force?
4. What is the significance of Jephthah's sacrifice of his daughter?
5. What can we learn from the judges in terms of leadership?

IV BIBLICAL RELEVANCE

A. Biblical Terms in Everyday English
1. put out a fleece (6:37): _____
2. shibboleth (12:6): _____

B. Biblical References in Literature

"Well," said he, "I will not be too urgent; but the sooner you fix, the more obliging shall think you. Mr Andrews, we must leave something to these Jephthah's daughters, in these cases, I suppose, the little bashful folly, which, in the happiest circumstances, may give a kind of regret to a thoughtful mind, on quitting the maiden state, is a reason with Pamela; and so she shall name her day."

(Samuel Richardson, *Pamela*, 1740)

C. The Bible and Arts
1. *Gideon and the Angel*, Matthaeus Merian, the Elder (1593—1650)
2. *Jephthah's Daughter*, Bon Boullogne, the Elder (1649—1717)
3. *Lament of Jephthah's Daughter*, 1846, Diaz de la Pena, Narcisse

V SOURCES FOR REFERENCE

1. Kuo, S. M. (1990). *Journeying through the Bible*. Nanjing: Nanjing University Press.
2. Black, M. (ed.) (2001). *Peake's Commentary on the Bible*. London: Routledge.

12. SAMSON AND THE PHILISTINES

I POINTS OF DEPARTURE

The Samson stories portray a hero who was quite different from the judges who preceded him. The other judges consistently appeared as charismatic leaders who rallied their tribes and delivered Israel from the enemy threat. Samson, too, was filled with Yahweh's spirit, but he emerged primarily as a heroic individual whose major preoccupation was loving Philistine women and fighting Philistine men. It was his weakness in the hands of women, combined with his prodigious feats of strength against his enemies, that fascinated the storytellers of Israel. Thus the figure of Samson, more than any of the other judges, has been enshrined and shrouded by the process of folklore. Samson is the hero of an entire cycle of traditions. The cycle can be roughly divided into three parts: *Judges 13*, the story of Samson's birth; *Judges 14—15*, stories connected with his marriage to a Philistine woman; and *Judges 16*, other love adventures which culminated in his betrayal, capture, and death.

Some points can be summarized from Samson's career (Gottcent, 1986: 26—30). First, though Samson demonstrated such archetypical heroic traits as strength, vengeance and cleverness, they proved to be of little avail. He displayed amazing feats, like tearing a young lion apart with bare hands, burning the fields of the Philistines with torches tied to foxes' tails, killing 1,000 Philistines with the jawbone of an ass, carrying the gates of Gaza to the top of a hill, but soon after each flexing of his muscles, the Philistines pounced on him by burning his wife and father-in-law, or capturing and enslaving him. He did set the Philistines an ingenious riddle and put Delilah off three times with clever tall tales about how he could be weakened, yet he proved powerless in the face of his enemies' cheating and his wife's persistent nagging. Even when he was at his "heroic" best, there was always a visit from "Spirit of the Lord." So, the real hero was not Samson after all; it was God who stood behind him, ever ready to assert power. And Samson's dalliances with women and his juvenile squabbles with the Philistines only served to instigate them, making possible the final conflict.

The story of Samson was used by Handel for his oratorio, and there are many great pictures (by, e.g. Rubens, Rembrandt, Reni) that were inspired by the stories of Samson. John Milton's tragic poetic drama, *Samson Agonistes* (1671), depicts the biblical hero with the flavor of Greek tragedy while analogizing his own personal tragedy of blindness.

II SELECTED READINGS

The Birth of Samson

Judges 13

¹ And the children of Israel did evil again in the sight of the LORD, and the LORD delivered them into the hand of the Philistines forty years.

² And there was a certain man of Zorah, of the family of the Danites, whose name was Manoah; and his wife was barren and bore not. ³ And the angel of the LORD appeared unto the woman and said unto her, "Behold now, thou art barren and bearest not; but thou shalt conceive and bear a son. ⁴ Now therefore beware, I pray thee, and drink not wine nor strong drink, and eat not any unclean thing. ⁵ For, lo, thou shalt conceive and bear a son; and no razor shall come on his head, for the child shall be a Nazirite① unto God from the womb. And he shall begin to deliver Israel out of the hand of the Philistines."

⁶ Then the woman came and told her husband, saying, "A man of God came unto me, and his countenance was like the countenance of an angel of God, very fearsome; but I asked him not from whence he was, neither told me his name. ⁷ But he said unto me, 'Behold, thou shalt conceive and bear a son. And now drink no wine nor strong drink, neither eat any unclean thing; for the child shall be a Nazirite to God from the womb to the day of his death.'" ⁸ Then Manoah entreated the LORD, and said, "O my Lord, let the man of God which Thou didst send come again unto us and teach us what we shall do unto the child that shall be born."

⁹ And God hearkened to the voice of Manoah, and the angel of God came again unto the woman as she sat in the field; but Manoah her husband was not with her. ¹⁰ And the woman made haste and ran, and showed her husband and said unto him, "Behold, the man hath appeared unto me, that came unto me the other day."

¹¹ And Manoah arose and went after his wife, and came to the man and said unto him, "Art thou the man that spokest unto the woman?" And he said, "I am."

¹² And Manoah said, "Now let thy words come to pass. How shall we order the child, and how shall we do unto him?"

¹³ And the angel of the LORD said unto Manoah, "Of all that I said unto the woman let her beware. ¹⁴ She may not eat of any thing that cometh of the vine, neither let her drink wine or strong drink, nor eat any unclean thing. All that I commanded her let her observe."

¹⁵ And Manoah said unto the angel of the LORD, "I pray thee, let us detain thee until we shall have made ready a kid for thee."

¹⁶ And the angel of the LORD said unto Manoah, "Though thou detain me, I will not eat of thy bread; and if thou wilt offer a burnt offering, thou must offer it unto the LORD." For Manoah knew not that he was an angel of the LORD.

¹⁷ And Manoah said unto the angel of the LORD, "What is thy name, that when thy sayings come to pass we may do thee honor?"

¹⁸ And the angel of the LORD said unto him, "Why askest thou thus after my name, seeing it is secret?" ¹⁹ So Manoah took a kid with a meat offering, and offered it upon a rock unto the LORD; and the angel did wondrously, and Manoah and his wife looked on. ²⁰ For it came to pass, when the flame went up toward heaven from off the altar, that the angel of the LORD ascended in the flame of the altar. And Manoah and his wife looked on it, and fell on their faces to the ground. ²¹ But the angel of the LORD appeared no more to Manoah and to his wife. Then Manoah knew that he was an angel of the LORD.

---

① **Nazirite**(/ˈnæzəraɪt/, 拿细耳人) also **Nazarite** means *consecrated*. A Nazirite was an Israelite who was consecrated to the service of God and bound by the vows to abstain from alcohol, let the hair grow, and avoid defilement by contact with dead bodies.

^{22} And Manoah said unto his wife, "We shall surely die, because we have seen God."

^{23} But his wife said unto him, "If the LORD were pleased to kill us, he would not have received a burnt offering and a meat offering at our hands, neither would he have shown us all these things nor would He, as at this time, have told us such things as these."

^{24} And the woman bore a son, and called his name Samson②; and the child grew, and the LORD blessed him. ^{25} And the Spirit of the LORD began to move him at times in the camp of Dan between Zorah and Eshtaol.

Samson's Disastrous Marriage

Judges 14

^{1} And Samson went down to Timnah, and saw a woman in Timnah of the daughters of the Philistines. ^{2} And he came up and told his father and his mother, and said, "I have seen a woman in Timnah of the daughters of the Philistines. Now therefore get her for me for a wife."

^{3} Then his father and his mother said unto him, "Is there not a woman among the daughters of thy brethren or among all my people, that thou goest to take a wife of the uncircumcised Philistines?"

Fighting a Lion

And Samson said unto his father, "Get her for me, for she pleaseth me well." ^{4} But his father and his mother knew not that it was because of the LORD, and that he sought an occasion against the Philistines. For at that time the Philistines had dominion over Israel. ^{5} Then went Samson and his father and his mother down to Timnah, and came to the vineyards of Timnah; and behold, a young lion roared against him. ^{6} And the Spirit of the LORD came mightily upon him, and he rent him as he would have rent a kid, and he had nothing in his hand; but he told not his father or his mother what he had done. ^{7} And he went down and talked with the woman, and she pleased Samson well.

^{8} And after a time he returned to take her, and he turned aside to see the carcass of the lion; and behold, there was a swarm of bees and honey in the carcass of the lion. ^{9} And he took thereof in his hands and went on eating, and came to his father and mother; and he gave to them, and they ate. But he told them not that he had taken the honey out of the carcass of the lion.

The Wedding Feast and a Riddle

^{10} So his father went down unto the woman; and Samson made there a feast, for so used the young men to do. ^{11} And it came to pass, when they saw him, that they brought thirty companions to be with him.

^{12} And Samson said unto them, "I will now put forth a riddle unto you. If ye can with certainty explain it to me within the seven days of the feast and find it out, then I will give you thirty shirts and thirty changes of garments. ^{13} But if ye cannot explain it to me, then shall ye give me thirty shirts and thirty changes of garments."

And they said unto him, "Put forth thy riddle, that we may hear it."

^{14} And he said unto them,

"Out of the eater came forth meat,
and out of the strong came forth sweetness."

And they could not in three days expound the riddle.

---

② **Samson** (/ˈsæmsən/, 参孙) means *the sun*.

Samson Putting Forth His Riddles at the Wedding Feast, 1638, Harmenszoon van Rijn Rembrandt

¹⁵ And it came to pass on the seventh day that they said unto Samson's wife, "Entice thy husband, that he may explain unto us the riddle, lest we burn thee and thy father's house with fire. Have ye called us to take what we have? Is it not so?"

¹⁶ And Samson's wife wept before him, and said, "Thou dost but hate me, and lovest me not. Thou hast put forth a riddle unto the children of my people, and hast not told it me."

And he said unto her, "Behold, I have not told it to my father nor my mother, and shall I tell it to thee?" ¹⁷ And she wept before him the seven days while their feast lasted. And it came to pass on the seventh day that he told her, because she pressed sorely upon him; and she told the riddle to the children of her people.

¹⁸ And the men of the city said unto him on the seventh day before the sun went down:

"What is sweeter than honey?
And what is stronger than a lion?"
And he said unto them,
"If ye had not plowed with my heifer,
ye would not have found out my riddle."

¹⁹ And the Spirit of the LORD came upon him; and he went down to Ashkelon, and slew thirty men of them and took their apparel, and gave changes of garments unto those who expounded the riddle. And his anger was kindled, and he went up to his father's house. ²⁰ But Samson's wife was given to his companion, whom he had used as his friend.

Samson's Revenge on the Philistines

Judges 15

¹ But it came to pass within a while after, in the time of wheat harvest, that Samson visited his wife with a kid; and he said, "I will go in to my wife into the chamber." But her father would not suffer him to go in.

² And her father said, "I verily thought that thou hadst utterly hated her. Therefore I gave her to thy companion. Is not her younger sister fairer than she? Take her, I pray thee, instead of her."

300 Foxes with Tails Tied with Firebrands

³ And Samson said concerning them, "Now shall I be more blameless than the Philistines, though I do them a displeasure." ⁴ And Samson went and caught three hundred foxes, and took firebrands, and turned tail to tail, and put a firebrand in the midst between two tails. ⁵ And when he had set the brands on fire, he let them go into the standing corn of the Philistines, and burned up both the shocks and also the standing corn, with the vineyards and olives.

⁶ Then the Philistines said, "Who hath done this?" And they answered, "Samson, the son-in-law of the Timnite, because he had taken his wife and given her to his companion."

And the Philistines came up and burned her and her father with fire. ⁷ And Samson said unto them, "Though ye have done this, yet will I be avenged of you, and after that I will cease"; ⁸ And he smote them hip and thigh with a great slaughter. And he went down and dwelt in the top of the rock of Etam.

⁹ Then the Philistines went up and pitched camp in Judah, and spread themselves in Lehi. ¹⁰ And the men of Judah said, "Why have ye come up against us?"

And they answered, "To bind Samson have we come up, to do to him as he hath done to us."

¹¹ Then three thousand men of Judah went to the top of the rock of Etam, and said to Samson, "Knowest thou not that the Philistines are rulers over us? What is this that thou hast done unto us?"

And he said unto them, "As they did unto me, so have I done unto them."

¹² And they said unto him, "We have come down to bind thee, that we may deliver thee into the hand of the Philistines." And Samson said unto them, "Swear unto me that ye will not fall upon me yourselves."

Slaying 1,000 Philistines with the Jawbone of an Ass

¹³ And they spoke unto him, saying, "No, but we will bind thee fast and deliver thee into their hand; but surely we will not kill thee." And they bound him with two new cords, and brought him up from the rock. ¹⁴ And when he came unto Lehi, the Philistines shouted against him. And the Spirit of the LORD came mightily upon him; and the cords that were upon his arms became as flax that was burned with fire, and his bands loosed from off his hands. ¹⁵ And he found a new jawbone of an ass, and put forth his hand and took it, and slew a thousand men therewith.

¹⁶ And Samson said,
"With the jawbone of an ass,
heaps upon heaps,
with the jaw of an ass
have I slain a thousand men."

¹⁷ And it came to pass, when he had made an end of speaking, that he cast away the jawbone out of his hand, and called that place Ramathlehi [that is, The lifting up of the jawbone].

¹⁸ And he was sore athirst, and called on the LORD and said, " Thou hast given this great deliverance into the hand of Thy servant. And now shall I die for thirst and fall into the hand of the uncircumcised?" ¹⁹ But God cleaved a hollow place that was in the jaw, and there came water thereout; and when he had drunk, his spirit came again and he revived. Therefore he called the name thereof Enhakkore [that is, The well of him that called or cried], which is in Lehi unto this day.

²⁰ And he judged Israel in the days of the Philistines twenty years.

Samson and Delilah

Judges 16

¹ Then went Samson to Gaza and saw there a harlot, and went in unto her. ² And it was told the Gazites, saying, "Samson has come hither." And they compassed him in, and lay in wait for him all night in the gate of the city, and were quiet all the night, saying, "In the morning when it is day, we shall kill him."

Carrying the Gates of Gaza

³ And Samson lay till midnight, and arose at midnight and took the doors of the gate of the city and the two posts, and went away with them, bar and all, and put them upon his shoulders and carried them up to the top of a hill that is before Hebron.

⁴ And it came to pass afterward, that he loved a woman in the Valley

Samson Carrying Away the Gates of Gaza, Gustave Doré (1832—1883)

of Sorek, whose name was Delilah③. ⁵ And the lords of the Philistines came up unto her and said unto her, "Entice him, and see wherein his great strength lieth and by what means we may prevail against him, that we may bind him to afflict him; and we will give thee every one of us eleven hundred pieces of silver."

A Woman's Nagging

⁶ And Delilah said to Samson, "Tell me, I pray thee, wherein thy great strength lieth, and wherewith thou mightest be bound to afflict thee."

⁷ And Samson said unto her, "If they bind me with seven green withes that were never dried, then shall I be weak, and be as another man."

Samson and Delilah, 1608, Peter Paul Rubens

⁸ Then the lords of the Philistines brought up to her seven green withes which had not been dried, and she bound him with them. ⁹ Now there were men lying in wait, abiding with her in the chamber. And she said unto him, "The Philistines be upon thee, Samson." And he broke the withes as a thread of tow is broken when it toucheth the fire. So his strength was not known.

¹⁰ And Delilah said unto Samson, "Behold, thou hast mocked me and told me lies. Now tell me, I pray thee, wherewith thou mightest be bound."

¹¹ And he said unto her, "If they bind me fast with new ropes wherewith work hath not been done, then shall I be weak, and be as another man."

¹² Delilah therefore took new ropes and bound him therewith, and said unto him, "The Philistines be upon thee, Samson." And there were liers in wait abiding in the chamber. And he broke them from off his arms like a thread.

¹³ And Delilah said unto Samson, "Hitherto thou hast mocked me and told me lies. Tell me wherewith thou mightest be bound."

And he said unto her, "If thou weavest the seven locks of my head with the web." ¹⁴ And she fastened it with the pin, and said unto him, "The Philistines be upon thee, Samson." And he awakened out of his sleep, and went away with the pin of the beam and with the web.

¹⁵ And she said unto him, "How canst thou say, 'I love thee,' when thine heart is not with me? Thou hast mocked me these three times, and hast not told me wherein thy great strength lieth." ¹⁶ And it came to pass, when she pressed him daily with her words and urged him, so that his soul was vexed unto death.

¹⁷ That he told her all his heart and said unto her, "There hath not come a razor upon mine head, for I have been a Nazirite unto God from my mother's womb. If I be shaven, then my strength will go from me, and I shall become weak and be like any other man."

¹⁸ And when Delilah saw that he had told her all his heart, she sent and called for the lords of the Philistines, saying, "Come up this once, for he hath shown me all his heart." Then the lords of the Philistines came up unto her and brought money in their hand.

Samson Grinding at the Prison Mill

¹⁹ And she made him sleep upon her knees. And she called for a man, and she caused him to shave off the seven locks of his head; and she began to afflict him, and his strength went from him.

---

③ **Delilah** (/dɪˈlaɪlə/, 大利拉) sounds like the Hebrew for *night*.

²⁰ And she said, "The Philistines be upon thee, Samson."

And he awoke out of his sleep and said, "I will go out as at other times before, and shake myself." And he knew not that the LORD had departed from him.

²¹ But the Philistines took him and put out his eyes, and brought him down to Gaza and bound him with fetters of brass; and he did grinding in the prison house. ²² However the hair of his head began to grow again after he was shaven.

The Death of Samson

²³ Then the lords of the Philistines gathered together to offer a great sacrifice unto Dagon their god and to rejoice, for they said, "Our god hath delivered Samson our enemy into our hand!"
²⁴ And when the people saw him, they praised their god; for they said,

"Our god hath delivered
into our hands our enemy,
and the destroyer of our country
who slew many of us."

²⁵ And it came to pass, when their hearts were merry, that they said, "Call for Samson, that he may make sport for us."

And they called for Samson out of the prison house, and they made sport of him and they set him between the pillars.

Death of Samson, ca. 1605, Peter Paul Rubens

²⁶ And Samson said unto the lad who held him by the hand, "Suffer me that I may feel the pillars whereupon the house standeth, that I may lean upon them." ²⁷ Now the house was full of men and women, and all the lords of the Philistines were there; and there were upon the roof about three thousand men and women who beheld while they made sport of Samson. ²⁸ And Samson called unto the LORD and said, "O Lord GOD, remember me, I pray Thee, and strengthen me, I pray Thee, only this once, O God, that I may be at once avenged on the Philistines for my two eyes." ²⁹ And Samson took hold of the two middle pillars upon which the house stood and on which it was borne up, the one with his right hand and the other with his left. ³⁰ And Samson said, "Let me die with the Philistines." And he bowed himself with all his might; and the house fell upon the lords, and upon all the people who were therein. So the dead which he slew at his death were more than those whom he slew in his life.

³¹ Then his brethren and all the house of his father came down and took him, and brought him up and buried him between Zorah and Eshtaol in the burying place of Manoah his father. And he judged Israel twenty years.

III FOOD FOR THOUGHT

1. What was unusual about Samson's birth?
2. What does Samson's request of his parents for a wife show about his character?
3. Which motivated Delilah's betrayal?
4. Why do you think Samson finally told Delilah the secret of his strength?
5. How can you comment on the heroes in *Judges* as compared with Moses, Joshua?

IV BIBLICAL RELEVANCE

A. Biblical Terms in Everyday English
1. Nazarite hair: _____

2. Delilah: _____
3. Samson: _____
4. smite sb. hip and thigh (15:8): _____
5. Samson's jawbone of a donkey (15:15): _____

B. Biblical References in Literature
1. John Milton, *Samson Agonistes*, 1671
2. Aldous Huxley, *Eyeless in Gaza*, 1936
3. Well, Miss Matty! Men will be men. Every mother's son of them wishes to be considered Samson and Solomon rolled into one—too strong ever to be beaten or discomfited—too wise ever to be outwitted.

   (Elizabeth Gaskell, *Cranford*, 1851—1853)
4. He ran a hand through his black Samson hair.

   (Philip Roth, *The Conversion of the Jews*, 1959)
5. This is the very dilemma that once confronted a young Hick. Hailed as great before he'd achieved it, he lost the glow of youth with frightening rapidity. With the erosion of innocence went his power, weakened like Samson at the barber's shop.

   (*The Observer*, 1998)
6. "Lassiter!" Jane whispered, as she gazed from him to the black, cold guns. Without them he appeared shorn of strength, defenseless, a smaller man. Was she Delilah?

   (Zane Grey, *Riders of the Purple Sage*, 1912)

C. The Bible and Arts
1. *The Sacrifice of Menoah*, 1641, Harmenszoon van Rijn Rembrandt
2. *Samson Vanquishing the Lion*, c. 1520—c. 1525, Lucas Cranach, the Elder
3. *Samson Putting Forth his Riddles at the Wedding Feast*, 1638, Harmenszoon van Rijn Rembrandt
4. *Samson Accusing his Father-in-law*, 1635, ibid.
5. *Samson Carrying Away the Gates of Gaza*, Gustave Dore (1832—1883)
6. *Samson and Delilah*, 1608, Peter Paul Rubens
7. *The Blinding of Samson*, 1636, Harmenszoon van Rijn Rembrandt
8. *Death of Samson*, c. 1605, Peter Paul Rubens

V SOURCES FOR REFERENCE

1. http://en.wikipedia.org/wiki/Samson_Agonistes
2. http://www.dartmouth.edu/-milton/reading_room/samson/drama/index.shtml
   (The complete text of Samson Agonistes with study aides)
3. http://academicearth.org/lectures/samson-agonistes (Yale Lecture: Samson Agonistes, also available from iTunes U)
4. (1949). *Samson and Delilah*, a Paramount film Pictures produced and directed by Cecil B. DeMille and starring Victor Mature and Hedy Lamarr.
5. (1994). *The Bible Collection: Abraham*, a TV play by Turner Home Entertainment.
6. Gottcent, J. H. (1986). *The Bible: A Literary Study*. Boston: Twayne Publishers.

13. RUTH

I. POINTS OF DEPARTURE

Lauded by the German poet Goethe (1749—1832) as "the loveliest little epic and idyllic whole that tradition has given us," the Book of Ruth is a heart-warming story of hope shimmering through the savagery of a chaotic period of the judges, and, given its canonical situation between the books of Judges and 1 Samuel, it serves as a bridge between two epochs in Israelite history: the judges and the monarchy to be initiated by King Saul. The book can be read at different and yet convergent levels.

Ruth is a book of love, the romantic love between two lovers worthy of each other and the admirable bond between two people stereotypically at odds — a mother-in-law and a daughter-in-law. As a happy romantic love story, the book, despite its brevity, contains most of the archetypical ingredients of people (background observers, a confidante, obstacles including a rival, a matchmaker) and events (first meeting, prying into each other's eligibility, secret rendezvous, the bestowal of favours, betrothal, and a consummation of love in marriage) (Ryken & Ryken, 2007:364—365). As a tale of familial relationship, this book shows the filial piety of a daughter-in-law whose determined words to her mother-in-law have become synonymous with the commitment to loving relationship: "Intreat me not to leave thee, or to return from following after thee: for whither thou goest, I will go; and where thou lodgest, I will lodge: thy people shall be my people, and thy God my God. Where thou diest, will I die, and there will I be buried: the LORD do so to me, and more also, if ought but death part thee and me." (*Ru. 1:16—17*) And there is evidence in the story that Ruth's kindness was reciprocated by her mother-in-law who actually masterminded all the daring maneuver that eventually secured Ruth's betrothal and subsequent marriage. A cynic may quibble that the old fox certainly had her own interests to brood over.

The story of Ruth can also be read as a fulfillment of the deuteronomic obligation of *levirate marriage* that if a married man died childless, a brother or other near relative was to marry the widow, and the son of the union would be reckoned to be the son of the first husband (*Dt. 25:5—10*). Since Ruth was a Moabitess and established herself through marriage to Boaz as the great grandmother of King David (*Ru. 4:21—22*), from whom Jesus Christ was descended (*Mt. 1:5—16*), this book is supposed to have been written as a polemic against the narrow-minded nationalism that prohibited intermarriages with foreigners in the post-exilic period of Ezra and Nehemiah (Browning, 2009: 224).

II SELECTED READINGS

Naomi and Ruth

Ruth 1

¹ Now it came to pass, in the days when the judges ruled, that there was a famine in the land. And a certain man of Bethlehemjudah went to sojourn in the country of Moab, he and his wife and his two sons. ² And the name of the man was Elimelech and the name of his wife Naomi①, and the name of his two sons Mahlon and Chilion, Ephrathites of Bethlehemjudah. And they came into the country of Moab, and continued there.

³ And Elimelech, Naomi's husband, died; and she was left, and her two sons. ⁴ And they took themselves wives of the women of Moab: the name of the one was Orpah, and the name of the other Ruth②. And they dwelt there about ten years. ⁵ And Mahlon and Chilion died also, both of them; and the woman was left without her two sons and her husband.

⁶ Then she arose with her daughters-in-law, that she might return from the country of Moab, for she had heard in the country of Moab how the LORD had visited His people in giving them bread. ⁷ Therefore she went forth out of the place where she was, and her two daughters-in-law with her; and they went on the way to return unto the land of Judah.

⁸ And Naomi said unto her two daughters-in-law, "Go, return each to your mother's house. The LORD deal kindly with you, as ye have dealt with the dead and with me. ⁹ The LORD grant you that ye may find rest, each of you in the house of her husband."

Then she kissed them, and they lifted up their voice and wept. ¹⁰ And they said unto her, "Surely we will return with thee unto thy people."

¹¹ And Naomi said, "Turn back, my daughters. Why will ye go with me? Are there yet any more sons in my womb, that they may be your husbands? ¹² Turn back, my daughters, go your way; for I am too old to have a husband. If I should say I have hope, if I should have a husband also tonight and should also bear sons. ¹³ Would ye tarry for them until they were grown? Would ye refrain for them from having husbands? Nay, my daughters, for it grieveth me much for your sakes that the hand of the LORD has gone out against me."

¹⁴ And they lifted up their voice and wept again; and Orpah kissed her mother-in-law, but Ruth cleaved unto her.

¹⁵ And she said, "Behold, thy sister-in-law has gone back unto her people and unto her gods. Return thou after thy sister-in-law."

¹⁶ And Ruth said: "Entreat me not to leave thee, or to return from following after thee; for whither thou goest, I will go, and where thou lodgest, I will lodge. Thy people shall be my people, and thy God my God. ¹⁷ Where thou diest will I die, and there will I be buried; the LORD do so to me, and more also, if aught but death part thee and me." ¹⁸ When she saw that she was steadfastly minded to go with her, then she left off speaking unto her.

¹⁹ So the two went until they came to Bethlehem. And it came to pass, when they had come to Bethlehem, that all the city was moved concerning them; and they said, "Is this Naomi?"

²⁰ And she said unto them, "Call me not Naomi [that is, Pleasant]. Call me Mara [that is, Bitter], for the Almighty hath dealt very bitterly with me. ²¹ I went out full, and the LORD hath brought me home again empty. Why then call ye me Naomi, seeing the LORD hath testified against me and the Almighty hath afflicted me?"

---

① **Naomi** (/neiˈəumi/, 拿俄米) means *pleasant*.
② **Ruth** /ˈruːθ/, 路得。

²² So Naomi returned, and Ruth the Moabitess her daughter-in-law with her, who returned out of the country of Moab; and they came to Bethlehem in the beginning of barley harvest.

Ruth Meets Boaz

Ruth 2

¹ And Naomi had a kinsman of her husband's, a mighty man of wealth of the family of Elimelech, and his name was Boaz③.

² And Ruth the Moabitess said unto Naomi, " Let me now go to the field, and glean ears of corn after him in whose sight I shall find grace."

And she said unto her, " Go, my daughter." ³ And she went, and came and gleaned in the field after the reapers; and she happened to light on a part of the field belonging unto Boaz, who was of the kindred of Elimelech.

⁴ And behold, Boaz came from Bethlehem, and said unto the reapers, " The LORD be with you."

And they answered him, " The LORD bless thee."

⁵ Then said Boaz unto his servant who was set over the reapers, " Whose damsel is this?"

⁶ And the servant who was set over the reapers answered and said, " It is the Moabite damsel who came back with Naomi out of the country of Moab. ⁷ And she said, ' I pray you, let me glean and gather after the reapers among the sheaves.' so she came and hath continued even from the morning until now, except she tarried a little in the house."

⁸ Then said Boaz unto Ruth, " Hearest thou not, my daughter? Go not to glean in another field, neither go from hence, but abide here fast by my maidens. ⁹ Let thine eyes be on the field that they reap, and go thou after them. Have I not charged the young men that they shall not touch thee? And when thou art athirst, go unto the vessels and drink of that which the young men have drawn."

Ruth, 1835, Francesco Hayez

¹⁰ Then she fell on her face and bowed herself to the ground, and said unto him, " Why have I found grace in thine eyes, that thou shouldest take notice of me, seeing I am a stranger?"

¹¹ And Boaz answered and said unto her, " It hath fully been shown to me all that thou hast done unto thy mother-in-law since the death of thine husband, and how thou hast left thy father and thy mother and the land of thy nativity, and hast come unto a people whom thou knewest not heretofore. ¹² The LORD recompense thy work, and a full reward be given thee from the LORD God of Israel, under whose wings thou hast come to trust."

¹³ Then she said, " Let me find favor in thy sight, my lord; for thou hast comforted me, and thou hast spoken friendly unto thine handmaid, though I am not like unto one of thine handmaidens."

¹⁴ And Boaz said unto her, " At mealtime come thou hither, and eat of the bread and dip thy morsel in the vinegar."

And she sat beside the reapers; and he passed to her parched corn, and she ate and was sufficed, and left. ¹⁵ And when she had risen up to glean, Boaz commanded his young men, saying, " Let her glean even among the sheaves, and reproach her not. ¹⁶ And let fall also some of the handfuls purposely for her; and leave them, that she may glean them, and rebuke her not."

¹⁷ So she gleaned in the field until evening, and beat out what she had gleaned; and it was about an ephah of barley. ¹⁸ And she took it up, and went into the city; and her mother-in-law saw what she had gleaned; and

③ **Boaz** /ˈbəʊæz/, 波阿斯。

she brought it forth and gave to her what she had reserved after she was sufficed.

¹⁹ And her mother-in-law said unto her, "Where hast thou gleaned today? And where wroughtest thou? Blessed be he that took notice of thee."

And she showed her mother-in-law with whom she had worked, and said, "The man's name with whom I wrought today is Boaz."

²⁰ And Naomi said unto her daughter-in-law, "Blessed be he of the LORD, who hath not left off his kindness to the living and to the dead." And Naomi said unto her, "The man is near of kin unto us, one of our next kinsmen."

²¹ And Ruth the Moabitess said, "He said unto me also, 'Thou shalt keep fast by my young men until they have ended all my harvest.'"

²² And Naomi said unto Ruth her daughter-in-law, "It is good, my daughter, that thou go out with his maidens, that they meet thee not in any other field."

²³ So she kept fast by the maidens of Boaz to glean unto the end of barley harvest and wheat harvest, and dwelt with her mother-in-law.

Ruth and Boaz at the Threshing Floor

Ruth 3

¹ Then Naomi her mother-in-law said unto her, "My daughter, shall I not seek rest for thee, that it may be well with thee? ² And now is not Boaz of our kindred, with whose maidens thou wast? Behold, he winnoweth barley tonight at the threshing floor. ³ Wash thyself therefore and anoint thee, and put thy raiment upon thee, and get thee down to the floor; but make not thyself known unto the man until he shall have done eating and drinking. ⁴ And it shall be, when he lieth down, that thou shalt mark the place where he shall lie; and thou shalt go in and uncover his feet, and lay thee down, and he will tell thee what thou shalt do."

Ruth in Boaz's Field, 1828,
Julius Schnorr von Carolsfeld

⁵ And she said unto her, "All that thou sayest unto me I will do." ⁶ And she went down unto the floor, and did according to all that her mother-in-law bade her.

⁷ And when Boaz had eaten and drunk and his heart was merry, he went to lie down at the end of the heap of corn; and she came softly, and uncovered his feet and laid herself down. ⁸ And it came to pass at midnight that the man was afraid, and turned himself; and behold, a woman lay at his feet.

⁹ And he said, "Who art thou?"

And she answered, "I am Ruth, thine handmaid. Spread therefore thy skirt over thine handmaid, for thou art a near kinsman."

¹⁰ And he said, "Blessed be thou of the LORD, my daughter; for thou hast shown more kindness in the latter end than at the beginning, inasmuch as thou followed not young men, whether poor or rich. ¹¹ And now, my daughter, fear not. I will do for thee all that thou requirest, for all the city of my people doth know that thou art a virtuous woman. ¹² And now it is true that I am thy near kinsman; however that be, there is a kinsman nearer than I. ¹³ Tarry this night, and it shall be in the morning, that if he will perform unto thee the part of a kinsman, well. Let him do the kinsman's part. But if he will not do the part of a kinsman for thee, then will I do the part of a kinsman for thee, as the LORD liveth. Lie down until the morning."

¹⁴ And she lay at his feet until the morning; and she rose up before one could know another. And he said, "Let it not be known that a woman came unto the floor."

¹⁵ Also he said, "Bring the veil that thou hast upon thee and hold it." And when she held it, he measured

six measures of barley, and laid it on her; and she went into the city.

¹⁶ And when she came to her mother-in-law, she said, "Who art thou, my daughter?"

And she told her all that the man had done to her. ¹⁷ And she said, "These six measures of barley gave he me; for he said to me, ' Go not empty unto thy mother-in-law.' "

¹⁸ Then said she, "Sit still, my daughter, until thou know how the matter will fall; for the man will not be in rest until he hath finished the thing this day."

Boaz Marries Ruth

Ruth 4

¹ Then went Boaz up to the gate and sat himself down there; and behold, the kinsman of whom Boaz spoke came by, unto whom he said, "Ho, such a one! Turn aside, sit down here." And he turned aside and sat down.

² And he took ten men of the elders of the city, and said, "Sit ye down here." And they sat down. ³ And he said unto the kinsman, "Naomi, who hath come again out of the country of Moab, selleth a parcel of land which was our brother Elimelech's. ⁴ And I thought to advise thee, saying, ' Buy it before the inhabitants and before the elders of my people. If thou wilt redeem it, redeem it. But if thou wilt not redeem it, then tell me, that I may know; for there is none to redeem it besides thee, and I am after thee.' "

And he said, "I will redeem it."

⁵ Then said Boaz, "What day thou buyest the field from the hand of Naomi, thou must buy it also from Ruth the Moabitess, the wife of the dead, to raise up the name of the dead upon his inheritance."

⁶ And the kinsman said, "I cannot redeem it for myself, lest I mar mine own inheritance. Redeem thou my right for thyself, for I cannot redeem it."

⁷ Now this was the manner in former times in Israel concerning redeeming and concerning exchanging, to confirm all things: a man plucked off his shoe, and gave it to his neighbor; and this was a testimony in Israel.

⁸ Therefore the kinsman said unto Boaz, "Buy it for thyself." So he drew off his shoe.

⁹ And Boaz said unto the elders and unto all the people, "Ye are witnesses this day that I have bought all that was Elimelech's and all that was Chilion's and Mahlon's from the hand of Naomi. ¹⁰ Moreover Ruth the Moabitess, the wife of Mahlon, have I purchased to be my wife, to raise up the name of the dead upon his inheritance, that the name of the dead be not cut off from among his brethren and from the gate of his place. Ye are witnesses this day."

¹¹ And all the people who were at the gate and the elders, said, "We are witnesses. The LORD make the woman who hath come into thine house like Rachel and like Leah, which two built the house of Israel; and do thou worthily in Ephrathah and be famous in Bethlehem. ¹² And let thy house be like the house of Perez, whom Tamar bore unto Judah, of the seed which the LORD shall give thee by this young woman."

The Genealogy of David

¹³ So Boaz took Ruth, and she was his wife; and when he went in unto her, the LORD gave her conception and she bore a son. ¹⁴ And the women said unto Naomi, "Blessed be the LORD, who hath not left thee this day without a kinsman, that his name may be famous in Israel. ¹⁵ And he shall be unto thee a restorer of thy life and a nourisher of thine old age; for thy daughter-in-law who loveth thee, who is better to thee than seven sons, hath borne him." ¹⁶ And Naomi took the child and laid it in her bosom, and became nurse unto it.

¹⁷ And the women, her neighbors, gave it a name, saying, "There is a son born to Naomi"; and they called his name Obed. He is the father of Jesse, the father of David. ...

III FOOD FOR THOUGHT

1. What risk might Ruth have when she went with Naomi to the latter's home?
2. What kind of person was Ruth as seen from *Ruth 2*?
3. Why did Naomi ask Ruth to go to the threshing floor where Boaz lay?
4. What custom concerning marriage can be observed through *Ruth 4*?

IV BIBLICAL RELEVANCE

A. Biblical Terms in Everyday English
Ruth gleans heads of grain: _____

B. Biblical References in Literature
1. So Planchet related how Truchen had charmed the years of his advancing age, and brought good luck to his business, as Ruth did to Boaz.
   (Alexandre Dumas, *The Man in the Iron Mask*, 1840s)
2. "If one could have a fine house, full of nice girls, or go traveling, the summer would be delightful, but to stay at home with three selfish sisters and a grown-up boy was enough to try the patience of a Boaz," complained Miss Malaprop, after several days devoted to pleasure, fretting, and ennui.
   (Louisa May Alcott, *Little Women*, 1868)

C. The Bible and Arts
1. *Ruth*, 1835, Francesco Hayez
2. *Ruth Gleaning*, 1860, Randolph John Rogers
3. *Ruth and Boaz*, 1660, Fabritius Barent Peitersz
4. *Ruth in Boaz's Field*, 1828, Julius Schnorr von Carolsfeld
5. *Summer*, 1660—1664, Nicolas Poussin

V SOURCES FOR REFERENCE

1. Ryken, L. & P. G. Ryken. (2007). *The Literary Study of Bible*. Wheaton, Illinois: Crossway Bibles.
2. Browning, W. R. E. (2009). *A Dictionary of the Bible*. Oxford: Oxford University Press.

PART FOUR

THE KINGDOMS OF SAUL AND DAVID
(C.1,020—900 B.C.E.)
THE BOOKS OF 1 & 2 SAMUEL, PSALMS

14. SAMUEL AND SAUL

I POINTS OF DEPARTURE

In spite of the brief diversion through Samson's suicidal destruction of the temple packed full of the Philistines, the Israelites were constantly plagued by their strong and hostile neighbours. They went to Samuel their judge and begged for an earthly king who would centralize power, making the nation more efficient in defending itself. But this was a blatant rejection of God's authority. Reluctantly, God gave Israel the government they wanted through Samuel who warned them against the dangers of monarchy including despotism, taxation, military service and slavery (1 Sam. 8:10—18). The first Israelite king anointed by Samuel was Saul, who came to the judge in a donkey hunt. His reign began with a series of victories over the enemies of Israel, making him popular as a charismatic leader. Very soon, he lost God's favor because of his challenge to Samuel's authority and disobedience against Mosaic laws. Then David was anointed king over Israel, a king often cited as one of the best of the kings of Israel who nevertheless sinned against God by committing a double crime of adultery and murder though he did repent more vehemently than other princes. His son, Solomon, succeeded him as a sovereign of wisdom, wealth and power, but also sinned against God with his indiscriminate worship of his wives' and concubines' deities. As a matter of fact, the question of who has authority to govern and why is part and parcel of this part of the Hebrew Scriptures known as the History Books. Among the standard issues addressed are: the nature of leaders and of leadership, the rules of governance, the proper means of establishing authority, the proper limits of governmental power, the rights reserved for the individual, and the appropriate manner of changing leaders or overthrowing unjust government. These are real-life issues that the Israelites struggled to resolve in their own tumultuous history. (Tischler, 2007: 192)

II SELECTED READINGS

The Birth of Samuel

1 Samuel 1

¹ Now there was a certain man of Ramathaimzophim, of Mount Ephraim, and his name was Elkanah the son of Jeroham, the son of Elihu, the son of Tohu, the son of Zuph, an Ephraimite. ² And he had two wives: the name of the one was Hannah, and the name of the other Peninnah. And Peninnah had children, but Hannah had no children.

³ And this man went up out of his city yearly to worship and to sacrifice unto the LORD of hosts in Shiloh. And the two sons of Eli, Hophni and Phinehas, the priests of the LORD, were there. ⁴ And when the time was that Elkanah offered, he gave to Peninnah his wife and to all her sons and her daughters, portions.

⁵ But unto Hannah he gave a double portion, for he loved Hannah; but the LORD had shut up her womb. ⁶ And her adversary also provoked her sorely to make her fret, because the LORD had shut up her womb. ⁷ And as he did so year by year, when she went up to the house of the LORD, so she provoked her; therefore she wept and did not eat. ⁸ Then said Elkanah her husband to her, "Hannah, why weepest thou? And why eatest thou not? And why is thy heart grieved? Am not I better to thee than ten sons?"

⁹ So Hannah rose up after they had eaten in Shiloh and after they had drunk. (Now Eli the priest sat upon a seat by a post of the temple of the LORD.) ¹⁰ And she was in bitterness of soul, and prayed unto the LORD and wept sorely.

¹¹ And she vowed a vow and said, "O LORD of hosts, if Thou wilt indeed look on the affliction of Thine handmaid, and remember me and not forget Thine handmaid, but wilt give unto Thine handmaid a manchild, then I will give him unto the LORD all the days of his life, and there shall no razor come upon his head."

¹² And it came to pass, as she continued praying before the LORD, that Eli observed her mouth. ¹³ Now Hannah spoke in her heart; only her lips moved, but her voice was not heard. Therefore Eli thought she had been drunken. ¹⁴ And Eli said unto her, "How long wilt thou be drunken? Put away thy wine from thee."

¹⁵ And Hannah answered and said, "No, my lord, I am a woman of a sorrowful spirit. I have drunk neither wine nor strong drink, but have poured out my soul before the LORD. ¹⁶ Count not thine handmaid as a daughter of Belial, for out of the abundance of my complaint and grief have I spoken hitherto."

¹⁷ Then Eli answered and said, "Go in peace; and the God of Israel grant thee thy petition that thou hast asked of Him."

¹⁸ And she said, "Let thine handmaid find grace in thy sight." So the woman went her way and ate, and her countenance was no more sad.

¹⁹ And they rose up in the morning early and worshiped before the LORD, and returned and came to their house at Ramah. And Elkanah knew Hannah his wife, and the LORD remembered her. ²⁰ Wherefore it came to pass, when the time had come about after Hannah had conceived, that she bore a son and called his name Samuel [that is, Asked of God], saying, "Because I have asked him of the LORD."

Hannah Dedicates Samuel

²¹ And the man Elkanah and all his house went up to offer unto the LORD the yearly sacrifice and his vow. ²² But Hannah went not up; for she said unto her husband, "I will not go up until the child is weaned, and then I will bring him, that he may appear before the LORD and there abide for ever."

²³ And Elkanah her husband said unto her, "Do what seemeth to thee good. Tarry until thou have weaned him, only the LORD establish His word." So the woman remained, and gave her son suck until she weaned him.

²⁴ And when she had weaned him, she took him up with her, with three bullocks and one ephah of flour and a bottle of wine, and brought him unto the house of the LORD in Shiloh; and the child was young. ²⁵ And they slew a bullock, and brought the child to Eli. ²⁶ And she said, "Oh my lord, as thy soul liveth, my lord, I am the woman who stood by thee here, praying unto the LORD. ²⁷ For this child I prayed, and the LORD hath given me my petition which I asked of Him. ²⁸ Therefore also I have lent him to the LORD; as long as he liveth he shall be lent to the LORD." And he worshiped the LORD there.

The Lord Calls Samuel

1 Samuel 3

¹ And the child Samuel ministered unto the LORD before Eli. And the word of the LORD was precious in those days; there was no open vision. ² And it came to pass at that time, when Eli was lying down in his place, and his eyes began to wax dim so that he could not see. ³ And ere the lamp of God went out in the

temple of the LORD where the ark of God was, and Samuel was lying down to sleep, ⁴ That the LORD called Samuel.

Samuel Brought to Eli,
George Tinworth (1843—1913)

And he answered, "Here am I." ⁵ And he ran unto Eli and said, "Here am I, for thou called me." And he said, "I called not; lie down again." And he went and lay down.

⁶ And the LORD called yet again, "Samuel." And Samuel arose and went to Eli and said, "Here am I, for thou didst call me." And he answered, "I called not, my son; lie down again."

⁷ Now Samuel did not yet know the LORD, neither was the word of the LORD yet revealed unto him.

⁸ And the LORD called Samuel again the third time. And he arose and went to Eli and said, "Here am I, for thou didst call me."

And Eli perceived that the LORD had called the child. ⁹ Therefore Eli said unto Samuel, "Go, lie down; and it shall be, if He call thee, that thou shalt say, 'Speak, LORD, for Thy servant heareth.'" So Samuel went and lay down in his place.

¹⁰ And the LORD came and stood, and called as at other times, "Samuel, Samuel."

Then Samuel answered, "Speak, for Thy servant heareth."

¹¹ And the LORD said to Samuel, "Behold, I will do a thing in Israel at which both the ears of every one who heareth it shall tingle. ¹² In that day I will perform against Eli all things which I have spoken concerning his house. When I begin, I will also make an end; ¹³ For I have told him that I will judge his house for ever for the iniquity which he knoweth, because his sons made themselves vile, and he restrained them not. ¹⁴ And therefore I have sworn unto the house of Eli that the iniquity of Eli's house shall not be purged with sacrifice nor offering, for ever."

¹⁵ And Samuel lay until the morning, and opened the doors of the house of the LORD. And Samuel feared to show Eli the vision. ¹⁶ Then Eli called Samuel and said, "Samuel, my son."

And he answered, "Here am I."

¹⁷ And he said, "What is the thing that the LORD hath said unto thee? I pray thee, hide it not from me. God do so to thee, and more also, if thou hide any word from me of all the things that He said unto thee." ¹⁸ And Samuel told him every whit, and hid nothing from him. And he said, "It is the LORD. Let Him do what seemeth to Him good."

¹⁹ And Samuel grew, and the LORD was with him and let none of his words fall to the ground. ²⁰ And all Israel from Dan even to Beersheba knew that Samuel was established to be a prophet of the LORD. ²¹ And the LORD appeared again in Shiloh, for the LORD revealed Himself to Samuel in Shiloh by the word of the LORD.

Samuel Anoints Saul

1 Samuel 9

¹ Now there was a man of Benjamin, whose name was Kish, the son of Abiel, the son of Zeror, the son of Bechorath, the son of Aphiah, a Benjamite, a mighty man of power. ² And he had a son, whose name was Saul①, a choice young man, and a goodly: and there was not among the children of Israel a goodlier person than he: from his shoulders and upward he was higher than any of the people.

³ And the asses of Kish Saul's father were lost. And Kish said to Saul his son, "Take now one of the servants with thee, and arise, go seek the asses." ⁴ And he passed through mount Ephraim, and passed through

---

① Saul /sɔːl/, 扫罗。

the land of Shalisha, but they found them not: then they passed through the land of Shalim, and there they were not: and he passed through the land of the Benjamites, but they found them not.

⁵ And when they were come to the land of Zuph, Saul said to his servant that was with him, "Come, and let us return; lest my father leave caring for the asses, and take thought for us."

⁶ And he said unto him, "Behold now, there is in this city a man of God, and he is an honourable man; all that he saith cometh surely to pass: now let us go thither; peradventure he can shew us our way that we should go."

⁷ Then said Saul to his servant, "But, behold, if we go, what shall we bring the man? For the bread is spent in our vessels, and there is not a present to bring to the man of God: what have we?"

⁸ And the servant answered Saul again, and said, "Behold, I have here at hand the fourth part of a shekel of silver: that will I give to the man of God, to tell us our way." ⁹ (Beforetime in Israel, when a man went to enquire of God, thus he spake, "Come, and let us go to the seer," for he that is now called a Prophet was beforetime called a Seer.)

The Prophet Samuel, Claude Vignon (1593—1670)

¹⁰ Then said Saul to his servant, "Well said; come, let us go." So they went unto the city where the man of God was.

¹¹ And as they went up the hill to the city, they found young maidens going out to draw water, and said unto them, "Is the seer here?"

¹² And they answered them, and said, "He is; behold, he is before you: make haste now, for he came to day to the city; for there is a sacrifice of the people to day in the high place. ¹³ As soon as ye be come into the city, ye shall straightway find him, before he go up to the high place to eat: for the people will not eat until he come, because he doth bless the sacrifice; and afterwards they eat that be bidden. Now therefore get you up; for about this time ye shall find him.

¹⁴ And they went up into the city: and when they were come into the city, behold, Samuel came out against them, for to go up to the high place.

¹⁵ Now the LORD had told Samuel in his ear a day before Saul came, saying,

¹⁶ "To morrow about this time I will send thee a man out of the land of Benjamin, and thou shalt anoint him to be captain over my people Israel, that he may save my people out of the hand of the Philistines: for I have looked upon my people, because their cry is come unto me."

¹⁷ And when Samuel saw Saul, the LORD said unto him, "Behold the man whom I spake to thee of! This same shall reign over my people."

¹⁸ Then Saul drew near to Samuel in the gate, and said, "Tell me, I pray thee, where the seer's house is."

¹⁹ And Samuel answered Saul, and said, "I am the seer: go up before me unto the high place; for ye shall eat with me to day, and to morrow I will let thee go, and will tell thee all that is in thine heart. ²⁰ And as for thine asses that were lost three days ago, set not thy mind on them; for they are found. And on whom is all the desire of Israel? Is it not on thee, and on all thy father's house?"

²¹ And Saul answered and said, "Am not I a Benjamite, of the smallest of the tribes of Israel? And my family the least of all the families of the tribe of Benjamin? Wherefore then speakest thou so to me?"

²² And Samuel took Saul and his servant, and brought them into the parlour, and made them sit in the chiefest place among them that were bidden, which were about thirty persons. ²³ And Samuel said unto the cook, "Bring the portion which I gave thee, of which I said unto thee, set it by thee."

²⁴ And the cook took up the shoulder, and that which was upon it, and set it before Saul. And Samuel said, "Behold that which is left! Set it before thee, and eat: for unto this time hath it been kept for thee since I said, I have invited the people." So Saul did eat with Samuel that day.

²⁵ And when they were come down from the high place into the city, Samuel communed with Saul upon the top of the house. ²⁶ And they arose early: and it came to pass about the spring of the day, that Samuel called Saul to the top of the house, saying, " Up, that I may send thee away." And Saul arose, and they went out both of them, he and Samuel, abroad. ²⁷ And as they were going down to the end of the city, Samuel said to Saul, " Bid the servant pass on before us, (and he passed on), but stand thou still a while, that I may shew thee the word of God."

Saul Begins to Blunder

1 Samuel 14

...

Jonathan② Eats Honey

²⁴ And the men of Israel were distressed that day: for Saul had adjured the people, saying, " Cursed be the man that eateth any food until evening, that I may be avenged on mine enemies." So none of the people tasted any food.

²⁵ And all they of the land came to a wood; and there was honey upon the ground. ²⁶ And when the people were come into the wood, behold, the honey dropped; but no man put his hand to his mouth: for the people feared the oath.

²⁷ But Jonathan heard not when his father charged the people with the oath: wherefore he put forth the end of the rod that was in his hand, and dipped it in an honeycomb, and put his hand to his mouth; and his eyes were enlightened. ²⁸ Then answered one of the people, and said, " Thy father straitly charged the people with an oath, saying, ' Cursed be the man that eateth any food this day.' And the people were faint."

²⁹ Then said Jonathan, " My father hath troubled the land: see, I pray you, how mine eyes have been enlightened, because I tasted a little of this honey. ³⁰ How much more, if haply the people had eaten freely to day of the spoil of their enemies which they found? For had there not been now a much greater slaughter among the Philistines?"

³¹ And they smote the Philistines that day from Michmash to Aijalon: and the people were very faint. ³² And the people flew upon the spoil, and took sheep, and oxen, and calves, and slew them on the ground: and the people did eat them with the blood. ³³ Then they told Saul, saying, " Behold, the people sin against the LORD, in that they eat with the blood."

And he said, " Ye have transgressed: roll a great stone unto me this day."

³⁴ And Saul said, " Disperse yourselves among the people, and say unto them, ' Bring me hither every man his ox, and every man his sheep, and slay them here, and eat; and sin not against the LORD in eating with the blood.' "

Saul Offers a Sacrifice on his Own

And all the people brought every man his ox with him that night, and slew them there. ³⁵ And Saul built an altar unto the LORD: the same was the first altar that he built unto the LORD.

³⁶ And Saul said, " Let us go down after the Philistines by night, and spoil them until the morning light, and let us not leave a man of them."

And they said, " Do whatsoever seemeth good unto thee."

Then said the priest, " Let us draw near hither unto God."

³⁷ And Saul asked counsel of God, " Shall I go down after the Philistines? Wilt thou deliver them into the hand of Israel?" But he answered him not that day.

³⁸ And Saul said, " Draw ye near hither, all the chief of the people: and know and see wherein this sin

---

② Jonathan /ˈdʒɔnəθən/, 约拿单。

hath been this day. ³⁹ For, as the LORD liveth, which saveth Israel, though it be in Jonathan my son, he shall surely die." But there was not a man among all the people that answered him.

⁴⁰ Then said he unto all Israel, "Be ye on one side, and I and Jonathan my son will be on the other side."

And the people said unto Saul, "Do what seemeth good unto thee."

⁴¹ Therefore Saul said unto the LORD God of Israel, "Give a perfect lot." And Saul and Jonathan were taken: but the people escaped. ⁴² And Saul said, "Cast lots between me and Jonathan my son." And Jonathan was taken."

⁴³ Then Saul said to Jonathan, "Tell me what thou hast done."

And Jonathan told him, and said, "I did but taste a little honey with the end of the rod that was in mine hand, and, lo, I must die."

⁴⁴ And Saul answered, "God do so and more also: for thou shalt surely die, Jonathan."

⁴⁵ And the people said unto Saul, "Shall Jonathan die, who hath wrought this great salvation in Israel? God forbid: as the LORD liveth, there shall not one hair of his head fall to the ground; for he hath wrought with God this day." So the people rescued Jonathan, that he died not. ...

Saul's Third Blunder and Samuel's Break with Him

1 Samuel 15

¹ Samuel also said unto Saul, "The LORD sent me to anoint thee to be king over His people, over Israel. Now therefore hearken thou unto the voice of the words of the LORD. ² Thus saith the LORD of hosts: ' I remember that which Amalek did to Israel, how he lay in wait for him on the way when he came up from Egypt. ³ Now go and smite Amalek and utterly destroy all that they have, and spare them not; but slay both man and woman, infant and suckling, ox and sheep, camel and ass.' "

⁴ And Saul gathered the people together and numbered them in Telaim, two hundred thousand footmen and ten thousand men of Judah. ⁵ And Saul came to a city of Amalek, and lay in wait in the valley. ⁶ And Saul said unto the Kenites, " Go, depart, get you down from among the Amalekites, lest I destroy you with them; for ye showed kindness to all the children of Israel when they came up out of Egypt." So the Kenites departed from among the Amalekites.

Sparing the Life of Agag, King of Amalek

⁷ And Saul smote the Amalekites from Havilah until thou comest to Shur, which is over against Egypt. ⁸ And he took Agag the king of the Amalekites alive, and utterly destroyed all the people with the edge of the sword. ⁹ But Saul and the people spared Agag, and the best of the sheep and of the oxen, and of the fatlings and the lambs, and all that was good, and would not utterly destroy them; but every thing that was vile and refuse, that they destroyed utterly.

¹⁰ Then came the word of the LORD unto Samuel, saying, ¹¹ " I repent that I have set up Saul to be king, for he has turned back from following Me and hath not performed My commandments." And it grieved Samuel, and he cried unto the LORD all night.

¹² And when Samuel rose early to meet Saul in the morning, it was told Samuel, saying, "Saul came to Carmel, and behold, he set him up a place, and has gone about and passed on and gone down to Gilgal."

¹³ And Samuel came to Saul; and Saul said unto him, "Blessed be thou of the LORD. I have performed the commandment of the LORD."

¹⁴ And Samuel said, "What meaneth then this bleating of the sheep in mine ears and the lowing of the oxen which I hear?"

¹⁵ And Saul said, "They have brought them from the Amalekites; for the people spared the best of the sheep and of the oxen to sacrifice unto the LORD thy God, and the rest we have utterly destroyed."

¹⁶ Then Samuel said unto Saul, " Stay, and I will tell thee what the LORD hath said to me this night." And he said unto him, " Say on."

¹⁷ And Samuel said, " When thou wast little in thine own sight, wast thou not made the head of the tribes of Israel, and the LORD anointed thee king over Israel? ¹⁸ And the LORD sent thee on a journey and said, ' Go, and utterly destroy the sinners, the Amalekites, and fight against them until they be consumed.' ¹⁹ Why then didst thou not obey the voice of the LORD, but didst leap upon the spoil and didst evil in the sight of the LORD?"

²⁰ And Saul said unto Samuel, " Yea, I have obeyed the voice of the LORD and have gone the way which the LORD sent me, and have brought Agag the king of Amalek, and have utterly destroyed the Amalekites. ²¹ But the people took of the spoil, sheep and oxen, the chief of the things which should have been utterly destroyed, to sacrifice unto the LORD thy God in Gilgal."

²² And Samuel said,

" Hath the LORD as great delight in burnt offerings and sacrifices
as in obeying the voice of the LORD? Behold,
To obey is better than sacrifice,
and to hearken than the fat of rams.
²³ For rebellion is as the sin of witchcraft,
and stubbornness is as iniquity and idolatry.
Because thou hast rejected the word of the LORD,
He hath also rejected thee from being king."

²⁴ And Saul said unto Samuel, " I have sinned; for I have transgressed the commandment of the LORD and thy words, because I feared the people and obeyed their voice. ²⁵ Now therefore, I pray thee, pardon my sin, and return with me, that I may worship the LORD."

²⁶ And Samuel said unto Saul, " I will not return with thee; for thou hast rejected the word of the LORD, and the LORD hath rejected thee from being king over Israel."

A morte de Agag, Gustave Doré
(1832—1883)

²⁷ And as Samuel turned about to go away, he laid hold upon the skirt of his mantle, and it rent. ²⁸ And Samuel said unto him, " The LORD hath rent the kingdom of Israel from thee this day, and hath given it to a neighbor of thine, who is better than thou. ²⁹ And also the Strength of Israel will not lie nor repent; for He is not a man, that He should repent."

³⁰ Then he said, " I have sinned; yet honor me now, I pray thee, before the elders of my people and before Israel, and return with me, that I may worship the LORD thy God." ³¹ So Samuel turned back after Saul, and Saul worshiped the LORD.

³² Then said Samuel, " Bring ye hither to me Agag, the king of the Amalekites."

And Agag came unto him charily; and Agag said, " Surely the bitterness of death is past."

³³ And Samuel said,

" As thy sword hath made women childless, so shall thy mother be childless among women."
And Samuel hewed Agag in pieces before the LORD in Gilgal.

³⁴ Then Samuel went to Ramah; and Saul went up to his house to Gibeah of Saul. ³⁵ And Samuel came no more to see Saul until the day of his death. Nevertheless Samuel mourned for Saul; and the LORD repented that He had made Saul king over Israel.

III. FOOD FOR THOUGHT

1. What was the purpose of the journey of Elkanah and his family to Shiloh?
2. Compare the birth stories of Samson and Samuel.
3. What was the message the Lord delivered to Samuel?
4. What new phase of Israelite history was being introduced with Saul's anointment?
5. Why was Saul rejected by the Lord? Do you think that Saul was treated fairly?

IV. BIBLICAL RELEVANCE

A. Biblical Terms in Everyday English
1. every whit (3:18): _____
2. from Dan to Beersheba (3:20): _____

B. Biblical References in Literature
That night Amelia made the boy read the story of Samuel to her, and how Hannah, his mother, having weaned him, brought him to Eli the High Priest to minister before the Lord.
(William Makepeace Thackeray, *Vanity Fair*, 1848)

C. The Bible and Arts
1. *Samuel Brought to Eli*, George Tinworth (1843—1913)
2. *Samuel in the Temple*, 1839, Sir David Willie
3. *The Death of Eli*, 1625—1630, Matthaeus Merian, the Elder
4. *The Sacrifice of the Old Covenant*, c. 1626, Peter Paul Rubens
5. *Samuel and Saul*, Phillip Ratner

V. SOURCES FOR REFERENCE

Tischler, N.M. (2007). *Thematic Guide to Biblical Literature*. Westport, CT: Greenwood Press.

15. SAUL AND DAVID

I POINTS OF DEPARTURE

King Saul started off with enormous promise, tall and handsome, with leadership qualities oozing out of him. But very soon, he showed an inner weakness: rebellion against God's directions. Rejected by God and tormented by an evil spirit, he grew fearful, impulsive and jealous, and suffered from a chronic mental trauma. This was where David came on the stage who was sent for to soothe with his harp music the king's troubled mind. Apart from his musical talent, David also made a worthy warrior through his dispatch of the Philistine giant Goliath with just a slingshot. This great plot has inspired writers, poets, painters, and sculptors, including Michelangelo with his marble statue of the standing naked David. With Goliath fallen, the rest of the Philistines quickly scattered and the overjoyed Israelites began their celebrations saying that "Saul hath slain his thousands, and David his ten thousands" (*1 Sam. 18:7*). It was a recognition of David's qualities for potential kingship, which resulted in the jealousy of King Saul, the subsequent attempts on David's life and the latter's decade of a fugitive life.

The Bible's first portrayal of male friendship is that of David and Jonathan, the older son of King Saul. Tested by difficult times, the two young men found their shared friendship weightier than even familial love. Jonathan presented David with his robe, his armor, his sword, his bow, and even his belt — regalia symbolizing the heir apparent's abduction of his rights to the throne as well as his unquestioning devotion to David. The way he helped his friend escape by sending a token is also memorable. Their friendship was so deep that David sang a most poignant tribute song when Jonathan was killed with King Saul in a battle against the Philistines, leaving behind one of the most quoted sayings: "How are the mighty fallen, and the weapons of war perished!" (*2 Sam. 1:27*)

In David's harem, Abigail stood out as a woman of beauty and brains, who averted with her hospitality a dangerous confrontation between King Saul and her rude, drunken and stupid husband Nabal. The king well remembered this remarkable woman and married her when her husband died of heart failure as a punishment from God.

The fate of King Saul was sealed as he paid a visit to the Witch of Endor, and through her help, got to meet with the ghost of the recently deceased prophet Samuel, who berated him for disobeying God, and predicted that he and his sons were to die in battle the next day. Ironically, he had earlier banned mediums in his kingdom, but through his disobedience Saul had lost contact with God, and he was desperate to know the future, which turned out to be anything but encouraging.

II SELECTED READINGS

The Anointing of David

1 Samuel 16

¹ And the LORD said unto Samuel, "How long wilt thou mourn for Saul, seeing I have rejected him from reigning over Israel? Fill thine horn with oil, and go. I will send thee to Jesse the Bethlehemite, for I have provided Me a king among his sons."

² And Samuel said, "How can I go? If Saul hear it, he will kill me."

And the LORD said, "Take a heifer with thee, and say, ' I have come to sacrifice to the LORD.' ³ And call Jesse to the sacrifice, and I will show thee what thou shalt do; and thou shalt anoint unto Me him whom I name unto thee."

⁴ And Samuel did that which the LORD spoke, and came to Bethlehem. And the elders of the town trembled at his coming, and said, "Comest thou peaceably?"

⁵ And he said, "Peaceably; I have come to sacrifice unto the LORD. Sanctify yourselves, and come with me to the sacrifice." And he sanctified Jesse and his sons, and called them to the sacrifice.

⁶ And it came to pass, when they had come, that he looked on Eliab and said, "Surely the LORD's anointed is before Him."

⁷ But the LORD said unto Samuel, "Look not on his countenance or on the height of his stature, because I have refused him; for the LORD seeth not as man seeth. For man looketh on the outward appearance, but the LORD looketh on the heart."

⁸ Then Jesse called Abinadab and made him pass before Samuel. And he said, "Neither hath the LORD chosen this." ⁹ Then Jesse made Shammah to pass by. And he said, "Neither hath the LORD chosen this." ¹⁰ Again, Jesse made seven of his sons to pass before Samuel. And Samuel said unto Jesse, "The LORD hath not chosen these." ¹¹ And Samuel said unto Jesse, "Are here all thy children?"

And he said, "There remaineth yet the youngest, and behold, he keepeth the sheep."

And Samuel said unto Jesse, "Send and fetch him, for we will not sit down till he come hither."

¹² And he sent, and brought him in. Now he was ruddy, and altogether of a beautiful countenance and goodly to look upon.

And the LORD said, "Arise, anoint him; for this is he."

¹³ Then Samuel took the horn of oil and anointed him in the midst of his brethren; and the Spirit of the LORD came upon David from that day forward. So Samuel rose up and went to Ramah.

David in Saul's Service

¹⁴ But the Spirit of the LORD departed from Saul, and an evil spirit from the LORD troubled him.

¹⁵ And Saul's servants said unto him, "Behold now, an evil spirit from God troubleth thee. ¹⁶ Let our lord now command thy servants, who are before thee, to seek out a man who is a skillful player on the harp; and it shall come to pass, when the evil spirit from God is upon thee, that he shall play with his hand, and thou shalt be well."

¹⁷ And Saul said unto his servants, "Provide me now a man who can play well, and bring him to me."

¹⁸ Then answered one of the servants and said, "Behold, I have seen a son of Jesse the Bethlehemite who is skillful in playing, and a mighty valiant man, and a man of war, and prudent in matters, and a comely person, and the LORD is with him."

¹⁹ Therefore Saul sent messengers unto Jesse and said, "Send me David thy son, who is with the sheep."

David Playing before Saul, 1645,
Bernardo Cavallino

²⁰ And Jesse took an ass laden with bread and a bottle of wine and a kid, and sent them by David his son unto Saul. ²¹ And David came to Saul and stood before him; and he loved him greatly, and he became his armor bearer. ²² And Saul sent to Jesse, saying, "Let David, I pray thee, stand before me, for he hath found favor in my sight."

²³ And it came to pass, when the evil spirit from God was upon Saul, that David took a harp and played with his hand; so Saul was refreshed and was well, and the evil spirit departed from him.

David and Goliath

1 Samuel 17

¹ Now the Philistines gathered together their armies for battle and were gathered together at Shochoh, which belongeth to Judah, and pitched camp between Shochoh and Azekah in Ephesdammim. ² And Saul and the men of Israel were gathered together and pitched camp by the Valley of Elah, and set up in battle array against the Philistines. ³ And the Philistines stood on a mountain on one side and Israel stood on a mountain on the other side, and there was a valley between them.

⁴ And there went out a champion out of the camp of the Philistines named Goliath①, of Gath, whose height was six cubits and a span②. ⁵ And he had a helmet of brass upon his head, and he was armed with a coat of mail; and the weight of the coat was five thousand shekels of brass. ⁶ And he had greaves of brass upon his legs and a buckler of brass between his shoulders. ⁷ And the staff of his spear was like a weaver's beam, and his spear's head weighed six hundred shekels of iron; and one bearing a shield went before him.

⁸ And he stood and cried unto the armies of Israel and said unto them, "Why have ye come out to set up in battle array? Am not I a Philistine, and ye servants to Saul? Choose you a man for you, and let him come down to me. ⁹ If he be able to fight with me and to kill me, then will we be your servants; but if I prevail against him and kill him, then shall ye be our servants and serve us."

¹⁰ And the Philistine said, "I defy the armies of Israel this day! Give me a man, that we may fight together!" ¹¹ When Saul and all Israel heard those words of the Philistine, they were dismayed and greatly afraid.

...

³² And David said to Saul, "Let no man's heart fail because of him. Thy servant will go and fight with this Philistine." ³³ And Saul said to David, "Thou art not able to go against this Philistine to fight with him; for thou art but a youth, and he a man of war from his youth." ³⁴ And David said unto Saul, "Thy servant kept his father's sheep, and there came a lion and a bear and took a lamb out of the flock; ³⁵ And I went out after him and smote him, and delivered it out of his mouth. And when he arose against me, I caught him by his beard and smote him, and slew him. ³⁶ Thy servant slew both the lion and the bear; and this uncircumcised Philistine shall be as one of them, seeing he hath defied the armies of the living God." ³⁷ David said moreover, "The LORD who delivered me out of the paw of the lion and out of the paw of the bear, He will deliver me out of the hand of this Philistine."

And Saul said unto David, "Go, and the LORD be with thee."

David, Michelangelo
(1475—1564)

---

① **Goliath** /gəˈlaiəθ/, 歌利亚。
② **six cubits and a span** about 3 metres.

³⁸ And Saul armed David with his armor, and he put a helmet of brass upon his head; also he armed him with a coat of mail. ³⁹ And David girded his sword upon his armor, and he attempted to go, for he had not tested it.

And David said unto Saul, "I cannot go with these, for I have not tested them." And David put them off him. ⁴⁰ And he took his staff in his hand, and chose for himself five smooth stones out of the brook and put them in a shepherd's bag which he had, even in a pouch, and his sling was in his hand; and he drew near to the Philistine.

⁴¹ And the Philistine came on and drew near unto David, and the man who bore the shield went before him. ⁴² And when the Philistine looked about and saw David, he disdained him; for he was but a youth, and ruddy, and of a fair countenance. ⁴³ And the Philistine said unto David, "Am I a dog, that thou comest to me with staves?" And the Philistine cursed David by his gods. ⁴⁴ And the Philistine said to David, "Come to me, and I will give thy flesh unto the fowls of the air and to the beasts of the field."

⁴⁵ Then said David to the Philistine, "Thou comest to me with a sword and with a spear and with a shield; but I come to thee in the name of the LORD of hosts, the God of the armies of Israel, whom thou hast defied. ⁴⁶ This day will the LORD deliver thee into mine hand. And I will smite thee and take thine head from thee; and I will give the carcasses of the host of the Philistines this day unto the fowls of the air and to the wild beasts of the earth, that all the earth may know that there is a God in Israel. ⁴⁷ And all this assembly shall know that the LORD saveth not with sword and spear; for the battle is the LORD's, and He will give you into our hands."

⁴⁸ And it came to pass, when the Philistine arose and came and drew nigh to meet David, that David hastened and ran toward the army to meet the Philistine. ⁴⁹ And David put his hand in his bag and took thence a stone, and slung it and smote the Philistine in his forehead, so that the stone sunk into his forehead. And he fell upon his face to the earth.

⁵⁰ So David prevailed over the Philistine with a sling and with a stone, and smote the Philistine and slew him; but there was no sword in the hand of David.

⁵¹ Therefore David ran and stood upon the Philistine, and took his sword, and drew it out of the sheath thereof and slew him, and cut off his head therewith.

And when the Philistines saw their champion was dead, they fled. ⁵² And the men of Israel and of Judah arose, and shouted, and pursued the Philistines until thou come to the valley and to the gates of Ekron. ⁵³ And the children of Israel returned from chasing after the Philistines, and they spoiled their tents. ⁵⁴ And David took the head of the Philistine, and brought it to Jerusalem; but he put his armour in his tent.

...

Saul's Jealousy of David

1 Samuel 18

¹ And it came to pass, when he had made an end of speaking unto Saul, that the soul of Jonathan was knit with the soul of David, and Jonathan loved him as his own soul. ² And Saul took him that day and would let him go home no more to his father's house. ³ Then Jonathan and David made a covenant, because he loved him as his own soul. ⁴ And Jonathan stripped himself of the robe that was upon him and gave it to David, and his garments, even to his sword and to his bow and to his girdle.

⁵ And David went out whithersoever Saul sent him, and behaved himself wisely; and Saul set him over the men of war, and he was accepted in the sight of all the people and also in the sight of Saul's servants.

⁶ And it came to pass as they came, when David was returning from the slaughter of the Philistine, that the women came out of all cities of Israel, singing and dancing, to meet King Saul, with taborets, with joy, and with instruments of music. ⁷ And the women answered one another as they played, and said,

"Saul hath slain his thousands,
and David his ten thousands."

⁸ And Saul was very wroth, and the saying displeased him; and he said, "They have ascribed unto David ten thousands, and to me they have ascribed but thousands. And what can he have more but the kingdom?" ⁹ And Saul eyed David from that day and forward.

Saul Casts a Javelin at David

Saul Attacking David, 1646, Guercino

¹⁰ And it came to pass on the morrow that the evil spirit from God came upon Saul, and he prophesied in the midst of the house. And David played with his hand, as at other times. And there was a javelin in Saul's hand; ¹¹ And Saul cast the javelin, for he said, "I will smite David even to the wall with it." And David escaped out of his presence twice.

¹² And Saul was afraid of David, because the LORD was with him and had departed from Saul. ¹³ Therefore Saul removed him from him, and made him his captain over a thousand; and he went out and came in before the people. ¹⁴ And David behaved himself wisely in all his ways; and the LORD was with him. ¹⁵ Wherefore when Saul saw that he behaved himself very wisely, he was afraid of him. ¹⁶ But all Israel and Judah loved David, because he went out and came in before them.

¹⁷ And Saul said to David, "Behold my elder daughter Merab, her will I give thee to wife: only be thou valiant for me, and fight the LORD's battles." For Saul said, "Let not mine hand be upon him, but let the hand of the Philistines be upon him." ¹⁸ And David said unto Saul, "Who am I? And what is my life, or my father's family in Israel, that I should be son in law to the king?" ¹⁹ But it came to pass at the time when Merab Saul's daughter should have been given to David, that she was given unto Adriel the Meholathite to wife. ²⁰ And Michal Saul's daughter loved David: and they told Saul, and the thing pleased him. ²¹ And Saul said, "I will give him her, that she may be a snare to him, and that the hand of the Philistines may be against him." Wherefore Saul said to David, "Thou shalt this day be my son in law in the one of the twain."

²² And Saul commanded his servants, saying, "Commune with David secretly, and say, 'Behold, the king hath delight in thee, and all his servants love thee: now therefore be the king's son in law.'"

²³ And Saul's servants spake those words in the ears of David. And David said, "Seemeth it to you a light thing to be a king's son in law, seeing that I am a poor man, and lightly esteemed?"

²⁴ And the servants of Saul told him, saying, "On this manner spake David." ²⁵ And Saul said, "Thus shall ye say to David, 'The king desireth not any dowry, but an hundred foreskins of the Philistines, to be avenged of the king's enemies.'" But Saul thought to make David fall by the hand of the Philistines.

²⁶ And when his servants told David these words, it pleased David well to be the king's son in law: and the days were not expired. ²⁷ Wherefore David arose and went, he and his men, and slew of the Philistines two hundred men; and David brought their foreskins, and they gave them in full tale to the king, that he might be the king's son in law. And Saul gave him Michal his daughter to wife.

²⁸ And Saul saw and knew that the LORD was with David, and that Michal Saul's daughter loved him. ²⁹ And Saul was yet the more afraid of David; and Saul became David's enemy continually.

³⁰ Then the princes of the Philistines went forth: and it came to pass, after they went forth, that David behaved himself more wisely than all the servants of Saul; so that his name was much set by.

David and Jonathan

1 Samuel 20

¹ And David fled from Naioth in Ramah, and came and said before Jonathan, "What have I done? What is mine iniquity? And what is my sin before thy father, that he seeketh my life?"

²And he said unto him, "God forbid; thou shalt not die: behold, my father will do nothing either great or small, but that he will shew it me: and why should my father hide this thing from me? It is not so."

³And David sware moreover, and said, "Thy father certainly knoweth that I have found grace in thine eyes; and he saith, 'Let not Jonathan know this, lest he be grieved,' but truly as the LORD liveth, and as thy soul liveth, there is but a step between me and death."

⁴Then said Jonathan unto David, "Whatsoever thy soul desireth, I will even do it for thee."

⁵And David said unto Jonathan, "Behold, to morrow is the new moon, and I should not fail to sit with the king at meat: but let me go, that I may hide myself in the field unto the third day at even." ⁶If thy father at all miss me, then say, 'David earnestly asked leave of me that he might run to Bethlehem his city: for there is a yearly sacrifice there for all the family.' ⁷If he say thus, 'It is well; thy servant shall have peace: but if he be very wroth, then be sure that evil is determined by him.' ⁸Therefore thou shalt deal kindly with thy servant; for thou hast brought thy servant into a covenant of the LORD with thee: notwithstanding, if there be in me iniquity, slay me thyself; for why shouldest thou bring me to thy father?"

⁹And Jonathan said, "Far be it from thee: for if I knew certainly that evil were determined by my father to come upon thee, then would not I tell it thee?"

¹⁰Then said David to Jonathan, "Who shall tell me? Or what if thy father answer thee roughly?"

¹¹And Jonathan said unto David, "Come, and let us go out into the field. And they went out both of them into the field."

¹²And Jonathan said unto David, "O LORD God of Israel, when I have sounded my father about to morrow any time, or the third day, and, behold, if there be good toward David, and I then send not unto thee, and shew it thee;

The LORD do so and much more to Jonathan. ¹³But if it please my father to do thee evil, then I will shew it thee, and send thee away, that thou mayest go in peace: and the LORD be with thee, as he hath been with my father. ¹⁴And thou shalt not only while yet I live shew me the kindness of the LORD, that I die not. ¹⁵But also thou shalt not cut off thy kindness from my house for ever: no, not when the LORD hath cut off the enemies of David every one from the face of the earth."

¹⁶So Jonathan made a covenant with the house of David, saying, "Let the LORD even require it at the hand of David's enemies." ¹⁷And Jonathan caused David to swear again, because he loved him: for he loved him as he loved his own soul.

Jonathan's Token to David

¹⁸Then Jonathan said to David, "To morrow is the new moon: and thou shalt be missed, because thy seat will be empty. ¹⁹And when thou hast stayed three days, then thou shalt go down quickly, and come to the place where thou didst hide thyself when the business was in hand, and shalt remain by the stone Ezel. ²⁰And I will shoot three arrows on the side thereof, as though I shot at a mark. ²¹And, behold, I will send a lad, saying, 'Go, find out the arrows.' If I expressly say unto the lad, 'Behold, the arrows are on this side of thee,' take them; then come thou: for there is peace to thee, and no hurt; as the LORD liveth. ²²But if I say thus unto the young man, 'Behold, the arrows are beyond thee;' go thy way: for the LORD hath sent thee away. ²³And as touching the matter which thou and I have spoken of, behold, the LORD be between thee and me for ever."

²⁴So David hid himself in the field: and when the new moon was come, the king sat him down to eat meat. ²⁵And the king sat upon his seat, as at other times, even upon a seat by the wall: and Jonathan arose, and

Jonathan's Token to David, Exhibited 1868, Lord Frederic Leighton

Abner sat by Saul's side, and David's place was empty. ²⁶Nevertheless Saul spake not any thing that day: for he thought, something hath befallen him, he is not clean; surely he is not clean. ²⁷And it came to pass on the morrow, which was the second day of the month, that David's place was empty: and Saul said unto Jonathan his son, "Wherefore cometh not the son of Jesse to meat, neither yesterday, nor to day?"

²⁸And Jonathan answered Saul, "David earnestly asked leave of me to go to Bethlehem. ²⁹And he said, 'Let me go, I pray thee; for our family hath a sacrifice in the city; and my brother, he hath commanded me to be there: and now, if I have found favour in thine eyes, let me get away, I pray thee, and see my brethren.' Therefore he cometh not unto the king's table."

³⁰Then Saul's anger was kindled against Jonathan, and he said unto him, "Thou son of the perverse rebellious woman, do not I know that thou hast chosen the son of Jesse to thine own confusion, and unto the confusion of thy mother's nakedness③? ³¹For as long as the son of Jesse liveth upon the ground, thou shalt not be established, nor thy kingdom. Wherefore now send and fetch him unto me, for he shall surely die."

³²And Jonathan answered Saul his father, and said unto him, "Wherefore shall he be slain? What hath he done?" ³³And Saul cast a javelin at him to smite him: whereby Jonathan knew that it was determined of his father to slay David. ³⁴So Jonathan arose from the table in fierce anger, and did eat no meat the second day of the month: for he was grieved for David, because his father had done him shame.

³⁵And it came to pass in the morning, that Jonathan went out into the field at the time appointed with David, and a little lad with him. ³⁶And he said unto his lad, "Run, find out now the arrows which I shoot." And as the lad ran, he shot an arrow beyond him. ³⁷And when the lad was come to the place of the arrow which Jonathan had shot, Jonathan cried after the lad, and said, "Is not the arrow beyond thee?" ³⁸And Jonathan cried after the lad, "Make speed, haste, stay not." And Jonathan's lad gathered up the arrows, and came to his master. ³⁹But the lad knew not any thing: only Jonathan and David knew the matter. ⁴⁰And Jonathan gave his artillery unto his lad, and said unto him, "Go, carry them to the city."

⁴¹And as soon as the lad was gone, David arose out of a place toward the south, and fell on his face to the ground, and bowed himself three times: and they kissed one another, and wept one with another, until David exceeded.

⁴²And Jonathan said to David, "Go in peace, forasmuch as we have sworn both of us in the name of the LORD, saying, 'The LORD be between me and thee, and between my seed and thy seed for ever.'" And he arose and departed: and Jonathan went into the city.

David and Abigail

1 Samuel 25

¹And Samuel died; and all the Israelites were gathered together, and lamented him, and buried him in his house at Ramah.

And David arose, and went down to the wilderness of Paran. ²And there was a man in Maon, whose possessions were in Carmel; and the man was very great, and he had three thousand sheep, and a thousand goats: and he was shearing his sheep in Carmel. ³Now the name of the man was Nabal④; and the name of his wife Abigail⑤: and she was a woman of good understanding, and of a beautiful countenance: but the man was churlish and evil in his doings; and he was of the house of Caleb.

⁴And David heard in the wilderness that Nabal did shear his sheep. ⁵And David sent out ten young men, and David said unto the young men, "Get you up to Carmel, and go to Nabal, and greet him in my name. ⁶And thus shall ye say to him that liveth in prosperity, 'Peace be both to thee, and peace be to thine house, and peace be unto all that thou hast.'"

---

③ **to thine own confusion, and unto the confusion of thy mother's nakedness** to your own shame and to the shame of the mother who bore you.
④ **Nabal** /ˈneibl/，拿八。
⑤ **Abigail** /ˈæbigeil/，亚比该。

⁷ " 'And now I have heard that thou hast shearers: now thy shepherds which were with us, we hurt them not, neither was there ought missing unto them, all the while they were in Carmel. ⁸ Ask thy young men, and they will shew thee. Wherefore let the young men find favour in thine eyes: for we come in a good day: give, I pray thee, whatsoever cometh to thine hand unto thy servants, and to thy son David.' "

⁹ And when David's young men came, they spake to Nabal according to all those words in the name of David, and ceased.

David is Slighted by Nabal

¹⁰ And Nabal answered David's servants, and said, " Who is David? And who is the son of Jesse? There be many servants now a days that break away every man from his master. ¹¹ Shall I then take my bread, and my water, and my flesh that I have killed for my shearers, and give it unto men, whom I know not whence they be?"

¹² So David's young men turned their way, and went again, and came and told him all those sayings. ¹³ And David said unto his men, " Gird ye on every man his sword." And they girded on every man his sword; and David also girded on his sword: and there went up after David about four hundred men; and two hundred abode by the stuff.

¹⁴ But one of the young men told Abigail, Nabal's wife, saying, " Behold, David sent messengers out of the wilderness to salute our master; and he railed on them. ¹⁵ But the men were very good unto us, and we were not hurt, neither missed we any thing, as long as we were conversant with them, when we were in the fields. ¹⁶ They were a wall unto us both by night and day, all the while we were with them keeping the sheep. ¹⁷ Now therefore know and consider what thou wilt do; for evil is determined against our master, and against all his household: for he is such a son of Belial, that a man cannot speak to him."

Abigail Saves the Day

¹⁸ Then Abigail made haste, and took two hundred loaves, and two bottles of wine, and five sheep ready dressed, and five measures of parched corn, and an hundred clusters of raisins, and two hundred cakes of figs, and laid them on asses. ¹⁹ And she said unto her servants, " Go on before me; behold, I come after you." But she told not her husband Nabal.

²⁰ And it was so, as she rode on the ass, that she came down by the covert on the hill, and, behold, David and his men came down against her; and she met them. ²¹ Now David had said, " Surely in vain have I kept all that this fellow hath in the wilderness, so that nothing was missed of all that pertained unto him: and he hath requited me evil for good. ²² So and more also do God unto the enemies of David, if I leave of all that pertain to him by the morning light any that pisseth against the wall."

²³ And when Abigail saw David, she hasted, and lighted off the ass, and fell before David on her face, and bowed herself to the ground, ²⁴ And fell at his feet, and said, " Upon me, my lord, upon me let this iniquity be: and let thine handmaid, I pray thee, speak in thine audience, and hear the words of thine handmaid. ²⁵ Let not my lord, I pray thee, regard this man of Belial, even Nabal: for as his name is, so is he; Nabal is his name, and folly is with him: but I thine handmaid saw not the young men of my lord, whom thou didst send."

²⁶ " Now therefore, my lord, as the LORD liveth, and as thy soul liveth, seeing the LORD hath withholden thee from coming to shed blood, and from avenging thyself with thine own hand, now let thine enemies, and they that seek evil to my lord, be as Nabal. ²⁷ And now this blessing which thine handmaid hath brought unto my lord, let it even be given unto the young men that follow my lord. ²⁸ I pray thee, forgive the trespass of thine handmaid: for the LORD will certainly make my lord a sure house; because my lord fighteth the battles of the LORD, and evil hath not been found in thee all thy days. ²⁹ Yet a man is risen to pursue thee, and to seek thy soul: but the soul of my lord shall be bound in the bundle of life with the LORD thy God; and the souls of thine enemies, them shall he sling out, as out of the middle of a sling. ³⁰ And it shall come to

pass, when the LORD shall have done to my lord according to all the good that he hath spoken concerning thee, and shall have appointed thee ruler over Israel; That this shall be no grief unto thee, nor offence of heart unto my lord, either that thou hast shed blood causeless, or that my lord hath avenged himself: but when the LORD shall have dealt well with my lord, then remember thine handmaid."

David Meeting Abigail, 1620s, Workshop of Peter Paul Rubens

³² And David said to Abigail, " Blessed be the LORD God of Israel, which sent thee this day to meet me. ³³ And blessed be thy advice, and blessed be thou, which hast kept me this day from coming to shed blood, and from avenging myself with mine own hand. ³⁴ For in very deed, as the LORD God of Israel liveth, which hath kept me back from hurting thee, except thou hadst hasted and come to meet me, surely there had not been left unto Nabal by the morning light any that pisseth against the wall."

³⁵ So David received of her hand that which she had brought him, and said unto her, " Go up in peace to thine house; see, I have hearkened to thy voice, and have accepted thy person."

The Death of Nabal

³⁶ And Abigail came to Nabal; and, behold, he held a feast in his house, like the feast of a king; and Nabal's heart was merry within him, for he was very drunken: wherefore she told him nothing, less or more, until the morning light. ³⁷ But it came to pass in the morning, when the wine was gone out of Nabal, and his wife had told him these things, that his heart died within him, and he became as a stone. ³⁸ And it came to pass about ten days after, that the LORD smote Nabal, that he died.

³⁹ And when David heard that Nabal was dead, he said, " Blessed be the LORD, that hath pleaded the cause of my reproach from the hand of Nabal, and hath kept his servant from evil: for the LORD hath returned the wickedness of Nabal upon his own head."

And David sent and communed with Abigail, to take her to him to wife. ⁴⁰ And when the servants of David were come to Abigail to Carmel, they spake unto her, saying, " David sent us unto thee, to take thee to him to wife."

⁴¹ And she arose, and bowed herself on her face to the earth, and said, " Behold, let thine handmaid be a servant to wash the feet of the servants of my lord." ⁴² And Abigail hasted, and arose and rode upon an ass, with five damsels of hers that went after her; and she went after the messengers of David, and became his wife. ⁴³ David also took Ahinoam of Jezreel; and they were also both of them his wives. ⁴⁴ But Saul had given Michal his daughter, David's wife, to Phalti the son of Laish, which was of Gallim.

Saul and the Witch of Endor

1 Samuel 28

¹ And it came to pass in those days, that the Philistines gathered their armies together for warfare, to fight with Israel. And Achish said unto David, " Know thou assuredly, that thou shalt go out with me to battle, thou and thy men."

² And David said to Achish, " Surely thou shalt know what thy servant can do." And Achish said to David, " Therefore will I make thee keeper of mine head for ever."

³ Now Samuel was dead, and all Israel had lamented him, and buried him in Ramah, even in his own city. And Saul had put away those that had familiar spirits, and the wizards, out of the land.

⁴ And the Philistines gathered themselves together, and came and pitched in Shunem: and Saul gathered all Israel together, and they pitched in Gilboa. ⁵ And when Saul saw the host of the Philistines, he was afraid, and

his heart greatly trembled. ⁶And when Saul enquired of the LORD, the LORD answered him not, neither by dreams, nor by Urim, nor by prophets. ⁷Then said Saul unto his servants, "Seek me a woman that hath a familiar spirit, that I may go to her, and enquire of her."

And his servants said to him, "Behold, there is a woman that hath a familiar spirit at Endor."

⁸And Saul disguised himself, and put on other raiment, and he went, and two men with him, and they came to the woman by night: and he said, "I pray thee, divine unto me by the familiar spirit, and bring me him up, whom I shall name unto thee."

⁹And the woman said unto him, "Behold, thou knowest what Saul hath done, how he hath cut off those that have familiar spirits, and the wizards, out of the land: wherefore then layest thou a snare for my life, to cause me to die?"

Saul and the Witch of Endor, 1828, William Sidney Mount

¹⁰And Saul sware to her by the LORD, saying, "As the LORD liveth, there shall no punishment happen to thee for this thing."

¹¹Then said the woman, "Whom shall I bring up unto thee?" And he said, "Bring me up Samuel."

¹²And when the woman saw Samuel, she cried with a loud voice: and the woman spake to Saul, saying, "Why hast thou deceived me? For thou art Saul." ¹³And the king said unto her, "Be not afraid: for what sawest thou?" And the woman said unto Saul, "I saw gods ascending out of the earth."

¹⁴And he said unto her, "What form is he of?"

And she said, "An old man cometh up; and he is covered with a mantle."

And Saul perceived that it was Samuel, and he stooped with his face to the ground, and bowed himself.

¹⁵And Samuel said to Saul, "Why hast thou disquieted me, to bring me up?" And Saul answered, "I am sore distressed; for the Philistines make war against me, and God is departed from me, and answereth me no more, neither by prophets, nor by dreams: therefore I have called thee, that thou mayest make known unto me what I shall do."

¹⁶Then said Samuel, "Wherefore then dost thou ask of me, seeing the LORD is departed from thee, and is become thine enemy?" ¹⁷And the LORD hath done to him, as he spake by me: for the LORD hath rent the kingdom out of thine hand, and given it to thy neighbour, even to David. ¹⁸Because thou obeyedst not the voice of the LORD, nor executedst his fierce wrath upon Amalek, therefore hath the LORD done this thing unto thee this day. ¹⁹Moreover the LORD will also deliver Israel with thee into the hand of the Philistines: and to morrow shalt thou and thy sons be with me: the LORD also shall deliver the host of Israel into the hand of the Philistines."

²⁰Then Saul fell straightway all along on the earth, and was sore afraid, because of the words of Samuel: and there was no strength in him; for he had eaten no bread all the day, nor all the night.

²¹And the woman came unto Saul, and saw that he was sore troubled, and said unto him, "Behold, thine handmaid hath obeyed thy voice, and I have put my life in my hand, and have hearkened unto thy words which thou spakest unto me. ²²Now therefore, I pray thee, hearken thou also unto the voice of thine handmaid, and let me set a morsel of bread before thee; and eat, that thou mayest have strength, when thou goest on thy way."

²³But he refused, and said, "I will not eat." But his servants, together with the woman, compelled him; and he hearkened unto their voice. So he arose from the earth, and sat upon the bed.

²⁴And the woman had a fat calf in the house; and she hasted, and killed it, and took flour, and kneaded it, and did bake unleavened bread thereof. ²⁵And she brought it before Saul, and before his servants; and they did eat. Then they rose up, and went away that night.

The Death of Saul and Jonathan

1 Samuel 31

¹Now the Philistines fought against Israel: and the men of Israel fled from before the Philistines, and fell down slain in mount Gilboa. ²And the Philistines followed hard upon Saul and upon his sons; and the Philistines slew Jonathan, and Abinadab, and Melchishua, Saul's sons. ³And the battle went sore against Saul, and the archers hit him; and he was sore wounded of the archers.

⁴Then said Saul unto his armourbearer, "Draw thy sword, and thrust me through therewith; lest these uncircumcised come and thrust me through, and abuse me."

The Bible in Everyday English: *fall on one's own sword*

King Saul committed suicide by falling on his own sword. In modern-day English, the phrase "*fall on one's sword*" conveys how somebody resigns or accepts the consequences of some wrongdoing though it could be shirked or shared.

But his armourbearer would not; for he was sore afraid. Therefore Saul took a sword, and fell upon it. ⁵And when his armourbearer saw that Saul was dead, he fell likewise upon his sword, and died with him. ⁶So Saul died, and his three sons, and his armourbearer, and all his men, that same day together.

⁷And when the men of Israel that were on the other side of the valley, and they that were on the other side Jordan, saw that the men of Israel fled, and that Saul and his sons were dead, they forsook the cities, and fled; and the Philistines came and dwelt in them.

⁸And it came to pass on the morrow, when the Philistines came to strip the slain, that they found Saul and his three sons fallen in mount Gilboa. ⁹And they cut off his head, and stripped off his armour, and sent into the land of the Philistines round about, to publish it in the house of their idols, and among the people. ¹⁰And they put his armour in the house of Ashtaroth: and they fastened his body to the wall of Bethshan.

¹¹And when the inhabitants of Jabeshgilead heard of that which the Philistines had done to Saul; ¹²All the valiant men arose, and went all night, and took the body of Saul and the bodies of his sons from the wall of Bethshan, and came to Jabesh, and burnt them there. ¹³And they took their bones, and buried them under a tree at Jabesh, and fasted seven days.

III FOOD FOR THOUGHT

1. Why was King Saul rejected by God?
2. How come that David entered Saul's service?
3. What made David go to the battlefield?
4. What made Saul so jealous of David?
5. How can you describe the friendship between David and Saul?

IV. BIBLICAL RELEVANCE

A. Biblical Terms in Everyday English
1. David and Jonathan: _____
2. David's harp: _____
3. G/goliath: _____
4. Abigail: _____
5. wash sb's feet (*1 Sam. 25:41*): _____
6. fall on one's sword (*1 Sam. 31:4*): _____

B. Biblical References in Literature
1. Oh the road to En-dor is the oldest road
   And the craziest road of all!
   Straight it runs to the Witch's abode,
   As it did in the days of Saul,
   And nothing has changed of the sorrow in store
   For such as go down on the road to En-dor!
   (Rudyard Kipling, *En-Dor*, 1916)
2. That night when Beth played to Mr. Laurence in the twilight, Laurie standing in the shadow of the curtain, listened to the little David, whose simple music always quieted his moody spirit.
   (Louisa M. Alcott, *Little Women*, 1868)
3. Every day we hear of more Italian armies driven back or defeated, and we feel the jubilation of David with Goliath dead at his feet.
   (Louis de Bernières, *Captain Corelli's Mandolin*, 1994)
4. Among the members of his church there was one young man, a little older than himself, with whom he had long lived in such close friendship that it was the custom of their Lantern Yard brethren to call them David and Jonathan.
   (George Eliot, *Silas Marner*, 1861)
5. I merely lit that fire because I was dull, and thought I would get a little excitement by calling you up and triumphing over you as the Witch of Endor called up Samuel. I determined you should come; and you have come.
   (Thomas Hardy, *The Return of the Native*, 1880)

C. The Bible and Arts
1. *David*, Michelangelo (1475—1564)
2. *Saul and David*, c. 1635, Erasmus Quellin II
3. *David Playing before Saul*, 1645, Bernardo Cavallino
4. *David*, 1623—1634, Lorenzo Bernini
5. *David*, 1600, Caravaggio
6. *Saul Attacking David*, 1646, Guercino
7. *Jonathan's Token to David*, Exhibited 1868, Lord Frederic Leighton
8. *David Meeting Abigail*, 1620s, Workshop of Peter Paul Rubens
9. *Saul and the Witch of Endor*, 1828, William Sidney Mount

V. SOURCES FOR REFERENCE

1. (1997). *The Bible Collection: David*, a TV play by Turner Home Entertainment.
2. Schippe, C. & C. Stetson. (2005). *The Bible and Its Influence*. Front Royal, VA: BLP Publishing.

16. DAVID THE KING

I POINTS OF DEPARTURE

The Bible is filled with memorable personalities, but few beat David in the popularity rating. Reliving his life in one's mind is like taking a roller coaster ride that affords a whirlwind of striking images. He is seen playing his harp to calm Saul in his manic phases, writing poems with some of the earlier psalms to his name, fighting battles, dancing jubilantly in praise of God as the ark of covenant came into Jerusalem, an unseemly sight to his wife Michal. He reveals to us his tear-streaked face when he bemoaned his sworn brother Jonathan's death. He is also seen on the rooftop, gazing down lustfully on the bathing beauty Bathsheba. Nathan is seen pointing his finger at him for committing the double crime of adultery and murder, using a kind of didactic story called *parable*. The repentant David is heard crying his heart out to God for the life of his infant child. And he is seen stumbling with a bowed head out of Jerusalem, pursued by his murderous and rebellious son Absalom. King David was perhaps the most humane when he lamented his son's death with words that are as heart-wrenching as ever: "O my son Absalom, my son, my son Absalom! Would God I had died for thee, O Absalom, my son, my son!" (*2 Sam. 18:33*)

David is not painted as a flawless character, or a perfect model of strength and courage, with his own crimes and his failure to discipline his children who were let off with their vices of rape (of Tamar by her half-brother Amnon), murder (of Amnon by Absalom as a revenge on his sister Tamar's rape), rebellion (of Absalom against King David). Yet, he is celebrated in the Old Testament as Israel's ideal king and in the New Testament as an ancestor of the Messiah, the anointed one promised by God, known as the "Son of David." David's hold on the Western imagination is attributable to his personal charm, his whole-hearted commitment to his God, and his sincere and unreserved repentance, which was the most familiarly commented on by Benjamin Franklin in *Poor Richard's Almanac* (1754):

Many Princes sin with David, but few repent with him.

II SELECTED READINGS

David Dances Naked Before the Ark

2 Samuel 6

...

¹⁶And as the ark of the LORD came into the city of David, Michal Saul's daughter looked through a window, and saw king David leaping and dancing before the LORD; and she despised him in her heart. ¹⁷And they brought in the ark of the LORD, and set it in his place, in the midst of the tabernacle that David had pitched for it: and David offered burnt offerings and peace offerings before the LORD. ¹⁸And as

soon as David had made an end of offering burnt offerings and peace offerings, he blessed the people in the name of the LORD of hosts. ¹⁹ And he dealt among all the people, even among the whole multitude of Israel, as well to the women as men, to every one a cake of bread, and a good piece of flesh, and a flagon of wine. So all the people departed every one to his house.

²⁰ Then David returned to bless his household. And Michal the daughter of Saul came out to meet David, and said, " How glorious was the king of Israel to day, who uncovered himself to day in the eyes of the handmaids of his servants, as one of the vain fellows shamelessly uncovereth himself!"

²¹ And David said unto Michal, " It was before the LORD, which chose me before thy father, and before all his house, to appoint me ruler over the people of the LORD, over Israel: therefore will I play before the LORD. ²² And I will yet be more vile than thus, and will be base in mine own sight: and of the maidservants which thou hast spoken of, of them shall I be had in honour."

²³ Therefore Michal the daughter of Saul had no child unto the day of her death.

David and Bathsheba

2 Samuel 11

¹ And it came to pass, after the year was expired, at the time when kings go forth to battle, that David sent Joab①, and his servants with him, and all Israel; and they destroyed the children of Ammon, and besieged Rabbah. But David tarried still at Jerusalem.

The Toilet of Bathsheba

² And it came to pass in an eveningtide, that David arose from off his bed, and walked upon the roof of the king's house: and from the roof he saw a woman washing herself; and the woman was very beautiful to look upon. ³ And David sent and enquired after the woman. And one said, " Is not this Bathsheba②, the daughter of Eliam, the wife of Uriah③ the Hittite?" ⁴ And David sent messengers, and took her; and she came in unto him, and he lay with her; for she was purified from her uncleanness: and she returned unto her house. ⁵ And the woman conceived, and sent and told David, and said, " I am with child." ⁶ And David sent to Joab, saying, " Send me Uriah the Hittite." And Joab sent Uriah to David. ⁷ And when Uriah was come unto him, David demanded of him how Joab did, and how the people did, and how the war prospered. ⁸ And David said to Uriah, " Go down to thy house, and wash thy feet." And Uriah departed out of the king's house, and there followed him a mess of meat from the king. ⁹ But Uriah slept at the door of the king's house with all the servants of his lord, and went not down to his house.

¹⁰ And when they had told David, saying, " Uriah went not down unto his house." David said unto Uriah, " Camest thou not from thy journey? Why then didst thou not go down unto thine house?"

¹¹ And Uriah said unto David, " The ark, and Israel, and Judah, abide in tents; and my lord Joab, and the servants of my lord, are encamped in the open fields; shall I then go into mine house, to eat and to drink, and to lie with my wife? As thou livest, and as thy soul liveth, I will not do this thing."

¹² And David said to Uriah, " Tarry here to day also, and to morrow I will let thee depart." So Uriah abode in Jerusalem that day, and the morrow. ¹³ And when David had called him, he did eat and drink before him; and he

Bathsheba in the Bath, 1834, Francesco Hayez

---

① **Joab** (/ˈdʒəʊæb/, 约押) supreme commander of David's army.
② **Bathsheba** /bæθˈʃiːbə/, 拔示巴。
③ **Uriah** /jʊˈraɪə/, 乌利亚。

made him drunk; and at even he went out to lie on his bed with the servants of his lord, but went not down to his house.

Letter of Uriah

¹⁴ And it came to pass in the morning, that David wrote a letter to Joab, and sent it by the hand of Uriah. ¹⁵ And he wrote in the letter, saying, " Set ye Uriah in the forefront of the hottest battle, and retire ye from him, that he may be smitten, and die."

King David Handing the Letter to Uriah, Pieter Pietersz Lastman (1583—1633)

¹⁶ And it came to pass, when Joab observed the city, that he assigned Uriah unto a place where he knew that valiant men were. ¹⁷ And the men of the city went out, and fought with Joab: and there fell some of the people of the servants of David; and Uriah the Hittite died also. ¹⁸ Then Joab sent and told David all the things concerning the war; ¹⁹ And charged the messenger, saying, " When thou hast made an end of telling the matters of the war unto the king, ²⁰ And if so be that the king's wrath arise, and he say unto thee, ' Wherefore approached ye so nigh unto the city when ye did fight? Knew ye not that they would shoot from the wall, ²¹ Who smote Abimelech the son of Jerubbesheth? Did not a woman cast a piece of a millstone upon him from the wall, that he died in Thebez? Why went ye nigh the wall?' Then say thou, ' Thy servant Uriah the Hittite is dead also.' "

The Bible in Everyday English: *letter of Uriah*

Uriah is known for his undivided loyalty to David and uncompromising adherence to the code of honor expected of a soldier. He is also known as a conveyer of a message that is to bring about his own destruction. Today,"a letter of Uriah" often refers to a treacherous letter of friendship, but in reality a death-warrant.

²² So the messenger went, and came and shewed David all that Joab had sent him for. ²³ And the messenger said unto David, " Surely the men prevailed against us, and came out unto us into the field, and we were upon them even unto the entering of the gate. ²⁴ And the shooters shot from off the wall upon thy servants; and some of the king's servants be dead, and thy servant Uriah the Hittite is dead also."
²⁵ Then David said unto the messenger, " Thus shalt thou say unto Joab, ' Let not this thing displease thee, for the sword devoureth one as well as another: make thy battle more strong against the city, and overthrow it: and encourage thou him.' "
²⁶ And when the wife of Uriah heard that Uriah her husband was dead, she mourned for her husband. ²⁷ And when the mourning was past, David sent and fetched her to his house, and she became his wife, and bare him a son. But the thing that David had done displeased the LORD.

Amnon④ and Tamar⑤

2 Samuel 13

¹And it came to pass after this, that Absalom the son of David had a fair sister, whose name was Tamar; and Amnon the son of David loved her.

²And Amnon was so vexed, that he fell sick for his sister Tamar; for she was a virgin; and Amnon thought it hard for him to do anything to her.

³But Amnon had a friend, whose name was Jonadab, the son of Shimeah David's brother: and Jonadab was a very subtil man. ⁴And he said unto him, "Why art thou, being the king's son, lean from day to day? Wilt thou not tell me?"

And Amnon said unto him, "I love Tamar, my brother Absalom's sister."

⁵And Jonadab said unto him, "Lay thee down on thy bed, and make thyself sick; and when thy father cometh to see thee, say unto him, ' I pray thee, let my sister Tamar come, and give me meat, and dress the meat in my sight, that I may see it, and eat it at her hand.' "

⁶So Amnon lay down, and made himself sick: and when the king was come to see him, Amnon said unto the king, "I pray thee, let Tamar my sister come, and make me a couple of cakes in my sight, that I may eat at her hand."

⁷Then David sent home to Tamar, saying, "Go now to thy brother Amnon's house, and dress him meat." ⁸So Tamar went to her brother Amnon's house; and he was laid down. And she took flour, and kneaded it, and made cakes in his sight, and did bake the cakes. ⁹And she took a pan, and poured them out before him; but he refused to eat.

And Amnon said, "Have out all men from me." And they went out every man from him. ¹⁰And Amnon said unto Tamar, "Bring the meat into the chamber, that I may eat of thine hand." And Tamar took the cakes which she had made, and brought them into the chamber to Amnon her brother. ¹¹And when she had brought them unto him to eat, he took hold of her, and said unto her, "Come lie with me, my sister."

The Rape of Tamar, probably ca. 1640, Eustache de Sueur

¹²And she answered him, "Nay, my brother, do not force me; for no such thing ought to be done in Israel: do not thou this folly. ¹³And I, whither shall I cause my shame to go? And as for thee, thou shalt be as one of the fools in Israel. Now therefore, I pray thee, speak unto the king; for he will not withhold me from thee." ¹⁴Howbeit he would not hearken unto her voice: but, being stronger than she, forced her, and lay with her.

¹⁵Then Amnon hated her exceedingly; so that the hatred wherewith he hated her was greater than the love wherewith he had loved her. And Amnon said unto her, "Arise, be gone."

¹⁶And she said unto him, "There is no cause: this evil in sending me away is greater than the other that thou didst unto me."

But he would not hearken unto her. ¹⁷Then he called his servant that ministered unto him, and said, "Put now this woman out from me, and bolt the door after her." ¹⁸And she had a garment of divers colours upon her: for with such robes were the king's daughters that were virgins apparelled. Then his servant brought her out, and bolted the door after her. ¹⁹And Tamar put ashes on her head, and rent her garment of divers colours that was on her, and laid her hand on her head, and went on crying.

²⁰And Absalom her brother said unto her, "Hath Amnon thy brother been with thee? But hold now thy

---

④ **Amnon** /ˈæmnən/, 暗嫩。
⑤ **Tamar** /ˈteimɑː(r)/, 他玛。See another Tamar in *Genesis* 38.

peace, my sister: he is thy brother; regard not this thing." So Tamar remained desolate in her brother Absalom's house.
²¹ But when king David heard of all these things, he was very wroth. ²² And Absalom spake unto his brother Amnon neither good nor bad: for Absalom hated Amnon, because he had forced his sister Tamar.

Absalom Kills Amnon

The Banquet of Absalom, c.1650, Niccolo de Simone

²³ And it came to pass after two full years, that Absalom had sheepshearers in Baalhazor, which is beside Ephraim: and Absalom invited all the king's sons. ²⁴ And Absalom came to the king, and said, "Behold now, thy servant hath sheepshearers; let the king, I beseech thee, and his servants go with thy servant."
²⁵ And the king said to Absalom, "Nay, my son, let us not all now go, lest we be chargeable unto thee." And he pressed him: howbeit he would not go, but blessed him.
²⁶ Then said Absalom, "If not, I pray thee, let my brother Amnon go with us."

And the king said unto him, "Why should he go with thee?" ²⁷ But Absalom pressed him, that he let Amnon and all the king's sons go with him.
²⁸ Now Absalom had commanded his servants, saying, "Mark ye now when Amnon's heart is merry with wine, and when I say unto you, 'Smite Amnon,' then kill him, fear not: have not I commanded you? Be courageous, and be valiant." ²⁹ And the servants of Absalom did unto Amnon as Absalom had commanded. Then all the king's sons arose, and every man gat him up upon his mule, and fled.
³⁰ And it came to pass, while they were in the way, that tidings came to David, saying, "Absalom hath slain all the king's sons, and there is not one of them left." ³¹ Then the king arose, and tare his garments, and lay on the earth; and all his servants stood by with their clothes rent.
³² And Jonadab, the son of Shimeah David's brother, answered and said, "Let not my lord suppose that they have slain all the young men the king's sons; for Amnon only is dead: for by the appointment of Absalom this hath been determined from the day that he forced his sister Tamar. ³³ Now therefore let not my lord the king take the thing to his heart, to think that all the king's sons are dead: for Amnon only is dead."

Absalom Flees

³⁴ But Absalom fled.
And the young man that kept the watch lifted up his eyes, and looked, and, behold, there came much people by the way of the hill side behind him.
³⁵ And Jonadab said unto the king, "Behold, the king's sons come: as thy servant said, so it is."
³⁶ And it came to pass, as soon as he had made an end of speaking, that, behold, the king's sons came, and lifted up their voice and wept: and the king also and all his servants wept very sore.
³⁷ But Absalom fled, and went to Talmai, the son of Ammihud, king of Geshur. And David mourned for his son every day.
³⁸ So Absalom fled, and went to Geshur, and was there three years.
And the soul of king David longed to go forth unto Absalom: for he was comforted concerning Amnon, seeing he was dead.

The Revolt of Absalom

2 Samuel 15

¹And it came to pass after this, that Absalom prepared him chariots and horses, and fifty men to run before him. ²And Absalom rose up early, and stood beside the way of the gate: and it was so, that when any man that had a controversy came to the king for judgment, then Absalom called unto him, and said, "Of what city art thou?" And he said, "Thy servant is of one of the tribes of Israel." ³And Absalom said unto him, "See, thy matters are good and right; but there is no man deputed of the king to hear thee." ⁴Absalom said moreover, "Oh that I were made judge in the land, that every man which hath any suit or cause might come unto me, and I would do him justice!"

⁵And it was so, that when any man came nigh to him to do him obeisance, he put forth his hand, and took him, and kissed him. ⁶And on this manner did Absalom to all Israel that came to the king for judgment: so Absalom stole the hearts of the men of Israel.

⁷And it came to pass after forty years, that Absalom said unto the king, "I pray thee, let me go and pay my vow, which I have vowed unto the LORD, in Hebron. ⁸For thy servant vowed a vow while I abode at Geshur in Syria, saying, 'If the LORD shall bring me again indeed to Jerusalem, then I will serve the LORD.'"

⁹And the king said unto him, "Go in peace." So he arose, and went to Hebron.

¹⁰But Absalom sent spies throughout all the tribes of Israel, saying, "As soon as ye hear the sound of the trumpet, then ye shall say, 'Absalom reigneth in Hebron.'" ¹¹And with Absalom went two hundred men out of Jerusalem, that were called; and they went in their simplicity, and they knew not any thing. ¹²And Absalom sent for Ahithophel the Gilonite, David's counsellor, from his city, even from Giloh, while he offered sacrifices. And the conspiracy was strong; for the people increased continually with Absalom.

David Flees

¹³And there came a messenger to David, saying, "The hearts of the men of Israel are after Absalom."

¹⁴And David said to all his servants that were with him at Jerusalem, "Rise up and let us flee; for we shall not escape from Absalom. Be quick to depart, lest he overtake us quickly, and bring evil upon us, and smite the city with the edge of the sword."

¹⁵And the king's servants said unto the king, "Behold, thy servants are ready to do whatsoever my lord the king shall appoint."

¹⁶And the king went forth, and all his household after him. And the king left ten women, which were concubines, to keep the house. ¹⁷And the king went forth, and all the people after him, and tarried in a place that was far off. ¹⁸And all his servants passed on beside him; and all the Cherethites, and all the Pelethites, and all the Gittites, six hundred men which came after him from Gath, passed on before the king.

¹⁹Then said the king to Ittai the Gittite, "Wherefore goest thou also with us? Return to thy place, and abide with the king: for thou art a stranger, and also an exile. ²⁰Whereas thou camest but yesterday, should I this day make thee go up and down with us? Seeing I go whither I may, return thou, and take back thy brethren: mercy and truth be with thee."

²¹And Ittai answered the king, and said, "As the LORD liveth, and as my lord the king liveth, surely in what place my lord the king shall be, whether in death or life, even there also will thy servant be."

²²And David said to Ittai, "Go and pass over." And Ittai the Gittite passed over, and all his men, and all the little ones that were with him.

²³And all the country wept with a loud voice, and all the people passed over: the king also himself passed over the brook Kidron, and all the people passed over, toward the way of the wilderness.

²⁴And lo Zadok also, and all the Levites were with him, bearing the ark of the covenant of God: and they set down the ark of God; and Abiathar went up, until all the people had done passing out of the city.

^{25}And the king said unto Zadok, "Carry back the ark of God into the city: if I shall find favour in the eyes of the LORD, he will bring me again, and shew me both it, and his habitation. ^{26}"But if he thus say, I have no delight in thee; behold, here am I, let him do to me as seemeth good unto him."

^{27}The king said also unto Zadok the priest, "Art not thou a seer? Return into the city in peace, and your two sons with you, Ahimaaz thy son, and Jonathan the son of Abiathar. ^{28}See, I will tarry in the plain of the wilderness, until there come word from you to certify me." ^{29}Zadok therefore and Abiathar carried the ark of God again to Jerusalem: and they tarried there.

^{30}And David went up by the ascent of mount Olivet, and wept as he went up, and had his head covered, and he went barefoot: and all the people that was with him covered every man his head, and they went up, weeping as they went up. ^{31}And one told David, saying, "Ahithophel is among the conspirators with Absalom." And David said, "O LORD, I pray thee, turn the counsel of Ahithophel into foolishness."

^{32}And it came to pass, that when David was come to the top of the mount, where he worshipped God, behold, Hushai the Archite came to meet him with his coat rent, and earth upon his head. ^{33}Unto whom David said, "If thou passest on with me, then thou shalt be a burden unto me. ^{34}But if thou return to the city, and say unto Absalom, ' I will be thy servant, O king; as I have been thy father's servant hitherto, so will I now also be thy servant,' then mayest thou for me defeat the counsel of Ahithophel. ^{35}And hast thou not there with thee Zadok and Abiathar the priests? Therefore it shall be, that what thing soever thou shalt hear out of the king's house, thou shalt tell it to Zadok and Abiathar the priests. ^{36}Behold, they have there with them their two sons, Ahimaaz Zadok's son, and Jonathan Abiathar's son; and by them ye shall send unto me every thing that ye can hear."

^{37}So Hushai David's friend came into the city, and Absalom came into Jerusalem.

Absalom's Death

2 Samuel 18

^{1}And David numbered the people that were with him, and set captains of thousands, and captains of hundreds over them. ^{2}And David sent forth a third part of the people under the hand of Joab, and a third part under the hand of Abishai the son of Zeruiah, Joab's brother, and a third part under the hand of Ittai the Gittite. And the king said unto the people, "I will surely go forth with you myself also."

Death of Absalom,
Gustave Doré (1832—1883)

^{3}But the people answered, "Thou shalt not go forth: for if we flee away, they will not care for us; neither if half of us die, will they care for us: but now thou art worth ten thousand of us: therefore now it is better that thou succour us out of the city."

^{4}And the king said unto them, "What seemeth you best I will do."

And the king stood by the gate side, and all the people came out by hundreds and by thousands. ^{5}And the king commanded Joab and Abishai and Ittai, saying, "Deal gently for my sake with the young man, even with Absalom." And all the people heard when the king gave all the captains charge concerning Absalom.

^{6}So the people went out into the field against Israel: and the battle was in the wood of Ephraim; ^{7}Where the people of Israel were slain before the servants of David, and there was there a great slaughter that day of twenty thousand men. ^{8}For the battle was there scattered over the face of all the country: and the wood devoured more people that day than the sword devoured.

^{9}And Absalom met the servants of David. And Absalom rode upon a mule, and the mule went under the thick boughs of a great oak, and his head caught hold of the oak, and he was taken up between the heaven and the earth; and the mule that was under him went away.

¹⁰ And a certain man saw it, and told Joab, and said, "Behold, I saw Absalom hanged in an oak."

¹¹ And Joab said unto the man that told him, "And, behold, thou sawest him, and why didst thou not smite him there to the ground? And I would have given thee ten shekels of silver, and a girdle."

¹² And the man said unto Joab, "Though I should receive a thousand shekels of silver in mine hand, yet would I not put forth mine hand against the king's son: for in our hearing the king charged thee and Abishai and Ittai, saying, 'Beware that none touch the young man Absalom.' ¹³ Otherwise I should have wrought falsehood against mine own life: for there is no matter hid from the king, and thou thyself wouldest have set thyself against me."

¹⁴ Then said Joab, "I may not tarry thus with thee." And he took three darts in his hand, and thrust them through the heart of Absalom, while he was yet alive in the midst of the oak. ¹⁵ And ten young men that bare Joab's armour compassed about and smote Absalom, and slew him.

¹⁶ And Joab blew the trumpet, and the people returned from pursuing after Israel: for Joab held back the people. ¹⁷ And they took Absalom, and cast him into a great pit in the wood, and laid a very great heap of stones upon him: and all Israel fled every one to his tent.

¹⁸ Now Absalom in his lifetime had taken and reared up for himself a pillar, which is in the king's dale: for he said, "I have no son to keep my name in remembrance," and he called the pillar after his own name: and it is called unto this day, Absalom's place.

Absalom, Absalom!

¹⁹ Then said Ahimaaz the son of Zadok, "Let me now run, and bear the king tidings, how that the LORD hath avenged him of his enemies."

²⁰ And Joab said unto him, "Thou shalt not bear tidings this day, but thou shalt bear tidings another day: but this day thou shalt bear no tidings, because the king's son is dead."

²¹ Then said Joab to Cushi, "Go tell the king what thou hast seen." And Cushi bowed himself unto Joab, and ran.

²² Then said Ahimaaz the son of Zadok yet again to Joab, "But howsoever, let me, I pray thee, also run after Cushi."

And Joab said, "Wherefore wilt thou run, my son, seeing that thou hast no tidings ready?"

²³ "But howsoever," said he, "let me run." And he said unto him, "Run." Then Ahimaaz ran by the way of the plain, and overran Cushi.

²⁴ And David sat between the two gates: and the watchman went up to the roof over the gate unto the wall, and lifted up his eyes, and looked, and behold a man running alone. ²⁵ And the watchman cried, and told the king.

And the king said, "If he be alone, there is tidings in his mouth." And he came apace, and drew near.

²⁶ And the watchman saw another man running: and the watchman called unto the porter, and said, "Behold another man running alone."

And the king said, "He also bringeth tidings."

²⁷ And the watchman said, "Me thinketh the running of the foremost is like the running of Ahimaaz the son of Zadok."

And the king said, "He is a good man, and cometh with good tidings."

²⁸ And Ahimaaz called, and said unto the king, "All is well." And he fell down to the earth upon his face before the king, and said, "Blessed be the LORD thy God, which hath delivered up the men that lifted up their hand against my lord the king."

²⁹ And the king said, "Is the young man Absalom safe?"

The Bible in Literature: *Faulkner's Absalom, Absalom!*

Absalom, Absalom! (1936), a novel that helped William Faulkner win the Nobel Prize in Literature, parallels closely the stories of David and his children. For one thing, the title itself alludes to a wayward son (Henry Sutpen) fighting the empire his father (Thomas Sutpen) built. Another parallel to the Biblical story is that Absalom had his half-brother executed for raping Tamar, his sister. Faulkner's novel substitutes a seduction for the rape.

And Ahimaaz answered, "When Joab sent the king's servant, and me thy servant, I saw a great tumult, but I knew not what it was."

³⁰And the king said unto him, "Turn aside, and stand here." And he turned aside, and stood still.

³¹And, behold, Cushi came; and Cushi said, "Tidings, my lord the king: for the LORD hath avenged thee this day of all them that rose up against thee." ³²And the king said unto Cushi, "Is the young man Absalom safe?"

And Cushi answered, "The enemies of my lord the king, and all that rise against thee to do thee hurt, be as that young man is."

³³And the king was much moved, and went up to the chamber over the gate, and wept: and as he went, thus he said, "O my son Absalom, my son, my son Absalom! Would God I had died for thee, O Absalom, my son, my son!"

III FOOD FOR THOUGHT

1. Of what crimes was David guilty in *2 Samuel 11*?
2. What contrasts of character can be drawn between David and Uriah?
3. How was Absalom killed?
4. How do we know the agony in David's lament?
5. Read *Deuteronomy 17:14—24*. Make a list of qualities of a good king and explain how David and Saul lived up to these qualities or failed to do so.

IV BIBLICAL RELEVANCE

A. Biblical Terms in Everyday English
1. Bathsheba: _____
2. David and Bathsheba: _____
3. letter of Uriah: _____
4. Uriah: _____
5. Absalom: _____

B. Biblical References in Literature
1. John Dryden, *Absalom and Achitophel*, 1681.
2. William Faulkner, *Absalom! Absalom!*, 1936.
3. Alan Paton: "Cry, the Beloved Country," 1948.
4. However, sir, here is a guarantee. Look at its contents: I do not again carry the letters of Uriah.
(Sir W. Scott, *Redgauntlet*, 1824)

5. "Well, doctor, 'tis a mercy you wasn't a-drowned, or a-splintered, or a-hanged up to a tree like Absalom—also a handsome gentleman like yourself, as the prophets say!"
(Thomas Hardy, *The Woodlanders*, 1887)

6. Sometimes, the worthy gentleman would reprove my mother for being overindulgent to her sons, with a reference to old Eli, or David and Absalom, which was particularly galling to her feelings.
(Anne Brontë, *The Tenant of Wildfell Hall*, 1848)

C. The Bible and Arts
1. *The Suicide of Saul*, 1562, Pieter Bruegel, the Elder
2. *David Anointed to Be King Over Judah*, 1851—1860, Julius Schnorr von Carolsfeld
3. *Entry of David into Jerusalem*, 1630s, Frans Francken II
4. David and Bathsheba
   Bathsheba Artemesia, 1640's, Gentileschi
   Bathsheba in the Bath, 1834, Francesco Hayez
   The Toilet of Bathsheba, after 1705, Style of Luca Giordano
   Bathsheba with King David's Letter, 1659, Govert Teunisz Flinck
   Bathsheba at Her Bath, 1654, Rembrandt
   King David Handing the Letter to Uriah, Pieter Pietersz Lastman (1583—1633)
5. *The Rape of Tamar*, probably ca. 1640, Eustache de Sueur
6. *Amnon and Tamar*, 1649—1650, Guercino
7. *Death of Absalom*, 1851—1860, Julius Schnorr von Carolsfeld

V SOURCES FOR REFERENCE

1. http://en.wikipedia.org/wiki/Absalom,_Absalom!
2. (1997). *The Bible Collection: David*, a TV play by Turner Home Entertainment.
3. Browning, W. R. E. (2009). *A Dictionary of the Bible*. Oxford: Oxford University Press.

17. PSALMS

I POINTS OF DEPARTURE

At the heart of the Bible are songs that appeal to a wide spectrum of human emotions, ranging from joy and happiness, longing and grief, anger and impatience, patriotism and solitary love to fear and hope, gaining its long-lasting popularity both among Christians and pagans alike. This cathartic property of psalms was famously captured by John Calvin who called the Psalter (i.e. the Book of Psalms) "an anatomy of all the parts of the soul," adding that "there is not an emotion of which any one can be conscious that is not here represented as in a mirror." (*qtd.* in Ryken & Ryken, 2007: 744)

The Book of Psalms contains stuff of such nature. It is a collection of 150 self-contained poems and prayers, traditionally ascribed to King David, but regarded by modern scholarship as mostly anonymous compositions of various dates and for undeclared occasions. In spite of tremendous variation, readers can always get a sense of inner consistency who just glide from one psalm to another without ever realizing a change of scene or time frame. It is rightfully a beautiful cathedral built over centuries, with each wing and each window contributed by geniuses of different eras blending into each other so seamlessly and harmoniously (Yancey & Stafford, 1989: 574).

There are roughly three categories of psalms. Many are hymns celebrating deeds for which God is praised—the Creation (*Ps. 8*), the Exodus (*Ps. 114*), and the long course of events from Abraham to the invasion of Canaan. Another category is that of laments, sometimes in a personal form (*Ps. 22*), and sometimes in a communal cry of distress (*Ps. 44*). There are also personal thanksgivings, such as for recovery from illness (*Ps. 30*). One group of psalms relates to the king of the line of David but it is uncertain whether those were composed during the reign of King David, or whether the psalmists had in mind some future idealized king through whom divine blessings would be channeled to the nation.

By the 2nd century, C. E., the psalms were an established element in the Christian liturgy, and in due course became part of the daily office in religious houses whose members, both monks and nuns, were required to know the Latin psalms by heart before Johannes Gutenberg's invention of printing. Ever since then, the psalms have been an essential ingredient of both Jewish and Christian worship and the continuous liturgical usage has been a main factor in their being collected and preserved.

Psalms are designed to be sung. There are many references in the psalms to musical instruments and even to methods of singing. As Christianity moved westward, the psalms were sung in the musical styles of Constantinople and Rome, the most common chant called Gregorian Chant, named after Pope Gregory I (590—604). Much later, such great composers as Bach and Mozart also rendered versions of the psalms. With the advent of the Protestant Reformation came a renewed emphasis on congregational singing of the psalms. That gave rise to the creation of many popular hymns, most of which were based on the Psalter. Isaac Watts (1674—1748) and Charles Wesley (1707—1788) were two of the most prolific hymn writers, and much of their work was based on or inspired by the psalms. Though not as productive, John Newton (1725—1807), an ex-slave-trader-turned minister and abolitionist, is well remembered for his lyrics of the immensely popular hymn "Amazing Grace."

II SELECTED READINGS

Psalm 19

FOR THE DIRECTOR OF MUSIC. A PSALM OF DAVID.

[1] The heavens declare the glory of God; and the firmament sheweth his handywork.

[2] Day unto day uttereth speech, and night unto night sheweth knowledge.

[3] There is no speech nor language, where their voice is not heard.

[4] Their line is gone out through all the earth, and their words to the end of the world. In them hath he set a tabernacle for the sun.

[5] Which is as a bridegroom coming out of his chamber, and rejoiceth as a strong man to run a race.

[6] His going forth is from the end of the heaven, and his circuit unto the ends of it: and there is nothing hid from the heat thereof.

[7] The law of the LORD is perfect, converting the soul: the testimony of the LORD is sure, making wise the simple.

[8] The statutes of the LORD are right, rejoicing the heart: the commandment of the LORD is pure, enlightening the eyes.

[9] The fear of the LORD is clean, enduring for ever: the judgments of the LORD are true and righteous altogether.

[10] More to be desired are they than gold, yea, than much fine gold: sweeter also than honey and the honeycomb.

[11] Moreover by them is thy servant warned: and in keeping of them there is great reward.

[12] Who can understand his errors? Cleanse thou me from secret faults.

[13] Keep back thy servant also from presumptuous sins; let them not have dominion over me: then shall I be upright, and I shall be innocent from the great transgression.

[14] Let the words of my mouth, and the meditation of my heart, be acceptable in thy sight, O LORD, my strength, and my redeemer.

The Bible as Literature: *rhetorical devices*

The variety of English translations competing for faithfulness, elegance as well as user-friendliness testifies to the difficulties and ambiguities of the Hebrew Bible. Fortunately, the original Hebrew of psalms used no rhyme or strict rhythm as traditional English poems do. Instead, the psalmists employed the structural device of *parallelism* and figures of speech such as metaphors and similes, which can be translated at comparative ease without distortion or loss of meanings. The main types of parallelism are *synonymous parallelism* (in which the second line repeats the content of the first in different images but similar grammatical form, e.g. *Ps. 19:1*); *antithetic parallelism* or *chiasm* (in which the second line states a contrast to the first, e.g. *Ps. 124:7*); *climactic parallelism* (in which the second line repeats part of the preceding line and then adds to it, e.g. *Ps. 19:2*).

Psalm 23
A PSALM OF DAVID.

Psalm 23, Raoul Vitale (1955—)

¹ The LORD is my shepherd; I shall not want.
² He maketh me to lie down in green pastures: he leadeth me beside the still waters.
³ He restoreth my soul: he leadeth me in the paths of righteousness for his name's sake.
⁴ Yea, though I walk through the valley of the shadow of death, I will fear no evil: for thou art with me; thy rod and thy staff they comfort me.
⁵ Thou preparest a table before me in the presence of mine enemies: thou anointest my head with oil; my cup runneth over.
⁶ Surely goodness and mercy shall follow me all the days of my life: and I will dwell in the house of the LORD for ever.

Psalm 27
OF DAVID.

¹ The LORD is my light and my salvation; whom shall I fear? The LORD is the strength of my life; of whom shall I be afraid?
² When the wicked, even mine enemies and my foes, came upon me to eat up my flesh①, they stumbled and fell.
³ Though an host should encamp against me, my heart shall not fear: though war should rise against me, in this will I be confident.
⁴ One thing have I desired of the LORD, that will I seek after; that I may dwell in the house of the LORD all the days of my life, to behold the beauty of the LORD, and to enquire in his temple.
⁵ For in the time of trouble he shall hide me in his pavilion: in the secret of his tabernacle shall he hide me; he shall set me up upon a rock.
⁶ And now shall mine head be lifted up above mine enemies round about me: therefore will I offer in his tabernacle sacrifices of joy; I will sing, yea, I will sing praises unto the LORD.
⁷ Hear, O LORD, when I cry with my voice: have mercy also upon me, and answer me.
⁸ When thou saidst, Seek ye my face; my heart said unto thee, Thy face, LORD, will I seek.
⁹ Hide not thy face far from me; put not thy servant away in anger: thou hast been my help; leave me not, neither forsake me, O God of my salvation.
¹⁰ When my father and my mother forsake me, then the LORD will take me up.
¹¹ Teach me thy way, O LORD, and lead me in a plain path, because of mine enemies.
¹² Deliver me not over unto the will of mine enemies: for false witnesses are risen up against me, and such as breathe out cruelty.
¹³ I had fainted, unless I had believed to see the goodness of the LORD in the land of the living.
¹⁴ Wait on the LORD: be of good courage, and he shall strengthen thine heart: wait, I say, on the LORD.

Psalm 137

¹ By the rivers of Babylon, there we sat down, yea, we wept, when we remembered Zion②.
² We hanged our harps upon the willows in the midst thereof.

---

① **to eat up my flesh** Or *to slander me.*
② **Zion** /ˈzaiən/, 锡安山 a Jebusite fortress on a mountain near Jerusalem which was conquered by King David, named as the City of David and is synonymous with Jerusalem.

³ *For there they that carried us away captive required of us a song; and they that wasted us required of us mirth, saying, " Sing us one of the songs of Zion."*

⁴ *How shall we sing the LORD's song in a strange land?*

⁵ *If I forget thee, O Jerusalem, let my right hand forget her cunning.*

⁶ *If I do not remember thee, let my tongue cleave to the roof of my mouth; if I prefer not Jerusalem above my chief joy.*

⁷ *Remember, O LORD, the children of Edom in the day of Jerusalem; who said, " Rase it, rase it, even to the foundation thereof."*

⁸ *O daughter of Babylon, who art to be destroyed; happy shall he be, that rewardeth thee as thou hast served us.*

⁹ *Happy shall he be, that taketh and dasheth thy little ones against the stones.*

III FOOD FOR THOUGHT

Psalm 19
1. Why is nature described?
2. How can you account for the use of different names for God in Verses 1—6 and Verses 7—12?

Psalm 23
1. What might this psalm remind a Jew and a Christian of?
2. Why do you think this psalm is often recited at funerals?

Psalm 27
1. What does the psalm recall about the psalmist David's life?
2. What is meant by trusting in God?

Psalm 137
1. What is the setting for this psalm?
2. How can you reconcile the curse on Babylonian babies (v. 9) and the Christian idea of forgiveness?

IV BIBLICAL RELEVANCE

A. Biblical Terms in Everyday English
1. out of the mouth of babes (8:2): _____

2. as the apple of the eye (17:8): _____
3. the valley of the shadow of death (23:4): _____
4. my cup runneth (23:5): _____
5. bite the dust (72:9): _____
6. A thousand years in thy sight are but as yesterday. (90:4): _____
_____
7. we spend our years as a tale that is told (90:9): _____
8. a lamp unto my feet (119:105): _____
9. gone astray like a lost sheep (119:176): _____
10. the wings of the morning (139:9): _____
11. put not your trust in princes (146:3): _____

B. Biblical References in Literature
1. The boy drew his chubby face down to a formidable length, and commenced toning a psalm tune through his nose, with imperturbable gravity.
(Harriet Beecher Stowe, *Uncle Tom's Cabin*, 1852)
2. As the psalms of David exceed all other language, so does the psalmody that has been fitted to them by the divines and sages of the land, surpass all vain poetry.
(James Fenimore Cooper, *The Last of the Mohicans*, 1757)

C. The Bible and Arts
1. *By the Rivers of Babylon*, Evelyn de Morgan (1855—1919)
2. *Psalms*, Moshe Tzvi Berger (1929—   ) (http://www.museumofpsalms.com)
3. Psalms set music: http://en.wikipedia.org/wiki/Psalms

V SOURCES FOR REFERENCE

1. Yancey, P. & T. Stafford (notes by) (1989). *The New Student Bible*, New International Version. Grand Rapids, Mich: Zondervan Publishing House.
2. Ryken, L. & P. G. Ryken. (2007). *The Literary Study Bible*. Wheaton, Illinois: Crossway Bibles.

PART FIVE

THE KINGDOM OF SOLOMON
(C. 962—922 B.C.E.)
THE BOOKS OF 1 KINGS, PROVERBS, SONG
OF SONGS, ECCLESIASTES

18. SOLOMON

I POINTS OF DEPARTURE

1 and 2 Kings record the 400-odd-year history of the people of Israel from the death of King David to the start of the Babylonian captivity when the southern kingdom of Judah was destroyed and the Jews were taken to Babylon by Nebuchadnezzar II (*See* Appendices 2: A Chronology of Biblical Times). 1 Kings divides almost neatly in half, with the first half (Chs. 1—11) reporting mostly good tidings of Israel's Golden Age, when King Solomon ruled a nation of peace and prosperity. Chapter 12 marks the beginning of a civil war which ripped Israel apart into two nations: the northern kingdom of Israel (931 B.C.E. —722 B.C.E.) with its capital in Samaria and the southern kingdom of Judah (931 B.C.E. — 586 B.C.E.) with its capital in Jerusalem. The remainder of 1 and 2 Kings gives a snapshot of the reigns of 38 kings and one queen of the two divided kingdoms. In spite of the resultant confusion a reader might face, the rule is that the kings in the north were all unfaithful to God while almost half of those in the south remained faithful to God. But generally, the kings of Israel and Judah were cruel, foolish, weak, and sinful, who exploited and abused the people from within and left themselves vulnerable to attacks from without. Eventually, Israel was conquered by the Assyrian Empire but Judah held out for another 135 years before it too was destroyed by the Neo-Babylonian Empire.

In spite of its tragic end, Israel did have its good old days when Solomon was the king. Born with a silver spoon and endowed generously by God, he was the wisest, richest, and the most successful person of his time. In an incredible dream sequence, the precocious young Solomon chose wisdom, which was granted by God, together with bonus gifts of wealth, honor and peace. His wisdom was so well recognized that attributed to him are such different kinds of wisdom literature as the Book of Proverbs, the Book of Ecclesiastes, and the Song of Songs (also known as the Song of Solomon). The so-called "Solomonic wisdom" is shown at its best in the famous court ruling concerning the dispute over a baby between two prostitutes. Solomon is equally famous for his wealth gleaned from his maritime expeditions, showcased in the temple of God, his most outstanding accomplishment, and more so in his own palace. The stories of his wealth and magnificence went abroad, attracting curious dignitaries far and wide and the Queen of Sheba may have been the most illustrious of the visitors to Solomon's court at Jerusalem. The queen's visit may have been for commercial purposes as much as for the pleasure of seeing Solomon's splendor and listening to his wisdom. Because of the location of Sheba in sub-Saharan Africa and the association of the queen with the "black and beautiful" beloved of the Song of Songs celebrating erotic passion, a romantic liaison is often hinted at (Schippe & Stetson, 2005: 103).

With his God-given gift of wisdom and his devotion to the building of the temple, Solomon would just be the ruler to inaugurate a long reign of peace, unity and prosperity for Israel. But the fact of the matter was, soon after his death, his kingdom disintegrated into dynastic chaos culminating in the secession of 10 northern tribes. What went wrong was Solomon's polygamy

(700 wives and 300 concubines!) necessitated by political alliances, and its inevitable consequence of apostasy. Both are insurrections against the laws of God. Perhaps it was Solomon's penchant for excess that doomed the fate of his kingdom. Just as Jesus Christ (*Mt. 6:29*) judged Solomon who was bent on striving for glory by pointing to a wild lily in the field, *[E]ven Solomon in all his glory was not arrayed like one of these.*

II SELECTED READINGS

1 Kings 3

¹ And Solomon made affinity with Pharaoh king of Egypt, and took Pharaoh's daughter, and brought her into the city of David, until he had made an end of building his own house, and the house of the LORD, and the wall of Jerusalem round about. ² Only the people sacrificed in high places, because there was no house built unto the name of the LORD, until those days. ³ And Solomon loved the LORD, walking in the statutes of David his father: only he sacrificed and burnt incense in high places.

Solomon Asks for Wisdom

⁴ And the king went to Gibeon to sacrifice there; for that was the great high place: a thousand burnt offerings did Solomon offer upon that altar. ⁵ In Gibeon the LORD appeared to Solomon in a dream by night: and God said, "Ask what I shall give thee."

⁶ And Solomon said, "Thou hast shewed unto thy servant David my father great mercy, according as he walked before thee in truth, and in righteousness, and in uprightness of heart with thee; and thou hast kept for him this great kindness, that thou hast given him a son to sit on his throne, as it is this day."

Dream of Solomon, c. 1693, Luca Giordano

⁷ "And now, O LORD my God, thou hast made thy servant king instead of David my father: and I am but a little child: I know not how to go out or come in. ⁸ And thy servant is in the midst of thy people which thou hast chosen, a great people, that cannot be numbered nor counted for multitude. ⁹ Give therefore thy servant an understanding heart to judge thy people, that I may discern between good and bad: for who is able to judge this thy so great a people?"

¹⁰ And the speech pleased the LORD, that Solomon had asked this thing. ¹¹ And God said unto him, "Because thou hast asked this thing, and hast not asked for thyself long life; neither hast asked riches for thyself, nor hast asked the life of thine enemies; but hast asked for thyself understanding to discern judgment; ¹² Behold, I have done according to thy words: lo, I have given thee a wise and an understanding heart; so that there was none like thee before thee, neither after thee shall any arise like unto thee. ¹³ And I have also given thee that which thou hast not asked, both riches, and honour: so that there shall not be any among the kings like unto thee all thy days. ¹⁴ And if thou wilt walk in my ways, to keep my statutes and my commandments, as thy father David did walk, then I will lengthen thy days." ¹⁵ And Solomon awoke; and, behold, it was a dream.

And he came to Jerusalem, and stood before the ark of the covenant of the LORD, and offered up burnt offerings, and offered peace offerings, and made a feast to all his servants.

A Wise Ruling

Judgment of Solomon, c. 1620, the Workshop of Peter Paul Rubens

¹⁶ Then came there two women, that were harlots, unto the king, and stood before him. ¹⁷ And the one woman said, "O my lord, I and this woman dwell in one house; and I was delivered of a child with her in the house. ¹⁸ And it came to pass the third day after that I was delivered, that this woman was delivered also: and we were together; there was no stranger with us in the house, save we two in the house."

¹⁹ "And this woman's child died in the night; because she overlaid it. ²⁰ And she arose at midnight, and took my son from beside me, while thine handmaid slept, and laid it in her bosom, and laid her dead child in my bosom. ²¹ And when I rose in the morning to give my child suck, behold, it was dead: but when I had considered it in the morning, behold, it was not my son, which I did bear."

²² And the other woman said, "Nay; but the living is my son, and the dead is thy son."

And this said, "No; but the dead is thy son, and the living is my son."

²³ Thus they spake before the king. Then said the king, "The one saith, 'This is my son that liveth, and thy son is the dead,' and the other saith, 'Nay; but thy son is the dead, and my son is the living.'"

²⁴ And the king said, "Bring me a sword." And they brought a sword before the king. ²⁵ And the king said, "Divide the living child in two, and give half to the one, and half to the other."

²⁶ Then spake the woman whose the living child was unto the king, for her bowels yearned upon her son, and she said, "O my lord, give her the living child, and in no wise slay it."

But the other said, "Let it be neither mine nor thine, but divide it."

²⁷ Then the king answered and said, "Give her the living child, and in no wise slay it: she is the mother thereof."

²⁸ And all Israel heard of the judgment which the king had judged; and they feared the king: for they saw that the wisdom of God was in him, to do judgment.

Solomon in All His Glory

1 Kings 4
...
Solomon's Daily Provisions

²⁰ Judah and Israel were many, as the sand which is by the sea in multitude, eating and drinking, and making merry. ²¹ And Solomon reigned over all kingdoms from the river unto the land of the Philistines, and unto the border of Egypt: they brought presents, and served Solomon all the days of his life.

²² And Solomon's provision for one day was thirty measures of fine flour, and threescore measures of meal. ²³ Ten fat oxen, and twenty oxen out of the pastures, and an hundred sheep, beside harts, and roebucks, and fallowdeer, and fatted fowl. ²⁴ For he had dominion over all the region on this side the river, from Tiphsah even to Azzah, over all the kings on this side the river: and he had peace on all sides round about him. ²⁵ And Judah and Israel dwelt safely, every man under his vine and under his fig tree, from Dan even to Beersheba, all the days of Solomon.

²⁶ And Solomon had forty thousand stalls of horses for his chariots, and twelve thousand horsemen.

²⁷ And those officers provided victual for king Solomon, and for all that came unto king Solomon's table, every man in his month: they lacked nothing. ²⁸ Barley also and straw for the horses and dromedaries brought they unto the place where the officers were, every man according to his charge.

Solomon's Wisdom

²⁹ And God gave Solomon wisdom and understanding exceeding much, and largeness of heart, even as the sand that is on the sea shore. ³⁰ And Solomon's wisdom excelled the wisdom of all the children of the east country, and all the wisdom of Egypt. ³¹ For he was wiser than all men; than Ethan the Ezrahite, and Heman, and Chalcol, and Darda, the sons of Mahol: and his fame was in all nations round about. ³² And he spake three thousand proverbs: and his songs were a thousand and five. ³³ And he spake of trees, from the cedar tree that is in Lebanon even unto the hyssop that springeth out of the wall: he spake also of beasts, and of fowl, and of creeping things, and of fishes. ³⁴ And there came of all people to hear the wisdom of Solomon, from all kings of the earth, which had heard of his wisdom.

The Temple of Solomon

1 Kings 5

...

⁷ And it came to pass, when Hiram heard the words of Solomon, that he rejoiced greatly, and said, "Blessed be the LORD this day, which hath given unto David a wise son over this great people."

⁸ And Hiram sent to Solomon, saying,

"I have considered the things which thou sentest to me for: and I will do all thy desire concerning timber of cedar, and concerning timber of fir. ⁹ My servants shall bring them down from Lebanon unto the sea: and I will convey them by sea in floats unto the place that thou shalt appoint me, and will cause them to be discharged there, and thou shalt receive them: and thou shalt accomplish my desire, in giving food for my household."

¹⁰ So Hiram gave Solomon cedar trees and fir trees according to all his desire. ¹¹ And Solomon gave Hiram twenty thousand measures of wheat for food to his household, and twenty measures of pure oil: thus gave Solomon to Hiram year by year. ¹² And the LORD gave Solomon wisdom, as he promised him: and there was peace between Hiram and Solomon; and they two made a league together.

¹³ And king Solomon raised a levy out of all Israel; and the levy was thirty thousand men. ¹⁴ And he sent them to Lebanon, ten thousand a month by courses: a month they were in Lebanon, and two months at home: and Adoniram was over the levy. ¹⁵ And Solomon had threescore and ten thousand that bare burdens, and fourscore thousand hewers in the mountains; ¹⁶ Beside the chief of Solomon's officers which were over the work, three thousand and three hundred, which ruled over the people that wrought in the work. ¹⁷ And the king commanded, and they brought great stones, costly stones, and hewed stones, to lay the foundation of the house. ¹⁸ And Solomon's builders and Hiram's builders did hew them, and the stonesquarers: so they prepared timber and stones to build the house.

Solomon Builds the Temple

1 Kings 6

...

⁷ And the house, when it was in building, was built of stone made ready before it was brought thither: so that there was neither hammer nor axe nor any tool of iron heard in the house, while it was in building.

⁸ The door for the middle chamber was in the right side of the house: and they went up with winding stairs into the middle chamber, and out of the middle into the third. ⁹ So he built the house, and finished it; and covered the house with beams and boards of cedar. ¹⁰ And then he built chambers against all the house, five cubits high: and they rested on the house with timber of cedar.

¹¹ And the word of the LORD came to Solomon, saying, ¹² "Concerning this house which thou art in building, if thou wilt walk in my statutes, and execute my judgments, and keep all my commandments to walk

in them; then will I perform my word with thee, which I spake unto David thy father: ¹³ And I will dwell among the children of Israel, and will not forsake my people Israel."

The Temple of Solomon, 1625—1630, Matthaeus Merian, the Elder

¹⁴ So Solomon built the house, and finished it. ¹⁵ And he built the walls of the house within with boards of cedar, both the floor of the house, and the walls of the ceiling: and he covered them on the inside with wood, and covered the floor of the house with planks of fir. ¹⁶ And he built twenty cubits on the sides of the house, both the floor and the walls with boards of cedar: he even built them for it within, even for the oracle, even for the most holy place. ¹⁷ And the house, that is, the temple before it, was forty cubits long. ¹⁸ And the cedar of the house within was carved with knops and open flowers: all was cedar; there was no stone seen.

¹⁹ And the oracle he prepared in the house within, to set there the ark of the covenant of the LORD. ²⁰ And the oracle in the forepart was twenty cubits in length, and twenty cubits in breadth, and twenty cubits in the height thereof: and he overlaid it with pure gold; and so covered the altar which was of cedar. ²¹ So Solomon overlaid the house within with pure gold: and he made a partition by the chains of gold before the oracle; and he overlaid it with gold. ²² And the whole house he overlaid with gold, until he had finished all the house: also the whole altar that was by the oracle he overlaid with gold.

Cultural Connections: *Solomon's Temple*

Solomon's Temple as described in the Bible has had a firm hold on Western imagination and inspired the designers of Gothic cathedrals and Renaissance basilicas. Bernini's canopy over the altar in Saint Peter's (right) in Vatican was inspired by the image of the great pillars of the temple. This image together with that of others associated with the profession of Masons and builders were later incorporated into the philosophy and practice of the Freemasons. (left)

²³ And within the oracle he made two cherubims of olive tree, each ten cubits high. ²⁴ And five cubits was the one wing of the cherub, and five cubits the other wing of the cherub: from the uttermost part of the one wing unto the uttermost part of the other were ten cubits. ²⁵ And the other cherub was ten cubits: both the cherubims were of one measure and one size. ²⁶ The height of the one cherub was ten cubits, and so was it of the other cherub. ²⁷ And he set the cherubims within the inner house: and they stretched forth the wings of the cherubims, so that the wing of the one touched the one wall, and the wing of the other cherub touched the other wall; and their wings touched one another in the midst of the house. ²⁸ And he overlaid the cherubims with gold.

²⁹ And he carved all the walls of the house round about with carved figures of cherubims and palm trees and open flowers, within and without.

...

³⁷ In the fourth year was the foundation of the house of the LORD laid, in the month Zif. ³⁸ And in the eleventh year, in the month Bul, which is the eighth month, was the house finished throughout all the parts

thereof, and according to all the fashion of it. So was he seven years in building it.

Solomon Builds His Palace

1 Kings 7

...

^{13} *And king Solomon sent and fetched Hiram out of Tyre.* ^{14} *He was a widow's son of the tribe of Naphtali, and his father was a man of Tyre, a worker in brass: and he was filled with wisdom, and understanding, and cunning to work all works in brass. And he came to king Solomon, and wrought all his work.*

^{15} *For he cast two pillars of brass, of eighteen cubits high apiece: and a line of twelve cubits did compass either of them about.* ^{16} *And he made two chapiters of molten brass, to set upon the tops of the pillars; the height of the one chapiter was five cubits, and the height of the other chapiter was five cubits.* ^{17} *And nets of checker work, and wreaths of chain work, for the chapiters which were upon the top of the pillars; seven for the one chapiter, and seven for the other chapiter.* ^{18} *And he made the pillars, and two rows round about upon the one network, to cover the chapiters that were upon the top, with pomegranates: and so did he for the other chapiter.* ^{19} *And the chapiters that were upon the top of the pillars were of lily work in the porch, four cubits.* ^{20} *And the chapiters upon the two pillars had pomegranates also above, over against the belly which was by the network: and the pomegranates were two hundred in rows round about upon the other chapiter.* ^{21} *And he set up the pillars in the porch of the temple: and he set up the right pillar, and called the name thereof Jachin: and he set up the left pillar, and he called the name thereof Boaz.* ^{22} *And upon the top of the pillars was lily work: so was the work of the pillars finished.*

...

^{48} *And Solomon made all the vessels that pertained unto the house of the LORD:*
the altar of gold,
and the table of gold,
whereupon the shewbread was.
^{49} *And the candlesticks of pure gold,*
five on the right side, and five on the left,
before the oracle, with flowers, and the lamps, and the tongs of gold.
^{50} *And the bowls, and the snuffers,*
and the bassoons, and the spoons,
and the corners of pure gold;
and the hinges of gold, both for the doors of the inner house,
the most holy place, and for the doors of he house, to wit, of the temple.
^{51} *So was ended all the work that king Solomon made for the house of the LORD. And Solomon brought in the things which David his father had dedicated, even the silver, and the gold, and the vessels, did he put among the treasures of the house of the LORD.*

The Visit of the Queen of Sheba

1 Kings 10

^{1} *And when the queen of Sheba*① *heard of the fame of Solomon concerning the name of the LORD, she came to prove him with hard questions.* ^{2} *And she came to Jerusalem with a very great train, with camels that bare spices, and very much gold, and precious stones: and when she was come to Solomon, she communed with*

---

① **Sheba** (/'ʃiːbə/, 示巴) an ancient country of southern Arabia, whose people colonized Ethiopia in the tenth century B. C. E. and were known for their wealth and commercial prosperity.

him of all that was in her heart. ³ And Solomon told her all her questions: there was not any thing hid from the king, which he told her not. ⁴ And when the queen of Sheba had seen all Solomon's wisdom, and the house that he had built, ⁵ And the meat of his table, and the sitting of his servants, and the attendance of his ministers, and their apparel, and his cupbearers, and his ascent by which he went up unto the house of the LORD; there was no more spirit in her②.

Solomon and the Queen of Sheba, 1550—1570, Lambert Sustris

⁶ And she said to the king, "It was a true report that I heard in mine own land of thy acts and of thy wisdom. ⁷ Howbeit I believed not the words, until I came, and mine eyes had seen it: and, behold, the half was not told me: thy wisdom and prosperity exceedeth the fame which I heard. ⁸ Happy are thy men, happy are these thy servants, which stand continually before thee, and that hear thy wisdom. ⁹ Blessed be the LORD thy God, which delighted in thee, to set thee on the throne of Israel: because the LORD loved Israel for ever, therefore made he thee king, to do judgment and justice."

¹⁰ And she gave the king an hundred and twenty talents of gold, and of spices very great store, and precious stones: there came no more such abundance of spices as these which the queen of Sheba gave to king Solomon

¹¹ And the navy also of Hiram, that brought gold from Ophir, brought in from Ophir great plenty of almug trees, and precious stones. ¹² And the king made of the almug trees pillars for the house of the LORD, and for the king's house, harps also and psalteries for singers.

¹³ And king Solomon gave unto the queen of Sheba all her desire, whatsoever she asked, beside that which Solomon gave her of his royal bounty. So she turned and went to her own country, she and her servants.

...

Solomon's Sin

1 Kings 11

The Idolatry of Solomon, 1622, Frans Francken II

¹ But king Solomon loved many strange women, together with the daughter of Pharaoh, women of the Moabites, Ammonites, Edomites, Zidonians, and Hittites. ² Of the nations concerning which the LORD said unto the children of Israel, "Ye shall not go in to them, neither shall they come in unto you: for surely they will turn away your heart after their gods." Solomon clave unto these in love. ³ And he had seven hundred wives, princesses, and three hundred concubines: and his wives turned away his heart. ⁴ For it came to pass, when Solomon was old, that his wives turned away his heart after other gods: and his heart was not perfect with the LORD his

---

② **there was no more spirit in her** she was overwhelmed.

God, as was the heart of David his father. ⁵ For Solomon went after Ashtoreth the goddess of the Zidonians, and after Milcom the abomination of the Ammonites. ⁶ And Solomon did evil in the sight of the LORD, and went not fully after the LORD, as did David his father.

⁷ Then did Solomon build an high place for Chemosh, the abomination of Moab, in the hill that is before Jerusalem, and for Molech, the abomination of the children of Ammon. ⁸ And likewise did he for all his strange wives, which burnt incense and sacrificed unto their gods. ⁹ And the LORD was angry with Solomon, because his heart was turned from the LORD God of Israel, which had appeared unto him twice. ¹⁰ And had commanded him concerning this thing, that he should not go after other gods: but he kept not that which the LORD commanded. ¹¹ Wherefore the LORD said unto Solomon, " Forasmuch as this is done of thee, and thou hast not kept my covenant and my statutes, which I have commanded thee, I will surely rend the kingdom from thee, and will give it to thy servant. ¹² Notwithstanding in thy days I will not do it for David thy father's sake: but I will rend it out of the hand of thy son. ¹³ Howbeit I will not rend away all the kingdom; but will give one tribe to thy son for David my servant's sake, and for Jerusalem's sake which I have chosen."

...

⁴¹ And the rest of the acts of Solomon, and all that he did, and his wisdom, are they not written in the book of the acts of Solomon? ⁴² And the time that Solomon reigned in Jerusalem over all Israel was forty years. ⁴³ And Solomon slept with his fathers, and was buried in the city of David his father: and Rehoboam his son reigned in his stead.

III FOOD FOR THOUGHT

1. What situation brought the two women into the court of Solomon?
2. What do you think was the writer's purpose in *1 Kings 4: 29—34*?
3. What's so important about the Temple of Solomon?
4. Why did the Queen of Sheba make her famous visit to Solomon?
5. What was King Solomon's sin?

IV BIBLICAL RELEVANCE

A. Biblical Terms in Everyday English
1. as wise as Solomon: _____
2. no Solomon: _____
3. Solomonic: _____
4. Queen of Sheba: _____

B. Biblical References in Literature
It was beginning to dawn on me that I am the member of public to whom the public interest requirement refers. In effect, the police are saying, "You were there. Was it bad? Do you think that person deserves to be punished? But this requires the judgment of Solomon."

(*The Independent*, 1995)

C. The Bible and Arts
1. *David's Dying Charge to Solomon*, 1643, Ferdinand Bol
2. *Dream of Solomon*, c. 1693, Luca Giordano
3. The Judgment of Solomon

Judgment of Solomon, c. 1620, the Workshop of Peter Paul Rubens
   The Judgment of Solomon, 1649, Nicolas Poussin
   The Judgment of Solomon, 1726—1729, Giovanni Battista Tiepolo
4. The Visit of Queen of Sheba
   Seaport with the Embarkation of the Queen of Sheba, 1648, Lorrain Claude
   Solomon and the Queen of Sheba, 1550—1570, Lambert Sustris
5. *The Temple of Solomon*, 1625—1630, Matthaeus Merian, the Elder
6. *The Idolatry of Solomon*, 1622, Frans Francken II

V SOURCES FOR REFERENCE

1. Yancey, P. & T. Stafford (notes by) (1989). *The New Student Bible*, New International Version. Grand Rapids, Mich: Zondervan Publishing House.
2. Schippe, C. & C. Stetson. (2005). *The Bible and Its Influence*. Front Royal, VA: BLP Publishing.

19. PROVERBS

I POINTS OF DEPARTURE

The First Book of Kings notes that Solomon's wisdom excelled all the wisdom of Egypt and credits him with the composition of 3,000 proverbs (*1 Kgs. 4:30, 32*). In Hebrew, the word for *proverb* is *mashal*, meaning "to rule" or "to govern." The Book of Proverbs then is not just a collection of pithy sayings but rules or moral advice that dictate how life should be lived for the enjoyment of it. Contrary to the convenient biblical ascription, it is the result of a long process of continuous and cumulative growth, the deposit of Israel's wisdom literature.

Much of the Book of Proverbs is in Hebrew poetic form of *parallelism*, which describes the tendency of Hebrew poetry to repeat a thought in a slightly different way (Yancey & Stafford, 1989: 669). For example, *Proverbs 10: 10* uses synonymous parallelism, "He who winks maliciously causes grief, and a chattering fool comes to ruin." (New International Version, NIV) The second half of this proverb underscores and embellishes the message of the first half. However, most of the proverbs in Chapter 10 employ *antithetical* parallelism, which contrasts one thought with its opposite, as in "He becometh poor that dealeth with a slack hand; but the hand of the diligent maketh rich." (*Prov. 10:4*) The parable, or didactic story, also appears in the Book of Proverbs, as in the famous admonition addressed to the "sluggard" — the biblical embodiment of foolishness (*Prov. 6: 6—8*)[①].

Although the Book of Proverbs is a compendium of individual sayings and axioms, the central thesis is that all wisdom issues from respecting God. "The fear of the Lord is the beginning of knowledge," says *Proverbs 1: 7*. Here "the fear of the Lord" does not mean cowering in fright before God, but having respect for God's wisdom, justice, and love. The Book of Proverbs offers what many people would agree is a model of commonsense morality. The basic values underlying *Proverbs* reflect a common thread running throughout Western culture. In its simplest terms, the Book of Proverbs contrasts right and wrong, good and evil. It praises certain character traits and condemns others. The biblical response to the perennial human questions of what is right and what is wrong influenced the medieval notion of *cardinal virtues* (prudence, justice, temperance and fortitude) and *deadly sins* (pride, envy, anger, lust, sloth, avarice and gluttony) (Schippe & Stetson, 2005: 146—147). The influence of the tradition of wisdom literature can also be felt in Benjamin Franklin in his *Poor Richard's Almanac* (1732—1757), to which the English-speaking world is indebted for such familiar witticisms as:

Haste makes waste.
God helps them who help themselves.
Fish and visitors stink in three days.
Early to bed and early to rise, makes a man healthy, wealthy, and wise.

---

① Go to the ant, thou sluggard; consider her ways, and be wise: Which having no guide, overseer, or ruler, provideth her meat in the summer, and gathereth her food in the harvest.

Don't throw stones at your neighbors, if your own windows are made of glass.

From left to right:
Prudence, Piero del Pollaiolo (c. 1443—1496)
Justice, Paolo Veronese (1528—1588)
Fortitude, Sandro Botticelli (1445—1510)
Temperance, Sir Edward Burne-Jones (1833—1898)

II SELECTED READINGS

Prologue: Purpose and Theme

Chapter 1

¹ The proverbs of Solomon, the son of David, king of Israel;
² To know wisdom and instruction; to perceive the words of understanding;
³ To receive the instruction of wisdom, justice, and judgment, and equity;
⁴ To give subtilty to the simple, to the young man knowledge and discretion.
⁵ A wise man will hear, and will increase learning; and a man of understanding shall attain unto wise counsels:
⁶ To understand a proverb, and the interpretation; the words of the wise, and their dark sayings.
⁷ The fear of the LORD is the beginning of knowledge: but fools despise wisdom and instruction.

Moral Benefits of Wisdom

Proverbs 2

¹⁰ When wisdom entereth into thine heart, and knowledge is pleasant unto thy soul;
¹¹ Discretion shall preserve thee, understanding shall keep thee.

Further Benefits of Wisdom

Proverbs 3

¹³ Happy is the man that findeth wisdom, and the man that getteth understanding.
²⁷ Withhold not good from them to whom it is due, when it is in the power of thine hand to do it.
³⁴ The wise shall inherit glory: but shame shall be the promotion of fools.

Warning Against Adultery

Proverbs 5

³ For the lips of a strange woman drops as an honeycomb, and her mouth is smoother than oil:
⁴ But her end is bitter as wormwood, sharp as a two-edged sword.
¹⁵ Drink waters out of thine own cistern, and running waters out of thine own well.
¹⁸ Let thy fountain be blessed: and rejoice with the wife of thy youth.

Warnings Against Folly

Proverbs 6

²⁷ Can a man take fire in his bosom, and his clothes not be burned?
²⁸ Can one go upon hot coals, and his feet not be burned?

Warning Against the Adulteress

Proverbs 7

² Keep my commandments, and live; and my law as the apple of thine heart.
²² He goeth after her straightway, as an ox goeth to the slaughter, or as a fool to the correction of the stocks.
²³ Till a dart strike through his liver; as a bird hasteth to the snare, and knoweth not that it is for his life.

Invitations of Wisdom and Folly[2]

Proverbs 9

⁸ Reprove not a scorner, lest he hate thee: rebuke a wise man, and he will love thee.
¹³ A foolish woman is clamourous: she is simple, and knoweth nothing. ¹⁷ Stolen waters are sweet, and bread eaten in secret is pleasant.

Proverbs of Solomon

Proverbs 10

¹ A wise son maketh a glad father: but a floolish son is the heaviness of his mother.
⁴ He becometh poor that dealeth with a slack hand: but the hand of the diligent maketh rich.
⁵ He that gathereth in summer is a wise son: but he that sleepeth in harvest is a son that causeth shame.
¹² Hatred stirreth up strifes: but love covereth all sins.
¹⁴ Wise men lay up knowledge: but the mouth of the foolish is near destruction.
¹⁵ The rich man's wealth is his strong city: the destruction of the poor is their poverty.
²⁶ As vinegar to the teeth, and as smoke to the eyes, so is the sluggard to them that send them.

Proverbs 11

¹⁶ A gracious woman retaineth honour: and strong men retain riches.
²² As a jewel of gold in a swine's snout, so is a fair woman which is without discretion.
²⁴ There is that scattereth, and yet increaseth; and there is that withholdeth more than is meet, but it tendeth to poverty.

---

[2] More proverbs on God's relationship to wisdom: 1:7; 2: 5—9; 8: 22—31; 9:10; 22:17—19.

Proverbs 12

⁴ A virtuous woman is a crown to her husband: but she that maketh ashamed is as rottenness in his bones.

¹¹ He that tilleth his land shall be satisfied with bread: but he that followeth vain persons is void of understanding.

¹⁶ A fool's wrath is presently known: but a prudent man covereth shame.

¹⁸ There is that speaketh like the piercings of a sword: but the tongue of the wise is health.③

²⁵ Heaviness in the heart of man maketh it stoop: but a good word maketh it glad.

Proverbs 13

³ He that keepeth his mouth keepeth his life: but he that openeth wide his lips shall have destruction.

¹¹ Wealth gotten by vanity shall be diminished: but he that gathereth by labour shall increase.

²⁰ He that walketh with wise men shall be wise: but a companion of fools shall be destroyed.④

²⁴ He that spareth his rod hateth his son: but he that loveth him chasteneth him bedtimes.

Proverbs 14

¹⁰ The heart knoweth his own bitterness; and a stranger doth not intermeddle with is joy.

¹² There is a way which seemeth right unto a man, but the end thereof are the ways of death.⑤

¹³ Even in laughter the heart is sorrowful; and the end of that mirth is heaviness.

¹⁸ The simple inherit folly: but the prudent are crowned with knowledge.

²⁰ The poor is hated even of his own neighbour: but the rich hath many friends.

²⁹ He that is slow to wrath is of great understanding: but he that is hasty of spirit exalted folly.

³⁰ A sound heart is the life of the flesh: but envy the rottenness of the bones.

Proverbs 15

¹ A soft answer turneth away wrath: but grievous words stir up anger.

¹³ A merry heart maketh a cheerful countenance: but by sorrow of the heart the spirit is broken.

¹⁵ All the days of the afflicted are evil: but he that is of a merry heart hath a continual feast.

¹⁷ Better is a dinner of herbs where love is, than a stalled ox and hatred therewith.

²⁰ A wise son maketh a glad father: but a foolish man despiseth his mother.

Proverbs 16

⁸ Better is a little with righteousness than great revenues without right.

¹⁸ Pride goeth before destruction, and an haughty spirit before a fall.

²³ The heart of the wise teacheth his mouth, and addeth learning to his lips.

²⁴ Pleasant words are as an honeycomb, sweet to the soul, and healeth to the bones.

³² He that is slow to anger is better than the mighty; and he that ruleth his spirit than he that taketh a city.

³³ The lot is cast into the lap; but the whole disposing thereof is of the LORD.

---

③ More proverbs on the importance of words: 10:11, 20; 12:14; 15:4; 17:10; 18:21; 25:11. More proverbs on the wrong way to speak: 6:16—19; 11:9, 12—13; 12:18; 13:3; 16:27—28; 18:8, 13; 26:23—28; 29:5. More proverbs on the right way to speak: 10:14, 21, 32; 12:25; 15:1—2, 23, 28; 16:13, 23—24; 17:27—28; 25:12, 15; 27:5—6; 28:23. More proverbs on the dangers of words: 10:19; 14:23.

④ More proverbs on becoming a wise person: 2: 1—6; 9: 1—10; 10:1, 5, 8, 14, 19, 23; 11:2; 12:18; 13:10; 20; 14:8; 15: 7, 31; 16:23; 17:24; 18:15; 19:11, 20; 20:1; 21:11, 20, 30; 23:4; 29:3, 8, 11, 15; 30:5—6.

⑤ More proverbs on "real living" : 3:18, 21—22; 4:23; 8:34—36; 10:11, 16; 12:28; 13:12; 14:27, 30; 15:4, 27; 18:21; 19:23; 21:21; 28:16. More proverbs on "real dying" : 2:16—18; 5:3—6; , 22—23; 10:21; 14:12, 32; 15:10; 19: 16; 21:25; 27:20.

Proverbs 17

¹ Better is a dry morsel, and quietness therewith, than an house full of sacrifices with strife.
⁶ Children's children are the crown of old men; and the glory of children are their fathers.
⁷ Excellent speech becometh not a fool; less do lying lips a prince.
⁸ A gift is as a precious stone in the eyes of him that hath it: whithersoever it turneth, it prospereth.
¹³ Whoso rewardeth evil for good, evil shall not depart from his house.
²² A merry heart doeth good like a medicine: but a broken spirit drieth the bones.
²⁵ A foolish son is a grief to his father, and bitterness to her that bare him.

Proverbs 19

¹ Better is the poor that walketh in his integrity, than he that is perverse in his lips, and is a fool.
⁴ Wealth maketh many friends; but the poor is separated from his neighbour.
¹² The king's wrath is as the roaring of a lion; but his favour is as dew upon the grass.
¹³ A foolish son is the calamity of his father: and the contentions of a wife are a continual dropping.
¹⁷ He that hath pity upon the poor lendeth unto the LORD; and that which he hath given will he pay him again.⑥

Proverbs 20

¹⁷ Bread of deceit is sweet to a man, but afterwards his mouth shall be filled with gravel.
²⁹ The glory if young men is their strength: and the beauty of old men is the gray head.

Proverbs 21

⁹ It is better to dwell in a corner of the housetop, than with a brawling woman in a wide house.⑦
¹⁹ It is better to dwell in the wilderness, than with a contentious and an angry woman.
²³ Whoso keepeth his mouth and his tongue keepeth his soul from troubles.

Proverbs 22

⁶ Train up a child in the way he should go: and when he is old, he will not depart from it.⑧
¹⁵ Foolishness is bound in the heart of a child; but the rod of correction shall drive it far from him.
²⁹ Seest thou a man diligent in his business? He shall stand before kings; he shall not stand before mean men.

Proverbs 23

³¹ Look not thou upon the wine when it is red, when it giveth his colour in the cup, when it moveth itself aright.
³² At the last it biteth like a serpent, and stingeth like an adder.

Proverbs 24

³³ Yet a little sleep, a little slumber, a little folding of the hands to sleep.⑨

---

⑥ More proverbs on money: 10:4,15,22; 11:4,16,28; 13:8,18,22—23; 14:20,23,31; 15:16; 18:23; 19:1,4,17; 22:1—2,4,7,9,16,22—23; 23:5; 28:3,6,8,11,19,20,22,27; 29:7,14; 30:7—9.

⑦ More on sexual sin: 2:16—19; 5:1—23; 6:20—35; 7:6—27; 23:26—28. More proverbs on marriage: 5:15—19; 12:4; 14:1; 18:22; 19:13—14; 21:9,19; 27:15—16; 31:10—31.

⑧ More proverbs on parent-child relationships: 3:11—12; 10:1,5; 13:1,24; 14:26; 15:20; 17:6,21; 19:18,26—27; 20:20; 22:6,15; 23:13—16,22—25; 27:11; 29:15,17; 31:28.

⑨ More proverbs on laziness: 6:6—11; 10:4,26; 12:24,27; 13:4; 15:19; 19:15,24; 20:4; 21:25; 22:13; 24:30—34; 26:13—16.

Proverbs 25

³ The heaven for height, and the earth for depth, and the heart of kings is unsearchable.

¹¹ A word fitly spoken is like apples of gold in pictures of silver.

¹⁷ Withdraw thy foot from thy neighbour's house; lest he be weary of thee, and so hate thee.

¹⁹ Confidence in an unfaithful man in time of trouble is like a broken tooth, and a foot out of joint.

²⁴ It is better to dwell in the corner of the housetop, than with a brawling woman and in a wide house.

²⁵ As cold waters to a thirsty soul, so is good news from a far country.

Proverbs 26

¹ As snow in summer, and as rain in harvest, so honour is not seemly for a fool.

⁹ As a thorn goeth up into the hand of a drunkard, so is a parable in the mouth of fools.

¹¹ As a dog returneth to his vomit, so a fool returneth to his folly.⑩

¹⁴ As the door turneth upon his hinges, so doth the slothful upon his bed.

Proverbs 27

⁷ The full soul loatheth an honeycomb; but to the hungry soul every bitter thing is sweet.

⁸ As a bird that wandereth from her nest, so is a man that wandereth from his place.

⁹ Ointment and perfume rejoice the heart; so doth the sweetness of a man's friend by hearty counsel.

¹⁰ Thy own friend, and thy father's friend, forsake not; neither go into thy brother's house in the day of thy calamity: for better is a neighbour that is near than a brother far off.

¹⁸ Whoso keepeth the fig tree shall eat the fruit thereof: so he that waiteth on his master shall be honoured.

¹⁹ As in water face answereth to face, so the heart of man to man.

Proverbs 29

² When the righteousness are in authority, the people rejoice: but when the wicked beareth rule, the people mourn.

⁴ The king by judgment establisheth the land: but he that receiveth gifts overthroweth it.

¹⁵ The rod and reproof give wisdom: but a child left to himself bringeth his mother to shame.

III FOOD FOR THOUGHT

Reclassify the proverbs provided above (or go to the Bible for the whole of Proverbs) under the following headings and relate them to your personal life: To what extent do they apply?
1. wisdom; 2. wealth and poverty; 3. life and death; 4. the power of speech or silence;
5. marriage; 6. parenting; 7. diligence and laziness; 8. anger, pride, jealousy, fear and conceit.

IV BIBLICAL RELEVANCE

A. Biblical Terms in Everyday English
1. a two-edged sword (Prov. 5:4): _____
2. a soft answer turns away wrath (Prov. 15:1): _____

---

⑩ More proverbs on foolishness: 1:7; 10:8; 12:15—16,23; 14:8—9,16,24; 15:14; 17:10,12,16; 18:2,6; 20:3; 26:3,11; 27:22; 28:26; 29:11.

3. Pride goes before a fall (Prov. 16:18): _____
4. dried bones (Prov. 17:22): _____
5. fruit of the mouth (Prov. 18:20): _____
6. lamp will go out (Prov. 24:20): _____
7. a lion in the way (Prov. 26:13): _____

B. Biblical References in Literature

I think, since Angel has come, that it will be more appropriate to read the thirty-first of Proverbs than the chapter which we should have had in the usual course of our reading?
(Thomas Hardy, *Tess of the d'Urbervilles—A Pure Woman*, 1891)

C. The Bible and Arts
1. *Prudence*, Piero del Pollaiolo (c. 1443—1496)
2. *Justice*, Paolo Veronese (1528—1588)
3. *Fortitude*, Sandro Botticelli (1445—1510)
4. *Temperance*, Sir Edward Burne-Jones (1833—1898)
5. *The Seven Deadly Sins and the Four Last Things*, Hieronymus Bosch (1450—1516)

V SOURCES FOR REFERENCE

1. Yancey, P. & T. Stafford (notes by) (1989). *The New Student Bible*, New International Version. Grand Rapids, Mich: Zondervan Publishing House.
2. Schippe, C. & C. Stetson. (2005). *The Bible and Its Influence*. Front Royal, VA: BLP Publishing.

20. THE SONG OF SONGS

I. POINTS OF DEPARTURE

For many readers, the Song of Songs (alternatively, the Book of Canticles, or Song of Solomon), is something of an embarrassment for its uninhibited expression of romantic passion and physical attractiveness. As a result, time and again there have been attempts to purge the book from the Bible altogether. A telling instance is Luis de León's expulsion from his classroom and subsequent imprisonment for translating the Song of Songs into Spanish in the 16th century. Literally, it is a series of love poems in dialogue form between a man (Lover) and a woman (Beloved) who take turns in unbashfully metaphorizing each other's body. A progression can be seen in the poems from the woman's search of her lover, her dreams and reveries, to the eventual consummation of their love.

This uninhibited expression of human love had led both Jews and Christians to look for some meaning befitting its presence in the Bible and come up with the *allegorical interpretation*. This kind of reading identifies every poetic detail with some corresponding facet of love between God and his people. For example, *S. 1:2*, "Let him kiss me with the kisses of his mouth: for thy love is better than wine" is read as referring to God's gift of the Torah. Another example is Beloved's dream sequence (*S. 5:2—6*) about her lover's disappearance, her frantic search and her harsh treatment by sentinels. This is seen as a metaphor for the Babylonian exile (Schippe & Stetson, 2005: 155). Saint Bernard of Clairvaux, for example, wrote 80 sermons on the first two chapters, using this allegorical approach. But the ingenuity required and the diversity of results raise doubts about this mode of interpretation. Then there have been attempts to read the book as a *drama*, that, in spite of variations, tells the story of how a maiden successfully withstands the attractions of the court of King Solomon and is finally reunited with her rustic lover.

These literal, allegorical and dramatic interpretations are not as irreconcilable as they are purported to be. In the biblical context, human love and marriage are just part of God's will (*Gen. 1:27f., 2:24; Ps. 45:11f.*); through love's fulfillment in marriage human nature reaches the greatest heights of earthly experience. Judaism has always celebrated the body as God's good creation, and marital sexuality as both a sign and an example of the covenant between God and his people. Christianity, too, sees marriage as a holy relationship. Just for this reason, poems from the Song of Songs are often read at both Jewish and Christian wedding ceremonies.

II. SELECTED READINGS

Song of Songs 1

¹ *The song of songs, which is Solomon's.*

Beloved

² " *Let him kiss me with the kisses of his mouth, for thy love is better than wine.*
³ *Because of the savor of thy good ointments, thy name is as ointment poured forth; therefore do the virgins love thee.*
⁴ *Draw me, we will run after thee. The king hath brought me into his chambers.*"

Friends

" *We will be glad and rejoice in thee; we will remember thy love more than wine;*

Beloved

the upright love thee."
⁵ " *I am black, but comely, O ye daughters of Jerusalem, as the tents of Kedar, as the curtains of Solomon.*
⁶ *Look not upon me because I am black, because the sun hath looked upon me. My mother's children were angry with me; they made me the keeper of the vineyards, but mine own vineyard have I not kept.*
⁷ *Tell me, O thou whom my soul loveth, where thou feedest, where thou makest thy flock to rest at noon; for why should I be as one that turneth aside by the flocks of thy companions?*"

Friends

⁸ " *If thou know not, O thou fairest among women, go thy way forth by the footsteps of the flock, and feed thy kids beside the shepherds' tents.*
⁹ *I have compared thee, O my love, to a company of horses in Pharaoh's chariots.*
¹⁰ *Thy cheeks are comely with rows of jewels, thy neck with chains of gold.*"
¹¹ " *We will make thee borders of gold with studs of silver.*"

Beloved

¹² " *While the king sitteth at his table, my spikenard sendeth forth the smell thereof.*
¹³ *A bundle of myrrh is my wellbeloved unto me; he shall lie all night between my breasts.*
¹⁴ *My beloved is unto me as a cluster of henna in the vineyards of Engedi.*"

Lover

¹⁵ " *Behold, thou art fair, my love; behold, thou art fair; thou hast doves' eyes.*"

Beloved

¹⁶ " *Behold, thou art fair, my beloved, yea, pleasant. Also our bed is green.*
¹⁷ *The beams of our house are cedar, and our rafters of fir.*

Beloved

Song of Songs 2

¹ " *I am the rose of Sharon, and the lily of the valleys.*"
² " *As the lily among thorns, so is my love among the daughters.*"

Beloved

³ "As the apple tree among the trees of the wood, so is my beloved among the sons. I sat down under his shadow with great delight, and his fruit was sweet to my taste.

⁴ He brought me to the banqueting house, and his banner over me was love.

⁵ Stay me with flagons, comfort me with apples; for I am sick with love.

⁶ His left hand is under my head, and his right hand doth embrace me.

⁷ I charge you, O ye daughters of Jerusalem, by the roes and by the hinds of the field, that ye stir not up nor awake my love till he please.

⁸ The voice of my beloved! Behold, he cometh leaping upon the mountains, skipping upon the hills.

⁹ My beloved is like a roe or a young hart. Behold, he standeth behind our wall; he looketh forth at the windows, showing himself through the lattice.

¹⁰ My beloved spoke and said unto me, ' Rise up, my love, my fair one, and come away.

¹¹ For lo, the winter is past, the rain is over and gone.

¹² The flowers appear on the earth; the time of the singing of birds is come, and the voice of the turtledove is heard in our land.

¹³ The fig tree putteth forth her green figs, and the vines with the tender grape give a good smell. Arise, my love, my fair one, and come away.' "

The Bible in Literature: *The Grapes of Wrath*

John Steinbeck named one of the main characters in *The Grapes of Wrath* "Rose of Sharon," a reference to *Song of Solomon 2:1*. With a similar beauty symbolism, its fictitious namesake is depicted as a childish and dreamy teenage daughter who develops as the novel progresses to become a mature and Virgin-Mary-like woman who breastfeeds a starving stranger at the end of the novel. The last sentence reads: "She looked up and across the barn, and her lips came together and smiled mysteriously." It is a Mona Lisa smile. Or rather, the smile of the Virgin Mary with her child Jesus — a paragon of feminine beauty.

Lover

¹⁴ " O my dove, that art in the clefts of the rock, in the secret places of the stairs, let me see thy countenance, let me hear thy voice; for sweet is thy voice, and thy countenance is comely."

¹⁵ " Take us the foxes, the little foxes, that spoil the vines; for our vines have tender grapes."

Beloved

¹⁶ " My beloved is mine, and I am his; he feedeth among the lilies.

¹⁷ Until the day break and the shadows flee away, turn, my beloved, and be thou like a roe or a young hart upon the mountains of Bether."

Song of Songs 3

¹ " By night on my bed I sought him whom my soul loveth; I sought him, but I found him not.

² I will rise now and go about the city in the streets, and in the broad ways I will seek him whom my

soul loveth. I sought him, but I found him not.

³ The watchmen that go about the city found me, to whom I said, ' Saw ye him whom my soul loveth?'

⁴ It was but a little that I passed from them, but I found him whom my soul loveth. I held him and would not let him go, until I had brought him into my mother's house, and into the chamber of her that conceived me.

⁵ I charge you, O ye daughters of Jerusalem, by the roes and by the hinds of the field, that ye stir not up nor awake my love, till he please."

⁶ "Who is this that cometh out of the wilderness like pillars of smoke, perfumed with myrrh and frankincense, with all powders of the merchant?

⁷ Behold his bed, which is Solomon's; threescore valiant men are about it, of the valiant of Israel.

⁸ They all hold swords, being expert in war; every man hath his sword upon his thigh, because of fear in the night.

⁹ King Solomon made himself a chariot of the wood of Lebanon;

¹⁰ He made the pillars thereof of silver, the bottom thereof of gold, the covering of it of purple, the midst thereof being paved with love for the daughters of Jerusalem.

¹¹ Go forth, O ye daughters of Zion, and behold King Solomon with the crown wherewith his mother crowned him on the day of his espousals, and in the day of the gladness of his heart."

Lover
Song of Songs 4

¹ "Behold, thou art fair, my love; behold, thou art fair. Thou hast doves' eyes within thy locks; thy hair is as a flock of goats that appear from Mount Gilead.

² Thy teeth are like a flock of sheep that are even shorn which came up from the washing, whereof every one bear twins, and none is barren among them.

³ Thy lips are like a thread of scarlet, and thy speech is comely; thy temples are like a piece of a pomegranate within thy locks.

⁴ Thy neck is like the tower of David builded for an armory, whereon there hang a thousand bucklers, all shields of mighty men.

⁵ Thy two breasts are like two young roes that are twins, which feed among the lilies.

⁶ Until the day break and the shadows flee away, I will get me to the mountain of myrrh and to the hill of frankincense.

⁷ Thou art all fair, my love; there is no spot in thee.

⁸ Come with me from Lebanon, my spouse, with me from Lebanon; look from the top of Amana, from the top of Senir and Hermon, from the lions' dens, from the mountains of the leopards.

⁹ Thou hast ravished my heart, my sister, my spouse; thou hast ravished my heart with one of thine eyes, with one chain of thy neck.

¹⁰ How fair is thy love, my sister, my spouse! How much better is thy love than wine, and the smell of thine ointments than all spices!

¹¹ Thy lips, O my spouse, drip as the honeycomb; honey and milk are under thy tongue, and the smell of thy garments is like the smell of Lebanon.

¹² A garden enclosed is my sister, my spouse, a spring shut up, a fountain sealed.

¹³ Thy plants are an orchard of pomegranates with pleasant fruits, henna with spikenard,

¹⁴ Spikenard and saffron, calamus and cinnamon, with all trees of frankincense, myrrh and aloes, with all the chief spices"

¹⁵ "A fountain of gardens, a well of living waters, and streams from Lebanon."

Beloved

¹⁶ "Awake, O north wind, and come, thou south! Blow upon my garden, that the spices thereof may

flow out. Let my beloved come into his garden and eat his pleasant fruits."

Lover
Song of Songs 5
¹ " I am come into my garden, my sister, my spouse; I have gathered my myrrh with my spice; I have eaten my honeycomb with my honey; I have drunk my wine with my milk."

Friends
"Eat, O friends; drink, yea, drink abundantly, O beloved."

Beloved
² " I sleep, but my heart waketh; it is the voice of my beloved that knocketh, saying, ' Open to me, my sister, my love, my dove, my undefiled; for my head is filled with dew and my locks with the drops of the night.'
³ I have put off my coat; how shall I put it on? I have washed my feet; how shall I defile them?
⁴ My beloved put in his hand by the hole of the door, and my heart was moved for him.
⁵ I rose up to open to my beloved, and my hands dripped with myrrh, and my fingers with sweet smelling myrrh, upon the handles of the lock.
⁶ I opened to my beloved, but my beloved had withdrawn himself and was gone. My soul failed when he spoke; I sought him, but I could not find him; I called him, but he gave me no answer.
⁷ The watchmen that went about the city found me. They smote me, they wounded me; the keepers of the walls took away my veil from me.
⁸ I charge you, O daughters of Jerusalem, if ye find my beloved, that ye tell him that I am sick with love."

Friends
⁹ "What is thy beloved more than another beloved, O thou fairest among women? What is thy beloved more than another beloved, that thou dost so charge us?"

Beloved
¹⁰ " My beloved is white and ruddy, the chiefest among ten thousand.
¹¹ His head is as the most fine gold; his locks are bushy, and black as a raven.
¹² His eyes are as the eyes of doves by the rivers of waters, washed with milk, and fitly set.
¹³ His cheeks are as a bed of spices, as sweet flowers; his lips like lilies, dropping sweetsmelling myrrh.
¹⁴ His hands are as gold rings set with the beryl; his belly is as bright ivory overlaid with sapphires.
¹⁵ His legs are as pillars of marble set upon sockets of fine gold; his countenance is as Lebanon, excellent as the cedars.
¹⁶ His mouth is most sweet; yea, he is altogether lovely. This is my beloved, and this is my friend, O daughters of Jerusalem."

Friends
Song of Songs 6
¹ " Whither is thy beloved gone, O thou fairest among women? Whither is thy beloved turned aside, that we may seek him with thee?"

Beloved
² " My beloved is gone down into his garden, to the beds of spices, to feed in the gardens and to gather lilies.

³ *I am my beloved's, and my beloved is mine; he feedeth among the lilies.*"

Lover
⁴ " *Thou art beautiful, O my love, as Tirzah, comely as Jerusalem, fearsome as an army with banners.*
⁵ *Turn away thine eyes from me, for they have overcome me. Thy hair is as a flock of goats that appear from Gilead.*
⁶ *Thy teeth are as a flock of sheep which go up from the washing, whereof every one beareth twins, and there is not one barren among them.*
⁷ *As a piece of a pomegranate are thy temples within thy locks.*
⁸ *There are threescore queens and fourscore concubines and virgins without number.*
⁹ *My dove, my undefiled is but one; she is the only one of her mother; she is the choice one of her that bore her.*" " *The daughters saw her and blessed her; yea, the queens and the concubines, and they praised her:*

Friends
¹⁰ " ' *Who is she that looketh forth as the morning, fair as the moon, clear as the sun, and fearsome as an army with banners?* ' "

Lover
¹¹ " *I went down into the garden of nuts to see the fruits of the valley, and to see whether the vine flourished and the pomegranates budded.*
¹² *Or ever I was aware, my soul made me like the chariots of Amminadib.*"

Friends
¹³ " *Return, return, O Shulamite; return, return, that we may look upon thee.*"

Lover
" *What will ye see in the Shulamite? As it were the company of two armies.*"

Song of Songs 7

¹ " *How beautiful are thy feet with shoes, O prince's daughter! The joints of thy thighs are like jewels, the work of the hands of a skillful workman.*
² *Thy navel is like a round goblet, which wanteth not liquor; thy belly is like a heap of wheat set about with lilies.*
³ *Thy two breasts are like two young roes that are twins;*
⁴ *Thy neck is as a tower of ivory. Thine eyes like the fishpools in Heshbon by the gate of Bathrabbim; thy nose is as the tower of Lebanon which looketh toward Damascus.*
⁵ *Thine head upon thee is like Carmel, and the hair of thine head like purple; the king is held in its galleries.*
⁶ *How fair and how pleasant art thou, O love, for delights!*
⁷ *This thy stature is like to a palm tree, and thy breasts to clusters of grapes.*
⁸ *I said, ' I will go up to the palm tree; I will take hold of the boughs thereof.*'
Now also thy breasts shall be as clusters of the vine, and the smell of thy nose like apples.
⁹ *And the roof of thy mouth like the best wine for my beloved, that goeth down sweetly, causing the lips of those that are asleep to speak.*"
¹⁰ " *I am my beloved's, and his desire is toward me.*
¹¹ *Come, my beloved, let us go forth into the field; let us lodge in the villages.*
¹² *Let us get up early to the vineyards; let us see if the vine flourish, whether the tender grape appear, and the pomegranates bud forth; there will I give thee my loves.*
¹³ *The mandrakes give a smell, and at our gates are all manner of pleasant fruits, new and old, which I*

have laid up for thee, O my beloved."

Song of Songs 8

¹ "O, that thou wert as my brother, that sucked the breasts of my mother! When I should find thee outside, I would kiss thee; yea, I should not be despised.

² I would lead thee, and bring thee into my mother's house, who would instruct me; I would cause thee to drink of spiced wine of the juice of my pomegranate.

³ His left hand should be under my head, and his right hand should embrace me.

⁴ I charge you, O daughters of Jerusalem, that ye stir not up nor awake my love, until he please."

Friends

⁵ "Who is this that cometh up from the wilderness, leaning upon her beloved?

Beloved

I raised thee up under the apple tree; there thy mother brought thee forth; there she brought thee forth that bore thee."

⁶ "Set me as a seal upon thine heart, as a seal upon thine arm; for love is strong as death; jealousy is cruel as the grave; the coals thereof are coals of fire, which hath a most vehement flame."

⁷ "Many waters cannot quench love, neither can the floods drown it; if a man would give all the substance of his house for love, it would utterly be contemned."

Friends

⁸ "We have a little sister, and she hath no breasts; what shall we do for our sister in the day when she shall be spoken for?

⁹ If she be a wall, we will build upon her a palace of silver; and if she be a door, we will enclose her with boards of cedar."

Song of Solomon, He Qi

Beloved

¹⁰ "I am a wall, and my breasts like towers; then was I in his eyes as one that found favor.

¹¹ Solomon had a vineyard at Baalhamon; he let out the vineyard unto keepers; every one for the fruit thereof was to bring a thousand pieces of silver.

¹² My vineyard, which is mine, is before me; thou, O Solomon, must have a thousand, and those that keep the fruit thereof two hundred."

Lover

¹³ "Thou that dwellest in the gardens, the companions hearken to thy voice; cause me to hear it."

Beloved

¹⁴ "Make haste, my beloved, and be thou like to a roe or to a young hart upon the mountains of spices."

III FOOD FOR THOUGHT

1. Why is a sexually-oriented book like *Song of Solomon* found in the Bible?
2. Which part of the book can be read as a drama involving an intruder and two lovers?
3. What do 2:7, 3:5 and 8:4 say about love?
4. Why does the girl wish that her lover were her brother (8:1)?
5. In what ways is love comparable to death (8:6)?

IV BIBLICAL RELEVANCE

A. Biblical Terms in Everyday English
1. rose of Sharon (2:1): _____
2. the lily of the valleys (*ibid.*): _____
3. the lily among thorns (2:2): _____
4. fair as the moon, clear as the sun (6:10): _____
5. tower of ivory (7:4): _____
6. like a gazelle or a young stag on the spice-laden mountains (8:14, NIV): _____

B. Biblical References in Literature
1. Geoffrey Chaucer, "The Miller's Tale," *The Canterbury Tales*, 1380s—1390s.
2. John Steinbeck, *The Grapes of Wrath*, 1939.
3. Toni Morrison, *Song of Solomon*, 1978.

C. The Bible and Arts
1. http://www.arthursussmangallery.com/index.htm
2. http://www.heqigallery.com

V SOURCES FOR REFERENCE

1. http://www.biblequery.org/sofs.htm
2. Schippe, C. & C. Stetson. (2005). *The Bible and Its Influence*. Front Royal, VA: BLP Publishing.

21. ECCLESIASTES

I POINTS OF DEPARTURE

In this world, there are only two tragedies, said Irish writer Oscar Wilde. "One is not getting what one wants, and the other is getting it." The latter part of the maxim is borne out by the experience of Solomon, the supposed author of the wisdom book Ecclesiastes①. As a great king, he had tasted just about everything life can offer: wisdom, wealth, power, fame, pleasures. But everything is pointless: You toil, but someone else gets the credit. You strive to be righteous, but evil people take advantage of you. You accumulate wealth, but it just goes to unworthy heirs. You seek pleasure, but it turns sour on you. It seems that however much or little one may try or enjoy, death, the great equalizer, is inevitable and no respecter of class, fame, or power; hence the initial proclamation, "Vanity of vanities, vanity of vanities; all is vanity." (*Ec. 1:2*) This is the observation of the Preacher, one of the two narrators, the other being the wise man that appears in 12:11. A key phrase in the book, "under the sun," which appears more than 30 times, indicates that the Preacher is confining his inquiry into meaning to what he can see and experience on earth, apart from God and without any belief in the afterlife. With the under-the-sun mentality, the Preacher reasonably concludes that everything is meaningless.

But the Preacher is not a complete nihilist—there is a message of faith and hope. One source of hope is *carpe diem* ("seize the day"), living life to the full: "Go thy way, eat thy bread with joy, and drink thy wine with a merry heart; for God now accepteth thy works." (*Ec. 9:7*) Hope also lies in respecting a life in which all things have their appropriate place, because "[t]o every thing there is a season, and a time to every purpose under the heaven." (*Ec. 3:1*) However, the Preacher's "under the sun" preaching does not represent the final viewpoint of the book. Rather, it is a vehicle employed by the wise man to warn his son against the dangers of searching for meaning the earthly way and to impress on him the obligation to "[f]ear God, and keep his commandments." (*Ec. 12:13*) All this being said, it is proper to quote from *Matthew 16:26* by way of summarizing the author's meaningless life:

[W]*hat is a man profited, if he shall gain the whole world, and lose his own soul?*

---

① **Ecclesiastes** (/iˌkliziˈæstiz; iˌkliːziˈæstiːz/, 传道书) the Latin translation of the Hebrew name *Qoheleth* (or *Kohelet*) literally meaning "one who assembles," which may refer to assembling a group of students to hear one's teaching. The association of the Preacher with Solomon is based on the superscription (1:1) and his descriptions of his great wealth, wisdom, and his harem (Comfort, 2006:253). But given the combination of skepticism and conventional moral advice in the book, multi-authorship is suggested (Schippe & Stetson, 2005:194).

II SELECTED READINGS

Everything Is Meaningless

Ecclesiastes 1

¹ The words of the Preacher, the son of David, king in Jerusalem.

² Vanity② of vanities, saith the Preacher, vanity of vanities; all is vanity.

³ What profit hath a man of all his labour which he taketh under the sun?

⁴ One generation passeth away, and another generation cometh: but the earth abideth for ever.

⁵ The sun also ariseth, and the sun goeth down, and hasteth to his place where he arose.

⁶ The wind goeth toward the south, and turneth about unto the north; it whirleth about continually, and the wind returneth again according to his circuits.

⁷ All the rivers run into the sea; yet the sea is not full; unto the place from whence the rivers come, thither they return again.

⁸ All things are full of labour; man cannot utter it: the eye is not satisfied with seeing, nor the ear filled with hearing.

⁹ The thing that hath been, it is that which shall be; and that which is done is that which shall be done: and there is no new thing under the sun.

¹⁰ Is there any thing whereof it may be said, "See, this is new? It hath been already of old time, which was before us."

¹¹ There is no remembrance of former things; neither shall there be any remembrance of things that are to come with those that shall come after.

Ecclesiastes, Gustave Doré (1832—1883)

Wisdom Is Meaningless

All Is Vanity, C. Allan Gilbert (1873—1929)

¹² I the Preacher was king over Israel in Jerusalem.

¹³ And I gave my heart to seek and search out by wisdom concerning all things that are done under heaven: this sore travail hath God given to the sons of man to be exercised therewith.

¹⁴ I have seen all the works that are done under the sun; and, behold, all is vanity and vexation of spirit.

¹⁵ That which is crooked cannot be made straight: and that which is wanting cannot be numbered.

¹⁶ I communed with mine own heart, saying, "Lo, I am come to great estate, and have gotten more wisdom than all they that have been before me in Jerusalem: yea, my heart had great experience of wisdom and knowledge."

¹⁷ And I gave my heart to know wisdom, and to know madness and folly: I perceived that this also is vexation of spirit.

¹⁸ For in much wisdom is much grief: and he that increaseth knowledge increaseth sorrow.

---

② **Vanity** Hebrew *hevel* meaning "vapor" or "wisp of smoke," alluding to the fleeting nature of life and its joys.

Pleasures Are Meaningless

Ecclesiastes 2

¹ I said in mine heart, " Go to now, I will prove thee with mirth, therefore enjoy pleasure: and, behold, this also is vanity."

² I said of laughter, " It is mad: and of mirth, what doeth it?"

³ I sought in mine heart to give myself unto wine, yet acquainting mine heart with wisdom; and to lay hold on folly, till I might see what was that good for the sons of men, which they should do under the heaven all the days of their life.

⁴ I made me great works; I builded me houses; I planted me vineyards:

⁵ I made me gardens and orchards, and I planted trees in them of all kind of fruits:

⁶ I made me pools of water, to water therewith the wood that bringeth forth trees:

⁷ I got me servants and maidens, and had servants born in my house; also I had great possessions of great and small cattle above all that were in Jerusalem before me:

⁸ I gathered me also silver and gold, and the peculiar treasure of kings and of the provinces: I gat me men singers and women singers, and the delights of the sons of men, as musical instruments, and that of all sorts.

⁹ So I was great, and increased more than all that were before me in Jerusalem: also my wisdom remained with me.

¹⁰ And whatsoever mine eyes desired I kept not from them, I withheld not my heart from any joy; for my heart rejoiced in all my labour: and this was my portion of all my labour.

¹¹ Then I looked on all the works that my hands had wrought, and on the labour that I had laboured to do: and, behold, all was vanity and vexation of spirit, and there was no profit under the sun.

¹² And I turned myself to behold wisdom, and madness, and folly: for what can the man do that cometh after the king? Even that which hath been already done.

¹³ Then I saw that wisdom excelleth folly, as far as light excelleth darkness.

¹⁴ The wise man's eyes are in his head; but the fool walketh in darkness: and I myself perceived also that one event happeneth to them all.

¹⁵ Then said I in my heart, " As it happeneth to the fool, so it happeneth even to me; and why was I then more wise?" Then I said in my heart, " that this also is vanity."

¹⁶ For there is no remembrance of the wise more than of the fool for ever; seeing that which now is in the days to come shall all be forgotten. And how dieth the wise man? As the fool.

Toil Is Meaningless

¹⁷ Therefore I hated life; because the work that is wrought under the sun is grievous unto me: for all is vanity and vexation of spirit.

¹⁸ Yea, I hated all my labour which I had taken under the sun: because I should leave it unto the man that shall be after me.

¹⁹ And who knoweth whether he shall be a wise man or a fool? Yet shall he have rule over all my labour wherein I have laboured, and wherein I have shewed myself wise under the sun. This is also vanity.

²⁰ Therefore I went about to cause my heart to despair of all the labour which I took under the sun.

²¹ For there is a man whose labour is in wisdom, and in knowledge, and in equity; yet to a man that hath not laboured therein shall he leave it for his portion. This also is vanity and a great evil.

²² For what hath man of all his labour, and of the vexation of his heart, wherein he hath laboured under the sun?

²³ For all his days are sorrows, and his travail grief; yea, his heart taketh not rest in the night. This is also vanity.

²⁴ There is nothing better for a man, than that he should eat and drink, and that he should make his soul

enjoy good in his labour. This also I saw, that it was from the hand of God.

²⁵ *For who can eat, or who else can hasten hereunto, more than I?*

²⁶ *For God giveth to a man that is good in his sight wisdom, and knowledge, and joy: but to the sinner he giveth travail, to gather and to heap up, that he may give to him that is good before God. This also is vanity and vexation of spirit.*

Ecclesiastes 3

¹ *To every thing there is a season, and a time to every purpose under the heaven:*

² *A time to be born, and a time to die; a time to plant, and a time to pluck up that which is planted;*

³ *A time to kill, and a time to heal; a time to break down, and a time to build up;*

⁴ *A time to weep, and a time to laugh; a time to mourn, and a time to dance;*

⁵ *A time to cast away stones, and a time to gather stones together; a time to embrace, and a time to refrain from embracing;*

⁶ *A time to get, and a time to lose; a time to keep, and a time to cast away;*

⁷ *A time to rend, and a time to sew; a time to keep silence, and a time to speak;*

⁸ *A time to love, and a time to hate; a time of war, and a time of peace.*

⁹ *What profit hath he that worketh in that wherein he laboureth?*

¹⁰ *I have seen the travail, which God hath given to the sons of men to be exercised in it.*

¹¹ *He hath made every thing beautiful in his time: also he hath set the world in their heart, so that no man can find out the work that God maketh from the beginning to the end.*

¹² *I know that there is no good in them, but for a man to rejoice, and to do good in his life.*

¹³ *And also that every man should eat and drink, and enjoy the good of all his labour, it is the gift of God.*

¹⁴ *I know that, whatsoever God doeth, it shall be for ever: nothing can be put to it, nor any thing taken from it: and God doeth it, that men should fear before him.*

¹⁵ *That which hath been is now; and that which is to be hath already been; and God requireth that which is past.*

¹⁶ *And moreover I saw under the sun the place of judgment, that wickedness was there; and the place of righteousness, that iniquity was there.*

¹⁷ *I said in mine heart, " God shall judge the righteous and the wicked: for there is a time there for every purpose and for every work."*

¹⁸ *I said in mine heart concerning the estate of the sons of men, that God might manifest them, and that they might see that they themselves are beasts.*

¹⁹ *For that which befalleth the sons of men befalleth beasts; even one thing befalleth them: as the one dieth, so dieth the other; yea, they have all one breath; so that a man hath no preeminence above a beast: for all is vanity.*

²⁰ *All go unto one place; all are of the dust, and all turn to dust again.*

²¹ *Who knoweth the spirit of man that goeth upward, and the spirit of the beast that goeth downward to the earth?*

²² *Wherefore I perceive that there is nothing better, than that a man should rejoice in his own works; for that is his portion: for who shall bring him to see what shall be after him?*

Cultural Connections: *Ecclesiastes 3*

Ec. 3 is the most enduring portion of the book's poetry. Folksinger Pete Seeger used the first part verbatim in a famous 1960s song titled *Turn! Turn! Turn!* It was also former United States president John F. Kennedy's favorite passage and the first 8 verses were read together with his entire Inaugural Speech in the funeral mass held at St. Matthew's Cathedral in Washington, D.C. on November 25, 1963 after his assassination.

A Common Destiny for All

Ecclesiastes 9

¹ For all this I considered in my heart even to declare all this, that the righteous, and the wise, and their works, are in the hand of God: no man knoweth either love or hatred by all that is before them.

² All things come alike to all: there is one event to the righteous, and to the wicked; to the good and to the clean, and to the unclean; to him that sacrificeth, and to him that sacrificeth not: as is the good, so is the sinner; and he that sweareth, as he that feareth an oath.

³ This is an evil among all things that are done under the sun, that there is one event unto all: yea, also the heart of the sons of men is full of evil, and madness is in their heart while they live, and after that they go to the dead.

⁴ For to him that is joined to all the living there is hope: for a living dog is better than a dead lion.

⁵ For the living know that they shall die: but the dead know not any thing, neither have they any more a reward; for the memory of them is forgotten.

⁶ Also their love, and their hatred, and their envy, is now perished; neither have they any more a portion for ever in any thing that is done under the sun.

⁷ Go thy way, eat thy bread with joy, and drink thy wine with a merry heart; for God now accepteth thy works.

⁸ Let thy garments be always white; and let thy head lack no ointment.

⁹ Live joyfully with the wife whom thou lovest all the days of the life of thy vanity, which he hath given thee under the sun, all the days of thy vanity: for that is thy portion in this life, and in thy labour which thou takest under the sun.

¹⁰ Whatsoever thy hand findeth to do, do it with thy might; for there is no work, nor device, nor knowledge, nor wisdom, in the grave, whither thou goest.

¹¹ I returned, and saw under the sun, that the race is not to the swift, nor the battle to the strong, neither yet bread to the wise, nor yet riches to men of understanding, nor yet favour to men of skill; but time and chance happeneth to them all.

¹² For man also knoweth not his time: as the fishes that are taken in an evil net, and as the birds that are caught in the snare; so are the sons of men snared in an evil time, when it falleth suddenly upon them.

Wisdom Better Than Folly

¹³ This wisdom have I seen also under the sun, and it seemed great unto me:

¹⁴ There was a little city, and few men within it; and there came a great king against it, and besieged it, and built great bulwarks against it:

¹⁵ Now there was found in it a poor wise man, and he by his wisdom delivered the city; yet no man remembered that same poor man.

¹⁶ Then said I, "Wisdom is better than strength: nevertheless the poor man's wisdom is despised, and his words are not heard."

¹⁷ The words of wise men are heard in quiet more than the cry of him that ruleth among fools.

Bread upon the Waters

Ecclesiastes 11

¹ Cast thy bread upon the waters: for thou shalt find it after many days.

² Give a portion to seven, and also to eight; for thou knowest not what evil shall be upon the earth.

³ If the clouds be full of rain, they empty themselves upon the earth: and if the tree fall toward the south, or toward the north, in the place where the tree falleth, there it shall be.

⁴ He that observeth the wind shall not sow; and he that regardeth the clouds shall not reap.

⁵ As thou knowest not what is the way of the spirit, nor how the bones do grow in the womb of her that is with child: even so thou knowest not the works of God who maketh all.

⁶ In the morning sow thy seed, and in the evening withhold not thine hand: for thou knowest not whether shall prosper, either this or that, or whether they both shall be alike good.

⁷ Truly the light is sweet, and a pleasant thing it is for the eyes to behold the sun:

⁸ But if a man live many years, and rejoice in them all; yet let him remember the days of darkness; for they shall be many. All that cometh is vanity.

⁹ Rejoice, O young man, in thy youth; and let thy heart cheer thee in the days of thy youth, and walk in the ways of thine heart, and in the sight of thine eyes: but know thou, that for all these things God will bring thee into judgment.

¹⁰ Therefore remove sorrow from thy heart, and put away evil from thy flesh: for childhood and youth are vanity.

Ecclesiastes 12

¹ Remember now thy Creator in the days of thy youth, while the evil days come not, nor the years draw nigh, when thou shalt say, I have no pleasure in them;

² While the sun, or the light, or the moon, or the stars, be not darkened, nor the clouds return after the rain:

³ In the day when the keepers of the house shall tremble, and the strong men shall bow themselves, and the grinders cease because they are few, and those that look out of the windows be darkened.

⁴ And the doors shall be shut in the streets, when the sound of the grinding is low, and he shall rise up at the voice of the bird, and all the daughters of musick shall be brought low;

⁵ Also when they shall be afraid of that which is high, and fears shall be in the way, and the almond tree shall flourish, and the grasshopper shall be a burden, and desire shall fail: because man goeth to his long home, and the mourners go about the streets:

⁶ Or ever the silver cord be loosed, or the golden bowl be broken, or the pitcher be broken at the fountain, or the wheel broken at the cistern.

⁷ Then shall the dust return to the earth as it was: and the spirit shall return unto God who gave it.

⁸ Vanity of vanities, saith the preacher; all is vanity.

Cultural Connections: *memento more*

Ecclesiastes inspired a genre of painting known as *memento more* (Latin for "Remember your mortality," "Remember you must die" or "Remember you will die"), which often depicts a skull surrounded by such earthly objects as a crown, a trophy, books, an hourglass, etc., intended to remind people of the inevitability of death and the meaninglessness of worldly pursuits. *Memento more* was originally uttered by a slave to his victorious master, a Roman general in triumphal march, warning him against vanity and pride.

The Conclusion of the Matter

⁹ And moreover, because the preacher was wise, he still taught the people knowledge; yea, he gave good heed, and sought out, and set in order many proverbs.

¹⁰ The preacher sought to find out acceptable words: and that which was written was upright, even words of truth.

¹¹ The words of the wise are as goads, and as nails fastened by the masters of assemblies, which are given from one shepherd.

¹² And further, by these, my son, be admonished: of making many books there is no end; and much study is a weariness of the flesh.

¹³ Let us hear the conclusion of the whole matter: Fear God, and keep his commandments: for this is the whole duty of man.

¹⁴ For God shall bring every work into judgment, with every secret thing, whether it be good, or whether it be evil.

III FOOD FOR THOUGHT

1. What is the theme of *Ecclesiates* as observed through the excerpts here? Do you agree or disagree?
2. Given the pessimistic view of life, does the author see any hope?
3. Compare *Ecclesiates* with the song of "All Good Things Must End" in Chapter 1, *A Dream of Red Mansions*.

好了歌   All Good Things Must End

世人都晓神仙好，	All men long to be immortals
只有功名忘不了！	Yet to riches and rank each aspires;
古今将相在何方？	The great ones of old, where are they now?
荒冢一堆草没了！	Their graves are a mass of briars.
世人都晓神仙好，	All men long to be immortals,
只有金银忘不了！	Yet silver and gold they prize
终朝只恨聚无多，	And grub for money all their lives

| 及到多时眼闭了！ | Till death seals up their eyes. |

世人都晓神仙好，	All men long to be immortals
只有娇妻忘不了！	Yet dote on the wives they've wed,
君生日日说恩情，	Who swear to love their husband evermore
君死又随人去了！	But remarry as soon as he's dead.

世人都晓神仙好，	All men long to be immortals
只有儿孙忘不了！	Yet with getting sons won't have done.
痴心父母古来多，	Although fond parents are legion,
孝顺儿孙谁见了？	Who ever saw a really filial son?

(English translation by Yang Hsien-yi and Gladys Yang)

IV. BIBLICAL RELEVANCE

A. Biblical Terms in Everyday English
1. All is vanity. (1:2): _____
2. under the sun (Ec. 1:14): _____
3. For everything there is a season. (3:1): _____
4. a fly in the ointment (Ec. 10:1): _____
5. a live dog is better than a dead lion (Ec. 9:4): _____
6. a little bird told me (Ec. 10:20): _____
7. cast bread upon the waters (11:1): _____

B. Biblical References in Literature
1. And to the question asked by Ecclesiastes three thousand years ago, "That which is far off and exceeding deep, who can find it out?"
   (Jules Verne, 20,000 *Leagues under the Sea*, 1870)
2. The truest of all men was the Man of Sorrows, and the truest of all books is Solomon's, and Ecclesiastes is the fine hammered steel of woe.
   (Herman Melville, *Moby Dick*, 1851)

C. The Bible and Arts
1. *Allegory of Vanity*, Trophime Bigot (1597—1650)
2. *Vanitas Vanitatum et Omnia Vanitas*, Evert Collier (between 1630 and 1650—1708)
3. *Still Life with Skull*, Paul Cezanne (1839—1906)
4. *All Is Vanity*, C. Allan Gilbert (1873—1929)

V. SOURCES FOR REFERENCE

1. Comfort, P. W. (ed.) (2006). *Cornerstone Biblical Commentary: Job, Ecclesiastes, Song of Songs.* Carol Stream, IL: Tyndale House Publishers, INC.
2. Schippe, C. & C. Stetson. (2005). *The Bible and Its Influence.* Front Royal, VA: BLP Publishing.

PART SIX

THE DIVIDED KINGDOM
(C. 933—800 B.C.E.)
THE BOOKS OF 1 & 2 KINGS

22. ELIJAH, THE ECSTATIC PROPHET

I POINTS OF DEPARTURE

The year 933 B. C. E. saw the death of Solomon and the succession of his son Rehoboam. Then ten northern tribes united together under Jeroboam rose up in rebellion to form a nation in the north called Israel. Only two tribes, Judah and Benjamin, remained loyal to Solomon's heir in Jerusalem. From then on, there started the period of divided kingdom. The evaluation of the various kings' reigns in the judgment of the biblical writers depended on the extent to which they encouraged worship in the Temple at Jerusalem. Under such a criterion all the northern kings naturally fell short because they had "made Israel sin" while the southern kings proved more loyal to God and "did that which was right in the eyes of the LORD."

Much of the next decades was spent in a smoldering rivalry between Judah and Israel, with Judah getting the worst of it, though Judah enjoyed the mixed blessing of the Davidic dynasty for three and a half centuries, whereas Israel lasted just over two with a succession of unrelated monarchs, of whom the most successful in bringing a measure of peace, prosperity, and international respect throughout Israel was Omri, its sixth king. It was he who founded a new capital for the Northern Kingdom at Samaria and who cemented a most useful alliance with the Phoenicians by marrying his son Ahab to the daughter of Ethbaal king of Sidon, Jezebel. And it was Jezebel who earned the hatred of the biblical writers by fostering the cult of Baal throughout Israel. The one who set out to challenge King Ahab and his wicked queen was the rigorously righteous warrior Elijah the Tishbite. Elijah was a desperate fugitive, hiding out in the wilderness fed by ravens. He was a miracle worker. Altogether, 1 and 2 Kings record eight amazing miracles through Elijah. Some, like his solo confrontation atop Mount Carmel with 850 priests of Jezebel's, were performed dramatically to the amazement of a large audience. Others, like his restoration of the widow's son, were familially heart-warming. When King Ahab stole Naboth's vineyard through Jezebel's intrigue, Elijah cursed the wicked couple and his condemnation eventually materialized.

Elijah holds an important place in modern Judaism. He is a symbolic guest at every circumcision and in observances of the Passover a place is regularly reserved for Elijah. The New Testament (*Mt. 17:10—13*) alludes to Elijah by describing John the Baptist as the new Elijah. Elijah, representing the prophets, is present along with Moses, giver of the law, at the Transfiguration of Jesus (*Mk. 9:4*).

II SELECTED READINGS

Israel Rebels Against Rehoboam

1 Kings 12

¹ And Rehoboam① went to Shechem: for all Israel were come to Shechem to make him king. ² And it came to pass, when Jeroboam② the son of Nebat, who was yet in Egypt, heard of it, (for he was fled from the presence of king Solomon, and Jeroboam dwelt in Egypt;) ³ That they sent and called him. And Jeroboam and all the congregation of Israel came, and spake unto Rehoboam, saying, ⁴ " Thy father made our yoke grievous: now therefore make thou the grievous service of thy father, and his heavy yoke which he put upon us, lighter, and we will serve thee."

⁵ And he said unto them, " Depart yet for three days, then come again to me. And the people departed."

⁶ And king Rehoboam consulted with the old men, that stood before Solomon his father while he yet lived, and said, " How do ye advise that I may answer this people?"

⁷ And they spake unto him, saying, " If thou wilt be a servant unto this people this day, and wilt serve them, and answer them, and speak good words to them, then they will be thy servants for ever." ⁸ But he forsook the counsel of the old men, which they had given him, and consulted with the young men that were grown up with him, and which stood before him. ⁹ And he said unto them, " What counsel give ye that we may answer this people, who have spoken to me, saying, ' Make the yoke which thy father did put upon us lighter?' "

The Israelites Refuse to Accept Rehoboam as Their King, 1851—1860, Julius Schnorr von Carolsfeld

¹⁰ And the young men that were grown up with him spake unto him, saying, " Thus shalt thou speak unto this people that spake unto thee, saying, ' Thy father made our yoke heavy, but make thou it lighter unto us,' thus shalt thou say unto them, ' My little finger shall be thicker than my father's loins. ¹¹ And now whereas my father did lade you with a heavy yoke, I will add to your yoke: my father hath chastised you with whips, but I will chastise you with scorpions.' "

¹² So Jeroboam and all the people came to Rehoboam the third day, as the king had appointed, saying, " Come to me again the third day." ¹³ And the king answered the people roughly, and forsook the old men's counsel that they gave him; ¹⁴ And spake to them after the counsel of the young men, saying, " My father made your yoke heavy, and I will add to your yoke: my father also chastised you with whips, but I will chastise you with scorpions." ¹⁵ Wherefore the king hearkened not unto the people; for the cause was from the LORD, that he might perform his saying, which the LORD spake by Ahijah the Shilonite unto Jeroboam the son of Nebat.

¹⁶ So when all Israel saw that the king hearkened not unto them, the people answered the king, saying,
" What portion have we in David?
Neither have we inheritance in the son of Jesse: to your tents,
O Israel: now see to thine own house, David."
So Israel departed unto their tents. ¹⁷ But as for the children of Israel which dwelt in the cities of Judah, Rehoboam reigned over them.

---

① **Rehoboam** /ˌriːəˈbəʊəm/, 罗波安。
② **Jeroboam** /ˌdʒerəˈbəʊəm/, 耶罗波安。

^{18}Then king Rehoboam sent Adoram, who was over the tribute; and all Israel stoned him with stones, that he died. Therefore king Rehoboam made speed to get him up to his chariot, to flee to Jerusalem. ^{19}So Israel rebelled against the house of David unto this day.

Jeroboam Becomes King of Israel

^{20}And it came to pass, when all Israel heard that Jeroboam was come again, that they sent and called him unto the congregation, and made him king over all Israel: there was none that followed the house of David, but the tribe of Judah only. ^{21}And when Rehoboam was come to Jerusalem, he assembled all the house of Judah, with the tribe of Benjamin, an hundred and fourscore thousand chosen men, which were warriors, to fight against the house of Israel, to bring the kingdom again to Rehoboam the son of Solomon. ^{22}But the word of God came unto Shemaiah the man of God, saying, ^{23}"Speak unto Rehoboam, the son of Solomon, king of Judah, and unto all the house of Judah and Benjamin, and to the remnant of the people, saying, ^{24}' Thus saith the LORD, Ye shall not go up, nor fight against your brethren the children of Israel: return every man to his house; for this thing is from me.' " They hearkened therefore to the word of the LORD, and returned to depart, according to the word of the LORD.

Jeroboam Builds Golden Calves at Bethel and Dan

Jeroboam's Sacrifice at Bethel,
1656, Gerbrandt van den Eeckhout

^{25}Then Jeroboam built Shechem in mount Ephraim, and dwelt therein; and went out from thence, and built Penuel. ^{26}And Jeroboam said in his heart, "Now shall the kingdom return to the house of David. ^{27}If this people go up to do sacrifice in the house of the LORD at Jerusalem, then shall the heart of this people turn again unto their lord, even unto Rehoboam king of Judah, and they shall kill me, and go again to Rehoboam king of Judah." ^{28}Whereupon the king took counsel, and made two calves of gold, and said unto them, "It is too much for you to go up to Jerusalem: behold thy gods, O Israel, which brought thee up out of the land of Egypt." ^{29}And he set the one in Bethel, and the other put he in Dan. ^{30}And this thing became a sin: for the people went to worship before the one, even unto Dan.

^{31}And he made an house of high places, and made priests of the lowest of the people, which were not of the sons of Levi. ^{32}And Jeroboam ordained a feast in the eighth month, on the fifteenth day of the month, like unto the feast that is in Judah, and he offered upon the altar. So did he in Bethel, sacrificing unto the calves that he had made: and he placed in Bethel the priests of the high places which he had made. ^{33}So he offered upon the altar which he had made in Bethel the fifteenth day of the eighth month, even in the month which he had devised of his own heart; and ordained a feast unto the children of Israel: and he offered upon the altar, and burnt incense.

Elijah and Ahab

1 Kings 17
Elijah Fed by Ravens

^{1}And Elijah③ the Tishbite, who was of the inhabitants of Gilead, said unto Ahab, "As the LORD God

---

③ Elijah /iˈlaidʒə/, 以利亚。

of Israel liveth, before whom I stand, there shall not be dew nor rain these years, except according to my word."

² And the word of the LORD came unto him, saying, ³ " Get thee hence and turn thee eastward, and hide thyself by the Brook Cherith, that is before the Jordan. ⁴ And it shall be that thou shalt drink of the brook, and I have commanded the ravens to feed thee there."

⁵ So he went and did according unto the word of the LORD; for he went and dwelt by the Brook Cherith, that is before the Jordan. ⁶ And the ravens brought him bread and flesh in the morning, and bread and flesh in the evening; and he drank from the brook.

Landscape with the Prophet Elijah in the Desert, 1610s, Abraham Bloemaert

The Widow at Zarephath

⁷ And it came to pass after a while that the brook dried up, because there had been no rain in the land. ⁸ And the word of the LORD came unto him, saying, ⁹ " Arise, get thee to Zarephath, which belongeth to Sidon, and dwell there. Behold, I have commanded a widow woman there to sustain thee." ¹⁰ So he arose and went to Zarephath. And when he came to the gate of the city, behold, the widow woman was there gathering sticks; and he called to her and said, " Fetch me, I pray thee, a little water in a vessel, that I may drink." ¹¹ And as she was going to fetch it, he called to her and said, " Bring me, I pray thee, a morsel of bread in thine hand."

Prophet Elijah and the Widow of Zarephath, 1630s, Bernardo Strozzi

¹² And she said, " As the LORD thy God liveth, I have not a cake, but a handful of meal in a barrel and a little oil in a cruse. And behold, I am gathering two sticks, that I may go in and dress it for me and my son, that we may eat it and die."

¹³ And Elijah said unto her, " Fear not; go and do as thou hast said, but make me thereof a little cake first, and bring it unto me, and afterward make for thee and for thy son. ¹⁴ For thus saith the LORD God of Israel: ' The barrel of meal shall not waste, neither shall the cruse of oil fail, until the day that the LORD sendeth rain upon the earth.' "

¹⁵ And she went and did according to the saying of Elijah, and she and he and her house ate for many days. ¹⁶ And the barrel of meal wasted not, neither did the cruse of oil fail, according to the word of the LORD which He spoke by Elijah.

¹⁷ And it came to pass after these things that the son of the woman, the mistress of the house, fell sick; and his sickness was so sore that there was no breath left in him. ¹⁸ And she said unto Elijah, " What have I to do with thee, O thou man of God? Art thou come unto me to call my sin to remembrance and to slay my son?"

¹⁹ And he said unto her, " Give me thy son." And he took him out of her bosom, and carried him up into a loft where he abode, and laid him upon his own bed. ²⁰ And he cried unto the LORD and said, " O LORD my God, hast Thou also brought evil upon the widow with whom I sojourn by slaying her son?" ²¹ And he stretched himself upon the child three times, and cried unto the LORD and said, " O LORD my God, I pray Thee, let this child's soul come into him again!"

²² And the LORD heard the voice of Elijah; and the soul of the child came into him again, and he revived. ²³ And Elijah took the child, and brought him down out of the chamber into the house, and delivered him unto his mother; and Elijah said, " See, thy son liveth."

^{24} And the woman said to Elijah, "Now by this I know that thou art a man of God, and that the word of the LORD in thy mouth is truth."

Elijah on Mount Carmel: One Prophet Against 850

1 Kings 18

...

^{16} So Obadiah④ went to meet Ahab, and told him; and Ahab went to meet Elijah. ^{17} And it came to pass, when Ahab saw Elijah, that Ahab said unto him, "Art thou he that troubleth Israel?"

^{18} And he answered, "I have not troubled Israel, but thou and thy father's house, in that ye have forsaken the commandments of the LORD, and thou hast followed the Baalim. ^{19} Now therefore, send and gather to me all Israel unto Mount Carmel, and the prophets of Baal four hundred and fifty, and the prophets of the Asherah⑤ four hundred, who eat at Jezebel's table."

^{20} So Ahab sent unto all the children of Israel, and gathered the prophets together unto Mount Carmel. ^{21} And Elijah came unto all the people and said, "How long halt ye between two opinions? If the LORD be God, follow Him; but if Baal, then follow him."

And the people answered him not a word.

^{22} Then said Elijah unto the people, "I, even I only, remain a prophet of the LORD, but Baal's prophets are four hundred and fifty men. ^{23} Let them therefore give us two bullocks. And let them choose one bullock for themselves and cut it in pieces, and lay it on wood and put no fire under it; and I will dress the other bullock, and lay it on wood, and put no fire under it. ^{24} And call ye on the name of your gods, and I will call on the name of the LORD; and the God that answereth by fire, let Him be God." And all the people answered and said, "It is well spoken."

^{25} And Elijah said unto the prophets of Baal, "Choose you one bullock for yourselves and dress it first, for ye are many; and call on the name of your gods, but put no fire under it." ^{26} And they took the bullock which was given them, and they dressed it, and called on the name of Baal from morning even until noon, saying, "O Baal, hear us!" But there was no voice, nor any that answered. And they leaped upon the altar which was made.

^{27} And it came to pass at noon that Elijah mocked them and said, "Cry aloud, for he is a god! Either he is talking, or he is pursuing, or he is on a journey, or perhaps he sleepeth and must be awakened." ^{28} And they cried aloud, and cut themselves according to their manner with knives and lancets, till the blood gushed out upon them. ^{29} And it came to pass, when midday was past, and they prophesied until the time of the offering of the evening sacrifice, that there was neither voice, nor any to answer, nor any that regarded.

^{30} And Elijah said unto all the people, "Come near unto me." And all the people came near unto him. And he repaired the altar of the LORD that was broken down. ^{31} And Elijah took twelve stones, according to the number of the tribes of the sons of Jacob, unto whom the word of the LORD came, saying, "Israel shall be thy name." ^{32} And with the stones he built an altar in the name of the LORD, and he made a trench about the altar as great as would contain two measures of seed. ^{33} And he put the wood in order, and cut the bullock in pieces, and laid him on the wood and said, "Fill four barrels with water, and pour it on the burnt sacrifice and on the wood."

^{34} And he said, "Do it the second time." And they did it the second time. And he said, "Do it the third time." And they did it the third time. ^{35} And the water ran round about the altar; and he filled the trench also with water.

^{36} And it came to pass at the time of the offering of the evening sacrifice, that Elijah the prophet came near and said, "LORD God of Abraham, Isaac, and of Israel, let it be known this day that Thou art God in Israel,

---

④ **Obadiah** (/ˌʊbəˈdaɪə/, 俄巴底) an official in charge of the palace of Ahab, king of Israel.

⑤ **Asherah** (/ɑːˈʃerə/, 亚舍拉) female equivalent of Baal.

and that I am Thy servant, and that I have done all these things at Thy word. ³⁷ Hear me, O LORD! Hear me, that this people may know that Thou art the LORD God, and that Thou hast turned their heart back again."

³⁸ Then the fire of the LORD fell and consumed the burnt sacrifice, and the wood and the stones and the dust, and licked up the water that was in the trench.

³⁹ And when all the people saw it, they fell on their faces and they said, " The LORD, He is the God! The LORD, He is the God!"

⁴⁰ And Elijah said unto them, " Take the prophets of Baal. Let not one of them escape!" And they took them; and Elijah brought them down to the Brook Kishon and slew them there.

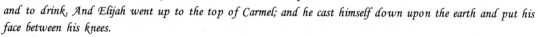

Elijah on Mt. Carmel
⟨http://thekingdomstory.org⟩

⁴¹ And Elijah said unto Ahab, " Get thee up, eat and drink; for there is a sound of abundance of rain." ⁴² So Ahab went up to eat and to drink. And Elijah went up to the top of Carmel; and he cast himself down upon the earth and put his face between his knees.

⁴³ And said to his servant, " Go up now, look toward the sea." And he went up and looked, and said, " There is nothing."

And he said, " Go again, seven times."

⁴⁴ And it came to pass at the seventh time, that he said, " Behold, there ariseth a little cloud out of the sea, like a man's hand."

And he said, " Go up, say unto Ahab, ' Prepare thy chariot, and get thee down, that the rain stop thee not.' "

⁴⁵ And it came to pass in the meantime, that the heaven was black with clouds and wind, and there was a great rain. And Ahab rode, and went to Jezreel. ⁴⁶ And the hand of the LORD was on Elijah; and he girded up his loins, and ran before Ahab to the entrance of Jezreel.

1 Kings 19

¹ And Ahab⑥ told Jezebel⑦ all that Elijah had done, and also how he had slain all the prophets with the sword. ² Then Jezebel sent a messenger unto Elijah, saying, " So let the gods do to me, and more also, if I make not thy life as the life of one of them by tomorrow about this time."

³ And when he saw that, he arose and went for his life and came to Beersheba, which belongeth to Judah, and left his servant there. ⁴ But he himself went a day's journey into the wilderness, and came and sat down under a juniper tree; and he requested for himself that he might die, and said, " It is enough! Now, O LORD, take away my life, for I am not better than my fathers." ⁵ And as he lay and slept under a juniper tree, behold, then an angel touched him and said unto him, " Arise and eat." ⁶ And he looked, and behold, there was a cake baked on the coals and a cruse of water at his head. And he ate and drank, and lay down again.

⁷ And the angel of the LORD came again the second time, and touched him and said, " Arise and eat, because the journey is too great for thee." ⁸ And he arose, and ate and drank, and went in the strength of that meat forty days and forty nights unto Horeb the mount of God.

The Lord Appears to Elijah

⁹ And he came thither unto a cave and lodged there; and behold, the word of the LORD came to him, and

---

⑥ **Ahab**(/ˈeihæb/, 亚哈) Israel's most wicked king.
⑦ **Jezebel** (/ˈdʒezəˌbel/, 耶洗別) Phoenician princess and the wife of Ahab, notorious for spreading her cult of Phoenician deities Baal and Ashtoreth.

He said unto him, "What doest thou here, Elijah?"

¹⁰ And he said, "I have been very jealous for the LORD God of hosts; for the children of Israel have forsaken Thy covenant, thrown down Thine altars, and slain Thy prophets with the sword. And I, even I only, am left; and they seek my life, to take it away."

¹¹ And He said, "Go forth, and stand upon the mount before the LORD."

And behold, the LORD passed by, and a great and strong wind rent the mountains and broke in pieces the rocks before the LORD, but the LORD was not in the wind; and after the wind an earthquake, but the LORD was not in the earthquake. ¹² And after the earthquake a fire, but the LORD was not in the fire; and after the fire a still small voice. ¹³ And it was so, when Elijah heard it, that he wrapped his face in his mantle, and went out and stood in the entrance of the cave.

And behold, there came a voice unto him and said, "What doest thou here, Elijah?"

¹⁴ And he said, "I have been very jealous for the LORD God of hosts, because the children of Israel have forsaken Thy covenant, thrown down Thine altars, and slain Thy prophets with the sword. And I, even I only, am left; and they seek my life, to take it away."

¹⁵ And the LORD said unto him, "Go, return on thy way to the Wilderness of Damascus. And when thou comest, anoint Hazael to be king over Syria; ¹⁶ And Jehu the son of Nimshi shalt thou anoint to be king over Israel; and Elisha the son of Shaphat of Abelmeholah shalt thou anoint to be prophet in thy stead. ¹⁷ And it shall come to pass that him that escapeth the sword of Hazael shall Jehu slay; and him that escapeth from the sword of Jehu shall Elisha slay. ¹⁸ Yet I have left Me seven thousand in Israel, all the knees which have not bowed unto Baal, and every mouth which hath not kissed him."

The Call of Elisha

¹⁹ So he departed from thence, and found Elisha⑧ the son of Shaphat, who was plowing with twelve yoke of oxen before him, and he with the twelfth; and Elijah passed by him, and cast his mantle upon him. ²⁰ And he left the oxen and ran after Elijah, and said, "Let me, I pray thee, kiss my father and my mother, and then I will follow thee."

And he said unto him, "Go back again, for what have I done to thee?"

²¹ And he returned back from him, and took a yoke of oxen and slew them and boiled their flesh with the instruments of the oxen, and gave unto the people, and they ate. Then he arose and went after Elijah, and ministered unto him.

Naboth's Vineyard

1 Kings 21

¹ And it came to pass after these things that Naboth⑨ the Jezreelite had a vineyard which was in Jezreel, hard by the palace of Ahab king of Samaria⑩. ² And Ahab spoke unto Naboth, saying, "Give me thy vineyard, that I may have it for a garden of herbs, because it is near unto my house. And I will give thee for it a better vineyard than it; or, if it seem good to thee, I will give thee the worth of it in money."

³ And Naboth said to Ahab, "The LORD forbid me that I should give the inheritance of my fathers unto thee."

⁴ And Ahab came into his house heavy and displeased because of the word which Naboth the Jezreelite had spoken to him; for he had said, "I will not give thee the inheritance of my fathers." And he lay down upon his bed, and turned away his face, and would eat no bread.

---

⑧ **Elisha** /iˈlaiʃə/, 以利沙。
⑨ **Naboth** /ˈneibɔθ/, 拿伯。
⑩ **Samaria** (/səˈmæriə/, 撒玛利亚) the capital of the northern kingdom of Israel in present-day northwest Jordan.

⁵ But Jezebel his wife came to him, and said unto him, "Why is thy spirit so sad, that thou eatest no bread?"

⁶ And he said unto her, "Because I spoke unto Naboth the Jezreelite and said unto him, 'Give me thy vineyard for money; or else, if it please thee, I will give thee another vineyard for it.' And he answered, 'I will not give thee my vineyard.'"

⁷ And Jezebel his wife said unto him, "Dost thou now govern the kingdom of Israel? Arise, and eat bread, and let thine heart be merry. I will give thee the vineyard of Naboth the Jezreelite."

Naboth Stoned to Death

⁸ So she wrote letters in Ahab's name and sealed them with his seal, and sent the letters unto the elders and to the nobles who were in his city, dwelling with Naboth. ⁹ And she wrote in the letters, saying,

Naboth in His Vineyard, 1856, James Smetham (1821—1889)

"Proclaim a fast, and set Naboth on high among the people. ¹⁰ And set two men, sons of Belial, before him to bear witness against him, saying, 'Thou didst blaspheme God and the king.' And then carry him out and stone him, that he may die."

¹¹ And the men of his city, even the elders and the nobles who were the inhabitants in his city, did as Jezebel had sent unto them and as it was written in the letters which she had sent unto them. ¹² They proclaimed a fast, and set Naboth on high among the people. ¹³ And there came in two men, children of Belial, and sat before him; and the men of Belial witnessed against him, even against Naboth, in the presence of the people, saying, "Naboth blasphemed God and the king." Then they carried him forth out of the city and stoned him with stones, so that he died. ¹⁴ Then they sent to Jezebel, saying, "Naboth has been stoned and is dead."

¹⁵ And it came to pass, when Jezebel heard that Naboth had been stoned and was dead, that Jezebel said to Ahab, "Arise, take possession of the vineyard of Naboth the Jezreelite, which he refused to give thee for money; for Naboth is not alive, but dead." ¹⁶ And it came to pass, when Ahab heard that Naboth was dead, that Ahab rose up to go down to the vineyard of Naboth the Jezreelite to take possession of it.

Elijah Curses Ahab and Jezebel

¹⁷ And the word of the LORD came to Elijah the Tishbite, saying, ¹⁸ "Arise, go down to meet Ahab king of Israel, who is in Samaria. Behold, he is in the vineyard of Naboth, whither he has gone down to possess it. ¹⁹ And thou shalt speak unto him, saying, 'Thus saith the LORD: Hast thou killed and also taken possession?' And thou shalt speak unto him, saying, 'Thus saith the LORD, In the place where dogs licked the blood of Naboth shall dogs lick thy blood, even thine.'"

²⁰ And Ahab said to Elijah, "Hast thou found me, O mine enemy?"

And he answered, "I have found thee, because thou hast sold thyself to work evil in the sight of the LORD. ²¹ 'Behold, I will bring evil upon thee, and will take away thy posterity, and will cut off from Ahab him that urinates against the wall, and him that is shut up and left in Israel. ²² And will make thine house like the house of Jeroboam the son of Nebat, and like the house of Baasha the son of Ahijah, for the provocation wherewith thou hast provoked Me to anger and made Israel sin.'

²³ And of Jezebel also spoke the LORD, saying, 'The dogs shall eat Jezebel by the wall of Jezreel.'

²⁴ Him of Ahab that dieth in the city the dogs shall eat, and him that dieth in the field shall the fowls of the air eat."

²⁵ But there was none like unto Ahab, who sold himself to work wickedness in the sight of the LORD, whom Jezebel his wife stirred up. ²⁶ And he did very abominably in following idols, according to all things as did the Amorites, whom the LORD cast out before the children of Israel.

²⁷ And it came to pass, when Ahab heard those words, that he rent his clothes and put sackcloth upon his

flesh, and fasted and lay in sackcloth, and went about dispiritedly.

²⁸ And the word of the LORD came to Elijah the Tishbite, saying, ²⁹ "Seest thou how Ahab humbleth himself before Me? Because he humbleth himself before Me, I will not bring the evil in his days; but in his son's days will I bring the evil upon his house."

The Curious Death of King Ahab

1 Kings 22

¹ And they continued three years without war between Syria and Israel. ² And it came to pass in the third year, that Jehoshaphat⑪ the king of Judah came down to the king of Israel. ³ And the king of Israel said unto his servants, "Know ye that Ramoth in Gilead is ours, and we be still, and take it not out of the hand of the king of Syria?"

⁴ And he said unto Jehoshaphat, "Wilt thou go with me to battle to Ramothgilead?"

And Jehoshaphat said to the king of Israel, "I am as thou art, my people as thy people, my horses as thy horses." ⁵ And Jehoshaphat said unto the king of Israel, "Enquire, I pray thee, at the word of the LORD to day."

⁶ Then the king of Israel gathered the prophets together, about four hundred men, and said unto them, "Shall I go against Ramothgilead to battle, or shall I forbear?"

And they said, "Go up; for the LORD shall deliver it into the hand of the king."

⁷ And Jehoshaphat said, "Is there not here a prophet of the LORD besides, that we might enquire of him?"

⁸ And the king of Israel said unto Jehoshaphat, "There is yet one man, Micaiah the son of Imlah, by whom we may enquire of the LORD: but I hate him; for he doth not prophesy good concerning me, but evil."

And Jehoshaphat said, "Let not the king say so."

⁹ Then the king of Israel called an officer, and said, "Hasten hither Micaiah the son of Imlah."

¹⁰ And the king of Israel and Jehoshaphat the king of Judah sat each on his throne, having put on their robes, in a void place in the entrance of the gate of Samaria; and all the prophets prophesied before them. ¹¹ And Zedekiah the son of Chenaanah made him horns of iron: and he said, "Thus saith the LORD, 'With these shalt thou push the Syrians, until thou have consumed them.'"

¹² And all the prophets prophesied so, saying, "Go up to Ramothgilead, and prosper: for the LORD shall deliver it into the king's hand."

¹³ And the messenger that was gone to call Micaiah spake unto him, saying, "Behold now, the words of the prophets declare good unto the king with one mouth: let thy word, I pray thee, be like the word of one of them, and speak that which is good."

¹⁴ And Micaiah said, "As the LORD liveth, what the LORD saith unto me, that will I speak."

¹⁵ So he came to the king. And the king said unto him, "Micaiah, shall we go against Ramothgilead to battle, or shall we forbear?"

And he answered him, "Go, and prosper: for the LORD shall deliver it into the hand of the king."

¹⁶ And the king said unto him, "How many times shall I adjure thee that thou tell me nothing but that which is true in the name of the LORD?"

¹⁷ And he said, "I saw all Israel scattered upon the hills, as sheep that have not a shepherd: and the LORD said, 'These have no master: let them return every man to his house in peace.'"

¹⁸ And the king of Israel said unto Jehoshaphat, "Did I not tell thee that he would prophesy no good concerning me, but evil?"

¹⁹ And he said, "Hear thou therefore the word of the LORD: I saw the LORD sitting on his throne, and all the host of heaven standing by him on his right hand and on his left. ²⁰ And the LORD said, "Who shall

---

⑪ **Jehoshaphat** (/dʒɪˈhɒʃəfæt/, 约沙法) king of the southern kingdom of Judah.

persuade Ahab, that he may go up and fall at Ramothgilead?

"And one said on this manner, and another said on that manner. ²¹And there came forth a spirit, and stood before the LORD, and said, ' I will persuade him.'

²²"And the LORD said unto him, ' Wherewith[12]?'

"And he said, ' I will go forth, and I will be a lying spirit in the mouth of all his prophets.'

"And he said, ' Thou shalt persude him, and prevail also: go forth, and do so.'

²³"Now therefore, behold, the LORD hath put a lying spirit in the mouth of all these thy prophets, and the LORD hath spoken evil concerning thee."

²⁴But Zedekiah the son of Chenaanah went near, and smote Micaiah on the cheek, and said, "Which way went the Spirit of the LORD from me to speak unto thee?"

²⁵And Micaiah said, "Behold, thou shalt see in that day, when thou shalt go into an inner chamber to hide thyself."

²⁶And the king of Israel said, "Take Micaiah, and carry him back unto Amon the governor of the city, and to Joash the king's son; ²⁷And say, ' Thus saith the king, Put this fellow in the prison, and feed him with bread of affliction and with water of affliction, until I come in peace.' "

²⁸And Micaiah said, " If thou return at all in peace, the LORD hath not spoken by me." And he said, "Hearken, O people, every one of you."

Ahab Killed by an Arrow Drawn at Random

²⁹So the king of Israel and Jehoshaphat the king of Judah went up to Ramothgilead. ³⁰And the king of Israel said unto Jehoshaphat, " I will disguise myself, and enter into the battle; but put thou on thy robes." And the king of Israel disguised himself, and went into the battle.

³¹But the king of Syria commanded his thirty and two captains that had rule over his chariots, saying, " Fight neither with small nor great, save only with the king of Israel." ³²And it came to pass, when the captains of the chariots saw Jehoshaphat, that they said, "Surely it is the king of Israel." And they turned aside to fight against him: and Jehoshaphat cried out. ³³And it came to pass, when the captains of the chariots perceived that it was not the king of Israel, that they turned back from pursuing him.

³⁴And a certain man drew a bow at a venture, and smote the king of Israel between the joints of the harness: wherefore he said unto the driver of his chariot, " Turn thine hand, and carry me

King Ahab is Killed by an Unaimed Arrow

out of the host; for I am wounded." ³⁵And the battle increased that day: and the king was stayed up in his chariot against the Syrians, and died at even: and the blood ran out of the wound into the midst of the chariot. ³⁶And there went a proclamation throughout the host about the going down of the sun, saying, "Every man to his city, and every man to his own country."

³⁷So the king died, and was brought to Samaria; and they buried the king in Samaria. ³⁸And one washed the chariot in the pool of Samaria; and the dogs licked up his blood; and they washed his armour; according unto the word of the LORD which he spake. ...

---

[12] **Wherewith** by what means.

Cultural Connections: *Mendelssohn's Elijah*

Felix Mendelssohn (1809—1847), wrote and conducted the premier of the Oratoria *Elijah*. Mendelssohn wrote a letter in 1836 to his collaborator on the libretto: "I imagined Elijah as a real prophet through and through, of the kind we could really do with today. Strong, zealous and yes, even bad-tempered, angry and brooding — in contrast to the riff-raff, whether of the court or of the people, and indeed at odds with almost the whole world — and yet borne aloft as if on angels' wings." (Schippe & Stetson, 2005: 104)

III FOOD FOR THOUGHT

1. How did Elijah survive the drought by the brook of Cherith?
2. What might be the narrator's purpose for telling the three stories: Elijah at the brook of Cherith, the jar of meal and the cruse of oil, and the revival of the widow's son?
3. What might the contest between Elijah and the prophets of Baal remind you about Moses before Pharaoh?
4. How would you characterize Ahab and Jezebel?
5. What characteristics do Moses and Elijah have in common and how do they differ?

IV BIBLICAL RELEVANCE

A. Biblical Terms in Everyday English
1. Naboth's vineyard(21): _____
2. draw a bow at random(22:34): _____

B. Biblical References in Literature
1. "Does Judith or either of the boys ever come down to hear you preach?"... "Nay, they strut like Ahab in their pride, and their eyes drip fatness, nor do they see the pit digged beneath their feet by the Lord."

   (Stella Gibbons, *Cold Comfort Farm*, 1932)

2. Canada, where Biblical references are still understood by quite a few people, sees itself suddenly as Naboth's Vineyard.

   (Robertson Davies, *Merry Heart*, 1998)

C. The Bible and Arts
1. *The Israelites Refuse to Accept Rehoboam as Their King*, 1851—1860, Julius Schnorr von Carolsfeld
2. *Elijah Fed by Ravens*, 1620, Guercino

3. *Prophet Elijah and the Widow of Zarephath*, 1630s, Bernardo Strozzi
4. *Elijah in the Wilderness*, c. 1878, Lord Frederic Leighton
5. *Naboth in His Vineyard*, 1856, James Smetham, 1821—1889

V SOURCES FOR REFERENCE

1. Browning, W. R. E. (2009). *A Dictionary of the Bible*. Oxford: Oxford University Press.
2. Roche, P. (2001). *The Bible's Greatest Stories*. New York: New American Library.

23. ELISHA

I. POINTS OF DEPARTURE

When time came for Elijah to ascend to heaven, he was taken up in a whirlwind accompanied by a chariot and horses of flame or riding in it. By taking the mantle let fall from Elijah, Elisha miraculously recrossed the Jordan, and won from the prophets at Jericho the recognition that "the spirit of Elijah doth rest on Elisha." (*2 Kings 2:15*) This symbolic transfer of responsibility is suggestive of the passing on of a mantle and an alms bowl (衣钵相传), a Buddhist ritual in which a monk hands down his knowledge to his favourite disciple.

Different from Elijah, who lived apart from the people, and preached judgment and the need for repentance, Elisha lived among the people, preferring the poor and outcast, and stressed life, hope and God's grace. But like Elijah, he was a miracle worker, dividing the waters of the Jordan, striking his enemies with blindness, recovering an axe-head from the water and making it float. But his healing of the Syrian commander Naaman's leprosy during a temporary lull in the sporadic conflicts between Israel and the Syrians was a demonstration of the power and mercy of God of Israel.

Anointed king of Israel after the death of King Ahab, Jehu was encouraged by Elisha to stage a coup which brought about the death of Jezebel. Jehu also slaughtered the worshippers of Baal. That is why Jehu is condemned by the prophet Hosea (*Hos. 1:4*).

II. SELECTED READINGS

Elijah Taken up to Heaven

2 Kings 2

¹ *And it came to pass, when the LORD would take up Elijah into heaven by a whirlwind, that Elijah went with Elisha from Gilgal.* ² *And Elijah said unto Elisha, "Tarry here, I pray thee; for the LORD hath sent me to Bethel."*

And Elisha said unto him, "As the LORD liveth and as thy soul liveth, I will not leave thee." So they went down to Bethel.

³ *And the sons of the prophets who were at Bethel came forth to Elisha and said unto him, "Knowest thou that the LORD will take away thy master from thy head today?"*

And he said, "Yea, I know it; hold ye your peace."

⁴ *And Elijah said unto him, "Elisha, tarry here, I pray thee; for the LORD hath sent me to Jericho."*

And he said, "As the LORD liveth and as thy soul liveth, I will not leave thee." So they came to Jericho.

⁵ And the sons of the prophets who were at Jericho came to Elisha and said unto him, "Knowest thou that the LORD will take away thy master from thy head today?"

And he answered, "Yea, I know it; hold ye your peace."

⁶ And Elijah said unto him, "Tarry, I pray thee, here; for the LORD hath sent me to the Jordan."

And he said, "As the LORD liveth and as thy soul liveth, I will not leave thee." And the two went on.

Elijah Stops the Jordan River

⁷ And fifty men of the sons of the prophets went and stood in sight to view afar off; and they two stood by the Jordan. ⁸ And Elijah took his mantle and wrapped it together and smote the waters, and they were divided hither and thither so that the two went over on dry ground.

⁹ And it came to pass, when they had gone over, that Elijah said unto Elisha, "Ask what I shall do for thee, before I be taken away from thee."

And Elisha said, "I pray thee, let a double portion of thy spirit be upon me."

¹⁰ And he said, "Thou hast asked a hard thing. Nevertheless, if thou see me when I am taken from thee, it shall be so unto thee; but if not, it shall not be so."

A Chariot of Fire

¹¹ And it came to pass, as they still went on and talked, that, behold, there appeared a chariot of fire and horses of fire, and parted them both asunder; and Elijah went up by a whirlwind into heaven. ¹² And Elisha saw it, and he cried, "My father, my father, the chariot of Israel and the horsemen thereof!" And he saw him no more. And he took hold of his own clothes, and rent them in two pieces.

¹³ He took up also the mantle of Elijah that fell from him, and went back and stood by the bank of the Jordan. ¹⁴ And he took the mantle of Elijah that fell from him, and smote the waters and said, "Where is the LORD God of Elijah?" And when he also had smitten the waters, they parted hither and thither; and Elisha went over.

Elijah Taken up in a Chariot of Fire, 1712, Giuseppe Angeli

¹⁵ And when the sons of the prophets who were in view at Jericho saw him, they said, "The spirit of Elijah doth rest on Elisha." And they came to meet him, and bowed themselves to the ground before him. ¹⁶ And they said unto him, "Behold now, there are with thy servants fifty strong men. Let them go, we pray thee, and seek thy master, lest perhaps the Spirit of the LORD hath taken him up and cast him upon some mountain or into some valley."

And he said, "Ye shall not send."

¹⁷ And when they urged him till he was ashamed, he said, "Send." They sent therefore fifty men, and they sought three days but found him not. ¹⁸ And when they came again to him (for he tarried at Jericho), he said unto them, "Did I not say unto you, 'Go not'?"

Healing of the Water

¹⁹ And the men of the city said unto Elisha, "Behold, I pray thee, the situation of this city is pleasant, as my lord seeth; but the water is nought, and the ground barren."

²⁰ And he said, "Bring me a new cruse, and put salt therein." And they brought it to him.

²¹ And he went forth unto the spring of the waters, and cast the salt in there and said, "Thus saith the LORD: 'I have healed these waters; there shall not be from thence any more death or barren land.'" ²² So the

waters were healed unto this day, according to the saying of Elisha which he spoke.

Cultural Connections: *the movie Chariots of Fire*

The 1981 film *Chariots of Fire*, tells the story of two athletes preparing for the 1924 Olympics. The film's title was inspired by the line, "Bring me my chariot of fire," from William Blake's poem "Jerusalem," though the phrase is biblical in origin. The titular theme music of the film was a 1980s hit and has been used in many films and television shows.

Elisha Mocked and His Revenge

²³ And he went up from thence unto Bethel. And as he was going up by the way, there came forth little children out of the city, and mocked him and said unto him, "Go up, thou bald head! Go up, thou bald head!" ²⁴ And he turned back and looked on them, and cursed them in the name of the LORD. And there came forth two shebears out of the wood and tore forty and two children of them. ²⁵ And he went from thence to Mount Carmel, and from thence he returned to Samaria.

Elisha's Miracles

2 Kings 4

The Widow's Oil Supply Amplified

¹ Now there cried a certain woman of the wives of the sons of the prophets unto Elisha, saying, "Thy servant my husband is dead; and thou knowest that thy servant did fear the LORD: and the creditor is come to take unto him my two sons to be bondmen."

² And Elisha said unto her, "What shall I do for thee? Tell me, what hast thou in the house?"

And she said, "Thine handmaid hath not any thing in the house, save a pot of oil."

³ Then he said, "Go, borrow thee vessels abroad of all thy neighbours, even empty vessels; borrow not a few." ⁴ And when thou art come in, thou shalt shut the door upon thee and upon thy sons, and shalt pour out into all those vessels, and thou shalt set aside that which is full."

⁵ So she went from him, and shut the door upon her and upon her sons, who brought the vessels to her; and she poured out. ⁶ And it came to pass, when the vessels were full, that she said unto her son, "Bring me yet a vessel."

And he said unto her, "There is not a vessel more." And the oil stayed.

⁷ Then she came and told the man of God. And he said, "Go, sell the oil, and pay thy debt, and live thou and thy children of the rest."

The Shunammite's Son Restored to Life

⁸ And it fell on a day, that Elisha passed to Shunem, where was a great woman; and she constrained him to eat bread. And so it was, that as oft as he passed by, he turned in thither to eat bread. ⁹ And she said unto her husband, "Behold now, I perceive that this is an holy man of God, which passeth by us continually. ¹⁰ Let us make a little chamber, I pray thee, on the wall; and let us set for him there a bed, and a table, and a stool,

and a candlestick; and it shall be, when he cometh to us, that he shall turn in thither."

^{11} And it fell on a day, that he came thither, and he turned into the chamber, and lay there. ^{12} And he said to Gehazi his servant, " Call this Shunammite." And when he had called her, she stood before him. ^{13} And he said unto him, " Say now unto her, Behold, thou hast been careful for us with all this care; what is to be done for thee? Wouldest thou be spoken for to the king, or to the captain of the host?"

And she answered, " I dwell among mine own people."

^{14} And he said, " What then is to be done for her?" And Gehazi answered, " Verily she hath no child, and her husband is old."

^{15} And he said, " Call her." And when he had called her, she stood in the door. ^{16} And he said, " About this season, according to the time of life, thou shalt embrace a son." And she said, " Nay, my lord, thou man of God, do not lie unto thine handmaid."

^{17} And the woman conceived, and bare a son at that season that Elisha had said unto her, according to the time of life.

^{18} And when the child was grown, it fell on a day, that he went out to his father to the reapers. ^{19} And he said unto his father, " My head, my head."

And he said to a lad, " Carry him to his mother." ^{20} And when he had taken him, and brought him to his mother, he sat on her knees till noon, and then died. ^{21} And she went up, and laid him on the bed of the man of God, and shut the door upon him, and went out.

^{22} And she called unto her husband, and said, " Send me, I pray thee, one of the young men, and one of the asses, that I may run to the man of God, and come again."

^{23} And he said, " Wherefore wilt thou go to him to day? It is neither new moon, nor sabbath."

And she said, " It shall be well."

^{24} Then she saddled an ass, and said to her servant, " Drive, and go forward; slack not thy riding for me, except I bid thee." ^{25} So she went and came unto the man of God to mount Carmel. And it came to pass, when the man of God saw her afar off, that he said to Gehazi his servant, " Behold, yonder is that Shunammite. ^{26} Run now, I pray thee, to meet her, and say unto her, ' Is it well with thee? Is it well with thy husband? Is it well with the child?' "

And she answered, " It is well."

^{27} And when she came to the man of God to the hill, she caught him by the feet: but Gehazi came near to thrust her away. And the man of God said, " Let her alone; for her soul is vexed within her: and the LORD hath hid it from me, and hath not told me."

^{28} Then she said, " Did I desire a son of my lord? Did I not say, do not deceive me?"

^{29} Then he said to Gehazi, " Gird up thy loins, and take my staff in thine hand, and go thy way: if thou meet any man, salute him not; and if any salute thee, answer him not again: and lay my staff upon the face of the child."

Elisha Raising the Son of the Shunamite, 1881, Frederic Leighton

^{30} And the mother of the child said, " As the LORD liveth, and as thy soul liveth, I will not leave thee." And he arose, and followed her.

^{31} And Gehazi passed on before them, and laid the staff upon the face of the child; but there was neither voice, nor hearing. Wherefore he went again to meet him, and told him, saying, " The child is not awaked."

^{32} And when Elisha was come into the house, behold, the child was dead, and laid upon his bed. ^{33} He went in therefore, and shut the door upon them twain, and prayed unto the LORD. ^{34} And he went up, and lay upon the child, and put his mouth upon his mouth, and his eyes upon his eyes, and his hands upon his hands: and stretched himself upon the child; and the flesh of the child waxed warm. ^{35} Then he returned, and walked in the house to and fro; and went up, and stretched himself upon him: and the child sneezed seven times, and the child opened his eyes.

³⁶ And he called Gehazi, and said, "Call this Shunammite." So he called her. And when she was come in unto him, he said, "Take up thy son." ³⁷ Then she went in, and fell at his feet, and bowed herself to the ground, and took up her son, and went out.

Death in the Pot

³⁸ And Elisha came again to Gilgal: and there was a dearth in the land; and the sons of the prophets were sitting before him: and he said unto his servant, "Set on the great pot, and seethe pottage for the sons of the prophets."

³⁹ And one went out into the field to gather herbs, and found a wild vine, and gathered thereof wild gourds his lap full, and came and shred them into the pot of pottage: for they knew them not. ⁴⁰ So they poured out for the men to eat. And it came to pass, as they were eating of the pottage, that they cried out, and said, "O thou man of God, there is death① in the pot." And they could not eat thereof.

⁴¹ But he said, "Then bring meal." And he cast it into the pot; and he said, "Pour out for the people, that they may eat." And there was no harm in the pot.

Feeding of a Hundred

⁴² And there came a man from Baalshalisha, and brought the man of God bread of the firstfruits, twenty loaves of barley, and full ears of corn in the husk thereof. And he said, "Give unto the people, that they may eat."

⁴³ And his servitor said, "What, should I set this before an hundred men?" He said again, "Give the people, that they may eat: for thus saith the LORD, 'They shall eat, and shall leave thereof.'" ⁴⁴ So he set it before them, and they did eat, and left thereof, according to the word of the LORD.

Naaman Healed of Leprosy

2 Kings 5

¹ Now Naaman, captain of the host of the king of Syria, was a great man with his master, and honourable, because by him the LORD had given deliverance unto Syria: he was also a mighty man in valour, but he was a leper.

² And the Syrians had gone out by companies, and had brought away captive out of the land of Israel a little maid; and she waited on Naaman's wife. ³ And she said unto her mistress, "Would God my lord were with the prophet that is in Samaria! For he would recover him of his leprosy."

⁴ And one went in, and told his lord, saying, "Thus and thus said the maid that is of the land of Israel." ⁵ And the king of Syria said, "Go to, go, and I will send a letter unto the king of Israel." And he departed, and took with him ten talents of silver, and six thousand pieces of gold, and ten changes of raiment. ⁶ And he brought the letter to the king of Israel, saying, "Now when this letter is come unto thee, behold, I have therewith sent Naaman my servant to thee, that thou mayest recover him of his leprosy."

⁷ And it came to pass, when the king of Israel had read the letter, that he rent his clothes, and said, "Am I God, to kill and to make alive, that this man doth send unto me to recover a man of his leprosy? Wherefore consider, I pray you, and see how he seeketh a quarrel against me."

---

① **death** colocynths (苦西瓜), which if taken in large quantities are poisonous (Black, 2001: 349)

Washing in Jordan 7 Times

⁸And it was so, when Elisha the man of God had heard that the king of Israel had rent his clothes, that he sent to the king, saying, "Wherefore hast thou rent thy clothes? Let him come now to me, and he shall know that there is a prophet in Israel." ⁹So Naaman came with his horses and with his chariot, and stood at the door of the house of Elisha. ¹⁰And Elisha sent a messenger unto him, saying, "Go and wash in Jordan seven times, and thy flesh shall come again to thee, and thou shalt be clean."

¹¹But Naaman was wroth, and went away, and said, "Behold, I thought, He will surely come out to me, and stand, and call on the name of the LORD his God, and strike his hand over the place, and recover the leper. ¹²Are not Abana and Pharpar, rivers of Damascus, better than all the waters of Israel? May I not wash in them, and be clean?" So he turned and went away in a rage.

The Prophet Elisha and Naaman, Lambert Jacobsz (1598—1636)

¹³And his servants came near, and spake unto him, and said, "My father, if the prophet had bid thee do some great thing, wouldest thou not have done it? How much rather then, when he saith to thee, 'Wash, and be clean?'" ¹⁴Then went he down, and dipped himself seven times in Jordan, according to the saying of the man of God: and his flesh came again like unto the flesh of a little child, and he was clean.

Naaman Converted

¹⁵And he returned to the man of God, he and all his company, and came, and stood before him: and he said, "Behold, now I know that there is no God in all the earth, but in Israel: now therefore, I pray thee, take a blessing of thy servant."

¹⁶But he said, "As the LORD liveth, before whom I stand, I will receive none." And he urged him to take it; but he refused.

¹⁷And Naaman said, "Shall there not then, I pray thee, be given to thy servant two mules' burden of earth? For thy servant will henceforth offer neither burnt offering nor sacrifice unto other gods, but unto the LORD. ¹⁸In this thing the LORD pardon thy servant, that when my master goeth into the house of Rimmon② to worship there, and he leaneth on my hand, and I bow myself in the house of Rimmon: when I bow down myself in the house of Rimmon, the LORD pardon thy servant in this thing."

Refusing Gifts from Naaman, 1630, Pieter De Grebber

¹⁹And he said unto him, "Go in peace."

The Greedy Gehazi

So he departed from him a little way. ²⁰But Gehazi, the servant of Elisha the man of God, said, "Behold, my master hath spared Naaman this Syrian, in not receiving at his hands that which he brought: but, as the LORD liveth, I will run after him, and take somewhat of him."

²¹So Gehazi followed after Naaman. And when Naaman saw him running after him, he lighted down from the chariot to meet him, and said, "Is all well?"

---

② **Rimmon** (/ˈrimən/, 临门) the Assyrian storm-god.

²² And he said, "All is well. My master hath sent me, saying, ' Behold, even now there be come to me from mount Ephraim two young men of the sons of the prophets: give them, I pray thee, a talent of silver, and two changes of garments.' "

²³ And Naaman said, " Be content, take two talents." And he urged him, and bound two talents of silver in two bags, with two changes of garments, and laid them upon two of his servants; and they bare them before him. ²⁴ And when he came to the tower, he took them from their hand, and bestowed them in the house: and he let the men go, and they departed. ²⁵ But he went in, and stood before his master.

And Elisha said unto him, " Whence comest thou, Gehazi?"

And he said, " Thy servant went no whither."

²⁶ And he said unto him, " Went not mine heart with thee, when the man turned again from his chariot to meet thee? Is it a time to receive money, and to receive garments, and oliveyards, and vineyards, and sheep, and oxen, and menservants, and maidservants? ²⁷ The leprosy therefore of Naaman shall cleave unto thee, and unto thy seed for ever." And he went out from his presence a leper as white as snow.

Jehu Anointed King of Israel

2 Kings 9

¹ And Elisha the prophet called one of the children of the prophets, and said unto him, " Gird up thy loins, and take this box of oil in thine hand and go to Ramothgilead. ² And when thou comest thither, seek out there Jehu the son of Jehoshaphat the son of Nimshi, and go in and make him arise up from among his brethren, and carry him to an inner chamber. ³ Then take the box of oil, and pour it on his head and say, ' Thus saith the LORD: I have anointed thee king over Israel.' Then open the door and flee, and tarry not."

⁴ So the young man, even the young man the prophet, went to Ramothgilead. ⁵ And when he came, behold, the captains of the host were sitting; and he said,

" I have a message for thee, O captain."

And Jehu said, " Unto which of us all?"

And he said, " To thee, O captain."

⁶ And he arose and went into the house; and he poured the oil on his head and said unto him, " Thus saith the LORD God of Israel: ' I have anointed thee king over the people of the LORD, even over Israel. ⁷ And thou shalt smite the house of Ahab thy master, that I may avenge the blood of My servants the prophets, and the blood of all the servants of the LORD, at the hand of Jezebel. ⁸ For the whole house of Ahab shall perish; and I will cut off from Ahab him that urinates against the wall, and him that is shut up and left in Israel. ⁹ And I will make the house of Ahab like the house of Jeroboam the son of Nebat and like the house of Baasha the son of Ahijah. ¹⁰ And the dogs shall eat Jezebel in the portion of Jezreel, and there shall be none to bury her.' " And he opened the door and fled.

¹¹ Then Jehu came forth to the servants of his lord; and one said unto him, " Is all well? Why came this mad fellow to thee?"

And he said unto them, " Ye know the man and his communication."

¹² And they said, " It is false; tell us now."

And he said, " Thus and thus spoke he to me, saying, ' Thus saith the LORD: I have anointed thee king over Israel.' "

¹³ Then they hastened and took every man his garment, and put it under him on the top of the stairs, and blew with trumpets, saying, " Jehu is king!"

Jehu Kills Joram and Ahaziah

¹⁴ So Jehu the son of Jehoshaphat the son of Nimshi conspired against Joram. (Now Joram had kept Ramothgilead, he and all Israel, because of Hazael king of Syria. ¹⁵ But King Joram had returned to be healed

in Jezreel of the wounds which the Syrians had given him when he fought with Hazael king of Syria.) And Jehu said, "If it be your minds, then let none go forth nor escape out of the city to go to tell it in Jezreel." ¹⁶ So Jehu rode in a chariot and went to Jezreel, for Joram lay there. And Ahaziah king of Judah had come down to see Joram.

¹⁷ And there stood a watchman on the tower in Jezreel, and he spied the company of Jehu as he came, and said, "I see a company."

And Joram said, "Take a horseman and send to meet them, and let him say, 'Is it peace?' "

¹⁸ So there went one on horseback to meet him, and said, "Thus saith the king: 'Is it peace?' "

And Jehu said, "What hast thou to do with peace? Turn thee in behind me." And the watchman told, saying, "The messenger came to them, but he cometh not back."

¹⁹ Then he sent out a second on horseback, who came to them and said, "Thus saith the king: 'Is it peace?' " And Jehu answered, "What hast thou to do with peace? Turn thee in behind me." ²⁰ And the watchman told, saying, "He came even unto them and cometh not back; and the driving is like the driving of Jehu the son of Nimshi, for he driveth furiously."

²¹ And Joram said, "Make ready." And his chariot was made ready. And Joram king of Israel and Ahaziah king of Judah went out, each in his chariot; and they went out against Jehu and met him in the portion of Naboth the Jezreelite. ²² And it came to pass, when Joram saw Jehu, that he said, "Is it peace, Jehu?"

And he answered, "What peace, so long as the whoredoms of thy mother Jezebel and her witchcrafts are so many?"

²³ And Joram turned his hands and fled, and said to Ahaziah, "There is treachery, O Ahaziah!"

²⁴ And Jehu drew a bow with his full strength and smote Joram between his arms, and the arrow went out at his heart, and he sank down in his chariot. ²⁵ Then said Jehu to Bidkar his captain, "Take him up, and cast him in the portion of the field of Naboth the Jezreelite; for remember how when I and thou rode together after Ahab his father, the LORD laid this burden upon him:

²⁶ ' Surely I have seen yesterday the blood of Naboth and the blood of his sons, saith the LORD, and I will requite thee in this plot, saith the LORD.' Now therefore take and cast him into the plot of ground, according to the word of the LORD."

²⁷ But when Ahaziah the king of Judah saw this, he fled by the way of the garden house. And Jehu followed after him and said, "Smite him also in the chariot." And they did so at the ascent to Gur, which is by Ibleam. And he fled to Megiddo, and died there. ²⁸ And his servants carried him in a chariot to Jerusalem, and buried him in his sepulcher with his fathers in the City of David.

²⁹ And in the eleventh year of Joram the son of Ahab, Ahaziah had begun to reign over Judah.

The Painted Jezebel Killed

³⁰ And when Jehu had come to Jezreel, Jezebel heard of it; and she painted her face and attired her head, and looked out at a window. ³¹ And as Jehu entered in at the gate, she said, "Had Zimri peace, who slew his master?"

³² And he lifted up his face to the window and said, "Who is on my side? Who?" And there looked out at him two or three eunuchs. ³³ And he said, "Throw her down!" So they threw her down, and some of her blood was sprinkled on the wall and on the horses; and he trod her underfoot.

³⁴ And when he had come in, he ate and drank, and said, "Go, see now this cursed woman, and bury her; for she is a king's daughter." ³⁵ And they went to bury her, but they found no more of her than the skull and the feet and the palms of her hands. ³⁶ Therefore they came back and told him. And he said, "This is the word of the LORD, which He spoke by His

The Death of Jezebel,
William Hole (1846—1917)

servant Elijah the Tishbite, saying, ' In the portion of Jezreel shall dogs eat the flesh of Jezebel.' "

^{37} And the carcass of Jezebel shall be as dung upon the face of the field in the portion of Jezreel, so that they shall not say, " This is Jezebel."

The Fall of Jerusalem

2 Kings 25

^{1} And it came to pass in the ninth year of his reign, in the tenth month, in the tenth day of the month, that Nebuchadnezzar king of Babylon came, he, and all his host, against Jerusalem, and pitched against it; and they built forts against it round about. ^{2} And the city was besieged unto the eleventh year of king Zedekiah. ^{3} And on the ninth day of the fourth month the famine prevailed in the city, and there was no bread for the people of the land. ^{4} And the city was broken up, and all the men of war fled by night by the way of the gate between two walls, which is by the king's garden: (now the Chaldees were against the city round about:) and the king went the way toward the plain. ^{5} And the army of the Chaldees pursued after the king, and overtook him in the plains of Jericho: and all his army were scattered from him. ^{6} So they took the king, and brought him up to the king of Babylon to Riblah; and they gave judgment upon him. ^{7} And they slew the sons of Zedekiah before his eyes, and put out the eyes of Zedekiah, and bound him with fetters of brass, and carried him to Babylon.

^{8} And in the fifth month, on the seventh day of the month, which is the nineteenth year of king Nebuchadnezzar king of Babylon, came Nebuzaradan, captain of the guard, a servant of the king of Babylon, unto Jerusalem: ^{9} And he burnt the house of the LORD, and the king's house, and all the houses of Jerusalem, and every great man's house burnt he with fire. ^{10} And all the army of the Chaldees, that were with the captain of the guard, brake down the walls of Jerusalem round about. ^{11} Now the rest of the people that were left in the city, and the fugitives that fell away to the king of Babylon, with the remnant of the multitude, did Nebuzaradan the captain of the guard carry away. ^{12} But the captain of the guard left of the door of the poor of the land to be vinedressers and husbandmen.

^{13} And the pillars of brass that were in the house of the LORD, and the bases, and the brasen sea that was in the house of the LORD, did the Chaldees break in pieces, and carried the brass of them to Babylon. ^{14} And the pots, and the shovels, and the snuffers, and the spoons, and all the vessels of brass wherewith they ministered, took they away. ^{15} And the firepans, and the bowls, and such things as were of gold, in gold, and of silver, in silver, the captain of the guard took away.

^{16} The two pillars, one sea, and the bases which Solomon had made for the house of the LORD; the brass of all these vessels was without weight. ^{17} The height of the one pillar was eighteen cubits, and the chapiter upon it was brass: and the height of the chapiter three cubits; and the wreathen work, and pomegranates upon the chapiter round about, all of brass: and like unto these had the second pillar with wreathen work.

^{18} And the captain of the guard took Seraiah the chief priest, and Zephaniah the second priest, and the three keepers of the door. ^{19} And out of the city he took an officer that was set over the men of war, and five men of them that were in the king's presence, which were found in the city, and the principal scribe of the host, which mustered the people of the land, and threescore men of the people of the land that were found in the city. ^{20} And Nebuzaradan captain of the guard took these, and brought them to the king of Babylon to Riblah. ^{21} And the king of Babylon smote them, and slew them at Riblah in the land of Hamath.

So Judah was carried away out of their land.

^{22} And as for the people that remained in the land of Judah, whom Nebuchadnezzar king of Babylon had left, even over them he made Gedaliah the son of Ahikam, the son of Shaphan, ruler. ^{23} And when all the captains of the armies, they and their men, heard that the king of Babylon had made Gedaliah governor, there came to Gedaliah to Mizpah, even Ishmael the son of Nethaniah, and Johanan the son of Careah, and Seraiah the son of Tanhumeth the Netophathite, and Jaazaniah the son of a Maachathite, they and their men. ^{24} And Gedaliah sware to them, and to their men, and said unto them, " Fear not to be the servants of the Chaldees:

dwell in the land, and serve the king of Babylon; and it shall be well with you."

²⁵ *But it came to pass in the seventh month, that Ishmael the son of Nethaniah, the son of Elishama, of the seed royal, came, and ten men with him, and smote Gedaliah, that he died, and the Jews and the Chaldees that were with him at Mizpah.* ²⁶ *And all the people, both small and great, and the captains of the armies, arose, and came to Egypt: for they were afraid of the Chaldees.*

²⁷ *And it came to pass in the seven and thirtieth year of the captivity of Jehoiachin king of Judah, in the twelfth month, on the seven and twentieth day of the month, that Evilmerodach king of Babylon in the year that he began to reign did lift up the head of Jehoiachin king of Judah out of prison;* ²⁸ *And he spake kindly to him, and set his throne above the throne of the kings that were with him in Babylon;* ²⁹ *And changed his prison garments: and he did eat bread continually before him all the days of his life.* ³⁰ *And his allowance was a continual allowance given him of the king, a daily rate for every day, all the days of his life.*

III FOOD FOR THOUGHT

1. Can you describe some of the miracles performed by Elisha?
2. What did Jezebel's actions reveal about her character?
3. What led to the destruction of Jerusalem?
4. What were the different styles of Elijah and Elisha?
5. What is meant by the "Babylonian captivity"?

IV BIBLICAL RELEVANCE

A. Biblical Terms in Everyday English
1. Elijah's mantle: _____
2. a painted Jezebel (9:30): _____
3. gird up one's loins (9:1): _____
4. Jehu: _____

B. Biblical References in Literature
1. But like the prophet in the chariot disappearing in heaven and dropping his mantle to Elisha, the withdrawing night transferred its pale robe to the breaking day.
   (Herman Melville, *Billy Budd, Foretopman*, 1891)
2. "Mr Slope," said Mrs Proudie, catching the delinquent at the door, "I'm surprised that you should leave my company to attend on such a painted Jezebel as that."
   (Anthony Trollope, *Barchester Towrs*, 1857)
3. I have been a Jezebel, a London prostitute, and what not.
   (Samuel Richardson, *Pamela*, 1740)
4. Red flames will lick round their feet like the dogs lickin' Jezebel's blood in the Good Book.
   (Stella Gibbons, *Cold Comfort Farm*, 1932)
5. And at last away he drove, Jehu-like, as they say, out of the courtyard.
   (Samuel Richardson, *Pamela*, 1740)

C. The Bible and Arts
1. *Elijah Taken up in a Chariot of Fire*, 1712, Giuseppe Angeli
2. *Prophet Elisha and the Woman of Shunem*, 1664, Gerbrandt van den Eeckhout

3. *The Prophet Elisha and Naaman*, Lambert Jacobsz (1598—1636)
4. *The Prophet Elisha*, c. 1566, Giorgio Vasari
5. *The Entry of Jehu into Jezebel*, Edward Corbould (1815—1905)

V SOURCES FOR REFERENCE

1. Black, M. (ed.) (2001). *Peake's Commentary on the Bible*. London: Routledge.
2. Yancey, P. & T. Stafford (notes by) (1989). *The New Student Bible*, *New International Version*. Grand Rapids, Mich: Zondervan Publishing House.

PART SEVEN

PALESTINE DURING THE ASSYRIAN, BABYLONIAN, PERSIAN AND GREEK DOMINATION

(C. 842—4 B.C.E.)

THE BOOKS OF ESTHER, JOB, ISAIAH, JEREMIAH, EZEKIEL, JONAH, DANIEL

24. ESTHER

I POINTS OF DEPARTURE

Harem politics, anti-semitism, and an audacious Jewish heroine combine to make the Book of Esther extremely popular among readers of the Bible. The time was the Persian period during the reign of Ahasuerus①. Esther, a Jewish beauty, became the Persian queen after the deposal of the Queen Vashti for her refusal to exhibit her charm. Influenced and instructed by her adoptive-father-like cousin Mordecai, she then pleaded successfully with her husband, for her people and Mordecai, and aborted the wicked plan of Haman who was intent on destroying all Jews in the land because of a supposed slight from Mordecai. After a series of banquets and intrigues behind them, the tables were unexpectedly turned: Haman was hanged on the very gallows he had erected for Mordecai and his people, and his own sons were killed on the very date he had set for the annihilation of Jews.

There is no mention of God or religion in the book, which is normally thought to provide a historical origin for the non-religious feast of Purim, when the Jewish people gather for good time of dancing, singing, feasting, rejoicing, and gift-giving. Patriotism is not the motivation for the book, either, since the indiscriminate tit-for-tat against Gentiles on Purim suggests a narrow nationalist sentiment. And Esther's patriotic heroism in risking her life for her people is somewhat downplayed by the fact that she refused to do so until her scheming cousin threatened her with an inescapable death in the event of an imminent genocide. In spite of its odd place in the supposedly religious Bible, Esther can be rightfully rated as a mature piece of literary work, replete with all the ingredients found in an engaging story—a beautiful and courageous heroine, a romantic love thread, a dire threat to the good characters, and ideally villainous villain, suspense, dramatic irony, evocative descriptions of exotic places, sudden reversal action, poetic justice, and a happy ending. (Ryken & Ryken, 2007:671) This tale has exerted a profound influence on Western literature, evidenced by the well-acclaimed tragedy *Esther* written in 1689 by the French dramatist, Jean Racine (朱维之, 2008:406).

To compensate for the lack of religious tone in the original Hebrew Bible, the LXX made some additions, which ascribed the reversal of fortunes, because of her beauty and her valor in the book, to her piety. These additions are now found in the Apocrypha in Protestant Bibles, but are only inserted in the appropriate places within the text of Catholic Bibles. (Browning, 2009:196)

---

① **Ahasuerus** (/əˌhæzjuˈiərəs/, 亚哈随鲁) a variant of Xerxes' Persian name. Xerxes (/ˈzɜːksiːz/, 薛西斯, c. 519—465 B. C. E.) I, son of Darius (/dəˈraiəs/, 大流士) I, was the king of Persian 486—465, famous for his victories in 480 B. C. E. at Artemisium and Thermopylae, but defeats at Salamis. He was killed in a court intrigue.

II SELECTED READINGS

Queen Vashti Deposed

Esther 1
Ahasuerus' Banquet

¹ Now it came to pass in the days of Ahasuerus, (this is Ahasuerus which reigned, from India even unto Ethiopia, over an hundred and seven and twenty provinces:) ² That in those days, when the king Ahasuerus sat on the throne of his kingdom, which was in Shushan the palace. ³ In the third year of his reign, he made a feast unto all his princes and his servants; the power of Persia and Media, the nobles and princes of the provinces, being before him.

⁴ When he shewed the riches of his glorious kingdom and the honour of his excellent majesty many days, even an hundred and fourscore days. ⁵ And when these days were expired, the king made a feast unto all the people that were present in Shushan the palace, both unto great and small, seven days, in the court of the garden of the king's palace; ⁶ Where were white, green, and blue, hangings, fastened with cords of fine linen and purple to silver rings and pillars of marble; the beds were of gold and silver, upon a pavement of red, and blue, and white, and black, marble. ⁷ And they gave them drink in vessels of gold, (the vessels being diverse one from another,) and royal wine in abundance, according to the

The Banquet of Ahasuerus, c. 1680s, Sellaio del Jacopo

state of the king. ⁸ And the drinking was according to the law; none did compel: for so the king had appointed to all the officers of his house, that they should do according to every man's pleasure.

⁹ Also Vashti② the queen made a feast for the women in the royal house which belonged to king Ahasuerus.

Queen Vashti Refuses to Display Her Royal Beauty

¹⁰ On the seventh day, when the heart of the king was merry with wine, he commanded Mehuman, Biztha, Harbona, Bigtha, and Abagtha, Zethar, and Carcas, the seven chamberlains that served in the presence of Ahasuerus the king. ¹¹ To bring Vashti the queen before the king with the crown royal, to shew the people and the princes her beauty: for she was fair to look on. ¹² But the queen Vashti refused to come at the king's commandment by his chamberlains. Therefore was the king very wroth, and his anger burned in him.

¹³ Then the king said to the wise men, which knew the times, (for so was the king's manner toward all that knew law and judgment. ¹⁴ And the next unto him was Carshena, Shethar, Admatha, Tarshish, Meres, Marsena, and Memucan, the seven princes of Persia and Media, which saw the king's face, and which sat the first in the kingdom.)

¹⁵ "What shall we do unto the queen Vashti according to law, because she hath not performed the commandment of the king Ahasuerus by the chamberlains?"

---

② **Vashti** /ˈvæʃtai/, 瓦实提.

Queen Vashti's Dismissal

Vashti Deposed, 1890, Ernest Normand

^{16} And Memucan answered before the king and the princes, "Vashti the queen hath not done wrong to the king only, but also to all the princes, and to all the people that are in all the provinces of the king Ahasuerus. ^{17} For this deed of the queen shall come abroad unto all women, so that they shall despise their husbands in their eyes, when it shall be reported, 'The king Ahasuerus commanded Vashti the queen to be brought in before him, but she came not.'"

^{18} Likewise shall the ladies of Persia and Media say this day unto all the king's princes, which have heard of the deed of the queen. Thus shall there arise too much contempt and wrath.

^{19} "If it please the king, let there go a royal commandment from him, and let it be written among the laws of the Persians and the Medes, that it be not altered, that Vashti come no more before king Ahasuerus; and let the king give her royal estate unto another that is better than she. ^{20} And when the king's decree which he shall make shall be published throughout all his empire, (for it is great,) all the wives shall give to their husbands honour, both to great and small."

^{21} And the saying pleased the king and the princes; and the king did according to the word of Memucan. ^{22} For he sent letters into all the king's provinces, into every province according to the writing thereof, and to every people after their language, that every man should bear rule in his own house, and that it should be published according to the language of every people.

Esther Made Queen

Esther 2

^{1} After these things, when the wrath of king Ahasuerus was appeased, he remembered Vashti, and what she had done, and what was decreed against her.

^{2} Then said the king's servants that ministered unto him, "Let there be fair young virgins sought for the king: ^{3} And let the king appoint officers in all the provinces of his kingdom, that they may gather together all the fair young virgins unto Shushan the palace, to the house of the women, unto the custody of Hege the king's chamberlain, keeper of the women; and let their things for purification be given them: ^{4} And let the maiden which pleaseth the king be queen instead of Vashti." And the thing pleased the king; and he did so.

^{5} Now in Shushan the palace there was a certain Jew, whose name was Mordecai③, the son of Jair, the son of Shimei, the son of Kish, a Benjamite, ^{6} who had been carried away from Jerusalem with the captivity which had been carried away with Jeconiah king of Judah, whom Nebuchadnezzar the king of Babylon had carried away. ^{7} And he brought up Hadassah, that is, Esther④, his uncle's daughter: for she had neither father nor mother, and the maid was fair and beautiful; whom Mordecai, when her father and mother were dead, took for his own daughter.

^{8} So it came to pass, when the king's commandment and his decree was heard, and when many maidens were gathered together unto Shushan the palace, to the custody of Hegai, that Esther was brought also unto the king's house, to the custody of Hegai, keeper of the women. ^{9} And the maiden pleased him, and she obtained kindness of him; and he speedily gave her her things for purification, with such things as belonged to her, and seven maidens, which were meet to be given her, out of the king's house: and he preferred her and her maids unto the best place of the house of the women.

---

③ **Mordecai** /ˈmɔːdəkaɪ/, 末底改。
④ **Esther** /ˈestə/, 以斯帖。

¹⁰ *Esther had not shewed her people nor her kindred⑤, for Mordecai had charged her that she should not shew it.* ¹¹ *And Mordecai walked every day before the court of the women's house, to know how Esther did, and what should become of her.*

One Night with the King

¹² *Now when every maid's turn was come to go in to king Ahasuerus, after that she had been twelve months, according to the manner of the women (for so were the days of their purifications accomplished, to wit, six months with oil of myrrh, and six months with sweet odours, and with other things for the purifying of the women).* ¹³ *Then thus came every maiden unto the king; whatsoever she desired was given her to go with her out of the house of the women unto the king's house.* ¹⁴ *In the evening she went, and on the morrow she returned into the second house of the women, to the custody of Shaashgaz, the king's chamberlain, which kept the concubines: she came in unto the king no more, except the king delighted in her, and that she were called by name.*

¹⁵ *Now when the turn of Esther, the daughter of Abihail, the uncle of Mordecai, who had taken her for his daughter, was come to go in unto the king, she required nothing but what Hegai the king's chamberlain, the keeper of the women, appointed. And Esther obtained favour in the sight of all them that looked upon her.* ¹⁶ *So Esther was taken unto king Ahasuerus into his house royal in the tenth month, which is the month Tebeth, in the seventh year of his reign.*

The Toilette of Esther, 1841, Théodore Chassériau

Esther the Queen

¹⁷ *And the king loved Esther above all the women, and she obtained grace and favour in his sight more than all the virgins; so that he set the royal crown upon her head, and made her queen instead of Vashti.* ¹⁸ *Then the king made a great feast unto all his princes and his servants, even Esther's feast; and he made a release to the provinces, and gave gifts, according to the state of the king.*

Mordecai Uncovers a Conspiracy

¹⁹ *And when the virgins were gathered together the second time, then Mordecai sat in the king's gate.* ²⁰ *Esther had not yet shewed her kindred nor her people; as Mordecai had charged her, for Esther did the commandment of Mordecai, like as when she was brought up with him.*

²¹ *In those days, while Mordecai sat in the king's gate, two of the king's chamberlains, Bigthan and Teresh, of those which kept the door, were wroth, and sought to lay hands on the king Ahasuerus.* ²² *And the thing was known to Mordecai, who told it unto Esther the queen; and Esther certified the king thereof in Mordecai's name.* ²³ *And when inquisition was made of the matter, it was found out; therefore they were both hanged on a tree: and it was written in the book of the chronicles before the king.*

---

⑤ **her people nor her kindred** her nationality and family background.

Haman's Plot to Destroy the Jews

Esther 3
Haman Slighted by Mordecai

¹After these things did king Ahasuerus promote Haman⑥ the son of Hammedatha the Agagite, and advanced him, and set his seat above all the princes that were with him. ²And all the king's servants, that were in the king's gate, bowed, and reverenced Haman, for the king had so commanded concerning him. But Mordecai bowed not, nor did him reverence. ³Then the king's servants, which were in the king's gate, said unto Mordecai, "Why transgressest thou the king's commandment?" ⁴Now it came to pass, when they spake daily unto him, and he hearkened not unto them, that they told Haman, to see whether Mordecai's matters would stand, for he had told them that he was a Jew.

⁵And when Haman saw that Mordecai bowed not, nor did him reverence, then was Haman full of wrath. ⁶And he thought scorn to lay hands on Mordecai alone; for they had shewed him the people of Mordecai, wherefore Haman sought to destroy all the Jews that were throughout the whole kingdom of Ahasuerus, even the people of Mordecai.

⁷In the first month, that is, the month Nisan, in the twelfth year of king Ahasuerus, they cast Pur, that is, the lot, before Haman from day to day, and from month to month, to the twelfth month, that is, the month Adar⑦.

License to Kill

⁸And Haman said unto king Ahasuerus, "There is a certain people scattered abroad and dispersed among the people in all the provinces of thy kingdom; and their laws are diverse from all people; neither keep they the king's laws: therefore it is not for the king's profit to suffer them. ⁹If it please the king, let it be written that they may be destroyed: and I will pay ten thousand talents of silver to the hands of those that have the charge of the business, to bring it into the king's treasuries."

¹⁰And the king took his ring from his hand, and gave it unto Haman the son of Hammedatha the Agagite, the Jews' enemy. ¹¹And the king said unto Haman, "The silver is given to thee, the people also, to do with them as it seemeth good to thee."

¹²Then were the king's scribes called on the thirteenth day of the first month, and there was written according to all that Haman had commanded unto the king's lieutenants, and to the governors that were over every province, and to the rulers of every people of every province according to the writing thereof, and to every people after their language; in the name of king Ahasuerus was it written, and sealed with the king's ring. ¹³And the letters were sent by posts into all the king's provinces, to destroy, to kill, and to cause to perish, all Jews, both young and old, little children and women, in one day, even upon the thirteenth day of the twelfth month, which is the month Adar, and to take the spoil of them for a prey. ¹⁴The copy of the writing for a commandment to be given in every province was published unto all people, that they should be ready against that day.

¹⁵The posts went out, being hastened by the king's commandment, and the decree was given in Shushan the palace. And the king and Haman sat down to drink; but the city Shushan was perplexed.

---

⑥ **Haman** (/ˈheimæn/, 哈曼) a descendant of the same Amalekite king Agag whom the prophet Samuel hewed to pieces (1 Sam. 15:32—33).

⑦ **Adar** /ɑːˈdɑː/, 亚达月。

Mordecai Persuades Esther to Help

Esther 4

¹ When Mordecai perceived all that was done, Mordecai rent his clothes, and put on sackcloth with ashes, and went out into the midst of the city, and cried with a loud and a bitter cry; ² and came even before the king's gate, for none might enter into the king's gate clothed with sackcloth. ³ And in every province, whithersoever the king's commandment and his decree came, there was great mourning among the Jews, and fasting, and weeping, and wailing; and many lay in sackcloth and ashes.

⁴ So Esther's maids and her chamberlains came and told it her. Then was the queen exceedingly grieved; and she sent raiment to clothe Mordecai, and to take away his sackcloth from him: but he received it not. ⁵ Then called Esther for Hatach, one of the king's chamberlains, whom he had appointed to attend upon her, and gave him a commandment to Mordecai, to know what it was, and why it was.

⁶ So Hatach went forth to Mordecai unto the street of the city, which was before the king's gate. ⁷ And Mordecai told him of all that had happened unto him, and of the sum of the money that Haman had promised to pay to the king's treasuries for the Jews, to destroy them. ⁸ Also he gave him the copy of the writing of the decree that was given at Shushan to destroy them, to shew it unto Esther, and to declare it unto her, and to charge her that she should go in unto the king, to make supplication unto him, and to make request before him for her people.

⁹ And Hatach came and told Esther the words of Mordecai. ¹⁰ Again Esther spake unto Hatach, and gave him commandment unto Mordecai, ¹¹ "All the king's servants, and the people of the king's provinces, do know, that whosoever, whether man or women, shall come unto the king into the inner court, who is not called, there is one law of his to put him to death, except such to whom the king shall hold out the golden sceptre, that he may live: but I have not been called to come in unto the king these thirty days."

Esther and Mordecai, 1685, Aert de Gelder

¹² And they told to Mordecai Esther's words. ¹³ Then Mordecai commanded to answer Esther, "Think not with thyself that thou shalt escape in the king's house, more than all the Jews. ¹⁴ For if thou altogether holdest thy peace at this time, then shall there enlargement and deliverance arise to the Jews from another place; but thou and thy father's house shall be destroyed: and who knoweth whether thou art come to the kingdom for such a time as this?"

¹⁵ Then Esther bade them return Mordecai this answer, ¹⁶ " Go, gather together all the Jews that are present in Shushan, and fast ye for me, and neither eat nor drink three days, night or day: I also and my maidens will fast likewise; and so will I go in unto the king, which is not according to the law: and if I perish, I perish."

¹⁷ So Mordecai went his way, and did according to all that Esther had commanded him.

Esther's Request to the King

Esther 5

¹ Now it came to pass on the third day, that Esther put on her royal apparel, and stood in the inner court of the king's house, over against the king's house: and the king sat upon his royal throne in the royal house, over against the gate of the house. ² And it was so, when the king saw Esther the queen standing in the court, that she obtained favour in his sight: and the king held out to Esther the golden sceptre that was in his hand. So Esther drew near, and touched the top of the sceptre.

³ Then said the king unto her, " What wilt thou, queen Esther? And what is thy request? It shall be even

given thee to the half of the kingdom."

⁴ And Esther answered, " If it seem good unto the king, let the king and Haman come this day unto the banquet that I have prepared for him."

⁵ Then the king said, " Cause Haman to make haste, that he may do as Esther hath said."

So the king and Haman came to the banquet that Esther had prepared.

⁶ And the king said unto Esther at the banquet of wine, " What is thy petition? And it shall be granted thee: and what is thy request? Even to the half of the kingdom it shall be performed."

⁷ Then answered Esther, and said, " My petition and my request is: ⁸ If I have found favour in the sight of the king, and if it please the king to grant my petition, and to perform my request, let the king and Haman come to the banquet that I shall prepare for them, and I will do to morrow as the king hath said."

Haman Has a Gallows Made for Mordecai

⁹ Then went Haman forth that day joyful and with a glad heart: but when Haman saw Mordecai in the king's gate, that he stood not up, nor moved for him, he was full of indignation against Mordecai. ¹⁰ Nevertheless Haman refrained himself: and when he came home, he sent and called for his friends, and Zeresh his wife.

¹¹ And Haman told them of the glory of his riches, and the multitude of his children, and all the things wherein the king had promoted him, and how he had advanced him above the princes and servants of the king. ¹² Haman said moreover, " Yea, Esther the queen did let no man come in with the king unto the banquet that she had prepared but myself; and to morrow am I invited unto her also with the king. ¹³ Yet all this availeth me nothing, so long as I see Mordecai the Jew sitting at the king's gate."

¹⁴ Then said Zeresh his wife and all his friends unto him, " Let a gallows be made of fifty cubits⑧ high, and to morrow speak thou unto the king that Mordecai may be hanged thereon: then go thou in merrily with the king unto the banquet." And the thing pleased Haman; and he caused the gallows to be made.

Mordecai Honored

Esther 6

¹ On that night could not the king sleep, and he commanded to bring the book of records of the chronicles; and they were read before the king. ² And it was found written, that Mordecai had told of Bigthana and Teresh, two of the king's chamberlains, the keepers of the door, who sought to lay hand on the king Ahasuerus.

³ And the king said, " What honour and dignity hath been done to Mordecai for this?" Then said the king's servants that ministered unto him, " There is nothing done for him."

⁴ And the king said, " Who is in the court?" Now Haman was come into the outward court of the king's house, to speak unto the king to hang Mordecai on the gallows that he had prepared for him.

⁵ And the king's servants said unto him, " Behold, Haman standeth in the court."

And the king said, " Let him come in."

⁶ So Haman came in. And the king said unto him, " What shall be done unto the man whom the king delighteth to honour?"

Now Haman thought in his heart, " To whom would the king delight to do honour more than to myself?" ⁷ And Haman answered the king, " For the man whom the king delighteth to honour, ⁸ let the royal apparel be brought which the king useth to wear, and the horse that the king rideth upon, and the crown royal which is set upon his head. ⁹ And let this apparel and horse be delivered to the hand of one of the king's most noble princes, that they may array the man withal whom the king delighteth to honour, and bring him on

---

⑧ **fifty cubits** about 23 metres.

horseback through the street of the city, and proclaim before him, thus shall it be done to the man whom the king delighteth to honour."

¹⁰ Then the king said to Haman, "Make haste, and take the apparel and the horse, as thou hast said, and do even so to Mordecai the Jew, that sitteth at the king's gate; let nothing fail of all that thou hast spoken."

The Royal Apparel and the Royal Horse

¹¹ Then took Haman the apparel and the horse, and arrayed Mordecai, and brought him on horseback through the street of the city, and proclaimed before him, "Thus shall it be done unto the man whom the king delighteth to honour."

¹² And Mordecai came again to the king's gate. But Haman hasted to his house mourning, and having his head covered. ¹³ And Haman told Zeresh his wife and all his friends every thing that had befallen him.

Then said his wise men and Zeresh his wife unto him, "If Mordecai be of the seed of the Jews, before whom thou hast begun to fall, thou shalt not prevail against him, but shalt surely fall before him." ¹⁴ And while they were yet talking with him, came the king's chamberlains, and hasted to bring Haman unto the banquet that Esther had prepared.

The Triumph of Mordecai,
1624, Pieter Pietersz Lastman

Haman Hanged on His Own Gallows

Esther 7
Esther's Banquet

The Banquet of Esther and Ahasuerus,
1640s, Jan Victors

¹ So the king and Haman came to banquet with Esther the queen. ² And the king said again unto Esther on the second day at the banquet of wine, "What is thy petition, queen Esther? And it shall be granted thee: and what is thy request? And it shall be performed, even to the half of the kingdom."

³ Then Esther the queen answered and said, "If I have found favour in thy sight, O king, and if it please the king, let my life be given me at my petition, and my people at my request. ⁴ For we are sold, I and my people, to be destroyed, to be slain, and to perish. But if we had been sold for bondmen and bondwomen, I had held my tongue, although the enemy could not countervail the king's damage."

⁵ Then the king Ahasuerus answered and said unto Esther the queen, "Who is he, and where is he, that durst presume in his heart to do so?"

⁶ And Esther said, "The adversary and enemy is this wicked Haman."

Then Haman was afraid before the king and the queen. ⁷ And the king arising from the banquet of wine in his wrath went into the palace garden: and Haman stood up to make request for his life to Esther the queen; for he saw that there was evil determined against him by the king.

⁸ Then the king returned out of the palace garden into the place of the banquet of wine; and Haman was fallen upon the bed whereon Esther was.

Then said the king, "Will he force the queen also before me in the house?"

As the word went out of king's mouth, they covered Haman's face. ⁹ And Harbonah, one of the chamberlains, said before the king, "Behold also, the gallows fifty cubits high, which Haman had made for

Mordecai, who spoken good for the king, standeth in the house of Haman."

Then the king said, "Hang him thereon." ¹⁰ So they hanged Haman on the gallows that he had prepared for Mordecai. Then was the king's wrath pacified.

The King's Edict in Behalf of the Jews

Esther 8

¹ On that day did the king Ahasuerus give the house of Haman the Jews' enemy unto Esther the queen. And Mordecai came before the king; for Esther had told what he was unto her. ² And the king took off his ring, which he had taken from Haman, and gave it unto Mordecai. And Esther set Mordecai over the house of Haman.

³ And Esther spake yet again before the king, and fell down at his feet, and besought him with tears to put away the mischief of Haman the Agagite, and his device that he had devised against the Jews. ⁴ Then the king held out the golden sceptre toward Esther.

⁵ So Esther arose, and stood before the king, and said, " If it please the king, and if I have favour in his sight, and the thing seem right before the king, and I be pleasing in his eyes, let it be written to reverse the letters devised by Haman the son of Hammedatha the Agagite, which he wrote to destroy the Jews which are in all the king's provinces, ⁶ for how can I endure to see the evil that shall come unto my people? Or how can I endure to see the destruction of my kindred?"

⁷ Then the king Ahasuerus said unto Esther the queen and to Mordecai the Jew, " Behold, I have given Esther the house of Haman, and him they have hanged upon the gallows, because he laid his hand upon the Jews. ⁸ Write ye also for the Jews, as it liketh you, in the king's name, and seal it with the king's ring, for the writing which is written in the king's name, and sealed with the king's ring, may no man reverse."

⁹ Then were the king's scribes called at that time in the third month, that is, the month Sivan, on the three and twentieth day thereof; and it was written according to all that Mordecai commanded unto the Jews, and to the lieutenants, and the deputies and rulers of the provinces which are from India unto Ethiopia, an hundred twenty and seven provinces, unto every province according to the writing thereof, and unto every people after their language, and to the Jews according to their writing, and according to their language. ¹⁰ And he wrote in the king Ahasuerus' name, and sealed it with the king's ring, and sent letters by posts on horseback, and riders on mules, camels, and young dromedaries:

¹¹ Wherein the king granted the Jews which were in every city to gather themselves together, and to stand for their life, to destroy, to slay and to cause to perish, all the power of the people and province that would assault them, both little ones and women, and to take the spoil of them for a prey. ¹² Upon one day in all the provinces of king Ahasuerus, namely, upon the thirteenth day of the twelfth month, which is the month Adar. ¹³ The copy of the writing for a commandment to be given in every province was published unto all people, and that the Jews should be ready against that day to avenge themselves on their enemies.

¹⁴ So the posts that rode upon mules and camels went out, being hastened and pressed on by the king's commandment. And the decree was given at Shushan the palace.

¹⁵ And Mordecai went out from the presence of the king in royal apparel of blue and white, and with a great crown of gold, and with a garment of fine linen and purple. And the city of Shushan rejoiced and was glad. ¹⁶ The Jews had light, and gladness, and joy, and honour. ¹⁷ And in every province, and in every city, whithersoever the king's commandment and his decree came, the Jews had joy and gladness, a feast and a good day. And many of the people of the land became Jews; for the fear of the Jews fell upon them.

Triumph of the Jews

Esther 9

¹ Now in the twelfth month, that is, the month Adar, on the thirteenth day of the same, when the king's

commandment and his decree drew near to be put in execution, in the day that the enemies of the Jews hoped to have power over them, (though it was turned to the contrary, that the Jews had rule over them that hated them;) ² The Jews gathered themselves together in their cities throughout all the provinces of the king Ahasuerus, to lay hand on such as sought their hurt: and no man could withstand them; for the fear of them fell upon all people. ³ And all the rulers of the provinces, and the lieutenants, and the deputies, and officers of the king, helped the Jews; because the fear of Mordecai fell upon them. ⁴ For Mordecai was great in the king's house, and his fame went out throughout all the provinces: for this man Mordecai waxed greater and greater.

⁵ Thus the Jews smote all their enemies with the stroke of the sword, and slaughter, and destruction, and did what they would unto those that hated them. ⁶ And in Shushan the palace the Jews slew and destroyed five hundred men. ⁷ And Parshandatha, and Dalphon, and Aspatha, ⁸ And Poratha, and Adalia, and Aridatha, ⁹ And Parmashta, and Arisai, and Aridai, and Vajezatha,

¹⁰ The ten sons of Haman the son of Hammedatha, the enemy of the Jews, slew they; but on the spoil laid they not their hand.

¹¹ On that day the number of those that were slain in Shushan the palace was brought before the king. ¹² And the king said unto Esther the queen, "The Jews have slain and destroyed five hundred men in Shushan the palace, and the ten sons of Haman; what have they done in the rest of the king's provinces? Now what is thy petition? And it shall be granted thee. Or what is thy request further? And it shall be done."

¹³ Then said Esther, "If it please the king, let it be granted to the Jews which are in Shushan to do to morrow also according unto this day's decree, and let Haman's ten sons be hanged upon the gallows."

¹⁴ And the king commanded it so to be done: and the decree was given at Shushan; and they hanged Haman's ten sons. ¹⁵ For the Jews that were in Shushan gathered themselves together on the fourteenth day also of the month Adar, and slew three hundred men at Shushan; but on the prey they laid not their hand.

¹⁶ But the other Jews that were in the king's provinces gathered themselves together, and stood for their lives, and had rest from their enemies, and slew of their foes seventy and five thousand, but they laid not their hands on the prey. ¹⁷ On the thirteenth day of the month Adar; and on the fourteenth day of the same rested they, and made it a day of feasting and gladness.

Purim Celebrated

¹⁸ But the Jews that were at Shushan assembled together on the thirteenth day thereof, and on the fourteenth thereof; and on the fifteenth day of the same they rested, and made it a day of feasting and gladness.

¹⁹ Therefore the Jews of the villages, that dwelt in the unwalled towns, made the fourteenth day of the month Adar a day of gladness and feasting, and a good day, and of sending portions one to another.

²⁰ And Mordecai wrote these things, and sent letters unto all the Jews that were in all the provinces of the king Ahasuerus, both nigh and far, ²¹ to establish this among them, that they should keep the fourteenth day of the month Adar, and the fifteenth day of the same, yearly. ²² As the days wherein the Jews rested from their enemies, and the month which was turned unto them from sorrow to joy, and from mourning into a good day: that they should make them days of feasting and joy, and of sending portions one to another, and gifts to the poor.

²³ And the Jews undertook to do as they had begun, and as Mordecai had written unto them. ²⁴ Because Haman the son of Hammedatha, the Agagite, the enemy of all the Jews, had devised against the Jews to destroy them, and had cast Pur, that is, the lot, to consume them, and to destroy them. ²⁵ But when Esther came before the king, he commanded by letters that his wicked device, which he devised against the Jews, should return upon his own head, and that he and his sons should be hanged on the gallows. ²⁶ Wherefore they called these days Purim⑨ after the name of Pur. Therefore for all the words of this letter, and of that which they had seen concerning this matter, and which had come unto them. ²⁷ The Jews ordained, and took upon them, and upon

---

⑨ **Purim** /ˈpjuərim/，普林节。

their seed, and upon all such as joined themselves unto them, so as it should not fail, that they would keep these two days according to their writing, and according to their appointed time every year. ²⁸ And that these days should be remembered and kept throughout every generation, every family, every province, and every city; and that these days of Purim should not fail from among the Jews, nor the memorial of them perish from their seed.

²⁹ Then Esther the queen, the daughter of Abihail, and Mordecai the Jew, wrote with all authority, to confirm this second letter of Purim. ³⁰ And he sent the letters unto all the Jews, to the hundred twenty and seven provinces of the kingdom of Ahasuerus, with words of peace and truth ³¹ to confirm these days of Purim in their times appointed, according as Mordecai the Jew and Esther the queen had enjoined them, and as they had decreed for themselves and for their seed, the matters of the fastings and their cry. ³² And the decree of Esther confirmed these matters of Purim; and it was written in the book.

Cultural Connections: *One Night with the King*

Based on the novel *Hadassah: One Night with the King* by Tommy Tenney and Mark Andrew Olsen, *One Night with the King* is a dramatization of the story of Esther, released in 2006 in the United States. In spite of its general adherence to the main plot of the Bible, the film adds stylistic elements not present in the biblical story. And different from the biblical version, the relationship between Hadassah and Ahasuerus is transformed into a love story instead of a forced marriage. The title of the film and the novel recalls in the *Arabian Nights* the oriental practice of preparing a young woman physically for just one night with the king, and the tribulation of a king who must nightly rise to the occasion until he is released from it by the one he truly loves.

III FOOD FOR THOUGHT

1. What was the time and geographical setting of this story?
2. Why was Queen Vashti deposed?
3. What "queenly" qualities did Esther display before she was made queen?
4. What perfect irony is involved in *Esther 6*?
5. How is dramatic tension built into the scene at the banquet table?

IV BIBLICAL RELEVANCE

A. Biblical Terms in Everyday English
1. Vashti: _____
2. hang as high as Haman: _____
3. Haman was hanged on the gallows he had prepared for Mordecai: _____

B. Biblical References in Literature

1. Presently my mother went to my father. I know I thought of Queen Esther and King Ahasuerus; for my mother was very pretty and delicate-looking, and my father looked as terrible as King Ahasuerus.

(Elizabeth Gaskell, Cranford, 1951—1953)

2. "Utter it, Jane: but I wish that instead of a mere inquiry into, perhaps, a secret, it was a wish for half my estate." "Now, king Ahasuerus! What do I want with half your estate?"

(Charlotte Brontë, Jane Eyre, 1847)

C. The Bible and Arts

1. Ahasuerus' Banquet
   The Banquet of Ahasuerus, c. 1680s, Aert de Gelder
   The Banquet of Ahasuerus, c. 1680s, Sellaio del Jacopo
2. *Vashti Deposed*, 1890, Ernest Normand
3. *The Toilette of Esther*, 1841, Théodore Chassériau
4. *Esther and Mordecai*, 1685, Aert de Gelder
5. *The Triumph of Mordecai*, 1624, Pieter Pietersz Lastman
6. Esther's Banquet
   The Banquet of Esther and Ahasuerus, 1640s, Jan Victors
   Feast of Esther, Frans Francken II (1581—1642)
7. *Punishment of Haman*, 1511, Buonarroti Michelangelo

V SOURCES FOR REFERENCE

1. Ryken, L. & P. G. Ryken. (2007). *The Literary Study Bible*. Wheaton, Illinois: Crossway Bibles.
2. Browning, W. R. E. (2009). *A Dictionary of the Bible*. Oxford: Oxford University Press.
3. 朱维之:《圣经文学十二讲》,北京:人民文学出版社,2008年。

25. JOB

I POINTS OF DEPARTURE

Pious, blameless, upright, and accidentally, prosperous, Job suddenly found himself struck by one calamity after another. First, all his belongings were stolen and his servants killed. Then a fire from the sky destroyed his sheep and the servants, and a mighty wind swept in, destroying his house and killing his sons and daughters. Finally, Job became afflicted with a horrible, painful skin ailment. "*What did I do to deserve such suffering?*" Job protested. The Book of Job is the classic study dealing with the so-called "problem of evil," the problem of why people, more specifically, the righteous, suffer.

The Book of Job attempts to solve the problem on three levels (Ryken & Ryken, 2007:684). On the literary level, it aims to be truthful to the human experience of suffering. A second level at which the book operates is to have various human characters offer their perspectives on the spectacle of exceptional calamity and suffering. Following the narration of Job's undeserved sufferings, *chs 3 to 42:6* are a dialogue of three cycles of speeches between Job and three friends who came to comfort him. These "comforters" of Job's explained that Job suffered the way he did simply because he had sinned against God, which only served to intensify his indignation. There is also a polemic level of the orthodox doctrine that argues for an automatic correspondence between good behavior and prosperity, a viewpoint that the Book of Job decisively refutes with its portrayal of a blameless man who suffers greatly. Finally, there is a divine perspective on human suffering that takes the form of God's interaction with Job in the voice from the whirlwind. What God said was very much what the friends had argued, but it reduced Job to repentance and his former prosperity was not only restored but doubled.

Job is praised in the New Testament (*Jas. 5:11*) for his "patience" in the face of adversity. Among modern readers of Job, feminist theologians might admire Job's wife and daughters; a Jewish reader will resonate with Job's first reply to Bildad (9—10) in complaining about God's arbitrary use of power; a Christian reader might see in the story of Job an illustration of the triumph of grace through obedience, rather than "patience," and of humility (42:3) rather than arrogance (23:6—7) (Browning, 2009:204).

II SELECTED READINGS

Prologue

Job 1

¹ There was a man in the land of Uz, whose name was Job[①]; and that man was perfect and upright,

---

① **Job** /dʒəub/, 约伯。

and one who feared God and eschewed evil.² And there were born unto him seven sons and three daughters. ³ His substance also was seven thousand sheep, and three thousand camels, and five hundred yoke of oxen, and five hundred sheasses, and a very great household, so that this man was the greatest of all the men of the East. ⁴ And his sons went and feasted in their houses, every one his day, and sent and called for their three sisters to eat and to drink with them. ⁵ And it was so, that when the days of their feasting were ended, Job sent and sanctified them, and rose up early in the morning and offered burnt offerings according to the number of them all; for Job said, "It may be that my sons have sinned and cursed God in their hearts." Thus did Job continually.

Job and His Family,
c. 1805—1806, William Blake

Job's First Test

⁶ Now there was a day when the sons of God came to present themselves before the LORD, and Satan② also came among them. ⁷ And the LORD said unto Satan, "From whence comest thou?"

Then Satan answered the LORD and said, "From going to and fro on the earth, and from walking up and down upon it."

⁸ And the LORD said unto Satan, "Hast thou considered My servant Job, that there is none like him on the earth, a perfect and an upright man, one who feareth God and escheweth evil?"

⁹ Then Satan answered the LORD and said, "Doth Job fear God for nought?

¹⁰ Hast not Thou made a hedge about him and about his house, and about all that he hath on every side? Thou hast blessed the work of his hands, and his substance hath increased in the land. ¹¹ But put forth Thine hand now and touch all that he hath, and he will curse Thee to Thy face!"

¹² And the LORD said unto Satan, "Behold, all that he hath is in thy power; only upon himself put not forth thine hand."

So Satan went forth from the presence of the LORD.

¹³ And there was a day when his sons and his daughters were eating and drinking wine in their eldest brother's house. ¹⁴ And there came a messenger unto Job and said, "The oxen were plowing and the asses feeding beside them.

¹⁵ And the Sabeans fell upon them and took them away. Yea, they have slain the servants with the edge of the sword, and I only have escaped alone to tell thee!"

¹⁶ While he was yet speaking, there came also another and said, "The fire of God hath fallen from heaven, and hath burned up the sheep and the servants, and consumed them; and I only have escaped alone to tell thee!"

¹⁷ While he was yet speaking, there came also another and said, "The Chaldeans made up three bands, and fell upon the camels and have carried them away, yea, and have slain the servants with the edge of the sword; and I only have escaped alone to tell thee!"

¹⁸ While he was yet speaking, there came also another and said, "Thy sons and thy daughters were eating and drinking wine in their eldest brother's house.

¹⁹ And behold, there came a great wind from the wilderness and smote the four corners of the house, and it fell upon the young men, and they are dead; and I only have escaped alone to tell thee!"

²⁰ Then Job arose, and rent his mantle and shaved his head, and fell down upon the ground and worshiped, ²¹ And said,

"Naked came I out of my mother's womb,

---

② **Satan** (/ˈseitən/, 撒旦) means in Hebrew *accuser*, *adversary*, *demon*.

and naked shall I return thither.
The LORD gave, and the LORD hath taken away;
blessed be the name of the LORD."

²² In all this Job sinned not, nor charged God foolishly.

Job's Second Test

Job 2

Job Castigated by his Wife, c1503—1504, Albrecht Durer

¹ Again there was a day when the sons of God came to present themselves before the LORD, and Satan came also among them to present himself before the LORD. ² And the LORD said unto Satan, " From whence comest thou?" And Satan answered the LORD and said, " From going to and fro on the earth, and from walking up and down upon it."

³ And the LORD said unto Satan, " Hast thou considered My servant Job, that there is none like him on the earth, a perfect and an upright man, one who feareth God and escheweth evil? And still he holdeth fast his integrity, although thou movedst Me against him to destroy him without cause."

⁴ And Satan answered the LORD and said, " Skin for skin, yea, all that a man hath will he give for his life. ⁵ But put forth Thine hand now and touch his bone and his flesh, and he will curse Thee to Thy face!"

⁶ And the LORD said unto Satan, " Behold, he is in thine hand; only spare his life."

⁷ So went Satan forth from the presence of the LORD, and smote Job with sore boils from the sole of his foot unto his crown. ⁸ And he took him a potsherd with which to scrape himself, and he sat down among the ashes.

⁹ Then said his wife unto him, " Dost thou still retain thine integrity? Curse God, and die!"

¹⁰ But he said unto her, " Thou speakest as one of the foolish women speaketh. What? Shall we receive good at the hand of God, and shall we not receive evil?"

In all this did not Job sin with his lips.

Job's Three Friends

¹¹ Now when Job's three friends heard of all this evil that had come upon him, they came every one from his own place: Eliphaz the Temanite, and Bildad the Shuhite, and Zophar the Naamathite. For they had made an appointment together to come to mourn with him and to comfort him. ¹² And when they lifted up their eyes afar off and knew him not, they lifted up their voice and wept; and they rent every one his mantle, and sprinkled dust upon their heads toward heaven. ¹³ So they sat down with him upon the ground seven days and seven nights, and none spoke a word unto him; for they saw that his grief was very great.

Wicked People Prosper

Job 21

¹ But Job answered and said:

² " Hear diligently my speech, and let this be your consolations.

³ Suffer me that I may speak; and after I have spoken, mock on.

⁴ " As for me, is my complaint to man? And if it were so, why should not my spirit be troubled?

⁵ Mark me, and be astonished, and lay your hand upon your mouth!

⁶ Even when I remember I am afraid, and trembling taketh hold on my flesh.

⁷ Why do the wicked live, become old, yea, are mighty in power?
⁸ Their seed is established in their sight with them, and their offspring before their eyes.
⁹ Their houses are safe from fear, neither is the rod of God upon them.
¹⁰ Their bull gendereth, and faileth not; their cow calveth and casteth not her calf.
¹¹ They send forth their little ones like a flock, and their children dance.
¹² They take the timbrel and harp, and rejoice at the sound of the organ.
¹³ They spend their days in wealth, and in a moment go down to the grave.
¹⁴ Therefore they say unto God, ' Depart from us, for we desire not the knowledge of Thy ways.
¹⁵ What is the Almighty, that we should serve Him? And what profit should we have, if we pray unto Him?'
¹⁶ Lo, their good is not in their hand; the counsel of the wicked is far from me.
¹⁷ " How oft is the candle of the wicked put out! And how oft cometh their destruction upon them! God distributeth sorrows in His anger.
¹⁸ They are as stubble before the wind, and as chaff that the storm carrieth away.
¹⁹ God layeth up his iniquity for his children; He rewardeth him, and he shall know it.
²⁰ His eyes shall see his destruction, and he shall drink of the wrath of the Almighty.
²¹ For what pleasure hath he in his house after him, when the number of his months is cut off in the midst?
²² " Shall any teach God knowledge, seeing He judgeth those that are high?
²³ One dieth in his full strength, being wholly at ease and quiet.
²⁴ His milk pails are full of milk, and his bones are moistened with marrow.
²⁵ And another dieth in the bitterness of his soul, and never eateth with pleasure.
²⁶ They shall lie down alike in the dust, and the worms shall cover them.
²⁷ " Behold, I know your thoughts, and the devices which ye wrongfully imagine against me.
²⁸ For ye say, ' Where is the house of the prince? And where are the dwelling places of the wicked?'
²⁹ Have ye not asked them that go along the way? And do ye not know their tokens.
³⁰ That the wicked are reserved for the day of destruction? They shall be brought forth on the day of wrath.
³¹ Who shall declare his way to his face? And who shall repay him what he hath done?
³² Yet shall he be brought to the grave, and shall remain in the tomb.
³³ The clods of the valley shall be sweet unto him, and every man shall draw after him, as there are innumerable before him.
³⁴ " How then comfort ye me in vain, seeing in your answers there remaineth falsehood?"

A Poem on Wisdom

Job 28

¹ " Surely there is a vein for the silver, and a place for gold where they refine it.
² Iron is taken out of the earth, and brass is smelted out of the stone.
³ Man setteth an end to darkness, and searcheth out all perfection, the stones of darkness, and the shadow of death.
⁴ The flood breaketh out from the inhabitant, even the waters forgotten by the foot; they are dried up, they are gone away from men.
⁵ As for the earth, out of it cometh bread, and under it is turned up as it were fire.
⁶ The stones of it are the place of sapphires, and it hath dust of gold.
⁷ There is a path which no fowl knoweth, and which the vulture's eye hath not seen.
⁸ The lion's whelps have not trodden it, nor the fierce lion passed by it.
⁹ Man putteth forth his hand upon the rock; he overturneth the mountains by the roots;

¹⁰ He cutteth out rivers among the rocks, and his eye seeth every precious thing;
¹¹ He bindeth the floods from overflowing; and the thing that is hid bringeth he forth to light.
¹² But where shall wisdom be found? And where is the place of understanding?
¹³ Man knoweth not the price thereof; neither is it found in the land of the living.
¹⁴ The deep saith, ' It is not in me;' and the sea saith, ' It is not with me.'
¹⁵ It cannot be gotten for gold; neither shall silver be weighed for the price thereof.
¹⁶ It cannot be valued with the gold of Ophir, with the precious onyx or the sapphire.
¹⁷ The gold and the crystal cannot equal it; and the exchange of it shall not be for jewels of fine gold.
¹⁸ No mention shall be made of coral or of pearls, for the price of wisdom is above rubies.
¹⁹ The topaz of Ethiopia shall not equal it; neither shall it be valued with pure gold.
²⁰ " Whence then cometh wisdom? And where is the place of understanding—
²¹ Seeing it is hid from the eyes of all living, and kept close from the fowls of the air?
²² Destruction and death say, ' We have heard the fame thereof with our ears.'
²³ God understandeth the way thereof, and He knoweth the place thereof.
²⁴ For He looketh to the ends of the earth, and seeth under the whole heaven,
²⁵ To make the weight for the winds, and He weigheth the waters by measure.
²⁶ When He made a decree for the rain, and a way for the lightning of the thunder,
²⁷ Then did He see it and declare it; He prepared it, yea, and searched it out.
²⁸ And unto man He said, ' Behold, the fear of the Lord: that is wisdom; and to depart from evil is understanding.' "

The Lord Finally Speaks

Job 38

¹ Then the LORD answered Job out of the whirlwind, and said:
² " Who is this that darkeneth counsel by words without knowledge? ³ Gird up now thy loins like a man; for I will demand of thee, and answer thou Me.
⁴ " Where wast thou when I laid the foundations of the earth? Declare, if thou hast understanding.
⁵ Who hath laid the measures thereof, if thou knowest? Or who hath stretched the line upon it?
⁶ " Whereupon are the foundations thereof fastened? Or who laid the cornerstone thereof,
⁷ When the morning stars sang together, and all the sons of God shouted for joy?
⁸ Or who shut up the sea with doors, when it broke forth as if it had issued out of the womb;
⁹ When I made the cloud the garment thereof and thick darkness a swaddling band for it,
¹⁰ And broke up for it My decreed place, and set bars and doors,
¹¹ And said, ' Hitherto shalt thou come, but no further; and here shall thy proud waves be stayed?'
¹² " Hast thou commanded the morning since thy days, and caused the dayspring to know his place,
¹³ That it might take hold of the ends of the earth, that the wicked might be shaken out of it?
¹⁴ It is turned as clay under the seal; and they stand out as a garment.
¹⁵ And from the wicked their light is withheld, and the high arm shall be broken.
¹⁶ " Hast thou entered into the springs of the sea? Or hast thou walked in the search of the depths?
¹⁷ Have the gates of death been opened unto thee? Or hast thou seen the doors of the shadow of death?
¹⁸ Hast thou perceived the breadth of the earth? Declare if thou knowest it all.
¹⁹ " Where is the way where light dwelleth? And as for darkness, where is the place thereof,
²⁰ That thou shouldest take it to the boundary thereof, and that thou shouldest know the paths to the house thereof?
²¹ Knowest thou it, because thou wast then born, or because the number of thy days is great?
²² " Hast thou entered into the treasure house of the snow, or hast thou seen the treasure house of the hail,

²³ Which I have reserved against the time of trouble, against the day of battle and war?
²⁴ By what way is the light parted, which scattereth the east wind upon the earth?
²⁵ "Who hath divided a watercourse for the overflowing of waters, or a way for the lightning of thunder,
²⁶ To cause it to rain on the earth where no man is, on the wilderness wherein there is no man;
²⁷ To satisfy the desolate and waste ground, and to cause the bud of the tender herb to spring forth?
²⁸ "Hath the rain a father? Or who hath begotten the drops of dew?
²⁹ Out of whose womb came the ice? And the hoary frost of heaven, who hath engendered it?
³⁰ The waters are hid as with a stone, and the face of the deep is frozen.
³¹ "Canst thou bind the sweet influences of Pleiades, or loose the bands of Orion?
³² Canst thou bring forth Mazzaroth in his season? Or canst thou guide Arcturus with his sons?
³³ Knowest thou the ordinances of heaven? Canst thou set the dominion thereof over the earth?
³⁴ "Canst thou lift up thy voice to the clouds, that abundance of waters may cover thee?
³⁵ Canst thou send lightnings, that they may go and say unto thee, 'Here we are?'
³⁶ Who hath put wisdom in the inward parts, or who hath given understanding to the heart?
³⁷ Who can number the clouds by wisdom? Or who can stay the bottles of heaven,
³⁸ When the dust groweth into hardness, and the clods cleave fast together?
³⁹ "Wilt thou hunt the prey for the lion, or fill the appetite of the young lions,
⁴⁰ When they crouch in their dens, and abide in the covert to lie in wait?
⁴¹ Who provideth for the raven his food, when his young ones cry unto God, and wander for lack of meat?

Job 39

¹ "Knowest thou the time when the wild goats of the rock bring forth? Or canst thou mark when the hinds do calve?
² Canst thou number the months that they fulfill? Or knowest thou the time when they bring forth?
³ They bow themselves, they bring forth their young ones; they cast out their sorrows.
⁴ Their young ones are sturdy; they grow up with corn; they go forth and return not unto them.
⁵ "Who hath sent out the wild ass free? Or who hath loosed the bands of the wild ass,
⁶ Whose house I have made the wilderness and the barren land his dwellings?
⁷ He scorneth the multitude of the city, neither regardeth he the crying of the driver.
⁸ The range of the mountains is his pasture, and he searcheth after every green thing.
⁹ Will the unicorn be willing to serve thee, or abide by thy crib?
¹⁰ Canst thou bind the unicorn with his band to the furrow? Or will he harrow the valleys behind thee?
¹¹ Wilt thou trust him because his strength is great? Or wilt thou leave thy labor to him?
¹² Wilt thou believe him, that he will bring home the seed and gather it into thy barn?
¹³ "Gavest thou the goodly wings unto the peacocks? Or wings and feathers unto the ostrich,
¹⁴ Which leaveth her eggs in the earth, and warmeth them in dust,
¹⁵ And forgetteth that the foot may crush them, or that the wild beast may break them?
¹⁶ She is hardened against her young ones, as though they were not hers; her labor is in vain without fear;
¹⁷ Because God hath deprived her of wisdom, neither hath He imparted to her understanding.
¹⁸ Yet when she lifteth up herself on high, she scorneth the horse and his rider.
¹⁹ "Hast thou given the horse strength? Hast thou clothed his neck with thunder?
²⁰ Canst thou make him afraid as a grasshopper? The glory of his nostrils is terrible.
²¹ He paweth in the valley, and rejoiceth in his strength; he goeth on to meet the armed men.
²² He mocketh at fear, and is not frightened, neither turneth he back from the sword.
²³ The quiver rattleth against him, the glittering spear and the shield.
²⁴ He swalloweth the ground with fierceness and rage, neither believeth he that it is the sound of the

trumpet.

²⁵ He saith among the trumpets, ' Ha, ha!' And he smelleth the battle afar off, the thunder of the captains, and the shouting.

²⁶ " Doth the hawk fly by thy wisdom, and stretch her wings toward the south?

²⁷ Doth the eagle mount up at thy command, and make her nest on high?

²⁸ She dwelleth and abideth on the rock, upon the crag of the rock and the strong place.

²⁹ From thence she seeketh the prey, and her eyes behold afar off.

³⁰ Her young ones also suck up blood; and where the slain are, there is she."

Behemoth

Job 40

¹ Moreover the LORD answered Job and said:

² " Shall he that contendeth with the Almighty instruct Him? He that reproveth God, let him answer it."

³ Then Job answered the LORD and said:

⁴ " Behold, I am vile. What shall I answer Thee? I will lay mine hand upon my mouth.

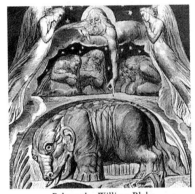

Behemoth, William Blake
(1757—1827)

⁵ Once have I spoken, but I will not answer; yea, twice, but I will proceed no further."

⁶ Then answered the LORD unto Job out of the whirlwind and said:

⁷ " Gird up thy loins now like a man; I will demand of thee, and declare thou unto Me.

⁸ Wilt thou also disannul My judgment? Wilt thou condemn Me, that thou mayest be righteous?

⁹ Hast thou an arm like God? Or canst thou thunder with a voice like Him?

¹⁰ " Deck thyself now with majesty and excellency; and array thyself with glory and beauty.

¹¹ Cast abroad the rage of thy wrath; and behold every one that is proud, and abase him.

¹² Look on every one that is proud, and bring him low; and tread down the wicked in their place.

¹³ Hide them in the dust together; and bind their faces in secret.

¹⁴ Then will I also confess unto thee that thine own right hand can save thee.

¹⁵ " Behold now Behemoth③, which I made with thee; he eateth grass as an ox.

¹⁶ Lo now, his strength is in his loins, and his force is in the navel of his belly.

¹⁷ He moveth his tail like a cedar; the sinews of his stones are wrapped together.

¹⁸ His bones are as strong pieces of brass; his bones are like bars of iron.

¹⁹ He is the chief of the ways of God; He that made him can make His sword to approach unto him.

²⁰ Surely the mountains bring him forth food, where all the beasts of the field play.

²¹ He lieth under the shady trees, in the covert of the reed and fens.

²² The shady trees cover him with their shadow; the willows of the brook compass him about.

²³ Behold, he drinketh up a river and hasteneth not; he trusteth that he can draw up the Jordan into his mouth.

²⁴ Will any take him with his sight, or bore his nose with a snare?

---

③ **Behemoth** /biˈhiːməθ/, possibly the hippopotamus or the elephant.

Leviathan

Job 41

¹ "Canst thou draw out Leviathan④ with a hook? Or his tongue with a cord which thou lettest down?
² Canst thou put a hook into his nose, or bore his jaw through with a thorn?
³ Will he make many supplications unto thee? Will he speak soft words unto thee?
⁴ Will he make a covenant with thee? Wilt thou take him as a servant for ever?
⁵ Wilt thou play with him as with a bird? Or wilt thou bind him for thy maidens?
⁶ Shall the companions make a banquet of him? Shall they parcel him among the merchants?
⁷ Canst thou fill his skin with barbed irons, or his head with fish spears?
⁸ Lay thine hand upon him; remember the battle, and do so no more!
⁹ Behold, the hope against him is in vain. Shall not one be cast down even at the sight of him?
¹⁰ None is so fierce that dare stir him up. Who then is able to stand before Me?
¹¹ Who hath come before Me, that I should repay him? Whatsoever is under the whole heaven is Mine.
¹² " I will not conceal his parts, nor his power, nor his comely proportion.
¹³ Who can uncover the face of his garment? Or who can come to him with his double bridle?
¹⁴ Who can open the doors of his face? His teeth are terrible round about.
¹⁵ His scales are his pride, shut up together as with a tight seal.
¹⁶ One is so near to another that no air can come between them.
¹⁷ They are joined one to another; they stick together, that they cannot be sundered.
¹⁸ By his sneezings a light doth shine, and his eyes are like the eyelids of the morning.
¹⁹ Out of his mouth go burning lamps, and sparks of fire leap out.
²⁰ Out of his nostrils goeth smoke, as out of a seething pot or caldron.
²¹ His breath kindleth coals, and a flame goeth out of his mouth.
²² In his neck remaineth strength, and sorrow is turned into joy before him.
²³ The folds of his flesh are joined together; they are firm in themselves; they cannot be moved.
²⁴ His heart is as firm as a stone, yea, as hard as a piece of the nether millstone.
²⁵ When he raiseth up himself, the mighty are afraid; by reason of breakings they purify themselves.
²⁶ The sword of him that layeth at him cannot hold the spear, the dart, nor the breastplate.
²⁷ He esteemeth iron as straw, and brass as rotten wood.

Cultural Connections: *Hobbes' Leviathan*

The English philosopher Thomas Hobbes (1588—1679) is best known for *Leviathan* (1651), based on the description of the leviathan in the Book of Job. He uses the biblical great beast subject to God alone as a metaphor for the power of the state, the only institution he believes is capable of offering security and stability in a chaotic world. It is one of the earliest and most influential examples of social contract theory, deemed as a classical western work on statecraft comparable to Machiavelli's *The Prince*.

²⁸ The arrow cannot make him flee; slingstones are turned by him into stubble.

---

④ **Leviathan** /lɪˈvaiəθən/, possibly the crocodile.

²⁹ Darts are counted as stubble; he laugheth at the shaking of a spear.

³⁰ Sharp potsherds are his undersides; he spreadeth sharp pointed things upon the mire.

³¹ He maketh the deep to boil like a pot; he maketh the sea like a pot of ointment.

³² He maketh a path to shine after him; one would think the deep to be hoary.

³³ Upon earth there is not his like, who is made without fear.

³⁴ He beholdeth all high things; he is a king over all the children of pride."

Job Is Blessed Manifold

Job 42

¹ Then Job answered the LORD and said:

² " I know that Thou canst do every thing, and that no thought can be withheld from Thee.

³ ' Who is he that hideth counsel without knowledge?' Therefore have I uttered what I understood not, things too wonderful for me, which I knew not.

⁴ ' Hear, I beseech thee, and I will speak; I will question thee, and declare thou unto Me.'

⁵ I have heard of Thee by the hearing of the ear, but now mine eye seeth Thee.

⁶ Therefore I abhor myself, and repent in dust and ashes."

Epilogue

⁷ And it was so, that after the LORD had spoken these words unto Job, the LORD said to Eliphaz the Temanite, " My wrath is kindled against thee and against thy two friends; for ye have not spoken of Me the thing that is right, as My servant Job hath.

⁸ Therefore take unto you now seven bullocks and seven rams, and go to My servant Job, and offer up for yourselves a burnt offering. And My servant Job shall pray for you; for him will I accept, lest I deal with you after your folly in that ye have not spoken of Me the thing which is right, like My servant Job."

⁹ So Eliphaz the Temanite and Bildad the Shuhite and Zophar the Naamathite went and did according as the LORD commanded them. The LORD also accepted Job.

¹⁰ And the LORD released Job from captivity when he prayed for his friends. Also the LORD gave Job twice as much as he had before.

¹¹ Then came there unto him all his brethren and all his sisters, and all those who had been of his acquaintance before, and ate bread with him in his house. And they bemoaned him and comforted him over all the evil that the LORD had brought upon him. Every man also gave him a piece of money, and every one an earring of gold.

¹² So the LORD blessed the latter end of Job more than his beginning; for he had fourteen thousand sheep, and six thousand camels, and a thousand yoke of oxen, and a thousand sheasses.

¹³ He had also seven sons and three daughters.

¹⁴ And he called the name of the first Jemimah, and the name of the second Keziah, and the name of the third Kerenhappuch.

¹⁵ And in all the land were no women found so fair as the daughters of Job, and their father gave them an inheritance among their brethren.

¹⁶ After this Job lived one hundred and forty years, and saw his sons and his sons' sons, even four generations.

¹⁷ So Job died, being old and full of days.

III FOOD FOR THOUGHT

1. According to *Job 1*, what are Job's virtues?
2. What misfortunes befell Job?
3. What phenomenon did Job observe in *Job 21* existent in human world?
4. Did Job find where wisdom dwells in *Job 28*?
5. How did Job respond to God's speeches?

IV BIBLICAL RELEVANCE

A. Biblical Terms in Everyday English
1. Job:
2. Job's news/post:
3. as poor as Job:
4. skin for skin (2:4):
5. Job's wife:
6. Job's comfort(er):
7. jobation:
8. the patience of Job:

B. Biblical References in Literature
1. Amiable as the old man was, prolonged exposure to him would test anyone's patience. But Dolly Harris would have made Job seem like a chain-smoking neurotic.
   (Martin Edwards, *Yesterday's Papers*, 1994)
2. "But stop nets do stop fish," I said, enjoying the novelty of his position enough to play devil's advocate. "Well, of course they do. But if they stopped all the fish, crews on the east would be richer'n Midas and those working the westernmost part of Bogue Banks would be poorer'n Job's house cat."
   (Margaret Maron, *Shooting at Loons*, 1994)
3. "That's splendid. One feels a certain pang of pity for whoever it is he's starting to work for, but that's splendid. The family were worried about him." "I don't wonder. I can't imagine anybody more capable of worrying a family than Eggy. Just suppose if Job had had him as well as boils."
   (P. G. Wodehouse, *Laughing Gas*, 1936)

C. The Bible and Arts
1. *Job and His Family*, c. 1805—1806, William Blake
2. *Satan Before God, and the First Calamities* (Left Wing), 1521, Bernaert van Orley
3. *Job's Sons and Daughters Killed* (Central Wing), 1521, Bernaert van Orley
4. *Job Castigated by his Wife*, c. 1503—1504, Albrecht Durer
5. *Job Mocked by his Wife*, 1630s, Georges de La Tour
6. *Job in Distress*, 1616, Hendrick Goltzius

V SOURCES FOR REFERENCE

1. Ryken, L. & P. G. Ryken. (2007). *The Literary Study Bible*. Wheaton, Illinois: Crossway Bibles.
2. Browning, W. R. E. (2009). *A Dictionary of the Bible*. Oxford: Oxford University Press.

26. THE PROPHETS: ISAIAH, JEREMIAH, EZEKIEL, JONAH

I POINTS OF DEPARTURE

Many ancient Near Eastern societies had a tradition of prophecy. The word *prophet* originates from the Greek word *prophetes*, meaning "to speak on behalf of another." It is defined in *Exodus 7:1ff* as a spokesperson for God. In that context, God spoke to Moses and Moses then spoke to his brother Aaron, who in turn spoke to the people. Aaron then was Moses' prophet. Prophets in the Bible were to speak exactly what God said to them.

Non-Israelite prophets were ordinarily employed by the religious and political establishment to seek favorable omens from the gods and to gain the support of the people for their institutions. Only in Israel, however, did the role of the prophet evolve after the reigns of King David and King Solomon to include social and religious criticism.

In the Hebrew Bible, the books of Prophets, or *Nebi'im*, fall into two groups—the Former Prophets (the books of Joshua, Judges, 1 and 2 Samuel, and 1 and 2 Kings) and the Latter Prophets (Isaiah, Jeremiah, Ezekiel, and the Twelve Minor Prophets including the Book of Jonah). Both groups share one consistent aim: to show that obedience to the terms of the covenant is rewarded and disobedience punished.

The prophet Isaiah was a giant of Jewish history. He was arguably the Shakespeare of Hebrew literature, noted for his rich vocabulary and use of imagery. Isaiah lived in the more pious southern kingdom of Judah though he did see his people beginning to abandon their covenant with God. He issued a volley of angry condemnations of the surrounding nations whose ways the Israelites had adopted and told them the inevitable consequences of Israel's infidelity — conquest and exile. But Isaiah's message was not wholly one of doom. Faced with ample evidence of humanity's inhumanity, injustice, and violence, Isaiah showed a vision of unshakeable peace where "they will beat their swords into plowshares and their spears into pruning hooks. Nation will not take up sword against nation, nor will they train for war anymore." (*Isa. 2:4*) Isaiah is quoted more often than all the other prophets combined in the New Testament. (Yancey & Stafford, 1989:711)

Shaggy-bearded, raggedly clothed, Jeremiah is often depicted as a prophet of doom. He was a contemporary of Isaiah, living in a time of relative prosperity and peace for Judah just before the fall of Jerusalem and the destruction of the First Temple (586 B.C.E.). It was a time when the people and their leaders were smugly comfortable in their mistreatment of the poor and their adoption of pagan religious practices. Accepting though reluctantly at first, Jeremiah assumed the mission assigned by God to sting the conscience of the people using his formidable gifts of eloquence and imagery. God's words flowed so freely from Jeremiah's mouth in a series of pointed attacks on idolatry and injustice, seasoned with terrible premonitions of devastation to come that the word *jeremiad* now is used to describe a mournful or fiercely critical speech, editorial, or other communication targeting social or political ills.

Ezekiel was one of the more dynamic individuals in Hebrew Scriptures. Serving as priest and prophet, Ezekiel's ideals for society were shaped by his duties to both offices. As a result, Ezekiel was a complex person. Equally bizarre was the way he communicated God's message. At times, he would act out his prophecy. He would also use metaphorical language, the most famous being comparing the religious infidelity of the people to marital infidelity and personifying Israel as the sexually voracious sister prostitutes Oholah and Oholibah (*Ezek. 23:1—49*). Ezekiel is best known for his visions, ranging from the "four living creatures," "wheels within wheels" (Ezekiel's vision of God's chariot which has found its way into Western art and the mystical traditions of Judaism and Christianity) to "dry bones" (*Ezek. 37*). At the core of his message was the unfolding of God's saving purpose in the history of the world — from God's withdrawal to the great redemption of God's people. Ezekiel's mission was to encourage the people to remain faithful while in Babylon. Though exile had its sorrows, Ezekiel urged the people to prosper in their new circumstances, lending their expertise as craftspeople to the imperial building programs under way in Nebuchadnezzar's kingdom.

The Book of Jonah tells the story of a man whom God instructed to love his enemies in Nineveh, the capital city of wickedness, the heart of Israel's oppressors, the Assyrians. Rather than carry out God's command, Jonah went in the opposite direction. After a storm and a subsequent narrow escape in the jaws of a big fish, Jonah obeyed a second command from God and went to proclaim God's message to the Ninevites, who later repented. The Book of Jonah contradicts the view that the Old Testament is racially narrow-minded and that the New Testament gives the first indication that God cares for non-Jewish people. For Jews, it is a reminder that each person is responsible for answering God's call and turning away from evil. For Christians, it conveys the message that the covenant extends to the Gentiles.

II SELECTED READINGS

ISAIAH[①]

Isaiah 2

¹The word that Isaiah the son of Amoz saw concerning Judah and Jerusalem.

²And it shall come to pass in the last days, that the mountain of the LORD's house shall be established in the top of the mountains, and shall be exalted above the hills; and all nations shall flow unto it.

³And many people shall go and say, "Come ye, and let us go up to the mountain of the LORD, to the house of the God of Jacob; and he will teach us of his ways, and we will walk in his paths: for out of Zion shall go forth the law, and the word of the LORD from Jerusalem.

⁴And he shall judge among the nations, and shall rebuke many people: and they shall beat their swords into plowshares, and their spears into pruninghooks: nation shall not lift up sword against nation, neither shall they learn war any more.

⁵O house of Jacob, come ye, and let us walk in the light of the LORD."

⁶Therefore thou hast forsaken thy people the house of Jacob, because they be replenished from the east,

---

① **ISAIAH** /aiˈzaiə/, 以赛亚(书)。

Let Us Beat Swords into Plowshares, a Soviet Union gift to the UN in 1959

and are soothsayers like the Philistines, and they please themselves in the children of strangers.

⁷ Their land also is full of silver and gold, neither is there any end of their treasures; their land is also full of horses, neither is there any end of their chariots:

⁸ Their land also is full of idols; they worship the work of their own hands, that which their own fingers have made:

⁹ And the mean man boweth down, and the great man humbleth himself: therefore forgive them not.

¹⁰ Enter into the rock, and hide thee in the dust, for fear of the LORD, and for the glory of his majesty.

¹¹ The lofty looks of man shall be humbled, and the haughtiness of men shall be bowed down, and the LORD alone shall be exalted in that day.

¹² For the day of the LORD of hosts shall be upon every one that is proud and lofty, and upon every one that is lifted up; and he shall be brought low:

¹³ And upon all the cedars of Lebanon, that are high and lifted up, and upon all the oaks of Bashan,

¹⁴ And upon all the high mountains, and upon all the hills that are lifted up,

¹⁵ And upon every high tower, and upon every fenced wall,

¹⁶ And upon all the ships of Tarshish, and upon all pleasant pictures.

¹⁷ And the loftiness of man shall be bowed down, and the haughtiness of men shall be made low: and the LORD alone shall be exalted in that day.

¹⁸ And the idols he shall utterly abolish.

¹⁹ And they shall go into the holes of the rocks, and into the caves of the earth, for fear of the LORD, and for the glory of his majesty, when he ariseth to shake terribly the earth.

²⁰ In that day a man shall cast his idols of silver, and his idols of gold, which they made each one for himself to worship, to the moles and to the bats;

²¹ To go into the clefts of the rocks, and into the tops of the ragged rocks, for fear of the LORD, and for the glory of his majesty, when he ariseth to shake terribly the earth.

²² Cease ye from man, whose breath is in his nostrils: for wherein is he to be accounted of?

The Branch from Jesse
Isaiah 11

¹ And there shall come forth a rod out of the stem of Jesse, and a Branch shall grow out of his roots:

² And the spirit of the LORD shall rest upon him, the spirit of wisdom and understanding, the spirit of counsel and might, the spirit of knowledge and of the fear of the LORD;

³ And shall make him of quick understanding in the fear of the LORD: and he shall not judge after the sight of his eyes, neither reprove after the hearing of his ears:

⁴ But with righteousness shall he judge the poor, and reprove with equity for the meek of the earth: and he shall smite the earth: with the rod of his mouth, and with the breath of his lips shall he slay the wicked.

⁵ And righteousness shall be the girdle of his loins, and faithfulness the girdle of his reins.

⁶ The wolf also shall dwell with the lamb, and the leopard shall lie down with the kid; and the calf and the young lion and the fatling together; and a little child shall

Peaceable Kingdom, Edward Hicks (1780—1849)

PART SEVEN PALESTINE DURING THE ASSYRIAN, BABYLONIAN, PERSIAN AND GREEK DOMINATION lead them.

⁷And the cow and the bear shall feed; their young ones shall lie down together: and the lion shall eat straw like the ox.

⁸And the sucking child shall play on the hole of the asp②, and the weaned child shall put his hand on the cockatrice'③ den.

⁹They shall not hurt nor destroy in all my holy mountain: for the earth shall be full of the knowledge of the LORD, as the waters cover the sea.

¹⁰And in that day there shall be a root of Jesse, which shall stand for an ensign of the people; to it shall the Gentiles seek; and his rest shall be glorious.

¹¹And it shall come to pass in that day, that the Lord shall set his hand again the second time to recover the remnant of his people, which shall be left, from Assyria, and from Egypt, and from Pathros④, and from Cush⑤, and from Elam⑥, and from Shinar⑦, and from Hamath⑧, and from the islands of the sea.

¹²And he shall set up an ensign for the nations, and shall assemble the outcasts of Israel, and gather together the dispersed of Judah from the four corners of the earth.

¹³The envy also of Ephraim shall depart, and the adversaries of Judah shall be cut off: Ephraim shall not envy Judah, and Judah shall not vex Ephraim.

¹⁴But they shall fly upon the shoulders of the Philistines toward the west; they shall spoil them of the east together: they shall lay their hand upon Edom and Moab; and the children of Ammon shall obey them.

¹⁵And the LORD shall utterly destroy the tongue of the Egyptian sea; and with his mighty wind shall he shake his hand over the river, and shall smite it in the seven streams, and make men go over dryshod.

¹⁶And there shall be an highway for the remnant of his people, which shall be left, from Assyria; like as it was to Israel in the day that he came up out of the land of Egypt.

The Suffering Servant Songs
Isaiah 53

¹Who hath believed our report? And to whom is the arm of the LORD revealed?

²For he shall grow up before him as a tender plant, and as a root out of a dry ground: he hath no form nor comeliness; and when we shall see him, there is no beauty that we should desire him.

³He is despised and rejected of men; a man of sorrows, and acquainted with grief: and we hid as it were our faces from him; he was despised, and we esteemed him not.

⁴Surely he hath borne our griefs, and carried our sorrows: yet we did esteem him stricken, smitten of God, and afflicted.

⁵But he was wounded for our transgressions, he was bruised for our iniquities: the chastisement of our peace was upon him; and with his stripes we are healed.

⁶All we like sheep have gone astray; we have turned every one to his own way; and the LORD hath laid on him the iniquity of us all.

⁷He was oppressed, and he was afflicted, yet he opened not his mouth: he is brought as a lamb to the slaughter, and as a sheep before her shearers is dumb, so he openeth not his mouth.

⁸He was taken from prison and from judgment: and who shall declare his generation? For he was cut off out of the land of the living: for the transgression of my people was he stricken.

⁹And he made his grave with the wicked, and with the rich in his death; because he had done no violence, neither was any deceit in his mouth.

---

② **asp** a venomous snake of Africa, Asia, and Europe.
③ **cockatrice** *mythology* a serpent hatched from a cock's egg and having the power to kill by its glance.
④ **Pathros** Upper Egypt.
⑤ **Cush** an ancient region of northeast Africa.
⑥ **Elam** east of Babylonia.
⑦ **Shinar** Babylonia.
⑧ **Hamath** a city of western Syria.

¹⁰ Yet it pleased the LORD to bruise him; he hath put him to grief: when thou shalt make his soul an offering for sin, he shall see his seed, he shall prolong his days, and the pleasure of the LORD shall prosper in his hand.

¹¹ He shall see of the travail of his soul, and shall be satisfied: by his knowledge shall my righteous servant justify many; for he shall bear their iniquities.

¹² Therefore will I divide him a portion with the great, and he shall divide the spoil with the strong; because he hath poured out his soul unto death: and he was numbered with the transgressors; and he bare the sin of many, and made intercession for the transgressors.

Cultural Connections: *Isaiah as a quotation book*

The popularity of the Book of Isaiah as a source of quotation continues into our modern times. In his memorable speech *I Have a Dream*, the civil rights activist Martin Luther King Jr. expressed his great hope and joy by drawing on *Isaiah 40:4—5*: "Every valley shall be exalted, and every mountain and hill shall be made low: and the crooked shall be made straight, and the rough places plain. And the glory of the LORD shall be revealed, and all flesh shall see it together." In the 1980s, a group dedicated to the eradication of nuclear weapons called itself the Plowshares Movement. When the space shuttle *Columbia* exploded in January 2003, the American president George W. Bush quoted *Isaiah 40:26* (NIV) to bring solace to the bereaved and people around the world: "Lift up your eyes and look to the heavens. Who created all these? He who brings out the starry host one by one and calls forth each of them by name. Because of his great power and mighty strength, not one of them is missing."

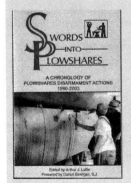

JEREMIAH⁹

Jeremiah 3

¹ They say, "If a man put away his wife, and she go from him, and become another man's, Shall he return unto her again? Shall not that land be greatly polluted? But thou hast played the harlot with many lovers; yet return again to me," saith the LORD.

² "Lift up thine eyes unto the high places, and see where thou hast not been lien with. In the ways hast thou sat for them, as the Arabian in the wilderness; and thou hast polluted the land with thy whoredoms and with thy wickedness.

³ Therefore the showers have been withholden, and there hath been no latter rain; and thou hadst a whore's forehead, thou refusedst to be ashamed.

⁴ Wilt thou not from this time cry unto me, 'My father, thou art the guide of my youth?'

⁵ Will he reserve his anger for ever? Will he keep it to the end?' Behold, thou hast spoken and done evil things as thou couldest."

---

⑨ **JEREMIAH** /dʒerəˈmaɪə/, 耶利米(书)。

Unfaithful Israel

⁶ The LORD said also unto me in the days of Josiah the king, "Hast thou seen that which backsliding Israel hath done? She is gone up upon every high mountain and under every green tree, and there hath played the harlot. ⁷ And I said after she had done all these things, "Turn thou unto me." But she returned not. And her treacherous sister Judah saw it. ⁸ And I saw, when for all the causes whereby backsliding Israel committed adultery I had put her away, and given her a bill of divorce; yet her treacherous sister Judah feared not, but went and played the harlot also. ⁹ And it came to pass through the lightness of her whoredom, that she defiled the land, and committed adultery with stones and with stocks. ¹⁰ And yet for all this her treacherous sister Judah hath not turned unto me with her whole heart, but feignedly," saith the LORD.

¹¹ And the LORD said unto me, " The backsliding Israel hath justified herself more than treacherous Judah. ¹² Go and proclaim these words toward the north, and say, " ' Return, thou backsliding Israel,' saith the LORD; ' and I will not cause mine anger to fall upon you: for I am merciful,' saith the LORD, ' and I will not keep anger for ever.'

¹³ ' Only acknowledge thine iniquity, that thou hast transgressed against the LORD thy God, and hast scattered thy ways to the strangers under every green tree, and ye have not obeyed my voice,'" saith the LORD.

¹⁴ " Turn, O backsliding children," saith the LORD; " for I am married unto you: and I will take you one of a city, and two of a family, and I will bring you to Zion: ¹⁵ And I will give you pastors according to mine heart, which shall feed you with knowledge and understanding. ¹⁶ And it shall come to pass, when ye be multiplied and increased in the land, in those days," saith the LORD, " they shall say no more, ' The ark of the covenant of the LORD:' neither shall it come to mind: neither shall they remember it; neither shall they visit it; neither shall that be done any more. ¹⁷ At that time they shall call Jerusalem the throne of the LORD; and all the nations shall be gathered unto it, to the name of the LORD, to Jerusalem: neither shall they walk any more after the imagination of their evil heart. ¹⁸ In those days the house of Judah shall walk with the house of Israel, and they shall come together out of the land of the north to the land that I have given for an inheritance unto your fathers.

¹⁹ " But I said, ' How shall I put thee among the children, and give thee a pleasant land, a goodly heritage of the hosts of nations?' and I said, ' Thou shalt call me, My father' ; and shalt not turn away from me. ²⁰ Surely as a wife treacherously departeth from her husband, so have ye dealt treacherously with me, O house of Israel," saith the LORD.

²¹ A voice was heard upon the high places, weeping and supplications of the children of Israel: for they have perverted their way, and they have forgotten the LORD their God.

²² " Return, ye backsliding children, and I will heal your backslidings." " Behold, we come unto thee; for thou art the LORD our God.

²³ Truly in vain is salvation hoped for from the hills, and from the multitude of mountains: truly in the LORD our God is the salvation of Israel.

²⁴ For shame hath devoured the labour of our fathers from our youth; their flocks and their herds, their sons and their daughters.

²⁵ We lie down in our shame, and our confusion covereth us: for we have sinned against the LORD our God, we and our fathers, from our youth even unto this day, and have not obeyed the voice of the LORD our God."

The Temple Sermon
Jeremiah 7

¹ The word that came to Jeremiah from the LORD, saying, ² " Stand in the gate of the LORD's house, and proclaim there this word, and say,

" ' Hear the word of the LORD, all ye of Judah, that enter in at these gates to worship the LORD. ³ Thus saith the LORD of hosts, the God of Israel, Amend your ways and your doings, and I will cause you to dwell in this place.'"

⁴Trust ye not in lying words, saying, "The temple of the LORD, The temple of the LORD, The temple of the LORD, are these." ⁵For if ye throughly amend your ways and your doings; if ye throughly execute judgment between a man and his neighbour; ⁶If ye oppress not the stranger, the fatherless, and the widow, and shed not innocent blood in this place, neither walk after other gods to your hurt: ⁷Then will I cause you to dwell in this place, in the land that I gave to your fathers, for ever and ever. ⁸Behold, ye trust in lying words, that cannot profit.

Jeremiah, the Sistine Chapel Ceiling paintings, Michelangelo (1475—1564)

⁹"'Will ye steal, murder, and commit adultery, and swear falsely, and burn incense unto Baal, and walk after other gods whom ye know not; ¹⁰And come and stand before me in this house, which is called by my name, and say, "We are delivered to do all these abominations? ¹¹Is this house, which is called by my name, become a den of robbers in your eyes? Behold, even I have seen it," saith the LORD.

¹²"'But go ye now unto my place which was in Shiloh, where I set my name at the first, and see what I did to it for the wickedness of my people Israel.

¹³And now, because ye have done all these works, saith the LORD, and I spake unto you, rising up early and speaking, but ye heard not; and I called you, but ye answered not; ¹⁴Therefore will I do unto this house, which is called by my name, wherein ye trust, and unto the place which I gave to you and to your fathers, as I have done to Shiloh. ¹⁵And I will cast you out of my sight, as I have cast out all your brethren, even the whole seed of Ephraim.'

¹⁶"Therefore pray not thou for this people, neither lift up cry nor prayer for them, neither make intercession to me: for I will not hear thee. ¹⁷Seest thou not what they do in the cities of Judah and in the streets of Jerusalem? ¹⁸The children gather wood, and the fathers kindle the fire, and the women knead their dough, to make cakes to the queen of heaven, and to pour out drink offerings unto other gods, that they may provoke me to anger. ¹⁹'Do they provoke me to anger?' saith the LORD: 'do they not provoke themselves to the confusion of their own faces?'"

²⁰"Therefore thus saith the Lord GOD; 'Behold, mine anger and my fury shall be poured out upon this place, upon man, and upon beast, and upon the trees of the field, and upon the fruit of the ground; and it shall burn, and shall not be quenched.'

²¹"Thus saith the LORD of hosts, the God of Israel;' Put your burnt offerings unto your sacrifices, and eat flesh. ²²For I spake not unto your fathers, nor commanded them in the day that I brought them out of the land of Egypt, concerning burnt offerings or sacrifices: ²³But this thing commanded I them, saying, Obey my voice, and I will be your God, and ye shall be my people: and walk ye in all the ways that I have commanded you, that it may be well unto you. ²⁴But they hearkened not, nor inclined their ear, but walked in the counsels and in the imagination of their evil heart, and went backward, and not forward. ²⁵Since the day that your fathers came forth out of the land of Egypt unto this day I have even sent unto you all my servants the prophets, daily rising up early and sending them: ²⁶Yet they hearkened not unto me, nor inclined their ear, but hardened their neck; they did worse than their fathers.'"

²⁷"'Therefore thou shalt speak all these words unto them; but they will not hearken to thee: thou shalt also call unto them; but they will not answer thee.'

²⁸"But thou shalt say unto them,' This is a nation that obeyeth not the voice of the LORD their God, nor receiveth correction: truth is perished, and is cut off from their mouth. ²⁹Cut off thine hair, O Jerusalem, and cast it away, and take up a lamentation on high places; for the LORD hath rejected and forsaken the generation of his wrath.'"

The Valley of Slaughter

³⁰" 'For the children of Judah have done evil in my sight, saith the LORD: they have set their abominations in the house which is called by my name, to pollute it. ³¹And they have built the high places of Tophet, which is in the valley of the son of Hinnom, to burn their sons and their daughters in the fire; which I commanded them not, neither came it into my heart. ³²Therefore, behold, the days come, saith the LORD, that it shall no more be called Tophet, nor the valley of the son of Hinnom, but the valley of slaughter: for they shall bury in Tophet, till there be no place. ³³And the carcases of this people shall be meat for the fowls of the heaven, and for the beasts of the earth; and none shall fray them away. ³⁴Then will I cause to cease from the cities of Judah, and from the streets of Jerusalem, the voice of mirth, and the voice of gladness, the voice of the bridegroom, and the voice of the bride: for the land shall be desolate.' "

Jeremiah Buys a Field
Jeremiah 32

¹The word that came to Jeremiah from the LORD in the tenth year of Zedekiah king of Judah, which was the eighteenth year of Nebuchadrezzar.

²For then the king of Babylon's army besieged Jerusalem: and Jeremiah the prophet was shut up in the court of the prison, which was in the king of Judah's house.

³For Zedekiah king of Judah had shut him up, saying, " Wherefore dost thou prophesy, and say, ' Thus saith the LORD, Behold, I will give this city into the hand of the king of Babylon, and he shall take it; ⁴And Zedekiah king of Judah shall not escape out of the hand of the Chaldeans, but shall surely be delivered into the hand of the king of Babylon, and shall speak with him mouth to mouth, and his eyes shall behold his eyes; ⁵And he shall lead Zedekiah to Babylon, and there shall he be until I visit him, saith the LORD: though ye fight with the Chaldeans, ye shall not prosper.' "

⁶And Jeremiah said, " The word of the LORD came unto me, saying, ⁷Behold, Hanameel the son of Shallum thine uncle shall come unto thee saying, ' Buy thee my field that is in Anathoth: for the right of redemption is thine to buy it.'

⁸" So Hanameel mine uncle's son came to me in the court of the prison according to the word of the LORD, and said unto me, ' Buy my field, I pray thee, that is in Anathoth, which is in the country of Benjamin: for the right of inheritance is thine, and the redemption is thine; buy it for thyself.'

" Then I knew that this was the word of the LORD.

⁹And I bought the field of Hanameel my uncle's son, that was in Anathoth, and weighed him the money, even seventeen shekels of silver. ¹⁰And I subscribed the evidence, and sealed it, and took witnesses, and weighed him the money in the balances. ¹¹So I took the evidence of the purchase, both that which was sealed according to the law and custom, and that which was open:

¹²And I gave the evidence of the purchase unto Baruch the son of Neriah, the son of Maaseiah, in the sight of Hanameel mine uncle's son, and in the presence of the witnesses that subscribed the book of the purchase, before all the Jews that sat in the court of the prison.

¹³" And I charged Baruch before them, saying, ¹⁴' Thus saith the LORD of hosts, the God of Israel; Take these evidences, this evidence of the purchase, both which is sealed, and this evidence which is open; and put them in an earthen vessel, that they may continue many days. ¹⁵For thus saith the LORD of hosts, the God of Israel; Houses and fields and vineyards shall be possessed again in this land.' " ...

EZEKIEL⑩

Ezekiel 1

¹Now it came to pass in the thirtieth year, in the fourth month, in the fifth day of the month, as I was

---

⑩ EZEKIEL /iźikiəl/, 以西结(书)。

among the captives by the river of Chebar, that the heavens were opened, and I saw visions of God. ²In the fifth day of the month, which was the fifth year of king Jehoiachin's captivity, ³The word of the LORD came expressly unto Ezekiel the priest, the son of Buzi, in the land of the Chaldeans by the river Chebar; and the hand of the LORD was there upon him.

The Vision of Ezekiel,
Raphael (1483—1520)

⁴And I looked, and, behold, a whirlwind came out of the north, a great cloud, and a fire infolding itself, and a brightness was about it, and out of the midst thereof as the colour of amber, out of the midst of the fire. ⁵Also out of the midst thereof came the likeness of four living creatures. And this was their appearance; they had the likeness of a man. ⁶And every one had four faces, and every one had four wings. ⁷And their feet were straight feet; and the sole of their feet was like the sole of a calf's foot: and they sparkled like the colour of burnished brass. ⁸And they had the hands of a man under their wings on their four sides; and they four had their faces and their wings. ⁹Their wings were joined one to another; they turned not when they went; they went every one straight forward.

¹⁰As for the likeness of their faces, they four had the face of a man, and the face of a lion, on the right side: and they four had the face of an ox on the left side; they four also had the face of an eagle. ¹¹Thus were their faces: and their wings were stretched upward; two wings of every one were joined one to another, and two covered their bodies. ¹²And they went every one straight forward: whither the spirit was to go, they went; and they turned not when they went. ¹³As for the likeness of the living creatures, their appearance was like burning coals of fire, and like the appearance of lamps: it went up and down among the living creatures; and the fire was bright, and out of the fire went forth lightning. ¹⁴And the living creatures ran and returned as the appearance of a flash of lightning.

¹⁵Now as I beheld the living creatures, behold one wheel upon the earth by the living creatures, with his four faces. ¹⁶The appearance of the wheels and their work was like unto the colour of a beryl: and they four had one likeness: and their appearance and their work was as it were a wheel in the middle of a wheel. ¹⁷When they went, they went upon their four sides: and they turned not when they went. ¹⁸As for their rings, they were so high that they were dreadful; and their rings were full of eyes round about them four.

¹⁹And when the living creatures went, the wheels went by them: and when the living creatures were lifted up from the earth, the wheels were lifted up. ²⁰Whithersoever the spirit was to go, they went, thither was their spirit to go; and the wheels were lifted up over against them: for the spirit of the living creature was in the wheels. ²¹When those went, these went; and when those stood, these stood; and when those were lifted up from the earth, the wheels were lifted up over against them: for the spirit of the living creature was in the wheels.

²²And the likeness of the firmament upon the heads of the living creature was as the colour of the terrible crystal, stretched forth over their heads above.

²³And under the firmament were their wings straight, the one toward the other: every one had two, which covered on this side, and every one had two, which covered on that side, their bodies. ²⁴And when they went, I heard the noise of their wings, like the noise of great waters, as the voice of the Almighty, the voice of speech, as the noise of an host: when they stood, they let down their wings.

²⁵And there was a voice from the firmament that was over their heads, when they stood, and had let down their wings. ²⁶And above the firmament that was over their heads was the likeness of a throne, as the appearance of a sapphire stone: and upon the likeness of the throne was the likeness as the appearance of a man above upon it. ²⁷And I saw as the colour of amber, as the appearance of fire round about within it, from the appearance of his loins even upward, and from the appearance of his loins even downward, I saw as it were the appearance of fire, and it had brightness round about. ²⁸As the appearance of the bow that is in the cloud in the day of rain, so was the appearance of the brightness round about.

This was the appearance of the likeness of the glory of the LORD. And when I saw it, I fell upon my face, and I heard a voice of one that spake.

The Valley of Dry Bones
Ezekiel 37

¹ The hand of the LORD was upon me, and carried me out in the spirit of the LORD, and set me down in the midst of the valley which was full of bones, ² And caused me to pass by them round about: and, behold, there were very many in the open valley; and, lo, they were very dry. ³ And he said unto me, "Son of man, can these bones live?"

And I answered, "O Lord GOD, thou knowest."

⁴ Again he said unto me, "Prophesy upon these bones, and say unto them, 'O ye dry bones, hear the word of the LORD. ⁵ Thus saith the Lord GOD unto these bones; Behold, I will cause breath to enter into you, and ye shall live: ⁶ And I will lay sinews upon you, and will bring up flesh upon you, and cover you with skin, and put breath in you, and ye shall live; and ye shall know that I am the LORD.'"

⁷ So I prophesied as I was commanded: and as I prophesied, there was a noise, and behold a shaking, and the bones came together, bone to his bone.

⁸ And when I beheld, lo, the sinews and the flesh came up upon them, and the skin covered them above: but there was no breath in them.

⁹ Then said he unto me, "Prophesy unto the wind, prophesy, son of man, and say to the wind, 'Thus saith the Lord GOD; Come from the four winds, O breath, and breathe upon these slain, that they may live.'" ¹⁰ So I prophesied as he commanded me, and the breath came into them, and they lived, and stood up upon their feet, an exceeding great army.

Valley of the Dry Bones, etching, Gustave Doré (1832—1883)

¹¹ Then he said unto me, "Son of man, these bones are the whole house of Israel: behold, they say, 'Our bones are dried, and our hope is lost: we are cut off for our parts.' ¹² Therefore prophesy and say unto them,' Thus saith the Lord GOD; Behold, O my people, I will open your graves, and cause you to come up out of your graves, and bring you into the land of Israel. ¹³ And ye shall know that I am the LORD, when I have opened your graves, O my people, and brought you up out of your graves, ¹⁴ And shall put my spirit in you, and ye shall live, and I shall place you in your own land: then shall ye know that I the LORD have spoken it, and performed it, saith the LORD.'"

¹⁵ The word of the LORD came again unto me, saying, ¹⁶ " Moreover, thou son of man, take thee one stick, and write upon it, 'For Judah, and for the children of Israel his companions' : then take another stick, and write upon it, 'For Joseph, the stick of Ephraim and for all the house of Israel his companions' : ¹⁷ And join them one to another into one stick; and they shall become one in thine hand."

¹⁸ "And when the children of thy people shall speak unto thee, saying, 'Wilt thou not shew us what thou meanest by these?' ¹⁹ Say unto them, 'Thus saith the Lord GOD; Behold, I will take the stick of Joseph, which is in the hand of Ephraim, and the tribes of Israel his fellows, and will put them with him, even with the stick of Judah, and make them one stick, and they shall be one in mine hand.' ²⁰ And the sticks whereon thou writest shall be in thine hand before their eyes. ²¹ And say unto them, 'Thus saith the Lord GOD; Behold, I will take the children of Israel from among the heathen, whither they be gone, and will gather them on every side, and bring them into their own land: ²² And I will make them one nation in the land upon the mountains of Israel; and one king shall be king to them all: and they shall be no more two nations, neither shall they be divided into two kingdoms any more at all. ²³ Neither shall they defile themselves any more with their idols, nor with their detestable things, nor with any of their transgressions: but I will save them out of all their dwelling places, wherein they have sinned, and will cleanse them: so shall they be my people, and I will be their God.

²⁴ "'And David my servant shall be king over them; and they all shall have one shepherd: they shall also walk in my judgments, and observe my statutes, and do them. ²⁵ And they shall dwell in the land that I have given unto Jacob my servant, wherein your fathers have dwelt; and they shall dwell therein, even they, and their children, and their children's children for ever: and my servant David shall be their prince for ever. ²⁶ Moreover I will make a covenant of peace with them; it shall be an everlasting covenant with them: and I will place them, and multiply them, and will set my sanctuary in the midst of them for evermore. ²⁷ My tabernacle also shall be with them: yea, I will be their God, and they shall be my people. ²⁸ And the heathen shall know that I the LORD do sanctify Israel, when my sanctuary shall be in the midst of them for evermore.'"

JONAH

Jonah Flees from the Lord
Jonah 1

¹ Now the word of the LORD came unto Jonah the son of Amittai, saying,

² "Arise, go to Nineveh①, that great city, and cry out against it; for their wickedness has come up before Me."

³ But Jonah rose up to flee unto Tarshish from the presence of the LORD; and he went down to Joppa, and found a ship going to Tarshish. So he paid the fare thereof, and went down into it to go with them unto Tarshish from the presence of the LORD.

A Storm at Sea

⁴ But the LORD sent out a great wind into the sea, and there was a mighty tempest in the sea, so that the ship was likely to be broken. ⁵ Then the mariners were afraid, and cried every man unto his god, and cast forth the wares that were in the ship into the sea to lighten it of them.

But Jonah had gone down into the inner parts of the ship, and he lay and was fast asleep. ⁶ So the shipmaster came to him and said unto him, "What meanest thou, O sleeper? Arise, call upon thy God, if it so be that God will think upon us, that we perish not."

⁷ And they said every one to his fellow, "Come, and let us cast lots, that we may know for whose cause this evil is upon us." So they cast lots, and the lot fell upon Jonah.

⁸ Then said they unto him, "Tell us, we pray thee, for whose cause this evil is upon us: What is thine occupation? And from whence comest thou? What is thy country? And of what people art thou?"

⁹ And he said unto them, "I am a Hebrew; and I fear the LORD, the God of heaven, who hath made the sea and the dry land."

¹⁰ Then were the men exceedingly afraid, and said unto him, "Why hast thou done this?" For the men knew that he fled from the presence of the LORD, because he had told them.

¹¹ Then said they unto him, "What shall we do unto thee, that the sea may be calm unto us?" For the sea grew more and more tempestuous.

¹² And he said unto them, "Take me up and cast me forth into the sea. So shall the sea be calm unto you, for I know that for my sake this great tempest is upon you."

¹³ Nevertheless the men rowed hard to bring it to the land; but they could not, for the sea was wrought, and was tempestuous against them. ¹⁴ Therefore they cried unto the LORD and said, "We beseech Thee, O LORD, we beseech Thee, let us not perish for this man's life, and lay not upon us innocent blood! For Thou, O LORD, hast done as it pleased Thee." ¹⁵ So they took up Jonah and cast him forth into the sea, and the sea ceased from her raging. ¹⁶ Then the men feared the LORD exceedingly, and offered a sacrifice unto the LORD and made vows.

---

① **Nineveh** (/ˈninivi/, 尼尼微) capital of Assyria on the Tigris River near what is now Mosul, Iraq.

In the belly of a Whale

¹⁷ Now the LORD had prepared a great fish to swallow up Jonah. And Jonah was in the belly of the fish three days and three nights.

Jonah Goes to Nineveh
Jonah 3

¹ And the word of the LORD came unto Jonah the second time, saying, ² "Arise, go unto Nineveh, that great city, and preach unto it the preaching that I bid thee."

³ So Jonah arose and went unto Nineveh, according to the word of the LORD. Now Nineveh was an exceeding great city of three days' journey. ⁴ And Jonah began to enter into the city a day's journey, and he cried and said, "Yet forty days, and Nineveh shall be overthrown." ⁵ So the people of Nineveh believed God, and proclaimed a fast and put on sackcloth, from the greatest of them even to the least of them.

⁶ For word came unto the king of Nineveh; and he arose from his throne, and he laid his robe from him, and covered himself with sackcloth and sat in ashes. ⁷ And he caused it to be proclaimed and published through Nineveh by the decree of the king and his nobles, saying,

Jonah Awaits the Fate of Nineveh, 1625—1630, Matthaeus Merian, the Elder

"Let neither man nor beast, herd nor flock, taste anything; let them not feed, nor drink water. ⁸ But let man and beast be covered with sackcloth and cry mightily unto God. Yea, let them turn every one from his evil way, and from the violence that is in their hands. ⁹ Who can tell if God will turn and repent, and turn away from His fierce anger, that we perish not?"

¹⁰ And God saw their works, that they turned from their evil way. And God repented of the evil that He had said that He would do unto them, and He did it not.

Jonah's Gourd
Jonah 4

Jonah Asleep under a Vine, Jonah Marbles, late 3rd c. central Turkey

¹ But it displeased Jonah exceedingly, and he was very angry. ² And he prayed unto the LORD and said, "I pray Thee, O LORD, was not this what I said when I was yet in my country? Therefore I fled before unto Tarshish; for I knew that Thou art a gracious God and merciful, slow to anger and of great kindness, and repentest of the evil.³ Therefore now, O LORD, take, I beseech Thee, my life from me, for it is better for me to die than to live."

⁴ Then said the LORD, "Doest thou well to be angry?"

⁵ So Jonah went out of the city and sat on the east side of the city, and there made himself a booth and sat under it in the shadow till he might see what would become of the city. ⁶ And the LORD God prepared a gourd, and made it to come up over Jonah, that it might be a shadow over his head to deliver him from his grief. So Jonah was exceeding glad for the gourd. ⁷ But God prepared a worm when the morning rose the next day, and it smote the gourd so that it withered. ⁸ And it came to pass, when the sun arose, that God prepared a vehement east wind; and the sun beat upon the head of Jonah, so that he grew faint and wished in himself to die, and said, "It is better for me to die than to live."

⁹ And God said to Jonah, "Doest thou well to be angry over the gourd?" And he said, "I do well to be

angry, even unto death."

¹⁰ Then said the LORD, "Thou hast had pity on the gourd for which thou hast not labored, neither madest it grow, which came up in a night and perished in a night.¹¹ And should not I spare Nineveh, that great city, wherein are more than sixscore thousand persons who cannot discern between their right hand and their left hand, and also many cattle?"

III FOOD FOR THOUGHT

ISAIAH
1. What does *Isaiah 2* show about the prophet's visions of the future?
2. Who is the suffering servant (ch. 53)?

JEREMIAH
3. How does God describe his relationship with his people (ch. 3)?
4. What does the purchase of a field symbolize (ch. 32)?

EZEKIEL
5. Why did God choose to appear to Ezekiel in Babylon?
6. What is the meaning of the metaphor of "dry bones"?

JONAH
7. What is the implied meaning of the incident of Jonah being swallowed by a great fish?
8. Can you feel the bitter satire in the story of Jonah?

IV BIBLICAL RELEVANCE

A. Biblical Terms in Everyday English

ISAIAH
1. beat swords into ploughshares (2:4): _____
2. Immanuel (7:14): _____
3. see eye to eye (52:8): _____

JEREMIAH
4. jeremiad: _____
5. a den of robbers/thieves (7:11): _____

EZEKIEL
6. set one's teeth on edge (18:2): _____

JONAH
7. Jonah: _____
8. Jonah's gourd (4:6): _____
9. Jonah trip: _____
10. Jonah word: _____

B. Biblical References in Literature

ISAIAH
1. Beauty from ashes, he quoted from Isaiah.

(W. Somerset Maugham, *Of Human Bondage*, 1915)

JEREMIAH
2. She was like Rachel, "mourning over her children, and would not be comforted."
(Washington Irving, *The Sketch-Book of Geoffrey Crayton*, Cent., 1820)

EZEKIEL
3. At night we could hear from amid the trees the long-drawn cry, as some primitive Ezekiel mourned for fallen greatness and recalled the departed glories of Ape Town.
(Sir Arthur Conan Doyle, *The Lost World*, 1912)

JONAH
4. His presence was a perpetual reminder of bad luck, and soon he was suffering the cold shoulder that had been my lot when Happy Hannah first decided I was a Jonah.
(Robertson Davies, *World of Wonders*, 1975)
5. I am back: again and again I am back, from the belly of the whale disgorged.
(J. M. Coetzee, *Age of Iron*, 1990)

C. The Bible and Arts
ISAIAH
1. *Peaceable Kingdom*, Edward Hicks (1780—1849)
2. *Let us Beat Swords into Plowshares*, a Soviet Union gift to the UN in 1959

JEREMIAH
3. *Jeremiah*, the Sistine Chapel, Michelangelo (1475—1564)

EZEKIEL
4. *Ezekiel*, the Sistine Chapel, Michelangelo (1475—1564)
5. *The Vision of Ezekiel*, Raphael (1483—1520)
6. *Valley of the Dry Bones*, etching, Gustave Doré (1832—1883)

JONAH
7. *Jonah*, c. 1885, Albert Pinkham Ryder
8. *Jonah Asleep under a Vine*, Jonah Marbles, late 3rd c. central Turkey
9. *Jonah Awaits the Fate of Nineveh*, 1625—1630, Matthaeus Merian, the Elder

V SOURCES FOR REFERENCE

1. (2002). *Jonah: A Veggie Tales Movie*. An American computer-animated comedy film based on the story of Jonah, produced by Big Idea Productions, Lions Gate Films and FHE Pictures.
2. Alter, R. & R. Kermode (ed.) (1987). *The Literary Guide to the Bible*. Cambridge, MA: The Belknap Press of Harvard University Press.
3. Black, M. (ed.) (2001). *Peake's Commentary on the Bible*. London: Routledge.

27. DANIEL

I POINTS OF DEPARTURE

Daniel is a legendary figure of wisdom and righteousness. The Book of Daniel is placed by Christians, following the LXX, in the section of the Old Testament after the major prophets of Isaiah, Jeremiah and Ezekiel; but in the Hebrew Bible it is included among the writings (others being Psalms, Proverbs, Job, Song of Songs, Ruth, Lamentations, Ecclesiastes, Esther, Ezra, Nehemiah, and 1 and 2 Chronicles). Different from other prophets, Daniel is half narrative (chs. 1—6) and half visionary and apocalyptic (chs. 7—12).

The narrative section contains the popular stories of the Burning Fiery Furnace, Belshazzar's Feast, and the Lion's Den. These stories are about the Jewish community as it lived in exile in Babylon and Persia. Daniel as depicted in the book is a trusted and outspoken adviser to three famous sovereigns (Nebuchadnezzar, Belshazzar, and Darius). The second group of chapters takes the form of visions of the future which purport to be predictions at the time of Babylonian supremacy of what would happen to the four kingdoms of Babylon, Media, Persia, and Greece. Finally, the culmination of all history is proclaimed with God reigning supreme over a kingdom of the saints. Both the stories and the visions follow a chronological order denoted by the reigns of Nebuchadnezzar to Cyrus.

Daniel's visions reflects a post-exilic interest in life after death, a concept that entered into Judaism late in the scriptural era. These ideas were taken up by some Jewish groups and, through them, influenced Christian theology, particularly as expressed in the New Testament Book of Revelation. From the Book of Daniel, then, come images that are associated with the end of the world, the resurrection of the dead, and the coming of God's universal, eternal kingdom.

In the apocryphal Book of Susanna, Daniel is portrayed as a wise judge, proving the falsely accused Susanna to be innocent. Throughout this book there are references to Daniel and to episodes from the Book of Daniel.

II SELECTED READINGS

Daniel's Training in Babylon

Daniel 1

¹ *In the third year of the reign of Jehoiakim king of Judah, came Nebuchadnezzar*[①] *king of Babylon unto*

[①] **Nebuchadnezzar** (/ˌnɛbjukədˈnezə/, 尼布甲尼撒) i. e. Nebuchadnezzar II (c. 630—562 B. C. E.), king of Babylon c. 605—562 B. C. E. In 586 B. C. E., he captured and destroyed Jerusalem and deported many Israelites, beginning a historical period known as the Babylonian Captivity ("巴比伦囚房"时期) (586—539 B. C. E.).

Jerusalem and besieged it.² And the Lord gave Jehoiakim king of Judah into his hand, with part of the vessels of the house of God, which he carried into the land of Shinar to the house of his god; and he brought the vessels into the treasure house of his god.

³ And the king spoke unto Ashpenaz, the master of his eunuchs, that he should bring certain of the children of Israel and of the king's seed and of the princes, ⁴ Youths in whom was no blemish, but well favored, and skillful in all wisdom, and cunning in knowledge, and understanding science, and such as had ability in them to stand in the king's palace, and whom they might teach the learning and the tongue of the Chaldeans. ⁵ And the king appointed them a daily provision of the king's meat and of the wine which he drank, so nourishing them three years, that at the end thereof they might stand before the king.

⁶ Now among these of the children of Judah were: Daniel②, Hananiah, Mishael, and Azariah, ⁷ Unto whom the prince of the eunuchs gave names: for he gave unto Daniel the name of Belteshazzar; and to Hananiah, Shadrach; and to Mishael, Meshach; and to Azariah, Abednego.

⁸ But Daniel purposed in his heart that he would not defile himself with the portion of the king's meat, nor with the wine which he drank. Therefore he requested of the prince of the eunuchs that he might not defile himself. ⁹ Now God had brought Daniel into favor and tender love with the prince of the eunuchs. ¹⁰ And the prince of the eunuchs said unto Daniel, " I fear my lord the king, who hath appointed your meat and your drink. For why should he see your faces sadder than the youths who are of your sort? Then shall ye make me endanger my head before the king."

¹¹ Then said Daniel to Melzar, whom the prince of the eunuchs had set over Daniel, Hananiah, Mishael, and Azariah, ¹² " Test thy servants, I beseech thee, ten days, and let them give us pulse to eat and water to drink. ¹³ Then let our countenances be looked upon before thee, and the countenance of the youths who eat of the portion of the king's meat. And as thou seest, deal with thy servants." ¹⁴ So he consented to them in this matter, and tested them ten days.

¹⁵ And at the end of ten days their countenances appeared fairer and fatter in flesh than all the youths who ate the portion of the king's meat. ¹⁶ Thus Melzar took away the portion of their meat and the wine that they should drink, and gave them pulse.

¹⁷ As for these four youths, God gave them knowledge and skill in all learning and wisdom; and Daniel had understanding in all visions and dreams.

¹⁸ Now at the end of the days that the king had said he should bring them in, then the prince of the eunuchs brought them in before Nebuchadnezzar. ¹⁹ And the king communed with them, and among them all was found none like Daniel, Hananiah, Mishael, and Azariah. Therefore stood they before the king.

²⁰ And in all matters of wisdom and understanding that the king inquired of them, he found them ten times better than all the magicians and astrologers who were in all his realm.

²¹ And Daniel continued even unto the first year of King Cyrus.

The Three Young Men in the Burning Fiery Furnace

Daniel 3
Nebuchadnezzar's Image of Gold

¹ Nebuchadnezzar the king made an image of gold, whose height was threescore cubits and the breadth thereof six cubits. He set it up in the plain of Dura, in the province of Babylon. ² Then Nebuchadnezzar the king sent to gather together the princes, the governors, and the captains, the judges, the treasurers, the counselors, the sheriffs, and all the rulers of the provinces to come to the dedication of the image which Nebuchadnezzar the king had set up. ³ Then the princes, the governors, and captains, the judges, the treasurers, the counselors, the sheriffs, and all the rulers of the provinces were gathered together unto the dedication of the image that Nebuchadnezzar the king had set up; and they stood before the image that Nebuchadnezzar had set up.

---

② **Daniel** /ˈdænjəl/，但以理。

⁴ Then a herald cried aloud: "To you it is commanded, O people, nations, and languages, ⁵ That at the time ye hear the sound of the cornet, flute, harp, sackbut, psaltery, dulcimer, and all kinds of music, ye fall down and worship the golden image that Nebuchadnezzar the king hath set up. ⁶ And whoso falleth not down and worshipeth shall the same hour be cast into the midst of a burning fiery furnace."

⁷ Therefore at that time when all the people heard the sound of the cornet, flute, harp, sackbut, psaltery, and all kinds of music, all the people, the nations, and the languages fell down and worshiped the golden image that Nebuchadnezzar the king had set up.

⁸ Therefore at that time certain Chaldeans came near and accused the Jews. ⁹ They spoke and said to King Nebuchadnezzar, "O king, live for ever! ¹⁰ Thou, O king, hast made a decree that every man who shall hear the sound of the cornet, flute, harp, sackbut, psaltery, and dulcimer, and all kinds of music, shall fall down and worship the golden image; ¹¹ And whoso falleth not down and worshipeth, that he should be cast into the midst of a burning fiery furnace. ¹² There are certain Jews whom thou hast set over the affairs of the province of Babylon: Shadrach, Meshach, and Abednego. These men, O king, have not regarded thee. They serve not thy gods, nor worship the golden image which thou hast set up."

¹³ Then Nebuchadnezzar in his rage and fury commanded to bring Shadrach, Meshach, and Abednego. Then they brought these men before the king. ¹⁴ Nebuchadnezzar spoke and said unto them, "Is it true, O Shadrach, Meshach, and Abednego, that ye do not serve my gods, nor worship the golden image which I have set up? ¹⁵ Now if ye be ready so that at the time ye hear the sound of the cornet, flute, harp, sackbut, psaltery, and dulcimer, and all kinds of music, ye fall down and worship the image which I have made, it is well; but if ye worship not, ye shall be cast the same hour into the midst of a burning fiery furnace. And who is that God that shall deliver you out of my hands?"

¹⁶ Shadrach, Meshach, and Abednego answered and said to the king, "O Nebuchadnezzar, we do not fear to answer thee in this matter. ¹⁷ If it be so, our God whom we serve is able to deliver us from the burning fiery furnace, and He will deliver us out of thine hand, O king. ¹⁸ But if not, be it known unto thee, O king, that we will not serve thy gods, nor worship the golden image which thou hast set up."

Shadrach, Meshach, and Abednego Walking in Fire Unscathed

¹⁹ Then was Nebuchadnezzar full of fury, and the form of his visage was changed against Shadrach, Meshach, and Abednego. Therefore he spoke, and commanded that they should heat the furnace seven times more than it was wont to be heated. ²⁰ And he commanded the most mighty men who were in his army to bind Shadrach, Meshach, and Abednego, and to cast them into the burning fiery furnace. ²¹ Then these men were bound in their coats, their breeches, and their hats, and their other garments, and were cast into the midst of the burning fiery furnace. ²² Therefore because the king's commandment was urgent and the furnace exceedingly hot, the flame of the fire slew those men who took up Shadrach, Meshach, and Abednego. ²³ And these three men, Shadrach, Meshach, and Abednego, fell down bound into the midst of the burning fiery furnace.

²⁴ Then Nebuchadnezzar the king was astonished, and rose up in haste and spoke, and said unto his counselors, "Did not we cast three men bound into the midst of the fire?"

They answered and said unto the king, "True, O king."

²⁵ He answered and said, "Lo, I see four men loose, walking in the midst of the fire, and they have no hurt; and the form of the fourth is like the Son of God."

²⁶ Then Nebuchadnezzar came near to the mouth of the burning fiery furnace, and spoke and said, "Shadrach, Meshach, and Abednego, ye servants of the Most High God, come forth and come hither."

Then Shadrach, Meshach, and Abednego came forth from the midst of the fire. ²⁷ And the princes, governors, and captains, and the king's counselors, being gathered together, saw these men upon whose bodies the fire had no power, nor was a hair of their head singed, neither were their coats changed nor had the smell of fire passed onto them.

²⁸ Then Nebuchadnezzar spoke and said, "Blessed be the God of Shadrach, Meshach, and Abednego, who

hath sent His angel and delivered His servants who trusted in Him, and have changed the king's word, and yielded their bodies, that they might not serve nor worship any god except their own God. ²⁹ Therefore I make a decree that every people, nation, and language which speak any thing amiss against the God of Shadrach, Meshach, and Abednego shall be cut in pieces and their houses shall be made a dunghill, because there is no other God who can deliver in this way." ³⁰ Then the king promoted Shadrach, Meshach, and Abednego in the province of Babylon.

Belshazzar's Feast

Daniel 5

¹ Belshazzar③ the king made a great feast for a thousand of his lords, and drank wine before the thousand. ² Belshazzar, while he tasted the wine, commanded to bring the golden and silver vessels which his father Nebuchadnezzar had taken out of the temple which was in Jerusalem, that the king and his princes, his wives, and his concubines might drink therein. ³ Then they brought the golden vessels that were taken out of the temple of the house of God which was at Jerusalem; and the king and his princes, his wives, and his concubines drank from them. ⁴ They drank wine, and praised the gods of gold and of silver, of brass, of iron, of wood, and of stone.

The Writing on the Wall

⁵ In the same hour came forth fingers of a man's hand, and wrote opposite the candlestick upon the plaster of the wall of the king's palace; and the king saw the part of the hand that wrote. ⁶ Then the king's countenance was changed and his thoughts troubled him, so that the joints of his loins were loosed and his knees smote one against another.

⁷ The king cried aloud to bring in the astrologers, the Chaldeans, and the soothsayers. And the king spoke and said to the wise men of Babylon, "Whosoever shall read this writing and show me the interpretation thereof, shall be clothed with scarlet and have a chain of gold about his neck, and shall be the third ruler in the kingdom."

Belshazzar's Feast, c. 1635,
Harmenszoon van Rijn Rembrandt

⁸ Then came in all the king's wise men; but they could not read the writing, nor make known to the king the interpretation thereof. ⁹ Then was King Belshazzar greatly troubled, and his countenance was changed in him, and his lords were dismayed.

¹⁰ Now the queen, by reason of the words of the king and his lords, came into the banquet house. And the queen spoke and said, " O king, live for ever! Let not thy thoughts trouble thee, nor let thy countenance be changed. ¹¹ There is a man in thy kingdom in whom is the spirit of the holy gods. And in the days of thy father, light and understanding and wisdom, like the wisdom of the gods, was found in him whom King Nebuchadnezzar thy father — the king, I say, thy father — made master of the magicians, astrologers, Chaldeans, and soothsayers.

¹² " Inasmuch as an excellent spirit, and knowledge, and understanding, interpreting of dreams, and interpreting of hard sentences, and dissolving of doubts were found in the same Daniel whom the king named Belteshazzar, now let Daniel be called and he will show the interpretation."

¹³ Then was Daniel brought in before the king. And the king spoke and said unto Daniel, "Art thou that Daniel who art of the children of the captivity of Judah, whom the king my father brought out of Jewry?

---

③ **Belshazzar** (/bel'ʃæzə/, 伯沙撒) son of Nebuchadnezzar II and last king of Babylon.

Nebuchadnezzar, 1795, William Blake

¹⁴ I have even heard of thee that the spirit of the gods is in thee, and that light and understanding and excellent wisdom are found in thee. ¹⁵ And now the wise men, the astrologers, have been brought in before me, that they should read this writing and make known unto me the interpretation thereof; but they could not show the interpretation of the thing. ¹⁶ And I have heard of thee that thou canst make interpretations and dissolve doubts. Now if thou canst read the writing and make known to me the interpretation thereof, thou shalt be clothed with scarlet, and have a chain of gold about thy neck, and shalt be the third ruler in the kingdom."

¹⁷ Then Daniel answered and said before the king, " Let thy gifts be to thyself, and give thy rewards to another; yet I will read the writing unto the king, and make known to him the interpretation.

¹⁸ " O thou king, the Most High God gave Nebuchadnezzar thy father a kingdom, and majesty and glory and honor. ¹⁹ And for the majesty that He gave him, all people, nations, and languages trembled and feared before him. Whomever he would he slew; and whomever he would he kept alive; and whomever he would he set up; and whomever he would he put down. ²⁰ But when his heart was lifted up and his mind hardened in pride, he was deposed from his kingly throne, and they took his glory from him.²¹④ And he was driven from the sons of men; and his heart was made like the beasts, and his dwelling was with the wild asses. They fed him with grass like oxen, and his body was wet with the dew of heaven, till he knew that the Most High God ruled in the kingdom of men, and that He appointeth over it whomsoever He will."

²² " And thou his son, O Belshazzar, hast not humbled thine heart though thou knewest all this, ²³ But hast lifted up thyself against the Lord of heaven. And they have brought the vessels of His house before thee, and thou and thy lords, thy wives, and thy concubines have drunk wine from them; and thou hast praised the gods of silver and gold, of brass, iron, wood, and stone, which see not nor hear nor know. And the God in whose hand thy breath is, and whose are all thy ways, hast thou not glorified. ²⁴ Then was the part of the hand sent from Him, and this writing was written.

²⁵ " And this is the writing that was written:
MENE, MENE, TEKEL, UPHARSIN⑤.
²⁶ " This is the interpretation of the thing.
Mene⑥: God hath numbered thy kingdom, and finished it.
²⁷ Tekel⑦: Thou art weighed in the balances, and art found wanting.
²⁸ Peres⑧: Thy kingdom is divided, and given to the Medes and Persians."
²⁹ Then commanded Belshazzar, and they clothed Daniel with scarlet and put a chain of gold about his neck, and made a proclamation concerning him, that he should be the third ruler in the kingdom.
³⁰ In that night was Belshazzar the king of the Chaldeans slain. ³¹ And Darius the Mede took the kingdom, being about threescore and two years old.

---

④ 21 Nebuchadnezzar was driven mad by God and his insanity is first described in *Daniel 4:33*: "[H] e was driven from men, and did eat grass as oxen, and his body was wet with the dew of heaven, till his hairs were grown like eagles' feathers, and his nails like birds' claws."

⑤ **UPHARSIN** (/juːˈfɑːsin/, 乌法珥新) Aramaic, i. e. *AND PHARSIN*.

⑥ **Mene** (/ˈmiːniː/, 弥尼) can mean *numbered* or *mina* (a unit of money).

⑦ **Tekel** (/ˈtekəl/, 提客勒) can mean *weighed* or *shekel*.

⑧ **Peres** (/ˈperez/, 毗勒斯) (the singular of *Pharsin*) can mean *divided* or *Persia* or *a half mina* or *a half shekel*.

Daniel in the Lion's Den

Daniel 6

¹ It pleased Darius to set over the kingdom a hundred and twenty princes, who should be over the whole kingdom; ² And over these, three presidents, of whom Daniel was first, that the princes might give account unto them and the king should have no damage. ³ Then this Daniel was preferred above the presidents and princes, because an excellent spirit was in him; and the king thought to set him over the whole realm. ⁴ Then the presidents and princes sought to find occasion against Daniel concerning the kingdom, but they could find no occasion nor fault, inasmuch as he was faithful; neither was there any error or fault found in him. ⁵ Then said these men, "We shall not find any occasion against this Daniel unless we find it against him concerning the law of his God."

Daniel in the Lions' Den, c. 1615, Peter Paul Rubens

⁶ Then these presidents and princes assembled together before the king, and said thus unto him, "King Darius, live for ever! ⁷ All the presidents of the kingdom, the governors and the princes, the counselors and the captains, have consulted together to establish a royal statute and to make a firm decree, that whosoever shall ask a petition of any god or man for thirty days, except of thee, O king, he shall be cast into the den of lions. ⁸ Now, O king, establish the decree and sign the writing, that it be not changed, according to the law of the Medes and Persians, which altereth not." ⁹ Therefore King Darius signed the writing and the decree.

¹⁰ Now when Daniel knew that the writing was signed, he went into his house; and his windows being open in his chamber toward Jerusalem, he kneeled upon his knees three times a day, and prayed and gave thanks before his God, as he did formerly. ¹¹ Then these men assembled, and found Daniel praying and making supplication before his God. ¹² Then they came near, and spoke before the king concerning the king's decree: "Hast thou not signed a decree, that every man that shall ask a petition of any god or man within thirty days, except of thee, O king, shall be cast into the den of lions?"

The king answered and said, "The thing is true, according to the law of the Medes and Persians, which altereth not."

¹³ Then answered they and said before the king, "That Daniel, who is of the children of the captivity of Judah, regardeth not thee, O king, nor the decree that thou hast signed, but maketh his petition three times a day." ¹⁴ Then the king, when he heard these words, was sorely displeased with himself, and set his heart on Daniel to deliver him; and he labored till the going down of the sun to deliver him.

¹⁵ Then these men assembled unto the king, and said unto the king, "Know, O king, that the law of the Medes and Persians is: that no decree nor statute which the king establisheth may be changed."

¹⁶ Then the king commanded, and they brought Daniel and cast him into the den of lions. Now the king spoke and said unto Daniel, "Thy God whom thou servest continually, He will deliver thee."

¹⁷ And a stone was brought and laid upon the mouth of the den, and the king sealed it with his own signet and with the signet of his lords, that the purpose might not be changed concerning Daniel. ¹⁸ Then the king went to his palace and passed the night fasting; neither were instruments of music brought before him, and his sleep went from him.

¹⁹ Then the king arose very early in the morning and went in haste unto the den of lions. ²⁰ And when he came to the den, he cried with a lamentable voice unto Daniel; and the king spoke and said to Daniel, "O Daniel, servant of the living God, is thy God, whom thou servest continually, able to deliver thee from the lions?"

²¹ Then said Daniel unto the king, "O king, live for ever! ²² My God hath sent His angel, and hath shut the lions' mouths, that they have not hurt me, inasmuch as before Him innocency was found in me; and also before thee, O king, have I done no hurt."

²³ Then was the king exceeding glad for him, and commanded that they should take Daniel up out of the

den. So Daniel was taken up out of the den, and no manner of hurt was found upon him, because he believed in his God.

^{24} And the king commanded, and they brought those men who had accused Daniel, and they cast them into the den of lions — them, their children, and their wives; and the lions had the mastery of them, and broke all their bones in pieces before they came to the bottom of the den.

^{25} Then King Darius wrote unto all people, nations, and languages that dwell in all the earth:
"Peace be multiplied unto you.
^{26} I make a decree that in every dominion of my kingdom men tremble and fear before the God of Daniel.
"For He is the living God
and steadfast for ever,
and His Kingdom, that which shall not be destroyed,
and His dominion shall be even unto the end.
^{27} He delivereth and rescueth,
and He worketh signs and wonders
in heaven and in earth, who hath delivered Daniel from the power of the lions."
^{28} So this Daniel prospered in the reign of Darius and in the reign of Cyrus the Persian.

Daniel's Dream of Four Beasts

Daniel 7

^{1} In the first year of Belshazzar king of Babylon Daniel had a dream and visions of his head upon his bed: then he wrote the dream, and told the sum of the matters.

Visions of Daniel 2 & Daniel 7 Compared
〈http://www.wrestedscriptures.com〉

^{2} Daniel spake and said, "I saw in my vision by night, and, behold, the four winds of the heaven strove upon the great sea. ^{3} And four great beasts came up from the sea, diverse one from another.

^{4} "The first was like a lion, and had eagle's wings: I beheld till the wings thereof were plucked, and it was lifted up from the earth, and made stand upon the feet as a man, and a man's heart was given to it.

^{5} "And behold another beast, a second, like to a bear, and it raised up itself on one side, and it had three ribs in the mouth of it between the teeth of it: and they said thus unto it, Arise, devour much flesh.

^{6} "After this I beheld, and lo another, like a leopard, which had upon the back of it four wings of a fowl; the beast had also four heads; and dominion was given to it.

^{7} "After this I saw in the night visions, and behold a fourth beast, dreadful and terrible, and strong exceedingly; and it had great iron teeth: it devoured and brake in pieces, and stamped the residue with the feet of it: and it was diverse from all the beasts that were before it; and it had ten horns.

^{8} "I considered the horns, and, behold, there came up among them another little horn, before whom there were three of the first horns plucked up by the roots: and, behold, in this horn were eyes like the eyes of man, and a mouth speaking great things.

^{9} "I beheld till
"the thrones were cast down,
and the Ancient of days did sit,
whose garment was white as snow,
and the hair of his head like the pure wool.
His throne was like the fiery flame, and his wheels as burning fire.
^{10} A fiery stream issued
and came forth from before him.

Thousand thousands ministered unto him,
and ten thousand times ten thousand stood before him.
The judgment was set, and the books were opened.

^{11} " I beheld then because of the voice of the great words which the horn spake: I beheld even till the beast was slain, and his body destroyed, and given to the burning flame. ^{12} As concerning the rest of the beasts, they had their dominion taken away: yet their lives were prolonged for a season and time.

^{13} " I saw in the night visions, and, behold, one like the Son of man came with the clouds of heaven, and came to the Ancient of days, and they brought him near before him. ^{14} And there was given him dominion, and glory, and a kingdom, that all people, nations, and languages, should serve him: his dominion is an everlasting dominion, which shall not pass away, and his kingdom that which shall not be destroyed."

The Interpretation of the Dream

^{15} " I Daniel was grieved in my spirit in the midst of my body, and the visions of my head troubled me. ^{16} I came near unto one of them that stood by, and asked him the truth of all this.

"So he told me, and made me know the interpretation of the things. ^{17} ' These great beasts, which are four, are four kings, which shall arise out of the earth. ^{18} But the saints of the most High shall take the kingdom, and possess the kingdom for ever, even for ever and ever.'

^{19} " Then I would know the truth of the fourth beast, which was diverse from all the others, exceeding dreadful, whose teeth were of iron, and his nails of brass; which devoured, brake in pieces, and stamped the residue with his feet;

^{20} And of the ten horns that were in his head, and of the other which came up, and before whom three fell; even of that horn that had eyes, and a mouth that spake very great things, whose look was more stout than his fellows. ^{21} I beheld, and the same horn made war with the saints, and prevailed against them; ^{22} Until the Ancient of days came, and judgment was given to the saints of the most High; and the time came that the saints possessed the kingdom.

^{23} " Thus he said, ' The fourth beast shall be the fourth kingdom upon earth, which shall be diverse from all kingdoms, and shall devour the whole earth, and shall tread it down, and break it in pieces. ^{24} And the ten horns out of this kingdom are ten kings that shall arise: and another shall rise after them; and he shall be diverse from the first, and he shall subdue three kings. ^{25} And he shall speak great words against the most High, and shall wear out the saints of the most High, and think to change times and laws: and they shall be given into his hand until a time and times and the dividing of time.'

^{26} ' But the judgment shall sit, and they shall take away his dominion, to consume and to destroy it unto the end. ^{27} And the kingdom and dominion, and the greatness of the kingdom under the whole heaven, shall be given to the people of the saints of the most High, whose kingdom is an everlasting kingdom, and all dominions shall serve and obey him.'

^{28} " Hitherto is the end of the matter. As for me Daniel, my cogitations much troubled me, and my countenance changed in me, but I kept the matter in my heart."

III FOOD FOR THOUGHT

1. Why were Daniel and his three friends favored by Nebuchadnezzar?
2. What is the purpose of the "fiery furnace" episode?
3. What did the handwriting on the wall imply according to Daniel?
4. What is the purpose of the story of Daniel in the den of lions?
5. The second part of the Book of Daniel (*Daniel 7—12*) records Daniel's visions. The literary genre represented therein is known as *apocalyptic*. In what ways did Daniel's visions point to possible future happenings?

IV. BIBLICAL RELEVANCE

A. Biblical Terms in Everyday English
1. Daniel:
2. Nebuchadnezzar:
3. writing on the wall:
4. Daniel in the den of lions:

B. Biblical References in Literature
1. Left to its own devices, the class tied Eunice Ann Simpson to a chair and placed her in the furnace room. We forgot her, trooped upstairs to church, and were listening quietly to the sermon when a dreadful banging issued from the radiator pipe, persisting until someone investigated and brought forth Eunice Ann saying she didn't want to play Shadrach any more—Jem Finch said she wouldn't get burnt if she had enough faith, but it was hot down there.
(Harper Lee, *To Kill a Mockingbird*, 1960)
2. You have a "faux air" of Nebuchadnezzar in the fields about you, that is certain: your hair reminds me of eagles' feathers; whether your nails are grown like birds' claws or not, I have not yet noticed.
(Charlotte Brontë, *Jane Eyre*, 1847)
3. He watched her walk firmly towards the Incident Room, where all lights were on. At the entrance, she turned and waved. She wouldn't be welcome in that room, as she well knew. Daniel into the lion's den.
(Jennie Melville, *Baby Drop*, 1994)
4. "I always like this room," said Spandrell as they entered. "It's like a scene for Belshazzar's feast."
(Aldou Huxley, *Point Counter Point*, 1928)
5. This inexplicable incident, this reversal of my previous experience, seemed like the Babylonian finger on the wall, to be spelling out the letters of my judgment.
(Robert Louis Stevenson, *The Strange Case of Dr Jekyll and Mr Hyde*, 1886)

C. The Bible and Arts
1. *Shadrach, Meshach, and Abednego in the Burning Fiery Furnace*, Exhibited 1832, Joseph Mallord William Turner
2. *Nebuchadnezzar*, 1795, William Blake
3. Writing on the Wall
   Belshazzar's Feast, 1826, John Martin
   Belshazzar's Feast, c. 1635, Harmenszoon van Rijn Rembrandt
4. Daniel in the lions' den
   Daniel and the Lion, 1650, Gian Lorenzo Bernini
   Daniel in the Lions' Den, c. 1615, Peter Paul Rubens
5. *The Vision of Daniel*, 1650, Willem Drost

V. SOURCES FOR REFERENCE

1. Browning, W. R. E. (2009). *A Dictionary of the Bible*. Oxford: Oxford University Press.
2. Schippe, C. & C. Stetson. (2005). *The Bible and Its Influence*. Front Royal, VA: BLP Publishing.

PART EIGHT

PALESTINE UNDER THE ROMANS
(C. 4 B.C.E. — 67 C.E.)
THE FOUR GOSPELS, THE ACTS OF
APOSTLES, REVELATION

THE FOUR GOSPELS

28. BIRTH OF JOHN AND JESUS

I POINTS OF DEPARTURE

Gospel is an Anglo-Saxon word that translates from the Greek word *evangelion*, meaning "good tidings" or "good news." The four gospels in the New Testament are named after their supposed authors, or *evangelists*—Mark, Matthew, Luke and John. Compiled in the second half of the 1st c. C. E., each gospel describes the life, teaching, death, and resurrection of Jesus, catering to the spiritual needs of a particular community in which each evangelist resided. At first there was the oral tradition with Jesus' teaching and acts remembered and passed on through word of mouth. Memory and rote repetition were so greatly valued that the Talmud, the body of Jewish statutes, described the good discipline as a "plastered cistern that loses not a drop." (Schippe & Stetson, 2005:209)

Rising to the occasion, Mark committed to writing those recollections of Jesus' sayings and miracles in a fast-paced, action-packed journalistic style. His gospel gives a detailed account of the trials and execution of Jesus, with an introduction containing excerpts of teaching and examples of about a dozen miracles.

The gospel of Matthew generally follows Mark's order, but incorporates into it such unique features as the genealogy of Jesus, the infancy narrative, parts of the resurrection narrative as well as the five great discourses, including the Sermon on the Mount (*Mt. 5—7*), the Missionary Discourse (*Mt. 10*), the Parable Discourse (*Mt. 13*), the Church Order Discourse (*Mt. 18*), and the Discourse on the End Times (*Mt. 24—28*). Known as "the gospel of the church," it is placed first in the canon of the New Testament because of its elaborate discussion of the church and its persistent use in the Christian liturgy.

Though sharing a similar structure and much material with Mark and Matthew, the gospel of Luke has several unique and defining features of its own. The infancy narrative from the perspective of Mary, the mother of Jesus; an emphasis on meal sharing; a focus on mercy and healing; a long teaching section using parables; and the resurrection narrative are all characteristically Luke. Because of the much ground shared, the gospels of Mark, Matthew and Luke are often called "synoptics," (同观福音书) able to be "viewed alongside," word for word and paragraph for paragraph, in three parallel columns.

With "In the beginning was the Word, and the Word was with God, and the Word was God," John announces his gospel is going to be different from the other three which focus on events, following Jesus through the bustling marketplaces and villages. Assuming that readers know the basic facts about Jesus, it mulls over the profound meaning of what Jesus had said and done. The Book of John reads as if it were written under a great, shady tree by an author who had a world of time for contemplation.

For the sake of comfortable and smooth reading, this part will be organized along the biographical line of Jesus, drawing chapters, wholesale or piecemeal, from the four gospels. Where parallels occur, chapters and verses of the synoptic gospels and other relevant books will be marked alongside the selected version. Readers are encouraged to find out how the same event is narrated from different perspectives.

II SELECTED READINGS

John the Baptist's Birth Foretold

Luke 1

...

⁵ There was in the days of Herod①, the king of Judea②, a certain priest named Zacharias③, of the priestly course of Abijah; and his wife was of the daughters of Aaron, and her name was Elizabeth. ⁶ And they were both righteous before God, walking blameless in all the commandments and ordinances of the Lord.

⁷ And they had no child because Elizabeth was barren, and they both were now well stricken in years.

⁸ And it came to pass that while he executed the priest's office before God in the order of his course, ⁹ According to the custom of the priest's office, his lot was to burn incense when he went into the temple of the Lord. ¹⁰ And the whole multitude of the people were praying outside at the time of incense.

The Visit of an Angel

¹¹ And there appeared unto him an angel of the Lord, standing on the right side of the altar of incense. ¹² And when Zacharias saw him he was troubled, and fear fell upon him. ¹³ But the angel said unto him, "Fear not, Zacharias, for thy prayer is heard, and thy wife Elizabeth shall bear thee a son, and thou shalt call his name John. ¹⁴ And thou shalt have joy and gladness, and many shall rejoice at his birth. ¹⁵ For he shall be great in the sight of the Lord, and shall drink neither wine nor strong drink, and he shall be filled with the Holy Ghost④ even from his mother's womb. ¹⁶ And many of the children of Israel shall he turn to the Lord their God. ¹⁷ And he shall go before Him in the spirit and power of Elijah, to turn the hearts of the fathers to the children, and the disobedient to the wisdom of the just, to make ready a people prepared for the Lord."

¹⁸ And Zacharias said unto the angel, "Whereby shall I know this? For I am an old man, and my wife

---

① **Herod** (/ˈherəd/, 希律王). The Herod family ruled on behalf of Rome. The New Testament records four different Herods, who all clashed with Jesus or his disciples.
Herod the Great (希律一世) reigned when Jesus was born, and, in order to kill the baby king, had all the baby boys killed (i.e. the Massacre of the Innocents) (*Mt.* 2; *Lk.* 1).
Herod Archelaus (/ˌɑːkiˈleiəs/, 阿基劳斯), son of Herod the Great; Joseph moved to Galilee in fear of him (*Mt.* 2:22).
Herod Antipas (/ˈæntipæs/, 安提帕) (also known as Herod the tetrarch), son of Herod the Great, was responsible for having John the Baptist imprisoned and beheaded. He was also involved in the trial of Jesus (*Mk.* 6; 8:15; *Lk.* 13:31).
Herod Agrippa I (/ˈherədəˈgripə/, 希律·亚基帕一世), grandson of Herod the Great, ruled Jerusalem when the Christian church began growing underground. He clamped down on the early Christians, executing James and arresting some others, including Peter (*Ac.* 12).
Herod Agrippa II (希律·亚基帕二世) was the last of the series of Herods who served as puppets of Rome. True to his family tradition of brutality, Agrippa had to pass judgment on the apostle Paul (*Ac.* 25:23—27, 26:1—32).
② **Judea** (/dʒuːˈdiə/, 犹太) the southern part of ancient Palestine.
③ **Zacharias** /zækəˈraiəs/, 撒迦利亚。
④ **the Holy Ghost** another term for **Holy Spirit** (圣灵).

well stricken in years."

¹⁹ And the angel answering said unto him, "I am Gabriel⑤ who stands in the presence of God, and am sent to speak unto thee and to show thee these glad tidings. ²⁰ And behold, thou shalt be dumb and not able to speak until the day that these things shall be performed, because thou believest not my words which shall be fulfilled in their season."

Zacharias Becomes Mute

²¹ And the people waited for Zacharias, and marveled that he tarried so long in the temple. ²² And when he came out, he could not speak unto them, and they perceived that he had seen a vision in the temple; for he beckoned unto them and remained speechless.

²³ And it came to pass that as soon as the days of his ministration were accomplished, he departed to his own house.

...

The Annunciation (天使报喜) and the Birth of John the Baptist

²⁶ And in the sixth month the angel Gabriel was sent from God unto a city of Galilee⑥, named Nazareth⑦? ²⁷ To a virgin espoused to a man whose name was Joseph⑧, of the house of David; and the virgin's name was Mary⑨. ²⁸ And the angel came in unto her and said, "Hail, thou that art highly favored, the Lord is with thee; blessed art thou among women."

The Annunciation, 1758, Giambattista Pittoni

²⁹ And when she saw him, she was troubled at his saying and cast about in her mind what manner of salutation this should be. ³⁰ And the angel said unto her, "Fear not, Mary, for thou hast found favor with God. ³¹ And behold, thou shalt conceive in thy womb and bring forth a Son, and shalt call His name JESUS. ³² He shall be great and shall be called the Son of the Highest; and the Lord God shall give unto Him the throne of His father David. ³³ And He shall reign over the house of Jacob for ever; and of His Kingdom there shall be no end."

³⁴ Then said Mary unto the angel, "How shall this be, seeing I know not a man?"

³⁵ And the angel answered and said unto her, "The Holy Ghost shall come upon thee, and the power of the Highest shall overshadow thee. Therefore also that Holy Being who shall be born of thee shall be called the Son of God. ³⁶ And behold, thy cousin Elizabeth: she hath also conceived a son in her old age, and this is the sixth month with her, who was called barren. ³⁷ For with God nothing shall be impossible."

³⁸ And Mary said, "Behold the handmaid of the Lord; be it unto me according to thy word." And the angel departed from her.

Mary Visits Elizabeth

³⁹ And Mary arose in those days and went into the hill country with haste, into a city of Judah, ⁴⁰ And

---

⑤ **Gabriel** (/ˈgeibriəl/, 加百利) an archangel acting as the messenger of God.
⑥ **Galilee** (/ˈgælili:/, 加利利) the northernmost part of Palestine, the center of Jesus' ministry.
⑦ **Nazareth** (/ˈnæzəriθ/, 拿撒勒) a town in lower Galilee.
⑧ **Joseph** /ˈdʒəuzif/, 约瑟.
⑨ **Mary** 玛利亚.

entered into the house of Zacharias and saluted Elizabeth. [41] And it came to pass, when Elizabeth heard the salutation of Mary, that the babe leaped in her womb, and Elizabeth was filled with the Holy Ghost. [42] And she spoke out with a loud voice and said, "Blessed art thou among women, and blessed is the fruit of thy womb. [43] And why is it granted to me that the mother of my Lord should come to me? [44] For lo, as soon as the voice of thy salutation sounded in mine ears, the babe leaped in my womb for joy. [45] And blessed is she that believed; for there shall be a fulfillment of those things which were told her from the Lord."

Visitation, 1486—1490, Domenico Ghirlandaio

Mary's Song: the "Magnificat"

[46] And Mary said, "My soul doth magnify the Lord,

[47] And my spirit hath rejoiced in God my Saviour.

[48] For he hath regarded the low estate of his handmaiden: for, behold, from henceforth all generations shall call me blessed.

[49] For he that is mighty hath done to me great things; and holy is his name.

[50] And his mercy is on them that fear him from generation to generation.

[51] He hath shewed strength with his arm; he hath scattered the proud in the imagination of their hearts.

[52] He hath put down the mighty from their seats, and exalted them of low degree.

[53] He hath filled the hungry with good things; and the rich he hath sent empty away.

[54] He hath helped his servant Israel, in remembrance of his mercy;

[55] As he spake to our fathers, to Abraham, and to his seed for ever."

Cultural Connections: *the Magnificat in music*

Perhaps no other New Testament has provided a richer source of inspiration for composers than the Magnificat. The Magnificat appears as a song in the earliest Christian liturgies and has been set to music by numerous composers, the most famous of whom is Johann Sebastian Bach (1685—1750). Bach's Magnificat in D Major was written for the Christmas service of 1723 at St. Thomas's Church in Leipzig. The form of Bach's music is the cantata, a genre of vocal chamber music in the Baroque period and a key part of the German Lutheran service. In Germany, the cantata was primarily a form of sacred music based on an actual biblical text or a paraphrase. Bach was a deeply religious man who signed his cantatas "S.D.G.," which stands for Soli Deo Gloria, "to God alone the glory."

The Birth of John the Baptist

[56] And Mary abode with her about three months, and returned to her own house.

[57] Now Elizabeth's full time came that she should be delivered, and she brought forth a son. [58] And her neighbors and her kindred heard how the Lord had shown great mercy upon her, and they rejoiced with her.

⁵⁹ And it came to pass that on the eighth day they came to circumcise the child, and they called him Zacharias, after the name of his father. ⁶⁰ But his mother answered and said, "Not so, but he shall be called John."

⁶¹ And they said unto her, "There is none of thy kindred that is called by this name."

⁶² And they made signs to his father, how he would have him called. ⁶³ And he asked for a writing tablet and wrote, saying, "His name is John." And they marveled all. ⁶⁴ And his mouth was opened immediately, and his tongue loosed, and he spoke and praised God. ⁶⁵ And fear came on all who dwelt round about them; and all these sayings were noised abroad throughout all the hill country of Judea. ⁶⁶ And all those who heard them laid them up in their hearts, saying, "What manner of child shall this be?" And the hand of the Lord was with him.

...

The Genealogy of Jesus

Matthew 1

¹ The book of the generation of Jesus Christ, the son of David, the son of Abraham.
² Abraham begat Isaac;
and Isaac begat Jacob;
and Jacob begat Judas and his brethren;
³ And Judas begat Phares and Zara of Thamar;
and Phares begat Esrom; and Esrom begat Aram;
⁴ And Aram begat Aminadab;
and Aminadab begat Naasson;
and Naasson begat Salmon;
⁵ And Salmon begat Booz of Rachab;
and Booz begat Obed of Ruth;
and Obed begat Jesse;
⁶ And Jesse begat David the king;
and David the king begat Solomon of her that had been the wife of Urias;
⁷ And Solomon begat Roboam;
and Roboam begat Abia;
and Abia begat Asa;
⁸ As Asa begat Josaphat;
and Josaphat begat Joram;
and Joram begat Ozias;
⁹ And Ozias begat Joatham;
and Joatham begat Achaz;
and Achaz begat Ezekias;
¹⁰ And Ezekias begat Manasses;
and Manasses begat Amon;
and Amon begat Josias;
¹¹ And Josias begat Jechonias and his brethren,
about the time they were carried away to Babylon:
¹² And after they were brought to Babylon,
Jechonias begat Salathiel;
and Salathiel begat Zorobabel;
¹³ And Zorobabel begat Abiud;

and Abiud begat Eliakim;
and Eliakim begat Azor;
^{14} And Azor begat Sadoc;
and Sadoc begat Achim;
and Achim begat Eliud;
^{15} And Eliud begat Eleazar;
and Eleazar begat Matthan;
and Matthan begat Jacob;
^{16} And Jacob begat Joseph the husband of Mary,
of whom was born Jesus,
who is called Christ.
^{17} So all the generations from Abraham to David are fourteen generations; and from David until the carrying away into Babylon are fourteen generations; and from the carrying away into Babylon unto Christ are fourteen generations.

The Birth of Jesus Christ

^{18} Now the birth of Jesus Christ was in this way: When His mother Mary was espoused to Joseph, before they came together, she was found with child of the Holy Ghost. ^{19} And Joseph her husband, being a just man and not willing to make her a public example, was minded to put her away privily.
^{20} But while he thought on these things, behold, the angel of the Lord appeared unto him in a dream, saying, "Joseph, thou son of David, fear not to take unto thee Mary thy wife, for that which is conceived in her is of the Holy Ghost. ^{21} And she shall bring forth a Son, and thou shalt call His name JESUS, for He shall save His people from their sins."
^{22} Now all this was done, that it might be fulfilled which was spoken of the Lord by the prophet, saying, ^{23} "Behold, a

Nativity, Lorenzo Costa (c. 1460—1535)

virgin shall be with child and shall bring forth a Son, and they shall call His name Emmanuel" (which being interpreted is, "God with us").
^{24} Then Joseph, being raised from sleep, did as the angel of the Lord had bidden him, and took unto him his wife, ^{25} And knew her not until she had brought forth her firstborn Son. And he called His name JESUS.

The Visit of the Magi

Matthew 2

^{1} Now when Jesus was born in Bethlehem⑩ of Judea in the days of Herod the king, behold, there came wise men⑪ from the East to Jerusalem, ^{2} Saying, "Where is He that is born King of the Jews? For we have seen His star in the East and have come to worship Him."
^{3} When Herod the king had heard these things, he was troubled, and all Jerusalem with him. ^{4} And when

---

⑩ **Bethlehem** (/ˈbeθlihem/, 伯利恒) a town in the West Bank south of Jerusalem, the native city of King David.
⑪ **wise men** although the names and number of the wise men are not mentioned, later tradition attributed variations of three kings: Balthasar, Melchior, and Casper, evidenced by their three gifts and through reflections on *Psalm 72* and *Isaiah 63* (*Biblica*: *The Bible Atlas*, 2007:414). The gifts they bore of gold, incense, and myrrh are literary symbols. Gold was a gift fit for a king. Frankincense was used to honor the deity. Myrrh was used in the preparation of a body for burial. The narrative uses the symbols to suggest a realization on the Magi's part that Jesus was a king and God and that he would suffer death. (Schippe & Stetson, 2005:228)

The Journey of the Magi, c. 1435, Sassetta

he had gathered all the chief priests and scribes of the people together, he demanded of them where Christ should be born. ⁵ And they said unto him, " In Bethlehem of Judea, for thus it is written by the prophet:

⁶ ' And thou, Bethlehem, in the land of Judah, art not the least among the princes of Judah; for out of thee shall come a Governor, that shall rule My people Israel.' "

The Star of Bethlehem

⁷ Then Herod, when he had privily called the wise men, inquired of them diligently what time the star appeared. ⁸ And he sent them to Bethlehem and said, " Go and search diligently for the young child, and when ye have found him, bring me word again, that I may come and worship him also."

⁹ When they had heard the king, they departed; and lo, the star which they saw in the East went before them until it came and stood over where the young Child was. ¹⁰ When they saw the star, they rejoiced with exceeding great joy. ¹¹ And when they had come into the house, they saw the young Child with Mary His mother, and fell down and worshiped Him. And when they had opened their treasures, they presented unto Him gifts: gold and frankincense and myrrh. ¹² And being warned by God in a dream that they should not return to Herod, they departed into their own country another way.

Adoration of the Shepherds, 1459—1461, Giorgione

The Escape to Egypt

¹³ And when they had departed, behold, the angel of the Lord appeared to Joseph in a dream, saying, " Arise, and take the young Child and His mother, and flee into Egypt, and be thou there until I bring thee word; for Herod will seek the young Child to destroy Him."

¹⁴ When he arose, he took the young Child and His mother by night and departed into Egypt? ¹⁵ And was there until the death of Herod, that it might be fulfilled which was spoken of the Lord by the prophet, saying, " Out of Egypt have I called My Son."

¹⁶ Then Herod, when he saw that he was mocked by the wise men, was exceeding wroth, and sent forth and slew all the children who were in Bethlehem and in all the region thereof, from two years old and under, according to the time which he had diligently inquired of the wise men. ¹⁷ Then was fulfilled that which was spoken by Jeremiah the prophet, saying,

¹⁸ " In Ramah was there a voice heard, lamentation and weeping and great mourning, Rachel weeping for her children and would not be comforted, because they are no more.

The Return to Nazareth

¹⁹ " But when Herod was dead, behold, an angel of the Lord appeared in a dream to Joseph in Egypt, ²⁰ Saying, " Arise, and take the young Child and His mother, and go into the land of Israel, for they are dead who sought the young Child's life."

²¹ And he arose and took the young Child and His mother, and came into the land of Israel. ²² But when he heard that Archelaus reigned in Judea in place of his father Herod, he was afraid to go thither.

Notwithstanding, being warned by God in a dream, he turned aside into the region of Galilee. ²³ *And he came and dwelt in a city called Nazareth, that it might be fulfilled which was spoken by the prophets: "He shall be called a Nazarene."*

The Boy Jesus at the Temple

Luke 2

...

Madonna of the Meadows,
1505/1506, Raphael

³⁹ *And when they (Joseph and Mary) had performed all things according to the law of the Lord, they returned into Galilee to their own city, Nazareth.* ⁴⁰ *And the Child grew and waxed strong in spirit, filled with wisdom, and the grace of God was upon Him.*

⁴¹ *Now His parents went to Jerusalem every year at the Feast of the Passover.* ⁴² *And when He was twelve years old, they went up to Jerusalem according to the custom of the Feast.* ⁴³ *And when they had fulfilled the days, as they returned, the child Jesus tarried behind in Jerusalem; and Joseph and His mother knew not of it.* ⁴⁴ *But they, supposing Him to have been in the company, went a day's journey; and they sought Him among their kinsfolk and acquaintances.* ⁴⁵ *And when they found Him not, they turned back again to Jerusalem, seeking Him.* ⁴⁶ *And it came to pass that after three days they found Him in the temple, sitting in the midst of the doctors, both hearing them and asking them questions.* ⁴⁷ *And all who heard Him were astonished at His understanding and answers.* ⁴⁸ *And when they saw Him they were amazed, and His mother said unto Him, "Son, why hast Thou thus dealt with us? Behold, Thy father and I have sought Thee sorrowing."*

The Boy Jesus, Friedrich Overbeck
(1789—1869)

⁴⁹ *And He said unto them, "How is it that ye sought Me? Knew ye not that I must be about My Father's business?"* ⁵⁰ *And they understood not the saying which He spoke unto them.*

⁵¹ *And He went down with them and came to Nazareth, and was subject unto them. But His mother kept all these things in her heart.* ⁵² *And Jesus increased in wisdom and stature, and in favor with God and man.*

FOOD FOR THOUGHT

1. Compare the beginning chapters of the three gospels. Do the differences show the nature of each of them?
2. Why does Matthew begin with the genealogy of Jesus? And why does it, different from many Jewish genealogies, include women of disreputable character?
3. What was Joseph's attitude towards Mary's immaculate conception (圣灵怀胎)? And what does this show about his personality?
4. What were the circumstances surrounding the birth of Jesus in Bethlehem of Nazareth?

IV. BIBLICAL RELEVANCE

A. Biblical Terms in Everyday English
1. annunciation: _____
2. nativity: _____
3. the Magi: _____
4. virgin birth: _____

B. Biblical References in Literature
1. O. Henry, *The Gift of the Magi*, 1906.
2. T. S. Eliot, *The Journey of the Magi*, 1927.
3. All babies start off looking like the last tomato in the fridge, but "cute," "gorgeous" and "adorable," which were the adjectives Lucy was throwing about the place with gay abandon, struck me as the raving of an insane and blind woman. Quite frankly, I began to see King Herod in a wholly different light.

   (Ben Elton, *Inconceivable*, 1999)

C. The Bible and Arts
1. *Zechariah and Elizabeth*, 1913—1914, Sir Stanley Spencer
2. the Visitation
   Visitation, 1486—1490, Domenico Ghirlandaio
   The Visitation, Juan Vicente Masip (1500—1579)
3. *Birth of St. John the Baptist*, 1486—1490, Domenico Ghirlandaio
4. Immaculate Conception
   Immaculate Conception, 1660s, Filippo Parodi
   The Esquilache Immaculate Conception, Between 1645 and 1655, Bartolom Esteban Murillo
5. The Annunciation
   Annunciation, c. 1420, ra Angelico
   Annunciation, Simone Martini (c. 1284—1344)
   The Annunciation to the Shepherds, Benjamin Gerritsz Cuyp (1612—1652)
   The Annunciation, 1472—1475, Leonardo da Vinci
   The Annunciation, 1486—1490, Francesco Albani
   The Annunciation, 1758, Giambattista Pittoni
6. *The Census at Bethlehem*, 1566, Pieter Bruegel, the Elder
7. The Nativity
   The Nativity, 1643, Philippe de Champaigne
   Nativity, Lorenzo Costa (c. 1460—1535)
8. *The Journey of the Magi*, c. 1435, Sassetta
9. The Adoration
   The Adoration of the Magi, Early 1480s, Sandro Botticelli
   Vigil of the Shepherds 1/2, 1459—1461, Gozzoli, Benozzo
   Adoration of the Shepherds, 1459—1461, Giorgione
   Adoration of the Shepherds, 1482—1485, Domenico Ghirlandaio
   Adoration of the Trinity, Albrecht Dürer (1471—1528)
10. The Holy Family
    The Holy Family, 1456, Michelangelo

The Alba Madonna, c. 1510, Raphael
Madonna of the Meadows, 1505/6, Raphael

V SOURCES FOR REFERENCE

1. (2006). *The Nativity Story*. A drama film based on the nativity of Jesus starring Keisha Castle-Hughes and Shohreh Aghdashloo.
2. (2009). *Nativity*! A British comedy directed by Debbie Isitt, starring Martin Freeman and Ashley Jensen.
3. Schippe, C. & C. Stetson. (2005). *The Bible and Its Influence*. Front Royal, VA: BLP Publishing.
4. (2007). *Biblica: The Bible Atlas*. London: New Holland Publications (UK) Ltd.

29. THE MINISTRY OF JOHN AND THE LAUNCH OF JESUS' CAREER

I POINTS OF DEPARTURE

Related to Jesus as his cousin and born to Elizabeth late in her life and a priest Zechariah, John was mostly famous for baptisms in the river Jordon, offering the hope of salvation. Therefore, he was called John the Baptist. John's preaching preceded that of Jesus, who aligned himself with John's ministry. The gospels betray an increasing reluctance to say without qualification that John baptized Jesus. They do not wish their readers to be in doubt that John was merely a forerunner, probably because for some time there existed disciples of John and it was important to establish a distance between the Messiah of Christian belief and the prophet who preceded him (attired in clothing made of camel's hair and a leather belt, John was indeed in the prophetic style), as scripture had anticipated (*Mal. 4:5*).

Once baptized by John, Jesus began his ministry, mostly concentrated in Galilee, though he did occasionally stray outside its borders, to the Decapolis or Tyre and Sidon. His milieu was that of the synagogue and his fellow Galilean Jews. The gospel of John records Jesus' several trips to Jerusalem while the other gospels record only one journey to Jerusalem — his final and fateful visit. Jesus' ministry was full of miraculous signs and engaging didactic sayings and stories known as parables. One of the most significant collections of teaching is recorded in the Sermon on the Mount in *Matthew 5—7*. Similar to Moses who delivered the Ten Commandments from Mount Sinai, Jesus delivered his sermon, consisting largely of ethical guidelines, from a mountain.

The first section of the Sermon on the Mountain has come to be called the *beatitudes*, meaning in Latin "happiness" or "blessedness." These are nine qualities that Jesus considered characteristics of people who are to be blessed by God. Following the beatitudes are two strong metaphors of "salt of the earth" and "a city built on a hill" to set the audience's mind darting off on a religious tangent. Next, the Sermon deals with various guidelines for worship, the most familiar aspect of which is Jesus' teaching on prayer. Then the Sermon ends with the well-known Golden Rule: "[A]ll things whatsoever ye would that men should do to you, do ye even so to them." (*Mt. 7:12*)

II SELECTED READINGS

John the Baptist Prepares the Way

Matthew 3

¹ In those days came John the Baptist, preaching in the wilderness of Judea, ² And saying, "Repent ye, for the Kingdom of Heaven is at hand." ³ For this is he that was spoken of by the prophet Isaiah, saying,
"The voice of one crying in the wilderness:
'Prepare ye the way of the Lord,
make His paths straight.'"①

⁴ And the same John had his raiment of camel's hair, and a leather girdle about his loins; and his meat was locusts and wild honey. ⁵ Then there went out to him Jerusalem and all Judea and all the region round about the Jordan. ⁶ And they were baptized by him in the Jordan, confessing their sins.

⁷ But when he saw many of the Pharisees② and Sadducees③ coming to his baptism, he said unto them, "O generation of vipers, who hath warned you to flee from the wrath to come? ⁸ Bring forth therefore fruits meet for repentance, ⁹ And think not to say to yourselves, 'We have Abraham as our father.' For I say unto you that God is able from these stones to raise up children unto Abraham. ¹⁰ And now also the ax is laid unto the root of the trees; therefore every tree which bringeth not forth good fruit is hewn down and cast into the fire.

St. John the Baptist in the Wilderness, 1504—1505, Hieronymus Bosch

¹¹ "I indeed baptize you with water unto repentance, but He that cometh after me is mightier than I, whose shoes I am not worthy to bear. He shall baptize you with the Holy Ghost and with fire. ¹² His fan is in His hand, and He will thoroughly purge His threshing floor and gather His wheat into the garner; but He will burn up the chaff with unquenchable fire."

The Baptism of Jesus

¹³ Then came Jesus from Galilee to the Jordan unto John to be baptized by him. ¹⁴ But John forbad Him, saying, "I have need to be baptized by Thee, and comest Thou to me?"

¹⁵ And Jesus answering said unto him, "Suffer it to be so now, for thus it becometh us to fulfill all righteousness." Then John suffered Him.

¹⁶ And Jesus, when He had been baptized, went up straightway out of the water. And lo, the heavens were opened unto Him, and He saw the Spirit of God descending like a dove and lighting upon Him. ¹⁷ And lo, a voice came from Heaven, saying, "THIS IS MY BELOVED SON, IN WHOM I AM WELL PLEASED."

---

① 3 *Isaiah* 40:3.
② **Pharisee** (/ˈfærisiː/, 法利赛人) a member of an ancient Jewish sect that emphasized strict interpretation and observance of the Mosaic law.
③ **Sadducee** (/ˈsædjusiː/, 撒都该人,文士) a member of a priestly, aristocratic Jewish sect of Christ's time that accepted only the written Mosaic law.

The Temptation in the Desert

Matthew 4

The Baptism of Christ, 1473—1478, Leonardo da Vinci et al.

^{1} Then was Jesus led up by the Spirit into the wilderness to be tempted by the devil. ^{2} And when He had fasted forty days and forty nights, He afterward hungered. ^{3} And when the tempter came to Him, he said, "If Thou be the Son of God, command that these stones be made bread."

^{4} But He answered and said, "It is written: 'Man shall not live by bread alone, but by every word that proceedeth out of the mouth of God.'"④

^{5} Then the devil took Him up into the holy city, and set Him on a pinnacle of the temple, ^{6} And said unto Him, "If Thou be the Son of God, cast Thyself down. For it is written: 'He shall give His angels charge concerning thee; and in their hands they shall bear thee up, lest at any time thou dash thy foot against a stone.'"⑤

^{7} Jesus said unto him, "It is written again: 'Thou shalt not tempt the Lord thy God.'"⑥

^{8} Again, the devil took Him up onto an exceeding high mountain, and showed Him all the kingdoms of the world and the glory of them, ^{9} And said unto Him, "All these things will I give Thee if Thou wilt fall down and worship me."

^{10} Then said Jesus unto him, "Get thee hence, Satan! For it is written: 'Thou shalt worship the Lord thy God, and Him only shalt thou serve.'"

^{11} Then the devil left Him, and behold, angels came and ministered unto Him.

Sermon on the Mount（登山宝训）

The Beatitudes⑦（八福词）

Matthew 5

^{1} And seeing the multitudes, He went up onto a mountain; and when He was set, His disciples came unto Him. ^{2} And He opened His mouth and taught them, saying,

^{3} "Blessed are the poor in spirit,
for theirs is the Kingdom of Heaven.⑧

^{4} Blessed are they that mourn,
for they shall be comforted.⑨

^{5} Blessed are the meek,
for they shall inherit the earth.⑩

^{6} Blessed are they that hunger and thirst after righteousness,
for they shall be filled.⑪

---

④ 4 *Deuteronomy* 8:3.
⑤ *Psalm* 91:11, 12.
⑥ 7 *Deuteronomy* 6:16.
⑦ **Beatitude** /biˈætitjuːd/, supreme blessedness or happiness.
⑧ 3：虚心的人有福了，因为天国是他们的。译文据中国基督教协会印发之《新旧约全书》(1984)，以下同。
⑨ 4：哀恸的人有福了，因为他们必受安慰。
⑩ 5：温柔的人有福了，因为他们必承受地土。
⑪ 6：饥渴慕义的人有福了，因为他们必得饱足。

⁷ Blessed are the merciful,
for they shall obtain mercy.⑫
⁸ Blessed are the pure in heart,
for they shall see God.⑬
⁹ Blessed are the peacemakers,
for they shall be called the children of God.⑭
¹⁰ Blessed are they that are persecuted for righteousness' sake,
for theirs is the Kingdom of Heaven.⑮
¹¹ Blessed are ye when men shall revile you and persecute you, and shall say all manner of evil against you falsely for My sake. ¹² Rejoice and be exceeding glad, for great is your reward in Heaven; for so persecuted they the prophets who were before you.⑯

Salt and Light

¹³ "Ye are the salt of the earth, but if the salt has lost his savor, wherewith shall it be salted? It is thenceforth good for nothing, but to be cast out and to be trodden under foot of men.

¹⁴ "Ye are the light of the world. A city that is set on a hill cannot be hid. ¹⁵ Neither do men light a candle and put it under a bushel, but on a candlestick, and it giveth light unto all that are in the house. ¹⁶ Let your light so shine before men, that they may see your good works, and glorify your Father who is in Heaven."

Cultural Connections: *a City on a Hill*

The notion of *a city on a hill* has captured the American imagination from colonial times when the Puritan John Winthrop used the phrase in a speech aboard the flagship Arabella in 1630. Winthrop's sermon gave rise to the widespread belief in American folklore that the United States is God's country because metaphorically it is a Shining City upon a Hill, an early example of American exceptionalism. In the twentieth century, the image was used a number of times in American politics. On 9 January, 1961, President-elect John F. Kennedy made this biblical phrase alive during an address delivered to the General Court of Massachusetts. President Ronald Reagan used the image again in his 1984 acceptance of the Republican Party nomination and in his January 11, 1989 farewell speech to the nation:

... I've spoken of the shining city all my political life, but I don't know if I ever quite communicated what I saw when I said it. But in my mind it was a tall proud city built on rocks stronger than oceans, wind-swept, God-blessed, and teeming with people of all kinds living in harmony and peace, a city with free ports that hummed with commerce and creativity, and if there had to be city walls, the walls had doors and the doors were open to anyone with the will and the heart to get here. That's how I saw it and see it still ...

---

⑫ 7：怜恤人的人有福了,因为他们必蒙怜恤。
⑬ 8：清心的人有福了,因为他们必得见神。
⑭ 9：使人和睦的人有福了,因为他们必称为神的儿子。
⑮ 10：为义受逼迫的人有福了,因为天国是他们的。
⑯ 11—12：人若因我辱骂你们,逼迫你们,捏造各样坏话毁谤你们,你们就有福了。应当欢喜快乐,因为你们在天上的赏赐是大的。在你们以前的先知,人也是这样逼迫他们的。

The Fulfillment of the Law

¹⁷ "Think not that I am come to destroy the Law or the Prophets. I am not come to destroy, but to fulfill. ¹⁸ For verily I say unto you, till heaven and earth pass away, not one jot or one tittle shall in any wise pass from the law till all be fulfilled. ¹⁹ Whosoever therefore shall break one of these least commandments and shall teach men so, he shall be called the least in the Kingdom of Heaven; but whosoever shall do and teach them, the same shall be called great in the Kingdom of Heaven. ²⁰ For I say unto you that unless your righteousness shall exceed the righteousness of the scribes and Pharisees, ye shall in no case enter into the Kingdom of Heaven."

Murder

²¹ "Ye have heard that it was said by them of old, 'Thou shalt not kill,'⑰ and 'Whosoever shall kill shall be in danger of the judgment.' ²² But I say unto you, that whosoever is angry with his brother without a cause shall be in danger of the judgment; and whosoever shall say to his brother, 'Raca,'⑱ shall be in danger of the council; but whosoever shall say, 'Thou fool,' shall be in danger of hell fire.

²³ Therefore if thou bring thy gift to the altar and there rememberest that thy brother hath aught against thee, ²⁴ Leave there thy gift before the altar, and go thy way. First be reconciled to thy brother, and then come and offer thy gift.

²⁵ "Agree with thine adversary quickly while thou art on the way with him, lest at any time the adversary deliver thee to the judge, and the judge deliver thee to the officer, and thou be cast into prison. ²⁶ Verily I say unto thee, thou shalt by no means come out thence until thou hast paid the uttermost farthing."

Adultery

²⁷ "Ye have heard that it was said by them of old, 'Thou shalt not commit adultery.'⑲ ²⁸ But I say unto you, that whosoever looketh on a woman to lust after her hath committed adultery with her already in his heart. ²⁹ And if thy right eye cause thee to fall, pluck it out and cast it from thee; for it is profitable for thee that one of thy members should perish, and not that thy whole body should be cast into hell. ³⁰ And if thy right hand cause thee to fall, cut it off and cast it from thee; for it is profitable for thee that one of thy members should perish, and not that thy whole body should be cast into hell."

Divorce

³¹ "It hath been said, 'Whosoever shall put away his wife, let him give her a writing of divorcement.' ⑳ ³² But I say unto you, that whosoever shall put away his wife, except for the cause of fornication, causeth her to commit adultery; and whosoever shall marry her that is divorced committeth adultery."

Oaths

³³ "Again, ye have heard that it hath been said by them of old times, 'Thou shalt not forswear thyself, but shalt perform unto the Lord thine oaths.' ³⁴ But I say unto you, swear not at all: neither by Heaven, for

---

⑰ **Thou shalt not kill** *Exodus* 20:13.
⑱ **Raca** an Aramaic term of contempt.
⑲ **Thou shalt not commit adultery** *Exodus* 20:14.
⑳ **Whosoever shall put away his wife, let him give her a writing of divorcement** *Deuteronomy* 24:1.

it is God's throne; ³⁵ Nor by the earth, for it is His footstool; neither by Jerusalem, for it is the city of the great King. ³⁶ Neither shalt thou swear by thy head, because thou canst not make one hair white or black. ³⁷ But let your communication be ' yea, yea' or ' nay, nay' ; for whatsoever is more than these cometh of evil."

An Eye for an Eye

³⁸ " Ye have heard that it hath been said, ' An eye for an eye, and a tooth for a tooth.' ㉑ ³⁹ But I say unto you that ye resist not evil, but whosoever shall smite thee on thy right cheek, turn to him the other also㉒. ⁴⁰ And if any man will sue thee at the law and take away thy coat, let him have thy cloak also. ⁴¹ And whosoever shall compel thee to go a mile, go with him two. ⁴² Give to him that asketh thee; and from him that would borrow of thee, turn not thou away."

Love for Enemies

⁴³ " Ye have heard that it hath been said, ' Thou shalt love thy neighbor and hate thine enemy.' ㉓ ⁴⁴ But I say unto you, love your enemies, bless them that curse you, do good to them that hate you, and pray for them that despitefully use you and persecute you, ㉔ ⁴⁵ That ye may be the children of your Father who is in Heaven. For He maketh His sun to rise on the evil and on the good, and sendeth rain on the just and on the unjust.㉕ ⁴⁶ For if ye love them that love you, what reward have ye? Do not even the publicans the same? ⁴⁷ And if ye salute your brethren only, what do ye more than others? Do not even the publicans so? ⁴⁸ Be ye therefore perfect, even as your Father who is in Heaven is perfect."

Giving to the Needy

Matthew 6

¹ " Take heed that ye do not your almsgiving before men, to be seen by them; otherwise ye have no reward from your Father who is in Heaven. ² Therefore when thou givest thine alms, do not sound a trumpet before thee, as the hypocrites do in the synagogues and in the streets, that they may have glory of men. Verily I say unto you, they have their reward. ³ But when thou givest alms, let not thy left hand know what thy right hand doeth? ⁴ That thine almsgiving may be in secret; and thy Father who seeth in secret, Himself shall reward thee openly."

Prayer

⁵ " And when thou prayest, thou shalt not be as the hypocrites are. For they love to pray standing in the synagogues and on the corners of the streets, that they may be seen by men. Verily I say unto you, they have their reward. ⁶ But thou, when thou prayest, enter into thy closet, and when thou hast shut thy door, pray to thy Father who is in secret; and thy Father who seeth in secret shall reward thee openly. ⁷ But when ye pray, use not vain repetitions as the heathen do, for they think that they shall be heard for their much speaking. ⁸ Be not ye therefore like unto them, for your Father knoweth what things ye have need of before ye ask Him.
⁹ " In this manner therefore pray ye:

㉑ **An eye for an eye, and a tooth for a tooth** *Exodus* 21:24; *Leviticus* 24:20; *Deuteronomy* 19:21.
㉒ whosoever shall smite thee on thy right cheek, turn to him the other also 有人打你的右脸，连左脸也转过来由他打。
㉓ **Thou shalt love thy neighbor and hate thine enemy** *Leviticus* 19:18.
㉔ love your enemies, bless them that curse you, do good to them that hate you, and pray for them that despitefully use you and persecute you 要爱你们的仇敌，为那逼迫你们的祷告。
㉕ He maketh His sun to rise on the evil and on the good, and sendeth rain on the just and on the unjust 他叫日头照好人，也照歹人；降雨给义人，也给不义之人。

" ' Our Father who art in Heaven,
hallowed be Thy name.
^{10} Thy Kingdom come.
Thy will be done on earth,
as it is in Heaven.
^{11} Give us this day our daily bread.
^{12} And forgive us our debts,
as we forgive our debtors.
^{13} And lead us not into temptation,
but deliver us from evil.
For Thine is the Kingdom,
and the power and the glory for ever. Amen.'
^{14} For if ye forgive men their trespasses, your heavenly Father will also forgive you. ^{15} But if ye forgive not men their trespasses, neither will your Father forgive your trespasses."

Fasting

^{16} "Moreover when ye fast, be not, as the hypocrites, of a sad countenance. For they disfigure their faces, that they may appear unto men to fast. Verily I say unto you, they have their reward. ^{17} But thou, when thou fastest, anoint thine head and wash thy face, ^{18} That thou appear not unto men to fast, but unto thy Father who is in secret; and thy Father, who seeth in secret, shall reward thee openly."

Treasure in Heaven

^{19} "Lay not up for yourselves treasures upon earth, where moth and rust doth corrupt, and where thieves break through and steal.㉖ ^{20} But lay up for yourselves treasures in Heaven, where neither moth nor rust doth corrupt, and where thieves do not break through nor steal. ^{21} For where your treasure is, there will your heart be also. ^{22} "The light of the body is the eye. If therefore thine eye be single, thy whole body shall be full of light. ^{23} But if thine eye be evil, thy whole body shall be full of darkness. If therefore the light that is in thee be darkness, how great is that darkness! ^{24} "No man can serve two masters; for either he will hate the one and love the other, or else he will hold to the one and despise the other. Ye cannot serve God and mammon㉗."

Do Not Worry

The Metaphor of the Fowls of the Air

^{25} "Therefore I say unto you, take no thought for your life, what ye shall eat, or what ye shall drink; nor yet for your body, what ye shall put on. Is not the life more than meat, and the body than raiment? ^{26} Behold the fowls of the air, for they sow not, neither do they reap, nor gather into barns; yet your heavenly Father feedeth them. Are ye not much better than they? ^{27} "Which of you by taking thought can add one cubit unto his stature?"

The Metaphor of the Lilies of the Field

^{28} And why take ye thought for raiment? Consider the lilies of the field, how they grow. They toil not, neither do they spin, ^{29} And yet I say unto you that even Solomon in all his glory was not arrayed like one of these. ^{30} Therefore, if God so clothe the grass of the field, which today is, and tomorrow is cast into the oven,

---

㉖ **Lay not up for yourselves treasures upon earth, where moth and rust doth corrupt, and where thieves break through and steal** 不要在地上为自己积攒财宝,地上有虫子咬,能锈坏,也有贼挖窟窿来偷。

㉗ **mammon** the Aramaic for *riches*.

shall He not much more clothe you, O ye of little faith? ³¹ Therefore take no thought, saying, 'What shall we eat?' or 'What shall we drink?' or 'Wherewith shall we be clothed?' ³² (For after all these things do the Gentiles seek,) For your heavenly Father knoweth that ye have need of all these things. ³³ But seek ye first the Kingdom of God and His righteousness, and all these things shall be added unto you. ³⁴ "Take therefore no thought for the morrow, for the morrow shall take thought for the things of itself. Sufficient unto the day is the evil thereof.

Judging Others

Matthew 7

¹ "Judge not, that ye be not judged.㉘ ² For with what judgment ye judge, ye shall be judged; and with what measure ye mete, it shall be measured to you again.

³ And why beholdest thou the mote that is in thy brother's eye, but considerest not the beam that is in thine own eye?㉙ ⁴ Or how wilt thou say to thy brother, 'Let me pull out the mote out of thine eye,' and behold, a beam is in thine own eye? ⁵ Thou hypocrite, first cast out the beam out of thine own eye, and then shalt thou see clearly to cast out the mote out of thy brother's eye.

⁶ "Give not that which is holy unto the dogs, neither cast ye your pearls before swine, lest they trample them under their feet, and turn again and rend you.㉚

Ask, Seek, Knock

⁷ "Ask, and it shall be given you; seek, and ye shall find; knock, and it shall be opened unto you.㉛ ⁸ For every one that asketh receiveth; and he that seeketh findeth; and to him that knocketh it shall be opened.

⁹ "Or what man is there among you whom, if his son ask for bread, will give him a stone? ¹⁰ Or if he ask for a fish, will give him a serpent? ¹¹ If ye then, being evil, know how to give good gifts unto your children, how much more shall your Father who is in Heaven give good things to them that ask Him? ¹² Therefore, all things whatsoever ye would that men should do to you, do ye even so to them; for this is the Law and the Prophets."

The Narrow and Wide Gates

¹³ "Enter ye in at the strait gate, for wide is the gate and broad is the way that leadeth to destruction, and many there be who go in thereat. ¹⁴ Because strait is the gate, and narrow is the way which leadeth unto life, and few there be that find it."

The Metaphor of a Tree and Its Fruit

¹⁵ "Beware of false prophets, who come to you in sheep's clothing, but inwardly they are ravening wolves.㉜ ¹⁶ Ye shall know them by their fruits. Do men gather grapes from thorns, or figs from thistles? ¹⁷ Even so, every good tree bringeth forth good fruit, but a corrupt tree bringeth forth evil fruit. ¹⁸ A good tree cannot bring forth evil fruit, neither can a corrupt tree bring forth good fruit. ¹⁹ Every tree that bringeth not forth good fruit is hewn down and cast into the fire. ²⁰ Therefore, by their fruits ye shall know them.

²¹ "Not every one that saith unto Me, 'Lord, Lord,' shall enter into the Kingdom of Heaven, but he that doeth the will of My Father who is in Heaven. ²² Many will say to Me in that Day, 'Lord, Lord, have we not prophesied in Thy name, and in Thy name have cast out devils, and in Thy name done many wonderful works?' ²³ And then will I profess unto them, 'I never knew you: depart from Me, ye that work iniquity.'"

㉘ Judge not, that ye be not judged 你们不要论断人，免得你们被论断。

㉙ why beholdest thou the mote that is in thy brother's eye, but considerest not the beam that is in thine own eye? 为什么看见你弟兄眼中有刺，却不想自己眼中有梁木呢？

㉚ Give not that which is holy unto the dogs, neither cast ye your pearls before swine, lest they trample them under their feet, and turn again and rend you 不要把圣物给狗，也不要把你们的珍珠丢在猪前，恐怕它们践踏了珍珠，转过来咬你们。

㉛ Ask, and it shall be given you; seek, and ye shall find; knock, and it shall be opened unto you 你们祈求，就给你们；寻找，就寻见；叩门，就给你们开门。

㉜ Beware of false prophets, who come to you in sheep's clothing, but inwardly they are ravening wolves 你们要防备假先知，他们到你们这里来，外面披着羊皮，里面却是残暴的狼。

The Wise and Foolish Builders

²⁴ "Therefore, whosoever heareth these sayings of Mine and doeth them, I will liken him unto a wise man, who built his house upon a rock. ²⁵ And the rain descended and the floods came, and the winds blew and beat upon that house; and it fell not, for it was founded upon a rock. ²⁶ And every one that heareth these sayings of Mine and doeth them not, shall be likened unto a foolish man, who built his house upon the sand; ²⁷ And the rain descended, and the floods came, and the winds blew, and beat upon that house; and it fell, and great was the fall of it." ²⁸ And it came to pass, when Jesus had ended these sayings, the people were astonished at His doctrine; ²⁹ For He taught them as one having authority, and not as the scribes.

III FOOD FOR THOUGHT

1. With what did Satan tempt Jesus?
2. What are the 9 declarations of blessedness made by Jesus? Do you find these surprising?
3. Was Jesus' sermon on the Mount meant to abolish Moses' Law?
4. How much do you agree or disagree with Jesus' preaching here?
5. Other religions had some form of *Matthew 7:12* but stated it negatively: "Don't do to others what you wouldn't want them to do to you." Which is more open-ended and challenging?
6. The Sermon on the Mount is considered a single cornerstone to Matthew's gospel. Can you find some sayings which may serve as your maxims?

IV BIBLICAL RELEVANCE

A. Biblical Terms in Everyday English
1. the salt of the earth (5:13): _____
2. a city set/built on a hill (*ibid.*): _____
3. not one jot or one title (5:18): _____
4. an eye for an eye, and a tooth for a tooth (5:38): _____
5. serve two masters (6:24): _____
6. judge not that you be judged (7:1): _____
7. cast pearls before swine (7:6): _____
8. a wolf in sheep's clothing (7:15): _____
9. be built upon a rock (7:24): _____
10. build … upon the sand (7:26): _____

B. Biblical References in Literature
1. He was a John the Baptist who took ennoblement rather than repentance for his text.
   (Thomas Hardy, *The Return of the Native*, 1880)
2. "I been thinkin'," he said. "I been in the hills thinkin', almost you might say like Jesus went into the wilderness to think His way out of a mess of troubles!"
   (John Steinbeck, *The Grapes of Wrath*, 1939)
3. They listened to the words of the man in their midst, who was preaching, while they abstractedly pulled heather, stripped ferns, or tossed pebbles down the slope. This was the first of a series of moral lectures or Sermons on the Mount, which were to be delivered from the same place every Sunday afternoon as long as the fine weather lasted.
   (Thomas Hardy, *The Return of the Native*, 1880)

4. Charles felt himself, under the first impact of this attractive comparison, like Jesus of Nazareth tempted by Satan. He too had had his days in the wilderness to make the proposition more tempting.

(John Fowles, *The French Lieutenant's Woman*, 1969)

C. The Bible and Arts
1. *St. John the Baptist in the Wilderness*, 1504—1505, Hieronymus Bosch
2. *Landscape with St. John the Baptist Preaching*, 1473—1478, Jan Bruegel, the Elder
3. *The Baptism of Christ*, 1473—1478, Leonardo da Vinci *et al.*
4. *Landscape on the Coast*, with the Calling of St. Peter and St. Andrew, c. 1608, Jan Bruegel, the Elder
5. *The Sermon on the Mount*, Fra Angelico (1395—1455)

V SOURCES FOR REFERENCE

1. (1961). *King of Kings*. An American motion picture epic directed by Nicholas Ray, noted for the youthful idol image of Jesus, depicted by Jeffrey Hunter and a mesmerizing scene of the Sermon on the Mount.
2. Schippe, C. & C. Stetson. (2005). *The Bible and Its Influence*. Front Royal, VA: BLP Publishing.
3. Browning, W. R. E. (2009). *A Dictionary of the Bible*. Oxford: Oxford University Press.

30. MIRACLES AND HEALINGS

I. POINTS OF DEPARTURE

Miracles are surprising events supposedly caused by God directly or indirectly through a chosen human intermediary. Writers of both the Old and the New Testament believed that God who created the world could and did intervene in the lives of people and in the course of nature. In the Old Testament, mighty acts were performed by God at vital moments in the history of Israel. The crossing of the sea (*Exod.* 14), for example, was seen as a confirmation of God's promise to his people. Healing miracles were performed by God as a response to the prayer of prophets.

The evangelists continue the Hebrew tradition of miracles and healings in describing Jesus' "Mighty Works." Jesus' ministry is two-fold in nature: preaching the "gospel to the poor" and carrying out the implications of such preaching in the form of philanthropic work calculated to ameliorate man's distress at every level of his life. Throughout his ministry word and work supplemented each other in a remarkable fashion. (Black, 2001: 737) Characteristic of the miracles of Jesus is the framework of eschatology in which they are related; they are indications of the coming of the kingdom of God; they are fulfillments of expectations of the Old Testament as when the Feeding of the 5,000 (*Mk.* 6:30—44) echoes the miraculous feeding of Israel in the wilderness; they are done in a context of faith and prayer; they represent the conquest of evil.

The readers of the gospels saw healings as authentic works of God in which believers received the power of the Kingdom which had begun to come already in the person of Jesus. Modern readers might argue that human bodies are more than machines which can be manipulated by medicines and surgery, and positive spiritual and mental influence from Jesus could have been therapeutic. Attempts have also been made to explain "scientifically" those familiar miracles and healings of Jesus, and BBC jumped on the bandwagon in 2006 with its documentary *The Miracles of Jesus* to reenact some of the famous miracles through dramatization, CGI, illusionistic techniques as well as scientific theories and historical facts.

II. SELECTED READINGS

The Man with Leprosy

See also *Mk.* 1:40—44; *Lk.* 5:12—14
Matthew 8

¹ When He had come down from the mountain, great multitudes followed Him. ² And behold, there came a leper and worshiped Him, saying, "Lord, if Thou wilt, Thou canst make me clean."

³ And Jesus put forth His hand and touched him, saying, "I will. Be thou clean." And immediately his leprosy was cleansed. ⁴ And Jesus said unto him, "See thou tell no man; but go thy way, show thyself to the priest, and offer the gift that Moses commanded for a testimony unto them."

The Faith of the Centurion

⁵ And when Jesus had entered into Capernaum, there came unto Him a centurion, beseeching Him. ⁶ And saying, "Lord, my servant lieth at home sick with the palsy and grievously tormented."

⁷ And Jesus said unto him, "I will come and heal him."

⁸ The centurion answered and said, "Lord, I am not worthy that Thou shouldest come under my roof. But speak the word only, and my servant shall be healed. ⁹ For I am a man under authority, having soldiers under me. And I say to this man, 'Go!' and he goeth; and to another, 'Come!' and he cometh; and to my servant, 'Do this!' and he doeth it."

¹⁰ When Jesus heard it, He marveled and said to those who followed, "Verily I say unto you, I have not found such great faith, no, not in Israel. ¹¹ And I say unto you, that many shall come from the east and west, and shall sit down with Abraham and Isaac and Jacob in the Kingdom of Heaven. ¹² But the children of the kingdom shall be cast out into outer darkness: there shall be weeping and gnashing of teeth." ¹³ And Jesus said unto the centurion, "Go thy way, and as thou hast believed, so be it done unto thee." And his servant was healed in that selfsame hour.

Jesus Heals Peter's Mother-in-law

¹⁴ And when Jesus had come into Peter's house, He saw his wife's mother lying and sick with a fever. ¹⁵ And He touched her hand, and the fever left her, and she arose and ministered unto them.

¹⁶ When the evening had come, they brought unto Him many who were possessed with devils, and He cast out the spirits with His word and healed all who were sick, ¹⁷ That it might be fulfilled which was spoken by Isaiah the prophet, who said,

"He Himself took our infirmities
and bore our sicknesses."①

The Cost of Following Jesus

¹⁸ Now when Jesus saw great multitudes about Him, He gave commandment to depart unto the other side. ¹⁹ And a certain scribe came and said unto Him, "Master, I will follow Thee whithersoever Thou goest."

²⁰ And Jesus said unto him, "The foxes have holes, and the birds of the air have nests, but the Son of Man hath nowhere to lay His head."

²¹ And another of His disciples said unto Him, "Lord, suffer me first to go and bury my father."

²² But Jesus said unto him, "Follow Me, and let the dead bury their dead."

Jesus Calms the Storm

²³ And when He had entered into a boat, His disciples followed Him. ²⁴ And behold, there arose a great tempest on the sea, insomuch that the boat was covered with the waves; but He was asleep. ²⁵ And His disciples came to Him and awoke Him, saying, "Lord, save us! We perish!"

²⁶ And He said unto them, "Why are ye fearful, O ye of little faith?" Then He arose and rebuked the winds and the sea, and there was a great calm.

---

① 17 Isaiah 53:4.

²⁷ But the men marveled, saying, "What manner of man is this, that even the winds and the sea obey Him?"

The Healing of Two Demon-possessed Men

²⁸ And when He had come to the other side into the country of the Gergesenes, there met Him two possessed with devils, coming out of the tombs, exceedingly fierce, so that no man might pass by that way. ²⁹ And behold, they cried out, saying, "What have we to do with Thee, Jesus, Thou Son of God? Art Thou come hither to torment us before the time?" ³⁰ Now there was a good way off from them a herd of many swine feeding. ³¹ So the devils besought Him, saying, "If Thou cast us out, suffer us to go away into the herd of swine." ³² And He said to them, "Go." And when they had come out, they went into the herd of swine, and behold, the whole herd of swine ran violently down a steep place into the sea and perished in the waters. ³³ And those who kept them fled and went their ways into the city, and told everything and what had befallen the ones possessed with the devils. ³⁴ And behold, the whole city came out to meet Jesus. And when they saw Him, they besought Him that He would depart out of their borders.

The Miracle of the Gadarene Swine, 1883, Briton Rivière

Jesus Heals a Paralytic

See also Mk. 2:3—12; Lk. 5:18—26

Matthew 9

¹ And He entered into a boat, and passed over and came into His own city. ² And behold, they brought to Him a man sick with the palsy, lying on a bed. And Jesus, seeing their faith, said unto the one sick with the palsy, "Son, be of good cheer; thy sins be forgiven thee." ³ And behold, certain of the scribes said within themselves, "This man blasphemeth." ⁴ And Jesus, knowing their thoughts, said, "Why think ye evil in your hearts? ⁵ For which is easier: to say, 'Thy sins be forgiven thee,' or to say, 'Arise and walk' ? ⁶ But that ye may know that the Son of Man hath power on earth to forgive sins," — (then said He to the one sick with palsy) "Arise, take up thy bed and go unto thine house." ⁷ And he arose and departed to his house. ⁸ But when the multitudes saw it, they marveled and glorified God, who had given such power unto men.

The Calling of Matthew

See also Mk. 2:14—17; Lk. 5:27—32

⁹ And as Jesus passed forth from thence, He saw a man named Matthew, sitting in the customhouse. And He said unto him, "Follow Me." And he arose and followed Him.

¹⁰ And it came to pass as Jesus sat at meat in the house, behold, many publicans and sinners came and sat down with Him and His disciples. ¹¹ And when the Pharisees saw it, they said unto His disciples, "Why eateth your master with publicans and sinners?"

¹² But when Jesus heard that, He said unto them, "They that be whole need not a physician, but they that are sick. ¹³ But go ye and learn what this meaneth: 'I will have mercy and not sacrifice.' For I am not come to call the righteous, but sinners to repentance."

Jesus Questioned about Fasting

See also Mk. 2:18—22; Lk. 5:33—39

The Calling of St. Matthew, 1599—1600, Carvaggio

¹⁴ Then the disciples of John came to Him, saying, "Why do we and the Pharisees fast often, but Thy disciples fast not?"

¹⁵ And Jesus said unto them, "Can the attendants of the bridechamber mourn as long as the bridegroom is with them? But the days will come when the bridegroom shall be taken from them, and then shall they fast.

¹⁶ "No man putteth a piece of new cloth upon an old garment, for that which is put in to fill it up taketh from the garment, and the rent is made worse.

¹⁷ Neither do men put new wine into old wineskins, else the wineskins burst and the wine runneth out and the skins perish. But they put new wine into new wineskins, and both are preserved."

A Dead Girl and a Sick Woman

See also Mk. 5:22—43; Lk. 8:41—56

Christ and the Woman with the Issue of Blood, 1565—1570, Paolo Veronese

¹⁸ While He spoke these things unto them, behold, there came a certain ruler and worshiped Him, saying, "My daughter is even now dead, but come and lay Thy hand upon her, and she shall live." ¹⁹ And Jesus arose and followed him, and so did His disciples.

²⁰ And behold, a woman who was diseased with an issue of blood for twelve years came up behind Him and touched the hem of His garment; ²¹ For she said to herself, "If I may but touch His garment, I shall be whole."

²² But Jesus turned about, and when He saw her, He said, "Daughter, be of good comfort; thy faith hath made thee whole." And the woman was made whole from that hour.

²³ And when Jesus came into the ruler's house and saw the minstrels and the people making a noise. ²⁴ He said unto them, "Give way, for the maid is not dead, but sleepeth." And they laughed Him to scorn. ²⁵ But when the people were put outside, He went in and took her by the hand, and the maid arose. ²⁶ And the fame thereof went abroad throughout all the land.

Jesus Heals the Blind and Mute

²⁷ And when Jesus departed thence, two blind men followed Him, crying and saying, "Thou Son of David, have mercy on us!"

²⁸ And when He had come into the house, the blind men came to Him, and Jesus said unto them, "Believe ye that I am able to do this?" They said unto Him, "Yea, Lord." ²⁹ Then He touched their eyes, saying, "According to your faith, be it unto you." ³⁰ And their eyes were opened, and Jesus strictly charged them, saying, "See that no man know it." ³¹ But they, when they had departed, spread abroad His fame in all that country.

³² As they went out, behold, they brought to Him a man, dumb and possessed with a devil. ³³ And when the devil was cast out, the dumb spoke; and the multitudes marveled, saying, "It was never so seen in Israel."

³⁴ But the Pharisees said, "He casteth out the devils through the prince of the devils."

The Workers Are Few

³⁵ And Jesus went about all the cities and villages, teaching in their synagogues and preaching the Gospel of the Kingdom, and healing every sickness and every disease among the people. ³⁶ But when He saw the multitudes, He was moved with compassion for them, because they were faint and were scattered abroad, as sheep having no shepherd. ³⁷ Then said He unto His disciples, "The harvest truly is plenteous, but the laborers are few. ³⁸ Pray ye therefore the Lord of the harvest, that He will send forth laborers into His harvest."

The Marriage in Cana

The Wedding at Cana, William Hole (1846—1917)

John 2

¹ And on the third day there was a marriage in Cana of Galilee, and the mother of Jesus was there; ² And both Jesus and His disciples were called to the marriage. ³ And when they lacked wine, the mother of Jesus said unto Him, "They have no wine."

⁴ Jesus said unto her, "Woman, what have I to do with thee? Mine hour is not yet come."

⁵ His mother said unto the servants, "Whatsoever He saith unto you, do it."

⁶ And there were set there six waterpots of stone, according to the manner of the purifying of the Jews, holding twenty to thirty gallons apiece.

Jesus Changes Water to Wine

⁷ Jesus said unto them, "Fill the waterpots with water." And they filled them up to the brim.

⁸ And He said unto them, "Draw some out now, and bear it unto the governor of the feast." And they took it. ⁹ When the ruler of the feast had tasted the water that was made wine, not knowing from whence it had come (but the servants who drew the water knew), the governor of the feast called the bridegroom

¹⁰ And said unto him, "Every man at the beginning doth set forth good wine, and when men have drunk well, then that which is worse; but thou hast kept the good wine until now."

¹¹ This beginning of miracles Jesus did in Cana of Galilee, and manifested forth His glory; and His disciples believed in Him.

...

The Raising of Lazarus

John 11

¹ Now a certain man was sick named Lazarus②, of Bethany, the town of Mary and her sister Martha. ² (It was that Mary who had anointed the Lord with ointment and wiped His feet with her hair, whose brother Lazarus was sick.) ³ Therefore his sisters sent unto Him, saying, "Lord, behold, he whom Thou lovest is sick."

⁴ When Jesus heard that, He said, "This sickness is not unto death, but for the glory of God, that the

---

② **Lazarus** /ˈlæzərəs/，拉撒路。

Son of God might be glorified thereby." ⁵ Now Jesus loved Martha and her sister and Lazarus. ⁶ When He heard therefore that Lazarus was sick, He stayed two days still in the same place where He was.

⁷ Then after that He said to His disciples, " Let us go into Judea again."

⁸ His disciples said unto Him, " Master, the Jews of late sought to stone Thee, and goest Thou thither again?"

⁹ Jesus answered, " Are there not twelve hours in the day? If any man walk in the day he stumbleth not, because he seeth the light of this world. ¹⁰ But if a man walk in the night, he stumbleth because there is no light in him."

¹¹ These things said He, and after that He said unto them, " Our friend Lazarus sleepeth; but I go, that I may awaken him out of sleep."

¹² Then said His disciples, " Lord, if he sleep he shall do well." ¹³ However Jesus spoke of his death, but they thought that He had spoken of the taking of rest in sleep.

¹⁴ Then Jesus said unto them plainly, " Lazarus is dead. ¹⁵ And I am glad for your sakes that I was not there, to the intent that ye may believe. Nevertheless let us go unto him."

¹⁶ Then Thomas, who was called Didymus, said unto his fellow disciples, " Let us also go, that we may die with Him."

Jesus Comforts the Sisters

¹⁷ Then when Jesus came, He found that he had lain in the grave four days already. ¹⁸ Now Bethany was nigh unto Jerusalem, about two miles away. ¹⁹ And many of the Jews came to Martha and Mary to comfort them concerning their brother. ²⁰ Then Martha, as soon as she heard that Jesus was coming, went and met Him; but Mary sat still in the house.

²¹ Then Martha said unto Jesus, " Lord, if Thou hadst been here, my brother would not have died. ²² But I know that even now, whatsoever Thou wilt ask of God, God will give it Thee."

²³ Jesus said unto her, " Thy brother shall rise again."

²⁴ Martha said unto Him, " I know that he shall rise again at the resurrection on the Last Day."

²⁵ Jesus said unto her, " I am the resurrection and the Life. He that believeth in Me, though he were dead, yet shall he live; ²⁶ And whosoever liveth and believeth in Me shall never die. Believest thou this?"

²⁷ She said unto Him, " Yea, Lord, I believe that Thou art the Christ, the Son of God, who should come into the world."

²⁸ And when she had so said, she went her way and called Mary her sister secretly, saying, " The Master has come, and calleth for thee." ²⁹ As soon as she heard that, she arose quickly and came unto Him. ³⁰ Now Jesus had not yet come into the town, but was in that place where Martha met Him. ³¹ The Jews then, who were with her in the house and comforting her, when they saw that Mary rose up hastily and went out, followed her, saying, " She goeth unto the grave to weep there."

³² Then when Mary had come where Jesus was and saw Him, she fell down at His feet, saying unto Him, " Lord, if Thou hadst been here, my brother would not have died."

³³ When Jesus therefore saw her weeping, and the Jews also weeping who came with her, He groaned in the spirit and was troubled, ³⁴ And said, " Where have ye laid him?" They said unto Him,

" Lord, come and see."

³⁵ Jesus wept.

³⁶ Then said the Jews, " Behold, how he loved him!"

³⁷ And some of them said, " Could not this man, who opened the eyes of the blind, have caused that even this man should not have died?"

Jesus Raises Lazarus from the Dead

³⁸ Jesus therefore again, groaning in Himself, came to the grave. It was a cave, and a stone lay against it. ³⁹ Jesus said, "Take ye away the stone." Martha, the sister of him that was dead, said unto Him, "Lord, by this time there is a stench, for he hath been dead four days." ⁴⁰ Jesus said unto her, "Said I not unto thee that if thou would believe, thou should see the glory of God?"

Raising of Lazarus, 1461, Nicolas Froment

⁴¹ Then they took away the stone from the place where the dead was laid. And Jesus lifted up His eyes and said, "Father, I thank Thee that Thou hast heard Me. ⁴² And I knew that Thou hearest Me always, but because of the people who stand by I said it, that they may believe that Thou hast sent Me."

⁴³ And when He thus had spoken, He cried with a loud voice, "Lazarus, come forth!" ⁴⁴ And he that was dead came forth, bound hand and foot with graveclothes, and his face was bound about with a napkin.

Jesus said unto them, "Loose him, and let him go."

...

A Collection of Miracles and Healings of Jesus

Healings

Man with leprosy, *Matthew 8:1—4; Mark 1:40—44; Luke 5:12—14*
Roman centurion's servant, *Matthew 8:5—13; Luke 7:1—10*
Peter's mother-in-law, *Matthew 8:14—15; Mark 1:30—31; Luke 4:38—39*
Two demon-possessed men from Gadara, *Matthew 8:28—34; Mark 5:1—15; Luke 8:27—39*
Paralyzed man, *Matthew 9:2—7; Mark 2:3—12; Luke 5:18—26*
Two blind men, *Matthew 9:27—31*
Man mute and possessed, *Matthew 9:32—33*
Man with a shriveled hand, *Matthew 12:10—13; Mark 3:1—5; Luke 6:6—11*
Man blind, mute, and possessed, *Matthew 12:23; Luke 11:14*
Canaanite woman's daughter, *Matthew 15:21—28; Mark 7:24—30*
Boy with epilepsy, *Matthew 17:14—21; Mark 9:17—29; Luke 9:38—43*
Two blind men, *Matthew 20:29—34; Mark 10:46—52; Luke 18:35—43*
Man with an evil spirit, *Mark 1:21—28; Luke 4:31—37*
Deaf mute, *Mark 7:31—37*
Blind man, *Mark 8:22—26*
Bartimaeus, or one blind man, *Mark 10:46—52; Luke 18:35—43*
Woman with bleeding, *Matthew 8:19; Luke 8:43—48*
Crippled woman, *Luke 13:11—13*
Man with dropsy, *Luke 14:1—4*
Ten men with leprosy, *Luke 17:11—19*
The high priest's servant, *Luke 22:50—51*
Royal official's son, *John 4:46—54*
Man at the pool of Bethesda, *John 5:1—9*

Miracles in nature
Calming of storm, *Matthew 8:22—27; Mark 4:35—41; Luke 8:22—25*
Feeding of 5,000, *Matthew 14:1—21; Mark 6:35—44; Luke 9:12—17; John 6:5—15*
Walking on water, *Matthew 14:22—23; Mark 6:45—52; John 6:16—21*
Feeding of 4,000, *Matthew 15:29—39; Mark 8:1—9*
Fish with coin, *Matthew 17:24—27*
Fig tree withers, *Matthew 21:18—22; Mark 11:12—14, 20—25*
Huge catch of fish, *Luke 5:1—11; John 21:1—11*
Water into wine, *John 2:1—11*

Raising the dead
Jairus's daughter, *Mark 5:22—42*
Widow at Nain's son, *Luke 7:11—15*
Lazarus, *John 11:1—44*

III FOOD FOR THOUGHT

1. What distinguishes *Matthew 8—10* from *Matthew 3—7*?
2. What does the healing of a centurion's servant show?
3. How did Jesus respond when the Pharisees challenged him on his sitting at the table with sinners (*Mt. 9:10—13*)?
4. What is the meaning of the parable, "No man putteth a piece of new cloth upon an old garment" (*Mt. 9:14—17*)?

IV BIBLICAL RELEVANCE

A. Biblical Terms in Everyday English
1. gnash one's/the teeth (*Mt. 8:12*): _____
2. let the dead bury their dead (*Mt. 8:22*): _____
3. between the devil and the deep (blue) sea (*Mt. 8:28—32*): _____
4. put new wine into old wineskins/bottles (*Mt. 9:17*): _____
5. sheep having no shepherd (*Mt. 9:36*): _____
6. be wise as serpents and harmless as doves (*Mt. 10:16*): _____
7. shake off the dust off one's feet (*Mt. 10:14*): _____
8. Lazarus syndrome/phenomenon (*Jn. 11:1—16*): _____

B. Biblical References in Literature
1. She has sent her here to be healed, even as the Jews of old sent their diseased to the troubled pool of Bethesda.

    (Charlotte Brontë, *Jane Eyre*, 1847)

2. He placed himself protectively by his mother. He was a lanky lad, as tall as she was, with bright blue eyes and a crest of reddish hair. Otherwise they were not alike, and he prided himself on taking after his dead father. If he was dead, he cherished the ideas that what Alfred had told him of the death in an accident was a lie, and that Dad would turn up, rich and

famous. He had to be both or need not bother acting Lazarus.

(Gwendoline Butler, *A Dark Coffin*, 1995)

C. The Bible and Arts
1. *The Miracle of the Gadarene Swine*, 1883, Briton Rivière
2. The Calling of Matthew
   The Calling of St. Matthew, 1599—1600, Caravaggio
   The Calling of St. Matthew, 1616, Hendrick Terbrugghen
   Jesus Summons Matthew to Leave the Tax Office, 1536, Jan Sanders van Hemessen
3. *Christ and the Woman with the Issue of Blood*, 1565—1570, Paolo Veronese
4. *Christ Healing the Blind*, 1565—1570, El Greco
5. *The Storm on the Sea of Galilee*, 1633, Harmenszoon van Rijn Rembrandt
6. *Raising of Jairus's Daughter*, 1871, Ilya Repin
7. Water into Wine
   The Marriage at Cana, Tintoretto (1518—1594)
   The Marriage at Cana, 1596—1597, Marten de Vos
8. *The Pool*, 1592, Giovane Palma
9. The Raising of Lazarus
   Raising of Lazarus, 1461, Nicolas Froment
   The Raising of Lazarus, c. 1517—1519, Piombo del Sebastiano
10. A Huge Catch of Fish
    Wonderful Catch of Fish, 1762, Anton Losenko
    The Miraculous Draught of Fishes, 1443—1444, Konrad Witz
    The Miraculous Draught of Fishes, 1618—1619, Peter Paul Rubens

V SOURCES FOR REFERENCE

1. www.bbc.co.hk/religion/religions/christianity/history/miraclesofjesus
2. (2006). *The Miracles of Jesus*. A BBC documentary film made to explain some of Jesus' famous miracles.
3. Black, M. (ed.) (2001). *Peake's Commentary on the Bible*. London: Routledge.

31. JESUS' PARABLES: THE KINGDOM OF HEAVEN

I POINTS OF DEPARTURE

According to *Matthew 13:34—35*, Jesus preached mainly through parables. The range of meaning of the term "parable" in the New Testament closely parallels that of the Hebrew *māsāl* in the OT and related Hebrew literature. Etymologically, *māsāl* is a "comparison," derived from a verb meaning "to become like" (*Ps. 28:1, 49:12, 143:7; Isa. 14:10*) or "to be comparable with" (*Isa. 46:5*). In the Greek version of the Bible, the Septuagint, the term *māsāl* became *parabole*, meaning "discourse, allegory." In the NT, the word *parabole* is almost confined to the Synoptic Gospels of Matthew, Mark, Luke and John, totaling around 60. The parables told by Jesus are often described as "earthly stories with a heavenly message," i. e. stories based on nature or real life that assert the supreme value of entering God's kingdom by believing the gospel.

The history of parable interpretation dates back to St. Augustine (354—430 C. E.) who attempted to assign a religious meaning to every single element in a parable. This allegorical interpretation had dominated parable interpretation for well over 1500 years until the publication of Adolf Jülicher's *Gleichnisreden Jesus* (the Parables of Jesus) in 1899, which maintained that the essence of a genuine parable is that it has but one single, discoverable point. After more than a century of further discussion, Jülicher's one-point approach has to be somewhat modified. There are allegorical elements in some parables (e. g. the Wicked Husbandmen, *Mt. 21:33ff.*).

Apart from how parables can be interpreted, there has been a debate on the paradox in *Mark 4:11* that the meaning of the Kingdom is veiled to outsiders but is being disclosed to the disciples by God's revelation though the express purpose of Jesus' parables was to teach and to persuade. One suggestion is that it is in line with the principle that Jesus did not compel belief by an irrefutable argument; faith and responsibility are left to people themselves because Jesus was committed to freedom.

II SELECTED READINGS

The Parable of the Sower

See also Mk. 4:1—20; Lk. 8:4—15
Matthew 13

¹*The same day, Jesus went out of the house and sat by the seaside.* ²*And great multitudes were gathered together unto Him, so that He went into a boat and sat, and the whole multitude stood on the shore.* ³*And He spoke many things unto them in parables, saying,* "*Behold, a sower went forth to sow.*" ⁴*And when he*

sowed, some seeds fell by the wayside; and the fowls came and devoured them up. ⁵ Some fell upon stony places where they had not much earth; and forthwith they sprang up, because they had no deepness of earth. ⁶ And when the sun was up they were scorched, and because they had no root they withered away. ⁷ And some fell among thorns; and the thorns sprang up and choked them. ⁸ But others fell into good ground and brought forth fruit, some a hundredfold, some sixtyfold, some thirtyfold. ⁹ Who hath ears to hear, let him hear."

¹⁰ And the disciples came and said unto Him, "Why speakest Thou unto them in parables?"

¹¹ He answered and said unto them, "Because it is given unto you to know the mysteries of the Kingdom of Heaven, but to them it is not given. ¹² For whosoever hath, to him shall be given, and he shall have more abundance. But whosoever hath not, from him shall be taken away even that which he hath. ¹³ Therefore speak I to them in parables, because seeing, they see not, and hearing, they hear not, neither do they understand.

¹⁴ And in them is fulfilled the prophecy of Isaiah, which saith,

'By hearing ye shall hear, and shall not understand; and seeing ye shall see, and shall not perceive.

¹⁵ For this people's heart has waxed gross, and their ears are dull of hearing, and their eyes they have closed; lest at any time they should see with their eyes, and hear with their ears, and should understand with their heart, and should be converted, and I should heal them.' ①

¹⁶ But blessed are your eyes, for they see; and your ears, for they hear. ¹⁷ For verily I say unto you, that many prophets and righteous men have desired to see those things which ye see, and have not seen them, and to hear those things which ye hear, and have not heard them.

¹⁸ "Hear ye therefore the parable of the sower: ¹⁹ When any one heareth the Word of the Kingdom and understandeth it not, then cometh the wicked one and catcheth away that which was sown in his heart. This is he that received seed by the wayside. ²⁰ But he that received the seed into stony places, the same is he that heareth the Word and at once with joy receiveth it; ²¹ Yet hath he not root in himself, but endureth for a while. For when tribulation or persecution ariseth because of the Word, by and by he loses faith. ²² He also that received the seed among the thorns is he that heareth the Word; and the cares of this world and the deceitfulness of riches choke the Word, and he becometh unfruitful. ²³ But he that received seed into the good ground is he that heareth the Word and understandeth it; who also beareth fruit and bringeth forth, some a hundredfold, some sixty, some thirty.'"

The Parable of the Weeds

²⁴ Another parable put He forth before them, saying, "The Kingdom of Heaven is likened unto a man who sowed good seed in his field; ²⁵ but while men slept, his enemy came and sowed tares among the wheat, and went his way. ²⁶ But when the blades had sprung up and brought forth fruit, then appeared the tares also.

²⁷ So the servants of the householder came and said unto him, 'Sir, didst not thou sow good seed in thy field? From whence then hath come the tares?'

²⁸ He said unto them, 'An enemy hath done this.' The servants said unto him, 'Wilt thou then have us go and gather them up?'

²⁹ But he said, 'Nay, lest while ye gather up the tares, ye root up also the wheat with them. ³⁰ Let both grow together until the harvest, and in the time of harvest I will say to the reapers, "Gather ye together first the tares, and bind them in bundles to burn them, but gather the wheat into my barn.'"

The Parable of the Mustard Seed

³¹ Another parable put He forth before them, saying, "The Kingdom of Heaven is like a grain of mustard seed, which a man took and sowed in his field, ³² Which indeed is the least of all seeds; but when it is grown it is the greatest among herbs and becometh a tree, so that the birds of the air come and lodge in the branches

---

① 15 Isaiah 6:9, 10.

thereof."³³ Another parable spoke He unto them: "The Kingdom of Heaven is like unto leaven, which a woman took and hid in three measures of meal till the whole was leavened."

³⁴ All these things spoke Jesus unto the multitude in parables; and without a parable spoke He not unto them, ³⁵ That it might be fulfilled which was spoken by the prophet, saying,

"I will open My mouth in parables; I will utter things which have been kept secret from the foundation of the world."②

The Parable of the Weeds Explained

³⁶ Then Jesus sent the multitude away and went into the house, and His disciples came unto Him, saying, "Explain unto us the parable of the tares of the field." ³⁷ He answered and said unto them, "He that soweth the good seed is the Son of Man. ³⁸ The field is the world, the good seed are the children of the Kingdom, but the tares are the children of the wicked one. ³⁹ The enemy that sowed them is the devil, the harvest is the end of the world, and the reapers are the angels.

⁴⁰ As therefore the tares are gathered and burned in the fire, so shall it be at the end of this world. ⁴¹ The Son of Man shall send forth His angels, and they shall gather out of His Kingdom all things that offend and them that do iniquity, ⁴² And shall cast them into a furnace of fire: there shall be wailing and gnashing of teeth. ⁴³ Then shall the righteous shine forth as the sun in the Kingdom of their Father. Who hath ears to hear, let him hear."

The Parable of the Hidden Treasure and the Pearl

⁴⁴ "Again, the Kingdom of Heaven is like unto treasure hid in a field, which, when a man hath found, he hideth; and for the joy thereof goeth and selleth all that he hath, and buyeth that field.

⁴⁵ "Again, the Kingdom of Heaven is like unto a merchant man, seeking goodly pearls, ⁴⁶ Who, when he had found one pearl of great price, went and sold all that he had and bought it."

The Parable of the Net

⁴⁷ "Again, the Kingdom of Heaven is like unto a net that was cast into the sea, and gathered of every kind, ⁴⁸ Which, when it was full, they drew to shore, and sat down and gathered the good into vessels, but cast the bad away. ⁴⁹ So shall it be at the end of the world: the angels shall come forth and sever the wicked from among the just, ⁵⁰ And shall cast them into the furnace of fire: there shall be wailing and gnashing of teeth."

⁵¹ Jesus said unto them, "Have ye understood all these things?" They said unto Him, "Yea, Lord."

⁵² Then said He unto them, "Therefore every scribe who is instructed unto the Kingdom of Heaven is like unto a man that is a householder, who bringeth forth out of his treasure things new and old."

A Prophet without Honor

See also Mk. 6:1—6.

⁵³ And it came to pass that when Jesus had finished these parables, He departed thence. ⁵⁴ And when He had come into His own country, He taught them in their synagogue, insomuch that they were astonished and said, "From whence hath this man this wisdom and these mighty works? ⁵⁵ Is not this the carpenter's son? Is not his mother called Mary and his brethren James and Joseph, and Simon and Judas? ⁵⁶ And his sisters, are they not all with us? From whence then hath this man all these things?" ⁵⁷ And they were offended at Him.

---

② **35** Psalm 78:2.

But Jesus said unto them, "A prophet is not without honor, save in his own country and in his own house."③

⁵⁸ And He did not many mighty works there, because of their unbelief.

Good Samaritan

See also Mt. 22:34—40; Mk. 12:28—31
Luke 10

...

²⁵ And, behold, a certain lawyer stood up, and tempted him, saying, "Master, what shall I do to inherit eternal life?"

²⁶ He said unto him, "What is written in the law? How readest thou?"

²⁷ And he answering said, "Thou shalt love the Lord thy God with all thy heart, and with all thy soul, and with all thy strength, and with all thy mind; and thy neighbour as thyself."

²⁸ And he said unto him, "Thou hast answered right: this do, and thou shalt live." ²⁹ But he, willing to justify himself, said unto Jesus, "And who is my neighbour?"

Cultural Connections: Good Samaritan laws

There are often news reports about passers-by who were sued by those they had intended to help but who suffered because of unexpected injury. Many people attribute these bitter-sweet occurrences to the ever deteriorating moral situation of our society. To reduce bystanders' hesitation to assist for fear of being sued or prosecuted, the so-called Good Samaritan laws are passed in many countries of the world. Good Samaritan laws vary from jurisdiction to jurisdiction, as do their interactions with various other legal principles, such as consent, parental rights and the right to refuse treatment. Such laws generally do not apply to medical professionals' or career emergency responders' on-the-job conduct, but some extend protection to professional rescuers when they are acting in a volunteer capacity.

³⁰ And Jesus answering said, "A certain man went down from Jerusalem to Jericho, and fell among thieves, which stripped him of his raiment, and wounded him, and departed, leaving him half dead. ³¹ And by chance there came down a certain priest that way: and when he saw him, he passed by on the other side. ³² And likewise a Levite, when he was at the place, came and looked on him, and passed by on the other side. ³³ But a certain Samaritan, as he journeyed, came where he was: and when he saw him, he had compassion on him, ³⁴ And went to him, and bound up his wounds, pouring in oil and wine, and set him on his own beast, and brought him to an inn, and took care of him. ³⁵ And on the morrow when he departed, he took out two pence, and gave them to the host, and said unto him, 'Take care of him; and whatsoever thou spendest more, when I come again, I will repay thee.'

³⁶ Which now of these three, thinkest thou, was neighbour unto him that fell among the thieves?"

³⁷ And he said, "He that shewed mercy on him." Then said Jesus unto him, "Go, and do thou likewise."

---

③ **A prophet is not without honor, save in his own country and in his own house** 大凡先知，除了本地本家之外，没有不被人尊敬的。

Mary and Martha

Christ in the House of Mary and Martha, Vincenzo Campi (1536—1591)

³⁸ Now it came to pass, as they went, that he entered into a certain village: and a certain woman named Martha④ received him into her house. ³⁹ And she had a sister called Mary, which also sat at Jesus' feet, and heard his word. ⁴⁰ But Martha was cumbered about much serving, and came to him, and said, "Lord, dost thou not care that my sister hath left me to serve alone? Bid her therefore that she help me."

⁴¹ And Jesus answered and said unto her, "Martha, Martha, thou art careful and troubled about many things: ⁴² But one thing is needful: and Mary hath chosen that good part, which shall not be taken away from her."

The Prodigal/Lost Son

Luke 15

...

¹¹ And he said, "A certain man had two sons: ¹² And the younger of them said to his father, 'Father, give me the portion of goods that falleth to me.' And he divided unto them his living.

The Prodigal Son, Gerrit van Honthorst (1592—1656)

¹³ "And not many days after the younger son gathered all together, and took his journey into a far country, and there wasted his substance with riotous living. ¹⁴ And when he had spent all, there arose a mighty famine in that land; and he began to be in want. ¹⁵ And he went and joined himself to a citizen of that country; and he sent him into his fields to feed swine. ¹⁶ And he would fain have filled his belly with the husks that the swine did eat: and no man gave unto him.

¹⁷ "And when he came to himself, he said, 'How many hired servants of my father's have bread enough and to spare, and I perish with hunger! ¹⁸ I will arise and go to my father, and will say unto him, Father, I have sinned against heaven, and before thee, ¹⁹ And am no more worthy to be called thy son: make me as one of thy hired servants.' ²⁰ And he arose, and came to his father.

"But when he was yet a great way off, his father saw him, and had compassion, and ran, and fell on his neck, and kissed him.

²¹ "And the son said unto him, 'Father, I have sinned against heaven, and in thy sight, and am no more worthy to be called thy son.'

²² "But the father said to his servants, 'Bring forth the best robe, and put it on him; and put a ring on his hand, and shoes on his feet: ²³ And bring hither the fatted calf, and kill it; and let us eat, and be merry: ²⁴ For this my son was dead, and is alive again; he was lost, and is found.' And they began to be merry.

²⁵ "Now his elder son was in the field: and as he came and drew nigh to the house, he heard musick and dancing. ²⁶ And he called one of the servants, and asked what these things meant. ²⁷ And he said unto him, 'Thy brother is come; and thy father hath killed the fatted calf, because he hath received him safe and sound.'

²⁸ "And he was angry, and would not go in: therefore came his father out, and intreated him. ²⁹ And he answering said to his father, 'Lo, these many years do I serve thee, neither transgressed I at any time thy

---

④ **Martha** /ˈmɑːθə/, 马大。

The Return of the Prodigal Son, 1662—1669, Rembrandt

commandment: and yet thou never gavest me a kid, that I might make merry with my friends: ³⁰ But as soon as this thy son was come, which hath devoured thy living with harlots, thou hast killed for him the fatted calf.'

³¹ "And he said unto him, 'Son, thou art ever with me, and all that I have is thine. ³² It was meet that we should make merry, and be glad: for this thy brother was dead, and is alive again; and was lost, and is found.'"

Rich man and Lazarus

Luke 16

...

¹⁹ There was a certain rich man, which was clothed in purple and fine linen, and fared sumptuously every day: ²⁰ And there was a certain beggar named Lazarus, which was laid at his gate, full of sores, ²¹ And desiring to be fed with the crumbs which fell from the rich man's table: moreover the dogs came and licked his sores.

²² And it came to pass, that the beggar died, and was carried by the angels into Abraham's bosom: the rich man also died, and was buried; ²³ And in hell he lift up his eyes, being in torments, and seeth Abraham afar off, and Lazarus in his bosom. ²⁴ And he cried and said, "Father Abraham, have mercy on me, and send Lazarus, that he may dip the tip of his finger in water, and cool my tongue; for I am tormented in this flame."

Lazarus at the Rich Man's Gate, 1886, Fedor Bronnikov

²⁵ But Abraham said, "Son, remember that thou in thy lifetime receivedst thy good things, and likewise Lazarus evil things: but now he is comforted, and thou art tormented. ²⁶ And besides all this, between us and you there is a great gulf fixed: so that they which would pass from hence to you cannot; neither can they pass to us, that would come from thence." ²⁷ Then he said, " I pray thee therefore, father, that thou wouldest send him to my father's house: ²⁸ For I have five brethren; that he may testify unto them, lest they also come into this place of torment." ²⁹ Abraham saith unto him, "They have Moses and the prophets; let them hear them."

³⁰ And he said, "Nay, father Abraham: but if one went unto them from the dead, they will repent." ³¹ And he said unto him, "If they hear not Moses and the prophets, neither will they be persuaded, though one rose from the dead."

Women Taken in Adultery

John 8

¹ Jesus went unto the mount of Olives. ² And early in the morning he came again into the temple, and all the people came unto him; and he sat down, and taught them. ³ And the scribes and Pharisees brought unto him a woman taken in adultery; and when they had set her in the midst, ⁴ They say unto him, "Master, this woman was taken in adultery, in the very act. ⁵ Now Moses in the law commanded us, that such should be stoned: but what sayest thou?" ⁶ This they said, tempting him, that they might have to accuse him.

But Jesus stooped down, and with his finger wrote on the ground, as though he heard them not. ⁷ So when they continued asking him, he lifted up himself, and said unto them, "He that is without sin among you, let him first cast a stone at her." ⁸ And again he stooped down, and wrote on the ground.

⁹ And they which heard it, being convicted by their own conscience, went out one by one, beginning at the eldest, even unto the last: and Jesus was left alone, and the woman standing in the midst. ¹⁰ When Jesus had

lifted up himself, and saw none but the woman, he said unto her, "Woman, where are those thine accusers? Hath no man condemned thee?"

¹¹She said, "No man, Lord." And Jesus said unto her, "Neither do I condemn thee: go, and sin no more."

...

Christ and the Adulteress, 1532, Lucas Cranach, the Elder

A Collection of Parables of Jesus

Canceled debts, *Luke 7:41—43*
Cost of discipleship, *Luke 14:28—33*
Faithful servant, *Luke 12:42—48*
Fig tree, *Matthew 21:18—22; Mark 13:28—29; Luke 21:29—31*
Good Samaritan, *Luke 10:30—37*
The great banquet, *Luke 14:16—24*
Growing seed, *Mark 4:26—29*
Hidden treasure and pearl, *Matthew 13:44—46*
Honor at a banquet, *Luke 14:7—14*
Light of the world, *Matthew 5:14—15*
Lost coin, *Luke 15:8—10*
Lost sheep, *Matthew 18:12—14; Luke 15:3—7*
Mary and Martha, *Luke 10:38—42*
Mustard seed, *Matthew 13:31—32*
New wine in old wineskins, *Matthew 9:16—17; Mark 2:21—22; Luke 5:36—39*
Net, *Matthew 13:47—50*
Obedient servants, *Luke 17:7—10*
Persistent friend, *Luke 11:5—8*
Persistent widow, *Luke 18:2—8*
Pharisee and the tax collector, *Luke 18:10—14*
Prodigal/Lost son, *Luke 15:11—32*
Rich fool, *Luke 12:16—21*
Rich man and Lazarus, *Luke 16:19—31*
Sheep and the goats, *Matthew 25:31—46*
Shrewd manager, *Luke 16:1—8*
Sower, *Matthew 13:1—8,18—23; Mark 4:3—8,14—20; Luke 8:5—8,11—15*
Talents, *Matthew 25:14—30*
Tenants, *Matthew 21:33—44; Mark 12:1—12; Luke 20:9—18*
Ten minas, *Luke 19:11—27*
Ten virgins, *Matthew 25:1—13*
Two sons, *Matthew 21:28—31*
Unfruitful fig tree, *Luke 13:6—9*
Unmerciful servant, *Matthew 18:23—34*
Watchful servants, *Luke 12:35—40*
Wedding banquet, *Matthew 22:2—14*
Weeds, *Matthew 13:24—30,36—43*
Women taken in adultery, *John 8:1—11*
Wise and foolish builders, *Matthew 7:24—27; Luke 6:47—49*

Workers in the vineyard, *Matthew 20:1—16*
Yeast, *Matthew 13:33*; *Luke 13:20—21*

III FOOD FOR THOUGHT

1. According to Jesus, why did he preach in parables?
2. Why were the Pharisees offended by Jesus?
3. How can you understand the parable of the sower? Can it be applied to your life?
4. How did St. Augustine interpret the parable of the Good Samaritan (*Lk. 10:30—37*)?
5. How can you understand Jesus' parables as "earthly stories with a heavenly message" (属天意义的属地故事)?

IV BIBLICAL RELEVANCE

A. Biblical Terms in Everyday English
1. a grain of mustard seed (*Mt. 13:31*): _____
2. good Samaritan (*Lk. 10*): _____
3. prodigal son/daughter (*Lk. 15*): _____
4. the crumbs which fell from the rich man's table (*Lk. 16:21*): _____
5. Abraham's bosom (*Lk. 16:22*): _____

B. Biblical References in Literature
1. The earl living down at Guetwick did not understand that the Income-tax Office in the City, and the General Committee Office at Whitehall, were as far apart as Dives and Lazarus, and separated by as impassable a gulf.
   (Anthony Trollope, *The Small House at Allington*, 1862)
2. "Aye, she'll git tired of deh life after a while an'den she'll wanna be a-comin'home, won' she, deh beast! I'll let'er in den, won't I?" "Well, I didn't mean none of dis prod'gal bus'ness anyway," explained Jimmie. "It wa'nt no prod'gal dauter, yeh fool," said the mother. "It was prod'gal son, anyway."
   (Stephen Crane, *Maggie, A Girl of the Streets*, 1893)
3. I told her that I had had a fall — I didn't say how — and she saw by my looks that I was pretty sick. Like a true Samaritan she asked no questions, but gave me a bowl of milk with a dash of whisky in it, and let me sit for a little by her kitchen fire.
   (John Buchan, *The Thirty-Nine Steps*, 1915)
4. "Trying to help women who've come to grief." Old Jolyon did not quite understand. "To grief?" he repeated; then realized with a shock that she meant exactly what he would have meant himself if he had used that expression. Assisting the Magdalenes of London! What a weird and terrifying interest!
   (John Galsworth, *A Man of Property*, 1906)

C. The Bible and Arts
1. *Christ and the Woman of Samaria*, 1496—1504, Flandes de Juan
2. Mary and Martha
   Christ in the House of Mary and Martha, Vincenzo Campi (1536—1591)

Christ in the House of Martha and Mary, 1628, Peter Paul Rubens
3. *Feast in the House of Simon the Pharisee*, 1618 — 1620, Peter Paul Rubens
4. The Prodigal Son
   The Prodigal Son, Gerrit van Honthorst (1592—1656)
   Return of the Prodigal Son, 1619, Guercino
   The Return of the Prodigal Son, 1662—1669, Rembrandt
5. *Lazarus at the Rich Man's Gate*, 1886, Fedor Bronnikov
6. The Woman Taken in Adultery
   The Woman Taken in Adultery, Jobst Harrich (1586—1617)
   Christ and the Sinner; the First meeting of Christ and Mary Magdalene, 1873, Henryk Hector Siemiradaki
   Christ and the Adulteress, 1532, Lucas Cranach, the Elder
   Christ and Mary Magdalene, 1618, Peter Paul Rubens

V SOURCES FOR REFERENCE

1. Dodd, C. H. (1961). *The Parables of the Kingdom*. New York: Scribners.
2. Jeremias, J. (1963). *The Parables of Jesus*. London: SCM Press Ltd.

32. THE CHURCH

I   POINTS OF DEPARTURE

In John the Baptist's day, the Holy Land was ruled by Herod the tetrarch, or Herod Antipas (for other Herods, see the first footnote in Chapter 28) and a Roman governor. This Herod was one of the sons of Herod the Great who survived his father's spell of murderous madness. Antipas divorced his first wife in favour of Herodias, who had been his sister-in-law. For this indecency, he was condemned by John, who was eventually arrested and beheaded under the influence of Herodias and her daughter Salome. Salome has now become a symbol of *femme fatale* noted for her lightheartedness, cold foolishness and destructive power.

All the synoptic gospels give an account of the supernatural transformation into glory of the appearance of Jesus, known as the *transfiguration*. This episode should be understood against its Old Testament background, especially with regard to Moses, whose face shone with the reflected glory of God (*Exod. 34:29*); on the mount Jesus' figure shone with its own glory, and his clothes were "dazzling white" (*Mk. 9:3*). Jesus selected Peter, James, and John to accompany him up the Mount of Transfiguration and share the glorious vision possibly because only the three disciples were ready for it. Jesus' choice was also prophetic: these three were later to become the pillars of the infant Church in Jerusalem (Roche, 2001:415). As for the presence of Moses and Elijah in the vision, the former stands for the Old Testament Law and the exemplar of the great prophet who led his people out of the land of bondage. Jesus, too, was about to lead a new people. The latter is a representative of the prophets, the exponent of the type of moral decision, a similar role to be played by Jesus. The transfiguration interpreted this way finds its chief significance as staging the "call" of the Church.

II   SELECTED READINGS

John the Baptist Beheaded

See also Mk. 6:14—29
Matthew 14

¹ At that time Herod the tetrarch heard of the fame of Jesus, ² And said unto his servants, "This is John the Baptist. He is risen from the dead, and therefore mighty works show forth themselves in him."

³ For Herod had laid hold on John, and bound him and put him in prison for the sake of Herodias[①], his

---

[①] **Herodias** (/hɪˈrəʊdɪəs/, 希罗底) the niece and second wife of Herod Antipas and the mother of Salome.

The Bible and Western Culture

brother Philip's wife. ⁴ For John said unto him, "It is not lawful for thee to have her." ⁵ And when he would have put him to death, he feared the multitude, because they counted him as a prophet.

⁶ But when Herod's birthday was kept, the daughter of Herodias② danced before them and pleased Herod. ⁷ Whereupon he promised with an oath to give her whatsoever she would ask. ⁸ And she, being beforehand instructed by her mother, said, "Give me here John the Baptist's head on a charger." ⁹ And the king was sorry; nevertheless for the oath's sake, and those who sat with him at meat, he commanded it to be given her. ¹⁰ And he sent, and beheaded John in the prison. ¹¹ And his head was brought on a charger and given to the damsel, and she brought it to her mother. ¹² And his disciples came, and took up the body and buried it, and went and told Jesus.

Salome With the Head of St. John the Baptist, Bernardino Luini (1485—1532)

Cultural Connections: *Salome*

Salome is often remembered as a pampered, cold-blooded, coquettish dancer who charmed her stepfather Herod Antipas into granting her whatever she wished for, even the head of John the Baptist. A new ramification was added by Oscar Wilde, who in his play *Salome* portrayed her as something of a femme fatale. This interpretation was made even more memorable by Richard Strauss's opera based on Oscar Wilde, though neither of the two interpretations is consistent with Josephus's account. According to the Romanized Jewish historian, she lived long enough to marry twice and raise several children.

Jesus Feeds the Five Thousand

See also Mk. 6:32—44; Lk. 9:10—17; Jn. 6:1—13

Miracle of the Bread and Fish, c. 1607, Giovanni Lanranco

¹³ When Jesus heard of it, He departed thence by boat into a desert place apart. And when the people had heard thereof, they followed Him on foot out of the cities.

¹⁴ And Jesus went forth and saw a great multitude, and was moved with compassion toward them, and He healed their sick.

¹⁵ And when it was evening, His disciples came to Him, saying, "This is a desert place and the time is now past. Send the multitude away, that they may go into the villages and buy themselves victuals."

¹⁶ But Jesus said unto them, "They need not depart. Give ye them to eat."

---

② **the daughter of Herodias** i. e. **Salome** (/sə'ləumi/, 萨乐美). Her name is not given in the New Testament. Flavius Josephus (37 c. — 100 A. D.), Romano-Jewish historian, gives her name and some details about her family relations in his *Antiquities of the Jews*.

¹⁷ And they said unto Him, "We have here but five loaves and two fishes."
¹⁸ And He said, "Bring them hither to Me." ¹⁹ And He commanded the multitude to sit down on the grass, and took the five loaves and the two fishes; and looking up to Heaven, He blessed and broke the loaves and gave them to His disciples, and the disciples to the multitude. ²⁰ And they all ate and were filled. And they took up the fragments that remained, twelve baskets full. ²¹ And those who had eaten were about five thousand men, besides women and children.

Jesus Walks on the Water

See also Mk. 6:45—51; Jn. 6:16—21

²² And straightway Jesus constrained His disciples to get into a boat and to go before Him unto the other side, while He sent the multitudes away. ²³ And when He had sent the multitudes away, He went up onto a mountain apart to pray. And when evening had come, He was there alone. ²⁴ But the boat was now in the midst of the sea, tossed by the waves, for the wind was contrary.

²⁵ And in the fourth watch of the night, Jesus went unto them, walking on the sea. ²⁶ And when the disciples saw Him walking on the sea, they were troubled, saying, "It is a spirit"; and they cried out for fear.

²⁷ But straightway Jesus spoke unto them, saying, "Be of good cheer. It is I; be not afraid."

²⁸ And Peter answered Him and said, "Lord, if it be Thou, bid me come unto Thee on the water."

²⁹ And He said, "Come."

And when Peter had come down out of the boat, he walked on the water to go to Jesus. ³⁰ But when he saw that the wind was boisterous, he was afraid; and beginning to sink, he cried, saying, "Lord, save me!"

Saint Peter Attempting to Walk on Water, 1766, François Boucher

³¹ And immediately Jesus stretched forth His hand and caught him and said unto him, "O thou of little faith, why didst thou doubt?"

³² And when they had come into the boat, the wind ceased. ³³ Then those who were in the boat came and worshiped Him, saying, "In truth Thou art the Son of God."

³⁴ And when they had gone over, they came into the land of Gennesaret. ³⁵ And when the men of that place learned of Him, they sent out into all that country round about, and brought unto Him all who were diseased. ³⁶ And they besought Him that they might only touch the hem of His garment. And as many as touched were made perfectly whole.

The Demand for a Sign

See also Mk. 8:11—21
Matthew 16

¹ The Pharisees also with the Sadducees came, and testing, desired Him that He would show them a sign from Heaven.

² He answered and said unto them, "When it is evening ye say, 'It will be fair weather, for the sky is red.' ³ And in the morning, 'It will be foul weather today, for the sky is red and lowering.' O ye hypocrites, ye can discern the face of the sky, but can ye not discern the signs of the times? ⁴ A wicked and adulterous generation seeketh after a sign, and there shall no sign be given unto it, but the sign of the prophet Jonah." And He left them and departed.

The Yeast of the Pharisees and Sadducees

⁵ And when His disciples had come to the other side, they had forgotten to take bread. ⁶ Then Jesus said unto them, " Take heed and beware of the leaven of the Pharisees and of the Sadducees."

⁷ And they reasoned among themselves, saying, " It is because we have taken no bread."

⁸ But when Jesus perceived this, He said unto them, " O ye of little faith, why reason ye among yourselves, ' because ye have brought no bread' ? ⁹ Do ye not yet understand, neither remember the five loaves of the five thousand, and how many baskets ye took up? ¹⁰ Nor the seven loaves of the four thousand, and how many baskets ye took up? ¹¹ How is it that ye do not understand that I spoke it not to you concerning bread, but that ye should beware of the leaven of the Pharisees and the Sadducees?" ¹² Then understood they that He bade them not to beware of the leaven of bread, but of the doctrine of the Pharisees and of the Sadducees.

Peter's Confession of Christ

See also Mk. 8:27—29; Lk. 9:18—20

¹³ When Jesus came into the region of Caesarea Philippi, He asked His disciples, saying, " Who do men say that I, the Son of Man, am?"

¹⁴ And they said, " Some say that Thou art John the Baptist, some Elijah, and others Jeremiah or one of the prophets."

¹⁵ He said unto them, " But who say ye that I am?"

¹⁶ And Simon Peter answered and said, " Thou art the Christ, the Son of the living God."

¹⁷ And Jesus answered and said unto him, " Blessed art thou, Simon Bar-Jonah, for flesh and blood hath not revealed it unto thee, but My Father who is in Heaven. ¹⁸ And I say also unto thee, that thou art Peter, and upon this rock I will build My church; and the gates of hell shall not prevail against it. ¹⁹ And I will give unto thee the keys of the Kingdom of Heaven. And whatsoever thou shalt bind on earth shall be bound in Heaven, and whatsoever thou shalt loose on earth

Christ Handing the Keys to St. Peter, 1481—1482, Pietro Perugino

shall be loosed in Heaven." ²⁰ Then He charged His disciples that they should tell no man that He was Jesus the Christ.

Jesus Predicts His Death

See also Mk. 8:31—9:1; Lk. 9:22—27

²¹ From that time forth began Jesus to show unto His disciples that He must go unto Jerusalem and suffer many things of the elders and chief priests and scribes, and be killed, and be raised again the third day.

²² Then Peter took Him and began to rebuke Him, saying, " Be it far from Thee, Lord; this shall not happen unto Thee."

²³ But He turned and said unto Peter, " Get thee behind Me, Satan! Thou art an offense unto Me; for thou savorest not the things that be of God, but those that be of men."

²⁴ Then Jesus said unto His disciples, " If any man will come after Me, let him deny himself and take up his cross and follow Me.²⁵ For whosoever will save his life shall lose it, and whosoever will lose his life for My sake shall find it. ²⁶ For what is a man profited, if he shall gain the whole world and lose his own soul? Or what shall a man give in exchange for his soul? ²⁷ For the Son of Man shall come in the glory of His Father with His angels, and then He shall reward every man according to his works. ²⁸ Verily I say unto you,

there are some standing here who shall not taste of death till they see the Son of Man coming in His Kingdom."

The Transfiguration (耶稣变容/荣)

See also Mk. 9:2—13; Lk. 9:28—36
Matthew 17

¹ And after six days Jesus took Peter, James, and John his brother, and brought them up onto a high mountain apart. ² And He was transfigured before them; and His face shone as the sun, and His raiment was white as the light. ³ And behold, there appeared unto them Moses and Elijah, talking with Him. ⁴ Then answered Peter and said unto Jesus, "Lord, it is good for us to be here. If Thou wilt, let us make here three tabernacles: one for Thee and one for Moses and one for Elijah."

⁵ While he yet spoke, behold, a bright cloud overshadowed them. And behold, a voice out of the cloud, said, "THIS IS MY BELOVED SON IN WHOM I AM WELL PLEASED. HEAR YE HIM!"

⁶ And when the disciples heard it, they fell on their faces and were sore afraid. ⁷ And Jesus came and touched them and said, "Arise, and be not afraid." ⁸ And when they had lifted up their eyes, they saw no man, save Jesus only.

⁹ And as they came down from the mountain, Jesus charged them, saying, "Tell the vision to no man until the Son of Man be risen again from the dead."

¹⁰ And His disciples asked Him, saying, "Why then say the scribes that Elijah must first come?"

¹¹ And Jesus answered and said unto them, "Elijah truly shall first come and restore all things. ¹² But I say unto you that Elijah is come already, and they knew him not, but have done unto him whatsoever they pleased. Likewise shall also the Son of Man suffer by them." ¹³ Then the disciples understood that He spoke unto them of John the Baptist.

Transfiguration, 1594, Lodovico Carracci

...

The Greatest in the Kingdom of Heaven

See also Mk. 9:33—37; Lk. 9:46—48
Matthew 18

¹ At the same time came the disciples unto Jesus, saying, "Who is the greatest in the Kingdom of Heaven?"

² And Jesus called a little child unto Him, and set him in the midst of them, ³ And said, "Verily I say unto you, unless ye be converted and become as little children, ye shall not enter into the Kingdom of Heaven. ⁴ Whosoever therefore shall humble himself as this little child, the same is greatest in the Kingdom of Heaven.

⁵ And whoso shall receive one such little child in My name, receiveth Me. ⁶ But whoso shall cause one of these little ones who believe in Me to fall, it were better for him that a millstone were hung about his neck, and that he were drowned in the depth of the sea.

⁷ "Woe unto the world because of offenses! For it must happen that offenses come, but woe to that man by whom the offense cometh. ⁸ Therefore if thy hand or thy foot cause thee to fall, cut them off and cast them from thee; it is better for thee to enter into life halt or maimed, rather than having two hands or two feet, to be cast into everlasting fire. ⁹ And if thine eye cause thee to fall, pluck it out and cast it from thee; it is better for thee to enter into life with one eye, rather than having two eyes, to be cast into hell fire.

The Parable of the Lost Sheep

See also Lk. 15:4—7

¹⁰ "Take heed that ye despise not one of these little ones; for I say unto you that in Heaven their angels do always behold the face of My Father who is in Heaven. ¹¹ "For the Son of Man is come to save that which was lost.

¹² How think ye? If a man have a hundred sheep and one of them be gone astray, doth he not leave the ninety and nine, and goeth into the mountains and seeketh that which is gone astray? ¹³ And if it so be that he find it, verily I say unto you, he rejoiceth more over that sheep than over the ninety and nine which went not astray. ¹⁴ Even so it is not the will of your Father who is in Heaven that one of these little ones should perish.

A Brother Who Sins against You

¹⁵ "Moreover, if thy brother shall trespass against thee, go and tell him his fault between thee and him alone. If he shall hear thee, thou hast gained thy brother. ¹⁶ But if he will not hear thee, then take with thee one or two more, that ' in the mouth of two or three witnesses every word may be established.' ¹⁷ And if he shall neglect to hear them, tell it unto the church; but if he neglect to hear the church, let him be unto thee as a heathen man and a publican.

¹⁸ Verily I say unto you, whatsoever ye shall bind on earth shall be bound in Heaven; and so whatsoever ye shall loose on earth shall be loosed in Heaven.

¹⁹ "Again I say unto you, that if two of you shall agree on earth concerning anything that they shall ask, it shall be done for them by My Father who is in Heaven. ²⁰ For where two or three are gathered together in My name, there am I in the midst of them."

The Parable of the Unmerciful Servant

²¹ Then Peter came to Him and said, "Lord, how often shall my brother sin against me, and I forgive him? Until seven times?"

²² And Jesus said unto him, "I say not unto thee, until seven times, but until seventy times seven."

²³ "Therefore is the Kingdom of Heaven likened unto a certain king who would settle accounts with his servants. ²⁴ And when he had begun to reckon, one was brought unto him who owed him ten thousand talents. ²⁵ But inasmuch as he could not pay, his lord commanded him to be sold, and his wife and children and all that he had, and payment to be made.

²⁶ The servant therefore fell down and did homage to him, saying, 'Lord, have patience with me, and I will pay thee all.' ²⁷ Then the lord of that servant was moved with compassion, and loosed him and forgave him the debt.

²⁸ But the same servant went out and found one of his fellow servants who owed him a hundred pence. And he laid hands on him, and took him by the throat, saying, 'Pay me what thou owest.'

²⁹ And his fellow servant fell down at his feet, and besought him, saying, 'Have patience with me, and I will pay thee all.'

³⁰ And he would not, but went and cast him into prison till he should pay the debt. ³¹ So when his fellow servants saw what was done, they were very sorry and came and told unto their lord all that was done.

³² Then his lord, after he had called him, said unto him, 'O thou wicked servant, I forgave thee all that debt, because thou desiredst me. ³³ Shouldest not thou also have had compassion on thy fellow servant, even as I had pity on thee?' ³⁴ And his lord was wroth, and delivered him to the tormentors till he should pay all that was due unto him.

³⁵ So likewise shall My heavenly Father do also unto you, if ye from your hearts forgive not every one his brother's trespasses."

III FOOD FOR THOUGHT

1. Why was Peter promised by Jesus the keys of the Kingdom of Heaven (*Mt.* 16:19)?
2. Can you describe the scene of transfiguration (*Mt.* 17)?
3. What is the moral of the parable of the unmerciful servant?

IV BIBLICAL RELEVANCE

A. Biblical Terms in Everyday English
1. the blind leading the blind (*Mt.* 15:13—14; *Lk.* 6:39—40): _____
2. a millstone about/around sb's neck (*Mt.* 18:6): _____
3. lost sheep (*Mt.* 18:12—14): _____

B. Biblical References in Literature
1. Oscar Wilde, *Salome*, 1893
2. I remembered that he considered all this to be pleasure, as Herod thought Salome's dance was fun until he heard what she wanted as a reward.
   (Edmund White, *A Boy's Own Story*, 1982)

C. The Bible and Arts
1. *St. John the Baptist before Herod*, c. 1665, Mattia Preti
2. *Herod's Banquet*, 1427, Donatello
3. *Salome with the Head of St. John the Baptist*, c. 1607, Caravaggio
4. A Miracle of Bread and Fish
   Miracle of the Bread and Fish, c. 1607, Giovanni Lanranco
   The Miracle of the Loaves and Fishes, Lambert Lombard (1505—1566)
5. Keys to Peter
   Christ's Charge to Peter, Designed by Ford Madox Brown, Manufactured by William Morris, Jesus Church, Troutbeck, Cumbria, UK
   Christ Handing the Keys to St. Peter, 1481—1482, Pietro Perugino
6. Transfiguration
   Transfiguration, 1510—1512, Lorenzo Lotto
   Transfiguration, 1594, Lodovico Carracci
7. *St. Peter Finding the Tribute Money*, c. 1618, Peter Paul Rubens

V SOURCES FOR REFERENCE

1. Roche, P. (2001). *The Bible's Greatest Stories*. New York: New American Library.
2. Black, M. (ed.) (2001). *Peake's Commentary on the Bible*. London: Routledge.

33. THE FINAL JUDGMENT

I POINTS OF DEPARTURE

Eschatology[①], or *ta eschata* in Greek, meaning "doctrine of the last things," is concerned with "the four last things: death, judgment, heaven, and hell." (*The Oxford English Dictionary*). There are a group of parables about eschatology which are discussed as Parousia-parables by Jeremias (1963:48—63). These parables depict the return (Parousia) of Jesus as the heavenly, supernatural Son of man, and speak of the final judgment of men and women. Some have thought this was just a picturesque way of presenting the challenge of Jesus' message as it came to his hearers. But, in view of the strongly apocalyptical tone of much of the language used, it is quite obvious that it would have been understood by Jesus' hearers as relating to a future time, when God's authority and sovereignty would be made visible in some kind of tangible way. This is typical of Jesus' eschatological teaching.

Some of these parables depict a great day of reckoning, when those who merely profess to serve God, but do not actually do so, will be sorted out from those who really carry out God's will. This is the main message of the parables of the Corn and the Dragnet (*Mt. 13:47—50*), the Weeds (*Mt. 13:24—30, 36—43*), and the Sheep and the Goats (*Mt. 25:31—46*). In other parables, the future climax of the kingdom is depicted as a feast, to which not everyone will gain admission. The parable of the Great Banquet (*Mt. 25:1—13; Lk. 14:16—24*) suggests that the conventionally religious will have no place in it at all, and those who share in its blessings are more likely to come in from the streets than from the sanctuaries.

Jesus' Parousia-parables emphasize the responsibilities that all this places on those who profess to be trying to live in God's way. Since *Parousia* will occur as unexpectedly as the bridegroom arrives at midnight (Ten Virgins, *Mt. 25:1—13*), the master of the house returns late from the wedding-feast (the Doorkeeper, *Mk. 13:33—37; Lk. 12:35—38; Mt. 24:42*), the nobleman returns from a far journey (Talents, *Mt. 25:14—30*), everyone must be in a state of constant readiness and always full of hope. The kingdom is just like a mustard seed, which may have small and insignificant origin but which will surely grow into one of the biggest plants of all (*Mt. 13:31—32; Mk. 4:30—44; Lk. 3:18—19*).

---

① **Eschatology** /ˌeskəˈtɔlədʒi/，末世论，来世论。

II SELECTED READINGS

Jesus Blessing the Children

See also Mk. 10:13—16; Lk. 18:15—17
Matthew 19

...

¹³ Then were there brought unto him little children, that he should put his hands on them, and pray: and the disciples rebuked them. ¹⁴ But Jesus said, " Suffer little children, and forbid them not, to come unto me: for of such is the kingdom of heaven." ¹⁵ And he laid his hands on them, and departed thence.

The Parable of the Workers in the Vineyard

Matthew 20

Christ Blessing the Children,
Edward Burne-Jones (1833—1898)

¹ " For the Kingdom of Heaven is like unto a man that is a householder, who went out early in the morning to hire laborers into his vineyard. ² And when he had agreed with the laborers for a penny a day, he sent them into his vineyard.

³ And he went out about the third hour and saw others standing idle in the marketplace. ⁴ And said unto them, ' Go ye also into the vineyard, and whatsoever is right I will give you.' And they went their way. ⁵ Again he went out about the sixth and the ninth hour and did likewise.

⁶ And about the eleventh hour he went out and found others standing idle, and said unto them, ' Why stand ye here all the day idle?' ⁷ They said unto him, ' Because no man hath hired us.' He said unto them, ' Go ye also into the vineyard, and whatsoever is right, that shall ye receive.'

⁸ So when evening had come, the lord of the vineyard said unto his steward, ' Call the laborers and give them their hire, beginning from the last unto the first.'

⁹ And when they came that were hired about the eleventh hour, they received every man a penny. ¹⁰ But when the first came, they supposed they should have received more; and they likewise received every man a penny. ¹¹ And when they had received it, they murmured against the master of the house.

¹² Saying, ' These last have wrought but one hour, and thou hast made them equal unto us who have borne the burden and the heat of the day.'

¹³ But he answered one of them and said, ' Friend, I do thee no wrong. Didst thou not agree with me for a penny? ¹⁴ Take that which is thine and go thy way. I will give unto this last, even as unto thee. ¹⁵ Is it not lawful for me to do what I will with mine own? Is thine eye evil, because I am good?'

¹⁶ So the last shall be first, and the first last. For many are called, but few are chosen."

...

The Triumphal Entry

See also Mk. 11:1—10; Lk. 19:29—38; Jn.12:12—15
Matthew 21

¹ And when they drew nigh unto Jerusalem and had come to Bethphage unto the Mount of Olives, then sent Jesus two disciples, ² Saying unto them, " Go into the village opposite you, and straightway ye shall find

an ass tied, and a colt with her. Loose them and bring them unto Me. ³ And if any man say aught unto you, ye shall say, ' The Lord hath need of them,' and straightway he will send them."

⁴ All this was done that it might be fulfilled which was spoken by the prophet, saying,

⁵ "Tell ye the daughter of Zion, ' Behold, thy King cometh unto thee, meek and sitting upon an ass, and a colt, the foal of an ass.' "

⁶ And the disciples went and did as Jesus commanded them. ⁷ And they brought the ass and the colt and put on them their clothes, and they set Him thereon. ⁸ And a very great multitude spread their garments in the way; and others cut down branches from the trees and strewed them in the way. ⁹ And the multitudes that went before, and that followed, cried out, saying,

Jesus Enters Jerusalem, 2010, Zhixu Chen

" Hosanna② to the Son of David!"
" Blessed is He that cometh in the name of the Lord!"
" Hosanna in the highest!"

¹⁰ And when He had come into Jerusalem, all the city was moved, saying, " Who is this?"
¹¹ And the multitude said, " This is Jesus, the prophet of Nazareth of Galilee."

Jesus at the Temple

See also Mk. 11:15—18; Lk. 19:45—47

The Purification of the Temple, c. 1580, Jacopo Bassano

¹² And Jesus went into the temple of God, and cast out all those who sold and bought in the temple, and overthrew the tables of the moneychangers and the seats of those who sold doves? ¹³ And said unto them, " It is written, ' My house shall be called the house of prayer,' ③ but ye have made it a den of thieves."

¹⁴ And the blind and the lame came to Him in the temple, and He healed them. ¹⁵ And when the chief priests and scribes saw the wonderful things that He did, and the children crying out in the temple and saying, " Hosanna to the Son of David," they were sore displeased, ¹⁶ And said unto Him, " Hearest thou what these say?" And Jesus said unto them, " Yea, have ye never read, ' Out of the mouth of babes and sucklings Thou hast perfected praise' ?"

¹⁷ And He left them and went out of the city into Bethany, and He lodged there.
...

The Authority of Jesus Questioned

See also Mk. 11:27—33; Lk. 20:1—8

²³ And when He had come into the temple, the chief priests and the elders of the people came unto Him as He was teaching and said, " By what authority doest thou these things? And who gave thee this authority?"
²⁴ And Jesus answered and said unto them, " I also will ask you one thing, which if ye tell Me, I in like

---

② **Hosanna** (/həʊˈzænə/, 和撒那) means the Hebrew for "Save!" which later became an exclamation of praise.
③ **13** Isaiah 56:7.

manner will tell you by what authority I do these things. ²⁵ The baptism of John: whence was it? From Heaven, or of men?"

And they reasoned among themselves, saying, " If we shall say, ' From Heaven,' he will say unto us, ' Why did ye not then believe him?' ²⁶ But if we shall say, ' Of men,' we fear the people, for all hold John to be a prophet."

²⁷ And they answered Jesus and said, " We cannot tell." And He said unto them, " Neither tell I you by what authority I do these things."

The Parable of the Two Sons

²⁸ " But what think ye? A certain man had two sons. And he came to the first and said, ' Son, go work today in my vineyard.'

²⁹ He answered and said, ' I will not,' but afterward he repented and went.

³⁰ And he came to the second and said likewise. And he answered and said, ' I go, sir,' and went not.

³¹ Which of those two did the will of his father?"

They said unto Him, " The first." Jesus said unto them, " Verily I say unto you, that the publicans and the harlots go into the Kingdom of God before you. ³² For John came unto you in the way of righteousness, and ye believed him not; but the publicans and harlots believed him. And ye, when ye had seen it, repented not afterward, that ye might believe him.

The Parable of the Tenants

See also Mk. 12:1—12; Lk. 20:9—19

³³ " Hear another parable: There was a certain householder who planted a vineyard, and hedged it round about, and dug a wine press in it, and built a tower, and let it out to husbandmen and went into a far country. ³⁴ And when the time of the fruit drew near, he sent his servants to the husbandmen, that they might receive the fruits of it.

³⁵ " And the husbandmen took his servants, and beat one and killed another and stoned another. ³⁶ Again, he sent other servants, more than the first; and they did unto them likewise. ³⁷ But last of all he sent unto them his son, saying, ' They will reverence my son.'

³⁸ " But when the husbandmen saw the son, they said among themselves, ' This is the heir. Come, let us kill him, and let us seize on his inheritance.' ³⁹ And they caught him and cast him out of the vineyard and slew him.

⁴⁰ " When therefore the lord of the vineyard cometh, what will he do unto those husbandmen?"

⁴¹ They said unto Him, " He will miserably destroy those wicked men, and will let out his vineyard unto other husbandmen, who shall render him the fruits in their seasons."

⁴² Jesus said unto them, " Did ye never read in the Scriptures:

' The stone which the builders rejected,

the same is become the head of the corner.

This is the Lord's doing, and it is marvelous in our eyes' ?

⁴³ " Therefore say I unto you, the Kingdom of God shall be taken from you and given to a nation bringing forth the fruits thereof. ⁴⁴ And whosoever shall fall on this stone shall be broken; but on whomsoever it shall fall, it will grind him to powder."

⁴⁵ And when the chief priests and the Pharisees had heard His parables, they perceived that He spoke of them. ⁴⁶ But when they sought to lay hands on Him, they feared the multitude, because they took Him for a prophet.

Paying Taxes to Caesar

See also Mk. 12:13—17; Lk. 20:20—26
Matthew 22

...

¹⁵ Then went the Pharisees and took counsel how they might entangle Him in His talk. ¹⁶ And they sent out unto Him their disciples with the Herodians, saying, " Master, we know that thou art true and teachest the way of God in truth; neither carest thou for any man, for thou regardest not the person of men. ¹⁷ Tell us therefore, what thinkest thou? Is it lawful to give tribute unto Caesar, or not?"

¹⁸ But Jesus perceived their wickedness and said, " Why tempt ye Me, ye hypocrites? ¹⁹ Show Me the tribute money." And they brought unto Him a penny. ²⁰ And He said unto them, " Whose is this image and superscription?"

²¹ And they said unto Him, " Caesar's." Then said He unto them, " Render therefore unto Caesar the things which are Caesar's, and unto God the things that are God's."④

Cultural Connections: *paying taxes*

The sentence "Render therefore unto Caesar the things which are Caesar's, and unto God the things that are God's" (*Mt. 22:21*) has become a widely quoted summary of the relationship between Christianity and secular authority. It gives rise to multiple possible interpretations about under what circumstances it is desirable for the Christian to submit to earthly authority, varying from justification for obeying authority, paying taxes (and its opposite — encouragement of tax resistance), highlighting the dangers of cooperating with the state to propagating a monetary for the people. The "penny" mentioned is thought to be the coin of a Roman denarius with the head of Tiberius, sold and collected as the "tribute penny."

²² When they had heard these words, they marveled, and left Him and went their way.
...

The Greatest Commandment

See also Mk. 12:28—31

³⁴ But when the Pharisees had heard that He had put the Sadducees to silence, they were gathered together. ³⁵ Then one of them, who was a lawyer, asked Him a question, tempting Him and saying, ³⁶ " Master, which is the great commandment in the law?"

³⁷ Jesus said unto him, " ' Thou shalt love the Lord thy God with all thy heart, and with all thy soul, and with all thy mind.' ³⁸ This is the first and great commandment. ³⁹ And the second is like unto it: ' Thou shalt love thy neighbor as thyself.' ⁴⁰ On these two commandments hang all the Law and the Prophets."

---

④ **Render therefore unto Caesar the things which are Caesar's, and unto God the things that are God's** 凯撒的物当归给凯撒；神的物当归给神。

Whose Son Is the Christ

See also Mk. 12:35—37; Lk. 20:41—44

⁴¹ While the Pharisees were gathered together, Jesus asked them, ⁴² Saying, "What think ye of Christ? Whose Son is He?" They said unto Him, "The son of David."

⁴³ He said unto them, "How then doth David in the Spirit call Him 'Lord,' saying,

⁴⁴ "The LORD said unto my Lord, 'Sit Thou on My right hand until I make Thine enemies Thy footstool'"?⑤

⁴⁵ "If David then call Him 'Lord,' how is He his son?" ⁴⁶ And no man was able to answer Him a word; neither dared any man from that day forth ask Him any more questions.

The Parable of the Ten Virgins

Matthew 25

¹ "Then shall the Kingdom of Heaven be likened unto ten virgins, who took their lamps and went forth to meet the bridegroom. ² And five of them were wise, and five were foolish. ³ They that were foolish took their lamps and took no oil with them. ⁴ But the wise took oil in their vessels with their lamps. ⁵ While the bridegroom tarried, they all slumbered and slept.

The Parable of the Wise and Foolish Virgins (detail), Friedrich Wilhelm Schadow (1789—1862)

⁶ And at midnight there was a cry made: 'Behold, the bridegroom cometh; go ye out to meet him.'

⁷ Then all those virgins arose and trimmed their lamps. ⁸ And the foolish said unto the wise, 'Give us of your oil, for our lamps are gone out.'

⁹ But the wise answered, saying, 'Not so, lest there be not enough for us and you; but go ye rather to them that sell, and buy for yourselves.'

¹⁰ And while they went to buy, the bridegroom came, and they that were ready went in with him to the marriage, and the door was shut.

¹¹ Afterward came also the other virgins, saying, 'Lord, lord, open to us!'

¹² But he answered and said, 'Verily I say unto you, I know you not.'

¹³ Watch therefore, for ye know neither the day nor the hour wherein the Son of Man cometh."

The Parable of the Talents

¹⁴ "For the Kingdom of Heaven is as a man traveling into a far country, who called his own servants and delivered unto them his goods. ¹⁵ And unto one he gave five talents, to another two, and to another one, to every man according to his several ability, and straightway took his journey. ¹⁶ Then he that had received the five talents went and traded with the same, and made them another five talents. ¹⁷ And likewise he that had received two, he also gained another two. ¹⁸ But he that had received one went and dug in the earth and hid his lord's money.

¹⁹ "After a long time the lord of those servants came and reckoned with them. ²⁰ And so he that had received five talents came and brought the other five talents, saying, 'Lord, thou deliveredst unto me five

---

⑤ 44 Psalm 110:1.

talents. Behold, I have gained beside them five talents more.'

²¹ "His lord said unto him, 'Well done, thou good and faithful servant. Thou hast been faithful over a few things; I will make thee ruler over many things. Enter thou into the joy of thy lord.'

²² "He also that had received two talents came and said, 'Lord, thou deliveredst unto me two talents; behold, I have gained two other talents beside them.'

²³ "His lord said unto him, 'Well done, good and faithful servant. Thou hast been faithful over a few things; I will make thee ruler over many things. Enter thou into the joy of thy lord.'

²⁴ "Then he that had received the one talent came and said, 'Lord, I knew thee, that thou art a hard man, reaping where thou hast not sown, and gathering where thou hast not strewed. ²⁵ And I was afraid, and went and hid thy talent in the earth. Lo, there thou hast what is thine.'

²⁶ "His lord answered and said unto him, 'Thou wicked and slothful servant, thou knewest that I reap where I sowed not, and gather where I have not strewed. ²⁷ Thou ought therefore to have placed my money with the exchangers, and then at my coming I should have received mine own with interest.

²⁸ "'Take therefore the talent from him, and give it unto him that hath ten talents. ²⁹ For unto every one that hath shall be given, and he shall have abundance; but from him that hath not, shall be taken away even that which he hath. ³⁰ And cast ye the unprofitable servant into outer darkness: there shall be weeping and gnashing of teeth.'"

...

III FOOD FOR THOUGHT

1. Does the parable of the workers in the vineyard make any economic sense?
2. What does the parable of the ten virgins teach people to do?
3. How can you interpret the meaning of "Render therefore unto Caesar the things which are Caesar's, and unto God the things that are God's?"

IV BIBLICAL RELEVANCE

A. Biblical Terms in Everyday English
1. needle's eye (*Mt.* 19:24): _____
2. drink of one's cup (*Mt.* 20:23): _____
3. a den of thieves (*Mt.* 21:13): _____
4. talent (*Mt.* 25:14—30): _____

B. Biblical References in Literature
The ordinary view — rendering unto Caesar the things that are Caesar's — looks to natural agencies for the actual distribution and perpetuation of species, to a supernatural for their origin.
(Asa Gray, "The Origin of Species by Means of Natural Selection," *American Journal of Science and Arts*, 1860)

C. The Bible and Arts
1. *Christ Blessing the Children*, Designed by Edward Burne-Jones, Manufactured by William Morris, Jesus Church, Troutbeck, Cumbria, UK
2. *Jesus Healing the Blind of Jericho*, 1650, Nicolas Poussin
3. *The Entry into Jerusalem*, 1308—1311, Buoninsegna di Duccio

4. *The Entry into Jerusalem*, c. 1520, Pedro Orrente
5. *Christ Driving the Traders from the Temple*, c. 1832, Joseph Mallord William Turner
6. *The Purification of the Temple*, c. 1580, Jacopo Bassano
7. *The Parable of the Wise and Foolish Virgins*, Friedrich Wilhelm Schadow (1789—1862)

V SOURCES FOR REFERENCE

1. Jeremias, J. (1963). *The Parables of Jesus.* London: SCM Press Ltd.
2. Kendall, R. T. (2004). *The Complete Guide to the Parables.* Grand Rapids, MI: Chosen Books.

34. THE PASSION

I. POINTS OF DEPARTURE

The Passion (from the Greek verb *paschō*, "suffer") refers to the events and physical and mental sufferings covering the whole period from the Last Supper (*Mk.* 14), the arrest, the trials, the crucifixion, and the burial of Jesus Christ recorded in the four gospels, but the word "passion" is only mentioned in *Ac.* 1:3. The term *the Agony of Jesus* is more specifically applied to the Agony in the Garden, Jesus' praying before his arrest in the Garden of Gethsemane.

The one who was responsible for Jesus' arrest was Judas who, according to the gospels, betrayed his master for 30 pieces of silver. In spite of his stigmatization as a hypocritical, double-dealing traitor, various suggestions have been made over the centuries as to the motivation of his betrayal. One suggestion is that Judas, a disillusioned patriot, betrayed Jesus simply because he loved his country and thought Jesus had failed it. Another regards this "shameful" act as a "conspiracy" of Jesus who tended to bring about the fulfillment of God's plan. This view is supported by a 2nd-century Coptic papyrus manuscript titled *the Gospel of Judas* discovered in the 1970s. A modern suggestion relates the betrayal to the need of the early Bible authors to ingratiate themselves with the Roman conquerors and distance themselves from the Jews they conquered.

The Last Supper, or Lord's Supper, was the final meal shared by Jesus and his disciples before his trials and crucifixion and initiated the tradition of the Eucharist (Greek, "thanksgiving"). There are two major themes much discussed and depicted in art. The first is Jesus' announcement of his betrayal. The second is the institution of the tradition of the Eucharist, in which Jesus gave his disciples bread as his body, and wine as his blood. The body and blood analogy may symbolize the new covenant and the coming sacrifice of Jesus. The Last Supper also inspired the legend of Holy Grail or Chalice, the vessel used by Jesus to serve the wine, which in turn ushered in a time-honored tradition of religion and literature. The following scene, the Agony in the Garden, shows the human side of Jesus: a man with the realization of his approaching death is undergoing an intense physical and mental suffering, praying and discussing with God in order for death to pass him over.

The Sanhedrin trial and Pilate's court demonstrate different attitudes towards Jesus. The Sanhedrin, the supreme court in Jerusalem made up of chief priests and elders, or possibly Pharisees and the aristocratic Sadducees, was manipulated into reaching a unanimous verdict of guilt. The charge was mainly of blasphemy, i.e. feigned priesthood punishable by death. With no legal right to inflict capital punishment, the Sanhedrin referred the case to the Roman Governor who acceded to the wishes of the Jewish leaders and condemned Jesus to death. But realizing the innocence of Jesus, the governor Pilate decided to publicly wash his hands as a symbol of not being privy to Jesus' death. Obviously, the authors of the gospels tended to put the blame for the Roman penalty squarely on the doorstep of the Jewish leaders and to mitigate the responsibility of the Roman governor. This tendency only served to intensify the enmity that had already been simmering between Christians and Jews, Church and Synagogue, and plant the seed of bias and hatred in the fertile soil of Western anti-Semitism.

After being flogged, mocked by Roman soldiers as the "King of the Jews," clothed in a purple robe, crowned with thorns, Jesus then had to make his way with a cross on his back to the place of his crucifixion at Golgotha. The soldiers affixed an INRI sign above his head representing "Iesus Nazarenus, Rex Iudaeorum (Latin, "Jesus of Nazareth, King of the Jews"). Then Jesus was crucified and his crucifixion was accompanied by such supernatural events as darkness, an earthquake, and (in Matthew) the resurrection of saints. Jesus thus died according to the Christian tradition to atone for humanity's sin and make salvation possible and the cross has become a key element of Christian symbolism and art.

II SELECTED READINGS

The Plot Against Jesus

See also Mk. 14:1—2; Lk. 22:1—2
Matthew 26
¹ And it came to pass, when Jesus had finished all these sayings, He said unto His disciples, ² "Ye know that after two days is the Feast of the Passover, and the Son of Man is betrayed to be crucified."
³ Then the chief priests and the scribes and the elders of the people assembled together unto the palace of the high priest, who was called Caiaphas①, ⁴ And consulted that they might take Jesus by stealth and kill Him. ⁵ But they said, "Not on the feast day, lest there be an uproar among the people."

Jesus Anointed at Bethany

See also Mk. 14:3—9
⁶ Now when Jesus was in Bethany in the house of Simon the leper, ⁷ There came unto Him a woman having an alabaster box of very precious ointment, and poured it on His head as He sat at meat.
⁸ But when His disciples saw it, they were indignant, saying, "To what purpose is this waste? ⁹ For this ointment might have been sold for much and given to the poor."
¹⁰ When Jesus perceived this, He said unto them, "Why trouble ye the woman? For she hath wrought a good work upon Me. ¹¹ For ye have the poor always with you, but Me ye have not always. ¹² For in that she hath poured this ointment on My body, she did it for My burial. ¹³ Verily I say unto you, wheresoever this Gospel shall be preached in the whole world, there shall also this, which this woman hath done, be told as a memorial of her."

Judas Agrees to Betray Jesus

See also Mk. 14:10—11; Lk. 22:3—6
¹⁴ Then one of the twelve, called Judas Iscariot②, went unto the chief priests,
¹⁵ And said unto them, "What will ye give me if I will deliver Him unto you?"
And they covenanted with him for thirty pieces of silver. ¹⁶ And from that time he sought opportunity to betray Him.

---

① **Caiaphas** /ˈkaiəfæs/, 该亚法。
② **Judas Iscariot** /ˈdʒuːdəs, isˈkæriət/, 加略人犹大。

The Bible and Western Culture

The Last Supper

See also Mk. 14:12—25; Lk. 22:7—13

[17] Now on the first day of the Feast of Unleavened Bread, the disciples came to Jesus, saying unto Him, "Where wilt Thou that we prepare for Thee to eat the Passover?"

[18] And He said, "Go into the city to a certain man and say unto him, ' The Master saith, "My time is at hand; I will keep the Passover at thy house with My disciples," [19] And the disciples did as Jesus had appointed them, and they made ready the Passover.

[20] Now when the evening had come, He sat down with the twelve. [21] And as they ate, He said, "Verily I say unto you, that one of you shall betray Me."

[22] And they were exceeding sorrowful, and began every one of them to say unto Him, "Lord, is it I?"

[23] And He answered and said, "He that dippeth his hand with Me in the dish, the same shall betray Me. [24] The Son of Man goeth as it is written of Him, but woe unto that man by whom the Son of Man is betrayed! It had been good for that man if he had not been born."

[25] Then Judas, who betrayed Him, answered and said, "Master, is it I?" He said unto him, "Thou hast said."

The Last Supper, 1495—1498, Leonardo da Vinci

[26] And as they were eating, Jesus took bread and blessed it and broke it, and gave it to the disciples and said, "Take, eat; this is My body."

[27] And He took the cup and gave thanks, and gave it to them, saying, "Drink ye all of it; [28] For this is My blood of the new testament, which is shed for many for the remission of sins. [29] But I say unto you, I will not drink henceforth of this fruit of the vine until that day when I drink it new with you in My Father's Kingdom."

[30] And when they had sung a hymn, they went out unto the Mount of Olives.

Jesus Washes His Disciples' Feet

John 13

[1] Now before the feast of the passover, when Jesus knew that his hour was come that he should depart out of this world unto the Father, having loved his own which were in the world, he loved them unto the end.

[2] And supper being ended, the devil having now put into the heart of Judas Iscariot, Simon's son, to betray him; [3] Jesus knowing that the Father had given all things into his hands, and that he was come from God, and went to God; [4] He riseth from supper, and laid aside his garments; and took a towel, and girded himself. [5] After that he poureth water into a bason, and began to wash the disciples' feet, and to wipe them with the towel wherewith he was girded.

[6] Then cometh he to Simon Peter: and Peter saith unto him, "Lord, dost thou wash my feet?"

[7] Jesus answered and said unto him, "What I do thou knowest not now; but thou shalt know hereafter."

[8] Peter saith unto him, "Thou shalt never wash my feet."

Jesus answered him, "If I wash thee not, thou hast no part with me."

[9] Simon Peter saith unto him, "Lord, not my feet only, but also my hands and my head."

[10] Jesus saith to him, "He that is washed needeth not save to wash his feet, but is clean every whit: and

ye are clean, but not all." ¹¹ For he knew who should betray him; therefore said he, "Ye are not all clean."

¹² So after he had washed their feet, and had taken his garments, and was set down again, he said unto them, "Know ye what I have done to you?"

...

Jesus Predicts Peter's Denial

See also Mk. 14:27—31; Lk. 22:31—34
Matthew 26

...

³¹ Then Jesus said unto them, "All ye shall be offended because of Me this night; for it is written:
'I will smite the Shepherd, and the sheep of the flock shall be scattered abroad.'
³² But after I am risen again, I will go before you into Galilee."
³³ Peter answered and said unto Him, "Though all men shall be offended because of Thee, yet I will never be offended."
³⁴ Jesus said unto him, "Verily I say unto thee, that this night before the cock crow, thou shalt deny Me thrice."
³⁵ Peter said unto Him, "Though I should die with Thee, yet will I not deny Thee." Likewise also said all the disciples.

The Agony in the Garden

See also Mk. 14:32—42; Lk. 22:40—46

³⁶ Then Jesus came with them unto a place called Gethsemane③, and said unto the disciples, "Sit ye here while I go and pray yonder." ³⁷ And He took with Him Peter and the two sons of Zebedee, and began to be sorrowful and very heavy. ³⁸ Then He said unto them, "My soul is exceeding sorrowful, even unto death; tarry ye here and watch with Me."

Agony in the Garden, c. 1459, Giovanni Bellini

³⁹ And He went a little farther, and fell on His face and prayed, saying, "O My Father, if it be possible, let this cup pass from Me; nevertheless, not as I will, but as Thou wilt."
⁴⁰ And He came unto the disciples and found them asleep, and said unto Peter, "What, could ye not watch with Me one hour? ⁴¹ Watch and pray, that ye enter not into temptation. The spirit indeed is willing, but the flesh is weak.④"

⁴² He went away again the second time and prayed, saying, "O My Father, if this cup may not pass away from Me, unless I drink it, Thy will be done."

⁴³ And He came and found them asleep again, for their eyes were heavy. ⁴⁴ And He left them and went away again, and prayed a third time, saying the same words.

⁴⁵ Then came He to His disciples and said unto them, "Sleep on now, and take your rest. Behold, the hour is at hand, and the Son of Man is betrayed into the hands of sinners. ⁴⁶ Rise, let us be going. Behold, he is at hand that doth betray Me."

---

③ **Gethsemane** (/geθ'semәni/, 客西马尼) a garden east of Jerusalem near the foot of the Mount of Olives.
④ **The spirit indeed is willing, but the flesh is weak** 心灵固然愿意，肉体却软弱了。

Jesus Arrested

See also Mk. 14:43—50; Lk. 22:47—53

⁴⁷ And while He yet spoke, lo, Judas, one of the twelve came, and with him a great multitude with swords and staves, from the chief priests and elders of the people. ⁴⁸ Now he that betrayed Him gave them a sign, saying, "Whomsoever I shall kiss, that same is He; hold Him fast." ⁴⁹ And forthwith he came to Jesus and said, "Hail, Master!" and kissed Him.

⁵⁰ And Jesus said unto him, "Friend, why art thou come?"

Then they came and laid hands on Jesus and took Him. ⁵¹ And behold, one of those who was with Jesus stretched out his hand and drew his sword, and struck a servant of the high priest and smote off his ear.

⁵² Then said Jesus unto him, "Put up again thy sword into his place, for all they that take the sword shall perish with the sword.⑤ ⁵³ Thinkest thou that I cannot now pray to My Father, and He shall at once give Me more than twelve legions of angels? ⁵⁴ But how then shall the Scriptures be fulfilled, that thus it must be?"

Kiss of Judas, 1304—1306, Bondone di Giotto

⁵⁵ In that same hour Jesus said to the multitudes, "Are ye come out as against a thief, with swords and staves to take Me? I sat daily with you teaching in the temple, and ye laid no hold on Me. ⁵⁶ But all this was done that the Scriptures of the prophets might be fulfilled." Then all the disciples forsook Him and fled.

Before the Sanhedrin⑥

See also Mk. 14:53—65; Jn. 18:12—13, 19—24

Christ before the High Priest, c. 1617, Gerrit Van Honthorst

⁵⁷ And those who had laid hold on Jesus led Him away to Caiaphas the high priest, where the scribes and the elders were assembled. ⁵⁸ But Peter followed Him afar off unto the high priest's palace, and went in and sat with the servants to see the end.

⁵⁹ Now the chief priests and elders and all the council sought false witness against Jesus to put Him to death, ⁶⁰ But found none. Yea, though many false witnesses came, yet found they none.

At the last came two false witnesses, ⁶¹ And said, "This fellow said, 'I am able to destroy the temple of God and to build it in three days.'"

⁶² And the high priest arose and said unto Him, "Answerest thou nothing? What is it which these witnesses say against thee?" ⁶³ But Jesus held His peace.

And the high priest answered and said unto Him, "I adjure thee by the living God that thou tell us whether thou be the Christ, the Son of God."

⁶⁴ Jesus said unto him, "Thou hast said; nevertheless I say unto you, hereafter shall ye see the Son of Man sitting at the right hand of Power, and coming in the clouds of heaven."

---

⑤ **they that take the sword shall perish with the sword** 凡动刀的,必死在刀下。
⑥ **Sanhedrin** /ˈsænidrin/, highest Jewish court during Roman times.

⁶⁵ Then the high priest rent his clothes, saying, "He hath spoken blasphemy! What further need have we of witnesses? Behold, now ye have heard his blasphemy! ⁶⁶ What think ye?"

They answered and said, "He is deserving of death!"

⁶⁷ Then they spit in His face and buffeted Him, and others smote Him with the palms of their hands, ⁶⁸ Saying, "Prophesy unto us, thou Christ! Who is he that smote thee?"

Peter Disowns Jesus

See also Mk. 14:66—72; Lk. 22:55—62; Jn. 18:16—18, 25—27

Repentance of St. Peter, 1610, Guido Reni

⁶⁹ Now Peter sat outside in the palace, and a damsel came unto him, saying, "Thou also wast with Jesus of Galilee."

⁷⁰ But he denied it before them all, saying, "I know not what thou sayest."

⁷¹ And when he had gone out onto the porch, another maid saw him and said unto those who were there, "This fellow was also with Jesus of Nazareth."

⁷² And again he denied with an oath, "I do not know the man!"

⁷³ And after a while came unto him those who stood by, and said to Peter, "Surely thou also art one of them, for thy speech betrayeth thee."

⁷⁴ Then he began to curse and to swear, saying, "I know not the man!"

And immediately the cock crowed. ⁷⁵ And Peter remembered the word of Jesus, when He said unto him, "Before the cock crow, thou shalt deny Me thrice." And he went out and wept bitterly.

Judas Hangs Himself

Matthew 27

¹ When the morning had come, all the chief priests and elders of the people took counsel against Jesus to put Him to death. ² And when they had bound Him, they led Him away and delivered Him to Pontius Pilate⑦, the governor.

³ Then Judas, who had betrayed Him, when he saw that He was condemned, repented and brought back the thirty pieces of silver to the chief priests and elders,

⁴ Saying, "I have sinned in that I have betrayed the innocent blood." And they said, "What is that to us? See thou to that!"

⁵ And he cast down the pieces of silver in the temple and departed, and went and hanged himself.

⁶ And the chief priests took the silver pieces and said, "It is not lawful to put them into the treasury, because it is the price of blood." ⁷ And they took counsel and bought with them the potter's field, to bury strangers in. ⁸ Therefore that field was called the Field of Blood unto this day. ⁹ Then was fulfilled that which was spoken by Jeremiah the prophet, saying, "And they took the thirty pieces of silver, the price of Him that was valued, whom they the children of Israel did value? ¹⁰ And gave them for the potter's field, as the Lord appointed me."

Jesus before Pontius Pilate

See also Mk. 15:2—15; Lk. 23:2—3; Jn. 18:29—19:16

¹¹ And Jesus stood before the governor, and the governor asked Him, saying, "Art thou the King of the

---

⑦ **Pontius Pilate** (/ˈpɒntiəs ˈpaɪələt/, 彼拉多) Roman procurator of Judaea c. 26—c. 36.

Jews?"

And Jesus said unto him, "Thou sayest."

¹² And when He was accused by the chief priests and elders, He answered nothing. ¹³ Then said Pilate unto Him, "Hearest thou not how many things they witness against thee?" ¹⁴ And He answered him never a word, insomuch that the governor marveled greatly.

¹⁵ Now at that feast, the governor was wont to release unto the people a prisoner, whom they would. ¹⁶ And they had then a notable prisoner called Barabbas⑧. ¹⁷ Therefore when they were gathered together, Pilate said unto them, "Whom will ye that I release unto you: Barabbas, or Jesus who is called Christ?" ¹⁸ For he knew that for envy they had delivered Him.

¹⁹ When he had sat down on the judgment seat, his wife sent unto him, saying, "Have thou nothing to do with that just man; for I have suffered many things this day in a dream because of him."

²⁰ But the chief priests and elders persuaded the multitude that they should ask for Barabbas and destroy Jesus.

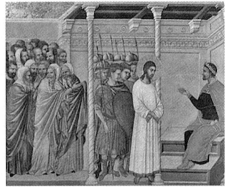

Pontius Pilate's Second Interrogation of Christ, 1308—1311, Buoninsegna di Duccio

²¹ The governor answered and said unto them, "Which of the two will ye that I release unto you?" They said, "Barabbas!"

²² Pilate said unto them, "What shall I do then with Jesus, who is called Christ?" They all said unto him, "Let him be crucified!"

²³ And the governor said, "Why, what evil hath he done?" But they cried out the more, saying, "Let him be crucified!"

²⁴ When Pilate saw that he could not prevail, but rather that a tumult was beginning, he took water and washed his hands before the multitude, saying, "I am innocent of the blood of this just person.⑨ See ye to it."

²⁵ Then answered all the people and said, "His blood be on us, and on our children!"

²⁶ Then released he Barabbas unto them; and when he had scourged Jesus, he delivered Him to be crucified.

The Soldiers Mock Jesus

See also Mk. 15:16—20

²⁷ Then the soldiers of the governor took Jesus into the common hall, and gathered unto Him the whole detachment of soldiers. ²⁸ And they stripped Him and put on Him a scarlet robe. ²⁹ And when they had plaited a crown of thorns, they put it upon His head and a reed in His right hand, and they bowed their knees before Him and mocked Him, saying, "Hail, King of the Jews!" ³⁰ And they spat upon Him, and took the reed and smote Him on the head. ³¹ And after they had mocked Him, they took the robe off from Him and put His own raiment on Him, and led Him away to crucify Him.

---

⑧ **Barabbas** /bəˈræbəs/, 巴拉巴。
⑨ **I am innocent of the blood of this just person** 流这义人的血,罪不在我。

Cultural Connections: *Ecce Homo*

Ecce Homo (/ˌekeɪˈhɔməʊ/, "Behold the Man") was what Pontius Pilate said to a hostile crowd when presenting a scourged Jesus Christ, bound and crowned with thorns (*Jn.* 19:5, the Vulgate). The scene is widely depicted in Christian art as a standard component of cycles illustrating the Passion and Life of Christ from the flagellation, the crowning with thorns and the mocking. The usual depiction shows Pilate and Christ, the mocking crowd against the background of the city of Jerusalem. In the 15th century, pictures began to portray Jesus alone with a purple robe, loincloth, crown of thorns and torture wounds. From the 19th century onwards, the meaning of *ecce homo* motif has been extended to the portrayal of suffering and the degradation of humans through violence and war. Following the Holocaust of World War II, the Jews were portrayed as the suffering Christ.

The Crucifixion

See also *Mk.* 15:22—32; *Lk.* 23:33—43; *Jn.* 19:17—24

Christ Carrying the Cross, 1737—1738, Giovanni Battista Tiepolo

^{32} And as they came out, they found a man of Cyrene, Simon by name; him they compelled to bear His cross. ^{33} And when they had come unto a place called Golgotha, that is to say, a Place of a Skull, ^{34} They gave Him vinegar to drink mingled with gall. And when He had tasted thereof, He would not drink. ^{35} And they crucified Him and parted His garments, casting lots, that it might be fulfilled which was spoken by the prophet: "They parted My garments among them, and upon My vesture did they cast lots." ⑩^{36} And sitting down, they watched Him there. ^{37} And set up over His head His accusation, written: THIS IS JESUS THE KING OF THE JEWS. ^{38} Then were there two thieves crucified with Him, one on the right hand and another on the left. ^{39} And those who passed by reviled Him, wagging their heads, ^{40} And saying, "Thou that destroyest the temple and buildest it in three days, save thyself! If thou be the Son of God, come down from the cross!"

^{41} Likewise also the chief priests mocking Him, with the scribes and elders said, ^{42} "He saved others; himself he cannot save. If he be the King of Israel, let him now come down from the cross, and we will believe him. ^{43} He trusted in God; let Him deliver him now, if He will have him. For he said, 'I am the Son of God.'" ^{44} The thieves also, who were crucified with Him, cast the same in His teeth.

---

⑩ They parted My garments among them, and upon My vesture did they cast lots. *Psalm* 22:18.

The Death of Jesus

See also Mk. 15:33—41; Lk. 23:44—49; Jn. 19:29—30

⁴⁵ *Now from the sixth hour there was darkness over all the land until the ninth hour.* ⁴⁶ *And about the ninth hour Jesus cried out with a loud voice, saying, "Eli, Eli, lama sabachthani?" That is to say, "My God, My God, why hast Thou forsaken Me?"*⑪

⁴⁷ *Some of those who stood there, when they heard that, said, "This man calleth for Elijah."*

⁴⁸ *And straightway one of them ran and took a sponge, and filled it with vinegar, and put it on a reed and gave Him to drink.* ⁴⁹ *The rest said, "Let be; let us see whether Elijah will come to save him."*

⁵⁰ *Jesus, when He had cried out again with a loud voice, yielded up the ghost.*

⁵¹ *And behold, the veil of the temple was rent in two from the top to the bottom, and the earth quaked and the rocks rent.* ⁵² *And the graves were opened; and many bodies of the saints who slept arose,* ⁵³ *And came out of the graves after His resurrection, and went into the Holy City and appeared unto many.*

⁵⁴ *Now when the centurion, and those who were with him watching Jesus, saw the earthquake and those things that were done, they feared greatly, saying, "Truly, this was the Son of God!"*

Crucifixion, 1583, Annibale Carracci

⁵⁵ *And many women were there beholding afar off, who followed Jesus from Galilee, ministering unto Him,* ⁵⁶ *Among whom were Mary Magdalene⑫, and Mary the mother of James and Joseph, and the mother of Zebedee's children.*

III FOOD FOR THOUGHT

1. Why did the chief priests and the elders have Jesus arrested at night?
2. Why did Jesus choose not to defend for himself when he was interrogated?
3. Describe Pilate's attitude towards Jesus. Was it different from that of the chief priests and the elders?
4. On what charges was Jesus arrested and crucified?
5. How can you comment on the characterization of Jesus in his passion?

IV BIBLICAL RELEVANCE

A. Biblical Terms in Everyday English
1. (Garden of) Gethsemane (*Mt. 26:36*): _____
2. The spirit indeed is willing, but the flesh is weak. (*Mt. 26:41*): _____
3. Judas kiss (*Mt. 26:49*): _____
4. sheathe/put up one's sword (*Mt. 26:52*): _____

---

⑪ **My God, My God, why hast Thou forsaken Me**? *Psalm 22:1*. 我的神,我的神！为什么离弃我？
⑫ **Mary Magdalene** (/ˈmæɡdəliːn/, 抹大拉的马利亚) c.f. *Luke 7:37*.

5. wash one's hands of (*Mt. 27:24*): _____
6. Peter's tears (*Mt. 26:75*): _____
7. Golgotha/Calvary (*Mt. 27:33*): _____
8. INRI: _____

B. Biblical References in Literature
1. "I been thinkin'," he said. "I been in the hills thinkin', almost you might say like Jesus went into the wilderness to think His way out of a mess of troubles."

(John Steinbeck, *The Grapes of Wrath*, 1939)

2. Well, he looks awfully nice. Of course you never really know someone till you've been married to them for a while and discover some of their scruffier habits. I remember how upset I was when I realized for the first time that after all Joe wasn't Jesus Christ. I don't know what it was, probably some silly thing like finding out he's crazy about Audrey Hepburn. Or that he's a philatelist.

(Margaret Atwood, *The Edible Woman*, 1969)

3. Are we to watch our words and stick out our necks to the knives of potential traitors here in this place where we meet to put our minds and hearts in the struggle … are we to sit with Judas in our midst?

(Nadine Gordimer, *My Son's Story*, 1990)

4. Chief Ranger Hull crossed the clearing, wiping his hands carefully on a clean white pocket hanky. … Hull never looked up from his hands while he talked, but continued to rub meticulously between each finger with the square of cotton. … Finally Norman Hull pocketed the handkerchief and Anna breathed a sign of relief. Till it stopped she'd not realized how much his Pontius Pilate routine was getting on her nerves.

(Neveda Barr, *Endangered Species*, 1997)

5. In a very special, very private sense DeQuincey is your Cross and your marriage is your Calvary.

(Edmund White, *A Boy's Own Story*, 1982)

C. The Bible and Arts
1. *Jesus Washing Peter's Feet*, 1852—1856, Ford Madox Brown
2. The Last Supper
   The Last Supper, 1495—1498, Leonardo da Vinci
   The Last Supper, 1560s, Juan de Juanes
   The Eucharist, 1647, Nicolas Poussin
3. Agony in the Garden
   Agony in the Garden, c. 1459, Giovanni Bellini
   Prayer in the Garden and Capture of Christ, 1482, Ercole de Robert
4. *Kiss of Judas*, 1304—1306, Bondone di Giotto
5. *Christ before the High Priest*, c. 1617
6. The Repentant Peter
   The Denial of St. Peter, 1610, Caravggio
   Repentance of St. Peter, 1635, Guido Reni
7. *Jesus before King Herod*, 1308—1311, Buoninsegna di Duccio
8. *Pontius Pilate's Second Interrogation of Christ*, 1308—1311, Buoninsegna di Duccio
9. *Pilate Washing His Hands*, Jan Lievens (1607—1674)
10. *Ecce Homo*, 1490, Hieronymus Bosch
11. Jesus Being Mocked

  Crowning with Thorns, 1618—1620
  Christ Crowned with Thorns, c. 1510, Giambattista Cima da Conegliano
  The Flagellation of Christ, 1308—1311, Gioacchino Assereto
12. The Road to Calvary
  Christ Carrying the Cross, 1737—1738, Giovanni Battista Tiepolo
  The Fall of Christ Under the Cross, Luc Faydherbe (1617—1697)
13. Crucifixion
  Crucifixion, 1617, Pieter Bruegel, the Younger
  Crucifixion, 1583, Annibale Carracci
14. *Pietà*, 1499, Michelangelo, Basilica di San Pietro, Vatican

V SOURCES FOR REFERENCE

1. http://www.haltadefinizione.com
2. (2004). *The Passion of the Christ*. An American drama film directed by Mel Gibson and starring Jim Caviezel as Jesus.
3. (2004). *The Passion of the Jew*. Episode 114 of the Comedy Central series *South Park*, a satire of Mel Gibson's 2004 movie.
4. (2004). *Judas*. A film directed by Charles Robert Carner, starring Johnathon Schaech and Jonathan Scarfe.
5. (2008). *The Passion*. A BBC One TV series.

35. THE RESURRECTION AND THEREAFTER

I POINTS OF DEPARTURE

Belief about life after death is not unique to Christianity, but Christians have some different ideas from their precursors Hebrews and Greeks. The ancient Hebrews rejected both the Canaanite Baal worship, which included in the cult the annual dying and rising again of the god, and also the Greek notion of the inherent immortality of the "soul." But the New Testament concept of resurrection has only the basest hints in the Old Testament.

The idea of a hopeless shadowy existence in *sheol* similar to the Greek conception of Hades is a state of misery where the dead survived as feeble shades. In later literature there is a richer conception of life after death that the human body is part of God's creation and life without "body" was incomplete and unsatisfying. Moreover, while existence in *sheol* might be a fair reward for the wicked, the faithful deserved something better. So there is a promise of resurrection for Israel as a nation; Yahweh's loyalists who have suffered will rise to an appropriate reward and apostates will endure shame and everlasting contempt. The death and resurrection of Jesus is the central focus of Christianity.

The resurrection of the body is part of Christian belief about life after death. The essence of the belief is that what has been of value on earth in the bodily, historical life is not wholly left behind but is transfigured. There have been three understandings of the resurrection of Jesus (Schippe & Stetson, 2005:276). One is the idea of *incarnation* articulated by Athanasius in the year 320 that Jesus rescued people from enslavement to sin and death first by coming to earth and then by going to the realm of Hades, destroying it, and conquering the evil one. His rescue was like the Passover of the Jews in the *Exodus*. Another is that Jesus died for others, an act known as *substitutionary atonement*. Jesus was also seen as an example of self-sacrifice that can be imitated and followed: "Greater love hath no man than this, that a man lay down his life for his friends." (Jn. 15:13) In the Middle Ages, Jesus' example was described as the *exemplary atonement*. Literature abounds with examples of Christ figures that rescue or stand in for others in self-sacrifice or whose selfless love saves the day and becomes an example to others. A case in point is Sydney Carton, a character in Charles Dickens' *A Tale of Two Cites* (1859). The guillotining scene that concludes the novel is especially suggestive of the sacrifice of Jesus.

II SELECTED READINGS

The Burial of Jesus

See also Mk. 15:42—47; Lk. 23:50—56; Jn. 19:38—42
Matthew 27

...

⁵⁷ When the evening had come, there came a rich man of Arimathea named Joseph, who himself also was Jesus' disciple. ⁵⁸ He went to Pilate, and begged the body of Jesus. Then Pilate commanded the body to be delivered. ⁵⁹ And when Joseph had taken the body, he wrapped it in a clean linen cloth, ⁶⁰ And laid it in his own new tomb, which he had hewn out in the rock. And he rolled a great stone to the door of the sepulcher and departed. ⁶¹ And Mary Magdalene was there, and the other Mary, sitting opposite the sepulcher.

The Guard at the Tomb

⁶² Now the next day, that following the Day of the Preparation, the chief priests and Pharisees came together unto Pilate, ⁶³ Saying, " Sir, we remember that that deceiver said while he was yet alive, ' After three days I will rise again.'

⁶⁴ Command therefore that the sepulcher be made secure until the third day, lest his disciples come by night and steal him away, and say unto the people ' He is risen from the dead,' so that the last error shall be worse than the first."

⁶⁵ Pilate said unto them, " Ye have a watch. Go your way, make it as secure as ye can." ⁶⁶ So they went and made the sepulcher secure, sealing the stone and setting up a watch.

The Empty Tomb

See also Mt. 28:1—8; Mk. 16:1—8; Lk. 24:1—10
John 20

¹ The first day of the week cometh Mary Magdalene early, when it was yet dark, unto the sepulchre, and seeth the stone taken away from the sepulchre. ² Then she runneth, and cometh to Simon Peter, and to the other disciple, whom Jesus loved, and saith unto them, " They have taken away the LORD out of the sepulchre, and we know not where they have laid him."

³ Peter therefore went forth, and that other disciple, and came to the sepulchre. ⁴ So they ran both together: and the other disciple did outrun Peter, and came first to the sepulchre. ⁵ And he stooping down, and looking in, saw the linen clothes lying; yet went he not in. ⁶ Then cometh Simon Peter following him, and went into the sepulchre, and seeth the linen clothes lie, ⁷ And the napkin, that was about his head, not lying with the linen clothes, but wrapped together in a place by itself. ⁸ Then went in also that other disciple, which came first to the sepulchre, and he saw, and believed. ⁹ For as yet they knew not the scripture, that he must rise again from the dead.

...

The Resurrection

See also Mk. 16:1—8; Lk. 24:1—10; Jn. 20:1—8
Matthew 28

¹ At the end of the Sabbath, as it began to dawn toward the first day of the week, came Mary Magdalene

and the other Mary to see the sepulcher.

^{2} And behold, there was a great earthquake, for the angel of the Lord descended from Heaven, and came and rolled back the stone from the door, and sat upon it. ^{3} His countenance was like lightning, and his raiment white as snow. ^{4} And for fear of him the guards shook, and became as dead men.

^{5} And the angel answered and said unto the women, "Fear ye not, for I know that ye seek Jesus, who was crucified. ^{6} He is not here, for He is risen, as He said. Come, see the place where the Lord lay. ^{7} And go quickly and tell His disciples that He is risen from the dead, and behold, He goeth before you into Galilee. There shall ye see Him. Lo, I have told you."

^{8} And they departed quickly from the sepulcher with fear and great joy, and ran to bring His disciples word. ^{9} And as they went to tell His disciples, behold, Jesus met them, saying, "All hail." And they came, and held Him by the feet, and worshiped Him. ^{10} Then said Jesus unto them, "Be not afraid. Go tell My brethren to go into Galilee, and there shall they see Me." ^{9} And as they went to tell his disciples, behold, Jesus met them, saying, "All hail." And they came and held him by the feet, and worshipped him. ^{10} Then said Jesus unto them, "Be not afraid: go tell my brethren that they go into Galilee, and there shall they see me."

The Guard's Report

^{11} Now when they were going, behold, some of the watch came into the city, and shewed unto the chief priests all the things that were done. ^{12} And when they were assembled with the elders, and had taken counsel, they gave large money unto the soldiers, ^{13} Saying, "Say ye, 'His disciples came by night, and stole him away while we slept.' ^{14} And if this come to the governor's ears, we will persuade him, and secure you." ^{15} So they took the money, and did as they were taught: and this saying is commonly reported among the Jews until this day.

The Great Commission

^{16} Then the eleven disciples went away into Galilee, into a mountain where Jesus had appointed them. ^{17} And when they saw him, they worshipped him: but some doubted. ^{18} And Jesus came and spake unto them, saying, "All power is given unto me in heaven and in earth. ^{19} Go ye therefore, and teach all nations, baptizing them in the name of the Father, and of the Son, and of the Holy Ghost: ^{20} Teaching them to observe all things whatsoever I have commanded you: and, lo, I am with you always, even unto the end of the world. Amen."

On the Road to Emmaus①

Luke 24

...

^{13} And, behold, two of them went that same day to a village called Emmaus, which was from Jerusalem about threescore furlongs. ^{14} And they talked together of all these things which had happened. ^{15} And it came to pass, that, while they communed together and reasoned, Jesus himself drew near, and went with them. ^{16} But their eyes were holden that they should not know him.

^{17} And he said unto them, "What manner of communications are these that ye have one to another, as ye walk, and are sad?"

^{18} And the one of them, whose name was Cleopas, answering said unto him, "Art thou only a stranger in

The Emmaus Disciples, 1622, Abraham Bloemaert

---

① **Emmaus** /iˈmeiəs/，以马忤斯。

Jerusalem, and hast not known the things which are come to pass there in these days?"

^{19}And he said unto them, "What things?"

And they said unto him, "Concerning Jesus of Nazareth, which was a prophet mighty in deed and word before God and all the people: ^{20}And how the chief priests and our rulers delivered him to be condemned to death, and have crucified him. ^{21}But we trusted that it had been he which should have redeemed Israel: and besides all this, to day is the third day since these things were done. ^{22}Yea, and certain women also of our company made us astonished, which were early at the sepulchre; ^{23}And when they found not his body, they came, saying, that they had also seen a vision of angels, which said that he was alive. ^{24}And certain of them which were with us went to the sepulchre, and found it even so as the women had said: but him they saw not." ^{25}Then he said unto them, "O fools, and slow of heart to believe all that the prophets have spoken: ^{26}Ought not Christ to have suffered these things, and to enter into his glory? ^{27}And beginning at Moses and all the prophets, he expounded unto them in all the scriptures the things concerning himself. ^{28}And they drew nigh unto the village, whither they went: and he made as though he would have gone further." ^{29}But they constrained him, saying, "Abide with us: for it is toward evening, and the day is far spent." And he went in to tarry with them.

^{30}And it came to pass, as he sat at meat with them, he took bread, and blessed it, and brake, and gave to them. ^{31}And their eyes were opened, and they knew him; and he vanished out of their sight. ^{32}And they said one to another, "Did not our heart burn within us, while he talked with us by the way, and while he opened to us the scriptures?"

^{33}And they rose up the same hour, and returned to Jerusalem, and found the eleven gathered together, and them that were with them, ^{34}Saying, "The Lord is risen indeed, and hath appeared to Simon." ^{35}And they told what things were done in the way, and how he was known of them in breaking of bread.

Jesus Appears to the Disciples

^{36}And as they thus spake, Jesus himself stood in the midst of them, and saith unto them, "Peace be unto you."

^{37}But they were terrified and affrighted, and supposed that they had seen a spirit. ^{38}And he said unto them, "Why are ye troubled? And why do thoughts arise in your hearts? ^{39}Behold my hands and my feet, that it is I myself: handle me, and see; for a spirit hath not flesh and bones, as ye see me have."

^{40}And when he had thus spoken, he shewed them his hands and his feet. ^{41}And while they yet believed not for joy, and wondered, he said unto them, "Have ye here any meat?" ^{42}And they gave him a piece of a broiled fish, and of an honeycomb. ^{43}And he took it, and did eat before them.

^{44}And he said unto them, "These are the words which I spake unto you, while I was yet with you, that all things must be

Christ Appearing to the Apostles after the Resurrection, c. 1795, William Blake

fulfilled, which were written in the law of Moses, and in the prophets, and in the psalms, concerning me." ^{45}Then opened he their understanding, that they might understand the scriptures, ^{46}And said unto them, "Thus it is written, and thus it behoved Christ to suffer, and to rise from the dead the third day: ^{47}And that repentance and remission of sins should be preached in his name among all nations, beginning at Jerusalem. ^{48}And ye are witnesses of these things. ^{49}And, behold, I send the promise of my Father upon you: but tarry ye in the city of Jerusalem, until ye be endued with power from on high."

^{50}And he led them out as far as to Bethany, and he lifted up his hands, and blessed them. ^{51}And it came to pass, while he blessed them, he was parted from them, and carried up into heaven. ^{52}And they worshipped him, and returned to Jerusalem with great joy: ^{53}And were continually in the temple, praising and blessing God. Amen.

Jesus Appears to Mary Magdalene

John 20

...

^{10}Then the disciples went away again unto their own home. ^{11}But Mary stood without at the sepulchre weeping: and as she wept, she stooped down, and looked into the sepulchre, ^{12}And seeth two angels in white sitting, the one at the head, and the other at the feet, where the body of Jesus had lain. ^{13}And they say unto her, "Woman, why weepest thou?" She saith unto them, "Because they have taken away my LORD, and I know not where they have laid him." ^{14}And when she had thus said, she turned herself back, and saw Jesus standing, and knew not that it was Jesus.

^{15}Jesus saith unto her, "Woman, why weepest thou? Whom seekest thou?"

She, supposing him to be the gardener, saith unto him, "Sir, if thou have borne him hence, tell me where thou hast laid him, and I will take him away."

^{16}Jesus saith unto her, "Mary." She turned herself, and saith unto him, "Rabboni; which is to say, Master."

The Appearance of Christ to Mary Magdalene, 1834—1836, Alexander Andreyevich Ivanov

^{17}Jesus saith unto her, "Touch me not; for I am not yet ascended to my Father: but go to my brethren, and say unto them, I ascend unto my Father, and your Father; and to my God, and your God."

^{18}Mary Magdalene came and told the disciples that she had seen the LORD, and that he had spoken these things unto her.

...

Doubting Thomas

^{24}But Thomas, one of the twelve, called Didymus, was not with them when Jesus came. ^{25}The other disciples therefore said unto him, "We have seen the LORD."

But he said unto them, "Except I shall see in his hands the print of the nails, and put my finger into the print of the nails, and thrust my hand into his side, I will not believe."

^{26}And after eight days again his disciples were within, and Thomas with them: then came Jesus, the doors being shut, and stood in the midst, and said, "Peace be unto you." ^{27}Then saith he to Thomas, "Reach hither thy finger, and behold my hands; and reach hither thy hand, and thrust it into my side: and be not faithless, but believing."

^{28}And Thomas answered and said unto him, "My LORD and my God."

^{29}Jesus saith unto him, "Thomas, because thou hast seen me, thou hast believed: blessed are they that have not seen, and yet have believed."

The Incredulity of St. Thomas, c. 1601—1602, Caravaggio

^{30}And many other signs truly did Jesus in the presence of his disciples, which are not written in this book: ^{31}But these are written, that ye might believe that Jesus is the Christ, the Son of God; and that believing ye might have life through his name.

The Bible in Everyday English: *Doubting Thomas*

For Thomas, Jesus' disciple, touching is believing. When he saw his resurrected master, he refused to believe his eyes and demanded to feel Jesus' wounds. A doubting Thomas now refers to a person who refuses to believe anything until concrete proof is provided.

Jesus Reinstates Peter

John 21

...

¹⁵ So when they had dined, Jesus saith to Simon Peter, "Simon, son of Jonas, lovest thou me more than these?"

He saith unto him, "Yea, Lord; thou knowest that I love thee."

He saith unto him, "Feed my lambs."

¹⁶ He saith to him again the second time, "Simon, son of Jonas, lovest thou me?"

He saith unto him, "Yea, Lord; thou knowest that I love thee."

He saith unto him, "Feed my sheep."

¹⁷ He saith unto him the third time, "Simon, son of Jonas, lovest thou me?"

Peter was grieved because he said unto him the third time, "Lovest thou me?" And he said unto him, "Lord, thou knowest all things; thou knowest that I love thee."

Jesus saith unto him, "Feed my sheep." ¹⁸ Verily, verily, I say unto thee, "When thou wast young, thou girdest thyself, and walkedst whither thou wouldest: but when thou shalt be old, thou shalt stretch forth thy hands, and another shall gird thee, and carry thee whither thou wouldest not." ¹⁹ This spake he, signifying by what death he should glorify God. And when he had spoken this, he saith unto him, "Follow me."

²⁰ Then Peter, turning about, seeth the disciple whom Jesus loved following; which also leaned on his breast at supper, and said, "Lord, which is he that betrayeth thee?" ²¹ Peter seeing him saith to Jesus, "Lord, and what shall this man do?"

²² Jesus saith unto him, "If I will that he tarry till I come, what is that to thee? Follow thou me." ²³ Then went this saying abroad among the brethren, that that disciple should not die: yet Jesus said not unto him, "He shall not die"; but, "If I will that he tarry till I come, what is that to thee?" ²⁴ This is the disciple which testifieth of these things, and wrote these things: and we know that his testimony is true. ²⁵ And there are also many other things which Jesus did, the which, if they should be written every one, I suppose that even the world itself could not contain the books that should be written. Amen.

III FOOD FOR THOUGHT

1. Who did Jesus first appear to after he arose from the dead? What is the significance of this?
2. What does the great commission (*Mt. 28:18—20*) show about the tradition of Christianity?
3. Read the guillotining scene of *A Tale of Two Cities* and relate it to the resurrection of Jesus.

IV BIBLICAL RELEVANCE

A. Biblical Terms in Everyday English
1. maudlin (from Magdalene): _____
2. doubting Thomas: _____

B. Biblical References in Literature
The love of country in all the Italian poets and romancers of the long period of the national resurrection ennobled their art in a measure which criticism has not yet taken account of.

(William Dean Howells, *My Literary Passions*, 1895)

C. The Bible and Arts
1. Resurrection
   The Resurrection, After Hans Memling
   The Walk to Emmaus, c. 1565—1575, Orsi Lelio
   The Emmaus Disciples, 1622, Abraham Bloemaert
   Christ Appearing to the Apostles after the Resurrection, c. 1795, William Blake
   The Appearance of Christ to Mary Magdalene, 1834—1836, Alexander Andreyevich Ivanov
   Landscape with Noli Me Tangere Scene, 1681, Lorrain Claude
   The Transfiguration, 1518—1520, Raphael
   The Incredulity of St. Thomas, Caravaggio
2. *Advent and Triumph of Christ*, 1480, Hans Memling
3. *Scenes from the Passion of Christ*, 1470—1471, Hans Memling

V SOURCES FOR REFERENCE

1. (1964). *The Gospel According to St. Matthew*. An Italian film directed by Pier Paolo Pasolini.
2. (1973). *Jesus Christ Superstar*. An American film adaptation of the Andrew Lloyd Webber/Tim Rice rock opera of the same name.
3. (1977). *Jesus of Nazareth*. An Anglo-Italian television miniseries co-written (with Anthony Burgess and Suso Cecchi d'Amico) and directed by Franco Zeffirelli.
4. (2007). *The Lost Tomb of Jesus*. A documentary co-produced and first broadcast on the Discovery Channel, covering the discovery of the Talpiot Tomb.
5. Maas, A. (1911). "Resurrection of Jesus Christ." In *The Catholic Encyclopedia*. New York: Robert Appleton Company. Retrieved January 25, 2012 from New Advent: http://www.newadvent.org/cathen/12789a.htm.
6. Schippe, C. & C. Stetson. (2005). *The Bible and Its Influence*. Front Royal, VA: BLP Publishing.

THE ACTS OF APOSTLES

36. APOSTLES EMPOWERED BY THE HOLY SPIRIT

I POINTS OF DEPARTURE

The Acts of the Apostles tells the story of the origin and growth of the Christian church from the time of Christ's ascension to Paul's final imprisonment in Rome. It follows an outward expansion of the early church from Jerusalem to Judea and Samaria to Rome, the capital of the Roman Empire. References to the Acts in early Christian literature regard it as the work of Luke, author of the third gospel, evidenced by the same Greek style, the dedication to Theophilus (*Lk. 1:3; Ac. 1:1*), and the author's slip into the first plural (*Ac. 16:10—17; 20:5—15; 21:1—18; 27:1—28:16*) suggesting Luke's presence at the events described, which fits in with Paul's reference to Luke in his letters (*Col. 4:14; Phm. 23—24*) (Browning, 2009:187). In point of fact, the Acts picks up the narrative threads and literary forms of the Gospel of Luke with lots of parallels. There are the journey theme in the *Acts* though of a larger scope and healings and the raising of people from the dead. It seems that the Book of Acts repeats what Jesus did except through his apostles, empowered by the Holy Spirit.

The Acts begins with the ascension of Jesus. There are two Old Testament stories of Enoch (*Gen. 5:24*) and Elijah (*2 Kgs. 2:11*) that form the background of the accounts. And a shorter version is found in *Luke 24:50—53*. Jesus' appearances after Easter as recorded by Luke have a more "solid" "corporeal" and evidential nature than elsewhere in the New Testament, even though the risen body could pass through doors. It was necessary for Luke to explain that the appearances would cease and be replaced by the presence in the Church of the Holy Spirit, and his solution was to use the Jewish Festival of Pentecost, which recalls the 50 days after the first Passover that Moses spent reaching Sinai and the making of the Sinai Covenant as the occasion for a renewal of that covenant and signifies the termination of resurrection appearances and the completion of Jesus' work of redemption and his ascendancy in a Messianic kingdom over all things.

II SELECTED READINGS

Christ's Ascension into Heaven

Acts 1

1 In the former treatise, O Theophilus, I have given an account of all that Jesus began both to do and teach, ² *Until the day in which He was taken up, after He had given commandments through the Holy Ghost unto the apostles, whom He had chosen.* ³ *To these also He showed Himself alive after His passion by many infallible proofs, being seen by them forty days, and speaking of the things pertaining to the Kingdom of God.* ⁴ *And being assembled together with them, He commanded them that they should not depart from Jerusalem, but wait for the promise of the Father,* " *which,*" *saith He,* " *ye have heard from Me;* ⁵ *For John truly baptized with water, but ye shall be baptized with the Holy Ghost not many days hence.*"

The Ascension, 1636,
van Rijn Rembrandt

⁶ *When they therefore had come together, they asked of Him, saying,* " *Lord, wilt Thou at this time restore again the kingdom to Israel?*"
⁷ *And He said unto them,* " *It is not for you to know the times or the seasons which the Father hath put in His own power.* ⁸ *But ye shall receive power after the Holy Ghost is come upon you; and ye shall be witnesses unto Me both in Jerusalem, and in all Judea and in Samaria, and unto the uttermost part of the earth.*"
⁹ *And when He had spoken these things, while they beheld, He was taken up, and a cloud received Him out of their sight.*
¹⁰ *And while they looked steadfastly toward heaven as He went up, behold, two men stood by them in white apparel,* ¹¹ *Who also said,* " *Ye men of Galilee, why stand ye gazing up into heaven? This same Jesus, who is taken up from you into Heaven, shall so come in like manner as ye have seen Him go into Heaven.*"

...

The Descent of the Holy Ghost

Acts 2

¹ *And when the day of Pentecost*① *was fully come, they were all with one accord in one place.* ² *And suddenly there came a sound from heaven as of a rushing mighty wind, and it filled all the house where they were sitting.* ³ *And there appeared unto them cloven tongues as of fire, and it sat upon each of them.* ⁴ *And they were all filled with the Holy Ghost and began to speak in other tongues, as the Spirit gave them utterance.*

⁵ *And there were dwelling at Jerusalem Jews, devout men out of every nation under heaven.* ⁶ *Now when this was noised abroad, the multitude came together and were confounded, because every man heard them speaking in his own language.* ⁷ *And they were all amazed and marveled, saying one to another,* " *Behold, are not all these who speak Galileans?* ⁸ *And how then do we each hear them speaking in our own tongue wherein we were born?* ⁹ *Parthians, Medes, Elamites and the dwellers in Mesopotamia, and in Judea and Cappadocia, Pontus and Asia,* ¹⁰ *Phrygia and Pamphylia, in Egypt and in the parts of Libya about Cyrene, and strangers from Rome, both Jews and proselytes,* ¹¹ *Cretans and Arabians — we hear them speak in our own tongues the wonderful works of God.*" ¹² *And they were all amazed and were in doubt, saying one to another,* " *What meaneth this?*"

¹³ *Others mocking said,* " *These men are full of new wine.*"

Peter's Sermon

¹⁴ *But Peter, standing up with the eleven, lifted up his voice and said unto them,* " *Ye men of Judea and all ye who dwell in Jerusalem, be this known unto you, and hearken to my words.* ¹⁵ *For these are not drunken as ye suppose, seeing it is but the third hour of the day;* ¹⁶ *but this is that which was spoken by the prophet Joel:*

---

① **Pentecost** (/ˈpentikɔst/, 圣灵降临节) Greek, "fiftieth," i. e. fifty days after Passover. It falls on the seventh Sunday after Easter, commemorating the descent of the Holy Spirit upon the disciples.

¹⁷ " ' And it shall come to pass in the last days, saith God,
I will pour out My Spirit upon all flesh;
and your sons and your daughters shall prophesy,
and your young men shall see visions,
and your old men shall dream dreams.
¹⁸ And on My servants and
on My handmaidens
I will pour out in those days My Spirit,
and they shall prophesy.
¹⁹ And I will show wonders in heaven above,
and signs in the earth beneath —
blood and fire and vapor of smoke.
²⁰ The sun shall be turned into darkness,
and the moon into blood
before that great and
notable Day of the Lord come.
²¹ And it shall come to pass that whosoever shall call
on the name of the Lord shall be saved.' ②
²² " Ye men of Israel, hear these words: Jesus of Nazareth, a Man approved of God among you by miracles, wonders, and signs, which God did through Him in the midst of you, as ye yourselves also know — ²³ Him, being delivered by the determinate will and foreknowledge of God, ye have taken and by wicked hands have crucified and slain. ²⁴ But God hath raised Him up, having loosed the pains of death, because it was not possible that He should be held by it. ²⁵ For David speaketh concerning Him:
' I beheld the Lord always before my face,
for He is on my right hand,
that I should not be moved.
²⁶ Therefore did my heart rejoice, and my tongue was glad;
moreover also my flesh shall rest in hope,
²⁷ Because Thou wilt not leave my soul in hell,
neither wilt Thou suffer Thine Holy One to see corruption.
²⁸ Thou hast made known to me the ways of life;
Thou shalt make me full of joy with Thy countenance.'
²⁹ " Men and brethren, let me freely speak unto you of the patriarch David, that he is both dead and buried, and his sepulcher is with us unto this day. ³⁰ Therefore, being a prophet and knowing that God had sworn an oath to him that from the fruit of his loins, according to the flesh He would raise up Christ to sit on his throne, ³¹ David, foreseeing this, spoke concerning the resurrection of Christ that ' His soul was not left in hell, neither did His flesh see corruption.' ³² This Jesus hath God raised up, of which we are all witnesses. ³³ Therefore, being exalted by the right hand of God, and having received from the Father the promise of the Holy Ghost, He hath shed forth this which ye now see and hear. ³⁴ For David is not ascended into the heavens, but he himself saith, ' The LORD said unto my Lord,
Sit Thou on My right hand
³⁵ Until I make Thy foes Thy footstool.' "
³⁶ " Therefore let all the house of Israel know assuredly that God hath made that same Jesus, whom ye have crucified, both Lord and Christ."
³⁷ Now when they heard this, they were pricked in their heart, and said unto Peter and to the rest of the apostles, " Men and brethren, what shall we do?"
³⁸ Then Peter said unto them, " Repent and be baptized, every one of you, in the name of Jesus Christ for

---

② 17—28 Joel 2:28—32.

the remission of sins; and ye shall receive the gift of the Holy Ghost. ³⁹ For the promise is unto you, and to your children, and to all who are afar off, even as many as the Lord our God shall call."

⁴⁰ And with many other words did he testify and exhort, saying, "Save yourselves from this untoward generation." ⁴¹ Then those who gladly received his words were baptized, and that same day there were added unto them about three thousand souls.

The Fellowship of the Believers

⁴² And they continued steadfastly in the apostles' doctrine and fellowship, and in the breaking of bread and in prayers. ⁴³ And fear came upon every soul, and many wonders and signs were done by the apostles. ⁴⁴ And all who believed were together and had all things in common, ⁴⁵ And they sold their possessions and goods and divided them among all men, as every man had need. ⁴⁶ And continuing daily with one accord in the temple, and breaking bread from house to house, they ate their meat with gladness and singleness of heart, ⁴⁷ Praising God and having favor with all the people. And the Lord added to the church daily such as should be saved.

III FOOD FOR THOUGHT

1. How can you account for the fact that the Acts begin with Jesus' ascension?
2. The beginning of Chapter 2 is reminiscent of the Tower of Babel (*Genesis 11:1—9*). But what is the difference?
3. How had Peter changed since the day when he denied Jesus three times?

IV BIBLICAL RELEVANCE

A. Biblical Terms in Everyday English
1. the Field of Blood, Akeldama (1:19): _____
2. go to one's own place (1:25): _____
3. speak in tongues (2:1—13): _____

B. Biblical References in Literature
From the chimneys of the farmhouses thin ascensions of blue smoke signaled preparations for a day's peaceful toil. (Ambrose Bierce, *Can Such Things Be*?)

C. The Bible and Arts
1. *Ascension of Christ*, 1520, Garofalo
2. *Pentecost*, c. 1597—1600, El Greco
3. *The Ascension*, 1636, van Rijn Rembrandt

V SOURCES FOR REFERENCE

1. (2007). *Biblica: The Bible Atlas*. London: New Holland Publications (UK) Ltd.
2. Browning, W. R. E. (2009). *A Dictionary of the Bible*. Oxford: Oxford University Press.
3. [加]菲(Gorden Fee),[美]斯图尔特(Douglas Stuart):《圣经导读》(下)(*How to Read the Bible Book by Book*),北京:北京大学出版社,2005年。

37. PREACHING IN JERUSALEM

POINTS OF DEPARTURE

In the stories of the early Jerusalem community that follow the Pentecost story, two apostles take particular priority: Simon Peter and John, son of Zebedee. Striking are the parallels between the activity of these apostles and the ministry of Jesus. The risen Christ continues his teaching and healing activity through the Church. Hence much of Peter and John's work occurs in Herodian Jerusalem, especially its Temple, echoing Jesus' activity there in *Luke 20—21*. The healing of the lame man echoes a similar healing by Jesus at *Luke 5:18—26*.

Religious communities held together by the gospel and by a rule of life were in the making (*Ac. 4*), which have inspired Western monastic tradition and profoundly influenced the history of Western civilization. *Ac. 5:1—11* is a "cautionary tale" of how the couple of Ananias and Sapp'ira met their unnatural deaths for violating the communal rule of the sharing of possessions. After the incident, Luke wrote how "great fear came upon all the church, and upon as many as heard these things." (*Ac. 5:11*)

The choosing of seven Grecian Jews to take care of serving the physical needs of the groups (*Ac. 6:1—6*) shows considerable diplomacy of the apostles intended to draw more followers to the Church. To prove the wisdom of their choice, the first Christian martyr, Stephen, was to come out of this group of seven.

As seen in the Book of Acts, the Roman government turned a blind eye as Jewish authorities persecuted and executed people who practiced a religion that deviated from the Jewish faith. Stephen's spiritual successes led the Jewish authorities to arrest him and bring him to trial. To defend himself, Stephen gave a long sermon, highlighting the Old Testament history with a list of names in the Hebraic hall of fame — Abraham, Joseph, Moses, Joshua, David, Solomon, and the prophets. He concluded his speech with a stinging rebuke of his accusers. Then Stephen was stoned to death, becoming the "first martyr of the Christian community," and also marking the discrete entry of Paul of Tarsus onto the stage of *Acts*.

II SELECTED READINGS

Peter and John before the Sanhedrin

Acts 4

⁸*Then Peter, filled with the Holy Ghost, said unto them, " Ye rulers of the people, and elders of Israel,* ⁹*If we this day be examined of the good deed done to the impotent man, by what means he is made whole;* ¹⁰*Be*

it known unto you all, and to all the people of Israel, that by the name of Jesus Christ of Nazareth, whom ye crucified, whom God raised from the dead, even by him doth this man stand here before you whole. ¹¹ This is the stone which was set at nought of you builders, which is become the head of the corner.

¹² Neither is there salvation in any other: for there is none other name under heaven given among men, whereby we must be saved."

...

Common Life

³² And the multitude of them that believed were of one heart and of one soul: neither said any of them that ought of the things which he possessed was his own; but they had all things common. ³³ And with great power gave the apostles witness of the resurrection of the Lord Jesus: and great grace was upon them all. ³⁴ Neither was there any among them that lacked: for as many as were possessors of lands or houses sold them, and brought the prices of the things that were sold, ³⁵ And laid them down at the apostles' feet: and distribution was made unto every man according as he had need.

³⁶ And Joses, who by the apostles was surnamed Barnabas, (which is, being interpreted, The son of consolation,) a Levite, and of the country of Cyprus, ³⁷ Having land, sold it, and brought the money, and laid it at the apostles' feet.

Ananias① and Sapp'ira②

Acts 5

¹ But a certain man named Ananias, with Sapphira his wife, sold a possession. ² And kept back part of the price, his wife also being privy to it, and brought a certain part, and laid it at the apostles' feet.

³ But Peter said, "Ananias, why hath Satan filled thine heart to lie to the Holy Ghost, and to keep back part of the price of the land? ⁴ Whiles it remained, was it not thine own? And after it was sold, was it not in thine own power? Why hast thou conceived this thing in thine heart? Thou hast not lied unto men, but unto God."

The Death of Ananias, c. 1515/1516, Raffaello Sanzio Raphael

⁵ And Ananias hearing these words fell down, and gave up the ghost: and great fear came on all them that heard these things. ⁶ And the young men arose wound him up, and carried him out, and buried him.

⁷ And it was about the space of three hours after, when his wife, not knowing what was done, came in. ⁸ And Peter answered unto her, "Tell me whether ye sold the land for so much?"

And she said, "Yea, for so much."

⁹ Then Peter said unto her, "How is it that ye have agreed together to tempt the Spirit of the Lord? Behold, the feet of them which have buried thy husband are at the door, and shall carry thee out."

¹⁰ Then fell she down straightway at his feet, and yielded up the ghost: and the young men came in, and found her dead, and, carrying her forth, buried her by her husband. ¹¹ And great fear came upon all the church, and upon as many as heard these things.

---

① **Ananias** /ˌænəˈnaɪəs/, 亚拿尼亚。
② **Sapp'ira** /sæˈfaɪərə/, 撒非喇。

The Apostles Heal Many

¹² And by the hands of the apostles were many signs and wonders wrought among the people, ¹³ And more believers were added to the Lord, multitudes both of men and women, ¹⁴ Insomuch that they brought forth the sick into the streets and laid them on beds and couches, ¹⁵ that at least the shadow of Peter passing by might overshadow some of them. ¹⁶ There came also a multitude out of the cities round about unto Jerusalem, bringing sick folks and those who were vexed with unclean spirits; and they were healed, every one.

The Apostles Persecuted

¹⁷ Then the high priest rose up and all those who were with him (which is the sect of the Sadducees); and they were filled with indignation, ¹⁸ And laid their hands on the apostles, and put them in the common prison. ¹⁹ But the angel of the Lord by night opened the prison doors, and brought them forth and said, ²⁰ " Go, stand and speak in the temple to the people all the words of this Life."

²¹ And when they heard that, they entered into the temple early in the morning and taught.

But the high priest came, and those who were with him, and called the council together with all the senate of the children of Israel, and sent to the prison to have them brought. ²² But when the officers came and found them not in the prison, they returned and reported, saying, ²³ " The prison truly found we shut with all safety and the keepers standing outside before the doors; but when we had opened them, we found no man within." ²⁴ Now when the high priest and the captain of the temple and the chief priests heard these things, they were in doubt about them as to where this would grow.

²⁵ Then there came one and told them, saying, " Behold, the men whom ye put in prison are standing in the temple and teaching the people." ²⁶ Then the captain went with his officers and brought them without violence, for they feared the people, lest they should be stoned.

²⁷ And when they had brought them, they set them before the council. And the high priest asked them, ²⁸ saying, " Did not we strictly command you that ye should not teach in this name? And behold, ye have filled Jerusalem with your doctrine and intend to bring this man's blood upon us."

²⁹ Then Peter and the other apostles answered and said, " We ought to obey God rather than men. ³⁰ The God of our fathers raised up Jesus, whom ye slew and hanged on a tree. ³¹ Him hath God exalted with His right hand to be a Prince and a Savior, to give repentance to Israel and forgiveness of sins. ³² And we are His witnesses of these things, and so is also the Holy Ghost, whom God hath given to those who obey Him."

³³ When they heard this, they were cut to the heart and took counsel to slay them. ³⁴ Then there stood up one in the council, a Pharisee named Gamaliel, a doctor of the law held in high repute among all the people, and commanded them to put the apostles outside a little while. ³⁵ And he said unto them, " Ye men of Israel, take heed to yourselves what ye intend to do concerning these men. ³⁶ For before these days Theudas rose up, boasting himself to be somebody, to whom a number of men, about four hundred, joined themselves. He was slain, and all who obeyed him were scattered and brought to nought. ³⁷ After this man, rose up Judas of Galilee in the days of the taxing, and drew away many people after him. He also perished, and all who obeyed him were dispersed. ³⁸ And now I say unto you, refrain from these men and let them alone, for if this counsel or this work be of men, it will come to nought; ³⁹ But if it be of God, ye cannot overthrow it, lest it may happen ye be found even to fight against God."

⁴⁰ And with him they agreed. And when they had called the apostles back and had beaten them, they commanded that they should not speak in the name of Jesus, and let them go.

⁴¹ And they departed from the presence of the council, rejoicing that they were counted worthy to suffer shame for His name. ⁴² And daily in the temple and in every house, they ceased not to teach and preach Jesus Christ.

The Choosing of the Seven

Acts 6

¹ And in those days when the number of the disciples was multiplied, there arose a murmuring of the Grecians against the Hebrews, because their widows were neglected in the daily ministration. ² Then the twelve called the multitude of the disciples unto them and said, "It is not fitting that we should leave the Word of God to serve tables. ³ Therefore, brethren, look ye out among you for seven men of honest report, full of the Holy Ghost and wisdom, whom we may appoint over this business. ⁴ But we will give ourselves continually to prayer and to the ministry of the Word."

⁵ And the saying pleased the whole multitude. And they chose Stephen, a man full of faith and of the Holy Ghost, and Philip and Prochorus and Nicanor, and Timon and Parmenas and Nicolaus, a proselyte of Antioch③, ⁶ Whom they set before the apostles. And when they had prayed, they laid their hands on them.

⁷ And the Word of God increased; and the number of the disciples multiplied in Jerusalem greatly, and a great company of the priests were obedient to the faith.

Stephen Seized

⁸ And Stephen④, full of faith and power, did great wonders and miracles among the people. ⁹ Then there arose certain from the synagogue which is called the Synagogue of the Libertines, and Cyrenians and Alexandrians, and those of Cilicia and of Asia, and they disputed with Stephen. ¹⁰ And they were not able to resist the wisdom and the Spirit by which he spoke.

¹¹ Then they suborned men who said, "We have heard him speak blasphemous words against Moses and against God."

¹² And they stirred up the people and the elders and the scribes, and came upon him and caught him, and brought him to the council. ¹³ And they set up false witnesses who said, "This man ceaseth not to speak blasphemous words against this holy place and the law; ¹⁴ For we have heard him say that this Jesus of Nazareth shall destroy this place, and shall change the customs which Moses delivered to us."

¹⁵ And all who sat on the council, looking steadfastly on him, saw his face as though it were the face of an angel.

Stephen's Speech to the Sanhedrin

Acts 7

¹ Then said the high priest, "Are these things so?"

² And he said, "Men, brethren and fathers, hearken! The God of glory appeared unto our father Abraham, when he was in Mesopotamia, before he dwelt in Charran. ³ And said unto him, 'Get thee out thy country, and thy kindred, and come into the land which I shall shew thee.'

⁴ "Then came he out of the land of the Chaldaeans, and dwelt in Charran; and from thence, when his father was dead, he removed him into this land, wherein ye now dwell. ⁵ And he gave him none inheritance in it, no, not so much as to set his foot on, yet he promised that he would give it to him for a possession, and to his seed after him, when as yet he had no child. ⁶ And God spake on this wise, that his seed should sojourn in a strange land; and that they should bring them into bondage, and entreat them evil four hundred years. ⁷ And the nation to whom they shall be in bondage will I judge, said God; and after that shall they come forth, and serve me in this place. ⁸ And he gave him the convenant of circumcision; and so Abraham begat Isaac, and

---

③ **Antioch** (/ˈæntiɔk/, 安提克) an ancient town of Phrygia, north of present-day Antalya, Turkey, once famous as a center of Hellenistic influence.

④ **Stephen** /ˈstiːvən/, 司提反。

circumcised him the eighth day; and Isaac begat Jacob; and Jacob begat the twelve patriarchs.

⁹ "And the patriarchs, moved with envy, sold Joseph into Egypt: but God was with him, ¹⁰ And delivered him out of all his afflictions, and gave him favour and wisdom in the sight of Pharaoh king of Egypt and all his house.

¹¹ "Now there came a dearth over all the land of Egypt and Chanaan, and great affliction: and our fathers found no sustenance. ¹² But when Jacob heard that there was corn in Egypt, he sent out our fathers first. ¹³ And at the second time Joseph was made known to his brethren; and Joseph's kindred was made known unto Pharaoh. ¹⁴ Then sent Joseph,

St. Stephen Preaching and St. Stephen Addressing the Council, 1447—1449, Fra Angelico

and called his father Jacob to him, and all his kindred, threescore and fifteen souls. ¹⁵ So Jacob went down into Egypt, and died, he, and our fathers. ¹⁶ And were carried over into Sychem, and laid in the sepulcher that Abraham bought for a sum of money of the sons of Emmor the father of Sychem.

¹⁷ "But when the time of the promise drew nigh, which God had sworn to Abraham, the people grew and multiplied in Egypt. ¹⁸ Till another king arose, which knew no Joseph. ¹⁹ The same dealt subtilly with our kindred, and evil entreated our fathers, so that they cast out their young children, to the end they might not live."

²⁰ "In which time Moses was born, and was exceedingly fair, and nourished up in his father's house three months. ²¹ And when he was cast out, Pharaoh's daughter took him up, and nourished him for her own son. ²² And Moses was learned in all the wisdom of the Egyptians, and was mighty in words and in deeds.

²³ "And when he was full forty years old, it came into his heart to visit his brethren the children of Israel. ²⁴ And seeing one of them suffer wrong, he defended him, and avenged him that was oppressed, and smote the Egyptian. ²⁵ For he supposed his brethren would have understood how that God by his hand would deliver them: but they understood him not. ²⁶ And the next day he shewed himself unto them as they strove, and would have set them at one again, saying, 'Sirs, ye are brethren; why do ye wrong one to another?'

²⁷ "But he that did his neighbour wrong thrust him away, saying, 'Who made thee a ruler and a judge over us? ²⁸ Wilt thou kill me, as thou diddest the Egyptian yesterday.' ²⁹ Then fled Moses at this saying, and was a stranger in the land of Madian, where he begat two sons.

³⁰ "And when forty years were expired, there appeared to him in the wilderness of mount Sina an angle of the Lord in a flame of fire in a bush. ³¹ When Moses saw it, he wondered at the sight: and as he drew near to behold it, the voice of the Lord came unto him? ³² Saying, 'I am the God of thy fathers, the God of Abraham, and the God of Isaac, and the God of Jacob. Then Moses trembled, and durst not behold.'

³³ "Then said the Lord to him, 'Put off thy shoes from thy feet, for the place where thou standest is holy ground. ³⁴ I have seen, I have seen the affliction of my people which is in Egypt, and I have heard their groaning, and am come down to deliver them. And now come, I will send thee into Egypt.'

³⁵ "This Moses whom they refused, saying, 'Who made thee a ruler and a judge? The same did God send to be ruler and a deliverer by the hand of the angel which appeared to him in the bush. ³⁶ He brought them out, after that he had shewed wonders and signs in the land of Egypt, and in the Red Sea, and in the wilderness forty years. ³⁷ This is what Moses, which said unto the children of Israel, 'A prophet shall the Lord your God raise up unto you of your brethren, like unto me; him shall ye hear.' ³⁸ "This is he, that was in the church in the wilderness with the angel which spake to him in the mount Sina, and with our fathers: who received the lively oracles to give unto us:

³⁹ "To whom our fathers would not obey, but thrust him from them, and in their hearts turned back again into Egypt. ⁴⁰ Saying unto Aaron, 'Make us gods to go before us: for as for this Moses, which brought

us out of the land of Egypt, we wot not what is become of him.'⑤ ⁴¹ And they made a calf in those days, and offered sacrifice unto the idol, and rejoiced in the works of their own hands. ⁴² Then God turned, and gave them up to worship the host of heaven; as it is written in the book of the prophets,

' O ye house of Israel,
have ye offered to me slain beasts and sacrifices
by the space of forty years in the wilderness.
⁴³ Yea, ye took up the tabernacle of Moloch,
and the star of your god Remphan,
figures which ye made to worship them,
and I will carry you away beyond Bebylon.'

⁴⁴ " Our fathers had the tabernacle of witness in the wilderness, as he had appointed, speaking unto Moses, that he should make it according to the fashion that he had seen. ⁴⁵ Which also our fathers that came after brought in with Jesus into the possession of the Gentiles, whom God drave out before the face of our fathers, unto the days of David; ⁴⁶ Who found favour before God, and desired to find a tabernacle for the God of Jacob. ⁴⁷ But Solomon built him an house.

⁴⁸ " Howbeit the most High dwelleth not in temples made with hands; as saith the prophet,
⁴⁹ ' Heaven is my throne,
and earth is my footstool.
What house will ye build me?
Saith the Lord.
Or what is the place of my rest?
⁵⁰ Hath not my hand made all these things?' ⑥

⁵¹ Ye stiffnecked and uncircumcised in heart and ears, ye do always resist the Holy Ghost: as your fathers did, so do ye. ⁵² Which of the prophets have your fathers not persecuted? And they have slain those who foretold the coming of the Just One. Of Him ye have now been the betrayers and murderers, ⁵³ Ye who have received the law by the disposition of angels, and have not kept it."

The Stoning of Stephen

⁵⁴ When they heard these things, they were cut to the heart, and they gnashed with their teeth at him. ⁵⁵ But he, being full of the Holy Ghost, looked up steadfastly into heaven, and saw the glory of God, and Jesus standing at the right hand of God, ⁵⁶ And he said, " Behold, I see the heavens opened, and the Son of Man standing at the right hand of God."

⁵⁷ Then they cried out with a loud voice, and stopped their ears, and ran upon him with one accord, ⁵⁸ And cast him out of the city and stoned him. And the witnesses laid down their clothes at the feet of a young man whose name was Saul.

⁵⁹ And they stoned Stephen as he called upon God and said, " Lord Jesus, receive my spirit!" ⁶⁰ And he kneeled down and cried with a loud voice, " Lord, charge not this sin against them." And when he had said this, he fell asleep.

The Stoning of Saint Stephen, 1625,
van Rijn Rembrandt

⑤ 40 *Exodus 32:1.*
⑥ 49—50 *Isaiah 66:1, 2.*

III FOOD FOR THOUGHT

1. What is the significance of the choosing of seven from among the Grecian Jews?
2. On what grounds was Stephen accused?
3. Which aspect of the Jewish religious establishment did Stephen denounce in his speech?
4. How was he killed? And by whom?
5. How does Stephen compare with Jesus?

IV BIBLICAL RELEVANCE

A. Biblical Terms in Everyday English
1. the beautiful gate (3:2): _____
2. bring /come to naught /nought (5:35): _____
3. footstool of the Almighty /God's footstool (7:49): _____
4. St. Stephen's bread/loaves: _____

B. Biblical References in Literature
It was so kind and tender of you to give up half a day's work to come and see me! ... You are Joseph the dreamer of dreams, dear Jude. And a tragic Don Quixote. And sometimes you are St. Stephen, who, while they were stoning him, could see Heaven opened.
(Thomas Hardy, *Jude the Obscure*, 1895)

C. The Bible and Arts
1. *The Death of Ananias*, c.1515/16, Raffaello Sanzio Raphael
2. *St. Stephen Preaching* and *St. Stephen Addressing the Council*, 1447—1449, Fra Angelico
3. *The Stoning of Saint Stephen*, 1625, van Rijn Rembrandt
4. *The Martyrdom of St. Stephen*, 1603—1604, Annibale Carracci

V SOURCES FOR REFERENCE

1. Martin, D. B. (2009). "The Acts of the Apostles." In *Introduction to New Testament History and Literature*. Retrieved January 27, 2012 from Academic Earth: http: // academicearth. org /speakers /dale-b-martin & Net Ease: http: //v. 163. com/movie/2010/ 1/L/5/M6GINEV5A_M6GIOCGL5. html
2. Black, M. (ed.) (2001). *Peake's Commentary on the Bible*. London: Routledge.

38. PREACHING IN SAMARIA AND JUDAEA

I POINTS OF DEPARTURE

Chapters 8—12 of the Acts connect the beginnings of the church in Jerusalem (Chs. 1—7), culminating in the martyrdom of Stephen, and the missionary journeys of Paul (Chs. 13—18), and explain how the Christian movement grew from being simply a local sect for Jews to being a distinct international faith for both Jews and Gentiles.

Philip, one of the seven appointed to administer the Church's charity, was the first character in this part, who centered his ministry in Samaria. He was known for extending his ministry to baptizing Simon the magician and a God-fearing Ethiopian eunuch. These events, among other things, show how, from the beginning, Christianity was not confined to one geographical location or culture but spread to the entire world.

The centerpiece of this part is the conversion of Paul. It all happened when Paul, otherwise known as Saul after the Israelite king, was traveling to the city Damascus to arrest the Christians there and bring them bound to Jerusalem. En route, he was struck blind by a light from heaven. Three days later, with the help of Ananias sent by God, he regained his sight; more importantly, he was converted and received the call to follow Jesus as Messiah and take the gospel to the Gentiles. Later in the Acts, he would be called Paul, a sign for his change of heart, recalling how Abram (*Gen. 17:5*) and Jacob (*Gen. 32:28*) acquired their new names. Then because of his effectiveness in bringing others to Christ, the former persecutor became the object of persecution himself. He had to flee Jerusalem.

Meanwhile, Peter, the apostle who had disowned his master Jesus three times, was busy converting people to Christianity, even a hated Roman centurion Cornelius. Before the conversion, Peter had a vision of a sheet full of animals, which God ordered him to kill and eat. This vision and the following conversion suggest that God had removed the barriers he once erected to separate his people from the surrounding nations and Gentile believers must be accepted as full members of the Christian Church (Kistemaker, 1990:378).

This part of the Acts ends in Chapter 12 with Herod Agrippa I's[1] persecution of followers of Jesus, among whom James was the first beheaded. Peter was also arrested and imprisoned but miraculously escaped through the midst of four sentries and the automatically opened iron city gates. It also describes the horrible death of Herod. Herod's persecution did not hinder the growth of early Christianity; instead, it helped win more adherents for the fledgling church.

---

[1] For other Herods, refer to the first footnote in Chapter 28.

II SELECTED READINGS

The Church Persecuted and Scattered

Acts 8

¹And Saul was consenting unto his death. And at that time there was a great persecution against the church which was at Jerusalem; and they were all scattered abroad throughout the regions of Judaea and Samaria, except the apostles. ²And devout men carried Stephen to his burial, and made great lamentation over him. ³As for Saul, he made havock of the church, entering into every house, and haling men and women committed them to prison.

Philip in Samaria

⁴Therefore they that were scattered abroad went every where preaching the word. ⁵Then Philip went down to the city of Samaria, and preached Christ unto them. ⁶And the people with one accord gave heed unto those things which Philip spake, hearing and seeing the miracles which he did. ⁷For unclean spirits, crying with loud voice, came out of many that were possessed with them: and many taken with palsies, and that were lame, were healed. ⁸And there was great joy in that city.

Simon the Sorcerer

⁹But there was a certain man, called Simon, which beforetime in the same city used sorcery, and bewitched the people of Samaria, giving out that himself was some great one: ¹⁰To whom they all gave heed, from the least to the greatest, saying, "This man is the great power of God." ¹¹And to him they had regard, because that of long time he had bewitched them with sorceries. ¹²But when they believed Philip preaching the things concerning the kingdom of God, and the name of Jesus Christ, they were baptized, both men and women. ¹³Then Simon himself believed also: and when he was baptized, he continued with Philip, and wondered, beholding the miracles and signs which were done.
¹⁴Now when the apostles which were at Jerusalem heard that Samaria had received the word of God, they sent unto them Peter and John: ¹⁵Who, when they were come down, prayed for them, that they might receive the Holy Ghost: ¹⁶(For as yet he was fallen upon none of them: only they were baptized in the name of the Lord Jesus.) ¹⁷Then laid they their hands on them, and they received the Holy Ghost.
¹⁸And when Simon saw that through laying on of the apostles' hands the Holy Ghost was given, he offered them money, ¹⁹Saying, "Give me also this power, that on whomsoever I lay hands, he may receive the Holy Ghost." ²⁰But Peter said unto him, "Thy money perish with thee, because thou hast thought that the gift of God may be purchased with money. ²¹Thou hast neither part nor lot in this matter: for thy heart is not right in the sight of God.
²²Repent therefore of this thy wickedness, and pray God, if perhaps the thought of thine heart may be forgiven thee. ²³For I perceive that thou art in the gall of bitterness, and in the bond of iniquity."
²⁴Then answered Simon, and said, "Pray ye to the LORD for me, that none of these things which ye have spoken come upon me."
²⁵And they, when they had testified and preached the word of the Lord, returned to Jerusalem, and preached the gospel in many villages of the Samaritans.

The Ethiopian Eunuch

^{26}And the angel of the Lord spake unto Philip, saying, "Arise, and go toward the south unto the way that goeth down from Jerusalem unto Gaza, which is desert." ^{27}And he arose and went: and, behold, a man of Ethiopia, an eunuch of great authority under Candace queen of the Ethiopians, who had the charge of all her treasure, and had come to Jerusalem for to worship, ^{28}Was returning, and sitting in his chariot read Esaias the prophet. ^{29}Then the Spirit said unto Philip, "Go near, and join thyself to this chariot."

^{30}And Philip ran thither to him, and heard him read the prophet Esaias, and said, "Understandest thou what thou readest?"

^{31}And he said, "How can I, except some man should guide me?" And he desired Philip that he would come up and sit with him.

^{32}The place of the scripture which he read was this,

"He was led as a sheep to the slaughter;
and like a lamb dumb before his shearer,
so opened he not his mouth.

^{33}In his humiliation his judgment was taken away: and who shall declare his generation?
For his life is taken from the earth." ②

The Baptism of the Ethiopian Eunuch, Oswald Fleuss

^{34}And the eunuch answered Philip, and said, "I pray thee, Of whom speaketh the prophet this? Of himself, or of some other man?" ^{35}Then Philip opened his mouth, and began at the same scripture, and preached unto him Jesus.

^{36}And as they went on their way, they came unto a certain water: and the eunuch said, "See, here is water; what doth hinder me to be baptized?" ^{37}And Philip said, "If thou believest with all thine heart, thou mayest." And he answered and said, "I believe that Jesus Christ is the Son of God."

^{38}And he commanded the chariot to stand still: and they went down both into the water, both Philip and the eunuch; and he baptized him. ^{39}And when they were come up out of the water, the Spirit of the Lord caught away Philip, that the eunuch saw him no more: and he went on his way rejoicing. ^{40}But Philip was found at Azotus: and passing through he preached in all the cities, till he came to Caesarea.

The Conversion of Saul

Acts 9

^{1}And Saul, yet breathing out threatenings and slaughter against the disciples of the Lord, went unto the high priest, ^{2}And asked of him letters to the synagogues at Damascus, that if he found any who were of this Way, whether they were men or women, he might bring them bound unto Jerusalem. ^{3}And as he journeyed he came near Damascus, and suddenly there shone round about him a light from heaven. ^{4}And he fell to the earth and heard a voice saying unto him, "Saul, Saul, why persecutest thou Me?"

^{5}And he said, "Who art Thou, Lord?"

And the Lord said, "I am Jesus whom thou persecutest; it is hard for

The Conversion on the Way to Damascus, 1600, Caravaggio

---

② 33 Isaiah 53:7, 8.

thee to kick against the goads." ⁶ And he, trembling and astonished, said, "Lord, what wilt Thou have me to do?" And the Lord said unto him, "Arise and go into the city, and it shall be told thee what thou must do."

⁷ And the men who journeyed with him stood speechless, hearing a voice but seeing no man. ⁸ And Saul arose from the earth, and when his eyes were opened, he could see no man; but they led him by the hand and brought him into Damascus. ⁹ And he was three days without sight, and neither did he eat nor drink.

¹⁰ And there was a certain disciple at Damascus named Ananias. And the Lord said to him in a vision, "Ananias." And he said, "Behold, I am here, Lord."

¹¹ And the Lord said unto him, "Arise and go into the street which is called Straight, and inquire in the house of Judas for the one called Saul of Tarsus; for behold, he prayeth, ¹² And hath seen in a vision a man named Ananias coming in and putting his hand on him, that he might receive his sight."

The Bible in Everyday English: *road to Damascus*

The sudden conversion of the Apostle Paul on the road from Jerusalem to Damascus to arrest Christians has inspired the expression *road to Damascus*, meaning "a sudden turning point in a person's life."

¹³ Then Ananias answered, "Lord, I have heard from many of this man, and how much evil he hath done to Thy saints in Jerusalem.

¹⁴ And here he hath authority from the chief priests to bind all who call on Thy name."

¹⁵ But the Lord said unto him, "Go thy way, for he is a chosen vessel unto Me, to bear My name before the Gentiles and kings and the children of Israel. ¹⁶ For I will show him what great things he must suffer for My name's sake."

¹⁷ And Ananias went his way and entered into the house, and putting his hands on him said, "Brother Saul, the Lord, even Jesus who appeared unto thee on the way as thou camest, hath sent me, that thou mightest receive thy sight and be filled with the Holy Ghost." ¹⁸ And immediately there fell from his eyes something like scales, and he received sight forthwith, and arose and was baptized. ¹⁹ And when he had received meat, he was strengthened.

Saul in Damascus and Jerusalem

Then was Saul certain days with the disciples who were at Damascus. ²⁰ And straightway he preached Christ in the synagogues, that He is the Son of God. ²¹ But all that heard him were amazed and said, "Is not this he that destroyed those who called on this name in Jerusalem, and came hither with the intent that he might bring them bound unto the chief priests?" ²² But Saul increased the more in strength and confounded the Jews who dwelt in Damascus, proving that Jesus is the very Christ.

²³ And after many days were fulfilled, the Jews took counsel to kill him. ²⁴ But their lying in wait became known to Saul. And they watched the gates day and night to kill him. ²⁵ Then the disciples took him by night, and let him down through the wall in a basket.

²⁶ And when Saul had come to Jerusalem, he attempted to join himself to the disciples, but they were all afraid of him and believed not that he was a disciple.

²⁷ But Barnabas③ took him and brought him to the apostles, and declared unto them how he had seen the Lord on the way and that He had spoken to him, and how he had preached boldly at Damascus in the name of Jesus. ²⁸ And he was with them, coming in and going out at Jerusalem. ²⁹ And he spoke boldly in the name

---

③ **Barnabas** /ˈbɑːnəbəs/, 巴拿巴。

of the Lord Jesus and disputed against the Grecians, but they went about to slay him. ³⁰ And when the brethren heard of this, they brought him down to Caesarea and sent him forth to Tarsus.

³¹ Then the churches throughout all Judea and Galilee and Samaria had rest and were edified, and, walking in the fear of the Lord and in the comfort of the Holy Ghost, were multiplied.

...

Cornelius Calls for Peter

Acts 10

¹ There was a certain man in Caesarea called Cornelius, a centurion of the band called the Italian band, ² A devout man, and one that feared God with all his house, which gave much alms to the people, and prayed to God alway. ³ He saw in a vision evidently about the ninth hour of the day an angel of God coming in to him, and saying unto him, " Cornelius."

⁴ And when he looked on him, he was afraid, and said, " What is it, Lord?"

And he said unto him, " Thy prayers and thine alms are come up for a memorial before God. ⁵ And now send men to Joppa, and call for one Simon, whose surname is Peter: ⁶ He lodgeth with one Simon a tanner, whose house is by the sea side: he shall tell thee what thou oughtest to do."

⁷ And when the angel which spake unto Cornelius was departed, he called two of his household servants, and a devout soldier of them that waited on him continually; ⁸ And when he had declared all these things unto them, he sent them to Joppa.

Peter's Vision of a Sheet Full of Animals

The Vision, Domenico Fetti (1589—1623)

⁹ On the morrow, as they went on their journey, and drew nigh unto the city, Peter went up upon the housetop to pray about the sixth hour: ¹⁰ And he became very hungry, and would have eaten: but while they made ready, he fell into a trance, ¹¹ And saw heaven opened, and a certain vessel descending upon him, as it had been a great sheet knit at the four corners, and let down to the earth: ¹² Wherein were all manner of fourfooted beasts of the earth, and wild beasts, and creeping things, and fowls of the air. ¹³ And there came a voice to him, " Rise, Peter; kill, and eat."

¹⁴ But Peter said, " Not so, Lord; for I have never eaten any thing that is common or unclean."

¹⁵ And the voice spake unto him again the second time, " What God hath cleansed, that call not thou common."

¹⁶ This was done thrice: and the vessel was received up again into heaven.

¹⁷ Now while Peter doubted in himself what this vision which he had seen should mean, behold, the men which were sent from Cornelius had made enquiry for Simon's house, and stood before the gate, ¹⁸ And called, and asked whether Simon, which was surnamed Peter, were lodged there.

¹⁹ While Peter thought on the vision, the Spirit said unto him, " Behold, three men seek thee. ²⁰ Arise therefore, and get thee down, and go with them, doubting nothing: for I have sent them."

²¹ Then Peter went down to the men which were sent unto him from Cornelius; and said, " Behold, I am he whom ye seek; what is the cause wherefore ye are come?"

²² And they said, " Cornelius the centurion, a just man, and one that feareth God, and of good report among all the nation of the Jews, was warned from God by an holy angel to send for thee into his house, and to hear words of thee." ²³ Then called he them in, and lodged them.

Peter at Cornelius's House

And on the morrow Peter went away with them, and certain brethren from Joppa accompanied him. [24] And the morrow after they entered into Caesarea. And Cornelius waited for them, and he had called together his kinsmen and near friends. [25] And as Peter was coming in, Cornelius met him, and fell down at his feet, and worshipped him. [26] But Peter took him up, saying, "Stand up; I myself also am a man."

[27] And as he talked with him, he went in, and found many that were come together. [28] And he said unto them, "Ye know how that it is an unlawful thing for a man that is a Jew to keep company, or come unto one of another nation; but God hath shewed me that I should not call any man common or unclean.

[29] Therefore came I unto you without gainsaying, as soon as I was sent for: I ask therefore for what intent ye have sent for me?"

[30] And Cornelius said, "Four days ago I was fasting until this hour; and at the ninth hour I prayed in my house, and, behold, a man stood before me in bright clothing, [31] And said, 'Cornelius, thy prayer is heard, and thine alms are had in remembrance in the sight of God. [32] Send therefore to Joppa, and call hither Simon, whose surname is Peter; he is lodged in the house of one Simon a tanner by the sea side: who, when he cometh, shall speak unto thee.' [33] Immediately therefore I sent to thee; and thou hast well done that thou art come. Now therefore are we all here present before God, to hear all things that are commanded thee of God."

St. Peter Baptizing Cornelius, Laurent Pécheux (1729—1821)

[34] Then Peter opened his mouth, and said, "Of a truth I perceive that God is no respecter of persons: [35] But in every nation he that feareth him, and worketh righteousness, is accepted with him. [36] The word which God sent unto the children of Israel, preaching peace by Jesus Christ: (he is Lord of all:) [37] That word, I say, ye know, which was published throughout all Judaea, and began from Galilee, after the baptism which John preached; [38] How God anointed Jesus of Nazareth with the Holy Ghost and with power: who went about doing good, and healing all that were oppressed of the devil; for God was with him.

[39] "And we are witnesses of all things which he did both in the land of the Jews, and in Jerusalem; whom they slew and hanged on a tree: [40] Him God raised up the third day, and shewed him openly; [41] Not to all the people, but unto witnesses chosen before God, even to us, who did eat and drink with him after he rose from the dead. [42] And he commanded us to preach unto the people, and to testify that it is he which was ordained of God to be the Judge of quick and dead. [43] To him give all the prophets witness, that through his name whosoever believeth in him shall receive remission of sins."

[44] While Peter yet spake these words, the Holy Ghost fell on all them which heard the word. [45] And they of the circumcision which believed were astonished, as many as came with Peter, because that on the Gentiles also was poured out the gift of the Holy Ghost. [46] For they heard them speak with tongues, and magnify God.

Then answered Peter, [47] "Can any man forbid water, that these should not be baptized, which have received the Holy Ghost as well as we?" [48] And he commanded them to be baptized in the name of the Lord. Then prayed they him to tarry certain days.

Peter's Miraculous Escape from Prison

Acts 12

[1] Now about that time Herod the king stretched forth his hands to vex certain of the church. [2] And he killed James the brother of John with the sword. [3] And because he saw that it pleased the Jews, he proceeded further to take Peter also. (This was during the Days of Unleavened Bread.) [4] And when he had apprehended him, he put him in prison and delivered him to four quaternions of soldiers to guard him, intending after Easter to bring him forth to the people.

The Liberation of St. Peter, 1722, Sebastiano Ricci

⁵Peter therefore was kept in prison, but prayer was made without ceasing by the church unto God for him. ⁶And when Herod would have brought him forth, that same night Peter was sleeping between two soldiers, bound with two chains; and the keepers were guarding the door of the prison. ⁷And behold, the angel of the Lord came upon him, and a light shined in the prison; and he smote Peter on the side and raised him up, saying, "Arise up quickly." And his chains fell off from his hands. ⁸And the angel said unto him, "Gird thyself and bind on thy sandals." And so he did. And the angel said unto him, "Cast thy garment about thee and follow me." ⁹And he went out and followed him, and knew not whether what was being done by the angel was real, but thought he saw a vision. ¹⁰When they had passed the first and the second guard, they came unto the iron gate that leadeth unto the city, which opened to them of his own accord. And they went out and passed on through one street, and forthwith the angel departed from him.

¹¹And when Peter had come to himself, he said, "Now I know in truth that the Lord hath sent His angel, and hath delivered me out of the hand of Herod and from all the expectations of the people of the Jews."

Peter at the Door of Mary's House

¹²And when he had considered this thing, he went to the house of Mary the mother of John, whose surname was Mark, where many were gathered together praying. ¹³And as Peter knocked at the door of the gate, a damsel named Rhoda came to ask who was there. ¹⁴And when she recognized Peter's voice, she opened not the gate for gladness, but ran in and told how Peter stood before the gate.

¹⁵And they said unto her, "Thou art mad." But she continued to affirm that it was even so. Then they said, "It is his angel."

¹⁶But Peter continued knocking, and when they opened the door and saw him, they were astonished. ¹⁷But he, beckoning unto them with his hand to hold their peace, declared unto them how the Lord had brought him out of the prison. And he said, "Go and tell these things unto James and to the brethren." And he departed and went into another place.

¹⁸Now as soon as it was day, there was no small stir among the soldiers over what had become of Peter. ¹⁹And when Herod had sought him and found him not, he examined the guards and commanded that they should be put to death.

Herod's Death

And he went down from Judea to Caesarea and there stayed. ²⁰And Herod was highly displeased with those from Tyre and Sidon. But they came with one accord to him and, having made Blastus the king's chamberlain their friend, they asked for peace, because their country was nourished by the king's country. ²¹And upon a set day Herod, arrayed in royal apparel, sat upon his throne and delivered an oration unto them. ²²And the people gave a shout, saying, "It is the voice of a god, and not of a man!" ²³And immediately the angel of the Lord smote him, because he gave not God the glory; and he was eaten by worms and gave up the ghost. ²⁴But the Word of God grew and multiplied.

²⁵And Barnabas and Saul returned from Jerusalem, when they had fulfilled their ministry, and took with them John, whose surname was Mark.

III FOOD FOR THOUGHT

1. How was Saul converted? Was the conversion complete?
2. Who helped restore Saul's sight?
3. What did the Jews think of the Gentiles at that time?
4. How did Peter escape from prison?
5. Make some comments on "If Stephen had not prayed, the church would not have had Paul." (St. Augustine)

IV BIBLICAL RELEVANCE

A. Biblical Terms in Everyday English
1. simony (8:6—23): _____
2. from Saul to Paul (9:1—22): _____
3. road to Damascus (9:3—7): _____
4. kick against the goads/pricks (9:5): _____
5. the scales fall from one's eyes (9:18): _____
6. Christians (11:26): _____

B. Biblical References in Literature
1. "You start Saul, and end up Paul," my grandfather had often said. "When you're a youngun, you Saul, but let life whup your head a bit and you starts to trying to be Paul—though you still Sauls around on the side."

   (Ralph Ellison, *Invisible Man*, 1952)

2. I remember a dramatic scene. I was Paul on the road to Damascus ... I was walking towards the museum along Fifth Avenue, thirty blocks, because there was a victory parade ... I kept walking, and there was a long-haired kid, nearer the bleachers, being assailed by this guy. The guy was yelling from the top of the bleachers: "You guys ought to be eliminated. In a democracy like this, you're not fit." I stopped and thought: if this is what Vietnams is doing to US, it's time it was over. I was anti-war from that day on.

   (Studs Terkel, *American Dreams: Lost and Found*, 1980)

C. The Bible and Arts
1. *The Conversion on the Way to Damascus*, 1600, Caravaggio
2. *Saul and Ananias*, Benjamin West (1738—1820)
3. *Healing of the Cripple and Raising of Tabitha*, 1426—1427, Panicale da Masolino
4. *The Vision*, Domenico Fetti (1589—1623)
5. *St. Peter and Cornelius the Centurion*, 1640s, Bernardo Cavallino
6. *The Liberation of St. Peter*, 1722, Sebastiano Ricci

V SOURCES FOR REFERENCE

1. Kistemaker, S. J. (1990). *Exposition of the Acts of the Apostles*. Grand Rapids, MI: Baker.
2. [加]菲(Gorden Fee),[美]斯图尔特(Douglas Stuart):《圣经导读》(下)(*How to Read the Bible Book by Book*),北京:北京大学出版社,2005年。
3. Kuo, S. M. (1990). *Journey through the Bible*. Nanjing: Nanjing University Press.

39. THE JOURNEYS OF PAUL

I   POINTS OF DEPARTURE

If Peter had labored on the boundaries of the Holy Land, Paul, together with his companions, would be the indefatigable globetrotter at least around the known world of the Mediterranean Sea, bringing the gospel not only to the Gentiles already attracted to Judaism, but his mission would also embrace worshippers of pagan Gods. Furthermore, the center of Luke's story will shift from the mother Church in Jerusalem to a new church in the city of Antioch, eventually to the very heart of the Empire, Rome. Altogether, Paul took three missionary journeys (*see* "Paul's Missionary" in **Appendices**), before he was taken in chains to Rome and began preaching there under guard.

The first journey (*Ac. 13:1—15:35*) took Paul and Barnabas from Antioch to Cyprus, then southern Asia Minor (Anatolia), and back to Antioch. Chapter 15 offers a fascinating glimpse into Jewish/Gentile politics in the early church, recounting a debate between such notable leaders as Peter, Paul and James. The leaders agreed on a compromise position that removed some of the barriers between the two groups. The outcome of the Jerusalem conference was that non-Jewish converts would be asked only to "abstain from meats offered to idols, and from blood, and from things strangled, and from fornication" (*Ac. 15:29*). They would not be circumcised, nor in large part would they keep the Torah. Instead, baptism would be the primary marker of entry into the community, and new rules of conduct based on the life and teachings of Jesus would guide the movement.

Acts 15:36—18:22 gives an account of Paul's second journey from Asia Minor to some Greek cities such as Philippi, Thessalonica, and especially Corinth. Chapter 17 contains one of the most famous events in the Book of Acts, Paul's debate with the philosophers at the Areopagus of the intellectual city of Athens. Nothing daunted, Paul stood before the skeptical audience and, in a burst of eloquence, delivered an extraordinary speech to an august assemblage of intellectuals, employing the oratorical skills familiar to them, but driving home the Christian idea of resurrection. Failure as his attempt was, Paul did manage to convert some elites, the most prominent among whom was Dionysius the Areopagite.

Paul's third missionary journey (*Ac. 18:23—21:26*) began at Antioch, retraced the Greek part of the second journey before the apostle went back to Jerusalem. While at Ephesus, there was a riot led by a silversmith named Demetrius whose business was being threatened by the Christians. Then Paul traveled again through Macedonia, then to Troas, where he raised the dead boy Eutychus, who fell from a window after he drifted off to sleep during a lengthy late-night session by Paul. As he traveled back towards Jerusalem, he passed Ephesius and gave a long farewell speech, predicting that he would suffer imprisonment, persecution, and death. Upon his return, Jews from Asia stirred up public sentiment against him and his life was constantly threatened. Then he was tried, first before the governor Felix and then a new governor Festus, who offered to send him to Jerusalem for trial. Paul requested instead to be tried by the Roman emperor.

The final section of Acts (Chs. 27—28) centers on Paul's adventurous journey by sea to Rome. Paul and his shipmates encountered severe weather, and finally had a shipwreck. When they were at last on the shore of the island of Malta, they remained there for three months, during which Paul took the opportunity to minister to the island's inhabitants. Once in Rome, Paul was put under house arrest, but the Jews of Rome frequented his cell in growing numbers. In Paul's final speech he applied *Isaiah 6:9—10* to the rejection of Jesus by the Jews:

Be it known therefore unto you, that the salvation of God is sent unto the Gentiles, and that they will hear it.

II SELECTED READINGS

The Council at Jerusalem

Acts 15

¹ *And certain men which came down from Judaea taught the brethren, and said, " Except ye be circumcised after the manner of Moses, ye cannot be saved."* ² *When therefore Paul and Barnabas had no small dissension and disputation with them, they determined that Paul and Barnabas, and certain other of them, should go up to Jerusalem unto the apostles and elders about this question.* ³ *And being brought on their way by the church, they passed through Phenice and Samaria, declaring the conversion of the Gentiles: and they caused great joy unto all the brethren.* ⁴ *And when they were come to Jerusalem, they were received of the church, and of the apostles and elders, and they declared all things that God had done with them.*

⁵ *But there rose up certain of the sect of the Pharisees which believed, saying, " That it was needful to circumcise them, and to command them to keep the law of Moses."*

⁶ *And the apostles and elders came together for to consider of this matter.*

⁷ *And when there had been much disputing, Peter rose up, and said unto them, " Men and brethren, ye know how that a good while ago God made choice among us, that the Gentiles by my mouth should hear the word of the gospel, and believe.* ⁸ *And God, which knoweth the hearts, bare them witness, giving them the Holy Ghost, even as he did unto us;* ⁹ *And put no difference between us and them, purifying their hearts by faith.* ¹⁰ *Now therefore why tempt ye God, to put a yoke upon the neck of the disciples, which neither our fathers nor we were able to bear?* ¹¹ *But we believe that through the grace of the LORD Jesus Christ we shall be saved, even as they."*

¹² *Then all the multitude kept silence, and gave audience to Barnabas and Paul, declaring what miracles and wonders God had wrought among the Gentiles by them.* ¹³ *And after they had held their peace, James answered, saying, " Men and brethren, hearken unto me.* ¹⁴ *Simeon hath declared how God at the first did visit the Gentiles, to take out of them a people for his name.* ¹⁵ *And to this agree the words of the prophets; as it is written,*

¹⁶ *" 'After this I will return, and will build again the tabernacle of David, which is fallen down; and I will build again the ruins thereof, and I will set it up,* ¹⁷ *That the residue of men might seek after the Lord, and all the Gentiles, upon whom my name is called, saith the Lord, who doeth all these things.'* ①*"*

¹⁸ *Known unto God are all his works from the beginning of the world.*

¹⁹ *" Wherefore my sentence is, that we trouble not them, which from among the Gentiles are turned to*

---

① **16—17** *Amos 9:11, 12.*

God: ^{20}But that we write unto them, that they abstain from pollutions of idols, and from fornication, and from things strangled, and from blood. ^{21}For Moses of old time hath in every city them that preach him, being read in the synagogues every Sabbath day."

The Council's Letter to Gentile Believers

^{22}Then pleased it the apostles and elders with the whole church, to send chosen men of their own company to Antioch with Paul and Barnabas; namely, Judas surnamed Barnabas and Silas, chief men among the brethren. ^{23}And they wrote letters by them after this manner;

The apostles and elders and brethren send greeting unto the brethren which are of the Gentiles in Antioch and Syria and Cilicia.

^{24}Forasmuch as we have heard, that certain which went out from us have troubled you with words, subverting your souls, saying, "Ye must be circumcised, and keep the law: to whom we gave no such commandment. ^{25}It seemed good unto us, being assembled with one accord, to send chosen men unto you with our beloved Barnabas and Paul, ^{26}Men that have hazarded their lives for the name of our Lord Jesus Christ. ^{27}We have sent therefore Judas and Silas, who shall also tell you the same things by mouth. ^{28}For it seemed good to the Holy Ghost, and to us, to lay upon you no greater burden than these necessary things; ^{29}that ye abstain from meats offered to idols, and from blood, and from things strangled, and from fornication: from which if ye keep yourselves, ye shall do well. Fare ye well.

^{30}So when they were dismissed, they came to Antioch: and when they had gathered the multitude together, they delivered the epistle: ^{31}which when they had read, they rejoiced for the consolation. ^{32}And Judas and Silas, being prophets also themselves, exhorted the brethren with many words, and confirmed them. ^{33}And after they had tarried there a space, they were let go in peace from the brethren unto the apostles. ^{34}Notwithstanding it pleased Silas to abide there still. ^{35}Paul also and Barnabas continued in Antioch, teaching and preaching the word of the Lord, with many others also.

...

Acts 17

The Debate at the Areopagus② of Athens

...

^{15}And those who conducted Paul brought him unto Athens and, having received direction for Silas and Timothy to come to him with all speed, they departed.

^{16}Now while Paul waited for them at Athens, his spirit was stirred within him when he saw the city wholly given to idolatry.

^{17}Therefore he disputed in the synagogue with the Jews, and with the devout persons, and in the marketplace daily with those who met with him. ^{18}Then certain philosophers of the Epicureans③ and of the Stoics④ encountered him. And some said, "What will this babbler say?" And some others said, "He seemeth to be a proclaimer of strange gods," because he preached unto them Jesus and the resurrection. ^{19}And they took him

---

② **the Areopagus** /ˌæriˈɔpəgəs/, the "Rock of Ares," a hill under the Acropolis. The word also referred to a council of advisors who met on the hill. The Agreopagus served as a kind of judicial council in ancient Greece.

③ **Epicurean** (/ˌɐpikjuˈriːən/, 伊壁鸠鲁学派) followers of the Greek philosophers, who taught that the gods did not intervene in human affairs and it was man's duty to free himself from such superstitions as punishment and reward, and there was no such thing as morality and immortality, only pleasure. The pursuit of pleasure was man's only true goal. (Dimont, 2004:76—77).

④ **Stoic** (/ˈstəuik/, 斯多葛学派) believed that God was a powerful energy that created and sustained the world. God was the world reason, or Logos, that was seen in the order and beauty of the world. Human duty was to live "naturally," according to the law of the universe, which was the embodiment of Divine Reason (Peterson, 1998:18).

and brought him unto the Areopagus, saying, "May we know what this new doctrine is whereof thou speakest? [20] For thou bringest certain strange things to our ears, and we would know therefore what these things mean." [21] (For all the Athenians and strangers who were there spent their time in nothing else than either telling or hearing some new thing.)

[22] Then Paul stood in the midst of Mars' Hill and said, "Ye men of Athens, I perceive that in all things ye are too superstitious. [23] For as I passed by and beheld your devotions, I found an altar with this inscription: 'To the Unknown God'. Whom therefore ye worship in ignorance, Him I declare unto you.

St. Paul Preaching in Athens, Raphael (1483—1520)

[24] "God who made the world and all things therein, seeing that He is Lord of Heaven and earth, dwelleth not in temples made with hands. [25] Neither is He worshiped with men's hands, as though He needed anything, seeing He giveth to all life, and breath, and all things. [26] And He hath made of one blood all nations of men to dwell on all the face of the earth, and hath determined the times before appointed, and the bounds of their habitation, [27] That they should seek the Lord, if perhaps they might feel after Him and find Him, though He be not far from every one of us. [28] For in Him we live, and move, and have our being; as also certain of your own poets have said, 'For we are also His offspring.'

[29] "For inasmuch, then, as we are the offspring of God, we ought not to think that the Godhead is like unto gold or silver or stone, graven by art and of man's devising. [30] The times of this ignorance God overlooked, but now He commandeth all men everywhere to repent, [31] Because He hath appointed a Day in which He will judge the world in righteousness by that Man whom He hath ordained. Of this He hath given assurance unto all men, in that He hath raised Him from the dead."

[32] But when they heard of the resurrection of the dead, some mocked and others said, "We will hear thee again on this matter." [33] So Paul departed from among them. [34] However, certain men cleaved unto him and believed, among whom were Dionysius the Areopagite, and a woman named Damaris, and others with them.

Acts 19

The Riot in Ephesus

...

[23] And the same time, there arose no small stir about that Way. [24] For a certain man named Demetrius, a silversmith who made silver shrines for Diana, brought no small gain unto the craftsmen. [25] These he called together with the workmen of like occupation, and said, "Sirs, ye know that by this craft we have our wealth. [26] Moreover, ye see and hear that, not alone at Ephesus but almost throughout all Asia, this Paul hath persuaded and turned away many people, saying that they are not gods which are made with hands, [27] So that not only this our craft is in danger of being set at nought, but also the temple of the great goddess Diana should be despised and her magnificence should be destroyed, whom all Asia and the world worshipeth."

[28] And when they heard these things, they were full of wrath and cried out, saying, "Great is Diana of the Ephesians!" [29] And the whole city was filled with confusion and, having seized Gaius and Aristarchus, men of Macedonia who were Paul's companions in his travel, they rushed with one accord into the theater. [30] And when Paul would have entered in unto the people, the disciples suffered him not. [31] And certain of the Asian chiefs, who were his friends, sent unto him, urging that he would not venture into the theater.

[32] Some therefore cried one thing and some another, for the assembly was in confusion, and the greater part knew not why they had come together. [33] And they drew Alexander out from the multitude, the Jews

putting him forward. And Alexander beckoned with his hand, and would have made his defense unto the people; ³⁴ But when they perceived that he was a Jew, all with one voice for about the space of two hours cried out, "Great is Diana of the Ephesians!"

³⁵ And when the town clerk had appeased the people, he said, "Ye men of Ephesus, what man is there who knoweth not that the city of the Ephesians is a worshiper of the great goddess Diana, and of the image which fell down from Jupiter? ³⁶ Seeing then that these things cannot be spoken against, ye ought to be quiet and do nothing rashly; ³⁷ For ye have brought hither these men who are neither robbers of churches, nor yet blasphemers of your goddess. ³⁸ Therefore if Demetrius and the craftsmen who are with him have a matter against any man, the law is open and there are deputies. Let them implead one another. ³⁹ But if ye inquire of anything concerning other matters, it shall be determined in a lawful assembly. ⁴⁰ For we are in danger of being called in question for this day's uproar, there being no cause whereby we can give an account of this concourse." ⁴¹ And when he had thus spoken, he dismissed the assembly.

Eutychus Raised from the Dead at Troas

Acts 20

...

⁷ And upon the first day of the week, when the disciples came together to break bread, Paul preached unto them, ready to depart on the morrow; and continued his speech until midnight. ⁸ And there were many lights in the upper chamber, where they were gathered together. ⁹ And there sat in a window a certain young man named Eutychus, being fallen into a deep sleep: and as Paul was long preaching, he sunk down with sleep, and fell down from the third loft, and was taken up dead. ¹⁰ And Paul went down, and fell on him, and embracing him said, "Trouble not yourselves; for his life is in him." ¹¹ When he therefore was come up again, and had broken bread, and eaten, and talked a long while, even till break of day, so he departed. ¹² And they brought the young man alive, and were not a little comforted.

Paul's Farewell to the Ephesian Elders

¹³ And we went before to ship, and sailed unto Assos, there intending to take in Paul: for so had he appointed, minding himself to go afoot. ¹⁴ And when he met with us at Assos, we took him in, and came to Mitylene. ¹⁵ And we sailed thence, and came the next day over against Chios; and the next day we arrived at Samos, and tarried at Trogyllium; and the next day we came to Miletus. ¹⁶ For Paul had determined to sail past Ephesus, because he would not spend the time in Asia; for he was in haste, that it might be possible for him to be at Jerusalem on the day of Pentecost.

¹⁷ And from Miletus he sent to Ephesus, and called for the elders of the church. ¹⁸ And when they had come to him, he said unto them, "Ye know, from the first day that I came into Asia, in what manner I have been with you in all seasons, ¹⁹ Serving the Lord in all humility of mind, and with many tears and temptations which befell me through the lying in wait of the Jews; ²⁰ And how I kept back nothing that was profitable for you, but have shown you and have taught you publicly and from house to house, ²¹ Testifying both to the Jews and also to the Greeks repentance toward God and faith toward our Lord Jesus Christ.

²² And now behold, bound by the Spirit, I go unto Jerusalem, not knowing the things that shall befall me there, ²³ Save that the Holy Ghost witnesseth in every city, saying that bonds and afflictions await me. ²⁴ But none of these things move me, neither count I my life dear unto myself, so that I might finish my course with joy, and the ministry which I have received from the Lord Jesus, to testify to the Gospel of the grace of God.

²⁵ "And now, behold, I know that ye all, among whom I have gone preaching the Kingdom of God, shall see my face no more. ²⁶ Therefore I attest to you this day that I am pure from the blood of all men, ²⁷ For I have not shrunk from declaring unto you all the counsel of God. ²⁸ "Take heed therefore unto yourselves and to all the flock, over which the Holy Ghost hath made you overseers, to feed the church of God which He hath

purchased with His own blood. ²⁹ For I know this: that after my departing shall grievous wolves enter in among you, not sparing the flock. ³⁰ Also from among your own selves shall men arise, speaking perverse things to draw away disciples after them. ³¹ Therefore watch, and remember that for the space of three years I ceased not to warn everyone night and day with tears.

³² "And now, brethren, I commend you to God and to the word of His grace, which is able to build you up and to give you an inheritance among all those who are sanctified. ³³ I have coveted no man's silver or gold or apparel. ³⁴ Yea, ye yourselves know that these hands have ministered unto my own necessities, and also to those who were with me. ³⁵ I have shown you all things, how that by so laboring ye ought to support the weak, and to remember the words of the Lord Jesus, how He said, ' It is more blessed to give than to receive.' "

³⁶ And when he had thus spoken, he kneeled down and prayed with them all. ³⁷ And they all wept sorely and fell on Paul's neck and kissed him, ³⁸ Sorrowing most of all because of the words which he had spoken, that they should see his face no more. And they accompanied him unto the ship.

Acts 21

Paul's Arrival at Jerusalem

...

¹⁷ And when we had come to Jerusalem, the brethren received us gladly. ¹⁸ And the day following, Paul went with us unto James, and all the elders were present. ¹⁹ And when he had saluted them, he declared particularly what things God had wrought among the Gentiles by his ministry.

²⁰ And when they heard it, they glorified the Lord and said unto him, " Thou seest, brother, how many thousands of Jews there are who believe, and they are all zealous for the law.²¹ And they are informed about thee, that thou teachest all the Jews who are among the Gentiles to forsake Moses, saying that they ought not to circumcise their children, nor walk according to the customs. ²² What is therefore to be done? The multitude must surely come together, for they will hear that thou art come.²³ Do therefore this which we say to thee: We have four men who have taken a vow upon themselves. ²⁴ Take them and purify thyself with them, and bear their charges with them, that they may shave their heads; and all may know that those things of which they have been informed concerning thee are nothing, but that thou thyself also walkest orderly and keepest the law. ²⁵ And as to the Gentiles who believe, we have written and concluded that they observe no such thing, save only that they keep themselves from things offered to idols, and from blood, and from things strangled, and from fornication." ²⁶ Then Paul took the men, and the next day, purifying himself with them, he entered into the temple to signify the accomplishment of the days of purification, until an offering should be offered for every one of them.

Paul Is Assaulted in the Temple and Arrested

²⁷ And when the seven days were almost ended, the Jews who were from Asia, when they saw him in the temple, stirred up all the people and laid hands on him, ²⁸ Crying out, " Men of Israel, help! This is the man who teacheth all men everywhere against the people and the law and this place, and furthermore brought Greeks also into the temple, and hath polluted this holy place." ²⁹ (For they had seen previously with him in the city Trophimus an Ephesian, whom they supposed that Paul had brought into the temple.)

³⁰ And all the city was moved and the people ran together, and they took Paul and dragged him out of the temple; and forthwith the doors were shut. ³¹ And as they went about to kill him, tidings came unto the chief captain of the garrison that all Jerusalem was in an uproar, ³² Who immediately took soldiers and centurions and ran down unto them; and when they saw the chief captain and the soldiers, they left off beating Paul.

³³ Then the chief captain came near, and took him and commanded that he be bound with two chains, and demanded who he was and what he had done. ³⁴ And some cried one thing, some another, among the multitude. And when he could learn nothing with certainty because of the tumult, he commanded him to be carried into the castle. ³⁵ And when Paul came upon the stairs, so it was that he had to be borne by the soldiers because of the violence of the people. ³⁶ For the multitude of the people followed after, crying, "Away with him!"

Paul Speaks to the Crowd

³⁷ And as Paul was to be led into the castle, he said unto the chief captain, "May I speak unto thee?"

Who said, "Canst thou speak Greek? ³⁸ Art not thou that Egyptian, which before these days madest an uproar, and leddest out into the wilderness four thousand men that were murderers?"

³⁹ But Paul said, "I am a man which am a Jew of Tarsus, a city in Cilicia, a citizen of no mean city: and, I beseech thee, suffer me to speak unto the people."

⁴⁰ And when he had given him licence, Paul stood on the stairs, and beckoned with the hand unto the people. And when there was made a great silence, he spake unto them in the Hebrew tongue, saying,

Acts 22

¹ "Men, brethren, and fathers, hear ye my defence which I make now unto you.

² (And when they heard that he spake in the Hebrew tongue to them, they kept the more silence: and he saith,) ³ "I am verily a man which am a Jew, born in Tarsus, a city in Cilicia, yet brought up in this city at the feet of Gamaliel, and taught according to the perfect manner of the law of the fathers, and was zealous toward God, as ye all are this day. ⁴ And I persecuted this way unto the death, binding and delivering into prisons both men and women. ⁵ As also the high priest doth bear me witness, and all the estate of the elders: from whom also I received letters unto the brethren, and went to Damascus, to bring them which were there bound unto Jerusalem, for to be punished.

⁶ "And it came to pass, that, as I made my journey, and was come nigh unto Damascus about noon, suddenly there shone from heaven a great light round about me. ⁷ And I fell unto the ground, and heard a voice saying unto me, Saul, Saul, why persecutest thou me?

⁸ "And I answered, 'Who art thou, Lord?'

"And he said unto me, 'I am Jesus of Nazareth, whom thou persecutest.' ⁹ And they that were with me saw indeed the light, and were afraid; but they heard not the voice of him that spake to me.

¹⁰ "And I said, 'What shall I do, LORD?'

"And the Lord said unto me, 'Arise, and go into Damascus; and there it shall be told thee of all things which are appointed for thee to do.' ¹¹ And when I could not see for the glory of that light, being led by the hand of them that were with me, I came into Damascus.

¹² "And one Ananias, a devout man according to the law, having a good report of all the Jews which dwelt there, ¹³ Came unto me, and stood, and said unto me, 'Brother Saul, receive thy sight.' And the same hour I looked up upon him.

¹⁴ "And he said, 'The God of our fathers hath chosen thee, that thou shouldest know his will, and see that Just One, and shouldest hear the voice of his mouth. ¹⁵ For thou shalt be his witness unto all men of what thou hast seen and heard. ¹⁶ And now why tarriest thou? Arise, and be baptized, and wash away thy sins, calling on the name of the Lord.'

¹⁷ "And it came to pass, that, when I was come again to Jerusalem, even while I prayed in the temple, I was in a trance; ¹⁸ and saw him saying unto me, 'Make haste, and get thee quickly out of Jerusalem: for they will not receive thy testimony concerning me.'

¹⁹ "And I said, 'Lord, they know that I imprisoned and beat in every synagogue them that believed on thee. ²⁰ And when the blood of thy martyr Stephen was shed, I also was standing by, and consenting unto his death, and kept the raiment of them that slew him.'

²¹ "And he said unto me, 'Depart: for I will send thee far hence unto the Gentiles.'"

Paul the Roman Citizen

²² And they gave him audience unto this word, and then lifted up their voices, and said, "Away with such a fellow from the earth: for it is not fit that he should live."

²³ And as they cried out, and cast off their clothes, and threw dust into the air, ²⁴ The chief captain commanded him to be brought into the castle, and bade that he should be examined by scourging; that he might know wherefore they cried so against him. ²⁵ And as they bound him with thongs, Paul said unto the centurion that stood by, "Is it lawful for you to scourge a man that is a Roman, and uncondemned?"

²⁶ When the centurion heard that, he went and told the chief captain, saying, "Take heed what thou doest: for this man is a Roman."

²⁷ Then the chief captain came, and said unto him, "Tell me, art thou a Roman?" He said, "Yea."

²⁸ And the chief captain answered, "With a great sum obtained I this freedom."

And Paul said, "But I was free born."

²⁹ Then straightway they departed from him which should have examined him: and the chief captain also was afraid, after he knew that he was a Roman, and because he had bound him.

Before the Sanhedrin

³⁰ On the morrow, because he would have known the certainty wherefore he was accused of the Jews, he loosed him from his bands, and commanded the chief priests and all their council to appear, and brought Paul down, and set him before them.

The Trial before Felix⑤

Acts 24

...

¹⁰ Then Paul, after that the governor had beckoned unto him to speak, answered, "Forasmuch as I know that thou hast been of many years a judge unto this nation, I do the more cheerfully answer for myself: ¹¹ Because that thou mayest understand, that there are yet but twelve days since I went up to Jerusalem for to worship. ¹² And they neither found me in the temple disputing with any man, neither raising up the people, neither in the synagogues, nor in the city: ¹³ Neither can they prove the things whereof they now accuse me. ¹⁴ But this I confess unto thee, that after the way which they call heresy, so worship I the God of my fathers, believing all things which are written in the law and in the prophets: ¹⁵ And have hope toward God, which they themselves also allow, that there shall be a resurrection of the dead, both of the just and unjust. ¹⁶ And herein do I exercise myself, to have always a conscience void to offence toward God, and toward men.

Antonius Felix

¹⁷ Now after many years I came to bring alms to my nation, and offerings. ¹⁸ Whereupon certain Jews from Asia found me purified in the temple, neither with multitude, nor with tumult. ¹⁹ Who ought to have been here before thee, and object, if they had ought against me. ²⁰ Or else let these same here say, if they have found any evil doing in me, while I stood before the council, ²¹ 'Except it be for this one voice, that I cried standing among them, Touching the resurrection of the dead I am called in question by you this day.'"

...

---

⑤ **Felix** full name **Antonius Felix** (/ænˈtəunjəs, ˈfiliks/, 安东尼厄斯·腓力斯) the Roman procurator of Judaea (52—58), in succession to Ventidius Cumanus.

The Trial before Festus[6]

Acts 25

¹ Now when Festus was come into the province, after three days he ascended from Caesarea to Jerusalem. ² Then the high priest and the chief of the Jews informed him against Paul, and besought him, ³ And desired favour against him, that he would send for him to Jerusalem, laying wait in the way to kill him. ⁴ But Festus answered, that Paul should be kept at Caesarea, and that he himself would depart shortly thither. ⁵ "Let them therefore," said he, "which among you are able, go down with me, and accuse this man, if there be any wickedness in him."

⁶ And when he had tarried among them more than ten days, he went down unto Caesarea; and the next day sitting on the judgment seat commanded Paul to be brought. ⁷ And when he was come, the Jews which came down from Jerusalem stood round about, and laid many and grievous complaints against Paul, which they could not prove.

⁸ While he answered for himself, "Neither against the law of the Jews, neither against the temple, nor yet against Caesar, have I offended any thing at all."

⁹ But Festus, willing to do the Jews a pleasure, answered Paul, and said, "Wilt thou go up to Jerusalem, and there be judged of these things before me?"

¹⁰ Then said Paul, "I stand at Caesar's judgment seat, where I ought to be judged: to the Jews have I done no wrong, as thou very well knowest. ¹¹ For if I be an offender, or have committed any thing worthy of death, I refuse not to die: but if there be none of these things whereof these accuse me, no man may deliver me unto them. I appeal unto Caesar."

¹² Then Festus, when he had conferred with the council, answered, "Hast thou appealed unto Caesar? Unto Caesar shalt thou go."

...

Paul Sails for Rome

Acts 27

¹ And when it was determined that we should sail into Italy, they delivered Paul and certain other prisoners unto one named Julius, a centurion of Augustus' band. ² And entering into a ship of Adramyttium, we launched, meaning to sail by the coasts of Asia; one Aristarchus, a Macedonian of Thessalonica, being with us.

³ And the next day we touched at Sidon. And Julius courteously entreated Paul, and gave him liberty to go unto his friends to refresh himself. ⁴ And when we had launched from thence, we sailed under Cyprus, because the winds were contrary. ⁵ And when we had sailed over the sea of Cilicia and Pamphylia, we came to Myra, a city of Lycia. ⁶ And there the centurion found a ship of Alexandria sailing into Italy; and he put us therein. ⁷ And when we had sailed slowly many days, and scarce were come over against Cnidus, the wind not suffering us, we sailed under Crete, over against Salmone; ⁸ And, hardly passing it, came unto a place which is called The fair havens; nigh whereunto was the city of Lasea.

⁹ Now when much time was spent, and when sailing was now dangerous, because the fast was now already past, Paul admonished them, ¹⁰ And said unto them, "Sirs, I perceive that this voyage will be with hurt and much damage, not only of the lading and ship, but also of our lives." ¹¹ Nevertheless the centurion believed the master and the owner of the ship, more than those things which were spoken by Paul. ¹² And because the haven was not commodious to winter in, the more part advised to depart thence also, if by any means they might attain to Phenice, and there to winter; which is an haven of Crete, and lieth toward the south west and north west.

---

⑥ **Festus** full name **Portius Festus** (/ˈpɔːʃəs, festəs/, 波求·非斯都) the Roman procurator of Judea from about C. E. 59 to 62, succeeding Antonius Felix.

The Storm

¹³ And when the south wind blew softly, supposing that they had obtained their purpose, loosing thence, they sailed close by Crete. ¹⁴ But not long after there arose against it a tempestuous wind, called Euroclydon①. ¹⁵ And when the ship was caught, and could not bear up into the wind, we let her drive. ¹⁶ And running under a certain island which is called Clauda, we had much work to come by the boat: ¹⁷ Which when they had taken up, they used helps, undergirding the ship; and, fearing lest they should fall into the quicksands, strake sail, and so were driven. ¹⁸ And we being exceedingly tossed with a tempest, the next day they lightened the ship; ¹⁹ And the third day we cast out with our own hands the tackling of the ship. ²⁰ And when neither sun nor stars in many days appeared, and no small tempest lay on us, all hope that we should be saved was then taken away.

²¹ But after long abstinence Paul stood forth in the midst of them, and said, " Sirs, ye should have hearkened unto me, and not have loosed from Crete, and to have gained this harm and loss. ²² And now I exhort you to be of good cheer: for there shall be no loss of any man's life among you, but of the ship. ²³ For there stood by me this night the angel of God, whose I am, and whom I serve.

²⁴ Saying, ' Fear not, Paul; thou must be brought before Caesar: and, lo, God hath given thee all them that sail with thee.' ²⁵ Wherefore, sirs, be of good cheer: for I believe God, that it shall be even as it was told me. ²⁶ Howbeit we must be cast upon a certain island."

The Shipwreck

²⁷ But when the fourteenth night was come, as we were driven up and down in Adria, about midnight the shipmen deemed that they drew near to some country; ²⁸ and sounded, and found it twenty fathoms: and when they had gone a little further, they sounded again, and found it fifteen fathoms. ²⁹ Then fearing lest we should have fallen upon rocks, they cast four anchors out of the stern, and wished for the day. ³⁰ And as the shipmen were about to flee out of the ship, when they had let down the boat into the sea, under colour as though they would have cast anchors out of the foreship, ³¹ Paul said to the centurion and to the soldiers, " Except these abide in the ship, ye cannot be saved." ³² Then the soldiers cut off the ropes of the boat, and let her fall off.

³³ And while the day was coming on, Paul besought them all to take meat, saying, " This day is the fourteenth day that ye have tarried and continued fasting, having taken nothing. ³⁴ Wherefore I pray you to take some meat: for this is for your health: for there shall not an hair fall from the head of any of you." ³⁵ And when he had thus spoken, he took bread,

St. Paul Shipwrecked, Gustave Doré (1832—1883)

and gave thanks to God in presence of them all: and when he had broken it, he began to eat. ³⁶ Then were they all of good cheer, and they also took some meat. ³⁷ And we were in all in the ship two hundred threescore and sixteen souls. ³⁸ And when they had eaten enough, they lightened the ship, and cast out the wheat into the sea.

³⁹ And when it was day, they knew not the land: but they discovered a certain creek with a shore, into the which they were minded, if it were possible, to thrust in the ship. ⁴⁰ And when they had taken up the anchors, they committed themselves unto the sea, and loosed the rudder bands, and hoised up the mainsail to the wind, and made toward shore. ⁴¹ And falling into a place where two seas met, they ran the ship aground; and the forepart stuck fast, and remained unmoveable, but the hinder part was broken with the violence of the waves.

⁴² And the soldiers' counsel was to kill the prisoners, lest any of them should swim out, and escape. ⁴³ But

---

① **Euroclydon** (/juˈrɒklidɔn/, 友拉革罗) the northeastern storm around the Mediterranean.

the centurion, willing to save Paul, kept them from their purpose; and commanded that they which could swim should cast themselves first into the sea, and get to land: ⁴⁴ And the rest, some on boards, and some on broken pieces of the ship. And so it came to pass, that they escaped all safe to land.

Ashore on Malta

Acts 28

¹ And when they were escaped, then they knew that the island was called Melita. ² And the barbarous people shewed us no little kindness: for they kindled a fire, and received us every one, because of the present rain, and because of the cold. ³ And when Paul had gathered a bundle of sticks, and laid them on the fire, there came a viper out of the heat, and fastened on his hand. ⁴ And when the barbarians saw the venomous beast hang on his hand, they said among themselves, " No doubt this man is a murderer, whom, though he hath escaped the sea, yet vengeance suffereth not to live." ⁵ And he shook off the beast into the fire, and felt no harm. ⁶ Howbeit they looked when he should have swollen, or fallen down dead suddenly: but after they had looked a great while, and saw no harm come to him, they changed their minds, and said that he was a god.

⁷ In the same quarters were possessions of the chief man of the island, whose name was Publius; who received us, and lodged us three days courteously. ⁸ And it came to pass, that the father of Publius lay sick of a fever and of a bloody flux: to whom Paul entered in, and prayed, and laid his hands on him, and healed him. ⁹ So when this was done, others also, which had diseases in the island, came, and were healed: ¹⁰ Who also honoured us with many honours; and when we departed, they laded us with such things as were necessary.

Arrival at Rome

¹¹ And after three months we departed in a ship of Alexandria, which had wintered in the isle, whose sign was Castor and Pollux. ¹² And landing at Syracuse, we tarried there three days. ¹³ And from thence we fetched a compass, and came to Rhegium: and after one day the south wind blew, and we came the next day to Puteoli: ¹⁴ Where we found brethren, and were desired to tarry with them seven days: and so we went toward Rome. ¹⁵ And from thence, when the brethren heard of us, they came to meet us as far as Appii forum, and the three taverns: whom when Paul saw, he thanked God, and took courage. ¹⁶ And when we came to Rome, the centurion delivered the prisoners to the captain of the guard: but Paul was suffered to dwell by himself with a soldier that kept him.

Paul Preaches at Rome under Guard

¹⁷ And it came to pass, that after three days Paul called the chief of the Jews together: and when they were come together, he said unto them, " Men and brethren, though I have committed nothing against the people, or customs of our fathers, yet was I delivered prisoner from Jerusalem into the hands of the Romans. ¹⁸ Who, when they had examined me, would have let me go, because there was no cause of death in me. ¹⁹ But when the Jews spake against it, I was constrained to appeal unto Caesar; not that I had ought to accuse my nation of. ²⁰ For this cause therefore have I called for you, to see you, and to speak with you: because that for the hope of Israel I am bound with this chain."

²¹ And they said unto him, " We neither received letters out of Judaea concerning thee, neither any of the brethren that came shewed or spake any harm of thee. ²² But we desire to hear of thee what thou thinkest: for as concerning this sect, we know that every where it is spoken against."

²³ And when they had appointed him a day, there came many to him into his lodging; to whom he expounded and testified the kingdom of God, persuading them concerning Jesus, both out of the law of Moses, and out of the prophets, from morning till evening. ²⁴ And some believed the things which were spoken, and

some believed not. ²⁵ And when they agreed not among themselves, they departed, after that Paul had spoken one word, " Well spake the Holy Ghost by Esaias the prophet unto our fathers, saying,

²⁶ ' Go unto this people, and say,
"Hearing ye shall hear, and shall not
understand;
and seeing ye shall see,
and not perceive."
²⁷ For the heart of this people
is waxed gross,
and their ears are dull of hearing,
and their eyes have they closed;
lest they should see with their eyes,
and hear with their ears,
and understand with their heart,
and should be converted, and I should heal them.' ⑧

St. Paul in Prison, Harmenszoon van Rijn Rembrandt (1606—1669)

²⁸ " Be it known therefore unto you, that the salvation of God is sent unto the Gentiles, and that they will hear it.
²⁹ And when he had said these words, the Jews departed, and had great reasoning among themselves."
³⁰ And Paul dwelt two whole years in his own hired house, and received all that came in unto him?
³¹ Preaching the kingdom of God, and teaching those things which concern the Lord Jesus Christ, with all confidence, no man forbidding him.

III FOOD FOR THOUGHT

1. What was the issue discussed in the council at Jerusalem?
2. Did they arrive at any decision?
3. What approach did Paul take to convince the Athenians to believe in God?
4. How did the riot in Ephesus start?
5. Why was Paul taken to Rome?

IV BIBLICAL RELEVANCE

A. Biblical Terms in Everyday English
1. put a yoke upon sb's neck (15:10): _____
2. turn the world upside down (17:6): _____

B. Biblical References in Literature
They then raised another cloth which it appeared covered Saint Paul falling from his horse, with all the details that are usually given in representations of his conversion.
(Miguel Cervantes, *Don Quixote*, 1605—1615)

---

⑧ 26—27 Isaiah 6:9, 10.

C. The Bible and Arts
1. *St. Paul Preaching in Athens*, Raphael (1483—1520)
2. *St. Paul in Prison*, Harmenszoon van Rijn Rembrandt (1606—1669)
3. *St. Paul at Malta*, Adam Elsheimer (1578—1610)

V SOURCES FOR REFERENCE

1. (2004). *Saint Paul*. A BBC documentary film directed by Jean-Claude Bragard.
2. Schippe, C. & C. Stetson. (2005). *The Bible and Its Influence*. Front Royal, VA: BLP Publishing.
3. Peterson, R. D. (1998). *The Concise History of Christianity*. Beijing: Peking University Press.
4. Dimont, M. I. (2004). *Jews, God and History*. New York: New American Library.
5. (2007). *Biblica: The Bible Atlas*. London: New Holland Publications (UK) Ltd.

REVELATION

40. REVELATION

I. POINTS OF DEPARTURE

The Christian Bible ends with the dramatically intimidating Book of Revelation, also called the Apocalypse (Greek, "unveiling" or "revelation"). Heavily indebted to such Jewish apocalyptic writings as Ezekiel, Zechariah, and Daniel, it uses symbols, numbers, and images to reveal the truth about the world, especially its future destiny. Revelation is commonly believed to have been written by John, possibly the author of the gospel that bears his name, during the time of Emperor Domitian (81—96). The emperor's policy towards Christians was that of ostracization and persecution. Just because Revelation was written at this time of persecution, the author used a great deal of symbolism to hide his meaning from civil authorities. As a result, without considerable knowledge of Hebrew Scriptures, it can be very challenging reading.

In spite of the seemingly unrelated images, visions, symbols and, accidentally, events, Revelation falls into four parts (Schippe, & Stetson, 2005:336). The first part (1:1—3:22) takes the form of letters to seven Churches in Asia Minor whose failings are sternly rebuked by John. The second part (4:1—20:15) consists of a scene in the heavenly throne room and the conflict between the dragon, representing evil, and the Lamb of God, a symbol of Jesus. The last part (21:1—22:21) presents a vision of a New Jerusalem and of eternal life with God.

The letters sent to the seven churches convey messages that encompass the whole of the Christian experience: faithful perseverance, loss of enthusiasm, internal problems caused by rival teachers, complacency. The terms and numbers used in this first vision though lost on contemporary readers had meaning for the audience at the time. *Son of Man* in the Book of Daniel to designate a future messiah-like figure was used by Jesus in the gospels to refer to himself. And the frequent use of the number seven in the Book of Revelation symbolizes a divine pattern of events.

The second part in depicting the great battle between good and the evil provides a riot of images, creatures, battles, and symbols, and has inspired writers, composers, artists, and filmmakers over the centuries. John introduced this part with his vision of heaven in which were found among other things a scroll closed with seven seals that was to be opened by an unusual lamb with seven horns and seven eyes. "The Lamb" is a reference to Jesus, who sacrificed himself for all humanity. As the seven seals were opened, a series of visions containing the number seven (seven seals, seven

Four Horsemen of the Apocalypse, Albrecht Dürer (1471—1528)

trumpets, and seven bowls) began. As the first four of the seven seals were opened, the four beasts that ride on white, red, black, and pale horses (known as "Four Horsemen of the Apocalypse") were summoned forth, which symbolize Conquest, War, Famine, and Death, respectively.

After the visions of the seals and trumpets, John came to a series of visions central to the meaning of the Book of Revelation. The first was that of the pregnant woman crowned with 12 stars and the red dragon with seven heads and ten horns. The woman has been identified variably as the people of Israel, the church, and Mary (her son, Jesus). Immediately afterwards, there is a conflict between the child and the dragon, which recalls the conflict predicted in *Genesis 3:15* concerning the enmity between the serpent and Eve's offspring. Chapter 13 describes two famous beasts of Revelation. The first was an unusual beast of the sea, with ten horns with crowns on them, seven heads, and the body of a leopard, the feet of a bear, and the mouth of a lion, identified as the devil of Satan in the previous chapter. The second was from the earth, with two horns like a lamb, the voice of a dragon, which rules on behalf of the first one. What is even more bizarre, this beast had number 666. Speculation on the identity of the beast has pervaded literature, art, and popular culture for two millennia. It is generally agreed, in line with the Hebrew tradition (e.g. *Daniel* 7), that grotesque monsters often symbolize oppressive kings and empires. In this context, the second beast may refer to "Nero Caesar," whose number value of Hebrew letters happens to be 666. This is reasonable enough, because Nero's brutality also extended to Christians. Other candidates for the beasts include the Roman Empire, the antichrist, as well as a false prophet. Next, John saw a lamb on Mount Zion, accompanied by 144,000 people. What follows it are images of the Son of Man and his angels reaping the earth with a sickle and gathering the vintage of the earth into the "wine press" of God's wrath. This scene calls to mind *Isaiah* 63 and inspired the American Nobel laureate John Steinbeck's novel *The Grapes of Wrath* (1939). The final cycle of seven is described next. The angels poured out God's wrath from seven bowls. When it came to the sixth bowl, the demonic spirits gathered all of the kings of the earth for a great battle at a place called Armageddon.

The Pope as the Whore of Babylon, from the 1545 edition of the Luther Bible

Chapter 17 shows the judgment of a prostitute now familiarly known as the Whore of Babylon for her fornication with many kings and people of the earth. The woman was seen sitting on a beast with seven heads and ten horns, clothed in purple and scarlet, holding a golden cup full of abominations and the impurities of her fornications. From the imagery described, the woman is seen as symbolizing Rome, with the beast representing seven hills that surround Rome and seven Roman emperors. The last two chapters of the second part show a sequence of battle and judgment scenes, in which Satan and his accomplices were definitely dispatched, giving way to a glorious vision of a new heaven and a new earth which would last 1,000 years (known as Millennium) before the Final Judgment.

In the last part of Revelation, John shared his vision of the New Jerusalem, which taps into the deepest longings of the human heart. First, it is an impregnable city in the form of a perfect cube, a place of security from the dangers outside, within which humanity may flourish. Secondly, the city itself is a temple, where all its citizens have direct access to God. Thirdly, the city is a garden, containing the tree of life and the river of the water of life. In John's vision, the end is as the beginning. Eden's Paradise, once so tragically lost to humanity, is now regained as humanity finds its true destiny in the purposes of God. The garden of perfection at the beginning of the Bible is here completed in a city of perfection, but with an expansive inclusiveness — it is a new garden that differs from an enclosed one inhabited by a restricted number of people (Ryken & Ryken, 2007:1877).

SELECTED READINGS

Prologue

Revelation 1

^{1} *The Revelation of Jesus Christ, which God gave unto him, to shew unto his servants things which must shortly come to pass; and he sent and signified it by his angel unto his servant John:* ^{2} *Who bare record of the word of God, and of the testimony of Jesus Christ, and of all things that he saw.* ^{3} *Blessed is he that readeth, and they that hear the words of this prophecy, and keep those things which are written therein: for the time is at hand.*

Greetings and Doxology

...
^{4} *John to the seven churches which are in Asia:*
Grace be unto you, and peace, from him which is, and which was, and which is to come; and from the seven Spirits which are before his throne; ^{5} *And from Jesus Christ, who is the faithful witness, and the first begotten of the dead, and the prince of the kings of the earth.*
Unto him that loved us, and washed us from our sins in his own blood, ^{6} *And hath made us kings and priests unto God and his Father; to him be glory and dominion for ever and ever. Amen.*
^{7} *Behold, he cometh with clouds;*
and every eye shall see him,
and they also which pierced him:
and all kindreds of the earth shall wail because of him.
Even so, Amen.

The Bible in Everyday English: *Alpha and Omega*

Alpha (A) and Omega (Ω) are the first and last letters of the Greek alphabet, signifying the first and last, or the most important part of something.

---

^{8} " *I am Alpha and Omega, the beginning and the ending, saith the Lord, which is, and which was, and which is to come, the Almighty.*"

One Like a Son of Man

^{9} *I John, who also am your brother, and companion in tribulation, and in the kingdom and patience of Jesus Christ, was in the isle that is called Patmos, for the word of God, and for the testimony of Jesus Christ.* ^{10} *I was in the Spirit on the Lord's day, and heard behind me a great voice, as of a trumpet,* ^{11} *Saying, " I am Alpha and Omega, the first and the last: and, What thou seest, write in a book, and send it unto the seven* churches which are in Asia; unto Ephesus, and unto Smyrna, and unto Pergamos, and unto Thyatira, and unto Sardis, and unto Philadelphia, and unto Laodicea."

Christ Testifies to John

^{12} And I turned to see the voice that spake with me. And being turned, I saw seven golden candlesticks; ^{13} And in the midst of the seven candlesticks one like unto " the Son of man,"① clothed with a garment down to the foot, and girt about the paps with a golden girdle. ^{14} His head and his hairs were white like wool, as white as snow; and his eyes were as a flame of fire; ^{15} And his feet like unto fine brass, as if they burned in a furnace; and his voice as the sound of many waters. ^{16} And he had in his right hand seven stars: and out of his mouth went a sharp twoedged sword: and his countenance was as the sun shineth in his strength.

^{17} And when I saw him, I fell at his feet as dead. And he laid his right hand upon me, saying unto me, " Fear not; I am the first and the last: ^{18} I am he that liveth, and was dead; and, behold, I am alive for evermore, Amen; and have the keys of hell and of death.

^{19} Write the things which thou hast seen, and the things which are, and the things which shall be hereafter; ^{20} The mystery of the seven stars which thou sawest in my right hand, and the seven golden candlesticks. The seven stars are the angels of the seven churches: and the seven candlesticks which thou sawest are the seven churches."

The Woman and the Dragon

Revelation 12

^{1} And there appeared a great wonder in heaven; a woman clothed with the sun, and the moon under her feet, and upon her head a crown of twelve stars: ^{2} And she being with child cried, travailing in birth, and pained to be delivered. ^{3} And there appeared another wonder in heaven; and behold a great red dragon, having seven heads and ten horns, and seven crowns upon his heads. ^{4} And his tail drew the third part of the stars of heaven, and did cast them to the earth: and the dragon stood before the woman which was ready to be delivered, for to devour her child as soon as it was born. ^{5} And she brought forth a man child, who was to rule all nations with a rod of iron: and her child was caught up unto God, and to his throne.

^{6} And the woman fled into the wilderness, where she hath a place prepared of God, that they should feed her there a thousand two hundred and threescore days.

^{7} And there was war in heaven: Michael and his angels fought against the dragon; and the dragon fought and his angels, ^{8} And prevailed not; neither was their place found any more in heaven. ^{9} And the great dragon was cast out, that old serpent, called the Devil, and Satan, which deceiveth the whole world: he was cast out into the earth, and his angels were cast out with him.

^{10} And I heard a loud voice saying in heaven,
" Now is come salvation, and strength,
and the kingdom of our God,
and the power of his Christ:
for the accuser of our brethren is cast down,
which accused them before our God day and night.
^{11} And they overcame him
by the blood of the Lamb,
and by the word of their testimony;

---

① " the Son of man" Daniel 7:13.

and they loved not their lives unto the death.
¹² Therefore rejoice, ye heavens,
and ye that dwell in them.
Woe to the inhabiters of the earth and of the sea!
For the devil is come down unto you, having great wrath,
because he knoweth that he hath but a short time.

¹³ And when the dragon saw that he was cast unto the earth, he persecuted the woman which brought forth the man child. ¹⁴ And to the woman were given two wings of a great eagle, that she might fly into the wilderness, into her place, where she is nourished for a time, and times, and half a time, from the face of the serpent. ¹⁵ And the serpent cast out of his mouth water as a flood after the woman, that he might cause her to be carried away of the flood. ¹⁶ And the earth helped the woman, and the earth opened her mouth, and swallowed up the flood which the dragon cast out of his mouth. ¹⁷ And the dragon was wroth with the woman, and went to make war with the remnant of her seed, which keep the commandments of God, and have the testimony of Jesus Christ.

The New Jerusalem

Revelation 21

¹ And I saw a new heaven and a new earth: for the first heaven and the first earth were passed away; and there was no more sea. ² and I John saw the holy city, new Jerusalem, coming down from God out of heaven, prepared as a bride adorned for her husband. ³ And I heard a great voice out of heaven saying, "Behold, the tabernacle of God is with men, and he will dwell with them, and they shall be his people, and God himself shall be with them, and be their God. ⁴ And God shall wipe away all tears from their eyes; and there shall be no more death, neither sorrow, nor crying, neither shall there be any more pain: for the former things are passed away."

⁵ And he that sat upon the throne said, "Behold, I make all things new." And he said unto me, "Write: for these words are true and faithful."

⁶ And he said unto me, "It is done. I am Alpha and Omega, the beginning and the end. I will give unto him that is athirst of the fountain of the water of life freely. ⁷ He that overcometh shall inherit all things; and I will be his God, and he shall be my son. ⁸ But the fearful, and unbelieving, and the abominable, and murderers, and whoremongers, and sorcerers, and idolaters, and all liars, shall have their part in the lake which burneth with fire and brimstone: which is the second death."

⁹ And there came unto me one of the seven angels which had the seven vials full of the seven last plagues, and talked with me, saying, "Come hither, I will shew thee the bride, the Lamb's wife." ¹⁰ And he carried me away in the spirit to a great and high mountain, and shewed me that great city, the holy Jerusalem, descending out of heaven from God, ¹¹ Having the glory of God: and her light was like unto a stone most precious, even like a jasper stone, clear as crystal; ¹² And had a wall great and high, and had twelve gates, and at the gates twelve angels, and names written thereon, which are the names of the twelve tribes of the children of Israel: ¹³ On the east three gates; on the north three gates; on the south three gates; and on the west three gates. ¹⁴ And the wall of the city had twelve foundations, and in them the names of the twelve apostles of the Lamb.

¹⁵ And he that talked with me had a golden reed to measure the city, and the gates thereof, and the wall thereof. ¹⁶ And the city lieth foursquare, and the length is as large as the breadth: and he measured the city with the reed, twelve thousand furlongs.② The length and the breadth and the height of it are equal.

¹⁷ And he measured the wall thereof, an hundred and forty and four cubits, according to the measure of a man, that is, of the angel. ¹⁸ And the building of the wall of it was of jasper: and the city was pure gold, like unto clear glass. ¹⁹ And the foundations of the wall of the city were garnished with all manner of precious stones. The first foundation was jasper; the second, sapphire; the third, a chalcedony; the fourth, an emerald;

---

② **twelve thousand furlongs** about 1,400 mils (about 2,200 kilometers).

²⁰ *The fifth, sardonyx; the sixth, sardius; the seventh, chrysolyte; the eighth, beryl; the ninth, a topaz; the tenth, a chrysoprasus; the eleventh, a jacinth; the twelfth, an amethyst.*

²¹ *And the twelve gates were twelve pearls: every several gate was of one pearl: and the street of the city was pure gold, as it were transparent glass.*

²² *And I saw no temple therein: for the Lord God Almighty and the Lamb are the temple of it.* ²³ *And the city had no need of the sun, neither of the moon, to shine in it: for the glory of God did lighten it, and the Lamb is the light thereof.* ²⁴ *And the nations of them which are saved shall walk in the light of it: and the kings of the earth do bring their glory and honour into it.* ²⁵ *And the gates of it shall not be shut at all by day: for there shall be no night there.*

²⁶ *And they shall bring the glory and honour of the nations into it.* ²⁷ *And there shall in no wise enter into it any thing that defileth, neither whatsoever worketh abomination, or maketh a lie: but they which are written in the Lamb's book of life.*

Revelation 22

¹ *And he shewed me a pure river of water of life, clear as crystal, proceeding out of the throne of God and of the Lamb.* ² *In the midst of the street of it, and on either side of the river, was there the tree of life, which bare twelve manner of fruits, and yielded her fruit every month: and the leaves of the tree were for the healing of the nations.* ³ *And there shall be no more curse: but the throne of God and of the Lamb shall be in it; and his servants shall serve him:* ⁴ *And they shall see his face; and his name shall be in their foreheads.* ⁵ *And there shall be no night there; and they need no candle, neither light of the sun; for the Lord God giveth them light: and they shall reign for ever and ever.*

John of Patmos Watches the Descent of the New Jerusalem from God, a 14th century tapestry

⁶ *And he said unto me, "These sayings are faithful and true: and the Lord God of the holy prophets sent his angel to shew unto his servants the things which must shortly be done."*

Jesus Is Coming

⁷ *"Behold, I come quickly: blessed is he that keepeth the sayings of the prophecy of this book."*

⁸ *And I John saw these things, and heard them. And when I had heard and seen, I fell down to worship before the feet of the angel which shewed me these things.* ⁹ *Then saith he unto me, "See thou do it not: for I am thy fellowservant, and of thy brethren the prophets, and of them which keep the sayings of this book: worship God."*

¹⁰ *And he saith unto me, "Seal not the sayings of the prophecy of this book: for the time is at hand.* ¹¹ *He that is unjust, let him be unjust still: and he which is filthy, let him be filthy still: and he that is righteous, let him be righteous still: and he that is holy, let him be holy still."*

¹² *"And, behold, I come quickly; and my reward is with me, to give every man according as his work shall be.* ¹³ *I am Alpha and Omega, the beginning and the end, the first and the last.*

¹⁴ *"Blessed are they that do his commandments, that they may have right to the tree of life, and may enter in through the gates into the city.*

¹⁵ *"For without are dogs, and sorcerers, and whoremongers, and murderers, and idolaters, and whosoever loveth and maketh a lie.*

¹⁶ *"I Jesus have sent mine angel to testify unto you these things in the churches. I am the root and the offspring of David, and the bright and morning star."*

¹⁷ And the Spirit and the bride say, "Come." And let him that heareth say, "Come." And let him that is athirst come. And whosoever will, let him take the water of life freely.

¹⁸ For I testify unto every man that heareth the words of the prophecy of this book, If any man shall add unto these things, God shall add unto him the plagues that are written in this book: ¹⁹ And if any man shall take away from the words of the book of this prophecy, God shall take away his part out of the book of life, and out of the holy city, and from the things which are written in this book.

²⁰ He which testifieth these things saith, "Surely I come quickly."
Amen. Even so, come, Lord Jesus.
²¹ The grace of our Lord Jesus Christ be with you all. Amen.

III FOOD FOR THOUGHT

1. What was the purpose of the Book of Revelation?
2. What do the woman and the dragon (*Rev.* 12) each represent and why?
3. How does *Revelation* 21—22 mirror Genesis in a story of a new creation?

IV BIBLICAL RELEVANCE

A. Biblical Terms in Everyday English
1. the Alpha and the Omega (1:8): _____
2. mark of the beast (13:17): _____
3. 666 (13:18): _____
4. the grapes of wrath (14:19—20): _____
5. Armageddon (16:16): _____
6. whore of Babylon (17:1, 5—6): _____

B. Biblical References in Literature
1. Filled with amazement and terror by this apparition of a horseman in the sky—half believing himself the chosen scribe of some new apocalypse, the officer was overcome by the intensity of his emotions; his legs failed him and he fell.
   (Ambrose Bierce, *A Horseman in the Sky*, 1889)
2. We expect Armageddon; the Bible has trained us well. We assume either annihilation or salvation, perhaps both. Millenarian beliefs are as old as time; the apocalypse has always been at hand.
   (Penelope Lively, *Moon Tiger*, 1988)
3. I'd marry the W—of Babylon rather than do anything dishonourable!
   (Thomas Hardy, *Jude the Obscure*, 1895)

C. The Bible and Arts
1. *Four Horsemen of the Apocalypse*, Albrecht Dürer (1471—1528)
2. *The Pope as the Whore of Babylon*, from the 1545 edition of the Luther Bible
3. *John of Patmos Watches the Descent of the New Jerusalem from God*, a 14th century tapestry

V SOURCES FOR REFERENCE

1. (1979). *Apocalypse Now*. An American epic war film set during the Vietnam War, directed and produced by Francis Ford Coppola.
2. (2005). "The Revelation: The End of the World?" In *Bible Mysteries*. A BBC and Discovery Channel co-production documentary series exploring great figures and events from biblical times.
3. Schippe, C. & C. Stetson. (2005). *The Bible and Its Influence*. Front Royal, VA: BLP Publishing.
4. Ryken, L. & P. G. Ryken. (2007). *The Literary Study Bible*. Wheaton, Illinois: Crossway Bibles.

BIBLIOGRAPHY

1. Ackerman, J. S. & A. W. Jenks, etc. (1973). *Teaching the Old Testament in English Classes*. Bloomington: Indiana University Press.
2. Alter, R. & R. Kermode (ed.) (1987). *The Literary Guide to the Bible*. Cambridge, MA: The Belknap Press of Harvard University Press.
3. (2007). *Biblica: The Bible Atlas*. London: New Holland Publications (UK) Ltd.
4. Black, M. (ed.) (2001). *Peake's Commentary on the Bible*. London: Routledge.
5. Browning, W. R. E. (2009). *A Dictionary of the Bible*. Oxford: Oxford University Press.
6. Bragg, M. (2011). *The Book of Books: The Radical Impact of the King James Bible 1611—2011*. London: Hodder & Stoughton Ltd.
7. Comfort, P. W. (ed.) (2006). *Cornerstone Biblical Commentary: Job, Ecclesiastes, Song of Songs*. Carol Stream, IL: Tyndale House Publishers, INC.
8. Delahunty, A,. S. Dignen & P. Stock. (2001). *The Oxford Dictionary of Allusions*. Oxford: Oxford University Press.
9. Dimont, M. I. (2004). *Jews, God and History*. New York: New American Library.
10. Dodd, C. H. (1961). *The Parables of the Kingdom*. New York: Scribners.
11. Evans, I. H. (1975). *Brewer's Dictionary of Phrase and Fable*. London: Cassell & Co., Ltd.
12. Hauer, C. E. & W. A. Young. (1986). *An Introduction to the Bible: A Journey into Three Worlds*. Englewood Cliffs, New Jersey: Prentice-Hall, Inc.
13. (1991). *The Holy Bible (King James Version)*. New York: Ivy Books.
14. Jeremias, J. (1963). *The Parables of Jesus*. London: SCM Press Ltd.
15. Keller, W., (transl.) (1974). *The Bible as History*. New York: Bantam Books.
16. Kendall, R. T. (2004). *The Complete Guide to the Parables*. Grand Rapids, MI: Chosen Books.
17. Kuo, S. M. (1990). *Journey through the Bible*. Nanjing: Nanjing University Press.
18. (1995). *Merriam-Webster's Encyclopedia of Literature*. Springfield, MA: Merriam-Webster, Inc.
19. Pearsall, J. (ed.) (1998). *The New Oxford Dictionary of English*. Oxford: Clarendon Press.
20. Peterson, R. D. (1998). *The Concise History of Christianity*. Beijing: Peking University Press.
21. (1981). *Reader's Digest Atlas of the Bible*. Pleasantville, NY: The Reader's Digest Association, Inc.
22. Roche, P. (2001). *The Bible's Greatest Stories*. New York: New American Library.
23. Ryken, L. & P. G. Ryken. (2007). *The Literary Study Bible*. Wheaton, Illinois: Crossway Bibles.
24. Schippe, C. & C. Stetson. (2005). *The Bible and Its Influence*. Front Royal, VA: BLP Publishing.
25. Van Loon, H. W. (1941). *The Story of the Bible*. New York: Garden City Publishing Co., Inc.

26. Yancey, P. & T. Stafford (notes by) (1989). *The New Student Bible*, *New International Version*. Grand Rapids, Mich: Zondervan Publishing House.
27. [加]菲(Gorden Fee),[美]斯图尔特(Douglas Stuart):《圣经导读》(上)(*How to Read the Bible for All Its Worth*),北京:北京大学出版社,2005年。
28. [加]菲(Gorden Fee),[美]斯图尔特(Douglas Stuart):《圣经导读》(下)(*How to Read the Bible Book by Book*),北京:北京大学出版社,2005年。
29. 刘意青:《〈圣经〉的文学阐释—理论与实践》,北京:北京大学出版社,2005年。
30. 陆谷孙:《英汉大词典》,上海:上海译文出版社,1993年。
31. 马超群:《基督教二千年》,北京:中国青年出版社,1988年。
32. 穆尔,G..F.:《基督教简史》,北京:商务印书馆,1981年。
33. 孙毅:《〈圣经〉导读》,北京:中国人民大学出版社,2005年。
34. 谭善余(译):《圣经是怎样一本书》,北京:生活·读书·新知三联书店,1988年。
35. 维尔纳·克勒尔著,林纪焘等译:《圣经:一部历史》,北京:三联书店,1998年。
36. 《新旧约全书》,南京:中国基督教协会印发,1994年。
37. 杨佑方:《英语圣经词源》,成都:四川人民出版社,2003年。
38. 张朝柯:《〈圣经〉与希伯来民间文学》,北京:东方出版社,2004年。
39. 朱维之:《圣经文学十二讲》,北京:人民文学出版社,2008年。

Internet resources
1. http://www.biblegateway.com/
2. http://www.bible-history.com
3. http://www.bibleliteracy.org
4. http://www.biblequery.org/
5. http://christiananswers.net
6. http://www.creationism.org/images/DoreBibleIllus/index.htm
7. http://www.fourmilab.ch/etexts/www/Bible/Bible.htm
8. http://www.preceptaustin.org/maps_page.htm
9. http://www.studylight.org/se/maps

APPENDICES

1. Maps

1.1 Map of the Ancient Near East

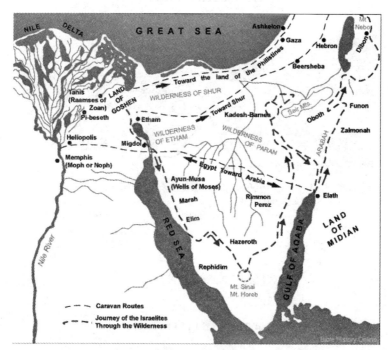

1.2 Route of the Exodus of the Israelites from Egypt

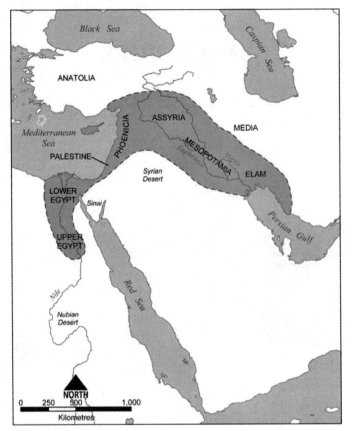

1.3 The Fertile Crescent

1.4 The World of Patriarchs

The Bible and Western Culture

1.5 Map of the Kingdoms of David and Solomon

1.6 The Divided Monarchy

APPENDICES 373

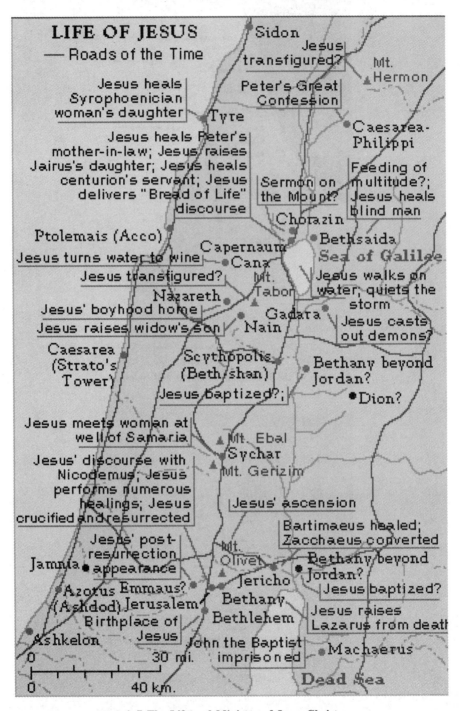

1.7 The Life and Ministry of Jesus Christ

The Bible and Western Culture

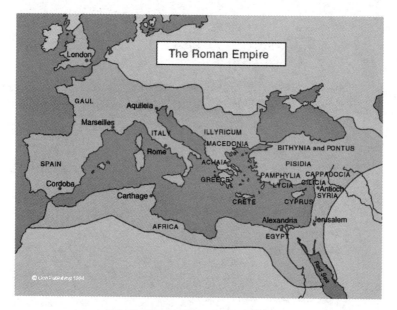

1.8 The Roman Empire at Its Zenith

1.9 Paul's Missionary Journeys (1)

APPENDICES 375

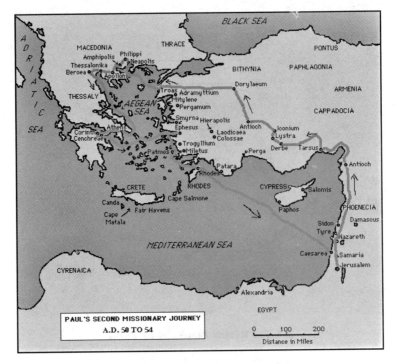

1.10 Paul's Missionary Journeys (2)

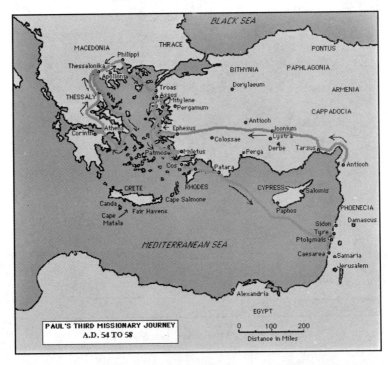

1.11 Paul's Missionary Journeys (3)

2. A Chronology of Biblical Times
(Based on *Reader's Digest*, 1981:42—43; 刘意青, 2005: 289—297)

2.1 Ancient-United Kingdom

	Egypt	Holy Land	Mesopotamia
2000	The 12th Kingdom	Abraham arrives in land of Canaan, Isaac → Jacob → Joseph	The tribes of Hurrians and Amorites Amorties establish dynasty in Babylon, 1830
1800		Abraham and his family leave Ur towards the west	Hammurabi reunifies Mesopotamia, issues Babylonian law code
1800—1700	The Hyksos invade Egypt		
1700—1600	Hyksos rule, c. 1650—1550	Joseph and Jacob in Egypt	the Fall of the Babylonian Kingdom
1500	Thutmose III, c. 1490—1436		
1400—1300	Akhenaton, c. 1366—1349		Emergence of Assyria
1300	Seti I, c. 1305—1290; Ramses II, c. 1290—1224; Extend border of Egypt northward	Moses leads Exodus of Hebrews from Egypt; Joshua invades Canaan	
1200—1100	Ramses III, c. 1183—1152	Prophet/Judge Samuel Saul named first king of Israel, c. 1020	Tiglath-pileser I establishes Assyrian empire
1000	Libyan dynasty, c. 935—725	David rules Judah, c. 1000—993; captures Jerusalem and rules united kingdom of Israel, c. 993—961./ Prophet Nathan Solomon, c. 961—922. Beginning of divided monarchy, c. 922	Period of Assyrian weakness

2.2 Divided Monarchy-Exile

	Israel/Judah	Assyrian Empire
900—800	House of Omri rules, 876—842; Revolt of Jehu, 842; Shalmaneser III, invades Syria, Israel	Shalmaneser III, c. 859—825, attempts to extend empire; his rule ends in revolt
700	Period of prophets: Amos 760—740, Hosea 750—735, Isaiah 740—701, Micah 725—690) Renaissance of Israel under Jeroboam II, 786—746, and Judah under Uzziah, 783—742. Assyrians capture Samaria, end of kingdom of Israel, 721. Sennacherib attacks Judah, 701	Tiglath-pileser III restores Assyrian power, 745 Chaldean dynasty rules in Babylon, 626—539. Babylonians conquer Nineveh, 612, end of Assyrian empire.
600	Babylonians take Jerusalem, end of kingdom of Judah, 587.	

The Exile	
Holy Land	**Babylon**

	Holy Land	Babylon
500	The 1st Exile 597 The 2nd Exile 586 Edict of Cyrus, 538; Jews return to Holy Land, Nehemiah builds Temple, Ezra brings the Law	Nebuchadrezzar invades Egypt, 568 Esther saves the Jews Cyrus conquers Babylonians, 539

2.3 The Greek Period

	Holy Land	Babylon	Greece/Rome
400—300	Alexander conquers Tyre en route to Egypt, 332 Septuagint（七十贤士译本）	Alexander the Great defeats Persians at Issus, 333; end of Persian empire After Alexander's death at Babylon, his generals divide empire	Alexander conquers Egypt, founds Alexandria, 332 Ptolemies begin Egyptian rule.
200	Four Syrian wars, 276—217; power struggle between Seleucids and Ptolemies to control Syria and Phoenicia. Battle of Paneas, 198; Seleucids rule of Holy Land. Beginning of Maccabean revolt, 167. the Essenes write the Qumran (Dead Sea) Scrolls		First Punic War between Rome and Carthage, 264—241. Hannibal crosses Alps at start of Third Punic War, 218—201. Carthage destroyed by Rome at end of Third Punic War, 149—146.
100	Parthians invade, put Antigonus II on throne, 40—37. Herod the Great, 37—4.		Julius Caesar conquers Gaul, Britain, 58—51. Caesar, Crassus, Pompey form first triumvirate, 60. Caesar assassinated, 44. Second triumvirate, 43.

2.4 The Roman Period/The New Testament

	Holy Land	The Roman Empire
0	Life of Jesus, c. 7 B.C. — c. A.D. 29. Pontius Pilate, governor of Judea, 26—36. Paul begins missionary journeys, c. 44; taken to Rome, 60, where he is martyred. First Jewish Revolt against Rome, 66—73.	Reign of Octavian as Augustus Caesar, 27 B.C. — A.D. 14. Reign of Tiberias, 14—37; Caligula, 37—41; Claudius, 41—54. Reign of Nero, 54—68; Christians persecuted after Roman fire, 64. Reign of Vespasian, 69—79; Titus, 79—81.
100	Second (Bar Kokhba) Jewish Revolt against Rome, 132—135; ends in complete Roman victory; Jews dispersed.	Persecution of Christians reaches peak during reign of Diocletian, 284—305. Constantine wins battle of Milvian Bridge, 312; issues Edict of Milan, 313.

3. An Overview of the Books of the Bible

(Based on Yancey & Stafford, 1989:xiv-xvii)

The Old Testament

Law/Pentateuch（律法书/摩西五经）

The first five books of the Bible tell the origins of the Jewish race and culture.

GENESIS（创世记）: The book of beginnings describes creation, the first rebellions against God, and God's choosing of Abraham and his offspring.
EXODUS（出埃及记）: God rescued the Israelites from slavery in Egypt and led them to the Desert of Sinai. There, he gave Moses the laws to govern the new nation.
LEVITICUS（利未记）: God set up laws for the Israelites, mostly regarding holiness and worship.
NUMBERS（民数记）: Because of their rebellion and disobedience, the Israelites had to wander in a wilderness for 40 years before entering the Promised Land.
DEUTERONOMY（申命记）: Just before his death, Moses made three emotional farewell speeches, recapping history and warning the Israelites against further mistakes.

History Books（历史书）

The next 12 books continue the history of the Israelites: they moved into the land of Canaan and established a kingdom that lasted almost 500 years.

JOSHUA（约书亚记）: After Moses' death, Joshua commanded the armies that conquered much of the territory in the Promised Land.
JUDGES（士师记）: The new nation fell into a series of dismal failures. God raised up leaders called "judges."
RUTH（路得记）: This story of love and loyalty between two widows shines out brightly in an otherwise dark period.
1 SAMUEL（撒母耳记上）: Samuel became a transition leader between the time of judges and that of the kings. He appointed Israel's first king, Saul. After his own failure, Saul tried violently to prevent God's king-elect David from taking the throne.
2 SAUMUEL（撒母耳记下）: David, a man after God's own heart, brought the nation together. But after committing adultery and murder, he was haunted by family and national crises.
1 KINGS（列王纪上）: Solomon succeeded David, with mixed success. At his death, a civil war tore apart the nation. Successive kings were mostly bad, and the prophet Elijah had dramatic confrontations with King Ahab.
2 KINGS（列王纪下）: This book continues the record of the rulers of the divided kingdom. None of the northern kings followed God constantly, and so Israel was finally destroyed by an invader. The South, Judah, lasted much longer, but finally Babylon conquered Judah and deported its citizens.
1 CHRONICLES（历代志上）: The book opens with the most complete genealogical record in the Bible, then adds many incidents from the life of David (often the same as those in 2 Samuel).

2 CHRONICLES（历代志下）：Often paralleling the books of Kings, this book records the history of the rulers of Judah, emphasizing the good kings.

EZRA（以斯拉记）：After being held captive in Babylon for decades, the Jews were allowed to return to their homeland. Ezra, a priest, emerged from one of the first waves of refugees.

NEHEMIAH（尼希米记）：Nehemiah returned from the Babylonian captivity after the temple had been rebuilt. He concentrated on restoring the protective wall around Jerusalem and joined Ezra in leading a religious revival.

ESTHER（以斯帖记）：This story is set among captive Jews in Persia. A courageous Jewish queen foiled a plan to exterminate her people.

Writings/Books of Wisdom（诗歌与智慧书）

Almost one-third of the Old Testament was originally written in poetry. These books concentrate on questions about pain, God, life, and love.

JOB（约伯记）：The best man of his day suffers the greatest personal tragedy. The entire book deals with the question, "Why?"

PSALMS（诗篇）：These prayers and hymns cover the full range of human emotion; together, they represent a personal journal of how to relate to God. Some were also used in public worship services.

PROVERBS（箴言）：The proverbs offer advice on every imaginable area of life. The style of wise living described here leads to a fulfilled life.

ECCLESIASTES（传道书）：A life without God, "under the sun," leads to meaninglessness and despair, says the Teacher in a strikingly modern book.

SONG OF SONGS（雅歌）：This beautiful poem celebrates romantic and physical love.

Books of the Prophets（先知书）

During the years when kings ruled Israel and Judah, God spoke through prophets. Though some prophets did predict future events, their primary role was to call God's people back to him.

ISAIAH（以赛亚书）：The most eloquent of the prophets, Isaiah analyzed the failures of all the nations around him and pointed to a future Messiah who would bring peace.

JEREMIAH（耶利米书）：Jeremiah led an emotionally tortured life, yet held to his stern message. He spoke to Judah in the last decades before Babylon destroyed the nation.

LAMENTATIONS（耶利米哀歌）：All Jeremiah's warnings about Jerusalem came true, and Lamentations records five poems of sorrow for the fallen city.

EZEKIEL（以西结书）：Ezekiel spoke to the Jews who were captive in Babylon. He often used dramatic stories and "enacted parables" to make his points.

DANIEL（但以理书）：A captive in Babylon, Daniel rose to the office of prime minister. Despite intense political pressure, he lived a model life of integrity and left highly symbolic prophecies about the future.

HOSEA（何西阿书）：By marrying a loose-living wife, Hosea lived out his message: that Israel had committed spiritual adultery against God.

JOEL（约珥书）：Beginning with a recent catastrophe in Judah (a locust plague), Joel foretold God's judgment on Judah.

AMOS（阿摩司书）：A country boy, Amos preached to Israel at the height of its prosperity.

His grim warnings focused on materialism.

OBADIAH（俄巴底亚书）: Obadiah warned Edom, a nation bordering Judah.

JONAH（约拿书）: Jonah reluctantly went to Nineveh and found Israel's enemies responsive to God's message.

MICAH（弥迦书）: Micah exposed corruption in every level of society, but closed with a promise of forgiveness and restoration.

NAHUM（那鸿书）: Long after Jonah had stirred Nineveh to repentance, Nahum foretold the mighty city's total destruction.

HABAKKUK（哈巴谷书）: Habakkuk addressed his book to God, not people. In a frank dialogue with God, he discussed problems of suffering and justice.

ZEPHANIAH（西番雅书）: Zephaniah focused on the coming day of the Lord, which would purge Judah, resulting in a remnant used to bless the entire world.

HAGGAI（哈该书）: After returning from the Babylonian captivity, the Jews began rebuilding the temple of God. But before long they set aside that task to work on their own homes. Haggai reminded them to put God first.

ZECHARIAH（撒迦利亚书）: Writing around the same time as Haggai, Zechariah also urged the Jews to work on the temple. He used a more uplifting approach, describing how the temple would point to the coming Messiah.

MALACHI（玛拉基书）: The last Old Testament prophet, Malachi faced a nation that had grown indifferent. He sought to stir them from apathy.

The New Testament

The Gospels（四福音书）

The word *gospel* means "good news." Almost half of the New Testament consists of four accounts of the life of Jesus and the good news he brought to earth. Each of these four books, or Gospels, has a different focus and a different audience; taken together, they give a complete picture of Jesus' life and teaching. About a third of their pages are devoted to the events of his last week on earth, including the crucifixion and resurrection.

MATTHEW（马太福音）: Written to a Jewish audience, this Gospel links the Old and New Testament. It presents Jesus as the Messiah and King promised in the Old Testament. Matthew emphasizes Jesus' authority and power.

MARK（马可福音）: Mark probably had pragmatic Roman readers in mind. His Gospel stresses action and gives a straightforward, blow-by-blow account of Jesus' work on earth.

LUKE（路加福音）: A doctor, Luke was also a fine writer. His Gospel provides many details of human interest, especially in Jesus' treatment of the poor and needy. A joyful tone characterizes Luke's book.

JOHN（约翰福音）: John has a different, more reflective style than the other Gospels. Its author selected seven signs that pointed to Jesus as the Son of God and wove together everything else to underscore that point.

The Acts of Apostles（使徒行传）

Acts tells what happened to Jesus' followers after he left them. Peter and Paul soon emerged as leaders of the rapidly spreading church.

The Letters（书信）

The young church was nourished by apostles who set down their beliefs and messages in a series of letters. The first 13 such letters (Romans through Philemon) were written by the apostle Paul who led the advance of Christianity to non-Jewish people.

Paul's Letters

ROMANS（罗马书）: Written to a sophisticated audience, Romans sets forth theology in a logical, organized form.

1 CORINTHIANS（哥林多前书）: A very practical book, 1 Corinthians takes up the problems of a tumultuous church in Corinth: marriage, factions, immorality, public worship, and lawsuits.

2 CORINTHIANS（哥林多后书）: Paul wrote this follow-up letter to defend himself against a rebellion led by certain false apostles.

GALATIANS（加拉太书）: A short version of the message of Romans, this book addresses legalism. It shows how Christ came to bring freedom, not bondage to a set of laws.

EPHESIANS（以弗所书）: Although written in jail, this letter is Paul's most optimistic and encouraging. It tells of the advantage a believer has in Christ.

PHILIPPIANS（腓立比书）: The church at Philippi ranked among Paul's favorites. This friendly letter stresses that joy can be found in any situation.

COLOSSIANS（歌罗西书）: Written to oppose certain cults, Colossians tells how faith in Christ is complete. Nothing needs to be added to what Christ did.

1 THESSALONIANS（帖撒罗尼迦前书）: Composed early in Paul's ministry, this letter gives a capsule history of one church, as well as Paul's direct advice about specific problems.

2 THESSALONIANS（帖撒罗尼迦后书）: Stronger in tone than his first letter to the Thessalonians, the sequel goes over the same topics, especially the church's questions about Christ's second coming.

1 TIMOTHY（提摩太前书）: As Paul neared the end of his life, he chose young men such as Timothy to carry on his work. His two letters to Timothy form a leadership manual for a young pastor.

2 TIMOTHY（提摩太后书）: Written just before Paul's death, 2 Timothy offers Paul's final words to his young assistant.

TITUS（提多书）: Titus was left in Crete, a notoriously difficult place to nurture a church. Paul's letter gave practical advice on how to go about it.

PHILEMON（腓利门书）: Paul urged Philemon, owner of runaway slave Onesimus, to forgive his slave and accept him as a brother in Christ.

Other Letters

HEBREWS（希伯来书）: No one knows who wrote Hebrews, but it probably first went to Christians in danger of slipping back into Judaism. It interprets the Old Testament, explaining many Jewish practices as symbols that prepared the way for Christ.

JAMES（雅各书）: James, a man of action, emphasized the right kind of behavior for a believer. Someone who calls himself or herself a Christian ought to act like it, James believed, and his letter spells out the specifics.

1 PETER（彼得前书）: Early Christians often met violent opposition, and Peter's letter comforted and encouraged Christians who were being persecuted for their faith.

2 PETER（彼得后书）: In contrast to Peter's first letter, this one focused on problems that sprang up from the inside. It warns against false teachers.

1 JOHN（约翰一书）: John could fill simple words - *light*, *love*, *life* - with deep meaning, and in this letter, he elegantly explains basic truths about the Christian life.

2 JOHN（约翰二书）: Warning against false teachers, John counseled churches on how to respond to them.

3 JOHN（约翰三书）: Balancing 2 John, this companion letter mentions the need to be hospitable to true teachers.

JUDE（犹大书）: Jude gave a brief but fiery exposé of heretics.

REVELATION（启示录）

A book of visions and symbols, Revelation is the only New Testament book that concentrates on prophecy. It completes the story, begun in Genesis, of the cosmic battle between good and evil being waged on earth. It ends with a picture of a new heaven and new earth.

《〈圣经〉与西方文化》

尊敬的老师：

　　您好！

　　为了方便您更好地使用《〈圣经〉与西方文化》，我们特向使用该书作为教材的教师赠送本书配套电子课件。如有需要，请完整填写"教师联系表"并加盖所在单位系（院）或培训中心公章，免费向出版社索取。

北京大学出版社

教 师 联 系 表

教材名称	《〈圣经〉与西方文化》						
姓名：		姓别：		职务：		职称：	
E-mail：		联系电话：			邮政编码：		
供职学校：			所在院系：				
学校地址：							（章）
教学科目与年级：			班级人数：				
通信地址：							

　　填写完毕后，请将此表邮寄给我们，我们将为您免费寄送本教材配套资料，谢谢！

北京市海淀区成府路205号
北京大学出版社外语编辑部　朱丽娜　　　邮购部电话：010-62534449
邮政编码：100871　　　　　　　　　　　　市场营销部电话：010-62750672
电子邮箱：zln0120@163.com　　　　　　　外语编辑部电话：010-62759634